Accurate Layer Selections Using Photoshop's Selection Tools

Use Photoshop and Illustrator to Refine Your Artwork

Jennifer Harder

Apress®

Accurate Layer Selections Using Photoshop's Selection Tools: Use Photoshop and Illustrator to Refine Your Artwork

Jennifer Harder
Delta, BC, Canada

ISBN-13 (pbk): 978-1-4842-7492-7   ISBN-13 (electronic): 978-1-4842-7493-4
https://doi.org/10.1007/978-1-4842-7493-4

Managing Director, Apress Media LLC: Welmoed Spahr
Acquisitions Editor: Spandana Chatterjee
Coordinating Editor: Mark Powers
Copyeditor : Kim Burton wiseman

Cover designed by eStudioCalamar

Cover image by Debby Hudson on Unsplash (www.unsplash.com)

Distributed to the book trade worldwide by Apress Media, LLC, 1 New York Plaza, New York, NY 10004, U.S.A. Phone 1-800-SPRINGER, fax (201) 348-4505, e-mail orders-ny@springer-sbm.com, or visit www.springeronline.com. Apress Media, LLC is a California LLC and the sole member (owner) is Springer Science + Business Media Finance Inc (SSBM Finance Inc). SSBM Finance Inc is a **Delaware** corporation.

For information on translations, please e-mail booktranslations@springernature.com; for reprint, paperback, or audio rights, please e-mail bookpermissions@springernature.com.

Apress titles may be purchased in bulk for academic, corporate, or promotional use. eBook versions and licenses are also available for most titles. For more information, reference our Print and eBook Bulk Sales web page at http://www.apress.com/bulk-sales.

Any source code or other supplementary material referenced by the author in this book is available to readers on GitHub via the book's product page, located at www.apress.com/9781484274927. For more detailed information, please visit http://www.apress.com/source-code.

Printed on acid-free paper

Table of Contents

About the Author

Jennifer Harder has worked in the graphic design industry for more than ten years. She has a degree in graphic communications and is currently teaching Adobe Acrobat, InDesign, and Dreamweaver courses at Langara College in Vancouver, British Columbia. As a freelancer, Jennifer frequently works with Adobe PDFs to help enhance websites. She enjoys talking about Adobe software, and her interests include writing, illustration, and working on her websites.

About the Technical Reviewers

PK Kaushal is a visual artist, a graphic designer, a photographer and has worked at an ad agency, print media house, and educational institute for about nine years. He has a post-graduate degree in applied arts from Kurukshetra University in Haryana, India. He currently runs a photo/video production company.

 **Bhuvnesh Kumar Varshney** has worked in the VFX industry for 14 years. He is trained in 3D graphics, visualization, and animation and has a personal interest in programming in Python. He has a bachelor's degree in computer science and finished his professional diploma in 3D. His main interest is key animation for VFX and gaming. He has worked at various companies as a team-lead and senior artist leading animation and visual effects studios, including Technicolor, Yash Raj Films, DQ Entertainment, and Anibrain Studio. He currently works at NY VFXWAALA as an animation supervisor. He has worked on numerous films, television series, and commercials during his career, including *How to Train Your Dragon, Penguins of Madagascar, Tell It to the Bees*, and many more. He has contributed to projects that have earned awards for their VFX. Bhuvnesh can be reached at bhuvnesh3danimator@gmail.com.

Acknowledgments

I'd like to thank some people for their assistance with writing this book. This includes my parents, from whom I inherited my drawing skills. They encouraged me to continue to find new ways to look at using Adobe applications. I am grateful for their assistance in selecting artwork for this book and doing some proofreading before I sent my notes to my editors. I thank Raymond Chow, my program coordinator at Langara College, for his suggestions and advice on what art and drawing in Photoshop and Illustrator should be about for students. I also thank my editors and technical reviewers at Apress. A special thank you to Spandana Chatterjee and Mark Powers for giving me the opportunity to continue my writing on topics that I enjoy, and I hope you, the readers, will too.

CHAPTER 1

Introduction and Pre-Photoshop Tools

Welcome to *Accurate Layer Selections Using Photoshop's Selection Tools*. As a graphic artist who enjoys drawing, I felt that it would be helpful to have a book explaining how to make your drawings portfolio ready and turn them into vector art. When I think about Photoshop, I sometimes focus too much on the digital photography aspect of the application or the fact that I can manipulate my photos using various filters to make them appear like drawings.

While these are all good skills to have, I also have hand-drawn sketches on paper. They may not be perfect, and they may have too many lines or smudges or were drawn on the wrong type of paper, but that doesn't mean that they can't be used in my portfolio or as preliminary drawings for a logo or an animation. This book focuses on using Photoshop tools beyond the eraser and paintbrush to clean up your artwork and sketches. The chapters look at a variety of Photoshop's selection tools, including the marquee and crop tools.

Note The projects for this book are at `www.github.com/apress/accurate-layer-selections-photoshop`.

Pre-Photoshop Tools for Drawing the Sketch and Importing Hardware

Before you open Photoshop, take a moment to consider what kind of hardware and software you might need to turn your sketches into a digital format. As an artist, some of

© Jennifer Harder 2022
J. Harder, *Accurate Layer Selections Using Photoshop's Selection Tools*,
https://doi.org/10.1007/978-1-4842-7493-4_1

these items may be very intuitive to you. Nevertheless, it is good to review them so that you achieve the desired results.

A Sketchbook

You may prefer a large or a small sketchbook depending on your style and what you like to draw. Refer to Figure 1-1.

Figure 1-1. *A graphic of a ring coil sketchbook and pencil*

Ideally, I recommend one with a ring coil at the top so that you can lay each page flat or cleanly tear it from the rings if you need a flatter surface while you are acquiring the digital scan, which I explain how to do shortly. Single sheets of paper and canvas are good as well. The paper should be a solid color, like white, gray, or black. White is ideal as it is easier to clean up in Photoshop.

I avoid using a lined notepad or graph paper with blue lines, for instance, because it's more difficult to extract the drawing from the page. Refer to Figure 1-2.

 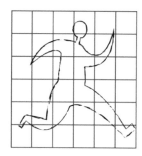 

Figure 1-2. *Drawing on paper that contains lines and one on the right without lines*

There are ways to work around this in Photoshop using adjustment layers, but it's best to start with blank paper to achieve the best results. Nevertheless, if you have sketches in this state, and the ink to draw the sketch is not blue, extraction is possible. This is covered in a later chapter. Also, paper that is so thin that it shows the drawing on the opposite side of the page is not ideal either. Refer to Figure 1-3.

Figure 1-3. *The paper is so thin the drawing on the opposite side of the page can be seen*

Remember, textured paper also scans some of the ridges, so paper with a smoother or matte finish is best.

There are many types of medium you can choose from to create your artwork: pencils, pens, acrylic paints, watercolors, oils, pastels, crayons, charcoal, and so on. Refer to Figure 1-4.

Figure 1-4. *A photo of various types of mediums you can use to create art and sketches*

When you create your drawing, make sure that the lines are not too faint and that you can see them clearly when you need to acquire the scan. Also, if you think that your medium might smear or flake if touched, you need to determine whether you need to spray a clear fixative over the sketch. Refer to Figure 1-5.

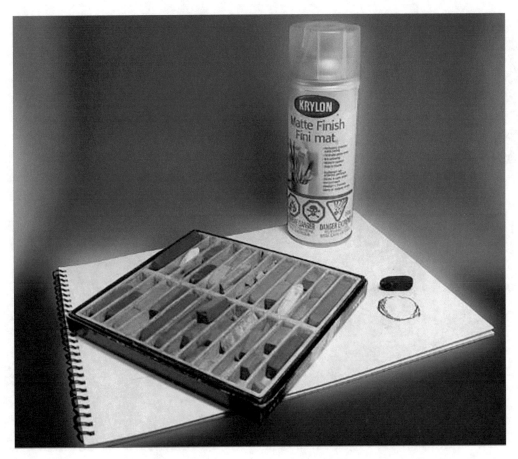

Figure 1-5. *A photo of a fixative to prevent smudging when using pastels*

You may need to acquire the image so that the surface of your art is not touched, which I discuss shortly.

If you're working with pencils or erasable ink, it's also good to have a kneadable eraser to prevent eraser shavings that can smudge your artwork. This clay eraser stays together and does not break off into little pieces as you erase areas of your sketch. Refer to Figure 1-6.

Figure 1-6. *A photo of various types of erasers that give off shavings, the kneadable one is on the right and does not smudge or give off shavings*

Other Materials and Methods

As an artist, you use a variety of other materials and methods to acquire your artwork. Refer to Figure 1-7.

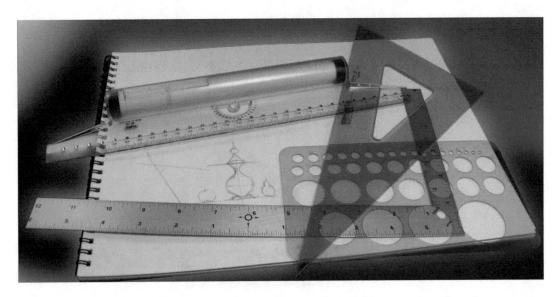

Figure 1-7. *A photo of various rulers and stencils used in creating sketches*

This may include rulers and straight edges. Keep in mind many of your sketch's design flaws can be corrected and enhanced in Photoshop. This book does not delve into any drawing methods. I present general information that a variety of artists can use with different skill levels and artistic abilities.

Once you have some sketches, you need to decide how you import the image digitally into your computer to begin working on it in Photoshop. Four affordable types of hardware come to mind.

- A flatbed scanner

- Photocopier or all-in-one printer/fax/scanner

- A digital camera

- Your smartphone camera

- An additional Adobe app

- A scanner bin

I'll talk about each of these next.

Flatbed Scanners and Scanner Basics

Most flatbed scanners can be acquired at an office supply store or online. For basic photos and artwork, flatbed scanners are affordable, and many brands are compatible with Photoshop. Refer to Figure 1-8.

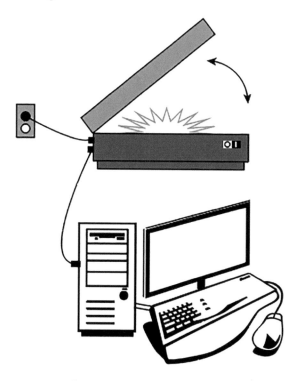

Figure 1-8. *An illustration of a flatbed scanner connected to the tower of a computer and wall power supply*

As with any electronic purchase, make sure you do some online research of the product first and check out the product's reviews before you buy. A flatbed scanner allows you to acquire the scan of a flat sheet of paper without the presence of outside light, which could cause color distortions to your artwork. Some flatbed scanners allow you to adjust the top lid to sit better on an art book with a higher raised surface. Other scanners have a hinged lid, so the bed might be exposed to outside light. Ultimately if you're dealing with a sketchbook that is either raised or has a binding that does not bend well, I recommend placing a dark cloth sheet over your scanner to prevent any outside light from coming into the scanner as well. Refer to Figure 1-9.

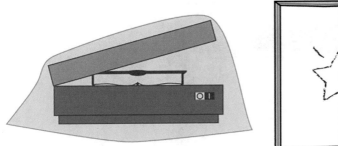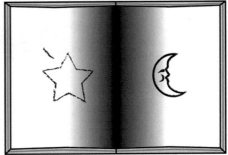

Figure 1-9. *An illustration of a flatbed scanner covered with a black cloth to prevent shadows and gutter shadow on a sketchbook near the spine*

With a book, you may get a gutter shadow between pages during the scan if it is not a coil bind that can lay flat. (Refer to Figure 1-9.) You may have to use the lid of the scanner and, with your hand, gently press down to press the book a bit flatter. Some scanners have software that can correct this gradient discoloration; however, you can use Photoshop and its adjustment layers afterward to clean up this and other issues, as shown in further chapters.

Scanners come in various sizes. The most affordable is usually a bit larger than a letter-size 8.5×11.7 inches. If you are planning to scan artwork larger than 11×17 inches, you need to check if the company you work for, your college, or your local print house might have a larger scanner you could use to scan the artwork. Later in this chapter, I provide some other options for how you can get around this issue. Alternately, you can scan your artwork in sections or separate images, but this requires you to "stitch" the image together again in Photoshop, as I show in Chapter 3. If you plan to do that, make sure you have enough area to move your artwork around the scanner to accommodate the paper size so that nothing collides or bends the paper. Refer to Figure 1-10.

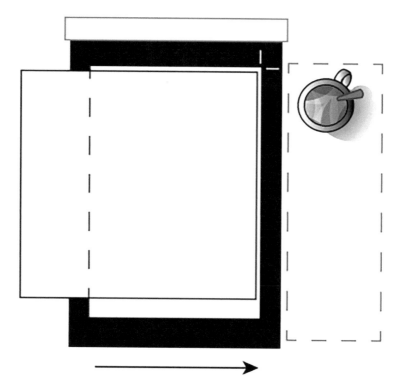

Figure 1-10. *Paper that is too large for the scanner needs to be moved to scan twice; here, a coffee cup in the way that should not be there, as they may collide*

If you have a scanner already, be aware that over time the light in the scanner ages. While it still may be operational, a scanner more than ten years old is very likely not the best for color photo scans where color is crucial for print or the web. However, artwork or sketches that are black and white, or where color reproduction is not critical, it may be fine to acquire images on an older scanner. I recommend that you upgrade your computer or monitor every five to ten years if it's within the budget. It's good to do the same with your scanner because the software and drivers may be out of date, and the scanner may cease to connect to your computer.

Scanner cleanliness is important. Make sure whatever scanner you are using that the scanner bed is free from dust and smudges. Refer to Figure 1-11.

Figure 1-11. *An illustration of a person cleaning the flatbed scanner glass and removing smudges and dust before use*

You can use a glasses lens cloth to clean the surface of the glass, and if required, a mild glass cleaner if recommended by the manufacture. Be careful not to scratch the glass since this can happen if you press down on the scanner lid and your booklet's coil has any rough metal edges. Also, you should not have your scanner in an area of high humidity as the glass surface inside the scanner can fog up, leaving streaks that are difficult to clean.

Take a moment to review your scanner's manual or online specs since scanners are built slightly differently depending on the manufacturer. Your scanner should be able to scan at least 300–600 dpi (dots per inch) or higher for good quality. Some scanners can also scan film slides or film negatives, but this is not a topic in this book. For this book, a scanner without that option is fine.

In Photoshop, to connect to your scanner, make sure your scanner is plugged in, turned on, and connected to a USB port and that your computer is recognizing the device and the drivers are up-to-date. Most scanners have a menu that you can access if you're unable to connect to Photoshop at first.

Adobe gives some helpful information on this topic of connecting to Photoshop. Depending on whether you are using a Mac or Windows computer go to `https://helpx.adobe.com/photoshop/using/acquiring-images-cameras-scanners.html`.

However, let me demonstrate how the typical image acquisition procedure might go, though there may be slight differences depending on your computer or scanner version. I demonstrate the steps I use for my scanner in Photoshop CC 2021 on a Windows 10 computer.

SCANNING A SKETCH

1. In Photoshop, go to File ➤ Import ➤ WIA Support. Refer to Figure 1-12.

Figure 1-12. *WIA Support dialog box*

You are presented with a dialog box where you use the Wizard or Windows Image Acquisition (WIA) to determine where you will place your scans. You can also use this area for compatible digital cameras if you use a USB cable to connect. Browse to the destination folder where the images will be stored and then enable the two options.

a. Open the acquired images in Photoshop.

b. Create a unique subfolder using today's date so that you can review them later. Refer to Figure 1-13.

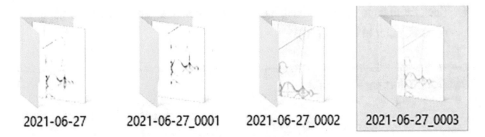

2021-06-27   2021-06-27_0001   2021-06-27_0002   2021-06-27_0003

Figure 1-13. *Subfolders containing individual scans*

2. Click the Start button to move to the next dialog box, or click the Cancel button
    to exit and not save your changes.

3. If you click the Start button, you are presented with the Select Device dialog
    box. It displays the selected scanner and its properties, which vary depending
    on the manufacturer and driver setup. If you have an older scanner, make sure
    that your drivers and software are up-to-date so the scanner is recognized.
    Refer to Figure 1-14.

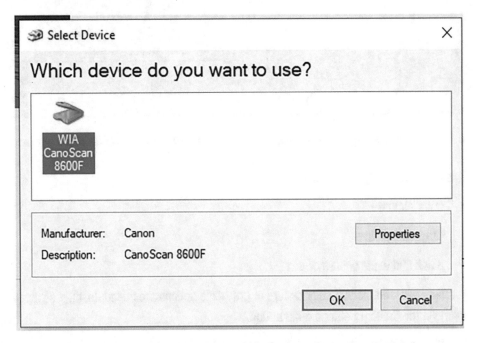

Figure 1-14. *Select Device dialog box where you can choose a digital camera or
scanner that you want to acquire images from*

4. Click OK to go to the Scan dialog box. You are presented with various scanning options. Refer to Figure 1-15.

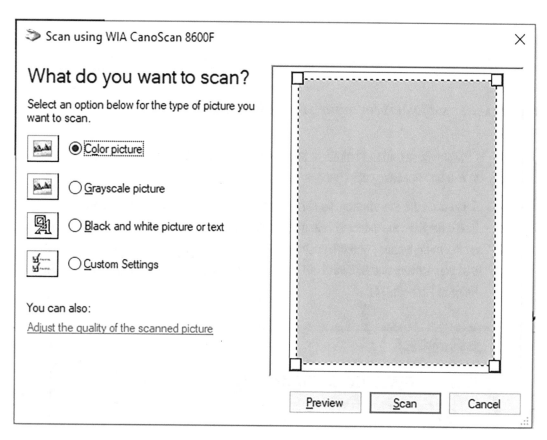

Figure 1-15. *Scan using WIA (scanner name) dialog box with its various options*

For this demonstration, I scanned a

- Color picture

- Grayscale picture

- Black and white picture or text

In most cases, the default color picture or grayscale options are adequate, but I selected them via the Custom Settings radio button.

5. Click the **Adjust the quality of the scanned picture** link. It brings up the Advanced Properties dialog box, which provides more options. You can adjust the resolution from 300 dpi (dots per inch) to 600 dpi and the brightness and

contrast. I generally leave those settings at 0 and do that type of appearance correction in Photoshop. But depending on your scanner, and after some experimentation, you may want to adjust these sliders or other settings available to you. Refer to Figure 1-16.

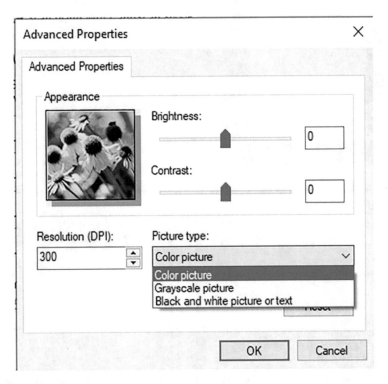

Figure 1-16. *Advanced Properties dialog box and various options*

6. In the Picture type drop-down menu, select your choice, and click OK to confirm.

7. Place the image you want to scan face down on the scanner bed, close the lid, and press the Preview button in the Scanner WIA dialog box. Refer to Figure 1-17.

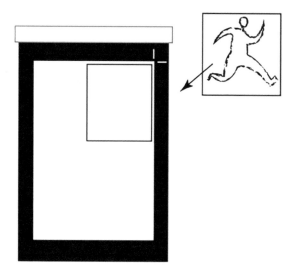

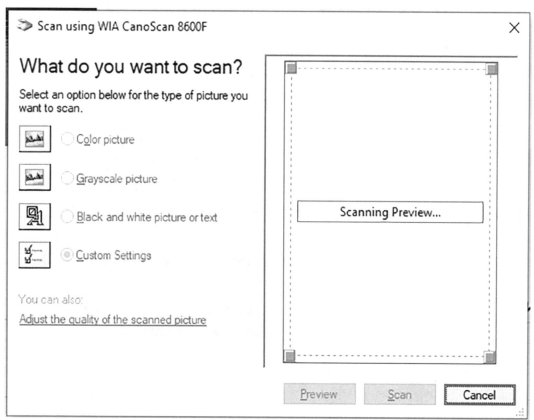

Figure 1-17. *The sketch is placed on the scanner face down, and then the Preview button in the dialog box is pressed to get a preview of the sketch*

The preview does not create a copy of the image. It is stored in memory until you are ready to press Scan. If you notice that your image is a bit slanted or rotated, open the lid, move the paper so it's against an edge, close the lid, and press the Preview button again. Some scanners recognize your artwork's area and use bounding box handles to crop or marquee to fit around that area, so you don't have to scan the whole bed. You should have the option to drag the handles to the area you want to scan. Some scanners allow you to scan more than one area on the page into separate files by allowing you to draw more than one bounding box. Refer to Figure 1-18.

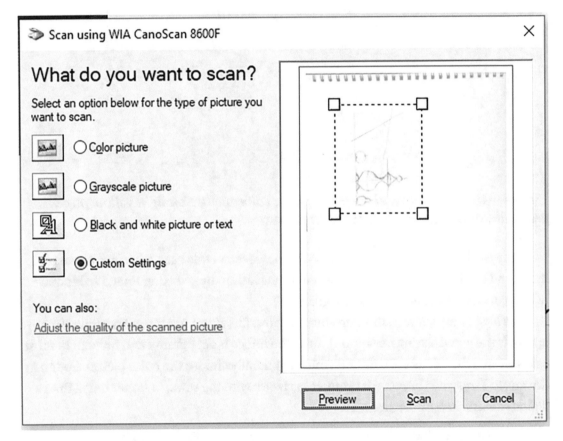

Figure 1-18. *A preview of the sketch appears. Use the bounding box to crop the sketch*

Scanner Color Modes

Different file color modes are generated via basic or advanced properties, depending on the setting you choose. For my scanner, a color picture produces an 8-bit bitmap file in RGB color mode. The file is generally larger than a camera .jpg file, but it is as good as a .tiff file. It does not lose quality like a .jpg would and can be stored for archival purposes. Refer to Figure 1-19.

Figure 1-19. *Scanner results left to right: a color picture on light yellow paper, grayscale, and black and white picture or text*

A grayscale picture produces a .bmp file; however, in this case, the color mode is Index and 8-bit. You can always convert it in Photoshop by selecting Image ➤ Mode ➤ RGB color from the menu. Refer to Figure 1-19.

The black-and-white picture produces a .bmp file; Bitmap is the color mode. This option is the worst setting for my sketches. The image is very grainy and broken. In most cases, even if the image is black and white, I generally choose the color picture option in Advanced Properties because it produces artwork with the same or better detail than a digital camera. Refer to Figure 1-19.

1. Once you have made your Settings choices, click the Scan button. The file is transferred and appears in Photoshop. It is saved in the destination subfolder that you set up earlier.

2. Check that 300 dpi is selected in the Image ➤ Image Size dialog box.

3. Click the Cancel button to exit the dialog box since you are not making any size adjustments. Refer to Figure 1-20.

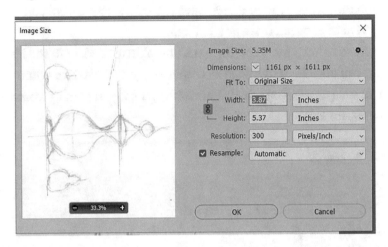

Figure 1-20. *Checking the resolution of the document using Image Size*

Note   If your scan is sideways, you can select Image ➤ Image Rotation and rotate the image 90° Clockwise or Counter Clockwise. Refer to Figure 1-21.

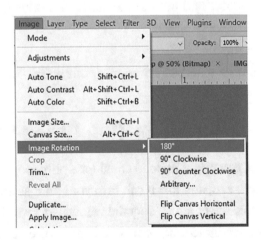

Figure 1-21. *Image Rotation menu in Image drop-down*

As you can see, acquiring an image of your sketch via a flatbed scanner is very easy. Repeat these steps if you have any additional sketches to scan.

Saving Scanned Files

At this point, you may want to go to File ➤ Save (Ctrl/Cmd+S) to save your scanned files to a USB flash drive or external drive as a backup.

You do not have to keep the .bmp format if you plan to work with the file in Photoshop. You can always go to Image ➤ Duplicate and click OK to confirm. Then go to File ➤ Save to save as a .tiff or a .psd (Photoshop) file if you plan to work with multiple layers. Refer to Figure 1-22.

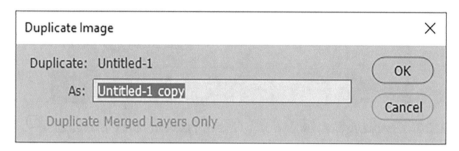

Figure 1-22. *Duplicate Image dialog box*

Note   You may be presented with options to save to your computer or the cloud. I usually save to my computer and then to the cloud or a drive later as a backup.

Click Save to confirm the file.

If you don't have room for a flatbed scanner in your office, consider other options.

A Photocopier or an All-in-One Office Printer

With limited office space, you might instead consider a photocopier or an office all-in-one printer that can copy, scan, and fax. It can turn your images into a PDF file format that could contain multiple pages stored together. However, I would not recommend using the auto document feeder to load your sketches into the machine since that could cause a jam and smear and ruin your artwork. Refer to Figure 1-23.

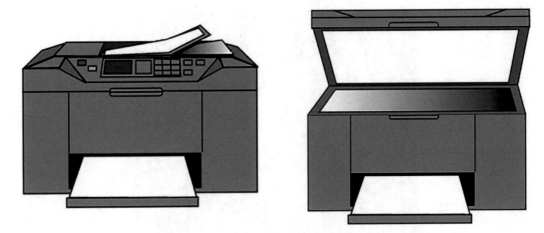

Figure 1-23. *An illustration of an all-in-one, scan/fax/print, and lid top to scan your drawings*

An all-in-one scanner with a lid that you can lift to place the scan on the glass as you do with a flatbed is best. Scan the artwork using the basic guidelines I described earlier and following the device's manual. You may be able to save the image on a USB drive or send it wirelessly to a computer drive on your network to store in a folder on your computer.

A Digital Camera

You can use a digital camera for larger artwork such as murals or art that cannot fit in your scanner. You may have to experiment with a few shots until you get the best quality.

For example, if the camera needs to be close or the surface is shiny, do not use a flash because it causes a reflection, and the image disappears. Use a tripod to avoid shaky images, even if your camera has an autostabilizer. Set up the image in a vertical position, or see if your tripod has an option where the camera can point straight down on the table without tipping over when taking the picture. Refer to Figure 1-24.

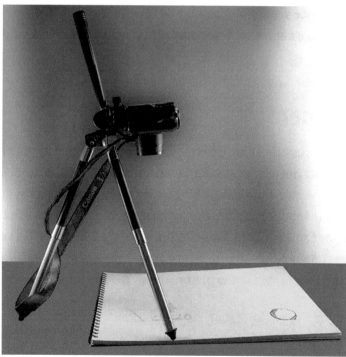

Figure 1-24. *Photo examples of how you could use a tripod and a digital camera as a scanner for larger sketches*

Your camera should be at least 12 megapixels or higher. You can also experiment on a macro setting as this may produce a better-quality resolution. The image is likely a .jpg (JPEG) in RGB color mode and 8-bit. To acquire the image, Adobe describes using a USB port drive connected to the camera (see `https://helpx.adobe.com/photoshop/using/acquiring-images-cameras-scanners.html`).

You could also remove the camera's memory card, insert it into your computer drive, and copy the images into a folder onto your computer.

Your Smartphone Camera, an Additional Adobe App, and a Scanner Bin

You can also use your smartphone in combination with the Adobe Scan app for mobile scanning and Scanner Bin or Scanbox, which you can purchase (or build cheaply).

Smartphones have a built-in camera app that can store and import photos and add them to the cloud. Adobe and other companies offer mobile scanning apps that you can use to scan documents. Adobe Scan comes included with your Creative Cloud subscription. Adobe provides instructions on setting up a link on your phone so you can download the app and use it for scanning. Refer to Figure 1-25.

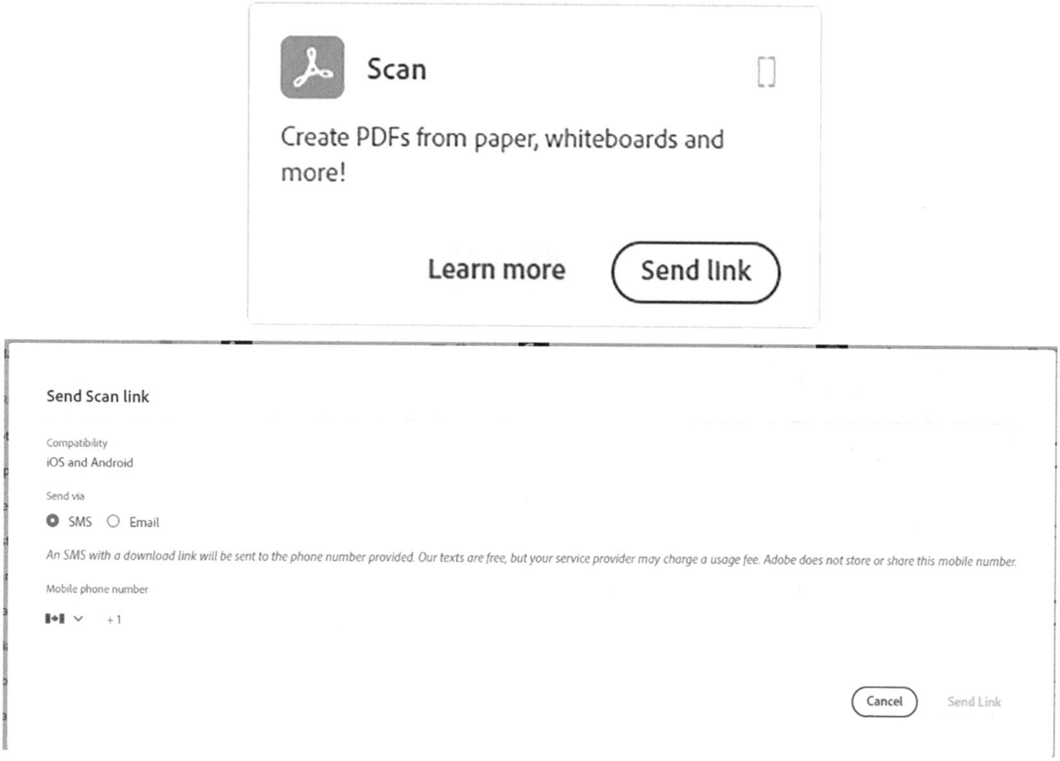

Figure 1-25. *Adobe Scan app that is part of your Creative Cloud subscription and can be added to your mobile phone or tablet*

You can find those instructions on the following web pages.

- `https://helpx.adobe.com/mobile-apps/help/adobe-scan-faq.html`

- `www.adobe.com/devnet-docs/adobescan/android/en/`

- `www.adobe.com/devnet-docs/adobescan/ios/en/`

In combination with the app, I suggest that you either make or purchase a scan box or scanner bin since this allows you to keep your smartphone steady and at the correct distance from the artwork so it does not become smudged as it might with pastels. You take the picture through a small hole in the top of the box. Refer to Figure 1-26.

Figure 1-26. *A scanner box keeps your smartphone steady and at the right distance when you take a picture*

Also, the scanner bin has several advantages. Like a scanner, it can block excess light from coming in on multiple sides, and in most cases, the box is collapsible, so it can be easily stored and takes up less space than a scanner. With the Adobe Scan app, the file is saved as a PDF and uploaded to your Adobe Document Cloud account, and you can retrieve it from there later. However, with the Mobile Scanner app, although you can resize images, apparently, there is no settings option for the scan resolution, so it is likely dependent on whatever your smartphone's resolution allows.

Note   A similar form of Adobe Scan is also available via Adobe Acrobat DC Pro. You can also access your scanner through the Create PDF or Scan & OCR features if you do not have access to Photoshop and only want to create PDF files. Refer to Figure 1-27.

Figure 1-27. *When you open Acrobat DC Pro on your computer, you have access to the following tools and can connect to your scanner*

Unlike the mobile app, you can reset Default Settings to a higher resolution because you are connecting to your scanner.

Although many settings are similar to Photoshop's, I am not delving deeper into Acrobat DC in this book. Should you want to explore this option on your own, refer to `https://helpx.adobe.com/acrobat/using/scan-documents-pdf.html`.

I have presented you with various options for acquiring a digital image of your sketches, and the choice is up to you.

Summary

If you do not have a flatbed scanner, I recommend researching your options to import your sketches and artwork into Photoshop. After you decide, practice acquiring images a few times until you feel comfortable with your workflow. Store your high-resolution images in a folder on your computer and a folder on an external drive for backup. Then you can move on to Chapter 2, which looks at how to clean up your scans in Photoshop. And from there, you work on using basic marquee tools and crop tools.

CHAPTER 2

Basic Photoshop Tools

This chapter gives an overview of the basic Photoshop panels, tools, adjustment layers, and filters to clean up sketches. It also explains how to set up a workspace so that you can work efficiently.

Getting Started in Photoshop

After you have scanned your artwork and acquired it as a digital file, you are ready to start working with a copy of the file in Photoshop. Use the projects in the Chapter 2 folder.

If you have an Adobe Creative Cloud subscription, then you should have this application available to you. Go to your Creative Cloud Desktop, choose All Apps, and click the Open button to start the app. In this book, I use CC 2022 or Version 23. Refer to Figure 2-1.

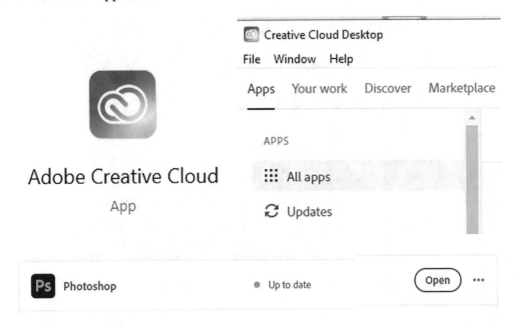

Figure 2-1. *Search for Photoshop in the Adobe Creative Cloud Desktop console*

J. Harder, *Accurate Layer Selections Using Photoshop's Selection Tools*,
https://doi.org/10.1007/978-1-4842-7493-4_2

Note   If you have an older computer, such as one that updated from a Windows
7 to 10, Photoshop version 22 or later may not run on your older graphic card.
Whether you have a macOS or Windows computer, check the system requirements
if the program is not opening or if you receive an error message after installation.
For more information, go to `https://helpx.adobe.com/photoshop/`
`system-requirements.html`.

Once Photoshop is open, select File ➤ Open and locate the scan2_1.psd file in the
Chapter 2 folder. I use this file for some basic touch up at the beginning of the lesson,
and then we'll use other images later.

I save a sketch file as .psd (Photoshop documents) if I plan to have multiple layers in
the document before I flatten the image. I use a .jpg copy of it in Illustrator for tracing.

Setting up the Workspace and Learning the Basic Tools

The workspace I use is Window ➤ Workspace ➤ Essentials (Default). Refer to Figure 2-2.

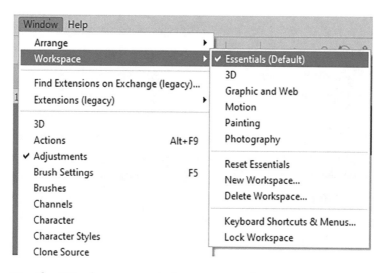

Figure 2-2. *Use the Window menu to locate a workspace*

You can always reset this workspace by choosing Reset Essentials. Later you may choose a different workspace that fits with your workflow, such as painting or creating a New Workspace.

Panels

The panels that you should see are from the Window menu.

Adjustments

The Adjustments panel features the various adjustment layers that you can add to your Layers panel to assist you in removing unwanted discolorations or marks in your artwork. You look at this in more detail later in the chapter. Refer to Figure 2-3.

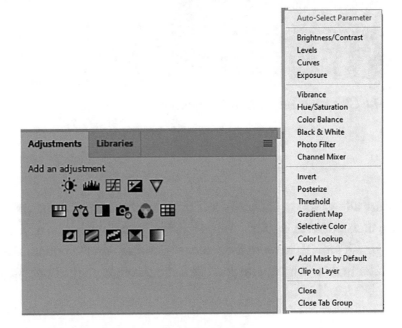

Figure 2-3. *The Adjustments panel and its menu*

Channels

The Channels panel displays your documents in various color channels, including RGB (red, green, blue). However, it can also store saved Alpha Channels or selections which I explain in Chapter 11. Refer to Figure 2-4.

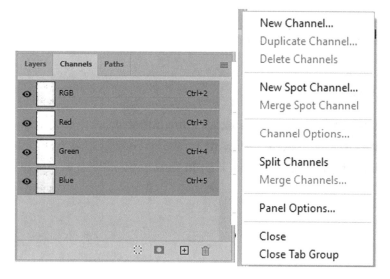

Figure 2-4. *The Channels panel and its menu*

Color

The Color feature allows you to choose colors that you can use with the Eyedropper tool (I) and are then stored in the foreground/background swatch area of your Tools panel. Use the Brush tool (B) to paint that color somewhere on the image. These tools are discussed later in this chapter, and you use them throughout the book. Refer to Figure 2-5.

Figure 2-5. *The Color panel and its menu*

History

The History panel records the various steps you have taken while working on your document. If you need to undo or go back several steps, you can open this panel and click a step higher on the list, and the image you are working on returns to that state. Likewise, pressing Ctrl/Cmd+Z or Edit ➤ Undo also moves the History panel up the list. Shift+Ctrl/Cmd+Z or Edit ➤ Redo moves you down the list to your last change. Refer to Figure 2-6.

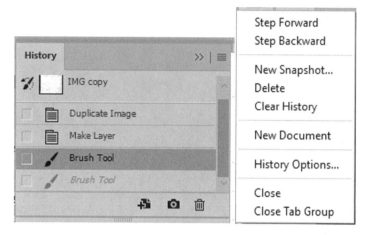

Figure 2-6. *The History panel and its menu*

Layers

The Layers panel displays the layers and layer adjustments within your .psd document. The purpose of these layers could be for color correction or to cover, using the Brush tool, small unwanted imperfections, or marks in your document. When a document is open, it generally has the background layer. You can double-click this layer and change it to layer 0 if you need to move it up (above) or down (below) another layer. Before you use the layer in Illustrator on a copy of your .psd file, you can choose Flatten Image from the Layers panel menu so that it is a small single background layer file. Then you can save (Ctrl/Cmd+S) this copy as a .tiff for printing or as a .jpg should you plan to place or embed it in Illustrator to use for tracing over. You see this later in Part 4 of the book. Refer to Figure 2-7.

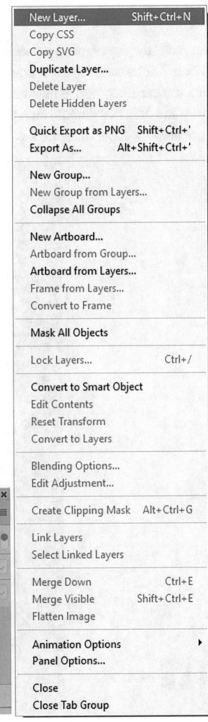

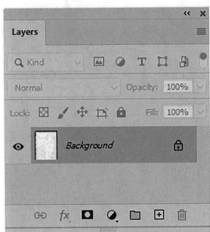

Figure 2-7. *The Layers panel and its menu*

Libraries

The Libraries panel displays various colors, styles, and graphics that you have created or acquired from Adobe stock. You can drag a layer into the libraries and save it as a graphic. Then you can open Adobe Illustrator. In the Window ➤ Libraries panel, you can locate a library and drag that graphic onto your artboard and place it. This is another way to import your artwork. Refer to Figure 2-8.

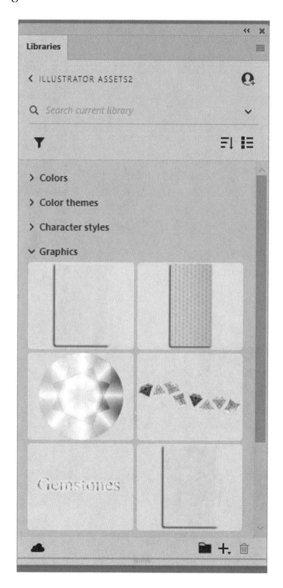

 Illustrator

Figure 2-8. *The Libraries panel looks the same in Illustrator as it does in Photoshop*

If you want to learn more about Creative Cloud libraries, you can check out my videos on this topic.

- **Introduction to Adobe's CC Libraries with Photoshop**

  https://link.springer.com/video/10.1007/978-1-4842-6000-5

- **Introduction to Adobe's CC Libraries in Illustrator and InDesign**

  https://link.springer.com/video/10.1007/978-1-4842-6092-0

- **Advanced Features for Adobe's CC Libraries**

  https://link.springer.com/video/10.1007/978-1-4842-6091-3

Keep in mind that some of the graphics have slightly changed since 2020, but this resource gives you a basic overview should you want to explore this topic further.

Gradients

The Gradients panel displays various gradients that are available or ones that you have created and saved. The book does not focus on this panel. But, if you want to use your selections later, such as the ones you create in Chapter 10 using a shape or Pen tool (P) to fill an area on a new layer with a gradient, this is where you find various gradients. Refer to Figure 2-9

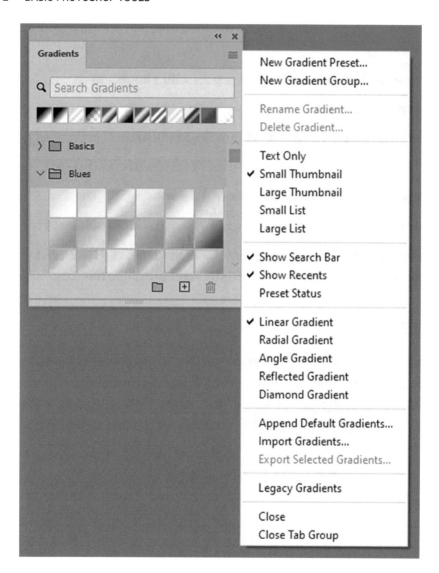

Figure 2-9. The Gradients panel and its menu

Patterns

The Patterns panel displays various patterns that are available or ones that you have created and saved. This book does not focus on this panel. But if you want to use your selections later, such as the ones you create in Chapter 10 in Photoshop using a shape or Pen tool (P) to fill an area on a new layer with a pattern to enhance your sketch, this is where you find various patterns. Refer to Figure 2-10.

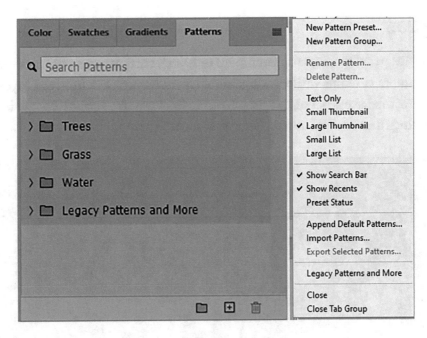

Figure 2-10. *The Patterns panel and its menu*

Paths

The Paths panel displays various vector paths you can create with your Pen tool (P) and save in this area. These paths can later be changed into selections and masks. I talk about this further in Chapters 10, 11, and 12. Refer to Figure 2-11.

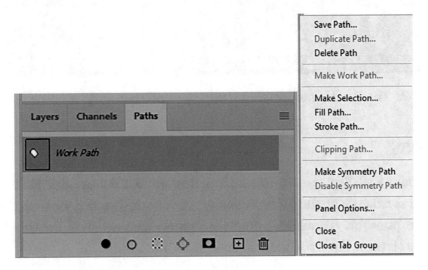

Figure 2-11. *The Paths panel and its menu*

Properties

The Properties panel displays the document or layer's current properties. For example, if your document contains various adjustment layers, as you click from one layer to another using the Layers panel, the properties in the Properties panel change to reveal various settings that you can adjust. Refer to Figure 2-12.

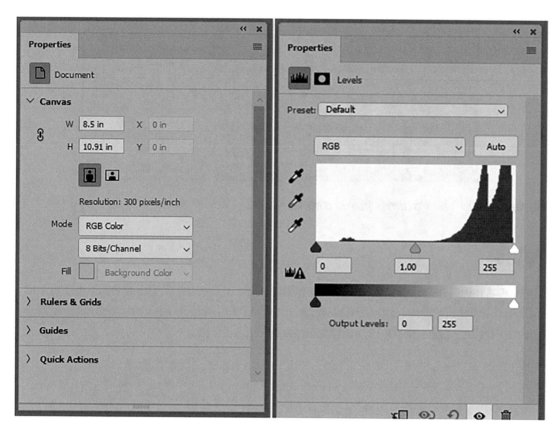

Figure 2-12. *The Properties panel and various options*

Swatches

The Swatches panel displays various swatches that are available or ones that you have created and saved. As with the Color panel, you can use the Eyedropper tool (I) to load a swatch into your Tools panel foreground/background and use your Brush tool (B) to paint on your layer or background layer. Refer to Figure 2-13.

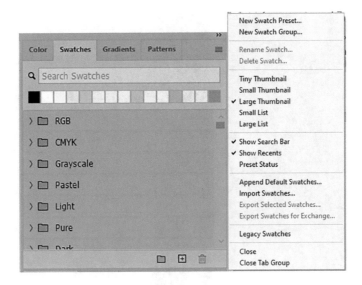

Figure 2-13. *The Swatches panel and its menu*

Options

The options are in a bar below the main drop-down menu. It shows the various options of each of your tools. Let's look at this in more detail in a moment but depending on what tool from the Tools panel you choose, your options change. Some tools are not in the Tools panel, only in the menu; for example, Edit ➤ Transform ➤ Scale. Refer to Figure 2-14.

Figure 2-14. *The options panel changes depending on the tool that is selected*

Tools

The Tools panel displays many of the tools that are available in Photoshop. Their options are mostly in the options panel and a few additional panels and menus for some. I discuss some of the key tools in this chapter. Refer to Figure 2-15.

Figure 2-15. *The Tools panel*

For now, let's stay with the Essential (default) workspace and introduce a few additional panels from the Window menu as required.

Note   You can mouse drag and dock these panels in different locations around Photoshop. Or, from the menu, choose Close if it is not needed in your workflow. Refer to Figure 2-16.

Figure 2-16. *Use the close option in the panel's menu to close it*

Working with the Basic Tools

The scan2_1.psd file is open, and you do not want to override it. Go to Image ➤ Duplicate and copy it. Refer to Figure 2-17.

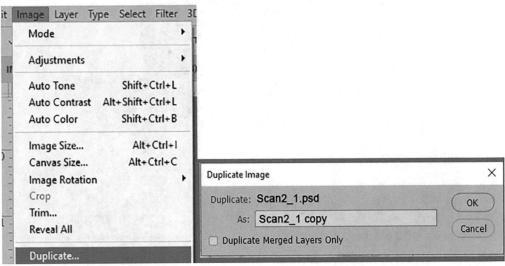

Figure 2-17. *The images scan was duplicated in Photoshop to preserve the original file*

Click OK to the dialog box message of creating a copy. You now use it to practice with the tools. Use the History panel to undo steps if you need to revert and try again.

Many of the tools used in this book are in the Window ➤ Tools panel. Refer to Figure 2-18.

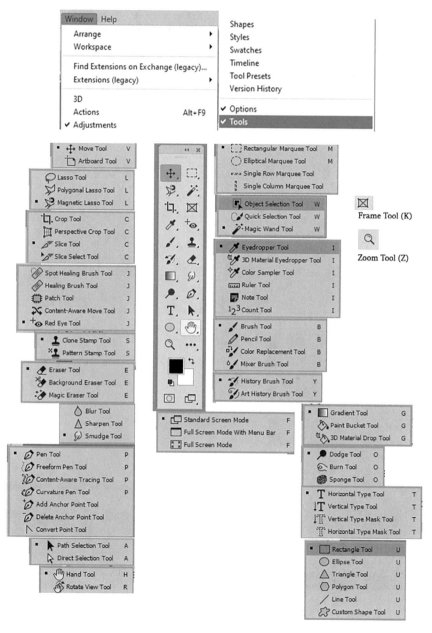

Figure 2-18.   *Window ➤ Tools presents many tool options*

As you can see there, are many tools. However, unlike when working with photos, not all are necessary for artwork and sketches.

Next, let's discuss the key tools that you need to work with.

Move Tool (V)

This tool is for moving images around on a selected layer in the Layers panel.

If you are only working in a file that in the Layers panel contains a background layer, the Move tool does not operate when you try to click and drag across it with the mouse. Refer to Figure 2-19.

Figure 2-19. *The Move tool*

The layer is locked. Instead, you get an informational warning that explains that this is a background layer and that you cannot move it or change its stacking order, blending mode or opacity. However, if you convert it to a normal layer, you can move it along with the ability to change its attributes. Refer to Figure 2-20.

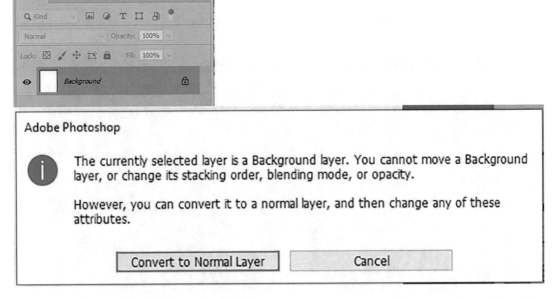

Figure 2-20. *Trying to move a locked background layer with the Move tool results in an informational message appearing*

If you click Convert to Normal Layer, it changes to layer 0, and you can freely move the layer in your file with the Move tool (V). When layer 0 is moved, you see a checkerboard pattern where no layer is present. Refer to Figure 2-21.

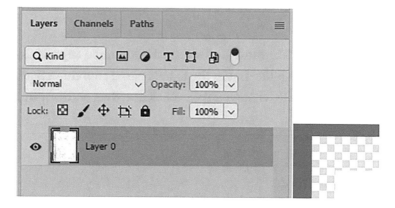

Figure 2-21. *When the layer is moved, it turns to layer 0, and you may see some areas behind it where there are no pixels*

As with most tools, they come with additional options in the options panel.

Move Tool Options

Look from left to right on the options panel. Refer to Figure 2-22.

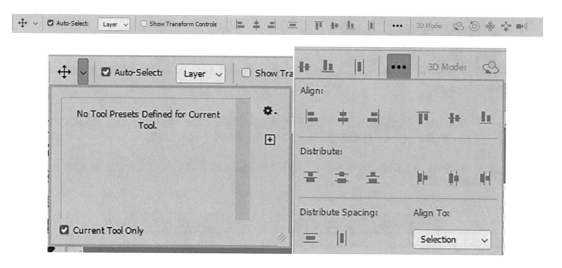

Figure 2-22. *Move tool options panel*

The **presets tool** drop-down menu lets you create additional saved settings. You can then use the preset in another project file. The preset tool area is blank by default, but you can add a New Tool preset by clicking the + icon. Name it and click OK. Refer to Figure 2-23.

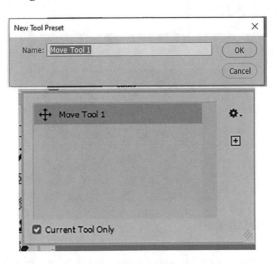

Figure 2-23. *Create a preset for the Move tool by clicking the plus symbol*

Add it to the list or manage your preset setting by clicking the gear on the right and revealing further menu options such as delete tool preset. Refer to Figure 2-24.

Figure 2-24. *Use the gear menu to manage your presets*

Note   If you want to view your presets in a separate panel, choose Window ➤ Tool Presets. The menu on the upper right of the panel has the same management options. Refer to Figure 2-25.

Figure 2-25.   *Tool Presets panel*

In the options panel, the **Auto-Select: Layer check box** lets you click the part of an exposed layer that you see on your artboard and select it rather and having to Ctrl/ Cmd-click the layer. The other option in the drop-down menu is a group in which, rather than selecting a single layer, you can auto-select a group folder that contains layers in the Layers panel. Refer to Figure 2-26.

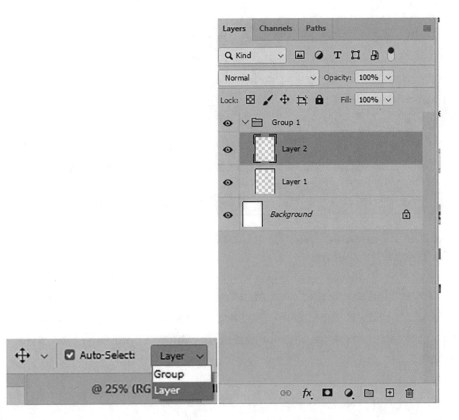

Figure 2-26. *Auto-select from the Move tool options and a group layer in the Layers panel*

Show Transform Controls adds a bounding box around the rectangular image layer. This is an alternative way to enter the Edit ➤ Transform Scale or Rotate options. Use such key commands as the Shift key to scale disproportionately and without the Shift key proportionately. Click the Commit button (the check mark) to confirm or the Cancel button (the slashed circle) to cancel the transformation and return to the dialog box options. Refer to Figure 2-27.

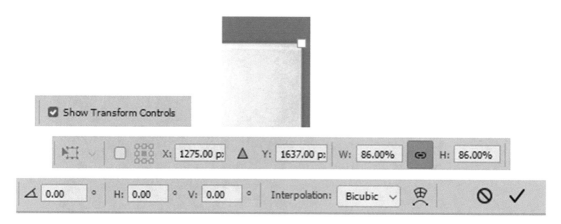

Figure 2-27. *When show Transform Controls is checked for the Move tool, you can enter the Transform options*

The next section in this tool's option is useful when you have two or more layers to select and **align** them, for example, either all to the left, center, or right. The dotted ellipse (…) reveals some more alignment and distribution options as well. Refer to Figure 2-28.

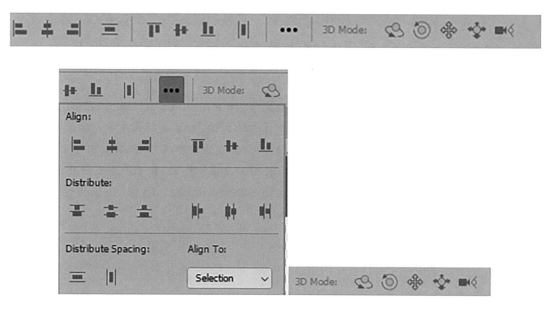

Figure 2-28. *Move tool, alignment layer options, and 3D mode*

3D Mode is for working with 3D files for rotation and movement, but it is grayed out. Although this topic is too vast to cover and does not apply to this book, you can check out a video that I created on this topic to create basic 3D drawings in Photoshop and Illustrator for a children's book. Refer to "Introduction to 3D Design with Adobe Photoshop and Illustrator" (**Apress,** 2019) (`https://link.springer.com/video/10.1007/978-1-4842-5396-0`).

3D options are gradually being transferred from newer versions of Photoshop to Adobe Substance for a more advanced experience.

Eyedropper Tool (I)

This tool selects colors in your artwork that you need to match so that you can later use your Brush tool to fill in gaps and breaks in your sketches. Click a line in this sketch or your sketch with the color picker. The color appears in the tool panel's foreground and background color picker (X). Refer to Figure 2-29.

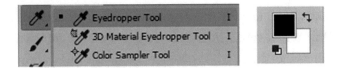

Figure 2-29. *The Eyedropper tool*

Eyedropper Tool Options

From left to right, besides creating a **preset**, the options panel allows you to do an exact or general **sample size**, where to **sample**, and **shows a ring of the area** when sampling. Refer to Figure 2-30.

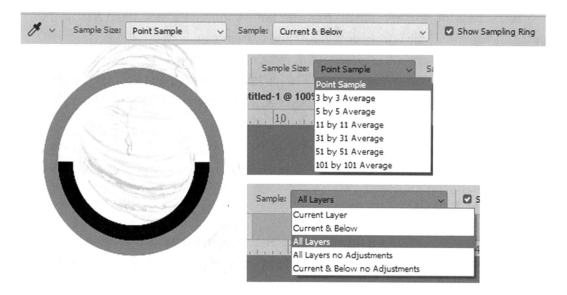

Figure 2-30. *Eyedropper tool options*

Generally, for sketches, I leave it at the **Sample Size: Point Sample** setting to get the exact color of the line in that spot. The 3 by 3 Average option samples the surrounding pixels. Higher numbers like the 51 by 51 Average option samples a broader range of pixels. I use Sample Current Layer if there is one. If there are multiple layers to sample, I use **Current & Below** or **All Layers**. Note that you can use **All Layers no Adjustments** if you are not getting an accurate color sample when those layers are present.

Brush Tool (B)

Using the Brush tool with the Tools panel foreground/background color picker (X) helps clean up breaks in artwork lines or painting over discolorations that you want to hide. Refer to Figure 2-31.

Figure 2-31. *The Brush tool*

Note   If you have a Wacom stylus, you can use this instead of the mouse to clean up your brush strokes.

If you want to paint over some of the yellow areas of this scan, press the (D) key first on your keyboard to reset to the default of black and white and then the (X) key to bring the white to the foreground in your Tools panel. If you need to switch back to black press (X) again to toggle. Refer to Figure 2-32.

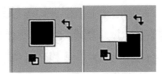

Figure 2-32. *Switching foreground and background colors in the Tools panel*

Brush Tool Options

Look from left to right in the options panel. You can create presets and adjust the **preset picker** drop-down menu. Refer to Figure 2-33.

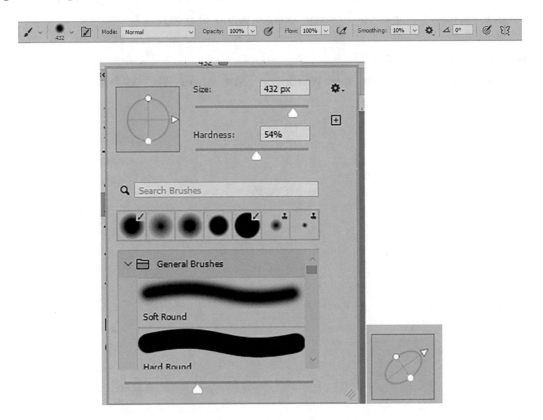

Figure 2-33. *Options for the Brush tool and the Brush Preset Picker, adjusting the roundness of the brush*

This lets you set the brush size (1 to 5000 px) and fuzziness or hardness (0%–100%), the angle (0°–360°), and the roundness.

Tip   Smaller-sized bushes are good for detail work and fine lines. Certain angles and hardness allow you to get a closer, clean edge. Use larger brushes for a larger area you need to cover quickly. 100% gives a clean edge for hardness adjustments, but the line you create may not blend in well. A hardness of 0% is very soft but may make the line too fuzzy and appear blurry and not give you an accurate trace when brought into Illustrator.

You can also search for default brushes or brushes that you created. These bushes you can access through the Brushes panel and zoom in to at a larger scale, and you can click them to select the one you want. Then click the artboard with your paintbrush to start panting or click the drop-down to collapse it and start to paint.

Brush Settings and Brushes Panel

The access the brush settings, open Window ➤ Brushes and Window ➤ Brushes Settings. Refer to Figure 2-34.

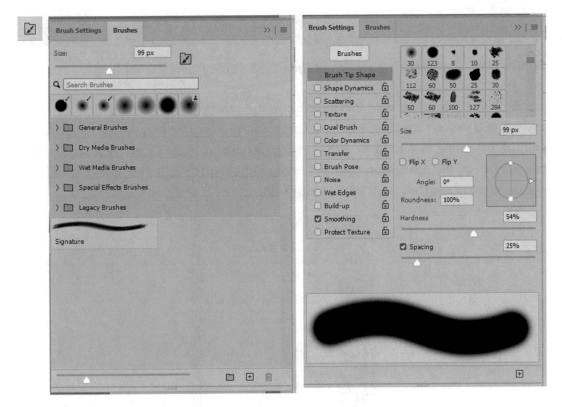

Figure 2-34. *Brushes and Brush Settings panel*

The Brushes panel acts as a library of all the default brushes that are stored in your application. You can load additional brushes that you created, or someone has supplied to you. The Brush settings let you manipulate a brush and add additional features, such as brush tip shape, shape dynamics, scattering, texture, dual brush, color dynamics, transfer, brush pose, noses, wet edges, smoothing, and protect texture. When Brush Tip Shape is enabled, you can see some additional options, these you did not see in the options menu, such as flipping on the horizontal (X) or vertical (y) axis and adjusting the spacing. Likewise, the other setting can be enabled when you check the check box beside them. You can then create a new brush from the Brush Settings panel by clicking the plus symbol in the lower right and adding it to the panel.

Brush Tool Options (continued)

Look at the options panel. Refer to Figure 2-35.

Figure 2-35. *Looking at a section of the Brush Tool options panel*

Mode is a type of blending that affects how the paint goes over other painted areas and can add various artistic effects. It controls how pixels in the image are affected by a painting or editing tool. It works with the original base color, the blend color applied by the paint, or as you can see later, the adjustment layer and the combination of the blend is known as the *result color.* Refer to Figure 2-36.

Figure 2-36. *Brush Blending modes*

The options are Normal (the default), Dissolve, Behind, Clear, Darken, Multiply, Color Burn, Linear Burn, Darker Color, Lighten, Screen, Color Dodge, Linear Dodge (Add), Lighter Color, Overlay, Soft Light, Hard Light, Vivid Light, Linear Light, Pin Light, Hard Mix, Difference, Exclusion, Subtract, Divide, Hue, Saturation, Color, and Luminosity.

For this book, while you can experiment with different blends if you are trying to fill in gaps, leaving it at Normal mode is the best to keep the original paint color.

For more information on how paint affects the background image, go to `https://helpx.adobe.com/photoshop/using/blending-modes.html`.

A brush's Opacity can be set from 0% to 100%. When painting solid lines that are to be traced, I leave the opacity at 100%. Refer to Figure 2-37.

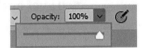

Figure 2-37. *Opacity Setting in the Brush tool options panel*

The icon next to Opacity is for pressure. *Always use pressure with opacity.* When it is turned off, the brush preset controls the pressure.

Flow can also be set from 0% to 100%. I usually leave it at 100% when cleaning up line art. Refer to Figure 2-38.

Figure 2-38. *Flow and Airbrush options in the Brush tool options panel*

Enable airbrush style build up effects add more paint if the mouse button is held down longer. I usually leave this off.

Depending on the brush you are using, you can set the **smoothing** for the stroke higher than the default of 10% if you find that the brush strokes appear to be shaky. After adjusting the percentage, you can find additional smoothing settings in the **gear icon**. Refer to Figure 2-39.

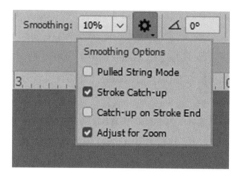

Figure 2-39. *Smoothing options in the Brush tool options panel*

According to Adobe these options can enhance the painting experience and allow for less jittery and smoother strokes while zoomed in or out on your artwork. You can find at this link more technical information on the following smoothing options:

`https://helpx.adobe.com/photoshop/using/whats-new/2018.html`

- Pulled String mode

- Stroke Catch-up

- Catch-up on Stroke End

- Adjust for Zoom

If you did not set the angle of your brush in the Brush presets picker, you can do that in **Angle**. Refer to Figure 2-40.

Figure 2-40. *Angle, pressure, and symmetry paint options for the Brush tool*

The target-shaped button is Always Use Pressure for Size. However, when it is turned off, the Brush presets control the pressure.

Note   The last option in the Brush option panel (looks like a butterfly) is Symmetry paint. Although not a topic in this book, options in this drop-down menu can create unusual symmetrical patterns, such as mandalas. Remember to return to normal brush mode and always click Symmetry Off when you are done to make the guide lines disappear. Refer to Figures 2-40 and 2-41.

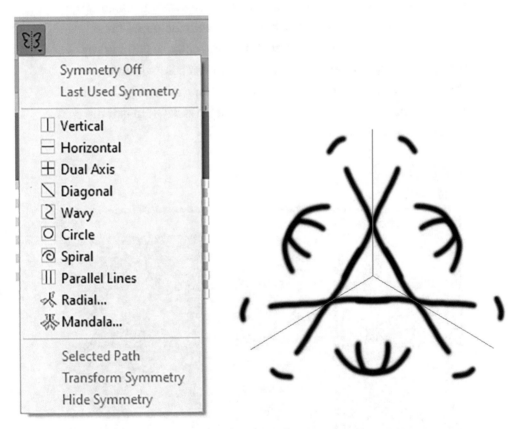

Figure 2-41. *Symmetry paint options and an example for the Brush tool*

The Brush tool has many different options that allow you to paint in artistic ways in Photoshop. When you paint with brushes in this book, however, it is usually to clean up a sketch.

The following are some things I do with the Brush tool that you can try.

- Use a soft or a hard-edged round brush as you zoom in or out using the Zoom and Hand tools.

- Change the brush size to get closer to the area I want to clean up. With color, I generally keep the black and white default. I press the (D) key and use the (X) key to switch the color to paint in my foreground. If you need to switch to a different color, double-click the foreground color in the Tools panel. Enter the color picker and choose a different color than white or black. Click OK to exit the color picker. Refer to Figure 2-42.

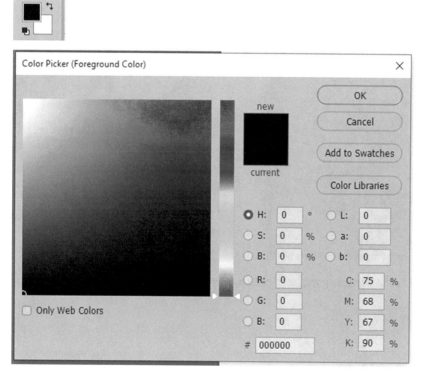

Figure 2-42. *Entering the Color Picker (Foreground Color) from the Tools panel*

- Another technique you can try with your brush, besides dragging with the mouse or stylus, is to click in one spot and Shift+click in another to create a line through that area. This speeds up your painting time. Refer to Figure 2-43.

Figure 2-43. *Drawing a straight line with the Brush tool*

Tip   If you are concerned while painting that you might accidentally paint on something on the layer you do not want to, in the Layers panel, click the create new layer button icon (+) to paint on a separate layer. You can then turn on/off the eye on the layer to compare what you have already done and see if you have missed anything. If you want to merge with the background layer or a normal layer 0 from the menu, choose Flatten Image. Refer to Figure 2-44.

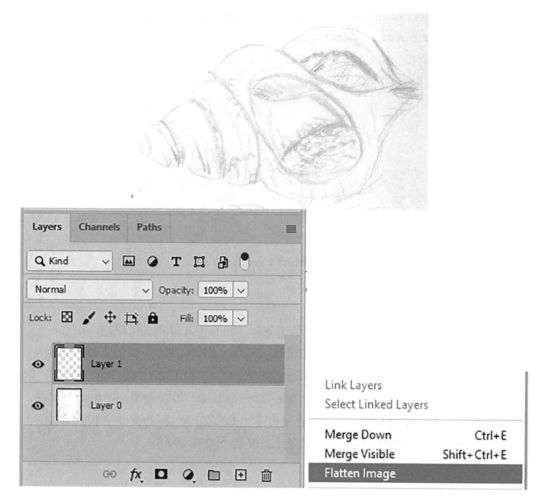

Figure 2-44. *Painting on an image and then merging the two layers using the Layers panel menu*

Pencil Tool (B)

This tool is similar to the Brush tool and can also access the brush settings, so I only point out key differences. Refer to Figure 2-45.

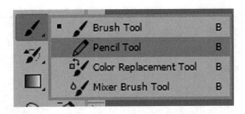

Figure 2-45. *The Pencil tool*

Pencil Tool Options

Look from left to right in the options panel. The **preset options** are first. (See the section on the Move tool for more information.) Refer to Figure 2-46.

Figure 2-46. *Pencil tool options*

Next is the **Brush preset picker**. The default is 1 px, which is ideal for thin lines. However, even if you adjust the hardness setting in the preset brush picker, the hard edge remains. Refer to Figure 2-47.

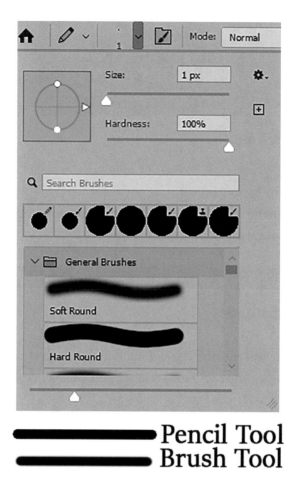

Figure 2-47. *The preset brushes picker for the Pencil tool and a comparison of the pencil and brush when painting*

If you enter the Brush Settings panel, some options like wet edge and buildup are grayed out. Certain brushes in the Brushes panel might not work the same as with the Brush tool. Refer to Figure 2-48.

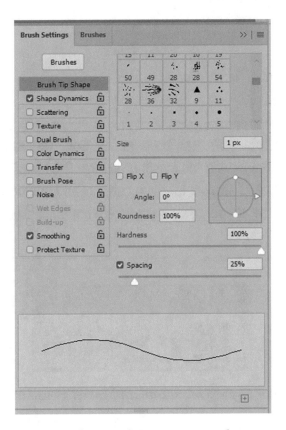

Figure 2-48. *Some settings in the Brush Settings panel are grayed out for the Pencil tool*

For information on mode, opacity, opacity pressure, smoothing, smoothing options, angle, size, pressure, and symmetry paint, refer to the Brush tool section in this chapter. Refer to Figure 2-49.

Figure 2-49. *Pencil tool options are similar to the Brush tool*

One additional setting in the pencil option panel is **Auto-Erase,** which draws the background color over the foreground color. By default, it is unchecked. Refer to Figure 2-50.

Figure 2-50. *Auto-Erase for the Pencil tool*

Note   There are two other brushes in menu. The Color Replacement tool (B) recolors areas while preserving the existing texture. The Mixer Brush tool (B) simulates traditional paint strokes that you can mix and smudge. Their purpose is not for cleaning up artwork, so these brushes are not discussed in any detail. Refer to Figure 2-51.

Figure 2-51. *The Color Replacement tool and Mixer Brush tool*

Eraser Tool (E)

This tool removes unwanted marks, scratches, and smudges from your layer. If you are painting on your background layer, it uses whatever color is currently the Tools panel background color. Refer to Figure 2-52.

Figure 2-52. *The Eraser tool and the foreground and background colors in the color picker*

As with the brush, you can use (X) to switch while erasing, which flips the Tools panel's color. Refer to Figure 2-53.

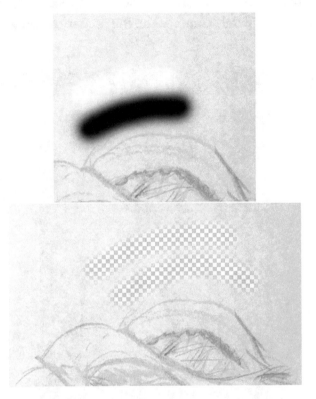

Figure 2-53. *Painting with Eraser tool on background layer and erasing on layer 0*

However, if you are painting on a normal layer or layer 0, then you can use the Eraser tool to show transparency through and remove actual pixels regardless of what the foreground or background colors are unless you are using a mask on your layer. This is covered in Chapter 12.

Eraser Tool Options

The Eraser tool options panel is like the Brush tool. They both have the same options, presets, and brushes, so I will only comment on the primary differences. Refer to Figure 2-54.

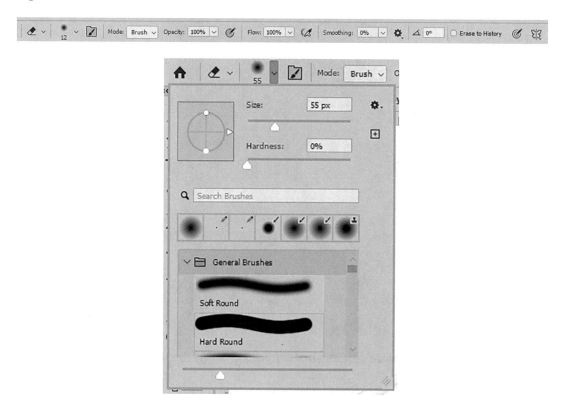

Figure 2-54. *Eraser tool options and the Brush preset picker*

Because this is an Eraser, some **Brush Settings panel** options are grayed out, including color dynamics and wet edges. Refer to Figure 2-55.

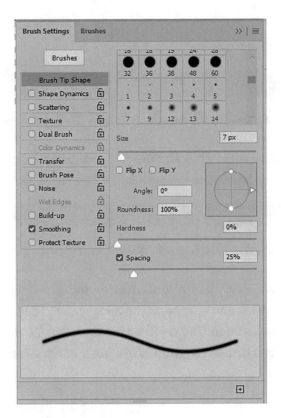

Figure 2-55. *Brush settings panel for the Eraser tool some options are grayed out*

In the options panel, **Mode** has three options in the drop-down menu. Refer to Figure 2-56.

Figure 2-56. *Choosing the Brush mode option in the Eraser options panel*

Brush mode allows the eraser to operate like a brush. I generally use this setting when touching up artwork and changing the size and hardness of the eraser as I zoom in and out of an area (as I would with a brush on the layer). Remember that you can't use a blank layer to erase on to preserve details if you make a mistake in erasing as you do with the Brush tool though you can erase the brush strokes you did make on your new blank layer. If you want to erase in a non-destructive way, you need to use a layer mask. This is covered in Chapter 12. Refer to Figure 2-56.

Pencil mode acts like a pencil, except some erasing options are grayed out in the options panel. Refer to Figure 2-57.

Figure 2-57. *Choosing the Pencil mode option in the Eraser options panel*

Block mode creates a square block eraser with no sizing options, and other than pressure and smoothing, few options are available. Refer to Figure 2-58.

Figure 2-58. *Choosing the Brush mode option in the Eraser options panel*

However, the block is a very handy tool when zooming in to erase in very tight spaces. Also, when you click and release on the image once. Then hold down the Shift key and click in another location. You can then create a straight line to square off areas. This technique can be used regardless of what mode your eraser is in. Refer to Figure 2-59.

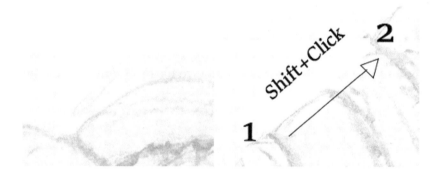

Figure 2-59. *Erasing in a straight line with the Eraser tool*

For information on opacity, opacity pressure, flow, airbrush style, smoothing, smoothing options, angle, size pressure, and symmetry paint, refer to the Brush tool section in this chapter. Refer to Figure 2-58.

Erase to history allows the eraser to erase from a designated history state using the History panel. Refer to Figure 2-60.

Figure 2-60. *Erase to history option in the Eraser options panel*

Other Erasers

Photoshop has two other eraser tools: the Background Eraser tool and the Magic Eraser tool. Refer to Figure 2-61.

Figure 2-61. *Less used eraser tools*

1. Open scan2_2.psd and make an Image ➤ Duplicate to practice on. Refer to Figure 2-62.

Figure 2-62. *Sketch of an elephant statue*

Background Eraser Tool (E)

The Background Eraser tool is generally used on photographs. But it can erase selected colors to transparency on a normal layer for any sketch.

Background Eraser Options

Look from left to right in the options panel. Refer to Figure 2-63.

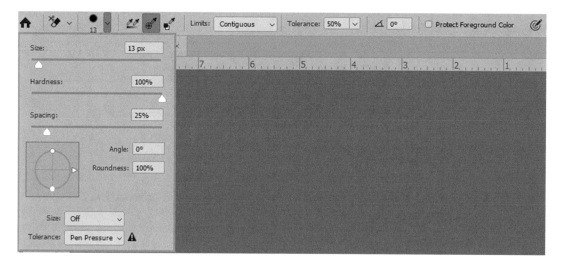

Figure 2-63. *Background Eraser tool options*

Create a preset (refer to Move tool on how to do that). Choose an eraser size from the Brush preset picker. It has similar settings as the Brush tool preset picker but has more pen and stylus options in the Size and Tolerance areas. Then from the options, choose Sampling: Continuous, Sampling Once, or Sampling: Background Swatch. I choose sampling background color (in my Tools panel, the background is white). With your eraser, click a whitish area outside the elephant. The layer changes to layer 0, and then you can begin erasing that sample color while other colors like blacks and grays are not erased and are preserved. Refer to Figure 2-64.

Figure 2-64. *The sampling option of background swatch white prevents the grays and black of the elephant from being erased and only the yellow paper, which is close to white*

You can also set **Limits** on how much is erased: Contiguous, Discontiguous, or Find Edges. Refer to Figure 2-65.

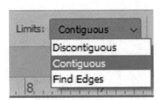

Figure 2-65. *Limits settings in the options menu for the background Eraser tool*

You can also set **Tolerance** (0%–100%) and **Angle** (0°–360°), and enable the **protect the area with the current foreground** swatch color. You can enable the **pressure** for the size of the eraser, as you can with the Brush tool. Refer to Figure 2-63.

Magic Eraser Tool (E)

Though it has no set brush size, the Magic Eraser lets you select large areas of color quickly and erase them instantly when you click that area. Although this method is fast, it is destructive, so set your tolerance correctly, or you may erase areas you don't want to.

Magic Eraser Tool Options

Look from left to right in the options panel. You have the option of creating a **preset.** You may have to use the History panel or Ctrl/Cmd+Z a few times to get the right number **Tolerance** setting (0–255). I leave it at the default setting of 32, but you can choose a higher or lower number to select and delete pixels. But when it comes to erasing pixels, I find using it in combination with a selection is much better, as you see in Chapter 3. This tool works best with closed shapes, so make sure your drawing has no small gaps. Use the Brush or Pencil tool with a black to fill in gaps if there are any. Refer to Figure 2-66.

Figure 2-66. *The Magic Eraser tool options panel setting and areas eraser outside of the elephant statue because it is a closed shape*

You can also set the **anti-alias** for smoothness, erase only **contiguous** pixels, **Sample All layers** if there is more than one, and adjust the **Opacity** (0%–100%).

Clone Stamp Tool (S)

The Clone Stamp tool, like the Brush tool, is useful for joining gaps in sketches and ensuring that you get similar colors in pixels. Refer to Figure 2-67.

Figure 2-67. *The Clone Stamp tool*

1. Return to your copy of the scan2_1.psd file to practice on. Refer to Figure 2-68.

Figure 2-68. *Sketch for practicing the Clone Stamp on*

Clone Stamp Options

Like the Brush tool, it can create **presets** and change settings in the **brushes preset picker** of the size, hardness, roundness, and angle. Refer to Figure 2-69.

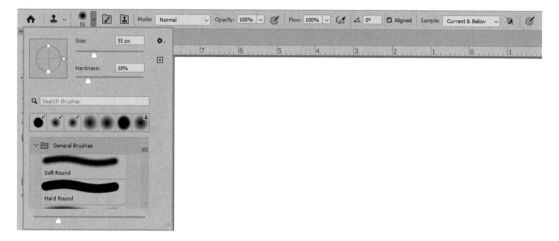

Figure 2-69.   *The Clone Stamp options and Brushes preset picker*

You can also access the **Brush Settings** panel options, though some settings like color dynamics and smoothing are unavailable. Refer to Figure 2-70.

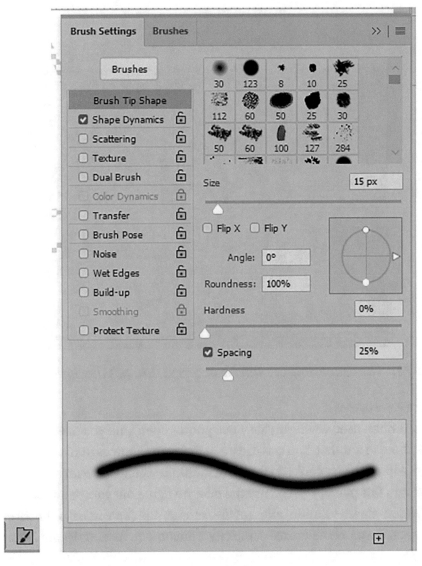

Figure 2-70. *Brush Settings for the Clone Stamp tool some options are grayed out*

Now you have an additional panel that you have access to Window ➤ Clone Source. Refer to Figure 2-71.

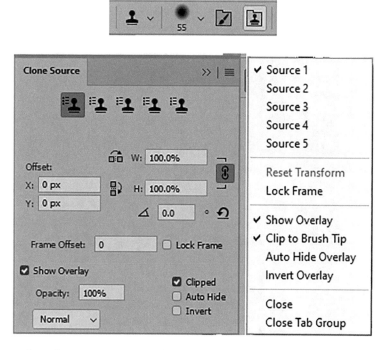

Figure 2-71. *The Clone Source panel is accessed through the options menu*

Clone Source Panel Options

This panel is often used when you have two photos open, and you need to clone details from one photo to another. You can use up to five clone sources until the documents are closed. Although you could do that with multiple sketches, I want to point out other useful items in this panel. You can use the offset to figure out your sampling point when you Alt/Option-click a location, angle of the sample, and flip vertical or horizontal or scale the area of your clone source within your document. Refer to Figure 2-72.

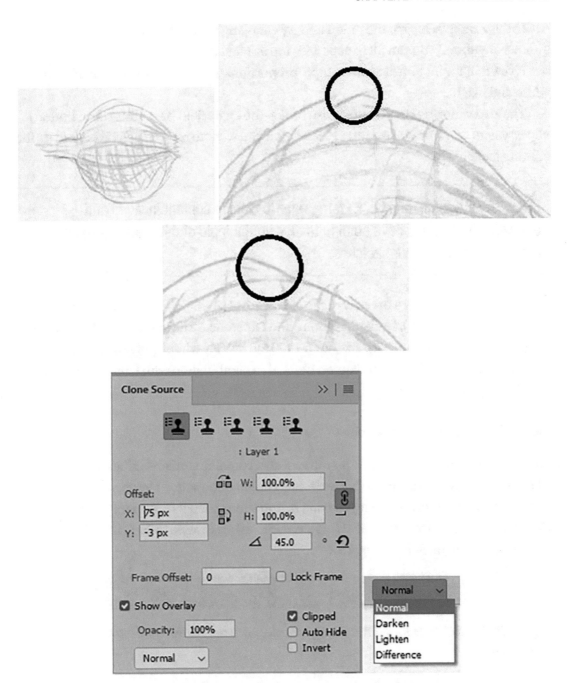

Figure 2-72. *Changing the angle and the overlay mode in the Clone Source panel and viewing the result with the Clone Stamp tool*

In this example, look at the onion and try changing the angle of the sample to 45° of another angle, and you can fill in gaps with the original pencil strokes.

If you don't want to scale your sample proportionately, disable the link icon for the width and height.

The arrow moving counterclockwise beside the angle field (reset transform button) allows you to reset the clone source. Click this if you want to reset the angle back to 0 ° for another location.

Note   Frame Offset and Lock Frame refer to cloning content in video and animation frames and have nothing to do with the topic of this book, so you can ignore that area for your sketches.

Show overlay shows a preview of the cloned pixels in the stamp. It has four viewing modes: Normal (default), Darken, Lighten, and Difference. The overlay preview can be clipped to the current brush tip size, auto-hide the overlay while applying the strokes, or invert the overlay. Show Overlay can be used in combination with Opacity settings (0%–100%). Refer to Figure 2-72.

Clone Stamp Options (continued)

Like the Brush tool (B), the Clone Stamp tool also contains similar settings for Mode: Blending. However, to get lines that are exactly colored the same, I leave at Normal. Refer to the Brush tool section if you need to know more details on **Opacity** (0%–100%), **Opacity pressure**, **Flow rate** (0%–100%), **Enable airbrush style to build up effects**, and **set the brush angle**. Refer to Figure 2-73.

Figure 2-73. *Settings for Clone Stamp mode, Opacity, pressure flow rate, airbrush, and angle*

Note   This is different from the Clone Sources angle in the Clone Source panel.

Selecting the **Aligned** check box allows you to sample pixels continuously without losing the current sampling point as you continue to drag the stroke. After you've released the mouse button and resume cloning, deselecting the Aligned box lets you continue to use the sampled pixels from the initial sampling point each time you stop and resume painting, rather than moving to the new location. Refer to Figure 2-74.

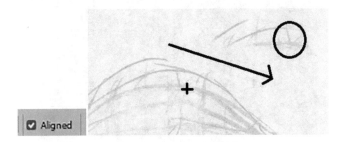

Figure 2-74. *Using the Aligned setting in the options panel*

You can set **Sample** for Current Layer, Current & Below, or All layers. The icon next to the menu lets you exclude or ignore adjustment layers while cloning, which I will talk about shortly. Refer to Figure 2-75.

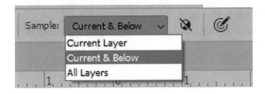

Figure 2-75. *Sample options for the Clone Stamp tool and pressure*

And as with the Brush tool, the final button allows you to **control pressure for size** if turned on. Refer to Figure 2-75.

Tips for Working with the Clone Stamp Tool

The following are tips for working with the Clone Stamp tool. Refer to Figure 2-76 and Figure 2-77.

- Choose a brush size with a set hardness.

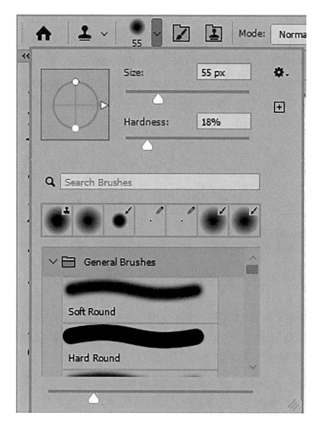

Figure 2-76. *Adjusting settings in the brush presets picker*

- Keep Normal mode.

- Keep Opacity at 100% and the pressure off.

- Keep the flow at 100% and the airbrush off.

- Keep the brush angle at 0°.

- Keep Aligned enabled.

Figure 2-77. *Mode, Opacity, Pressure Flow, Airbrush, Angle, and Aligned settings*

- I then either Sample in this example, the Current Layer or Current & Below if I am using a blank layer as I did with the Brush tool to paint on. Refer to Figure 2-78.

Figure 2-78. *Sample and pressure size settings*

- Press Alt/Option-click in the area to clone on the background.

- Create a new blank layer and then click that layer and start painting with a brush. That way, you do not destroy the artwork below. Refer to Figure 2-79 and Figure 2-80.

Figure 2-79. *Eraser tool*

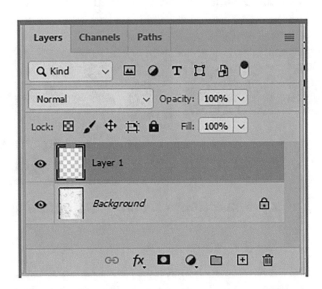

Figure 2-80. *The Layers panel cloning on a blank layer and then using the eraser to clean up*

At this point, you can use the Eraser tool to remove any of the excess cloning areas. When you are happy with the result from the Layers panel menu, select Flatten Image. Refer to Figure 2-81.

Link Layers
Select Linked Layers

Merge Down   Ctrl+E
Merge Visible   Shift+Ctrl+E
Flatten Image

Figure 2-81. *Choose Flatten Image from the Layers panel menu*

Note   I do not go into any detail on the topic of the Pattern Stamp tool for adding patterns or other healing tools in Photoshop because they are generally reserved for color photos. However, if you have realistic sketches or drawing that you have scanned, you can certainly experiment with them on your artwork to see if they improve the drawings. I recommend trying the Spot Healing Brush tool and Healing Brush tool for minor imperfections you want to blend in. Refer to Figure 2-82.

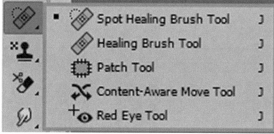

Figure 2-82. *Pattern Stamp and various healing tools, including Spot Healing tool and Healing Brush tool*

Note   You can learn more about them and how they can be used with the Clone Source panel at

https://helpx.adobe.com/photoshop/using/retouching-repairing-images.html

Hand Tool (H)

Use the Hand tool when you need to move around your image without accidentally moving a layer by mistake, which would happen with the Move tool. Refer to Figure 2-83.

Figure 2-83. *Use the Hand tool to move around your image rather than the Move tool*

Hand Tool Options

Holding down the spacebar on your keyboard while you click and drag, changes the cursor icon of any tool to the Hand tool instantly. In the options panel, you can add **presets** (see Move tool) and choose to **Scroll All Windows**. However, if you only have one document open, this can be left unchecked. You also have the option to zoom to **100%, fit the image on the screen, or fill the screen**.

Zoom Tool (Z)

The Zoom tool lets you zoom in and out of areas as you paint, erase, or clone on various layers.

Zoom Tool Options

In the options panel, look from left to right. First, you can set **presets**. Refer to Figure 2-84.

Figure 2-84. *The Zoom tool options*

When the cursor icon has a **plus (+)**, you can zoom in. The minus **(-)** icon allows you to zoom out. Holding down the Alt/Option key while clicking, change your mouse to zoom out. Most options are like the Hand tool's options. You can **Resize Windows to Fit** or **Zoom All Windows** if more than one is open. There is also **100%, Fit Screen, and Fill Screen**. If you have the **Scrubby Zoom option**, you can move left or right to scale.

In later chapters, I introduce additional tools for creating selections and cleaning up your artwork. Sometimes you need to use several tools in combination to clean up sketches.

Layers Panel Basics

Returning to the Layers panel, I want to point out a few additional basic things, but you learn more about the Layers panel in the chapters to come.

Besides the Create New Layers button, if you need to delete a layer, drag it on top of the trash can button in the lower right, or from the Layers menu, select Delete Layer. Refer to Figure 2-85.

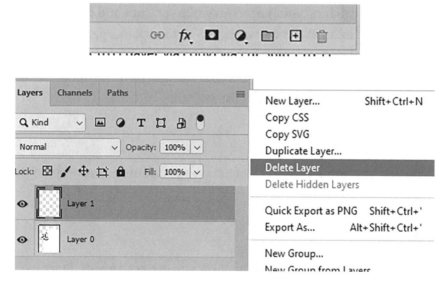

Figure 2-85. *Layers panel options use the trash can or the layer's menu to delete a layer*

You can turn the layer eye on and off to compare the layer above to the one below, but you can also drag the opacity slider from 100% to 0% and back if you need to check that the changes you have made cover the area they need to.

Adjustment Layers

The Layers panel lets you add adjustment layers to correct or remove unwanted colors. Generally, I use these for photos; however, I find three very helpful when cleaning up my sketches.

Levels

When you have a scanned sketch that is on paper that is light gray or yellowed with age.
Refer to Figure 2-86.

Figure 2-86. *Car sketch to be improved with Levels adjustment layers*

Open (Ctrl/Cmd+O) the scan2_3.psd file for this example. (Remember to make an
Image ➤ Duplicate so as not to destroy the original.)

Choose Levels from the adjustment layer panel or bottom of the Layers panel to add
it to the Layers panel. Refer to Figure 2-87.

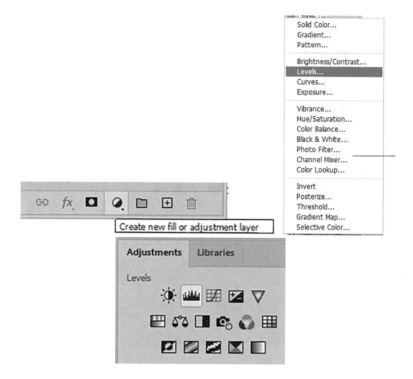

Figure 2-87. *Adding the Levels adjustments layer to the Layers panel*

Using the Levels adjustment layer in the Properties panel, click the white eyedropper to sample the image and set the white point. Press Alt/Option to display clipping preview if you need to see which area is affected before clicking. Then click in the yellowed area of your page, and it turns white. Refer to Figure 2-28 and Figure 2-89.

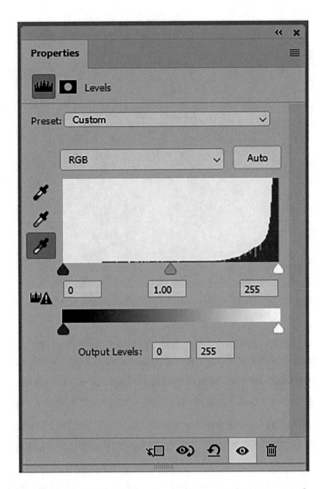

Figure 2-88. *Use the white eyedropper to create a white point from the lightest area of the yellow image*

Figure 2-89. *After clicking with the white Eyedropper tool, the yellow background is removed*

Likewise, you could use the black eyedropper to set the darkest point in your image if the lines were too faded, which would darken them. However, in some cases, that may make them too dark. If that happens, click the reset adjustment defaults (button to the left of the eye in the Properties panel) and move the shadow sliders instead. This resets the highlight, so you may need to repeat that step if you choose to reset.

Refer to scan2_4.psd, where a drawing is showing from the opposite side of the paper. Notice how on the levels, I moved the midtone slider to the left. This causes the image on the opposite side and any midtone lines on the elephant to become lighter. Refer to Figure 2-90.

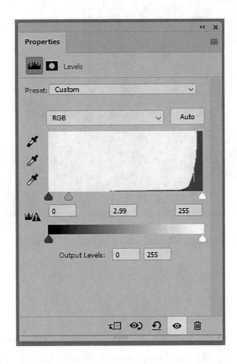

Figure 2-90. *Moving the Midtone slider in the Levels panel makes the reverse image fade*

This can also work for gutter shadows as well as. However, I only recommend using simple line art that does not contain any midtones because they disappear. You review this option in Chapter 12 and use selections and masks on the adjustment layer to refine what is faded so that the elephant lines remain dark. When you are happy with the result, choose Flatten Image in the Layers panel. Leave the layers intact if you want to return to this example later. Refer to Figure 2-91.

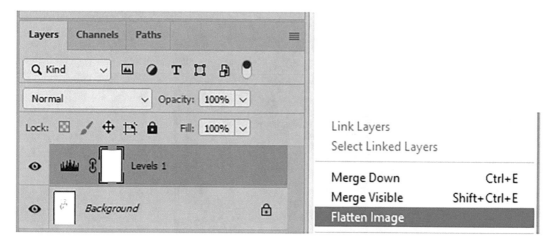

Figure 2-91. *Flatten the image in the Layers panel to apply the Levels adjustment layer*

Brightness/Contrast

This adjustment layer is also very useful for fading or darkening lines.

Return to example scan2_3.psd. This time, either from the Adjustments panel or Layers panel, choose Brightness/Contrast to add this adjustment layer on top of the levels. Refer to Figure 2-92.

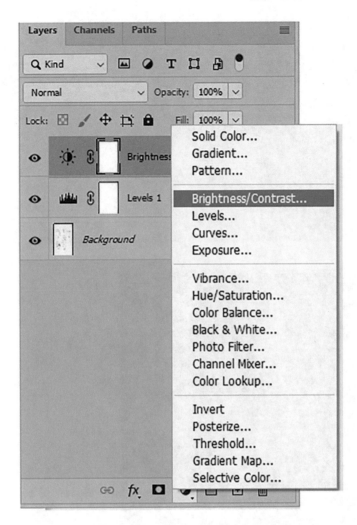

Figure 2-92. *Adding a Brightness/Contrast adjustment layer on top of the levels*

Move the brightness and contrast sliders as you did with the levels. Notice you can make the midtones disappear or soften depending on what settings you choose. Refer to Figure 2-93.

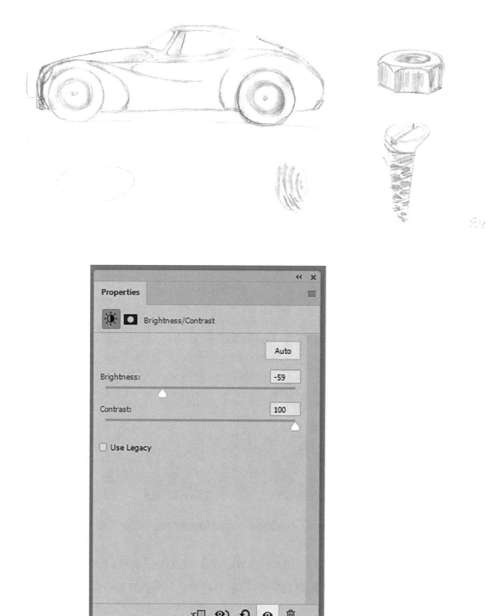

Figure 2-93. *Changing the Brightness/Contrast in the Properties panel*

When you are happy with the result from the Layers panel menu, choose Flatten Image or keep the layers intact to continue adding adjustment layers. Refer to Figure 2-94.

Black & White

This turns your sketch into what appears to be a black and white or grayscale image.

Continue working with scan2_3.psd. This time either from the Adjustments panel or Layers panel, choose Black & White to add this adjustment layer on top of Brightness/Contrast.

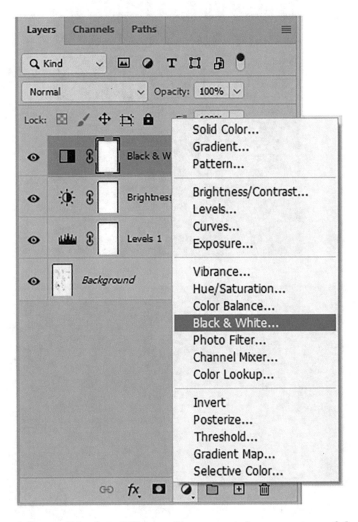

Figure 2-94. *Adding a Black & White adjustments layer on top of the Brightness/Contrast adjustments layer*

You can then use the sliders by dragging them to the right to remove color casts on the page, such as the yellows and blues that resulted from the scan, the paper, or another adjustment layer. Refer to Figure 2-95.

Figure 2-95. *Moving the sliders in the Black & White adjustment layer to remove color cast*

If you are working with graph or line paper that you sketched a doodle on, often the blue lines get in the way of your artwork. Refer to scan2_5.psd. Refer to Figure 2-96.

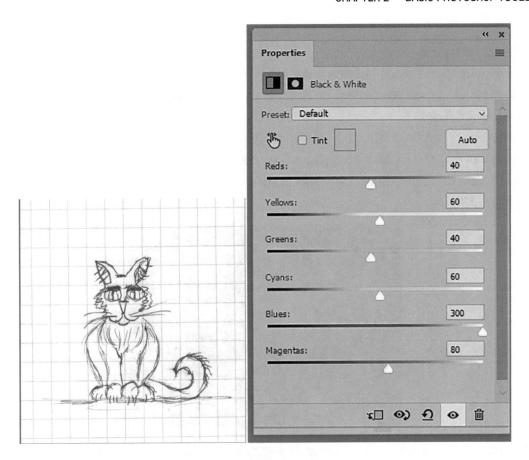

Figure 2-96. *Make the blue lines disappear by moving the sliders in the Black & White adjustment layer*

If the sketch is not in blue ink, you can remove all blue lines using this Black & White adjustment layer by dragging the blues or cyan sliders to the right. This may leave some tiny gaps in your artwork, but that is OK. When you are happy with the result from the Layers panel, choose Flatten Image. You can leave the layers intact if you want to return to review this later.

In scan2_3 and scan2_5, on a blank layer above the adjustment layers, use the Clone Stamp tool (S) to fill in the missing lines (sample current and below). Use the Brush tool to paint (white) and the Eraser tool (E) to remove any remaining marks. Refer to Figure 2-97.

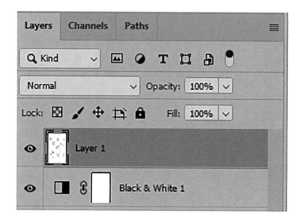

Figure 2-97. *Adding a Blank layer on top of the adjustment layers to do painting, cloning, and erasing*

Remember to use your Zoom tool and a smaller brush so that you can get in close to the car or the cat. Refer to Figure 2-98.

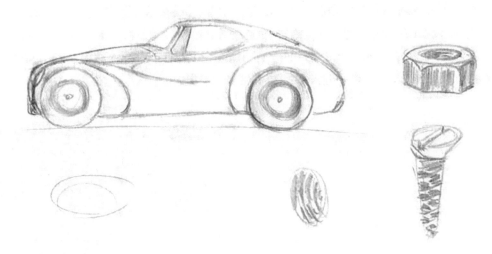

Figure 2-98. *After painting with the Brush tool in white and cloning, the image is much cleaner*

The adjustment I mentioned can be used in combination or separately to clean up your sketches. You may want to experiment with other adjustment layers like Curves or Invert to see if they improve your artwork. Refer to Figure 2-99.

Figure 2-99. *Explore other adjustment layers in your own project*

Note   While you are using your adjustment layers, you can also alter them using the layer's opacity and choose different blending modes from the drop-down, which may clean up the image further. You saw them with the brushes, but here they work with layers. More information and examples of how blending modes work with brushes and layers are at https://helpx.adobe.com/photoshop/using/blending-modes.html.

Althought it is impossible for me to know which blending modes work best for your specific project, in the scan2_5.psd black-and-white example, you could try Lighten, Screen, Lighter Color, or Overlay for the lines. But it all depends on the images and what you are trying to hide or improve. If a blending mode does not work for your project, leave Opacity at 100% and the default normal blending mode for that adjustment layer. Refer to Figure 2-100.

Figure 2-100. *Apply blending modes to your adjustment layers to see if they clean up your artwork further, as I did to the Black & White adjustment layer, and then set it back to the default*

Just remember that to fully apply the adjustment layer, you need to use Flatten Image from the Layers panel menu to confirm the final result.

Filters

There are also a few filters that you can use to fix layers where the lines are too thin or enhance the sketch. Note that if you do not want to destroy the original layer, drag that over the Create a New Layer icon in the Layers panel to duplicate it before applying your filter. Refer to Figure 2-101.

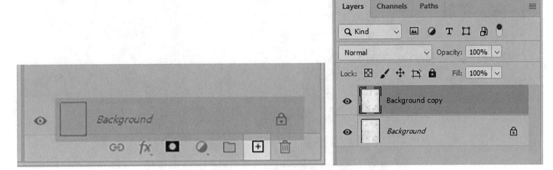

Figure 2-101. *Creating a duplicate Layer to try a filter on*

Try using Filter ➤ Sharpen ➤ Unsharp Mask to darken blurry or faint lines for easier tracing later in Illustrator. By moving the slider for the amount, radius, and threshold, you can achieve a darker crisper line enable and disable the preview check box to compare the change on the actual image and then click OK to apply the change. Refer to Figure 2-102.

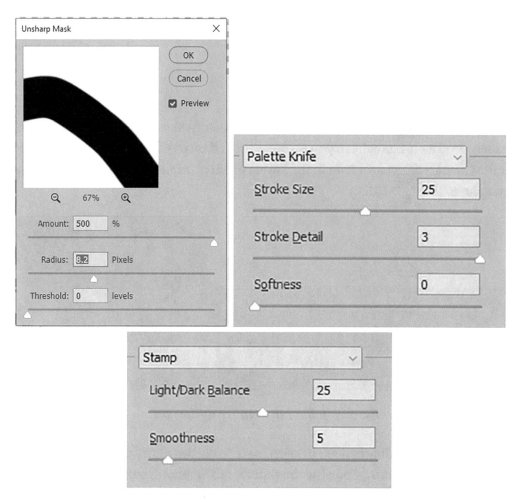

Figure 2-102. *Filters like Unsharp Mask, Palette Knife, and Stamp from the Filter Gallery may help you darken your sketches lines and make them less blurry*

Try the following to darken the lines in other drawings.

- Filter ➤ Filter Gallery

- Artistic ➤ Pallet knife

- Sketch ➤ Stamp

Click OK to confirm the changes on the layer.

You should try some of the other Artistic or Sketch filters in the Filter Gallery folders to enhance your work. Two or more can be combined in the Add New Effect Layer area. Try this before you click OK to confirm. Refer to Figure 2-103.

Figure 2-103. *Mixing filters in the Filter Gallery*

Saving Files

When you have completed cleaning up your artwork, make sure to save (Ctrl/Cmd+S) it as a .psd should you need to return to it later. Save another version as a .tiff file if you plan to print the file or as a .jpg to keep the file size small if you plan to place or embed later in Illustrator (See Chapter 13). You can see my files in the Chapter 2 folder.

Summary

This chapter covered a lot of tools and panels that you can use in Photoshop to clean up your sketches. You also examined some adjustment layers and filters that you can apply to your layers as well. The next chapter examines basic marquee tools that can make selections.

CHAPTER 3

Basic Marquee Tools

In this chapter, you learn how to use the basic marquee tools. Let's start by making selections in Photoshop. You can find the projects for this chapter in the Chapter 3 folder.

The marquee tools are in the Tools panel. Refer to Figure 3-1.

Figure 3-1. *Basic marquee tools*

There are four basic marquee tools.

- Rectangular Marquee tool (M)

- Elliptical Marquee tool (M)

- Single Row Marquee tool

- Single Column Marquee tool

Let's look at them one at a time.

1. Open the scan3_1.psd file, select Image ➤ Duplicate, and use the duplicate file for practice as you did in Chapter 2. Remember to use the History panel when you go back a step and use another marquee tool. Refer to Figure 3-2.

© Jennifer Harder 2022
J. Harder, *Accurate Layer Selections Using Photoshop's Selection Tools,*
https://doi.org/10.1007/978-1-4842-7493-4_3

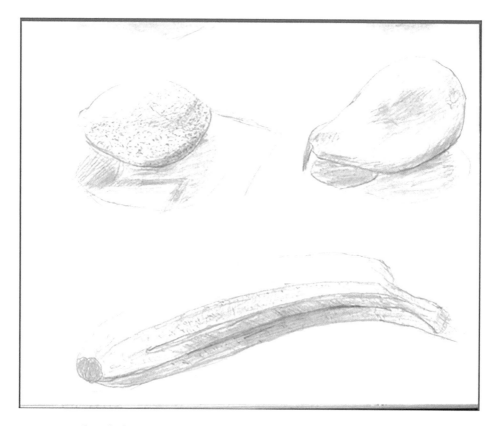

Figure 3-2. *A sketch for practicing with the basic marquee tools*

Rectangular Marquee Tool (M)

The Rectangular Marquee tool makes square or rectangular selections. Refer to Figure 3-3.

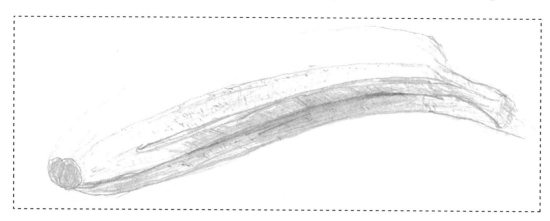

Figure 3-3. *A rectangular marquee around a banana sketch*

To make a rectangular selection in the background layer, click and drag over the area that you want to select. Transparent moving lines appear, which are sometimes called *marching ants*. If you use your Brush tool filled with a color like black and paint inside the selection, you find that the stroke you made with the brush stops when you go past the moving lines. This barrier prevents you from going further. Refer to Figure 3-4.

Figure 3-4. *A selection gives a clean edge. You can see this when the selection is hidden or removed*

Use the Rectangular Marquee tool to click somewhere else on the image. The marquee disappears, but you are left with a line with a clean edge. Without the marquee, you can paint anywhere you want.

To create a square marquee, hold down the Shift key while dragging. This creates a perfect square that you can paint inside of. Refer to Figure 3-5.

Figure 3-5. *A square marquee selection*

If you want to paint outside the marquee, go to the Select drop-down menu and choose Select ➤ Inverse (Ctrl/Cmd+Shift+I). Dotted lines appear around the border of the image as well as the square selection. You can paint anywhere except in the square. Refer to Figure 3-6.

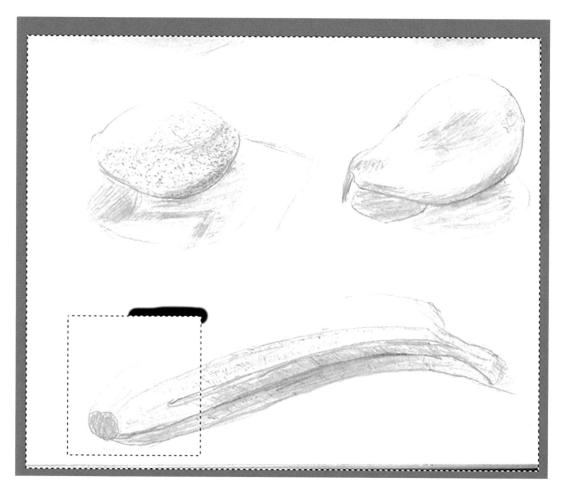

Figure 3-6. *Painting in the inverse of the selection*

You can hide the selection when working if you choose View ➤ Show ➤ Selection edges. It unhides if you choose that option again. I generally prefer to keep my selections shown, so I know that I am still in a selection. Refer to Figure 3-7.

Figure 3-7. *Hiding the inverse selection while painting*

To deselect the selection, choose Select ➤ Deselect (Ctrl/Cmd+D). If you need the selection, choose Select ➤ Reselect (Shift+Ctrl/Cmd+D). Refer to Figure 3-8.

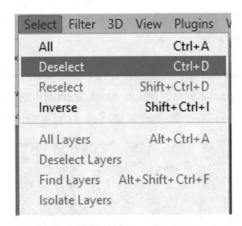

Figure 3-8. *The Select menu options*

Choose Select ➤ All (Ctrl/Cmd+A) to select the entire page.

Remember that Photoshop does not automatically save selections; before closing a file, you must save it.

Move and Transform Your Marquee

Drag out another marquee with the tool. You can move a selection with the Move tool by clicking and dragging the edge of the marquee. The scissor icon appears. Refer to Figure 3-9.

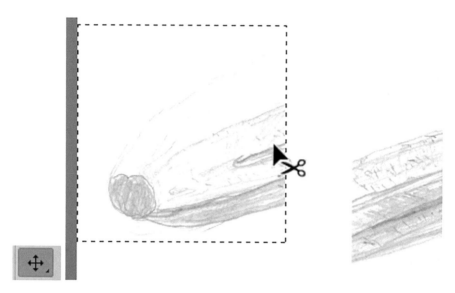

Figure 3-9. *Use the Move tool to move a selection and cut out pixels on a layer. I really do have a banana split!*

Remember that it cuts away the selected area when you do this on the background or normal layer. When you choose Select ➤ Deselect, those pixels are moved.

Use the History panel to undo the last step. Refer to Figure 3-10.

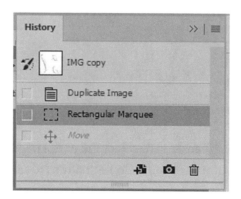

Figure 3-10. *Use the History panel to undo steps*

It is better to use the Rectangular Marquee tool to click and drag the edge of the selection to move the marquee, but not the pixels with it. Refer to Figure 3-11.

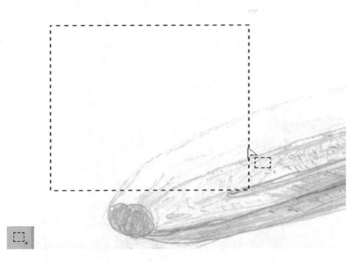

Figure 3-11. *Use the rectangular marquee to move your selection*

You can transform the selection using Select ➤ Transform Selection so that you can increase or decrease its size using the bounding box handles. Hold down the Shift key and drag for a disproportionate selection. Refer to Figure 3-12.

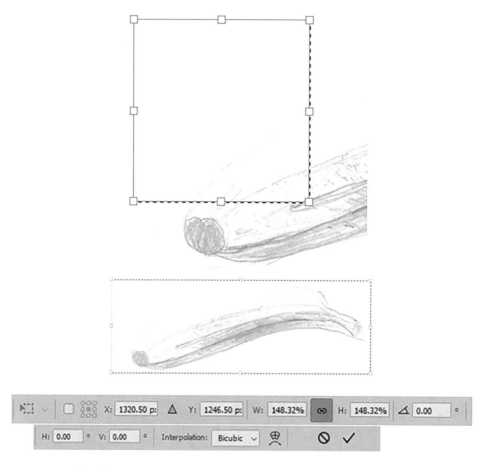

Figure 3-12. *The selection is transformed, and you can see transform options in the options panel*

Click the Commit button (the check mark) in the options panel to confirm. Only the selection is altered and not the surrounding pixels. You are returned to the Rectangular Marquee options.

Rectangular Marquee Options

Look at the options panel from left to right. The Rectangular Marquee tool offers several options to alter your selections. Refer to Figure 3-13.

Figure 3-13. *The Rectangular Marquee options panel*

On the left, there is an area to store **presets**.

Next, you have **four main selection options**. Refer to Figures 3-12 and 3-14.

Figure 3-14. *The four marquee selection options*

When you draw a marquee, the default is **New Selection**. With this setting, you can only create one selection at a time.

If you want to combine multiple selections, choose **Add to Section** or hold down the Shift key while dragging. Refer to Figure 3-15.

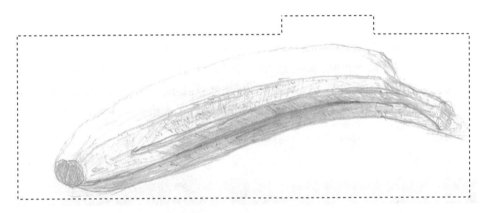

Figure 3-15. *Using add to selection in the options panel when I drag out a marquee*

To exclude a selection, choose the **subtract from selection** icon and then drag over the current selection. This removes part of the marquee. You can also hold down the Alt/ Option key while dragging to remove from the selection. Refer to Figure 3-16.

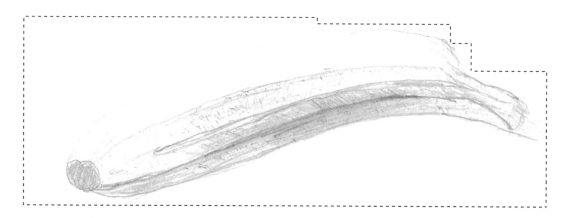

Figure 3-16. *Using subtract from selection in the options panel when I drag out a marquee multiple times*

Doing this multiple times helps you refine your selection area.

The fourth option in this set is **Intersect with Selection**. If you choose this option when you drag over a selection, only the area where the two selections overlap remains. Or, hold down the Alt/Option+Shift keys while dragging. Refer to Figure 3-17.

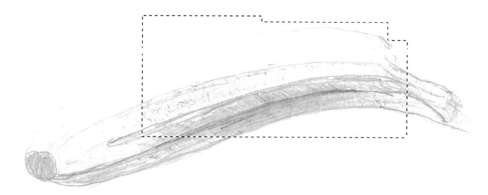

Figure 3-17. *Using Intersect with selection in the options panel*

After I make my selection, I usually reset back to the new selection so that it is ready the next time I return to Photoshop. Refer to Figure 3-18.

Figure 3-18. *The four marquee selection options reset back to New Selection*

Before you draw a marquee, the Feather setting allows you to soften the edges of a selection of pixels both inside and out so that when you paint or erase, the effect is feathered and blurry, and the selection is more rounded. Refer to Figure 3-19.

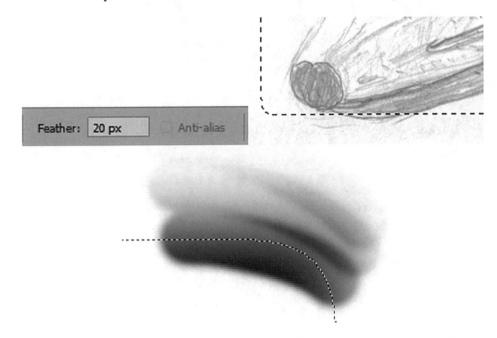

Figure 3-19. *Using a feathered marquee with a brush after setting it in the options panel*

If I want a clean edge for the selection, I leave the Feather at 0 px. However, you can set it up to 1000 px. Anti-alias can smooth further, but it is only available for the Elliptical Marquee tool, which you see later in the chapter.

Select ➤ Modify Menu

There are several ways to refine your selection. Go to Select ➤ Modify. Refer to Figure 3-20.

Figure 3-20. *Select ➤ Modify*

- **Border** creates a small border width of 1 to 200 pixels. Refer to Figure 3-21.

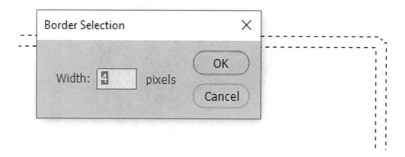

Figure 3-21. *Border Selection dialog box and result*

- **Smooth** allows you to round the sharp edges of the selection by 1 to 500 pixels. You can apply the effect at the image's canvas bounds. Refer to Figure 3-22.

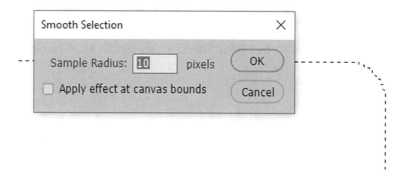

Figure 3-22. *Smooth Selection dialog box and result*

- **Expand** allows you to expand the selection by 1 to 500 pixels and apply the effect at the image's canvas bounds. Refer to Figure 3-23.

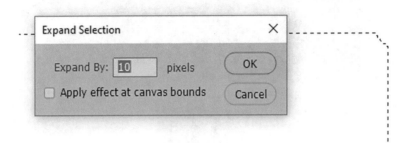

Figure 3-23. *Expand Selection dialog box and result*

- **Contract** allows you to shrink the selection by 1 to 500 pixels and apply the effect at the image's canvas bounds. Refer to Figure 3-24.

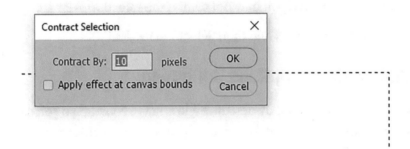

Figure 3-24. *Contract Selection dialog box and result*

- **Feather** is similar to the option that softens the selection, but it affects the edge of the selection. It also allows you to apply the effect at the image's canvas bounds. The feather radius ranges from 0.1 to 1000 pixels. Refer to Figure 3-25.

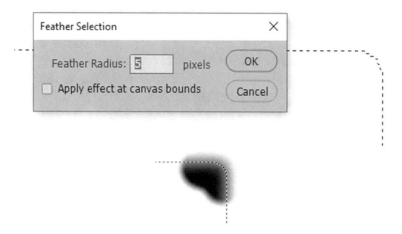

Figure 3-25. *Feather Selection dialog box and result*

- **Grow** causes the selection to fill the entire document but excludes smaller areas, which you may not want if the selection is small.

Try out each of these options and then Select ➤ Deselect.

Rectangular Marquee Options Continued

Let's return to the options panel. By default, Style is set to **Normal** so you can draw a rectangle any dimension you want. However, if you want a specific area, choose **Fixed Ratio** or **Fixed Size**. Refer to Figure 3-26.

Figure 3-26. *Rectangular Options setting for Fix Ratio and Fixed Size in the options panel*

Ratio allows you to enter a specific width and height ratio, like a 1:1 square or a 1:2 rectangle before dragging out your selection. You can reverse or swap this ratio using the arrows.

Fixed Size allows you to enter numbers for the width and height in increments. Right-click on the text box to access the increments. Refer to Figure 3-27.

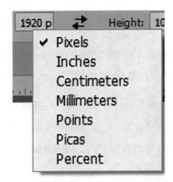

Figure 3-27. *Fixed Size increment options*

When you click the art board, a selection appears exactly that size; for example, a 100 px width and a 100px height. If you use this size frequently, you can save it as a preset. See Chapter 2's discussion on the Move tool on how to do that. Refer to Figure 3-28.

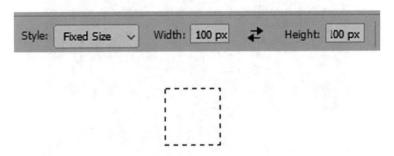

Figure 3-28. *A Fixed Size marquee*

Afterward, I reset Style to Normal so that I could draw rectangular marquees in any size I wanted. Refer to Figure 3-29.

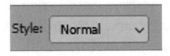

Figure 3-29. *Reset Style to Normal in the options panel*

Note   The last area in the options panel is Select and Mask. Refer to Figure 3-26. This is more of an intermediate topic and is covered in Chapter 9.

Copying and Pasting to Another Layer with Selections

There are a few more basic things to note with selections. You can also place a copy of the selection on a new layer. Select an area and layer, and try one of the following.

- Edit ➤ Copy (Ctrl/Cmd+C) and Edit ➤ Paste (Ctrl/Cmd+V) create a new layer of the selected pixels. As of version 2021, the new layer is in the same location. You can use the Move tool to move the section.

- Press Ctrl/Cmd+J or select Layer ➤ New ➤ Layer Via Copy to copy and paste on a new layer in one step and in the same place. Refer to Figure 3-30.

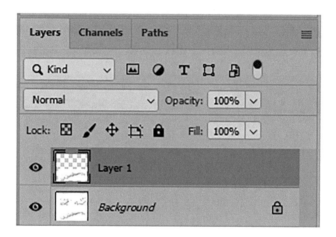

Figure 3-30. *Copy a selection to a new layer*

- Choose Edit ➤ Cut (Ctrl/Cmd+X) and then Edit ➤ Paste (Ctrl/Cmd+V) to cut out the pixels in that selection and paste them on a new layer—but not in the same place. To do that, select Edit ➤ Paste Special ➤ Paste in place (Shift+Ctrl/Cmd+V).

- Press Ctrl/Cmd+Shift+J or select Choose Layer ➤ New ➤ Layer Via Cut to cut and paste on a new layer in one step in the same location. The area cut out of the background is replaced by the current background color in the Tools panel. Refer to Figure 3-31.

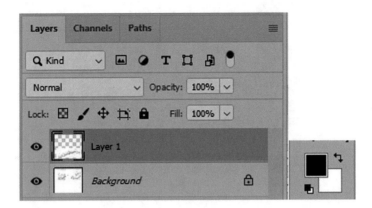

Figure 3-31. *Cutting a selection to a new layer*

You get an alert if there is nothing to copy or the selection area is blank. Refer to Figure 3-32.

Figure 3-32. *Alert message when no pixels are selected*

The selection remains as you move from layer to layer until you choose Select ➤ Deselect or click elsewhere on the image.

If you have a marquee selection on a background layer, you can press the Backspace/Delete key. Then from the Edit ➤ Fill dialog box, click the Contents drop-down menu. You can choose a color or content to fill that selection. Refer to Figure 3-33.

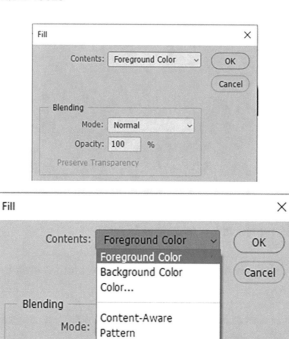

Figure 3-33. *Fill dialog box options*

The following are the options that apply to our work.

- **Foreground color**: The color that is currently in the Tools panel foreground.

- **Background color**: The color that is currently in the Tools panel background.

- **Color**: Choose a color from the color picker. Refer to Figure 3-34.

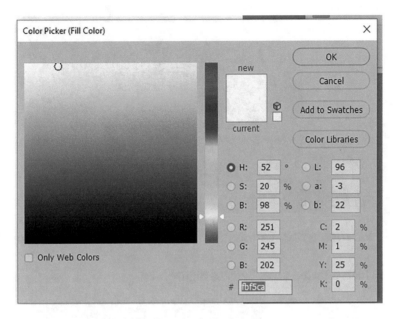

Figure 3-34. *The Color Picker (Fill Color) dialog box*

- **Black**: Fills the selection area with black

- **50% Gray**: Fills the selection area with gray

- **White**: Fills the selection area with white

Note   Content-Aware, pattern, and history do not apply to the content of this book and have more to do with photography and pattern creation.

The Fill dialog box also offers a Blending mode, similar to that in the Brush tool and Layers panel. Opacity is 0% to 100%. The Preserve Transparency option appears when transparent areas are on the layer; otherwise, it is grayed out. Refer to Figure 3-35.

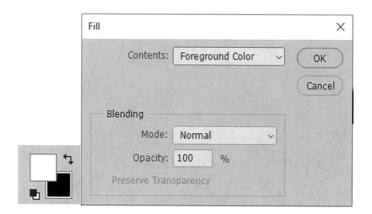

Figure 3-35. *Fill dialog box: Contents, Blending Mode, and Opacity options*

Click OK to fill a selected area. Refer to Figure 3-36.

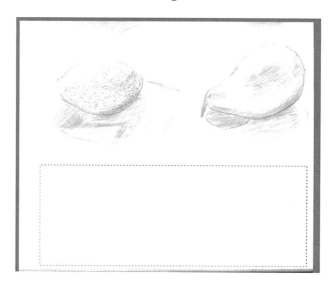

Figure 3-36. *The filled selection on a background layer*

On a normal layer or layer 0, pressing the Backspace/Delete key while the selection is active clears the area of all pixels. Refer to Figure 3-37.

If you want to fill that area with pixels on a normal layer, choose Edit ➤ Fill (Shift+F5) to bring up the dialog box.

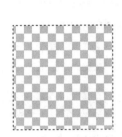

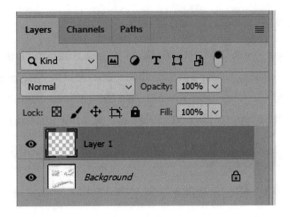

Figure 3-37. *Pixels are removed on a normal layer when you press the Backspace/Delete key*

Elliptical Marquee Tool (M)

Pretty much everything explained so far regarding the Rectangular Marquee tool can be applied to the Elliptical Marquee tool. However, there are a few differences. The Elliptical Marquee tool draws a circle or an ellipse.

Drag out an oval shape (as you would with the Rectangular Marquee tool). Refer to Figure 3-38.

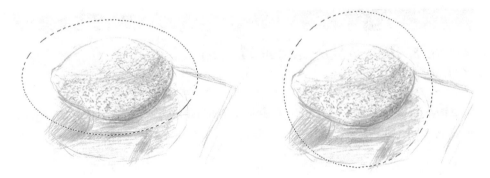

Figure 3-38. *Drawing a circle marquee*

If you want the shape to be circular, hold down the Shift key while dragging. Try Alt/Option+Shift and drag from a central location.

Elliptical Marquee Options

Anti-alias is available in the options panel. Enabling it allows for a smoother feathering selection. Adding **presets**, **selections**, and **feathering** and **style** options works the same way as the Marquee tool. You can use the two marquee tools together as you switch between them. Make sure the selection options are the same. Refer to Figure 3-39.

Figure 3-39. *The Elliptical Marquee tool options in the options panel*

Single Row Marquee Tool and Single Column Marquee Tool

The Single Row Marquee tool and the Single Column Marquee tool are nearly identical. The Row tool creates horizontal lines, and the Column tool creates vertical lines of 1 pixel width or height, respectively. Refer to Figure 3-40.

Figure 3-40. *Single Row Marquee tool and Single Column Marquee tool options in the options panel*

Using these tools is much easier and faster than using the Rectangular Marquee tool to draw a very thin line. Refer to Figure 3-41.

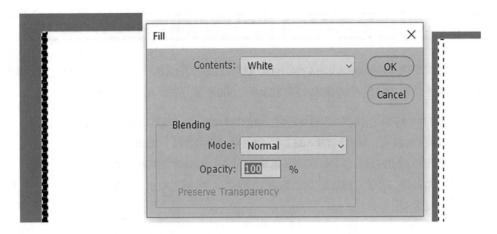

Figure 3-41. *The Fill dialog box after a column marquee has been chosen and then filled with white*

These tools are also very useful after scanning an image and you want to clear the very thin black line left on one edge (about a pixel in width or height).

1. Place the marquee over the area and press the Backspace/Delete key to enter the fill dialog box and fill it with white contents.

2. Click OK. The black line is gone.

3. Click Select ➤ Deselect to see the result.

These tools do not have style options, but you can add or subtract from the selection and feather. In addition, you could use Select ➤ Transform Selection if you need to make the selection wider or higher than a pixel.

Try these steps on the lower area of the scan3_1.psd file to clean up the edge with the Brush tool on a blank layer with a white foreground color. Refer to Figure 3-42.

Figure 3-42. *Expanding the row and painting white to cover dark line*

STITCHING A LARGE IMAGE TOGETHER WHILE WORKING WITH SELECTIONS

Let's review the tools and marquees you have looked at so far. Use a larger document to stitch two parts of a scan together because the scanner could not scan as one image.

1. Open the scan3_2a.psd and scan3_2b.psd files. The page in this sketch booklet was 11×14, which was too large for my 8.5×11 scanner. However, I found that by putting the sketch in landscape orientation and then moving the scan over once, I could complete the scanning in two scans. Refer to Figure 3-43.

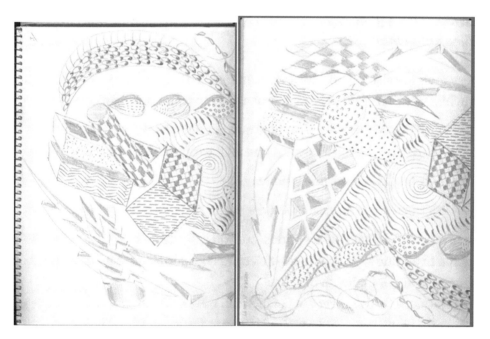

Figure 3-43. *The two sketch files that need to be put together as one*

2. I selected File ➤ New Document (Ctrl/Cmd+N) to create a new document with
    the Tabloid preset: 11 inch width, 17 inch height, 300 pixels/inch resolution,
    white background, and 8-bit RGB mode. Refer to Figure 3-44 and Figure 3-45.

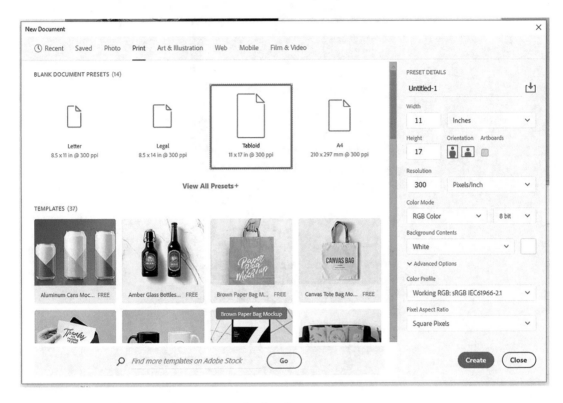

Figure 3-44. *The New Document dialog box*

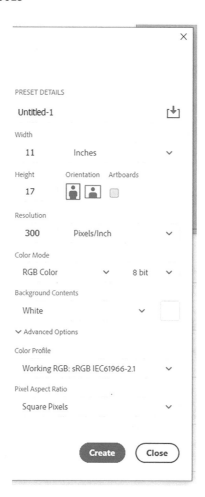

Figure 3-45. *Close up of the preset details*

3.   Click the Create button. The new blank untitled document appears. I made the
     document a bit larger so that if I needed to move or rotate the layers, it would
     be easier to see.

Do the following in the scan3_2a.psd file.

1.   Go to Image ➤ Image Rotation ➤ Rotate 90° Clockwise.

2.   Then Select ➤ All (Ctrl/Cmd+A) and Edit ➤ Copy.

3.   In your untitled 11×17 document, select Edit ➤ Paste to create layer 1. Use the
     Move tool (V) to move the image to the top.

4. Holding down the Shift key and dragging move it smoothly in a vertical
    direction. Refer to Figure 3-46 and Figure 3-47.

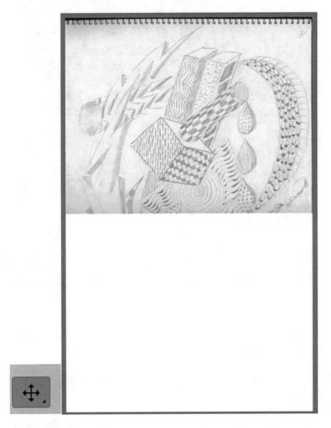

Figure 3-46. *Use the while holding down the Shift key; use the Move tool to drag*
layer 1 to the top of the page

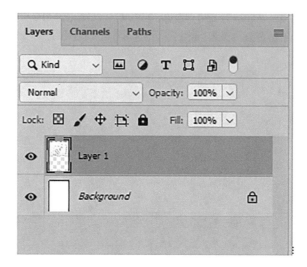

Figure 3-47. *Layer 1 in Layers panel*

5. You can close scan3_2a.psd without saving it at this point. Click No in the message, but keep your untitled document and scan3_2b.psd open. Refer to Figure 3-48.

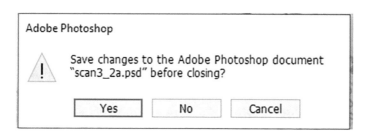

Figure 3-48. *Alert message when asked if you want to save changes to this altered file click No*

Do the following in the scan3_2b.psd file.

1. Go to Image ➤ Image Rotation ➤ Rotate 90° Counter Clockwise.

2. Then Select ➤ All and Edit ➤ Copy

3. In your untitled 11×17 document, select Edit ➤ Paste to create layer 2.

4. Use the Move tool (V) to move the image down to the point where the patterns overlap. Refer to Figure 3-49.

Figure 3-49. *Use Move tool to drag layer 2 to the bottom of the page and nudge into place and how it appears in the Layers panel on top of layer 1*

5. While still using the Move tool, use the arrows on your keyboard to nudge layer 2 slightly to the left as you need it to line up.

6. Save (Ctrl/Cmd+S) your document as project3_2.psd on your computer so that you can continue to adjust it.

7. Close the scan3_2.psd file without saving changes. Click No in the message box.

8. In the project3_2.psd file, select layer 2 and bring the opacity down to 65%. Use the Zoom tool to make sure that you have aligned the two layers. Refer to Figure 3-50.

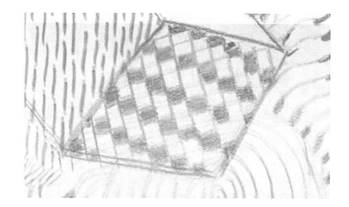

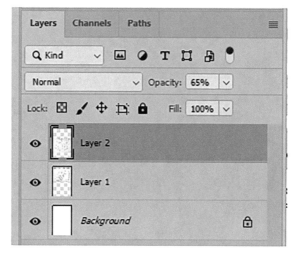

Figure 3-50. *Reduce the opacity of layer 2*

9. To fix the slight distortion that might happen when you hold down the scanner lid on a large document, go to Edit ➤ Transform ➤ Scale. Refer to Figure 3-51.

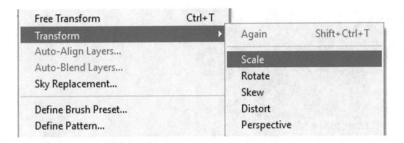

Figure 3-51. *Transform menu options*

Note   In the Transform tool options, use the Ctrl/Cmd + + and the Ctrl/Cmd + − keys to zoom in and out of the image. Use the spacebar to bring up the hand tool to move the image.

---

10. With the link icon disabled for the width and height in the Transform options panel, move the bounding box handle on the right inward and the top handle downward. Likewise, you can continue to use the arrows on your keyboard to nudge closer to the original shape. Refer to Figure 3-52.

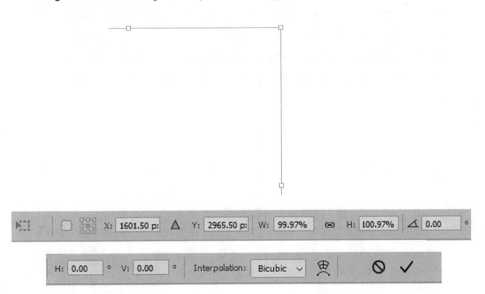

Figure 3-52. *With Transform Scale active, and width and height unlinked, drag the bounding box handles to scale the image*

11.   Click the Commit button in the options panel to confirm the change, and return the opacity of layer 2 to 100%. Refer to Figure 3-53.

Figure 3-53. *Changes made to layer 2 and opacity returned to 100%*

12.   Go to Edit ➤ Transform ➤ Rotate and use the upper right handle of the bounding box to rotate counterclockwise about –0.54°. Likewise, you can continue to use the arrows on your keyboard to nudge as close as you can to the original shape. If the rotation is not perfect on the right side, that is OK. Refer to Figure 3-54.

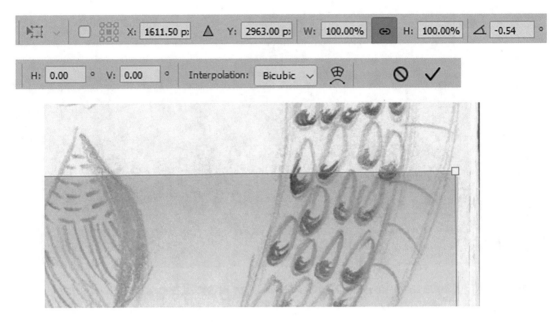

Figure 3-54. *Transform options to rotate and a close up of the rotation*

Note   Using the Up and Down arrow keys in a field in the options panel while a field is selected causes the number to increase or decrease, so make sure you have clicked out of a field if you do not want changes to occur.

---

13.   Click the Commit button in the options panel to confirm your settings. Return to the Move tool and nudge layer 2 as needed so that it fits as closely as possible. Refer to Figure 3-55.

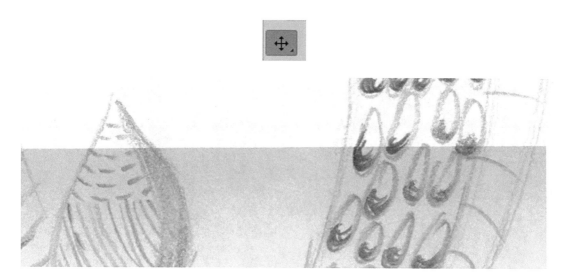

Figure 3-55. *Close up of layer 2 nudged with the arrow keys while using the Move tool*

While you can see my settings in the figures, yours might be slightly different depending on how you move the bounding box handles. Remember that you may need to do additional transformations, like Edit ➤ Transform ➤ Skew or Distort if something does not align exactly. Refer to Figure 3-56.

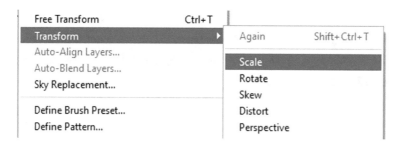

Figure 3-56. *Transform menu options*

That is why it is good to do as straight a scan as possible so that there is less to clean up when stitching.

14.   Now you need to use adjustment layers and stamping and brushing to get the paper white. For example, above layer 2, choose Image Adjustment in Levels. See Chapter 2 to review how to add adjustment layers. Refer to Figure 3-57.

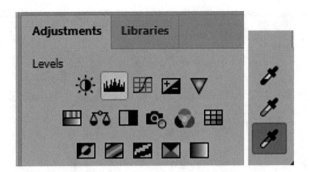

Figure 3-57. *Adjustments panel layer choices and the white eyedropper*

15. Select the white-point eyedropper and click somewhere on the left on a light-yellow area of layer 2 to change the background to white. Move the shadow slider.

16. Fix the gutter shadow. This lightens layer 1, which we don't want, so let's fix that next. Refer to Figure 3-58 and Figure 3-59.

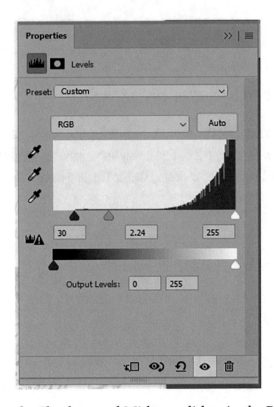

Figure 3-58. *Moving the Shadow and Midtone sliders in the Properties panel*

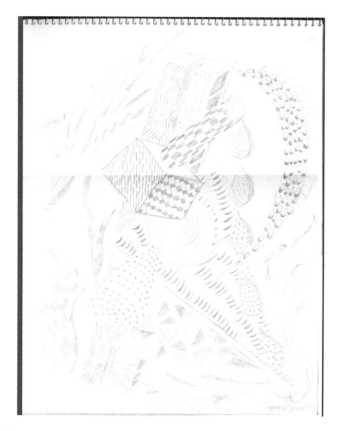

Figure 3-59. *Change to sketch after adding levels*

17. In the Layers panels, Alt/Option-click the dividing line between the level 1
     adjustment layer and layer 2 so that it only applies the adjustment layer to
     layer 2. This is the same as choosing Create Clipping Mask from the Layers
     menu. Refer to Figure 3-60.

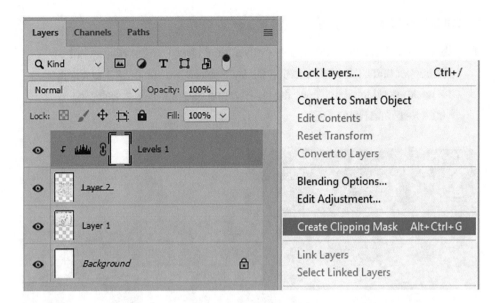

Figure 3-60. *Creating a levels clipping mask for layer 2 in the Layers panel*

A clipping mask can apply only a select adjustment layer to one normal layer. You learn more about this in Chapters 9 and 12. Refer to Figure 3-61.

Figure 3-61. *Levels are now only applied to layer 2*

You can see that the clipping mask is not applied to layer 1.

18.   Above layer 1, create another Levels adjustment layer. Use the white-point eyedropper and click somewhere in the light-yellow area on layer 1 to change the background to white. Move the shadow and midtone sliders. Refer to Figure 3-62 and Figure 3-63.

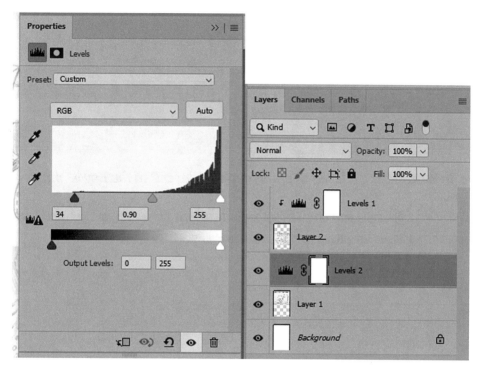

Figure 3-62. *Properties panel and creating another Levels adjustment layer for layer 1*

Figure 3-63. *The result of the adjustment*

Layer 2 appears lighter, so let's correct that.

19.   Return to the level 1 adjustment layer clipping mask and move the shadow
       slider back to the same dark tone. However, it has a slight red cast, and some
       of the gutter may reemerge. Refer to Figure 3-64 and Figure 3-65.

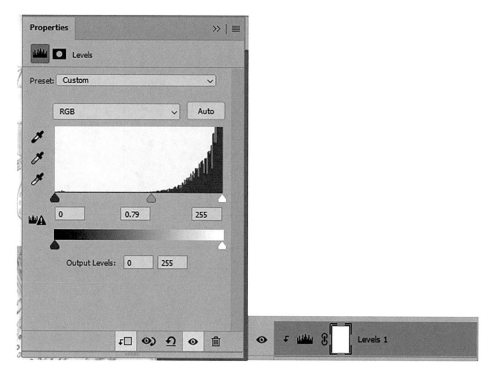

Figure 3-64. *Altering the clipping mask*

Figure 3-65. *The result of the adjustment*

20.   In the Layers panel, add another Black & White adjustment layer. Refer to
      Figure 3-66.

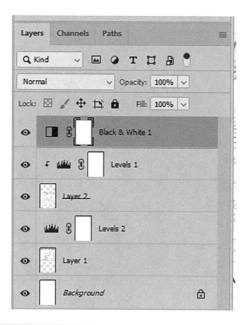

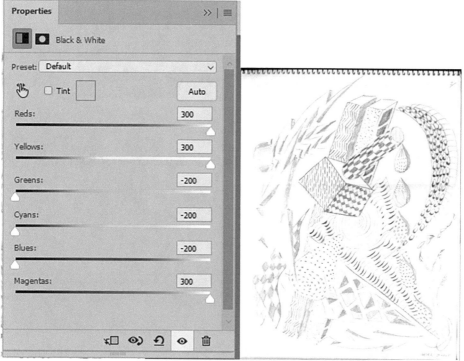

Figure 3-66. *Add the black and white adjustment layer and make alterations in the Properties panel—the result of the change on the sketch*

21. Try dragging the various siders left and right and notice how this eliminates color casts and most gutter shadow issues. I moved my Reds, Yellows, and Magentas sliders to the right and the Greens, Cyans, and Blues sliders to the left.

Keep in mind that your artwork may require other adjustments or adjustment layers like Brightness/Contrast. Review that area if you want to apply that adjustment layer to your artwork.

22. In the Layers panel, create a new blank layer on top of your artwork. Refer to Figure 3-67.

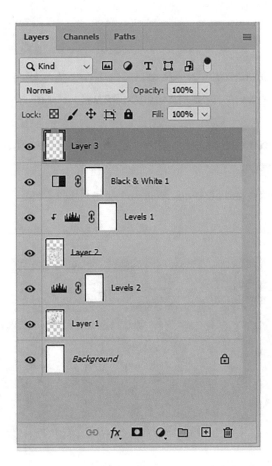

Figure 3-67. *Adding a New Blank Layer to the top of the Layers panel to paint on*

23.   Use the Rectangular Marque tool to create a selection to cover the coil bind. Refer to Figure 3-68.

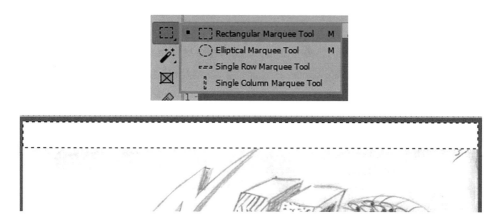

Figure 3-68.   *Use the Rectangular Marquee tool or other marquee tools to clean up and cover the coil bind with white using the paintbrush or Edit ➤ Fill*

24.   Use the single row or column marquee tools to remove the left, right, and bottom paper edges.

25.   Choose Edit ➤ Fill and Contents: White. Refer to Figure 3-69.

Figure 3-69.   *The Fill dialog box with Contents: White*

Remember that choosing Select ➤ Inverse allows you to paint in areas outside the marquee and prevent coloring over certain patterns.

26. Use the Brush tool with white in the foreground. Use large and small brush sizes of various degrees of hardness to clean up paper areas and make them white.

27. Use Shift-click with the Brush tool so that you can cover angled areas faster than painting and dragging.

28. Use the Eraser tool to clean up mistakes made with the brush when you accidentally cover something you did not intend to.

29. Use the Brush and Clone Stamp tools and remove the gutter shadow line where the two images meet.

30. Get close to the details by using the Zoom tool. When brushing or cloning, hold down the spacebar to reveal the Hand tool while dragging and moving to other areas as you work. Refer to Figure 3-70.

Figure 3-70. *Use the Brush tool, Clone Stamp tool, Eraser tool, Zoom tool, and Hand tool to clean up the sketch and remove the seam between the two parts of the image*

After using these various tools, the image is much cleaner than it was before. You can see my completed file (project3_2_final.psd) in the Chapter 3 folder.

31. Save (Ctrl/Cmd+S) the file.

32. From the Layers panel, choose Flatten Image, or leave the layers intact if you want to review or add to what you've done.

Summary

In this chapter, you learned about the four basic marquee tools and how to refine a selection. You can add to and subtract from selections in various ways. On a blank layer, you can paint, clone, or erase inside or outside (Select ➤ Inverse) a selection without destroying other areas of the sketch. The selection acts as a barrier. Feathering allows the brush or eraser strokes to escape through.

Chapter 4 looks at the Crop tool and the Perspective Crop tool.

CHAPTER 4

Using Crop Tools to Make Selections

This chapter shows how the crop tools make a selection to crop or straighten an image.

First, let's look at two basic features: the Crop tool and the Perspective Crop tool. Refer to Figure 4-1.

Figure 4-1. *Crop tool and Perspective Crop tool in the Tools panel*

This chapter has projects that are in the Chapter 4 projects folder.

Crop Tool (C)

The Crop tool is helpful when you have a scan, and you did not use the scanner's crop options to remove excess white areas. Refer to Chapter 1 for more on cropping in scanning.

When I stitch together two or more scanned images, I leave extra white space in the new file that combines the images. Once the scan is whole, that extra white area is unnecessary. Refer to Figure 4-2.

© Jennifer Harder 2022
J. Harder, *Accurate Layer Selections Using Photoshop's Selection Tools*,
https://doi.org/10.1007/978-1-4842-7493-4_4

Figure 4-2. *The earlier stitched sketch now has white space at the bottom that needs to be removed*

Cropping an Image

Practice the following steps.

1.   Choose Image ➤ Duplicate for the scan4_1.psd file, which is a flattened copy of project3_2.psd from the project we worked on in Chapter 3.

2.   Click OK in the Duplicate Image dialog box message.

3.   Select the Crop tool and drag the handles around the area that you want to crop. Give the image an equal top and bottom. Refer to Figure 4-3.

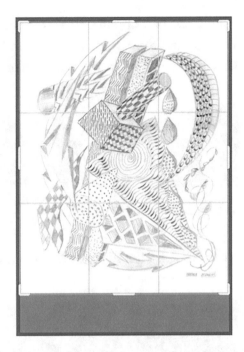

Figure 4-3. *Moving the crop tool handles up so that there is less white space at the bottom*

4. In the Crop preview, notice how it appears in the Layers panel. Refer to Figure 4-4.

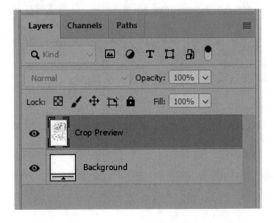

Figure 4-4. *Crop preview in the Layers panel while the crop is active*

Note   Holding down the Shift key allows you to scale proportionately.

---

5. In the options panel, click the Commit button (the check mark) to confirm that the crop and the excess pixels around the image were removed. Or select Image ➤ Crop in the main menu. Refer to Figure 4-5.

Figure 4-5. *Click the Commit button to confirm the crop*

6. If you don't like your crop, use the History panel to undo it. Refer to Figure 4-6.

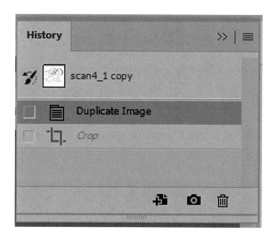

Figure 4-6. *History panel allows going back a step to cancel the crop*

7. Select the Crop tool again. Use the options panel to alter the settings.

8. Use this image and the History panel to continue practicing the various options.

Crop Tool Options

Let's look at the options in the options panel for the crop tool. From left to right: Refer to Figure 4-7.

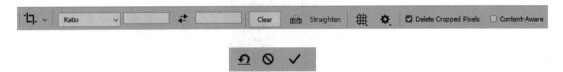

Figure 4-7. *Crop Tool options in the options panel*

Just like the Move tool, you can save or access **presets** for the tool. The Crop tool has default presets already stored in the drop-down menu, which you can access at any time. Refer to Figure 4-8.

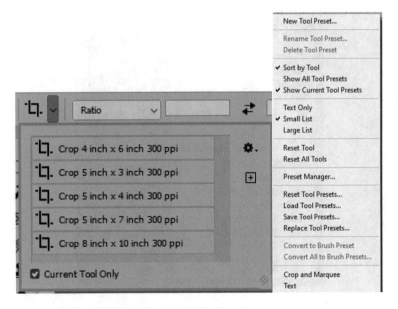

Figure 4-8. *Crop tool presets menu*

These are useful if you need to quickly scale your image to a set size, but you can add your own preset dimensions to this list by clicking the create **new preset (+)** symbol, and the gear menu helps you manage the presets.

By default, the **sizing** or aspect ratio fields for width and height are blank so that you can scale your crop to any size that you want while dragging the bounding box handles. Refer to Figure 4-9.

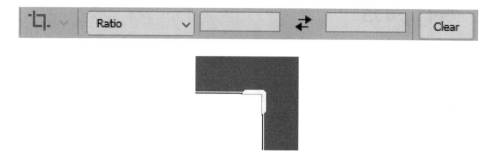

Figure 4-9. *The default Ratio options are blank so that you can scale the crop any size*

You can set the ratio in the Ratio drop-down menu just as you did with the Rectangular Marquee tool. Refer to Figure 4-10.

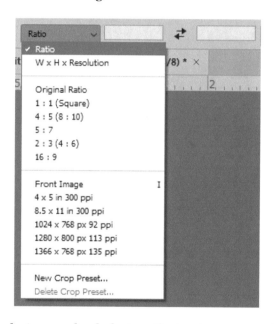

Figure 4-10. *Sizing choices and subchoices that act as presets for the Crop tool in the list*

There are other choices and subchoices in the drop-down menu.

Ratio subchoices are in the second part of the list. They function as presets.

- Original Ratio

- 1:1 (Square)

- 4:5 (8:10)

- 5:7

- 2:3 (4:6)

- 16:9

The ratio can be scaled proportionately on the canvas when you drag the bounding box handles.

Note   In Ratio, drag a bounding box handle outward to expand the crop. You can then scale the crop larger than the original page. It fills that area with whatever the current background color is in the Tools panel. So, make sure to set it to white if your paper is white. Use the Alt/Option key to enlarge from all sides. Refer to Figure 4-11.

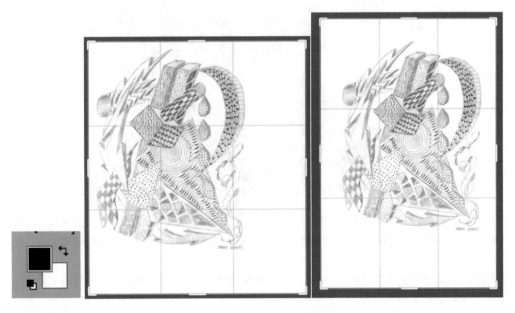

Figure 4-11. *In the Tools panel, make sure white is the background color when you expand your crop, or you may get an unwanted black border*

Crop Tool Rotation

You can also use the corner handles around the crop box to rotate on the background layer. Refer to Figure 4-12.

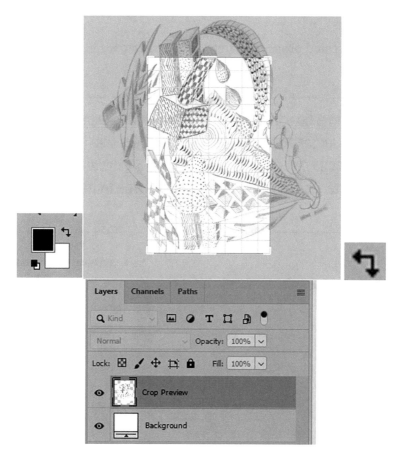

Figure 4-12. *While the background is white in the background layer, use a corner handle to rotate during crop preview. The icon changes to angled arrows*

If the background layer is made layer 0, you see the transparent areas under the shield. Refer to Figure 4-13.

Figure 4-13. *Rotations on a normal layer, or layer 0, shows the transparent pixels behind the rotation*

This is one way to straighten and get the area you want to crop at the same time.

Crop Tool Options Continued

The next option is the Size drop-down menu.

W × H × Resolution allows you to set the **width** and **height** and choose a **resolution** other than the 300 dpi/ppi you scanned in the original sketch. Refer to Figure 4-14.

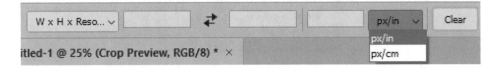

Figure 4-14. *Set a new width, height, and resolution of your image in the options menu*

The resolution can be in **pixels per inch** or **pixels per centimeter**. A different resolution does change the document's resolution after the crop if not set to 300 ppi. After you confirm the crop, you see the new resolution at the bottom of the document window. Refer to Figure 4-15.

Figure 4-15. *The new settings are reflected in the lower left of your document window*

Some suboptions act as presets for W × H × Resolution. Refer to Figure 4-16.

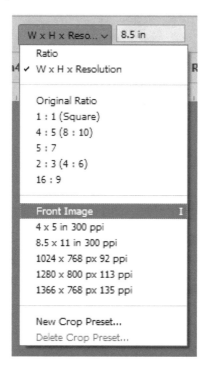

Figure 4-16. *Subchoices or presets for W × H × Resolution in the options panel*

The following are the presets.

- Front Image (crops to the size of an image that is already open for the currently opened second image)

- 4 ×5 in 300 ppi

- 8.5 × 11 in 300 ppi

- 1024 × 768 px 92 ppi

- 1280 × 800 px 113 ppi

- 1366 × 768 px 135 ppi

You can save your new crop or delete crop presets in the drop-down list in the fourth section.

Click the **Clear** button if you need to remove any numbers from the fields. Refer to Figure 4-17.

Figure 4-17. *The Clear button to clear fields in the Crop tool options panel*

The **Straighten** button straightens a sketch. Refer to Figure 4-18.

Figure 4-18. *The Straighten button in the options panel is enabled*

By enabling the Straighten button, you can draw a line next to an edge of the paper that you want to be the level edge of the sketch.

When you release the mouse button, Photoshop rotates the area based on that line.

Then you adjust and expand or contract the preview of the cropped pixels by moving the bounding box handles. Refer to Figure 4-19.

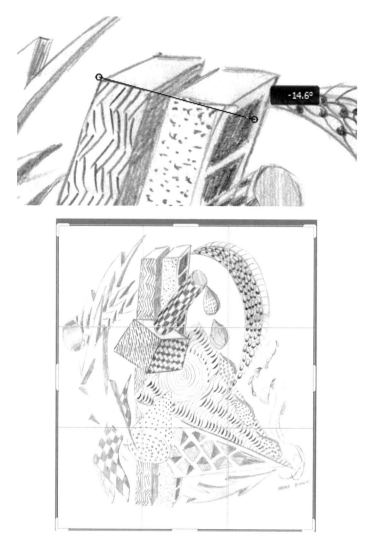

Figure 4-19. *Move the crop bounding box handles around the new area*

The next icon is a drop-down that lets you set the **crop overlay grid**. The grid is set to **Rule of Thirds** by default, as shown in Figure 4-19. Depending on what you are trying to line up accurately, you can also use the following.

- Grid

- Diagonal

- Triangle

- Golden Ratio

- Golden Spiral

Refer to Figure 4-20.

Figure 4-20. *Crop tool grid options*

The overlay is set to **Always Show Overlay** by default. The transparent background shield surrounding the overlay is gray to show you the area that disappears after cropping.

Auto Show Overlay and **Never Show Overlay** both hide the grid. **Cycle Overlay** allows you to cycle through the grid options by pressing the O key.

Cycle Orientation (Shift+O) is only available for the grids Triangle and Golden Spiral; you can cycle through how the grid appears in various orientations. Refer to Figure 4-21.

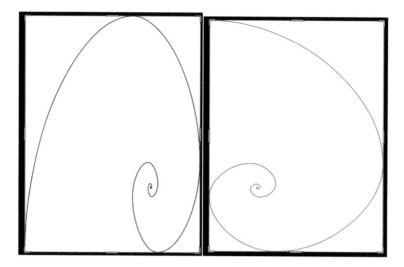

Figure 4-21. *Various orientations of the Golden Spiral Grid*

The **gear** drop-down menu next to the grid contains additional crop options. Refer to Figure 4-22.

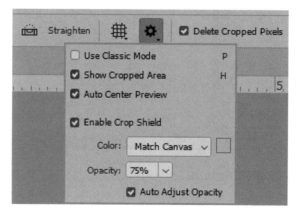

Figure 4-22. *Additional crop options under the gear*

- **Classic mode (P)** allows you to move and rotate the crop box itself instead of the image which you do when you chose Straighten and has no cropping preview, which Straighten does. Refer to Figure 4-23.

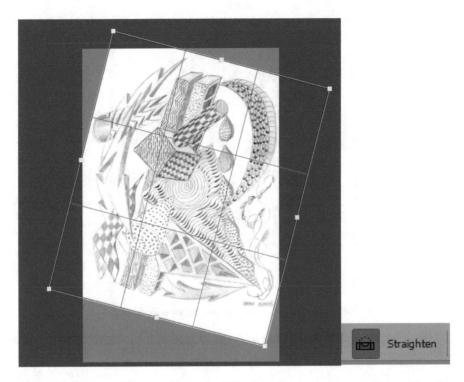

Figure 4-23. *Enabling Use Classic Mode hides the preview produced by the Straighten option. Uncheck this option to return to the Straighten setting*

This is how Photoshop did its cropping before the Straighten option was added. You might be familiar with this option from using older versions of Photoshop. It is disabled by default, and the Straighten option is preferred.

- **Show Cropped Area (H)**, when enabled, shows the gray shield.
  When disabled only shows the grid crop area but not the shield area.
  Enabling and disabling help you preview what you are cropping
  before you confirm. Refer to Figure 4-24.

Figure 4-24. *The gray shield is hidden when this check box is disabled, only showing the crop*

- **Auto Center Preview** allows you to keep the crop box centered on the canvas.

- **Enable Crop Shield** can be enabled or disabled and has color suboptions to match the canvas or custom color, which you can choose from the Color Picker dialog box. By default, the color is gray, and the opacity is 75%, but it can be set from 1% to 100%. Refer to Figure 4-25.

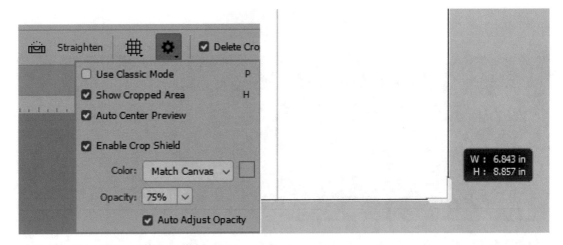

Figure 4-25. *The color of the crop shield and the opacity can be altered. The opacity is reduced by moving the bounding box handles*

- **Auto Adjust Opacity** reduces the shield opacity when using your mouse to drag and scale the crop. Refer to Figure 4-25.

- **Delete Cropped Pixels** is enabled by default. If you are on the background layer or normal layer, enable to remove the surrounding pixels. Refer to Figure 4-26.

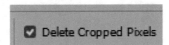

Figure 4-26. *Delete Cropped Pixels in the options panel is enabled*

If you simply want to crop the canvas area rather than the pixels themselves, uncheck the Delete Cropped Pixels on a normal layer or layer 0. Refer to Figure 4-27.

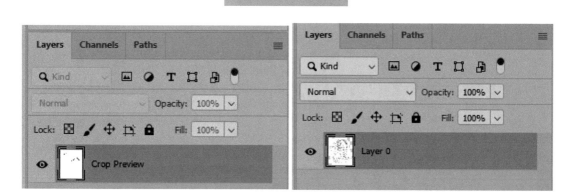

Figure 4-27. *Disable Delete Cropped Pixels to change the background layer to layer 0 and hide the pixels under the canvas*

You can then use the Move tool (V) to move the missing parts of the layer back onto the canvas if they were hidden but retained. Refer to Figure 4-28.

Figure 4-28. *Use the Move tool to move layer 0 around to display hidden pixels*

Depending on the purpose of your project, you can leave this option checked or unchecked.

- **Content-aware f**ills areas outside the original image when you expand the crop. This option is disabled by default. It allows you to fill the expanded area with the current background color in the layer, not the background color in the Tools panel, if there are enough selected pixels to work with. Refer to Figure 4-29.

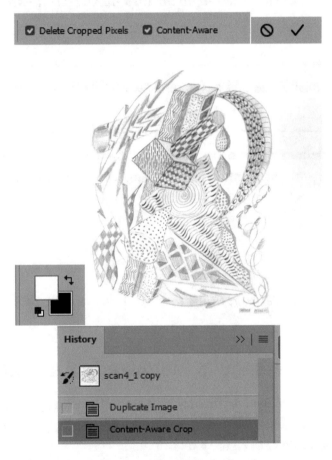

Figure 4-29. *Enabling Content-Aware to add pixels when you expand and confirm the crop even if the background color in the Tools panel is black. The History panel records the type of crop as Content-Aware*

If there are not enough source pixels on a normal layer, you get an alert. Click OK, but no fill is added. Refer to Figure 4-30.

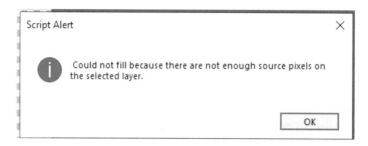

Figure 4-30. *If there are no pixels to fill the area during a content-aware crop, you get this message*

Note   This is similar to the Edit ➤ Content-Aware Fill option, which you look at in Chapter 7.

The last three buttons allow you to **reset** your crop settings (crop box, image rotation, and aspect ratio). Before you commit, you can **cancel** your crop by clicking the Cancel button (the slashed circle). You can **confirm** your crop by clicking the Commit button. Refer to Figure 4-31.

Figure 4-31. *Reset, Cancel, and Confirm buttons in the Crop tool's options panel*

Crop with the Rectangular Marquee Tool and Guides

In the background layer or layer 0, you may have started drawing using the Rectangular Marquee tool but realized you wanted to crop the image rather than choose Select ➤ Deselect the marquee. Refer to Figure 4-32.

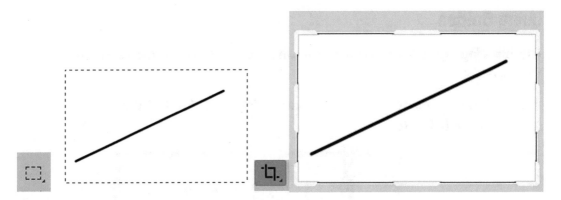

Figure 4-32. *After the Rectangular Marquee selection, click the Crop tool*

9. Click the Crop tool. A new Selection option appears in the options panel. Refer to Figure 4-33.

Figure 4-33. *The Selection option*

You can use the same settings as you did for the Ratio feature.

10. Press the Enter/Return key on your keyboard or select Ratio from the drop-down list. Refer to Figure 4-34.

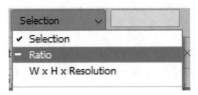

Figure 4-34. *Choose Ratio*

11. Click the Commit button to confirm the crop. Refer to Figure 4-35.

Figure 4-35. *Confirm the crop*

Using Guides

The following explains another way to get an accurate crop using the Rectangular Marquee tool.

    1.   Drag the guides from the upper and left rulers (View ➤ Rulers). Refer to Figure 4-36.

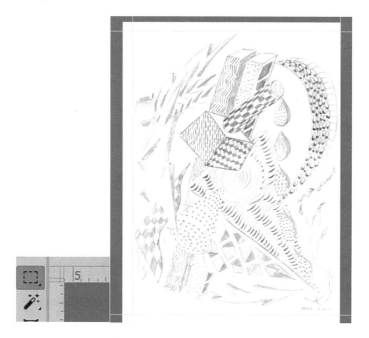

Figure 4-36. *Drag the guides from the rulers*

    2.   With the Rectangular Marquee tool selected, drag your marquee to snap to the guides (View ➤ Snap To Guides). Refer to Figure 4-37.

Figure 4-37. *Rectangular Marquee tool to drag a selection that snaps to guides*

3. Select the Crop tool and click the Commit button in the options
    panel to confirm the crop. Refer to Figure 4-38.

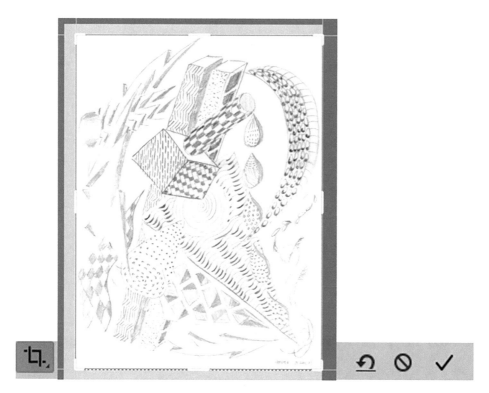

Figure 4-38. *Select the Crop tool and confirm the crop*

Note   If you use the Elliptical Marquee tool, followed by the Crop tool, and then press Enter/Return on the keyboard, the selection crops to a rectangular shape. Refer to Figure 4-39. Removing areas around non-rectangular shapes are best done with a mask, as discussed in Chapters 9 and 12.

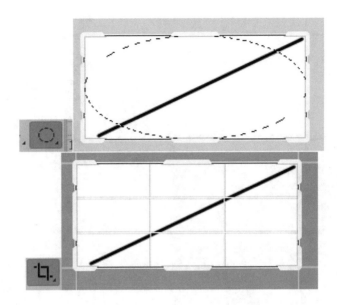

Figure 4-39. *The Elliptical Marquee is only rectangular*

4.   Choose View ➤ Clear Guides if you need to remove the guides.

Tip   For a sketch that needs to be cropped quickly, try Image ➤ Trim. Trimming is done based on Transparent Pixels or Pixel Color in the eyedropper. You can trim from the top, bottom, left, or right. In the dialog box, click a white area with the eyedropper and click OK. This trims closely and removes most of the excess white and transparent areas surrounding the sketch. Refer to Figure 4-40.

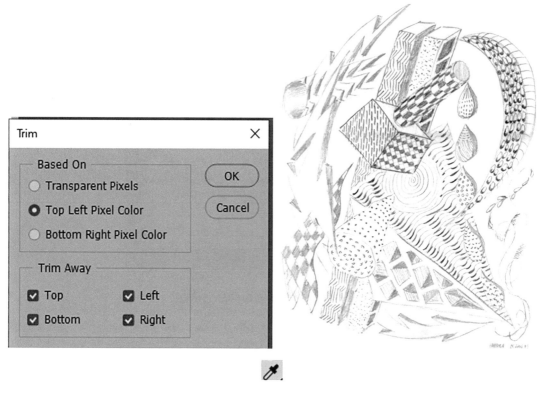

Figure 4-40. *The Trim dialog box, eyedropper, and results*

Perspective Crop Tool (C)

The Perspective Crop tool is also in the Tools panel. Refer to Figure 4-41.

Figure 4-41. *The Perspective Crop tool below the Crop tool*

This tool is generally used with photos to correct various keystone distortions. Let's try it on an artwork photo.

CORRECTING KEYSTONE DISTORTION

1. Open the scan4_2.psd file.

I took a picture of this painted wood-burned project on a grid background. Even though I did not stand directly over it, I could line up the points better. Refer to Figure 4-42.

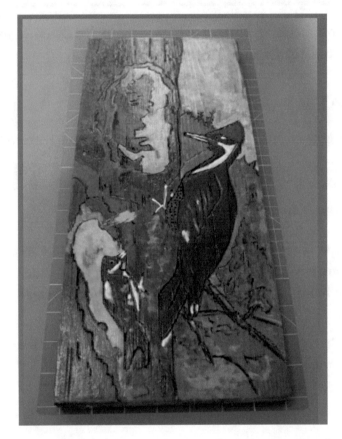

Figure 4-42. *A photo of a painted wood-burned project that has keystone distortion*

2. Go to Image ➤ Duplicate to make a practice on.

3. Click OK in the Duplicate Image dialog box. Refer to Figure 4-43.

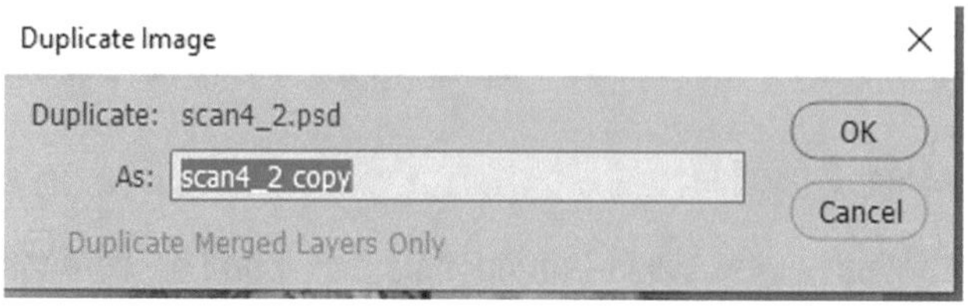

Figure 4-43. *Duplicate Image dialog box*

Refer to this tool and its options panel if you need to slightly adjust your artwork's perspective and crop it simultaneously.

Perspective Crop Options

The Perspective Crop tool has fewer options than the Crop tool. Refer to Figure 4-44.

Figure 4-44. *Perspective Crop tool options*

You can set a preset, swap the **width** or **height**, and change the **resolution** in **pixels per inch or** centimeters. The **Front Image** button takes its values from an earlier opened file; use the **Clear** button to remove data from the fields, and select the check box to hide or **show the grid**.

1. Select the tool. Click the four points of the area you want the crop grid to overlay. Refer to Figure 4-45.

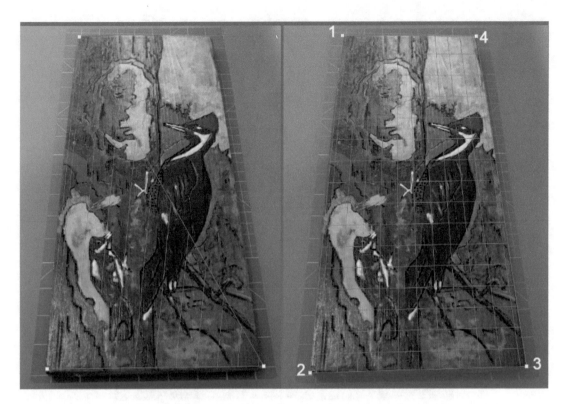

Figure 4-45. *Adding the four points of the perspective overlay grid*

This may be the four corners of a sheet of paper that scanned crookedly, or in this demo, a photo of a painting on a grid that I could not stand directly over. Now there is a visible keystone distortion.

2. Adjust the handles of the four points.

3. Click the Commit button to confirm the crop. Refer to Figure 4-46.

Figure 4-46. *Cancel or confirm the crop*

Photoshop corrects the distortion. The cropped area is now square and rotated. Refer to Figure 4-47.

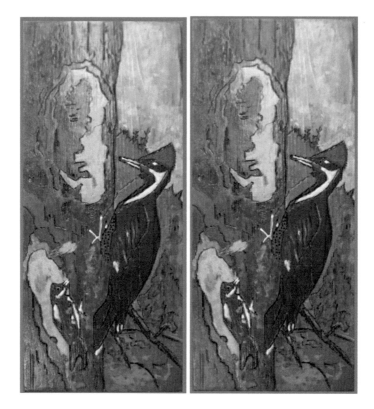

Figure 4-47. *The result of the corrected perspective: using a new layer and brush tool to clean up the image and remove some glare*

4. Use your Brush tool, Eraser tool, or Clone Stamp tool on a blank layer and the adjustment layers to touch up shininess or other imperfections. Refer to Figure 4-47.

Tip   For photos with keystone and lens distortion, I recommend Filter ➤ Lens Correction and tools like Edit ➤ Perspective Warp, Image ➤ Transform ➤ Distort, or Image ➤ Transform ➤ Perspective.

While these distortion correction options are not the topic of this book, I recommend exploring these topics further if you are working with larger pieces of artwork such as murals and large paintings. There may be situations where the artwork is not at eye level, and you must take the picture at an angle or in sections. I consider these extreme perspective distortions that require more advanced filters and transform options than the Perspective Crop tool.

---

5.   Save (Ctrl/Cmd+S) both documents you worked on in this chapter.

You can see an example of the completed scan4_2_final.psd file in this chapter's folder.

Summary

This chapter covered the two main selection tools that you can use to crop your photos from selections and remove unwanted white space around your images. Chapter 5 of this book moves on to intermediate-level selections that you can use to get closer to the edge of your sketches.

CHAPTER 5

Lasso Selection Tools

This chapter shows how to use the Lasso, Polygonal, and Magnetic Lasso tools to get a more accurate selection of the area depending on the background. We'll then review how to copy that selection on a new layer in the Layers panel.

Chapter 3 looked at basic selection tools, including the Rectangular Marquee, Elliptical Marque, and in Chapter 4, Crop tools. Those tools allow you to create a barrier around a sketch so that you can clean up selected areas with the Brush tool, Eraser tool, or Clone Stamp tool. However, the selections are likely not as close or accurate as you would like them to be. You need selection tools that allow you to get closer to more complex shape selections. Refer to Figure 5-1.

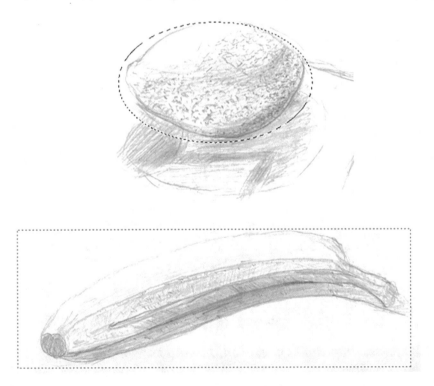

Figure 5-1. *Sketch of lemon and banana with elliptical and rectangular selections*

© Jennifer Harder 2022
J. Harder, *Accurate Layer Selections Using Photoshop's Selection Tools*,
https://doi.org/10.1007/978-1-4842-7493-4_5

Note   This chapter's projects are in the Chapter 5 projects folder.

Let's look at three of them below the Move tool (V). Refer to Figure 5-2.

- Lasso tool (L)

- Polygonal Lasso tool (L)

- Magnetic Lasso tool (L)

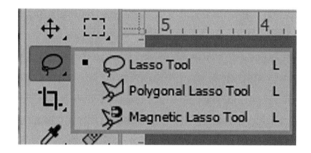

Figure 5-2. *Lasso tool, Polygonal Lasso tool, and Magnetic Lasso tool*

Note   If you read Chapter 3, much of what you have learned about selections can be applied to the following three tools. This chapter gives a basic overview, but you should return to Chapter 3 if you need more instruction on using tools we already discussed in the options panel, the Select ➤ Modify menu (Border, Smooth, Expand, Contract, Feather, and Grow) or Transform Selection. Refer to Figure 5-3.

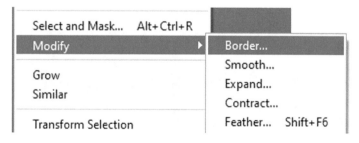

Figure 5-3. *Select drop-down menu options and suboptions*

1. Open the scan5_1.psd file, which you use for practice.

2. Go to Image ➤ Duplicate Copy to make a copy of the file. Click
    OK in the dialog box to confirm the copy. Refer to Figure 5-4.

Figure 5-4. *Baseball cap, garlic bulbs, and driftwood. The Duplicate Image dialog
box creates a duplicate of the file so you don't overwrite the original*

Note   I have already added the adjustment layers to this file in the Layers panel.
Leave the layer 3 eye turned off for now. Refer to Figure 5-5.

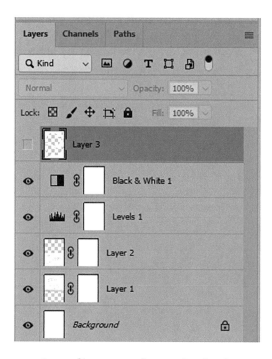

Figure 5-5. *This file contains adjustment layers in the Layers panel, and layer 3 has been hidden with the visibility eye turned off*

Lasso Tool (L)

The Lasso tool allows you to drag or loop around a sketch to create a selection before you paint with your Brush tool.

Try this by clicking once, then on mouse key down, dragging a loop around the cap until you touch the other end. The cursor adds an O to indicate a closed loop when you release the mouse. Refer to Figure 5-6.

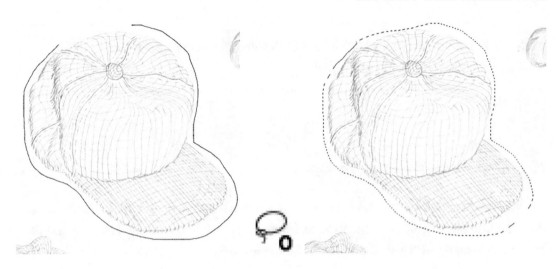

Figure 5-6. *Draw a selection around the baseball cap with the Lasso tool*

The dotted selection or "marching ants" is loose, but it is much closer than you could get with your rectangular or elliptical marquee tools. Refer to Figure 5-7.

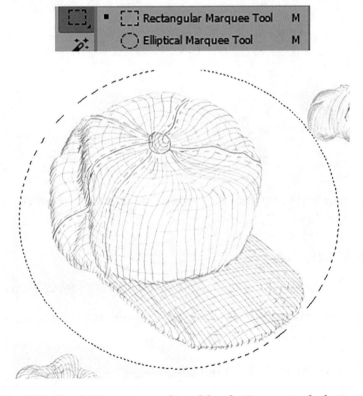

Figure 5-7. *The Elliptical Marquee tool, unlike the Lasso tool, does not create a very close selection*

Tip   Use your Zoom tool to get in closer before using your Lasso tool to get a tighter selection. Refer to Figure 5-8.

Figure 5-8. *Zoom tool in the Tools panel*

When you click away on the canvas, the selection disappears. If you do not complete the selection before releasing the mouse, Photoshop tries to complete it for you and fill in the gap, usually with a straight join. Refer to Figure 5-9.

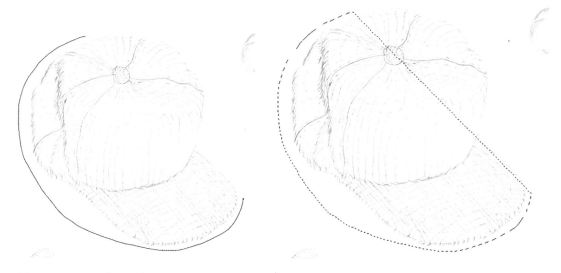

Figure 5-9. *Photoshop completes an incomplete selection when you release the mouse*

You can do the following.

- Paint or erase inside the selection with your Brush tool or Eraser tool

- Select ➤ Inverse (Shift+Ctrl/Cmd+I) and paint outside the selection with your Brush or Eraser tool

- Select ➤ Deselect (Ctrl/Cmd+D) to remove the selection

- Select ➤ Reselect (Shift+ Ctrl/Cmd+D) to bring the selection back right away.

Lasso Tool Options

From left to right, look at the options panel. Many of the settings should already have become familiar to you. Refer to Figure 5-10.

Figure 5-10. *Options for the Lasso tool*

As with all the other tools you have looked at so far, you can add **presets** by choosing various options. Click the plus (+) button, name the preset, click OK to confirm the name, and add it to the list. Or, use the gear menu to manage the current presets; by default, there are none. Refer to Figure 5-11.

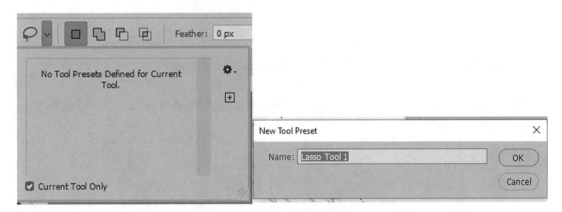

Figure 5-11. *Presets drop-down for the Lasso tool is empty by default until you create a new preset and click OK in the New Tool Preset dialog box*

The next section in the options panel offers four selection choices. Refer to Figure 5-12.

Figure 5-12. *Selection options*

The New Selection button drags out a new selection. It is the default. Refer to Figure 5-13.

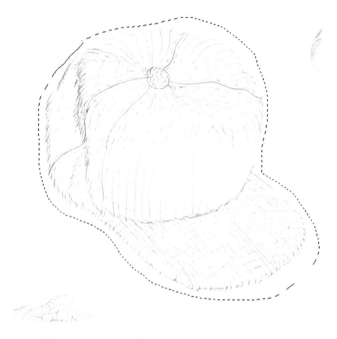

Figure 5-13. *A new selection around the baseball cap sketch*

The Add to Selection button adds to the selection (or hold down the Shift key while dragging). Refer to Figure 5-14.

Figure 5-14. *Addition of a selection added to the baseball cap sketch*

The Subtract from Selection button removes part of a selection (or hold down the Alt/Option key while dragging). Refer to Figure 5-15.

Figure 5-15. *Subtraction of a selection around the baseball cap sketch*

The Intersect with Selection button only retains the part of the selection that intersects. Alt/Option+Shift keys allow you to access this option. Refer to Figure 5-16.

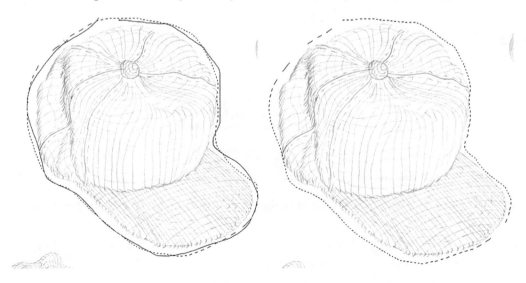

Figure 5-16. *Intersecting parts of the current selection with this option gets a tighter selection around the cap*

Refer to Chapter 3 if you need more information on how these selections work.

After working with a selection tool, I always reset the options to New Selection. Refer to Figure 5-17.

Figure 5-17. *Reset the selection back to New Selection*

Note   You can use these selection tool's options in combination with other selection tools discussed in this chapter and Chapter 3.

Feather allows you to create a feathered selection and softened edges. Refer to Figure 5-18.

Figure 5-18. *Feather and Anti-alias options*

On both the inside and outside of the selection, set a feather between 0 and 1000 px. You may get this warning if you set the setting too high in pixel number, such as 1000 pixels. Refer to Figure 5-19.

Figure 5-19. *Photoshop warning message about the current feathered selection*

Click OK in the message. It does not reveal the selection, so you should set your feather lower.

Draw another selection around the cap at 100 px. When you use the Brush tool, it paints a very soft edge beyond the borders. Refer to Figure 5-20.

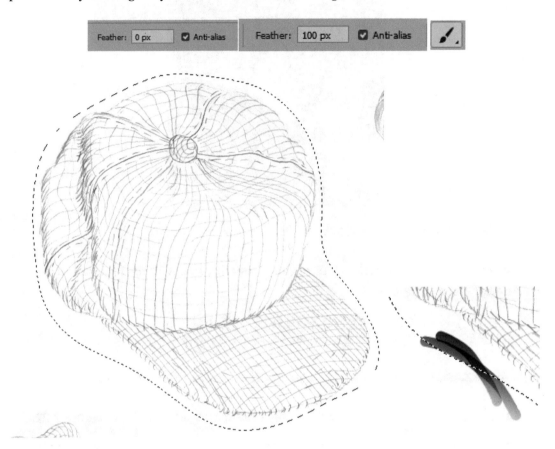

Figure 5-20. *After setting the feathering, a new selection is made, and then with the Brush tool, you can paint to see the result of the feather*

Note   To remove the brush strokes, use the History panel. See Chapter 2 if you need more information on how to do this. Refer to Figure 5-21.

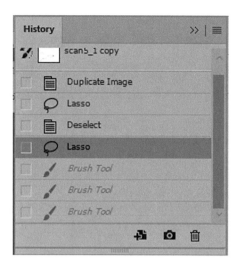

Figure 5-21. *Moving back a few steps in the History panel*

I usually reset Feather back to 0 pixels after I am finished with the tool, so it is ready next time. Refer to Figure 5-22.

Figure 5-22. *Reset Feather to 0 px before you make another selection*

Enabling **Anti-alias** also smooths the edges of the transition. Refer to Figure 5-22.

Note   Using Select ➤ Modify ➤ Feather on a selection, this command feathers more on the edge than on the inside of the selection. Refer to Figure 5-23.

Figure 5-23. *The result of Modify* ➤ *Feather on a selection is different from the Feather option*

The last button, Select and Mask, is covered in Chapter 9. Refer to Figure 5-24.

Figure 5-24. *Select and Mask button*

You have a new selection around the cap, and Feather is set to 0 px. In the Layers panel, choose New Layer (Shift +Ctrl/Cmd+N). Refer to Figure 5-25.

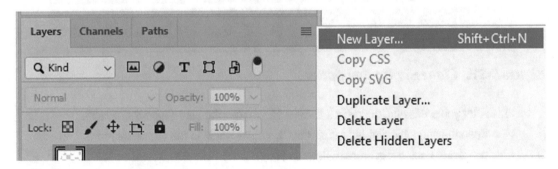

Figure 5-25. *Create a new layer*

Use the Brush tool to paint in white or use the Clone Stamp tool to clear up any imperfections around the hat on a blank layer.

WORKING WITH THE CLONE SOURCE PANEL

While working with your selection, you may notice that some of the lines in the hat are broken, and you want to use your Clone Stamp tool to correct this. Refer to Figure 5-26.

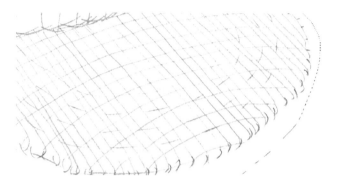

Figure 5-26. *Close up of edge around the baseball cap*

The Window ➤ Clone Source panel was introduced in Chapter 2. It allows you to change the angle of your clone. Try this on the blank layer you created and make sure the sample is set to Current & Below. Refer to Figure 5-27.

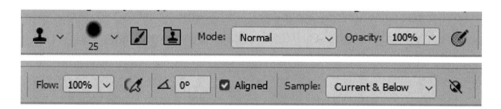

Figure 5-27. *Clone Stamp tool options*

1. After you press Alt/Option-click to select a source with your Clone Stamp tool. Keep the angle highlighted rather than typing an angle in the Clone Source panel and hoping it is correct. Refer to Figure 5-28.

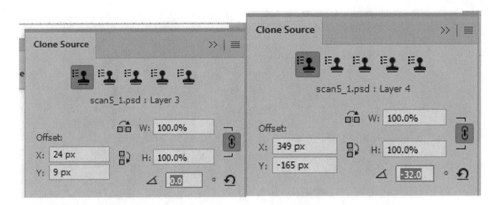

Figure 5-28. *Setting the angle in the Clone Source panel*

2. Fill in line areas around the curve. Use the Up and Down arrow keys on your keyboard to change the preview of the Clone Stamp tool rotation by a tenth of a degree. Or hold down the Shift key while using the arrows and rotate by a degree at a time. Refer to Figure 5-29.

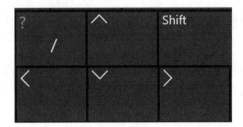

Figure 5-29. *Use the Up and Down arrow keys in combination with the Shift key to set the angle of the Clone Source preview*

3. Then click the new point you want to Clone Stamp. Refer to Figure 5-30.

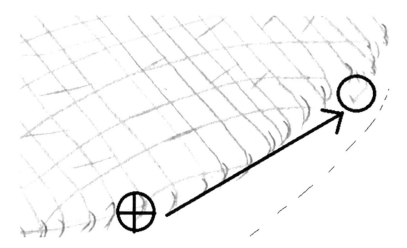

Figure 5-30. *Close up of Clone Source and new source to line up the edge of my sketch to add some of the original pencil strokes*

4. Repeat these steps to fill in the gaps alternating with the Eraser tool to remove part of the clone you don't need.

You can see the cloning before and after by turning off layer 4 and turning on the eye in layer 3 of this file to compare.

In addition, I painted in various areas with white using the Brush tool to cover up various lines around other areas of the image. Refer to Figure 5-31.

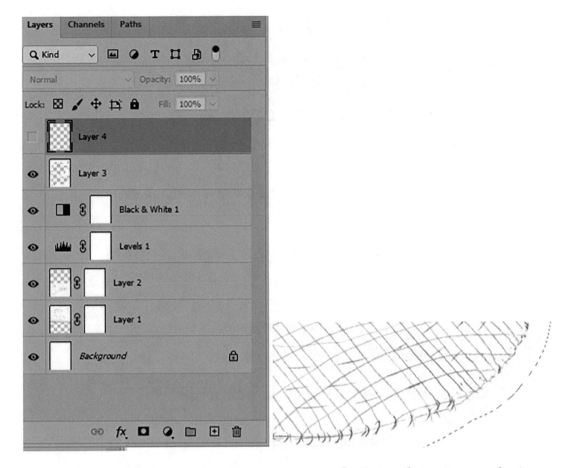

Figure 5-31. *In the Layers panel, compare your cloning on layer 4 to my cloning on layer 3 and see if you can add lines to the edge of the baseball cap*

5. After completing the selection, choose Select ➤ Deselect (Ctrl/Cmd+D) to try the next selection tool.

6. Save (Ctrl/Cmd+S) the document.

Polygonal Lasso Tool (L)

The Polygonal Lasso tool is under the Lasso tool. It is good for creating selections around angular shapes and selections with sharp edges. Refer to Figure 5-32.

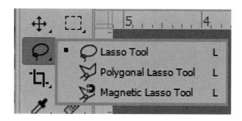

Figure 5-32. *Polygonal Lasso tool*

1. Go to File ➤ Open to open the scan5_2.psd practice file. Refer to Figure 5-33.

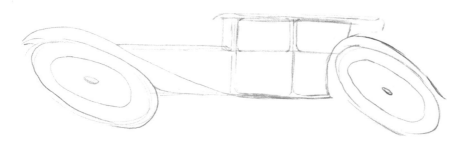

Figure 5-33. *Sketch of an old fast-moving car with big tires*

2. Click a starting point and go around a shape clicking at points to create an angular selection.

3. Hold down the Shift key to drag a straight line at a 45° or 90° angle as you click the next segment. Refer to Figure 5-34.

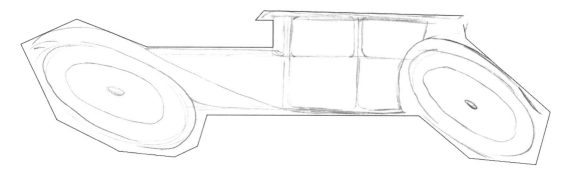

Figure 5-34. *Use the Polygonal Lasso tool to click around the car*

4.   While clicking and dragging, switch temporarily to the Lasso tool and draw freehand, hold down the Alt/Option key to change the cursor and then release that key to return to the Polygonal Lasso tool and continue clicking your next point on the path. Refer to Figure 5-35.

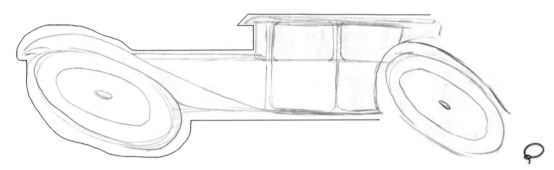

Figure 5-35.   *Using the Polygonal Lasso and the Lasso tool at the same time for sharp and freehand curves to make the selection*

5.   If you made a mistake, use the Backspace/Delete key to go back one or more clicks while creating the selection. Refer to Figure 5-36.

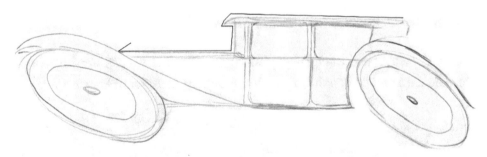

Figure 5-36.   *You can revert in your selection while creating it if you make a mistake*

Tip   Use the Hand tool while working with the Polygonal Lasso by pressing the spacebar so you can move around to the next point in your section. You can also use the key commands Ctrl/Cmd+ + (plus) and Ctrl/Cmd+ - (hyphen) to zoom in and out. Refer to Figure 5-37.

Figure 5-37. *Access the Hand tool while you hold down the spacebar on your keyboard*

6. To finish, click the starting point to close the selection. You see a small O by the Polygonal Lasso tool cursor, which indicates closure. Refer to Figure 5-38.

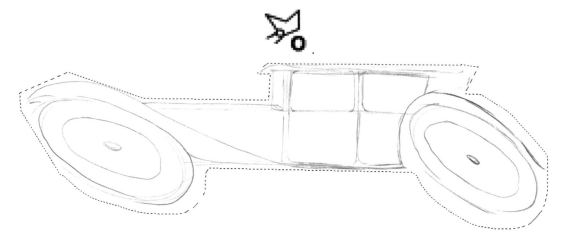

Figure 5-38. *Close the selection around the car*

If you don't complete the selection, double-click your canvas. Photoshop tries to finish the selection and bridge the gap with a straight join. Refer to Figure 5-39.

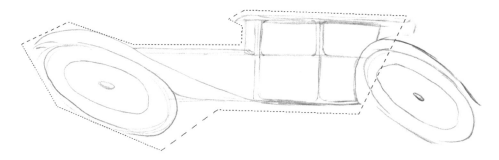

Figure 5-39. *Photoshop tries to close an incomplete selection*

Polygonal Lasso Options

The Lasso tool is very similar to the Polygonal Lasso tool. Refer to Chapter 3 if you need more information. Refer to Figure 5-40 for Polygonal Lasso tool options.

Figure 5-40. *Options for the Polygonal Lasso tool*

The following describes these options.

- **The Tool Presets** drop-down creates new presets.
- **The New Selection, Add to Selection, Subtract from Selection, and Intersect with Selection icons.**
- **Feather** selects from 0 to 1000 pixels.
- **Anti-alias** smoothing in combination with Feather when enabled.
- **Select and Mask** is covered in Chapter 9.

Note   If you need to combine or subtract selections, use the Polygonal Selection tool options in combination with other selection tools that were looked at in this chapter and Chapter 3.

As you did with the Lasso tool on a blank layer while your selection is active, use your Brush tool and Clone Stamp tool to clean up imperfections. Refer to Figure 5-41.

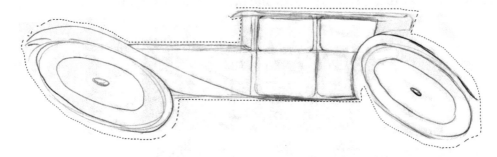

Figure 5-41. *Clean up areas of the sketch inside the selection or Select ➤ Inverse to clean up around the selection*

You can see that I did that on layer 1 of the file. Notice I have also included some adjustment layers, which you can review in Chapter 2. Refer to Figure 5-42.

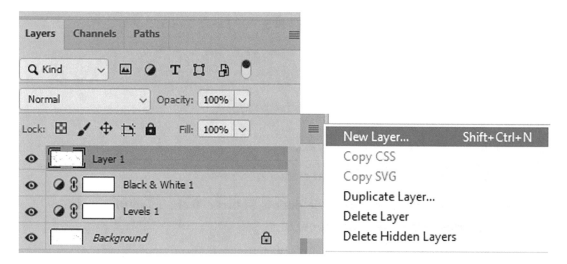

Figure 5-42. *Use your new layer to paint or Clone Stamp on. Two adjustment layers where added to the Layers panel by me*

After completing the selection, go to Select ➤ Deselect to try the last selection tool. Save (Ctrl/Cmd+S) the document.

Magnetic Lasso Tool (L)

The Magnetic Lasso tool in the collection is a helpful selection tool that acts as a combination of the Lasso tool and the Polygonal Lasso tool. It works best with a sketch with a distinct edge to follow with a path and points. Refer to Figure 5-43.

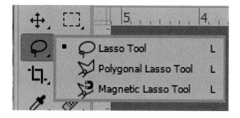

Figure 5-43. *The Magnetic Lasso tool in the Tools panel*

Return to Image ➤ Duplicate to open the scan5_1.psd file (copy). Use the garlic bulb in the lower left on the page this time for practice. Refer to Figure 5-44.

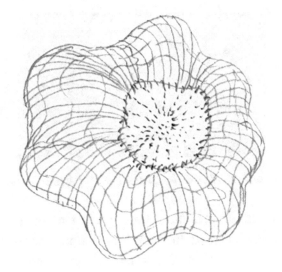

Figure 5-44. *Sketch of a garlic bulb*

If you click a fastening point and then move the mouse and hover or keep pressed around the edge of a sketch, the Magnetic Lasso tool lays down points and a path that snaps as closely to the edge to create a tight selection with both curved and angular edges. Refer to Figure 5-45.

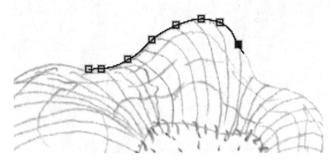

Figure 5-45. *Magnetic Lasso points and path*

Note   If a point does not fasten, you can click to add a point and then continue to let Photoshop lay down points as you hover over the sketch line.

While drawing the selection, if you find the points getting tangled up or sticking to lines you don't want them to, you can pause and move back points by pressing the Backspace/Delete Key on your keyboard. Refer to Figure 5-46.

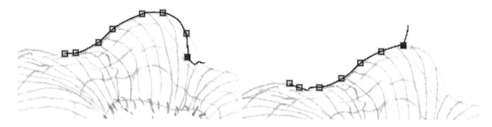

Figure 5-46. *Remove points if you find they are getting tangled up, and continue*

This removes some path points. Then you can return to that point and hover again around the selection until you reach the endpoint. Double-click to close.

As you near the end of the selection, an O should appear next to the tool's cursor. Click to close it. Double-click or press Enter/Return on your keyboard if you can't see the final point, and Photoshop closes the selection. Refer to Figure 5-47.

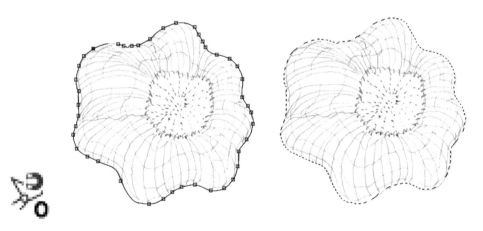

Figure 5-47. *Close the selection with the Magnetic Lasso tool*

To close a border with a straight segment, hold down the Alt/Option key and double-click.

Click away or choose Select ➤ Deselect if you want to deselect the selection.

Note   Paths are discussed in more detail in Chapters 10, 11, and 12.

Magnetic Lasso options

The Magnetic Lasso tool has many of the same options as the Lasso and Polygonal Lasso tools. It also has options that allow you to adjust the way the selection points appear.

Take a moment to compare the Magnetic Lasso tool's options to the Polygonal Lasso tool's options. If you need more information on how to use the various options, refer to the section on the Lasso tool in this chapter and the sections on the Rectangular and Elliptical Marquee tools in Chapter 3.

The Magnetic Lasso tool's options panel is shown from left to right in Figure 5-48.

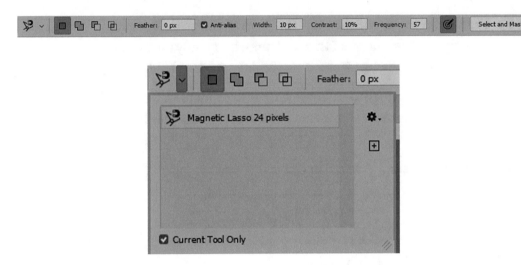

Figure 5-48. *Magnetic Lasso tool options*

- **Tool Presets** drop-down for creating new presets.

- **New Selection, Add to Selection, Subtract from Selection, Intersect with Selection**

- **Feather** selection from 0 to 1000 pixels. **Anti-alias** smoothing in combination with Feather when enabled.

- **Width sets** the distance from edge to consider for the path between 1 px and 256 px. Detection of edges occurs within the specified distance from the pointer. To see the lasso width, press the Caps Lock key on your keyboard. You can use the right bracket ( ]) to increase the width edge by 1 px and the left bracket ([ ) to decrease the width edge by 1 px at a time; the default is 10 px. Refer to Figure 5-49.

Figure 5-49. *Width, Contrast, Frequency, and Pressure settings*

- **Contrast** sets the edge to consider for the path (1% to 100%). High values detect edges that contrast sharply with the surrounding pixels and lower values can be used for lower contrast edges. Refer to Figure 5-49.

- **Frequency** sets at which points are added to the path (0 to 100). The higher the value, the faster and more frequently the anchor points appear and be placed. 57 is the default. Refer to Figure 5-49.

- **Use Tablet pressure to Change pen width** (optional if using a tablet and stylus) increases in pressure decreases the edge width. Refer to Figure 5-49.

- **Select and Mask** is covered in Chapter 9. Refer to Figure 5-50.

Figure 5-50. *Select and Mask button*

Note   Depending on your image, you must adjust the width, contrast, and frequency higher or lower to lay down accurate points Chapters 10, 11, and 12 explain how the Paths tool can assist in placing points exactly where you want them.

After selecting, you can use your Brush tool, Eraser tool, and Clone Stamp tool to clean up the sketch on a New Blank layer as I did on layer 3 earlier. Refer to Figure 5-51.

Figure 5-51. *Brush tool, Eraser tool, and Clone Stamp tool in the Tools panel*

COPY OR CUT TO ANOTHER LAYER USING SELECTIONS REVIEW

1. After you clean up your copy, go to the Layers panel and choose Flatten Image. Refer to Figure 5-52.

Create Clipping Mask	Alt+Ctrl+G
Link Layers	
Select Linked Layers	
Merge Down	Ctrl+E
Merge Visible	Shift+Ctrl+E
Flatten Image	

Figure 5-52. *Choose Flatten Image from the Layers panel if you need to make all the layers one layer*

2. Then create another selection using one of the Lasso tools used in this chapter. Refer to Figure 5-53.

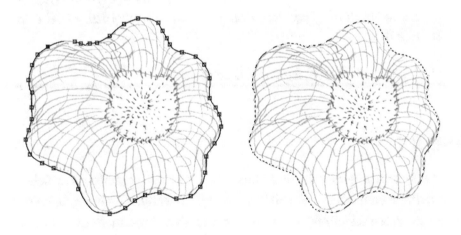

Figure 5-53. *Using the Magnetic Lasso tool, I again selected the garlic bulb*

3. Use one of the copying and pasting techniques from Chapter 3 to move parts of the image to a new layer.

- **Layer Via Copy** (Ctrl/Cmd+J) copies that selection from the Background layer and pastes it onto a new layer in the same location.

- **Layer Via Cut** (Ctrl/Cmd+Shift+J) cuts that selection from the background and pastes it onto a new layer in that same location. The area cut from the background is replaced with whatever the current background color is in the Tools panel. Make sure the background is white in this case. Refer to Chapter 2 if you need to review this.

Refer to Figure 5-54.

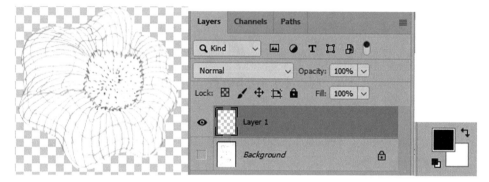

Figure 5-54. *Either copy or cut your selection from the background onto a new layer in the same location. If you cut, make sure your background in the Tools panel is set to white*

4. Save (Ctrl/Cmd+S) your project to your computer.

Summary

This chapter looked at three selection tools that you can use to refine your selection to get closer to the sketch rather than adding multiple selections together using rectangular or elliptical marquee selections. However, you can always use them in combination. The next section explores how to use the Magic Wand tool outside and inside of Quick Mask mode to get even closer to your selection edge and look at how to use the Type Mask tool for specialized selections.

CHAPTER 6

Selections with Magic Wand, Quick Mask Mode, and Type Mask Tools

This chapter shows how to use the Magic Wand and the Quick Mask mode to refine selections using the Brush or Eraser tool. You continue to look at various ways to control the type of selection using the main menu and copy selections to another layer. A brief reference at the end is made on how you can use the horizontal and vertical type mask tools to make a type selection.

So far, you have seen that you can get closer selections to a sketch if you use various lasso tools in the Tools panel. However, you may have also observed that while these selection tools are useful, they are not 100% accurate.

As well, if you click away from the selection, it disappears, and you need to choose Select ➤ Reselect right away to get it back if you want to continue to add to the selection using the options panel. This can get frustrating if you need to create a very accurate selection and not rush through the process. This chapter addresses that using the Quick Mask mode.

Note This chapter's projects are in the Chapter 6 project folder for this book.

213

© Jennifer Harder 2022
J. Harder, *Accurate Layer Selections Using Photoshop's Selection Tools*,
https://doi.org/10.1007/978-1-4842-7493-4_6

First, let's look at another selection tool in the Tools panel. Refer to Figure 6-1.

- The Magic Wand tool (W)

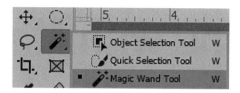

Figure 6-1. *Location of the Magic Wand tool in the Tools panel*

Let's examine how it compares to the other selection tools and how it can be used with **Quick Mask mode**. Refer to Figure 6-2.

Figure 6-2. *Edit in Quick Mask mode (Q) button in the Tools panel*

Note   Chapter 7 goes over the Quick Selection tool and the Object Selection tool.

Though not directly part of the sketch clean-up process, later, you look at a lesser-known set of selection tools. Refer to Figure 6-3.

- Vertical Type Mask tool (T)

- Horizontal Type Mask tool (T)

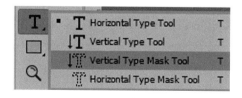

Figure 6-3. *Locations of Vertical Type Mask tool and Horizontal Type Mask tool in the Tools panel*

Magic Wand Tool (W)

Much of what you have learned so far about Selection tools in Chapters 3 and 5 can be applied to the Magic Wand tool once you have used it to create a selection.

1. File ➤ Open scan6_1.psd and make an Image ➤ Duplicate Copy as you did in Chapter 1 to work on as practice. Click OK in the dialog box. Refer to Figure 6-4.

Figure 6-4. *A sketch of a bird. Use the Duplicate Image dialog box to make a copy*

2. To create a selection on a sketch using this tool, click any area. For this practice, I clicked a white area. Refer to Figure 6-5.

Figure 6-5. *My selection result after clicking on the white area with the Magic Wand tool around the bird*

The tool selects those white pixels.

3.   You can paint with your Brush tool or erase with the Eraser tool within that selection, either on the background or a normal layer.

However, in some areas, the Magic Wand selects pixels that you do not want to, such as on the bird's wing or leg. This may be due to an area not being completely closed off by a line, or the color falls within a set Tolerance, which you look at in a moment.

Nevertheless, this is a useful tool for fast selection when you have imperfections on the paper and need to paint white over the spots to remove them.

Magic Wand Options

To understand more about the Magic Wand tool, look at its options panel from left to right. There are many similarities in this panel with previous selection tools. Refer to Figure 6-6.

Figure 6-6. *Magic Wand tool options in the options panel*

As with the other tools explored in Chapters 2, 3, 4, and 5, the **presets** allow you to save presets of your various tools options that you may want to use at various times in other files. Refer to Figure 6-7.

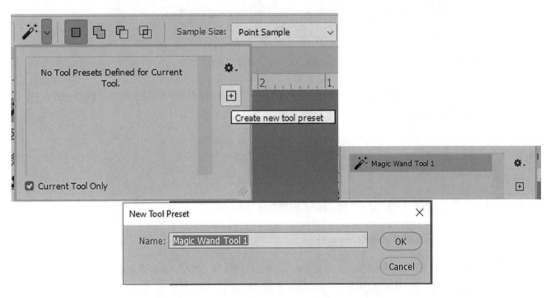

Figure 6-7. *Use the options panel to create a new tool preset*

By default, there are no presets, but you can create ones for the current tool by pressing the (+) plus icon and then naming the tool preset and clicking OK to exit the dialog box. The gear drop-down menu allows you to manage and delete tool presets. Refer to Figure 6-8.

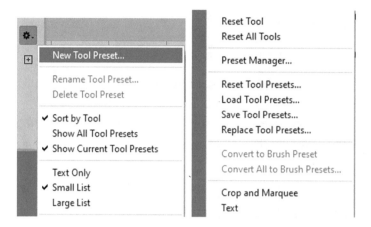

Figure 6-8. *Use the gear menu to manage your presets*

The next section allows you to adjust and add to your selections, as you saw in Chapter 3 and Chapter 5. Refer to Figure 6-9.

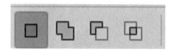

Figure 6-9. *Selection options in the Options panel*

Let's review as it relates to this tool.

- The **New Selection** button allows you to click areas of a sketch with a color of similar pixels and create a selection of that area. Refer to Figure 6-10.

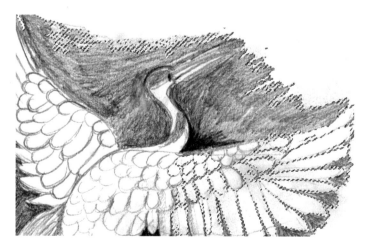

Figure 6-10. *New selection using the Magic Wand tool*

218

- The **Add to Selection** button allows you to click more than one area
  of a sketch to add more to the selection, increasing its size. If you hold
  down the Shift key while you click, you can add to the selection, and
  the cursor adds a plus symbol beside it. This is useful for holes and
  blank areas in a sketch. Refer to Figure 6-11.

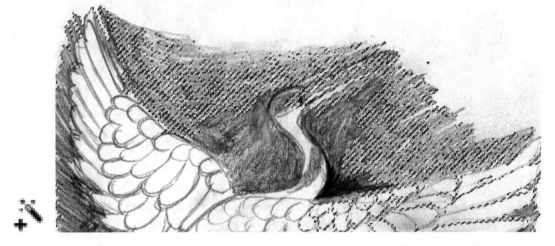

Figure 6-11. *The selection area is expanded by clicking another area while using
the Add to Selection button*

- The **Subtract from Selection** button allows you to click in more than
  one area of a sketch to subtract and decrease the selection size. If you
  hold down the Alt/Option key while you click, you can remove parts
  of the selection, and the cursor adds a minus symbol beside it. Refer
  to Figure 6-12.

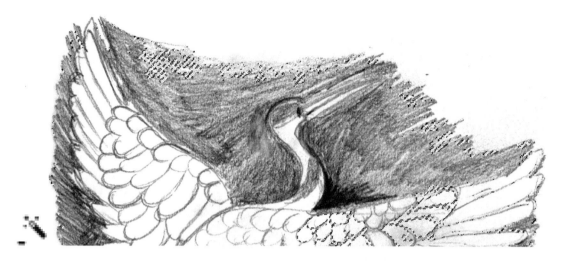

Figure 6-12. *The selection area is reduced by clicking another area using the Subtract From Selection button*

- The **Intersect with Selection** button allows you to intersect two selections and the center of the two selections is what remains. Using the Alt/Option+Shift keys allows you to access this option, and the cursor adds an X symbol beside it. Refer to Figure 6-13.

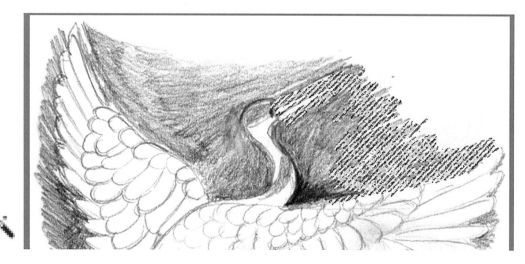

Figure 6-13. *Only the selection area that intersects with the first selection remains after clicking the second time*

After I am done using this selection tool, I set it back to the default of New Selection to use it for another sketch. Refer to Figure 6-14.

Figure 6-14. *Reset selection area*

As with the Rectangular Marquee tool, you can use the Select menu and Modify submenu to adjust your selection. Refer to Chapter 3 if you need to review. You can choose Select ➤ Inverse (Shift+Ctrl/Cmd+I) to select the inverse or outside the current selection. Refer to Figure 6-15.

Figure 6-15. *Inverse the selection to paint in the area containing the bird*

In the Select ➤ Modify submenu, use one of the following to alter the selection. Refer to Figure 6-16.

- **Border** adds a set pixel border selection around the sketch.

- **Smooth** rounds the corners of the current selection by a set number of pixels.

- **Contract** shrinks the current selection by a set number of pixels.

- **Expand** increases the area around the current selection by a set number of pixels.

- **Feather** softens the edge of the current selection by a set number of pixels.

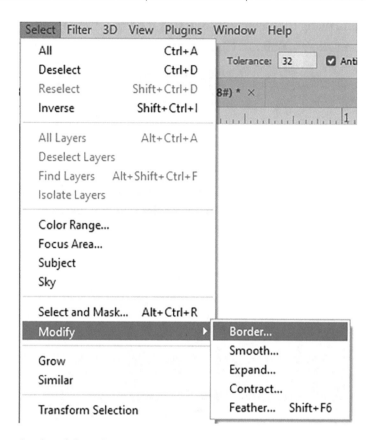

Figure 6-16. *The Modify submenu and its options*

Select ➤ Similar allows you to select similar colors to add to your selection. Refer to Figure 6-16 and Figure 6-17.

Figure 6-17. *Select ➤ Similar lets you select pixels of a similar color range*

Select ➤ Transform Selection lets you expand the selection using the bounding box handles, but this is not the best way to modify with the Magic Wand tool and get an accurate selection.

Note   In the Select menu, selecting all or some of layer(s)/deselect layers, find, and Isolate layers can help you with your correct selection process of layers, but they in no way modify the current selection. Refer to Figure 6-16.

Magic Wand Options Continued

The next section controls what pixels are selected. Refer to Figure 6-18.

Figure 6-18. *Magic Wand tool options*

Sample Size is the number of pixels sampled by the tool. In some ways, the Magic Wand tool is similar to the Eyedropper tool in that it samples colors and the current pixels to make a selection. Refer to Figure 6-19.

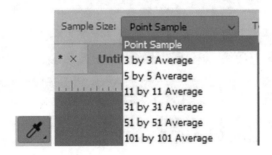

Figure 6-19. *Sample Size options are similar to the Eyedropper tool (I)*

You can choose an exact Point Sample size or broader ranges of 3 by 3 Average up to 101 by 101 Average. This is entirely dependent on how close the pixels blend, so every image is different in its selection size regardless of the Sample Size option.

In my graphic of a grayscale gradient (gradient_fill.psd), I demonstrate that when you click in a white area how much you could be expanding your selection. The blue guide mark helps you visualize where on the picture you are. Refer to Figure 6-20.

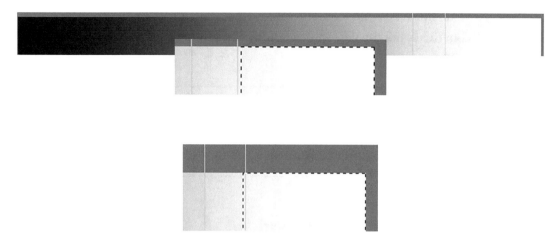

Figure 6-20. *Use of Sample Size: (Top) No Sample. (Middle) Point Sample,
(Bottom) 101 by 101 Average*

Tolerance sets the range while sampling color and can be set from 0 to 255. The
default is 32, but higher numbers sample more colors faster. You can see here how that
affects the selection in a grayscale gradient. Refer to Figure 6-21.

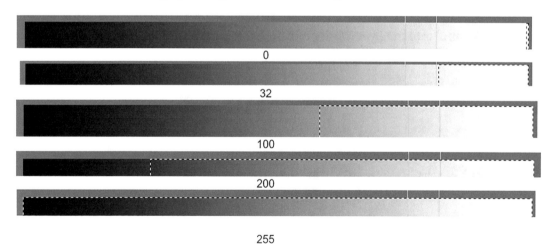

Figure 6-21. *Notice how setting the tolerance at various settings creates a larger
selection of colors in the grayscale 255 being the entire selection. Blue guides are
added for reference*

Anti-alias, when enabled, smooths the edge transition. Refer to Figure 6-22.

Figure 6-22. *Anti-alias, Contiguous, and Sample All Layers*

Contiguous allows you to sample those pixels that share a common border or are touching other pixels and is enabled by default. Refer to Figure 6-22.

Sample All Layers is used when your document has more than one layer, and you need to sample from all layers. This makes it easier to sample all pixels no matter what layer you're on, but leave this option unchecked if you need to sample only from one layer. Refer to Figure 6-22.

The following are the last buttons on the options panel. Refer to Figure 6-23.

Select Subject (Select ➤ Subject) creates a selection from prominent objects in the image. You look at this in more detail in Chapter 7.

The Select and Mask is button is covered in Chapter 9.

Figure 6-23. *Select Subject and Select and Mask buttons in the options panel*

Tip   If you are not using the Magic Wand tool, another way to quickly select an object on a normal layer or layer 0 is to click the Layers panel thumbnail preview while holding down the Ctrl/Cmd key. This is the same as right-click the layers thumbnail preview and choosing Select Pixels from the pop-up menu. Refer to Figure 6-24.

Figure 6-24. *Select pixels using the Layers panel*

Quick Mask Mode (Q)

When working on a complex selection, you want to edit the selection when some pixels are not selecting as they should. You should not have to worry that the selection disappears while you have your new selection active if you click somewhere else on your sketch.

Continue to work with the copy of scan6_1.psd with the active selection. Refer to Figure 6-25.

Figure 6-25. *Current Selection of the white background area around the bird*

To create the more accurate selection, press the Q button on your keyboard, click Edit in Quick Mask mode from the lower-left Tools panel, or Select ➤ Edit in Quick Mask mode. Refer to Figure 6-26.

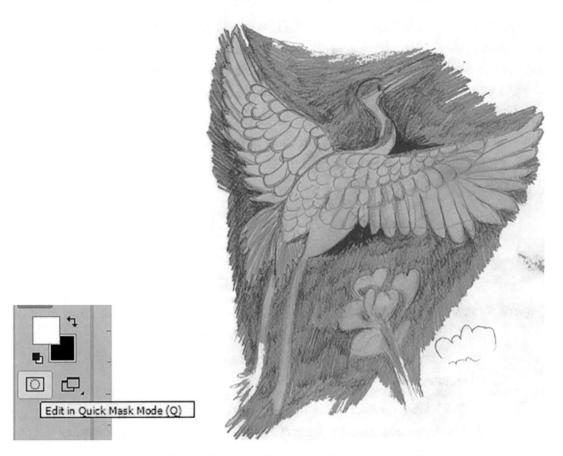

Figure 6-26. *Enter Quick Mask mode (Q) using the Tools panel*

This turns the area that is not part of the selection an opaque red and leaves the selected area clear, in this case, the white area around the sketch in its true color. The selected layer is red as well. Refer to Figure 6-27.

Figure 6-27. *The selected Background Layer in the Layer panel turns a red color*

Quick Mask mode allows you to use the Eraser tool or Brush tool only on the mask to get even closer to the selection to clean up an image. In this mode, you are not erasing anything in the image, only the mask which modifies the selection.

The following are things to know when working in Quick Mask mode.

- The Brush tool allows you to reveal with a white foreground and hide with a black foreground. In the Tools panel, use your X key to toggle between the two. Refer to Figure 6-28.

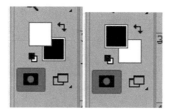

Figure 6-28. *Switching the foreground and background colors in the Tools panel*

- The Eraser tool reveals the black background and hides the white foreground in the Tools panel.

- In Quick Mask mode, I prefer to use the Brush tool. I use various Brush Sizes and Hardness to get closer to the selection edges. Refer to Figure 6-29.

Figure 6-29. *Access your Brush tool options in the options panel while in Quick Mask mode*

- If you want to fade or feather or anti-alias the mask while painting, choose another color that gives you a shade of gray. Just remember, to return to black and white, press the D key for default and the X to switch as you paint and erase. Refer to Figure 6-30.

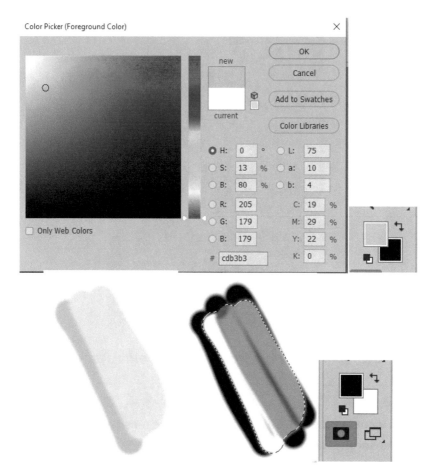

Figure 6-30. *Colors other than black and white produce a grayscale mask that can be used for feathering, later when painting with the Brush tool in a selection. Remember to set back to the default colors when done*

1. In the Tools panel, give your Brush tool a black foreground and cover areas of the bird's legs, wings, or anywhere you want to be excluded from the selection. Refer to Figure 6-31.

Figure 6-31. *In Quick Mask mode, paint over the leg and areas you want to exclude from the selection*

2. Press X and use white to remove the smudge on the right side that you want to remove and make it part of the selection. Refer to Figure 6-32.

Figure 6-32. *In Quick Mask mode, switch to white and paint over areas you want to include in the selection*

3. Remember to Zoom in with the Zoom tool and Use your Hand tool when you hold down the spacebar to maneuver around your image. Refer to Figure 6-33.

Figure 6-33. *Use your Zoom tool (Z) and Hand tool (H) to move around in Quick Mask mode while working with your Brush tool*

4. Once you have cleared the area you want for your selection, press the Q again, or Edit in Standard Mode button in the Tools panel, and your new selection will be visible. Refer to Figure 6-34.

Figure 6-34. Exit the Quick Mask mode using the Tools panel and return to Standard mode (Q)

Note   On your project, you may have to enter and exit the Quick Mask mode a few times if you notice you missed a few pixels. Don't start erasing in your selection area until you are happy with the results of your Quick Mask.

---

5.   Create a new layer in your Layers panel, and the selection remains
     active. Refer to Figure 6-35.

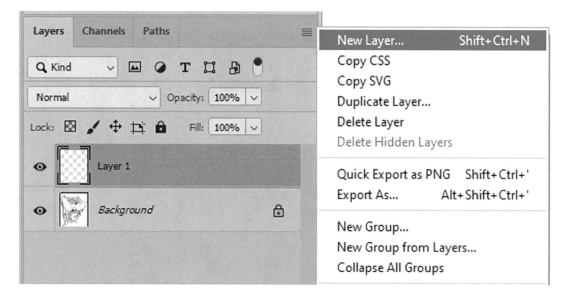

Figure 6-35.   *Add a new layer to paint over imperfections while using your
selection*

6.   You can continue to use your Brush tool, in this case in the white
     and Eraser tool or Clone Stamp tools, to clean up the area within
     the selection, which is the area surrounding the bird. Refer to
     Figure 6-36.

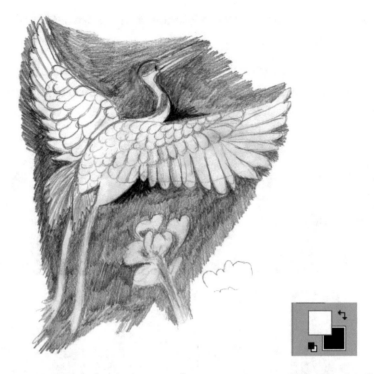

Figure 6-36. *Paint with white to cover the areas surrounding the bird*

Note   Because this is a complex selection, it is probably a good idea to save it. You learn how to do that with sketches in Chapters 9, 10, 11, and 12 of this book. However, I saved the selection in my scan6_1b.psd file. It is in the Window ➤ Channels panel. Masks are also discussed in those chapters. Refer to Figure 6-37.

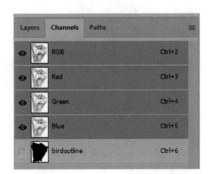

Figure 6-37. *The Channels panel storing saved selection*

7. Keep the selection active for the moment and choose Select ➤
    Inverse (Shift Ctrl/Cmd+I).

8. Clean up any areas inside the selection with your Clone stamp
    tool, like the lines on the feathers. Refer to that section Chapter 2 if
    you need to review. Refer to Figure 6-38.

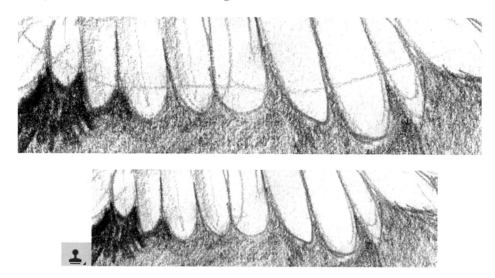

Figure 6-38. *Use your Clone Stamp tool to clean up some of the extra lines in the bird's wing*

9. Make sure your background color in the Tools panel is set to
    White. Refer to Figure 6-39.

Figure 6-39. *Set the background color to white in the Tools panel*

10. In the Layers panel, choose Flatten image. Refer to Figure 6-40.

Figure 6-40. *In the Layers panel, choose Flatten Image*

11. Use one of the following key commands to paste your selection to a new layer. Refer to Figure 6-41 and Figure 6-42.

- **Layer Via Copy** (Ctrl/Cmd+J)

- **Layer via Cut** (Ctrl/Cmd+Shift+J)

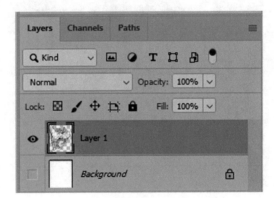

Figure 6-41. *The selected area is cut and pasted to a new layer*

12.   Turn off your background layer so that you can see the selection result.

Figure 6-42 *Location of the Magic Wand tool in the Tools panel*

13.   Save (Ctrl/Cmd+S) your document.

Quick Mask Mode and Selection Tools

While in Quick Mask mode, you can use all the selection tools discussed in previous chapters. This can be helpful when you need to quickly delete or fill part of the mask in the selection by pressing the Backspace/Delete key on your keyboard.

1.   For example, on layer 1, draw a rectangular marquee as you did in Chapter 3. Refer to Figure 6-43.

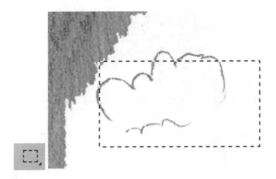

Figure 6-43. *The Rectangular Marquee tool can be used while in Quick Mask mode*

2. Switch to the Magic Wand tool in Quick Mask mode, and press Backspace/Delete on the keyboard and a black foreground clears, and a white foreground fills the selection. Refer to Figure 6-44.

Figure 6-44. *Depending on the foreground color of the Magic Wand tool, a selection can be filled or cleared of mask in Quick Mask mode*

3. When done, press Q to return to the selection's Standard mode and exit Quick Mask mode. The new selection is added to the current one. Refer to Figure 6-45.

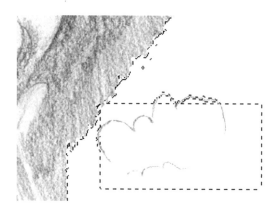

Figure 6-45. *The new selection is added to the current selection after exiting Quick Mask mode*

However, If the whole area was Red in Quick Mask mode, you might get a warning that no pixels were selected. Click OK to exit, and nothing is selected. Refer to Figure 6-46.

Figure 6-46. *Warning message if no selection is made and the entire area in Quick Mask mode is red*

Change the Color of the Quick Mask

You can change the mask's color if you do not want the Quick Mask to be red (maybe you're working with a sketch with red ink). Double-click the Quick Mask Mode button in the Tools panel to enter the dialog box. Refer to Figure 6-47.

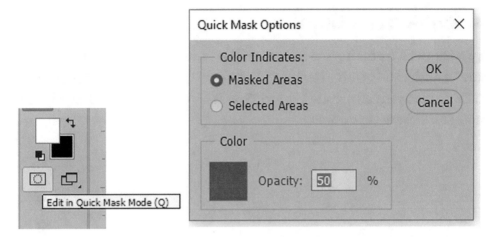

Figure 6-47. *Double-click the Edit Quick Mask mode (Q) button in the tool setting if you need to check if your options are the same as mine or change the color of the mask*

By default, the Color Indicates option is at Masked Areas. You can reverse it to Selected Areas. Under Color, select a new color and click OK. Refer to Figure 6-48.

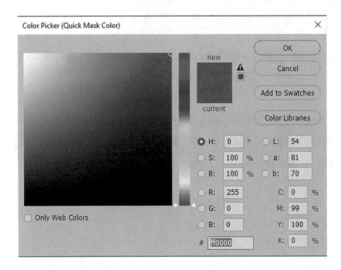

Figure 6-48. *Create a new color mask in the Color Picker (Quick Mask Color) window*

You can change the opacity 0%–100%; the default is 50%. Click OK to confirm, or click Cancel to exit. Refer to Figure 6-47.

Type Mask Selections

While working with type is not the topic of this book, there may be situations where you need to add a selection of text to remove (Backspace/Delete) or Edit ➤ Fill an area in a sketch. To do that, you can use the Vertical Type Mask tool (T) and the Horizontal Type Mask tool (T). Refer to Figure 6-49.

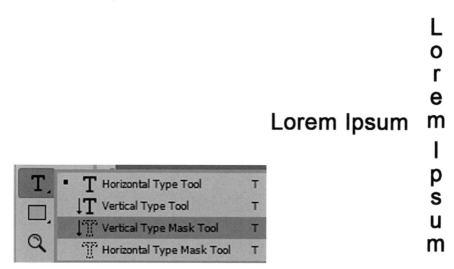

Figure 6-49. *Location of the Vertical and Horizontal Type Mask tools in the Tools panel*

4. Open scan6_2b.psd. You are using this file to practice with, so make a copy of it or Image ➤ Duplicate. Click OK in the dialog box to confirm. Refer to Figure 6-50.

Figure 6-50. *Sketch of a bowl of peeled fruit on a cluttered table*

Horizontal or Vertical Type Mask Options

Look from left to right in the options panel. Refer to Figure 6-51.

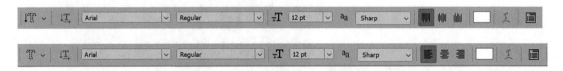

Figure 6-51. *Vertical and Horizontal Mask tool options*

The Type tools collection in the Tools panel lets you do the following.

- Create a new **Preset.**

- Toggle between **vertical and horizontal orientation.**

- Select from the list a specific **font** (Arial, Helvetica,...).

- Select **style** from the list (bold, italic...).

- Select a **size** from the list (other, 6 pt, 72 pt...).

- Select an **anti-alias** setting from the list (none, sharp, crisp, strong, smooth...).

- After creating a text layer or paragraph block, you can **align** horizontally (right, center, left) or vertically (top, center, bottom).

- Set a temporary **preview color** using the color picker. Note this color will not fill the selection after confirmation of selection.

- Create **warped text** using the dialog box.

- Open Window ➤ **Paragraph Panel** and Window ➤ **Character Panel** for additional options.

Except for the paragraph alignment options, the Vertical Type Mask tool and Horizontal Type Mask tool are the same.

One example is a watermark or signature. Let's talk about that briefly next.

CREATE A WATERMARK OR SIGNATURE SELECTION

1. While in the copy of your scan6_2b file, select the Horizontal Type Mask tool. Refer to Figure 6-52.

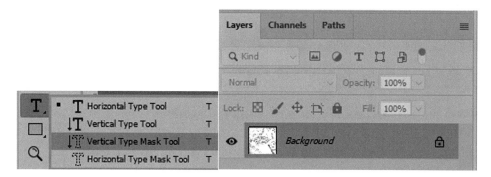

Figure 6-52. *Use the Horizontal Type tool and observe your Layers panel*

2. Click somewhere on the sketch as you would with the non-mask type tools.

Note   When requiring more than one line of text for a paragraph, click, and drag outward to create a type area. Refer to Figure 6-53.

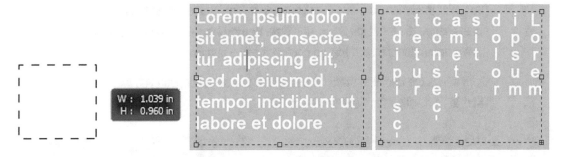

Figure 6-53. *Drag out an area for a paragraph box when you need to type more than one line, either for horizontal or vertical text*

In the Layers panel, no new type layer appears. However, you are now in **Type Quick Mask mode. It is** similar to Quick Mask mode but only for type. Refer to Figure 6-54.

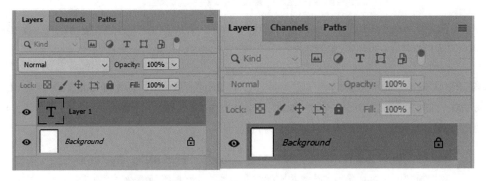

Figure 6-54. *In Type Quick Mask mode, the type never appears as its own type layer*

Some default Text appears highlighted and is surrounded by the red mask.

3. Press the Backspace/Delete key to remove the highlighted text.

4. Type your name. Refer to Figure 6-55.

Figure 6-55. *Delete the filler text and type your name*

5. Drag over the letters to make sure your text is highlighted. Using the options panel change the font type, style, and size. **Remember:** Your computer may have different fonts than mine, so choose the one you like.

    Color keeps the question mark (?) because it is a selection, and you can decide what to fill it with later. Refer to Figure 6-56.

Figure 6-56. *Choose a different font and size for the highlighted text and confirm the selection in the options panel*

Click the Cancel button to exit without saving changes, or click the Commit button to confirm the text. Refer to Figure 6-56. When you click the Commit button, a selection is made based on the chosen lettering, and the text cannot be edited.

6. You can move and drag the selection to a new location using any of the selections tools discussed in this chapter or previous chapters. Refer to Figure 6-57.

Figure 6-57. *The text now appears as a selection that I can move and drag with any selection tool*

7. Choose Edit ➤ Fill Contents with black, white, or another option. Click OK to confirm. Refer to Figure 6-58.

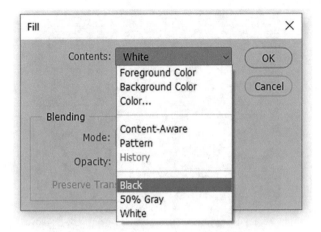

Figure 6-58. *Fill dialog box—Contents: Fill color for the selection*

8. The selection is filled. Select ➤ Deselect (Ctrl/Cmd+D) the selection. Refer to
    Figure 6-59.

Jennifer Harder

Figure 6-59. *The type selection is filled*

Warning   If you choose to fill the selection directly on the sketch, the result is
permanent. You can undo this fill step right away using the Window ➤ History
panel, as you saw in Chapter 2. Refer to Figure 6-60.

Figure 6-60. *Go back a few steps in the History panel if you filled the selection on the wrong layer*

9. Instead, while the section is active, you may want to fill the selection in a new layer, then use the Move tool (V) until you find an exact location to place the watermark. Refer to Figure 6-61.

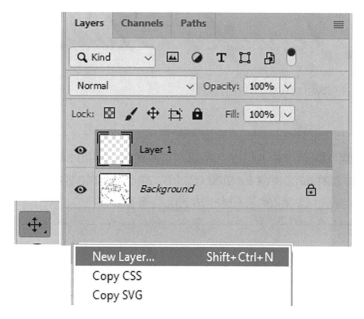

Figure 6-61. *Create a new layer and fill in your selection*

10. Once done, repeat fill steps 8 and 9 on the new layer 1. Later if you want, you can choose Flatten Image in the Layers panel. Refer to Figure 6-62.

Figure 6-62. *Flatten your text or leave it as two layers. The watermark signature is added to the sketch*

11. Save (Ctrl/Cmd+S) your document at this point.

Note   I do not condone adding your name to sketches that are not your own creation, or you do not have permission to use as practice for personal instruction. Doing that on other people's work and putting it into your online portfolio without permission is considered plagiarism and is not a good idea. Someone, including the actual artist, could find out. Use this exercise for your own sketches, or put the actual artist's name on the sketch to acknowledge their efforts when comparing to your creation.

Text Fringe

If you get fringe areas when copying a scanned image containing text, suggestions for removing fringe are at `https://helpx.adobe.com/photoshop/using/adjusting-pixel-selections.html#soften_the_edges_of_selections`.

Summary

This chapter explored using the Magic Wand tool in combination with Quick Mask mode. You saw that with Quick Mask mode and the Brush tool, you could create more accurate selections. You also created a type selection for a watermark using Type Quick Mask mode.

The next chapter looks at two more specialized selection tools in the Tools panel: the Quick Selection tool and the Object Selection tool.

CHAPTER 7

Quick Selection and Object Selection Tools

This chapter shows how to use the Quick Selection or Object Selection tools to refine selections in combination with the Brush tool or the Eraser tool.

The previous chapter explained using the Magic Wand tool (W) with Quick Mask mode (Q). However, in this pop-out menu of the Tools panel, two other related selection tools perform a similar function: the Object Selection tool (W) and the Quick Selection tool (W). Refer to Figure 7-1.

Figure 7-1. *Location of the Object Selection tool and Quick Selection tool in the Tools panel*

Much of what you have learned about the other selection tools in previous chapters can be applied to these tools. So, make sure to go back and review those chapters if you need more detail on a previously related topic. Nevertheless, these tools I am introducing now also have some specific settings that you have not seen yet, which you look at shortly.

Later in this chapter, you also look at another workspace Content-Aware Fill in which you can use these selection tools in combination. The Content-Aware option was briefly mentioned in Chapter 4.

© Jennifer Harder 2022
J. Harder, *Accurate Layer Selections Using Photoshop's Selection Tools*,
https://doi.org/10.1007/978-1-4842-7493-4_7

Note   This chapter's projects are in the Chapter 7 folder.

Let's start by looking at the Quick Selection tool.

Open the scan7_1.psd file and make an Image ➤ Duplicate to use as practice. Click OK in the message dialog box. Refer to Figure 7-2.

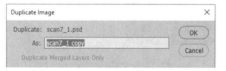

Figure 7-2. *Make sure you make a copy of my sketch of the frog statue so that you can practice with it*

Quick Selection Tool (W)

Like Quick Mask mode (Q) in combination with the Magic Wand tool (W), the Quick Selection tool acts like a brush and allows you to select a selection of a sketch very quickly without having to spend time painting over certain areas while in the mask if you do not have time. It also operates a bit like the Magnetic Lasso tool in Chapter 5 in that it snaps to various pixels as you drag.

You can try this by holding down the mouse key and dragging around an area of the frog statue to create a selection. Refer to Figure 7-3.

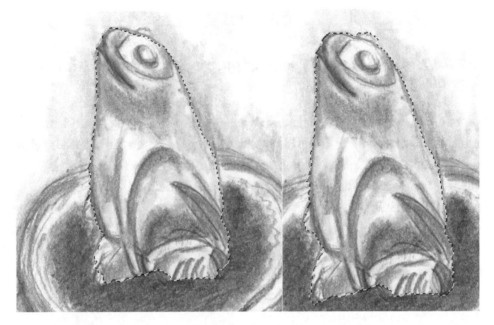

Figure 7-3. *Use the selection tool to drag a selection around areas of the frog statue*

You can release the mouse and then hold down the mouse key again and add to the selection.

Quick Selection Options

Now let's look at the options panel for the tool, from left to right. Refer to Figure 7-4.

Figure 7-4. *Quick Selection tool options in the options panel*

As with previous tools in the options panel, you can save a **preset** of your current tool options. Review the Magic Wand tool options panel in Chapter 6 if you are unsure how to do that.

Unlike the Magic Wand tool and other selection tools that you have looked at, the next section is divided into only three brush selection options. Refer to Figure 7-5.

Figure 7-5. *In the options panel, you find three selection tools. Add to Selection is set to the default*

New Selection creates a new selection by clicking and dragging around an area. Automatically it jumps over to the Add to Selection button when the mouse is released.

Add to Selection expands the selection while holding down the mouse and continues to paint larger selection areas. It is selected by default.

Subtract From Selection removes some or all selected areas when you hold down the mouse key. Likewise, you can hold down the Alt/Option key while dragging, which causes the cursor to change from a plus to a minus symbol within the brush. Refer to Figure 7-6.

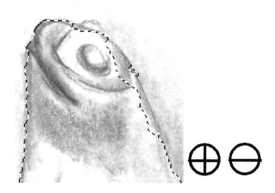

Figure 7-6. *Use Subtract From Selection when you want to remove part of your selection, the cursor has a minus crosshair*

You can always return to the Add Selection by releasing the Alt/Option key or clicking on the button in the options menu and continue adding the selection again. Refer to Figure 7-7.

Figure 7-7. *Add back areas to your selection using the Add to Selection option*

Like other brush tools that you saw in Chapter 2, you can **adjust** the options by using the slider or pressing the left or right bracket ([ ]) keys on your keyboard. In the menu, you can also change the brush's hardness, spacing, angle, and roundness, as well as the pen pressure if you have a stylus and tablet. Refer to Figure 7-8.

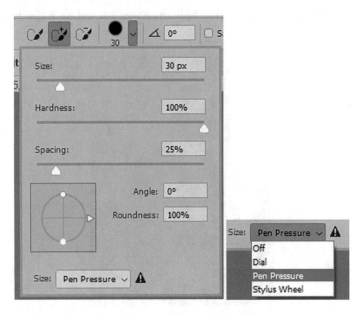

Figure 7-8. *The Brush options for the Quick Selection tool can be used optionally used with a stylus*

The angle in the drop-down brush options menu is the same as the angle in the main area of the options panel and changes in both areas if you switch it. Note that this type of brush is for creating selections and so there are not any specialized brush designs that you can choose from.

Sample All Layers allows you to make a selection that is larger than the selection on the currently selected layer by detecting other color boundaries on multiple layers. By default, it is unchecked to detect color boundaries on the current layer. Refer to Figure 7-9.

Figure 7-9. *Choose options like Sample All Layers, Enhance Edge, Select Subject, or Select and Mask from the options panel*

Enhance Edge offers a smoother and refined selection edge. It is unchecked by default as it can sometimes select more pixels than you intend to. Refer to Figure 7-10.

Figure 7-10. *Enhance Edge may give you a smoother edge selection, but it may not be as accurate as you want it to be*

The next section contains two buttons. Refer to Figure 7-11.

Figure 7-11. *Select Subject and Select and Mask buttons in the options panel*

Select Subject allows you to select well-defined dark or prominent areas or objects very quickly in the image. Refer to Figure 7-12.

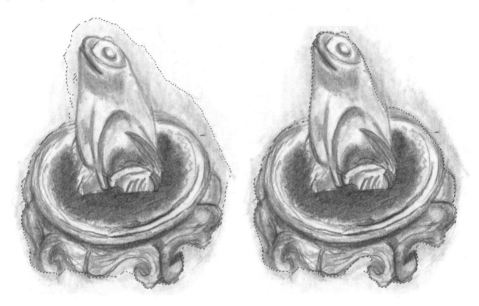

Figure 7-12. *Select Subject selects most of the statue and base, but you may need to use your Quick Selection tool to clean the selection further*

You can then use the Quick Selection tool options—Add to Selection and Subtract from Selection—to clean up the selection further. Refer to Figure 7-12. Adobe has made this tool more content-aware over time. You can learn more about it at `https://helpx.` `adobe.com/photoshop/using/making-quick-selections.html`.

As you saw in Chapter 3 and Chapter 6, you can use any options or commands in the Select menu (except for the Layers commands) to transform your selection further after using the Quick Selection tool. Refer to Figure 7-13.

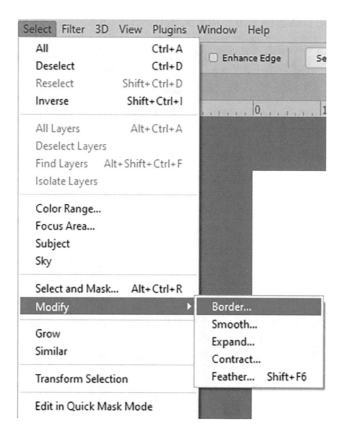

Figure 7-13. *Any selection can still use the options and commands in the Select menu*

Select and Mask is discussed in Chapter 9.

Also, if you make selections, as you did in Chapter 6, you can enter Quick Mask mode (Q) and use your Brush tool to refine the selection further. Refer to Figure 7-14.

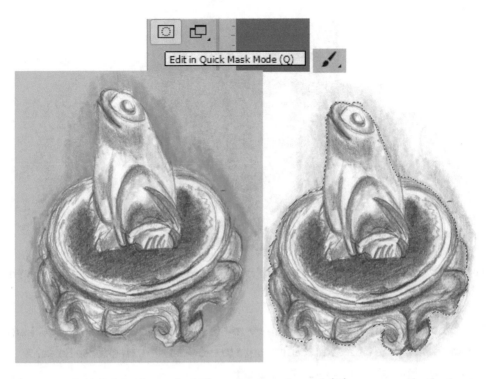

Figure 7-14. *Quick Mask mode (Q) and a Brush tool (B) are usually the best solutions when you need to refine your selection around the sketch*

If you make a mistake in your selection, you can either use the History panel to go back a few steps or Edit ➤ Undo (Ctrl/Cmd+Z) to undo the steps right away. Refer to Figure 7-15.

Figure 7-15. *Use the History panel when you need to go back a few steps in your selection process*

This Quick Selection tool does not allow you to deselect the selection by clicking somewhere else on the canvas as it adds more to the selection, so choose Select ➤ Deselect (Ctrl/Cmd+D) to remove the selection.

Next, let's look at another selection tool using the same copy of the scan7_1.psd file.

Object Selection Tool (W)

This Object Selection tool is generally used for photos to select recognizable areas and shapes such as people, furniture, and pets. However, it can be used for sketches as well. Refer to Figure 7-16.

Figure 7-16. *Location of the Object Selection tool and Quick Selection tool in the Tools panel*

It combines other selection tools in its options panel and, for certain subjects, may make the selection process faster.

Drag around the frog statue. The selection conforms or snaps very closely to that shape. Refer to Figure 7-17.

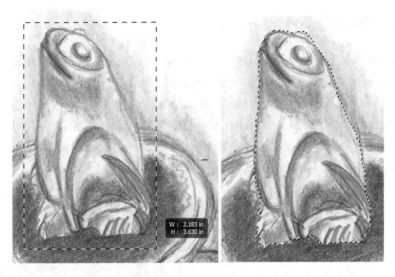

Figure 7-17. *Drag around the frog statue with the Object Selection tool, and much of the statue is selected*

Object Selection Options

Looking at the options panel from left to right, by now, many of the choices should become familiar to you as you have seen them in other previous tools. Refer to Chapters 3, 5, and 6 if you need more information on these options. Refer to Figure 7-18.

Figure 7-18. *Object Selection options panel*

As with the Magic Wand tool and the Quick Selection tool, you can set presets from the current tool.

The next section allows you to set four different selection options. Refer to Figure 7-19.

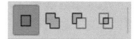

Figure 7-19. *Four selection options*

New Selection allows you to click and drag over areas of a sketch with a color of similar pixels and creates a selection of that area. Refer to Figure 7-17 and Figure 7-18.

Add to Selection allows you to click and drag more than one area of a sketch to add more to the selection, increasing its size. If you hold down the Shift key while you click, you can add to the selection, and the cursor adds a plus symbol beside it. This is useful for holes and blank areas in a sketch. Refer to Figure 7-19 and Figure 7-20.

Figure 7-20. *Add to the current selection the other foot off the frog in the upper left*

Drag around the frog's upper front foot since that was missing from my new selection. Refer to Figure 7-20.

Subtract From Selection allows you to click and drag over more than one area of a sketch to subtract and decrease the selection size. If you hold down the Alt/Option Key while you click, you can remove parts of the selection, and the cursor adds a minus symbol beside it. Refer to Figure 7-19 and Figure 7-21.

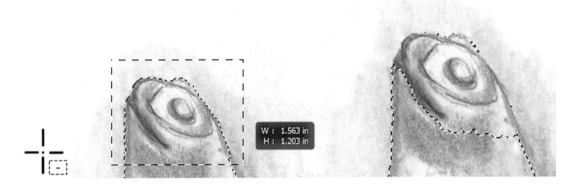

Figure 7-21. *Remove part of the selection using the Subtract from Selection option*

Intersect with Selection allows you to intersect two selections and the center of the two selections is what remains. Using the Alt/Option+Shift keys while you click and drag over an area allows you to access this option, and the cursor adds an X symbol beside it. Refer to Figure 7-19 and Figure 7-22.

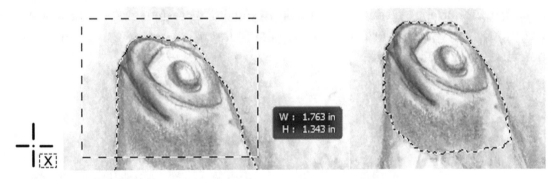

Figure 7-22. *Intersect with Selection leaving only part of the selection behind*

I generally reset this area back to a new selection after working with the tool, so I am ready for the next project. Refer to Figure 7-23.

Figure 7-23. *Reset your selection options back to New Selection after you have finished working with them for the next time*

Like the Rectangular Marquee tool, you can use the Select menu and Modify submenu to adjust your selection. Refer to Chapter 3 if you need to review. Refer to Figure 7-24.

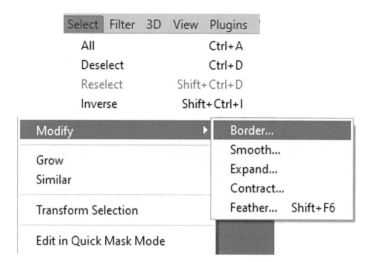

Figure 7-24. *There are many options and commands you can choose from in the Select menu*

Remember to use Select ➤ Inverse (Ctrl/Cmd+Shift+I) to select the inverse or outside of the current selection. For example, as you did in previous chapters on a new layer, you could, with your Brush tool, then paint white areas around the frog, removing the stand. Refer to Figure 7-25.

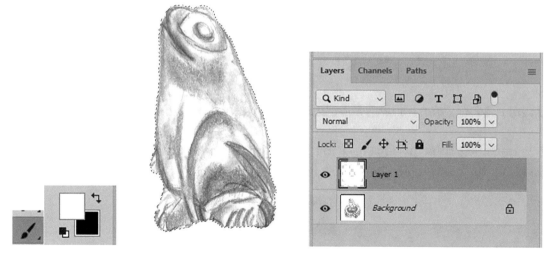

Figure 7-25. *While you have an Inverse selection, use your Brush tool and white foreground to paint a new layer around the statue*

Turn off the eye in layer 1, select the background layer again, and continue practicing with the Object Selection tool.

The next section allows you to choose a **selection mode** when dragging a selection around a sketch area. Refer to Figure 7-26.

In the 2022 version of the Photoshop App an additional feature has been added called Object Finder. When the checkbox is enabled it allows you to find your objects that you want to select more easily by hovering over them and they are highlighted in a blue overlay. At this point you can click to make a quick selection. This section in the options panel allows you to refresh the Object Finder, keep the object overlay visible, as well as change the Overlay options under the additional options gear. Refer to Figure 7-26.

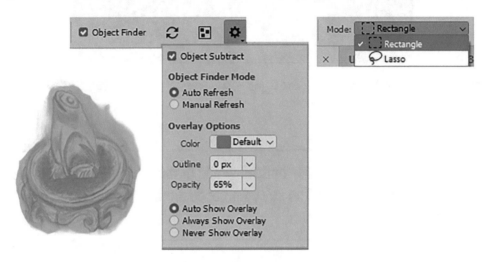

Figure 7-26. *Choose a mode to create your selection—Rectangle or Lasso*

You can use the **Rectangle** mode to select part of a sketch. However, the selection does not remain as a rectangle but snaps around the shape.

You can also use **Lasso** mode, which is similar to working with the Lasso tool. Drag a loop around the same area you want to select. Refer to Figure 7-27.

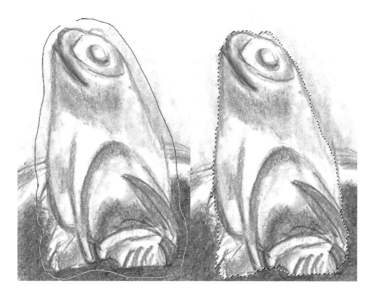

Figure 7-27. *Using Lasso mode may get you a better, tighter selection around the frog*

Note   You can use your selection options to add or remove part of the selection as you did in Rectangle mode. The key commands are the same as well. Refer to Figure 7-28.

Figure 7-28. *Lasso mode allows you to use the same four selection options*

Depending on the sketch and what you need to select closely, one mode may be better than another, so you have to experiment on your own sketches.

There are more familiar options in the next section of the options panel. Refer to Figure 7-26 and Figure 7-29.

Figure 7-29. *The Object Selection tool allows you to Sample All Layers, Create a Hard Edge, and Object Subtract in the options panel*

Sample All Layers makes a larger selection on the selected layer by detecting other color boundaries on multiple layers. By default, it is unchecked to detect color boundaries on the current layer.

Hard Edge provides a smoother and refined selection edge, and for this tool, it is checked by default. You may find that by disabling this option, you get a closer selection.

Object Subtract found under the set additional options gear is enabled by default. When you are working on a normal layer or layer 0, and the area outside the sketch is transparent, it finds and automatically subtracts the region inside a defined region. In this example, a hole inside a very dark area is excluded from the selection. Refer to Figure 7-30.

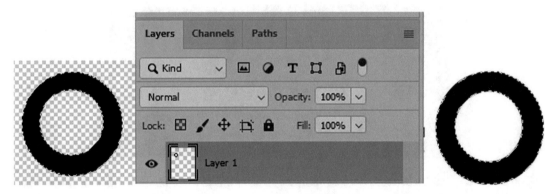

Figure 7-30. *Object Subtract works best on transparent areas on a normal layer over a background layer*

However, in some situations, if you're working in a background layer, this may not work, and the entire shape is selected, even the hole.

For this example, use the piece of driftwood sketch.

Open scan7_2.psd. You can see due to the color differences which I added to visually enhance the sketch, for the exclusion to work accurately, you need to:

Drag to create a New Selection around the wood in Rectangle mode. You should be able to exclude the hole at the same time. Refer to Figure 7-31.

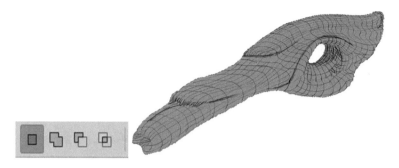

Figure 7-31. *A new selection around the driftwood sketch on the background layer selects both the wood and the hole*

However on your project if this did not occur, then from the options panel, Choose Subtract from Selection and then drag over the hole that you want to exclude. Refer to Figure 7-32.

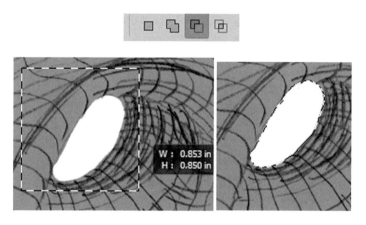

Figure 7-32. *Use Subtract from Selection to select the hole and remove it from the selection*

Note   In future version as this tool improves you can also provide feed back. Refer to icon in Figure 7-29.

To refine your selection further, you may need to enter Quick Mask mode (Q) and use your Brush tool. Refer to Figure 7-33.

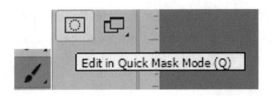

Figure 7-33. *Some selections are not perfect, so use Quick Mask mode if that is the case*

Object Selection Options continued

In the final section of the options panel, the **Select Subject** button allows you to select well-defined dark or prominent areas or objects very quickly in the image. Refer to Figure 7-34.

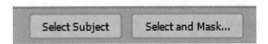

Figure 7-34. *The Object Selection tool also has the Select Subject and Select and Mask buttons*

Note   The **Select and Mask** button is covered in Chapter 9.

On a sketch, when you select an area that does not have any distinct pixels, or the selection is too small, you might receive the following warning. Click OK, and nothing is selected. Refer to Figure 7-35.

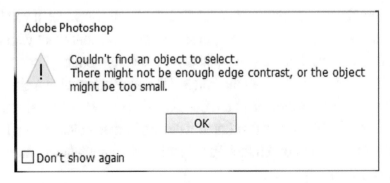

Figure 7-35. *Warning message when no pixels or object is selected*

As you can see in the copy of scan7_1, the Select Object tool is very useful when selecting one part of a subject rather than multiple subjects in a sketch. Refer to Figure 7-36.

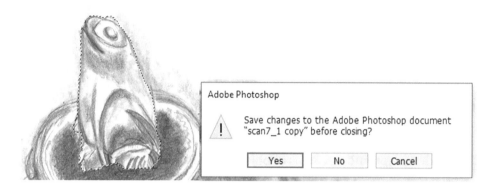

Figure 7-36. *You can save your statue file or click No in the warning message and close it without saving changes*

You can either save the document as a .psd file, or close without saving by clicking **No**. Refer to Figure 7-36.

Content-Aware Fill Workspace

As Adobe becomes more intuitive in recognizing areas of a picture for selection, here is a Photoshop workspace that you might be interested in that does not appear in the Tools panel. It's Content-Aware Fill.

Note   This workspace is better when applied to photos. However, if you have some realistic sketches with color or grayscale, you can experiment with this option to fill in the selected area with pixels from the surrounding image. Though not the topic of this book, besides the Edit ➤ Fill dialog box having a simplified version of the Content-Aware Fill in the Contents drop-down menu, at least three healing tools in the Tools panel use Content-Aware in their calculations. This includes the Spot Healing Brush tool, Patch tool, and Content-Aware Move tool. Refer to Figure 7-37.

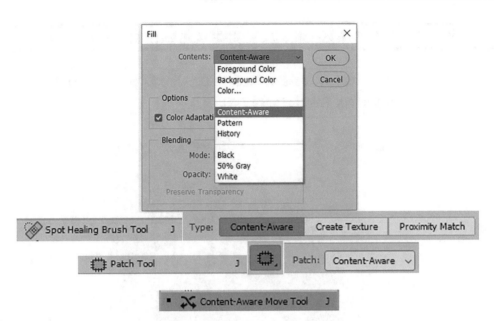

Figure 7-37. *A few tools and the Fill Dialog box offer Content-Aware options*

When using the Crop tool, you could use a simplified version in the options panel. Refer to Figure 7-38.

Figure 7-38. *The Crop tool allows you to fill an area with content when the Content-Aware check box is enabled*

However, the Edit menu contains a more complex workspace version, which you can use with some selection tools.

USING THE CONTENT-AWARE FILL WORKSPACE WITH SELECTION TOOLS

1. Open the scan7_3.psd file. Make an Image ➤ Duplicate for practice and click OK to confirm the copy. Refer to Figure 7-39.

Figure 7-39. *Make a copy of the sketch of some stray cats outside an autobody shop. One of the cats is going to a new home today*

I recommend saving your copy at this point as Content-Aware appears to use more of your computer's memory than some other workspaces, and you don't want to cause a stall or crash while working and lose your own file.

This image contains a group of cats. I want to remove the cat that appears in the lower area of the sketch and blend the grass into that area.

You can use one of the selection tools to create a selection, such as the Magic Wand tool, Quick Selection tool, Select ➤ Subject, or Object Selection tool.

2. Use the Object Selection tool and drag in Rectangle mode around the cat and then edit the section a bit more in Quick Mask mode (Q). I kept the selection loose so that none of the cat's fur is left behind and the area I plan to blend into the ground. Refer to Figure 7-40.

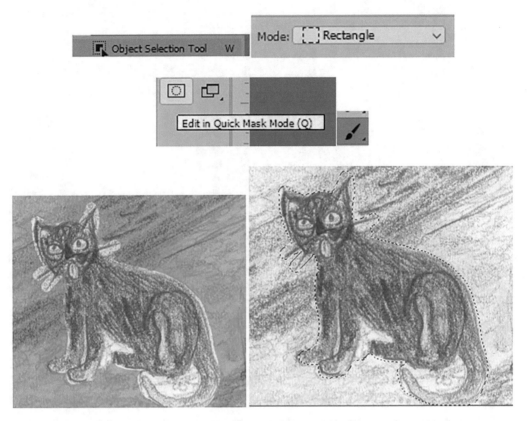

Figure 7-40. *After you have made your selection with the Object Selection tool in rectangle mode, make sure to clean it up further using Quick Mask mode and your Brush tool. I made a loose selection*

3. Now while in the Object Selection tool, either right-click within the selection or Choose Edit ➤ Content-Aware Fill, which brings up the Content-Aware Fill workspace, which contains tools and panels. Refer to Figure 7-41.

Figure 7-41. *When your selection is active, choosing Content-Aware Fill allows you to enter the workspace*

In the Image window, there is a green mask around the cat. In the preview, it has disappeared and is blended in with the ground. Photoshop has analyzed the surrounding area and, based on the settings in the Content-Aware Fill panel, made this the result of the fill blend.

Even if you like the result, before you click OK to confirm it, let's take a tour of the options and tools within this workspace.

Workspace Options

There are five tools in the options panel that are similar to tools outside this workspace. Refer to Figure 7-42.

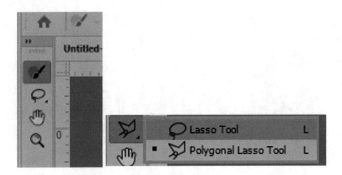

Figure 7-42. *On the left of the workspace are five tools: Sample Brush tool, Lasso tool, Polygonal Lasso tool, Hand tool, and Zoom tool*

The Sampling Brush tool (B) adds or removes the sampled image's masked areas that are green to fill the selected areas. Use Add mode when you brush over areas you want to include in the sampling overlay or Subtract mode when brushing over areas in the sketch you want to exclude from the sampling overlay. Holding down the Alt/Option key allows you to toggle between the mode. If you need to set the brush size, use the slider or the left [and right] bracket keys on the keyboard. Refer to Figure 7-43.

Figure 7-43. *The Sampling Brush tool has options in the options panel. If you add or subtract from the sample area, what fills the selection will change*

You can see that with less of a sample area, Photoshop does not have as many options to sample, and so the fill may not be what you want. It is better to leave as much of the sampling area as possible for this sketch. If you need to undo your sample brush strokes at this point, click Cancel and then reenter the Content-Aware Fill workspace again.

The Lasso tool (L) and the **Polygonal Lasso tool (L)** are helpful for refining edges and creating, adding, subtracting, or intersecting with your current selections, as well as feather by a pixel amount and anti-alias the feather. You can use the expand button to enlarge the selection by a set number of pixels and the contract button to shrink the selection. Click the reset button to undo the last few steps. Refer to Figure 7-44.

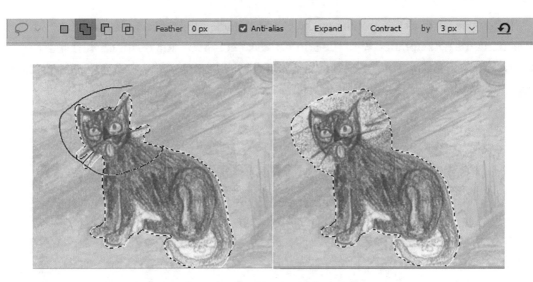

Figure 7-44. *Using the Lasso tool or Polygonal Lasso gives you similar options and allows you to increase or decrease your selection area*

If you alter the selection, the sampling area is reset, but previous brush strokes are preserved.

Note   Keep an eye on your Preview panel as you add to the selection, as sometimes it may add more to the fill than you want. As you adjust the selection, the preview updates and adjusts what is being previewed. Refer to Figure 7-45.

Figure 7-45. *The Preview panel may add a few more pixels to the bottom of the panel and then adjust as the selection area changes*

In most cases, I recommend creating your sample selection outside of this workspace before you enter the Content-Aware Fill dialog box.

When you do click OK, you leave the Content-Aware Fill workspace, and the selection area gets updated with the additional selections made by those workspace tools. If you make too large of a selection, you may get areas of the sketch you don't want from the green sample area. Refer to Figure 7-46.

Figure 7-46. *If you enlarge the selection, the new area is added, but you may add something to the sample you don't want, like another stray cat*

The Hand tool (H) allows you to pan over different parts of the sketch, and you can access it by holding down the spacebar key on your keyboard. You can use it in the Image window and Preview window. Refer to Figure 7-47.

Figure 7-47. *Hand tool options in the options panel*

The Zoom tool (Z) magnifies various areas of your image to get a closer selection or zoom out to see the whole picture in the Image window or Preview window. Refer to Figure 7-48 and Figure 7-49.

Figure 7-48. *The Zoom tool options in the options panel help you get close to the actual image and the preview*

Figure 7-49. *The Zoom tool options in the options panel help you get close to the actual image and the preview*

The Image window is where you preview the selection and green sample areas. Note that Content-Aware Fill is currently only sampling a rectangular area. This is based on my settings in the options, which you will look at shortly. Refer to Figure 7-50.

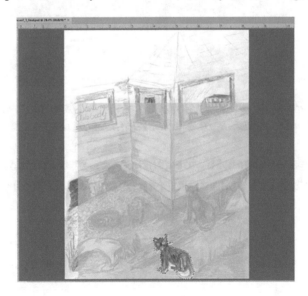

Figure 7-50. *The main window shows the sample mask area and the selection*

The **Preview** window displays how the currently selected area appears with changes. While changes are being made, it starts in a low-resolution and then renders in full resolution. You can use the slider below to zoom in and out. Refer to Figure 7-51.

Figure 7-51. *The Preview window shows that the cat is now removed from the scene and the ground is filled in, and I can zoom in on that area to inspect it*

The **Content-Aware Fill** panel on the right contains further options for Sampling Area Overlay, Sampling Area Options, Fill Settings, and Output Settings. Refer to Figure 7-52.

Figure 7-52. *On the Right is the Content-Aware Fill panel that helps you adjust sampling and fill settings*

Sampling Area Overlay shows or hides the sampling area in the document window or uses the Indicates drop-down list to show the excluded area, which is the inverse of the current sample mask. Sampling Area is the default. Refer to Figure 7-53.

Figure 7-53. *Adjust the sampling area to see the sample more clearly*

You can also alter the color by clicking on it to access the Color Picker dialog box. By default, the color is green, unlike Quick Mask mode, which is red. Set the sample opacity 0%–100%. Refer to Figure 7-53 and Figure 7-54.

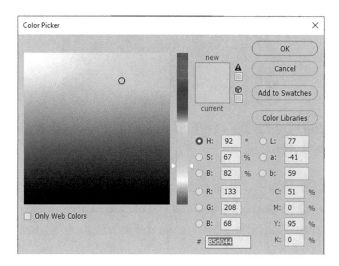

Figure 7-54. *Use the Color Picker dialog box when you want to alter the sample area color*

Sampling Area Options can be reset with the reset icon. You can use three options to determine where Photoshop should look for source pixels to fill the content. Refer to Figure 7-55.

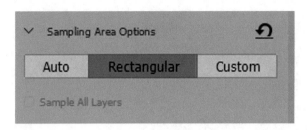

Figure 7-55. *Content-Aware Sampling Areas Options of Auto, Rectangle, Custom, Sample All Layer and Reset*

Auto is for sampling content that is like the surrounding fill area. Refer to Figure 7-56.

Figure 7-56. *Auto selects some areas that look similar to what surrounds the cat and what the preview area records*

Rectangular selects a rectangular sampling region around the fill area. It is the default setting. Refer to Figure 7-57.

Figure 7-57. *Rectangular selects a rectangle area around the cat and has a broader sample area, and you can see that the preview is a bit more accurate for this sketch*

Custom creates a manually defined sample area. You get an informational warning letting you know you need to use the Sampling Brush tool to add to the area. Click OK and then start painting a new green sample area on the sketch. Refer to Figure 7-58.

Figure 7-58. *Custom allows you to paint with the Sampling Brush tool any sized sample you want, but if the sampling area is not large enough, then you may get a ghost cat outline*

Note   Different sampling options alter the preview fill inside the selection. Refer to Figure 7-58.

Sample All Layers allows you to select source pixels from all visible layers in your document if there is more than one; otherwise, the option remains disabled. Refer to Figure 7-55.

Fill Settings can be reset using the reset icon. Refer to Figure 7-59.

Figure 7-59. *Fill Setting in the Content-Aware Fill panel of Color Adaption, Rotation Adaption, Scale, Mirror, and Reset icon*

Color Adaption allows you to fill the content with gradual color and texture changes: None, Default, High, or Very High. Refer to Figure 7-60.

Figure 7-60. *Color Adaption settings of None, Default, High, and Very High in the Preview panel of the same area with subtle changes*

Rotation Adaption allows you to rotate the content for a better match. Adobe states that it is useful for rotated and curved patterns. You can choose the following from the drop-down menu: None, Low, Medium, High, or Full. None is the default. Refer to Figure 7-61.

Figure 7-61. *Rotation Adaptation settings of None, Low, Medium, High, and Full in the Preview panel of the same area with subtle changes*

Scale allows content resizing for a better match. Refer to Figure 7-62.

Figure 7-62. *Scale setting enabled and the result in the Preview panel, some paws are showing*

Mirror allows you to fill with horizontal symmetry. Refer to Figure 7-63.

Figure 7-63. *Mirror setting enabled. There is a flip of the sample in the Preview window that shows a light outline of a cat*

As you can see, though the changes are subtle, you want to get the most accurate blending, so always zoom into the area in the preview panel while changing the settings, and sometimes leaving them on the default is best.

The Output Settings let you output your changes to the current layer, a new layer, or a duplicate layer. Refer to Figure 7-64.

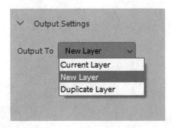

Figure 7-64. *Choose how you output the sample using the Content-Aware Fill panel Output Settings*

I chose **New Layer** because I do not want to destroy my background layer, and I may want to edit the section later.

The **Reset icon** on the lower left of the Content-Aware Fill panel allows you to reset all the settings in this panel, not only in select areas. When you click **OK**, the selection area is applied and based on the current Output Settings, it is filled with the generated random pattern from the preview, and the pixels are placed on the background layer copy. Refer to Figure 7-65.

Figure 7-65. *Reset, OK, Apply, or Cancel in the Content-Aware Fill panel*

Note   If you need to do multiple fills in the image, click **Apply**. Then use one of the lasso tools in the workspace to make a new selection to fill and click OK to exit. Each time you click Apply, a new output is generated on the current layer, a new layer, or duplicate layers, depending on choices made. Refer to Figure 7-65.

Cancel exits the workspace without making changes.

In this exercise, click OK and see how Content-Aware fills in the selection on the background layer copy. Refer to Figure 7-66.

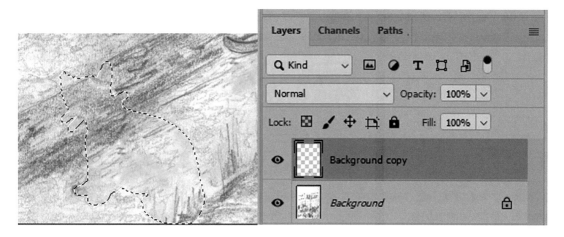

Figure 7-66. *The Sample selection is filled and added to a new layer in the Layers panel*

Note   If you do not like your selection, you can click the Delete Layer trash icon at the bottom of the Layers panel. Click Yes in the message. Then while the selection is active, try the Edit ➤ Content-Aware Fill process again. Nothing has been changed on the background layer. Refer to Figure 7-67.

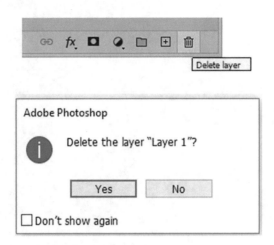

Figure 7-67. Delete your layer if you don't like the result. Click Yes in the message

If you are OK with the results, choose Select ➤ Deselect (Ctrl/Cmd+D) to deselect the selection.

If you like to, you can later use the Clone Stamp tool on a New Layer in the Layers panel to blend in additional areas. Refer to Figure 7-68.

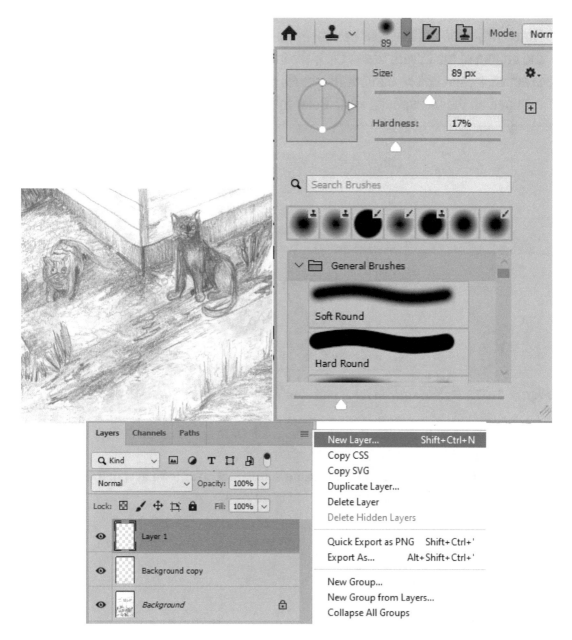

Figure 7-68. *One stray cat is no longer in the sketch. On a new layer, use the Clone Stamp tool to clean up any areas containing traces of the cat so that the ground blends in*

You can see how this looks in my scan7_3_final.psd file. Save (Ctrl/Cmd+S) your document as a .psd file on your computer.

Note   You can learn more about the Content-Aware Fill workspace if you are working with Photos at `https://helpx.adobe.com/photoshop/using/content-aware-fill.html`

Summary

Adobe has many selection tools. Some, such as the Quick Selection and the Object Selection tools, can select subjects within a sketch better and faster than other selection tools, depending on what you are trying to accomplish. You can adjust your sketch further and use these selection tools in combination with the Content-Aware Fill workspace.

The next chapter looks at two more specialized tools or commands that are not in the Tools panel. They make it easier to select an area based on the color range or on the color of the sky.

CHAPTER 8

Using Color Range and Sky

This chapter shows you how to use the Select menu's Color Range dialog box and Sky option to deal with images that have difficult color selections.

So far in this book, you have reviewed and explored many of the selection tools within the Tools panel. There are a few additional selection tools that you might not be aware of. You look at some of them starting in Chapter 10 of this book. You have also looked at many selection options and commands in Photoshop's Select menu and saw how they could be used interchangeably with selection tools. This chapter and the next look at four Select menu options. Refer to Figure 8-1.

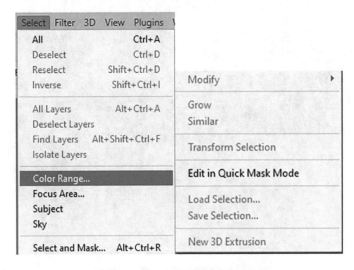

Figure 8-1. *Options and commands in the Select menu*

This chapter focuses on Color Range and Sky. Chapter 9 looks at Focus Area and Select and Mask.

© Jennifer Harder 2022
J. Harder, *Accurate Layer Selections Using Photoshop's Selection Tools*,
https://doi.org/10.1007/978-1-4842-7493-4_8

Note   Load and Save Selection are explored in more detail in Chapter 11. New 3D extrusion from a selection is not relevant to this book, but in Chapter 2 I provide a link to my video showing how it works in the Photoshop 3D workspace, should you want to learn more about it on your own. Also, much of the 3D workspace is being transferred from future Photoshop versions to Adobe Substance.

This chapter's projects are in the Chapter 8 folder.

Color Range

Select ➤ Color Range selects difficult selections of color in a photo. However, it can select certain color areas in a colored sketch or painting.

Open the scan8_1.psd file and go to Image ➤ Duplicate Copy for practice. Click OK in the dialog box message. Refer to Figure 8-2.

Figure 8-2. *A watercolor sketch of a boathouse on a river. Use the Duplicate Image dialog box to Create a copy of this file*

You do not have to have any prior selection tool to start using it. Refer to Figure 8-3.

Figure 8-3. *The Color Range dialog box can be opened even if you have not made a selection*

However, you can if use a marquee if you want to narrow the selection area.

Select the Rectangular Marquee tool (M) and drag a selection around the blue boat. Your goal is to select only the blue hull of the boat since you may want to adjust the color later. Refer to Figure 8-4.

Figure 8-4. *Use your Rectangular Marquee tool to create a selection around the boat to narrow the Color Range selection*

Go to Select ➤ Color Range to open the dialog box.

Color Range Dialog Box and Eyedropper Tool Options

Once the Color Range dialog box opens, the options bar automatically changes to the Eyedropper tool (I) regardless of what other tools you have been using. Refer to Figure 8-5.

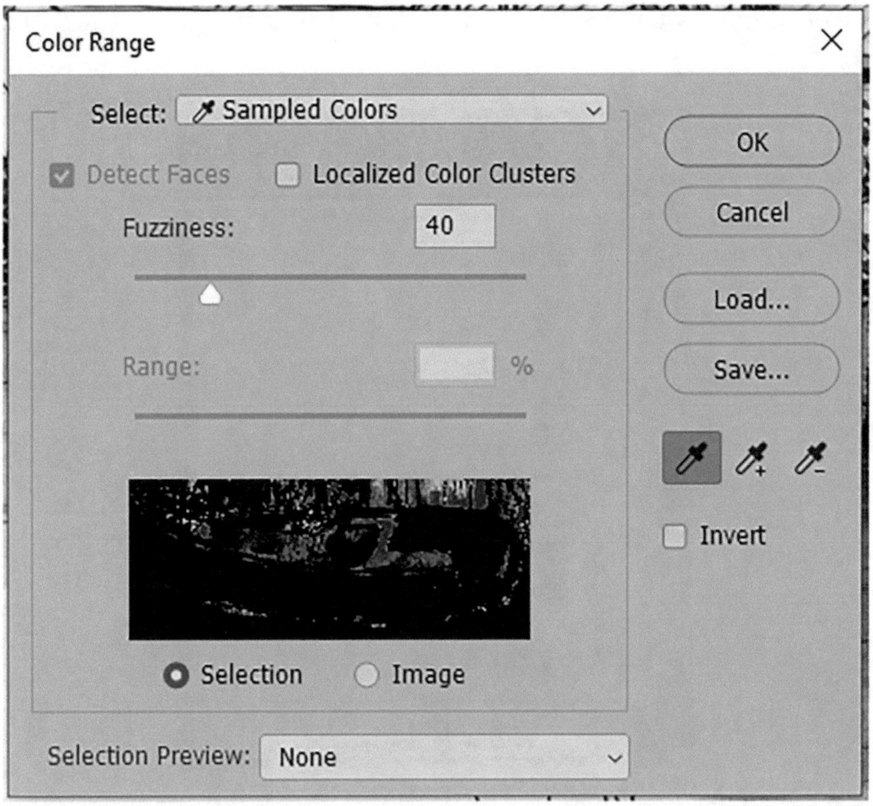

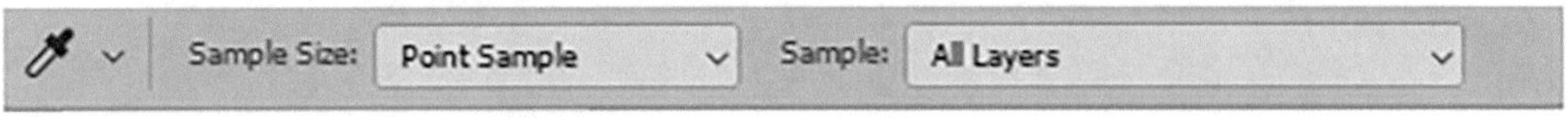

Figure 8-5. *The Color Range dialog box works with the Eyedropper tool in the options panel*

If you need to review the eyedropper sample size and sample area on layers, refer to Chapter 2.

Let's take a tour of the Color Range dialog box.

The **Select** drop-down menu has many options for selecting a color. Refer to Figure 8-6.

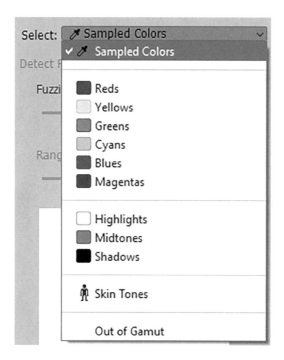

Figure 8-6. *The Select drop-down menu contains many sampling options divided into sections*

Sampled Colors are those that are sampled by the eyedropper, based on the settings in the options panel.

Click somewhere on the dark blue area of the boat in your picture and observe what colors become part of the selection. Refer to Figure 8-7.

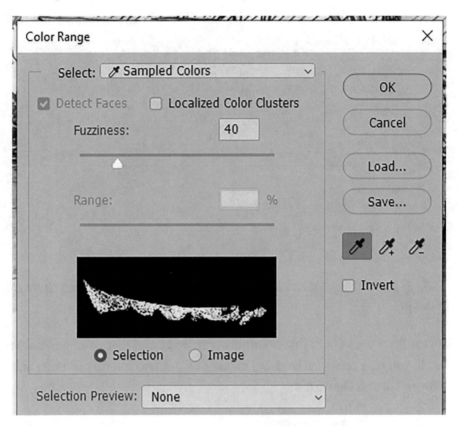

Figure 8-7. *The Color Range of the area of the dark blue boat in the preview*

You can also sample colors—**Reds, Yellows, Greens, Cyans, Blues**, or **Magentas**—in your sketch. Refer to Figure 8-6 and Figure 8-8.

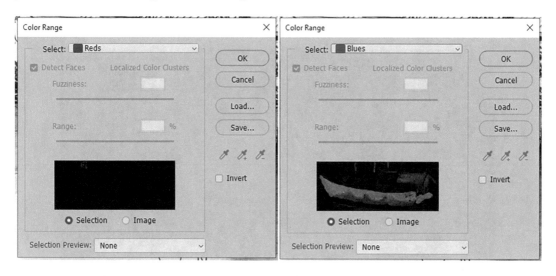

Figure 8-8. *If you try to find red in the boat's hull, there is none, but there are plenty of blues*

However, if you click OK in this example of the Reds, and that color was not present in the sketch, you may receive a warning message. Click OK, but no pixels are selected. Refer to Figure 8-8 and Figure 8-9.

Figure 8-9. *Warning message when no red pixels are selected*

In this case, Blues is a much better sample selection.

You can also sample by luminosity. **Highlights**, **Midtones**, or **Shadows** are useful if you are trying to correct an area that might have a gutter shadow when you scanned the sketch. For Midtones, there are two slider handles. Refer to Figure 8-6 and Figure 8-10.

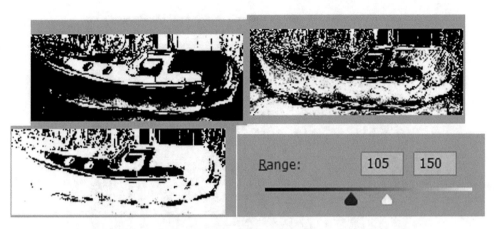

Figure 8-10. *Selections of Highlights, Midtones, and Shadows. The Midtones have some additional range settings you can adjust*

Skin Tones is generally used for photos or color sketches of people. Refer to Figure 8-6 and Figure 8-12.

Out of Gamut is generally used for colors that do not fit within the RGB and CMYK modes. It is typically used for photos. Refer to Figure 8-6.

Detect Faces is generally used when people are in the image. Refer to Figure 8-11.

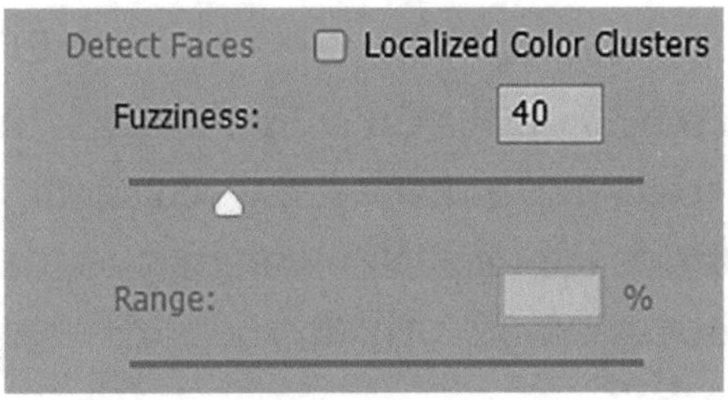

Figure 8-11. *Some Select options disable Detect Faces and Range*

To activate this option, you need to select Skin Tones from the menu. Enabling it provides more accurate skin tone selection. Refer to Figure 8-12.

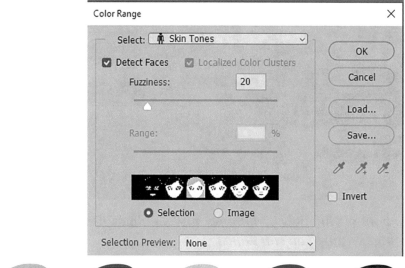

Figure 8-12.   Select Skin Tones and enable Detect Faces if you need to select areas within faces

In this example, I used the EmojiOne Color font to demo that most skin tones except the yellow skin turn up as selections with the setting enabled.

Localized Color Clusters is only available with the Sampled Colors menu option. It helps you make contiguous selections of colors near the one you clicked with the eyedropper. Refer to Figure 8-13.

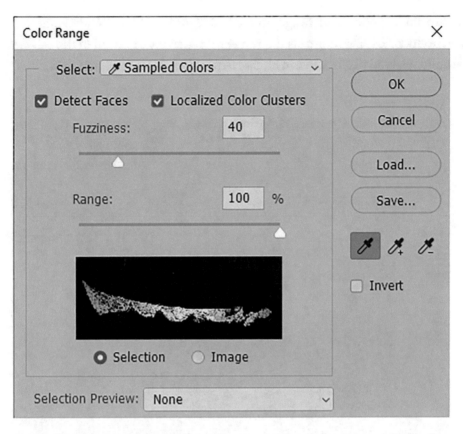

Figure 8-13. *Enable Localized Color Clusters in the Color Range dialog box to get a better selection of the boat's hull*

Note   In the Sample Colors option, you can select Detect Faces for more accurate skin tone selection while detecting other color samples.

The Fuzziness slider has a range from 0 to 200. Adjust the fallout beyond the selection boundaries. This controls the range from narrow or broad of the selected colors and partially selected pixels and is a bit like feathering. Refer to Figure 8-14.

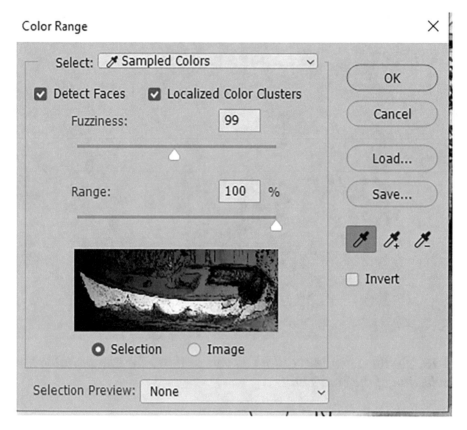

Figure 8-14. *Adjust the Fuzziness slider in the Color Range dialog box*

The **Range** slider is from 0% to 100%. It adjusts the range of the selection of similar colors or sampled points based on the Eyedropper settings. Refer to Figure 8-15.

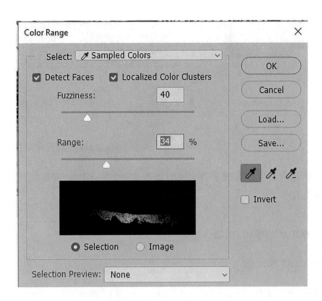

Figure 8-15. *Adjust the Range slider in the Color Range dialog box*

In the preview area, you can either sample colors from the image or use a predefined color range in the Select drop-down menu. The eyedropper only works if **Sampled Colors is** active.

You can view the **Selection** mask or the **Image**. Press the Ctrl/Cmd key if you want to toggle while your eyedropper is selected. Refer to Figure 8-16.

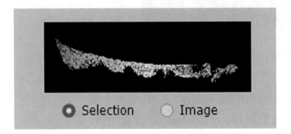

Figure 8-16. *A preview of Selection and Image in the Color Range dialog box*

Stay in Selection mode so you know which colors you are selecting. Selection Preview appears on the actual image behind the dialog box. Refer to Figure 8-17.

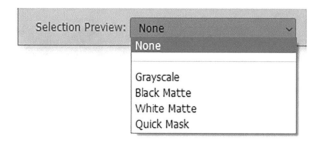

Figure 8-17. *Use your Selection Preview options to preview the image outside of the Color Range dialog box*

Selection Preview is in the following.

- **None** (original image).

- **Grayscale** shows select areas in white and unselected areas in black. Partially selected areas are gray, which is the same as the dialog box preview. Refer to Figure 8-18.

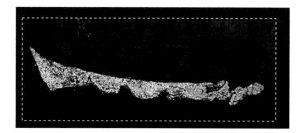

Figure 8-18. *Grayscale selection preview*

- **Black Matte** allows you to view the selection against a black background. Skin tones are in color. It is recommended for bright images. Refer to Figure 8-19.

Figure 8-19. *Black Matte selection preview*

- **White Matte** allows you to view the selection against a white background. Skin tones are in color. It is recommended for dark images. Refer to Figure 8-20.

Figure 8-20. *White Matte selection preview*

- **Quick Mask** has the same red overlay as Quick Mask mode. Refer to Figure 8-21.

Figure 8-21. *Quick Mask selection preview*

On the right side of the dialog box are a few other settings. Refer to Figure 8-22.

Figure 8-22. *Buttons in the Color Range dialog box and how they appear when the Alt/Option key is held down*

OK allows you to confirm the selection, and it appears on the canvas.

Click **Cancel** to exit the dialog box without applying the selection.

Note   If you need to reset the dialog box, hold down the Alt/Option key and press reset when the Cancel button changes. Then release the Alt/Option key. Refer to Figure 8-22.

You can **Load** a color range selection. If you have a color range selection from another document in the form of an .axt file, you can access it from here and then locate the file. Refer to Figure 8-23.

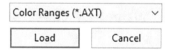

Figure 8-23. *Load a Color Ranges (*.AXT) file*

You can **Save** a color range selection. If you want to save your color range selection, you can save it as an .axt file for another Photoshop user in a folder on your computer or email to the other user, which they can then Load into their document. Refer to Figure 8-24.

:	Untitled.axt ⌄
:	Color Ranges (*.AXT) ⌄

Save   Cancel

Figure 8-24. *Save a Color Ranges (*.AXT) file*

This may be useful when dealing with skin tones in an image and want to record the preset.

Next are three eyedropper icons. The first is the default **Eyedropper tool** that you use to sample the image and create the selection. Then the eyedropper with the plus (+) lets you **add to the sample** selection. You can also hold down the Shift key while clicking and dragging in preview with the eyedropper tool to increase the area sample. The eyedropper with the minus (–) lets you **subtract from the sample** selection. You can hold down the Alt/Option Key while clicking and dragging in the preview with the eyedropper tool to decrease the sample area. Refer to Figure 8-25.

Figure 8-25. *Eyedropper options in the Color Range dialog box*

Enable the **Invert** check box if you want to Invert the selection of the blue color range, which is similar to Select ➤ Inverse (Shift+Ctrl/Cmd+I). Refer to Figure 8-26.

Figure 8-26. *Inverted selection of blue area of the boat hull*

On the boat, select Sampled Colors and deselect Detect Faces and Invert to disable them. Click the eyedropper and hold down the Shift key to sample more of the boat's blue hull until you have most of it selected. Refer to Figure 8-27.

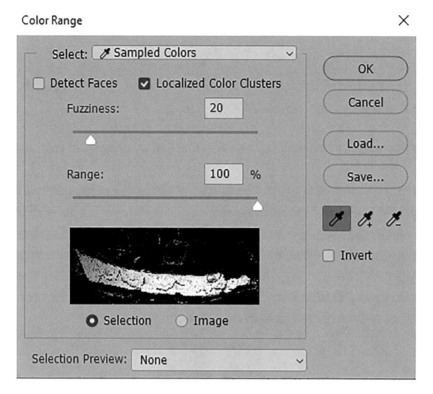

Figure 8-27.   *Adjust the settings in the Color Range dialog box*

Enable Localized Color Clusters. You can also lower the Fuzziness slider to about 20 to avoid extra selection areas. Keep the range at 100%.

Next, use the eyedropper with the minus or hold down Alt/Option to remove some of the selection. Refer to Figure 8-28.

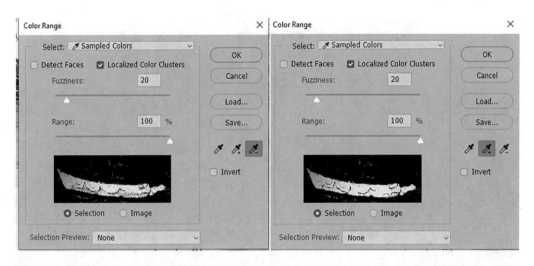

Figure 8-28. *Add and remove parts of the selection using the Eyedropper tools*

You may have to toggle between the two eyedroppers (plus and minus). It will not be perfect, but get as close as you can.

When you are happy with the results, click OK to exit, and the selection is applied. Refer to Figure 8-28 and Figure 8-29.

Figure 8-29. *The selection is applied to the boat after exiting the Color Range dialog box*

Now use the Quick Mask mode (Q) and your Paint Brush tool (B) with white to remove any selection areas you did not intend to add and black to mask over areas. Refer to Figure 8-30.

311

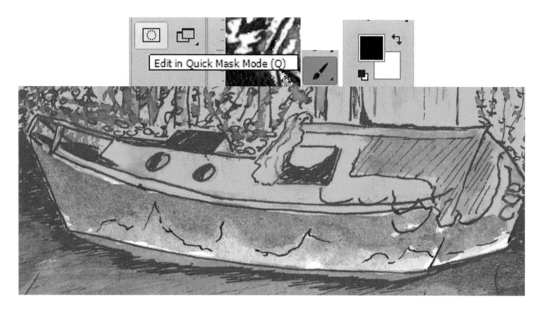

Figure 8-30. *Use Quick Mask mode to clean up your selection further*

Remember to zoom in with your Zoom tool to see that you have cleaned the area thoroughly.

Then exit the Quick Mask mode back to Standard mode (Q).

You can then paint a new color by selecting the blue on the top of the boat with the Eyedropper tool (I). Refer to Figure 8-31.

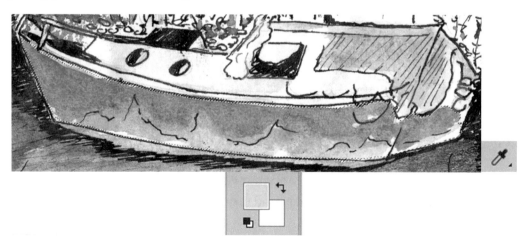

Figure 8-31. *While the selection is active, use your Eyedropper tool to select some of the light blues on top of the boat*

The color sample that appears in the foreground color picker is R:98 G:206 B: 252.

Next, choose New Layer in the Layers panel. Paint on the new layer 1 within that area of the selection. This covers up some of the detail on the boat. Refer to Figure 8-32.

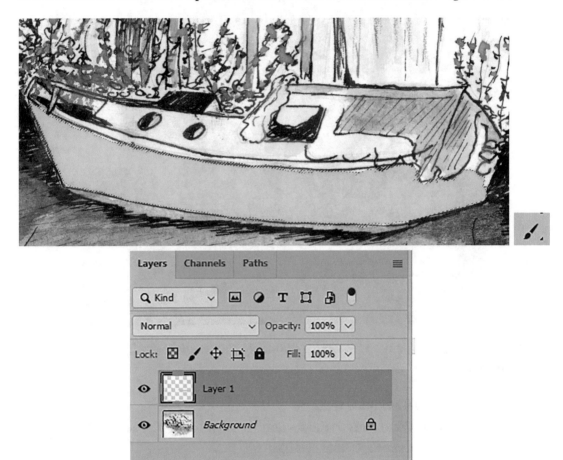

Figure 8-32. Paint on layer 1 some blue within the selection

On layer 1, set the **Blending Mode** to **Color** and the **Opacity** to about **67%**. Refer to Figure 8-33.

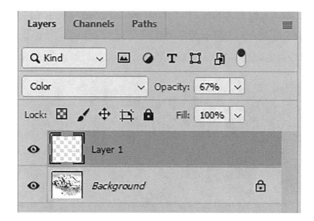

Figure 8-33. *Change selected layer 1's Blending mode and opacity in the Layers panel*

This blends the colors in quite well.

Select ➤ Deselect (Ctrl/Cmd+D) the section area. Save (Ctrl/Cmd+S) your file.

My results are in the scan8_1_boat.psd file.

Note   The Color Range setting you last used appears when you open the dialog box again. However, if you want to use the current foreground color in your Tools panel as the sampled color, hold down the spacebar as you open the dialog box.

If the selection is complex, you may want to save it in case you need to reapply it later. This is explored in Chapter 11, but I saved a copy of the selection in the Channels panel in the scan8_1.psd file. Refer to Figure 8-34.

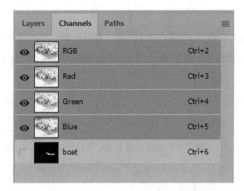

Figure 8-34. *The Channels panel saves a selection of the boat*

Sky

The Select ➤ Sky option or command has no dialog box. It only has one purpose: to select the sky area or blue/white color in photos, usually broken by the dark horizon line or a sudden luminosity transition from highlight to midtones.

Open ➤ scan8_2.psd to practice on. Refer to Figure 8-35.

Figure 8-35. *Simulated oil painting using Photoshop filters on the beach and sand cliffs*

Note   This is an image that I used several filters on, such as Filter Gallery ➤ Artistic ➤ Fresco and then Stylize ➤ Oil Paint. However, you can use your example instead of mine if you prefer.

Go to Select ➤ Sky. Because this command only does one thing, this does not mean it is not a useful tool. If your image or sketch has trees and branches, they often create a patchwork of blue and green areas that can take hours to select around if you must use the Magic Wand tool. Refer to Figure 8-36.

Figure 8-36. *Sky did a good job selecting the blue area, but there are a few blue areas in the middle of the trees not detected*

However, for a more accurate selection of sky areas between the trees, Select ➤ Color Range picks up more pixels of a certain blue. Refer to Figure 8-37.

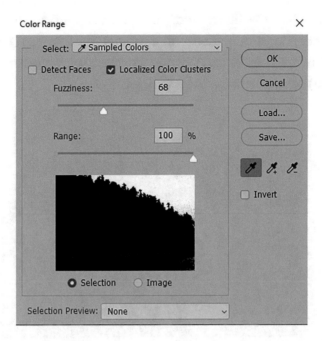

Figure 8-37. *In other situations, try using the Color Range dialog box to select your sky area, as you might pick up more of the blue between the trees*

In the dialog box, hold down the Shift key to add to your selection. Also, smears and indentations may cause parts of the sky to not be selected. Refer to Figure 8-38.

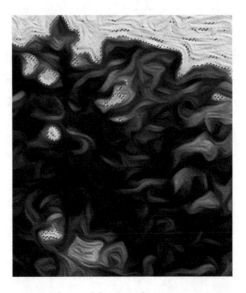

Figure 8-38. *Some blue was selected better, but impressions in the sky of the oil painting left some areas unselected*

317

Whether you use Select ➤ Sky or Color Range for a simple sketch, you can then use the create sky selection in combination with the Quick Mask mode (Q) and your Brush tool (B) as you did in this chapter and Chapter 6 to clean up areas that you do or do not want to have as part of the selection. Refer to Figure 8-39.

Figure 8-39. *Use Quick Mask mode when you need to clean up the selection further. You can see the result when you exit*

Close this file if you did not make any changes to it.

Note   The Sky command is different from the Edit ➤ Sky Replacement command and dialog box. However, it is very useful for photos where you need to replace a blue sky with a sunset. Although this is not a topic in this book, more information is at `https://helpx.adobe.com/photoshop/using/replace-sky.html`. Refer to Figure 8-40.

Figure 8-40. *Sky Replacement dialog box*

Summary

This chapter's focus was on two main selection tools: Color Range and Sky. You can use these tools independently or with other selection tools, like the Rectangular Marquee or Quick Mask mode and the Brush tool to clean up a selection.

The next chapter looks at two more tools that can help you clean up your selection: Focus Area and Select and Mask.

CHAPTER 9

Working with Focus Area and Select and Mask Properties

In this chapter, I demonstrate how to use the Focus Area dialog box and Select and Mask workspace with the Properties panel and a variety of selection tools.

In the previous chapter, you looked at some more complex selection tools that could select areas of color and then modified those selections to further adjust the color of the artwork or continue to refine the selection in Quick Mask mode. This chapter looks at two more selection tools in the Select menu: Focus Area and Select and Mask. Refer to Figure 9-1.

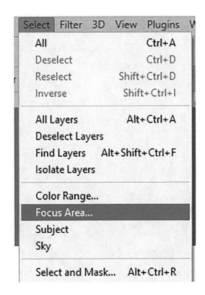

Figure 9-1. *The Select menu path to the Focus Area dialog box*

© Jennifer Harder 2022
J. Harder, *Accurate Layer Selections Using Photoshop's Selection Tools*,
https://doi.org/10.1007/978-1-4842-7493-4_9

Note   The projects in this chapter are in the Chapter 9 folder.

Focus Area

Unless you are a photographer, you may be unfamiliar with the Focus Area dialog box. Generally, it selects pixels in a photo that are in focus, but you can use it for sketches or artwork that you took with your camera. With photographs, unliked scanned images, there are generally areas in or out-of-focus depending on what the camera lens aperture determines is the main subject area versus the background depth of field. You also discover Focus Area has many features similar to Select and Mask. It also has a few tools within the dialog box that you should be familiar with now if you have read Chapter 7 on Quick Selection.

Open the photo9_1.psd file and make a copy (Image ➤ Duplicate) to practice on. Click OK in the dialog box to confirm the copy. Refer to Figure 9-2.

Figure 9-2. *The image with a painting on stone. Make a copy of the file for practice*

This is an acrylic painting that was done on a very jagged slate stone slab. I certainly would never place this on my scanner! So, I took a photo instead. Refer to Chapter 1. I placed it on some white paper on a carpeted floor, but you could use a white cloth sheet as well. Make sure the stone does not leave too much of a shadow on the sheet. I used no flash and did a macro shot. Later in Photoshop, I cropped the photo, and I used the adjustment layers of Levels as in Chapter 2 to balance out the white before making my selection. Your file has a flattened background layer. Refer to Figure 9-3.

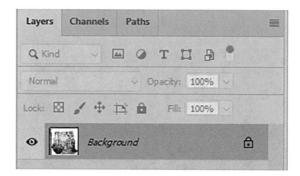

Figure 9-3. *In this file, there is only one background layer in the Layers panel*

Keep in mind, every image or sketch may require different preparatory work. In every case, you want to make the selection process as easy as possible, especially with complex selections.

To enter the dialog box, choose Select ➤ Focus Area.

I'll give a tour of this area as you adjust the selection. Refer to Figure 9-4.

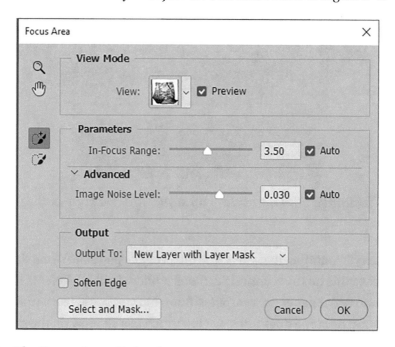

Figure 9-4. *The Focus Area dialog box*

Automatically, no matter what tool is selected, along with the open dialog box Focus Area, your options panel loads with the Focus Area Add tool (E) and its options. Looking from left to right, refer to Figure 9-5.

Figure 9-5. *Focus Area tool options in the options panel*

- **Focus Area Add tool (E)** with the + icon adds to the selection.
- **Focus Area Subtract tool (E)** with the – icon subtracts from the selection.
- **Brush size** sets a brush area for the selection between 1 and 5000. The default is 35.

In the Focus Area dialog box are the following additional tools.

Zoom tool (Z) zooms into your focus area. Options for the Zoom tool appear in the options panel when the tool is selected. See Chapter 2 for more details. Refer to Figure 9-6.

Figure 9-6. *Zoom tool options in the options panel*

Hand tool (H) moves around the focus area without disrupting the selection. Options for the Hand tool appear in the options panel when the tool is selected. See Chapter 2 for more details. Refer to Figure 9-7.

Figure 9-7. *Hand tool options in the options panel*

If nothing was selected with another selection tool before entering the Focus Area, then the whole page may be the focus area. However, in this case, Photoshop was aware of an area to focus on because I assisted it with the white paper background and earlier cropping of some of the carpet. Refer to Figure 9-8.

Figure 9-8. *The Focus Area tool was able to detect most of the edges around the stone. You can see what area is not part of the selection in red*

Use your Focus Area Subtract tool and click and drag over the carpet areas on the left and right to remove any area you don't want. If you drag over an area of the stone, then use the Focus Area Add tool, click and drag to add back to the selection, or Edit ➤ Undo (Ctrl/Cmd+Z) the last step. Refer to Figure 9-9.

Figure 9-9. *Note the path in red of the Focus Area Subtract tool over the carpet and then how it automatically masks that area*

In the options panel, Adjust the Brush size of the Focus Area tool if you find it too small or too large to get around a point like the rock tip on the lower right. Refer to Figure 9-10.

Figure 9-10. *Increase and decrease your Focus Area brush size as you paint around the rock. The red area shows what areas a no longer part of the selection and are masked*

Next, you can change the view of the selection in **View mode** in the dialog box.

From the **View** drop-down menu, you have the following options, but make sure your **Preview** check box is enabled so that you can view them. Hover over any modes if you need more details. Refer to Figure 9-11.

Figure 9-11. *View mode has several preview options to assist in making selections*

- **Marching Ants (M)** shows the Focus Area selection as a dotted line. View the selection with a standard selection border. On soft-edged selections, the border surrounds pixels that are greater than 50% selected. Refer to Figure 9-8 and Figure 9-11.

- **Overlay (V)** shows the Focus Area selection as it appears in Quick Mask mode. Masked areas appear red by default, while unmasked areas appear in normal color. Alt/Option-click while using your Focus Area Tools to edit the Quick Mask Settings. Refer to Figure 9-10 and Figure 9-11.

- **On Black (A)** shows the Focus Area selection on a black background, which is good for viewing lighter or colored lines. Refer to Figure 9-11.

- **On White (T)** shows the Focus Area selection on a white background, which is good for darker or colored lines. Refer to Figure 9-11.

- **Black & White (K)** shows the Focus Area selection as a mask, as you would see on a layer, which is discussed in Chapter 12. Refer to Figure 9-11.

- **On Layers (Y)** shows the Focus Area selection on its own layer and other layers if preset directly below it. Currently, this is how it would appear if it were masked by the selection and is surrounded by transparency. This is helpful if you plan to output this selection to a new layer with or without a mask. Refer to Figure 9-11.

- **Reveal layer (R)** views the entire layer without any masking. Refer to Figure 9-11.

Note   Press F to cycle through these views. Press X to temporarily disable all views. Press X again to reveal a view. Refer to Figure 9-11.

Keep your View on Overlay (V) as it is easiest to see the selection and mask area at the same time. You can then check if you missed any part of the selection and use the Focus Area tools to touch up the selection. Refer to Figure 9-12.

Figure 9-12.   *The selection in View mode Overlay*

Next are the **Parameters**. These sliders often adjust together when the **Auto** check box is enabled. Refer to Figure 9-13.

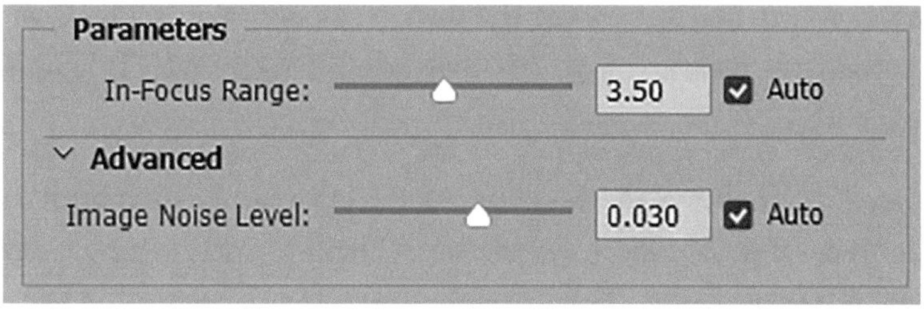

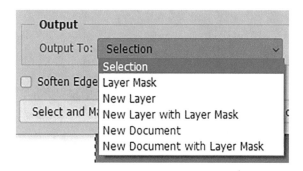

Figure 9-13. *The Parameters settings in the Focus Area dialog box*

- The **In-Focus Range** slider fine-tunes the Focus Area (0.00–7.50). You can let Photoshop do an automatic calculation when the Auto check is enabled. The default in this case is 3.50, but it could be different for you depending on your image.

- The **Advanced** settings control the **Image Noise Level** slider with a range of 0.002–0.100. Increase the image noise level if too much background is selected in a noisy image. You can let Photoshop do an automatic calculation when the Auto check is enabled. The default in this case is 0.030, but it could be different depending on your image.

I leave my Parameter settings at the Auto setting because it is a tight selection, but for your own image, try moving the sliders around to see if you can get better settings. Otherwise, enable Auto for each to reset. Refer to Figure 9-13.

The **Output** area was discussed in Chapter 7 when you looked at the Content-Aware Fill. Besides outputting to a new layer, you have some different options in the **Output To** drop-down list. Refer to Figure 9-14.

Figure 9-14. *Output Settings in the Focus Area dialog box*

The following are options under Output To.

- **Selection** creates a selection that is confirmed when you click OK.

- **Layer Mask** adds a layer mask to the current layer of that selection, and the background layer becomes layer 0. Refer to Figure 9-15.

Figure 9-15. *Output Settings create a mask around what was originally the background layer*

- **New Layer** copies what is in the selection to a new layer without a mask. Refer to Figure 9-16.

Figure 9-16. *The selection is applied to a new layer, and those pixels are copied to a new background layer*

- **New Layer with Layer Mask** copies the selection to a new layer but also adds a layer mask. Refer to Figure 9-17.

Figure 9-17. *The image and mask are copied to a new background layer*

- **New Document** copies what is within the selection to a new untitled document.

- **New Document with Layer Mask** copies the selection to a new untitled document with a layer mask on a layer 1.

Note   Layer Masks are discussed in Chapter 12.

Soften Edge runs additional processing to soften the edge. However, if you want a clean, rough edge to your selection, leave this setting disabled. Refer to Figure 9-18.

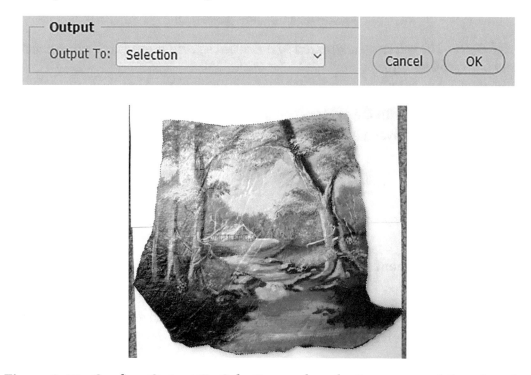

Figure 9-18. *The options of Soften Edge and Select and Mask in the Focus Area dialog box*

The Select and Mask button lets you enter the Select and Mask workspace to refine your selection further, which you look at in the next section of this chapter. Refer to Figure 9-18.

Cancel exit the dialog box with no selection confirmed. Refer to Figure 9-18.

In this case, remain in the dialog box, set Output To at **Selection**, and click **OK** to confirm your selection. Refer to Figure 9-19.

Figure 9-19. *Confirm Output To: Selection and a selection surround the edge of the painted stone upon exit*

While the selection is active, choose New Layer from the Layers panel menu. Refer to Figure 9-20.

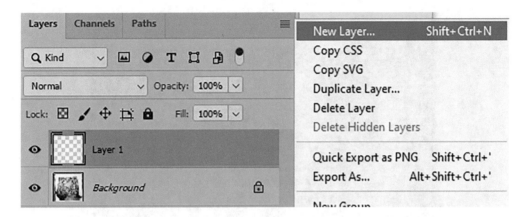

Figure 9-20. *Use the Layers panel to create a new layer 1 to paint on*

Choose Select ➤ Inverse. (Shift+Ctrl/Cmd+I). This now allows you to clean up the area around the rock. Refer to Figure 9-21.

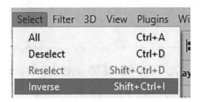

Figure 9-21. *Use the Select menu to create an inverse of the selection*

Then choose from the main menu Edit ➤ Fill and Fill Contents with White, leave the other settings as is, and click OK to confirm. Refer to Figure 9-22.

Figure 9-22. *Set Contents to White in the Fill dialog box*

The area around the stone is now filled with white on layer 1 in the Layers panel. Refer to Figure 9-23.

Note   In your own project, you may need to use the Brush tool (B) to touch up small areas that were missed or the Eraser tool (E) to remove some filled-over areas.

Figure 9-23. *The area around the stone on layer 1 is filled with white and covers the carpet*

Select ➤ Deselect (Ctrl/Cmd+D). Save (Ctrl/Cmd+S) your document as a .psd. You can refer to my photo9_1_finished.psd file.

Select and Mask

Select and Mask creates either a selection of an area and output the selection or output the selection as a layer mask.

Although you have not explored this workspace yet, you have worked with the following selection tools in past chapters.

- Rectangular Marquee tool

- Elliptical Marquee tool

- Single Row Marquee tool

- Single Column Marquee tool

- Lasso tool

- Polygonal Lasso tool

- Magnetic Lasso tool

- Magic Wand tool

- Quick Selection tool

- Object Selection tool

- Select ➤ Focus Area

This button appears in the tool's options panel or dialog box. Refer to Figure 9-24.

Figure 9-24.   *Select and Mask button*

Note   You also find it in the Properties panel in Chapter 12 when you work with layer masks.

So how does this workspace improve your selection any more than what you have seen already? As you have seen already, each workspace in Photoshop has its own skillset.

Working in the Select and Mask Workspace

Open the scan9_2.psd file. Make a copy (Image ➤ Duplicate) of the file and click OK in the dialog box to confirm. Refer to Figure 9-25.

Figure 9-25.   *A sketch of a furry cat in several poses*

Next, let's work with several sketches of a furry cat and use selections to assist in darkening the fur. This time, choose Select ➤ Select and Mask… (Alt/Option+Ctrl/Cmd+R) to enter the workspace. Refer to Figure 9-26.

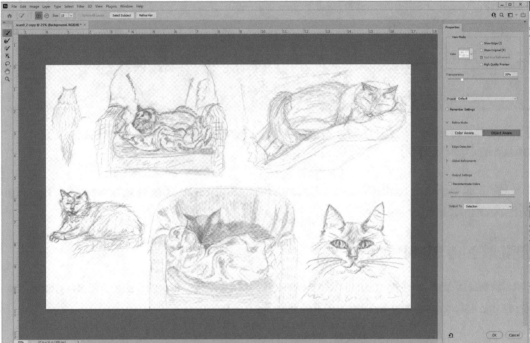

Figure 9-26. *Entering the Select and Mask workspace through the Select menu*

The Select and Mask Workspace is one of the most complex selection areas that you see in Photoshop. However, once again, if you read Chapter 7's descriptions of the Quick Selection, Object Selection, and Content-Aware Fill options, then many of these areas start to become familiar to you. Notice that some areas in the Properties panel on the left are similar to the Focus Area dialog box.

So, let's take a tour.

First, so that you can see changes, in the Properties panel on the right, switch the View mode from Onion Skin (O) to Overlay (V). Refer to Figure 9-27.

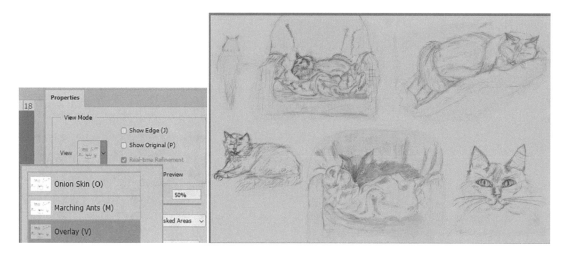

Figure 9-27. *As you did in the Focus Area, change your Properties panel View mode to Overlay (V)*

We'll come back to the View mode area later. Right now, nothing is selected, and the red mask covers the sketches.

Select and Mask Tools

On the left of the workspace, you find several tools with options in the options panel bar. They are listed from top to bottom. Refer to Figure 9-28.

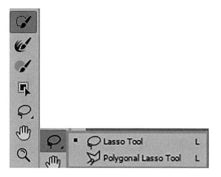

Figure 9-28. *Tools in the Select and Mask workspace*

The **Quick Selection tool (W)** tool was discussed in Chapter 7. Refer to Figure 9-29.

Figure 9-29. *Quick Selection tool options in the options panel*

The options panel shows you can use the following.

The **Add to Selection** icon (+) lets you click and drag to add large areas to the selection.

On the lower right of the sketch, drag inside the cat's head. Refer to Figure 9-30.

Figure 9-30. *Add to the selection by dragging the Quick Selection tool, Add to Selection around the cat's face*

The **Subtract from Selection** icon (–) lets you click and drag to remove large areas of the selection. Hold down the Alt/Option key to switch to this tool.

Drag around the cat's neck and subtract some of the selection. Refer to Figure 9-31.

Figure 9-31. *Subtract from selection by dragging the Quick Selection tool around parts of the selection you want to remove and return to mask*

Change the **brush size** using the slider or your left bracket [and right bracket]. Refer to Figure 9-32.

Figure 9-32. *Quick Selection tool change the brush size in the options panel*

Sample all layers can be enabled if more than one is preset to sample all colors from a composite image; otherwise, it is disabled. Refer to Figure 9-33.

Figure 9-33. *Sample All Layers enabled in the options panel*

Select Subject selects the most prominent objects in the sketch. Refer to Figure 9-34.

Figure 9-34. *The Select Subject button in the options panel, when clicked, can select more of the surrounding images*

Refine Hair finds and refines the hair around a selection; if no selection is present, you receive an alert message. You yield better results if you set the refine mode to Object Aware in the Properties panel. Refer to Figure 9-35.

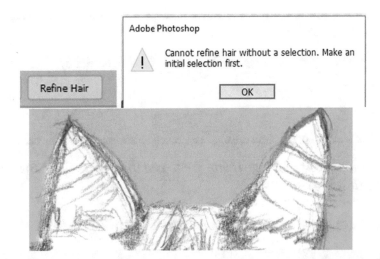

Figure 9-35. *Though very subtle, the Refine Hair button can assist with wisps of hair or fur. Make sure you have a selection started before you use it, or you get an alert message*

Once you have created a selection using the Quick Selection tool, you can then use the **Refine Edge Brush tool (R)** to make the edge smoother and feather the edge, which is good for hair and fur. Refer to Figure 9-36.

Figure 9-36. *The Refine Edge Brush tool*

Note   If you try to use this tool first, you receive a warning message. Click OK and select the Quick Selection tool. Refer to Figure 9-37.

Figure 9-37. *A warning message if you try to use the Refine Edge Brush tool without a selection present*

Looking at the options panel from left to right. Refer to Figure 9-38.

Figure 9-38. *Refined Edge Brush tool options*

The Refine Edge Brush tool contains two selection options.

- **Expand Detection Area** (+) expands the selection slightly when you click and drag on the area.

- **Restores Original Edge** (–) returns the selection to the original state when you click and drag over the same area. Alternatively, hold down the Alt/Option key when you need to toggle between the options.

- While using the brush, set the **Brush options** from the drop-down menu.

    - **Size** slider: 0 px – 5000 px

    - **Hardness** slider: 0%–100%

    - **Spacing** slider: 0%–1000%

    - **Angle:** 0°–360°

    - **Roundness:** 0%–100%

    - **Size Dynamic Control** is based on a stylus. Refer to Figure 9-39.

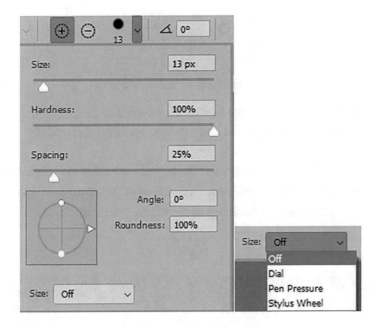

Figure 9-39. *Brush options settings in the options panel*

Note   Brush Angle is also present in the options panel bar. Refer to Figure 9-39.

Sample All Layers is enabled if more than one is present to sample all colors from a composite image; otherwise, it is disabled. Refer to Figure 9-40.

Figure 9-40. *Sample All Layers enabled in the options panel*

You can also use the **Select Subject** and **Refine Hair** buttons. Refer to Figure 9-38.

Use the **Refine Edge Brush tool** on the cat's whiskers and ear hairs. Expand the Detection Area (+) when you click and drag. The difference is very subtle and is much like feathering. Refer to Figure 9-41.

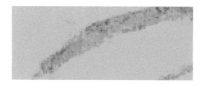

Figure 9-41. *Using the Refine Edge Brush tool might appear like it has done very little, but fur and hair are whispy, so only minor feathering occurs*

The **Brush tool (B)** has options similar to the Refine Brush tool. Refer to Chapter 2 if you need to know how to use it. However, it is a clean edge for making selections.

Looking at the options panel from left to right, refer to Figure 9-42.

Figure 9-42. *Brush tool options in the options panel*

- **Add to Selection** (+) is used when you click and drag over an area.

- **Subtract from Selection** (–) is used when you click and drag over an area. Alternately, use the Alt/Option key to toggle to subtract from a selection.

- Change the **Brush options** from the drop-down menu and brush angle. Refer to Figure 9-39 and Figure 9-42.

- **Sample All Layers** is enabled if more than one is preset to sample all colors from a composite image; otherwise, it is disabled. Refer to Figure 9-43.

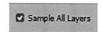

Figure 9-43. *Sample All Layers enabled in the options panel*

You can also use the **Select Subject** or **Refine Hair** buttons. Refer to Figure 9-42.

Use the Brush tool along the cat's ears to get a clean edge selection or other areas of the face for a more precise selection. Then subtract areas of the selection you don't want. Refer to Figure 9-44.

Figure 9-44. *Use the Brush tool to make a cleaner selection around some areas of the cat*

Refer to Chapter 7 if you need to use the **Object Selection tool (W)** tool. Refer to Figure 9-45.

Figure 9-45. *Object Selection tool in the options panel*

In the first section, you can do the following.

- Add to Selection

- Subtract from Selection

- Intersect with Selection

The next section allows you to use the Object Finder. For details on the new Object finder Options in the Options Panel see Chapter 7.

In **Mode**, select either **Rectangle** or **Lasso** to create a selection within a defined region when you click and drag around it. Refer to Figure 9-55 and Figure 9-46.

Figure 9-46. *Selection modes for the Object Selection tool*

Sample All Layers is enabled if more than one is present to sample all colors from a composite image; otherwise, it is disabled. Refer to Figure 9-47.

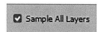

Figure 9-47. *Sample All Layers enabled in the options panel*

Object Subtract (located under the additional options gear).: enable or disable to automatically subtract an object within a defined region. For details on the enabled **Hard Edge** check box refer to Chapter 7. Refer to Figure 9-48.

Figure 9-48. *Object Subtract, Hard Edge, Select Subject, and Refine Hair*

You can also use the **Select Subject** or **Refine Hair** buttons. Refer to Figure 9-48.

Drag in Rectangle mode around the cat on the lower left, and a selection is created. Refer to Figure 9-49.

Figure 9-49. *Drag around the cat in Rectangle mode to select most of the cat's body*

You can then refine the selection around the cat's paw, ears, and hair using your **Brush tool** and **Refine Edge Brush tool**. Refer to Figure 9-50.

Figure 9-50. *The cat's paw now has no mask on it after using the Refine Edge Brush and Brush Tools, and it is a cleaner selection*

Note   There is no New Selection option, as you may have seen with the same selection tools outside of this workspace. This is because as you are adding, subtracting, or intersecting with the current selection. Refer to Figure 9-51.

Figure 9-51. *The Object Selection tool outside of the Select and Mask workspace has four rather than three options*

Note   This is the same for the following Lasso and Polygonal Lasso tools, and in this workspace, they also have the options of Sample All Layers, Select Subject and Refine Hair.

The **Lasso tool (L)** was described in Chapter 5 and Chapter 7. Drag around the area that you want as part of the selection. Release the mouse to create the selection. Refer to Figure 9-52.

Figure 9-52. *Lasso tool options in the options panel*

The **Polygonal Lasso tool (L)** was described in Chapter 5 and Chapter 7. Click around an area that you want as part of the selection. Double-click to complete the selection. Refer to Figure 9-53.

Figure 9-53. *Polygonal Lasso tool options*

Use either of these two tools to draw around the chair in the lower middle to select this area. I used the Lasso tool for a more rounded selection. Refer to Figure 9-54.

Figure 9-54. *Drag around the chair with a Lasso tool to create a selection*

Then use your **Brush tool (B)** to refine the selection around the chair. Use either Add to Selection or Subtract from Selection and change your brush size as required. Refer to Figure 9-55.

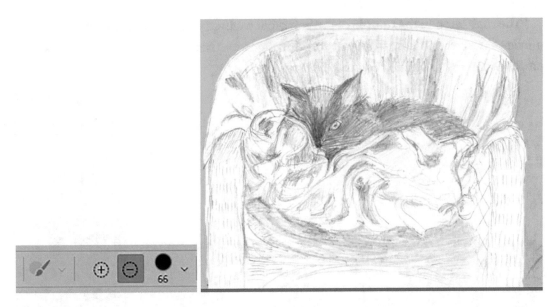

Figure 9-55. *Use the Brush tool to either add or subtract from the selection and get closer to the chair*

While you are doing the refinement, use the next two tools to assist you. Refer to Figures 9-56 and Figure 9-57.

The **Hand tool (H)** was described in Chapter 2 and Chapter 7. The hand lets you move around the viewing area and is useful when you are zoomed in. Hold down the spacebar to switch to the Hand tool temporarily. Refer to Figure 9-56.

Figure 9-56. *Hand tool options*

The **Zoom tool (Z)** was described in Chapter 2 and Chapter 7. Zoom in or out of areas while selecting. Remember, you can also use Ctrl/Cmd++(plus) or Ctrl/Cmd+- (hyphen) to zoom in and out. Refer to Figure 9-57.

Figure 9-57. *Zoom tool options*

The main area in the middle of the workspace where you have been working previews the selection changes, but you can alter them further using the **Properties panel** on the right. Refer to Figure 9-58.

Figure 9-58. *Preview the Current Selections in your Select and Mask workspace and then edit them further using the Properties panel*

Select and Mask Properties Panel

The Properties panel, as you saw in Chapter 2, stores many of the editing properties for a layer. In this case, it stores the editing properties for the Select and Mask workspace. There are similarities between the Content-Aware Fill panel in Chapter 7 and the Focus Area dialog box.

View Mode

The following are the view mode options.

- Marching Ants (M)

- Overlay (V)

- On Black (A)

- On White (T)

- Black and White (K)

- On Layers (Y)

- Press F to cycle views

- Press X to disable all views

However, there are a few more additional features. I point out the new features and differences. Refer to Figure 9-59.

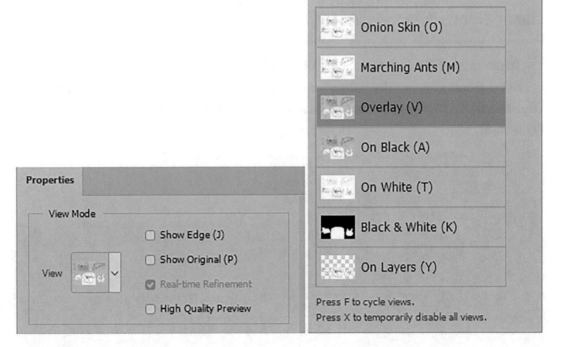

Figure 9-59. *Properties panel View mode and its various settings for selection viewing*

In View, you can choose the following.

Onion Skin (O) lets you view layers masked by the selection. Selected areas are solid, while masked areas are transparent. Refer to Figure 9-60.

Figure 9-60. *The checkerboard pattern behind the cat's head shows the area is masked or transparent*

Note   There is no Reveal layer (R) in the menu.

To the right of View are some check boxes.

Show Edge (J) shows the refinement area in the areas that you use the Refine Edge Brush tool (R). You can see this best in the View mode of Overlay (V). Refer to Figure 9-61.

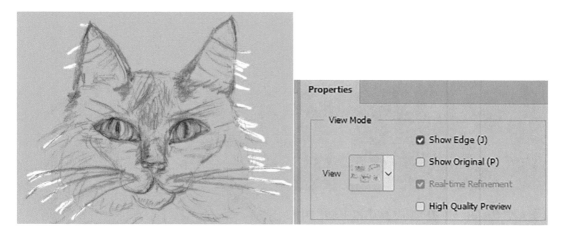

Figure 9-61. *Show Edge Brush tool on cat's whiskers and ear hairs*

Show Original (P) lets you view the original area before the selection was made. In this case, there was no prior selection, so nothing appears. Refer to Figure 9-62.

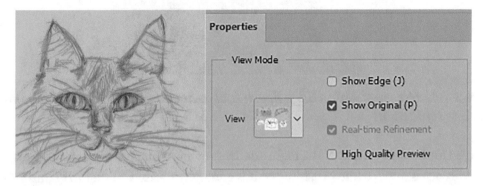

Figure 9-62. *Shows how the selection appeared before it was made in Select and Mask*

The preview might look like this if a selection was made before entering the Select and Mask workspace. Refer to Figure 9-63.

Figure 9-63. *This is how the Show Original area would appear if a selection had already been made before I entered Select and Mask*

Real-time Refinement previews updates while brushing. This setting is only accessible when the Refine Edge Brush tool is chosen and enabled or disabled. Refer to Figure 9-64.

Figure 9-64. *Use your Refine Edge Brush tool to access the Properties View mode Real-time refinement*

High Quality Preview shows a high-quality preview while working, but this might slow the process down while brushing, so it is generally disabled. Refer to Figure 9-64.

Below the View mode is an area for you to alter the settings.

Use the slider to set the viewing **Transparency** of the masked areas. (0%–100% in Onion Skin View mode.) Refer to Figure 9-65.

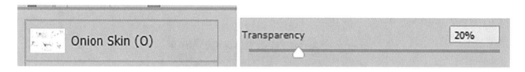

Figure 9-65. *Transparency option in Onion Skin View mode*

When you change the View mode, other options or no options appear depending on the View mode. For example, Overlay (V) allows you to change the mask's **Opacity** and **Color** using the Color Picker dialog box and whether it **Indicates** the Masked Areas or the Selected Areas. Refer to Figure 9-66.

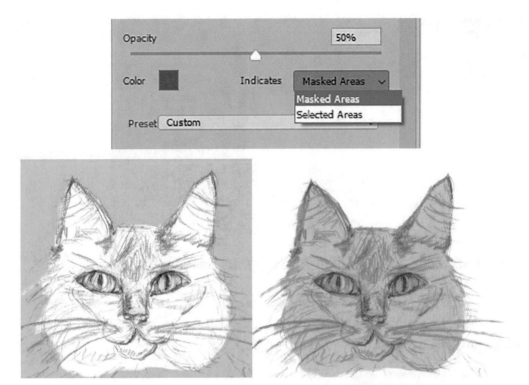

Figure 9-66. *Overlay Viewing mode lets you change the color and opacity of the mask or change the selection view*

The On Black (A) or On White (T) modes allow you to change the **Opacity** of Matte. But Marching Ants (M), Black & White (K), and On Layers (Y) have no Transparency or Opacity options. Refer to Figure 9-67.

Figure 9-67. *Some Viewing modes have Opacity Setting while others have no other settings*

Select a preset or the **Default** setting from the drop-down list. When you change settings in the Properties panel, this area changes to read **Custom**. To select a preset, choose **Load Preset** and locate a Select and Mask (.slm) file. Refer to Figure 9-68.

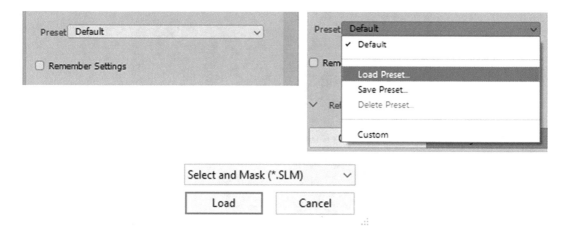

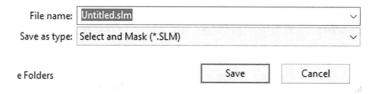

Figure 9-68. *Load Select and Mask presets from the Preset drop-down list*

Likewise, if you need to save a preset, you can choose **Save Preset** from the list and save it as a Select and Mask (.slm) file that you can use later or share with other users in your group. Refer to Figure 9-78 and Figure 9-69.

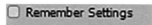

Figure 9-69. *Save Select and Mask Presets*

If additional presets are stored in the list, they can also be deleted by choosing **Delete Preset**. Refer to Figure 9-68.

Note   Saving a selection within a file is discussed later in Chapter 12.

Remember Settings lets you always use certain settings when you enter the Select and Mask workspace. By default, it is disabled as you may want to use different settings each time. Refer to Figure 9-70.

Figure 9-70. *Properties panel Remember Settings option*

Refine Mode

Refine mode has two settings buttons: **Color Aware** and **Object Aware**. Refer to Figure 9-71.

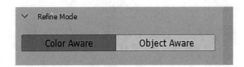

Figure 9-71. *Properties panel Refine mode settings of Color Aware and Object Aware*

Although most selections might turn out fine with Color Aware, which deals with contrasts, use Object Aware when working with the Quick Selection tool or Object Selection tool if you must refine hair or very thin lines in a complex background.

If you are on Color or Object Aware and click another mode to switch, you receive a warning message that switching to Refine mode may alter the edge. Click **OK** to proceed or **Cancel** to remain in the current mode. Refer to Figure 9-72.

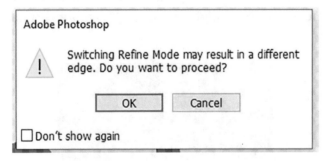

Figure 9-72. *An alert message appears when you change your refine mode*

Depending on the sketch or image, the changes may be subtle in the selection. Refer to Figure 9-73.

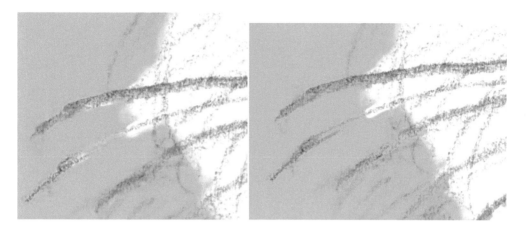

Figure 9-73. *Color Aware and Object Aware modes can affect the selection of sketches of fur in subtle ways*

Edge Detection

This next section lets you define the **Radius** of the edge refinement area (0 px – 250 px). 0 px leaves the refinement sharp. A higher number gives a more feathered refined edge. Refer to Figure 9-74.

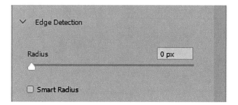

Figure 9-74. *Edge Detection Radius setting*

Drag the radius up to 7 px while in **Color Aware Refine mode** and notice how it affects the selection around the whiskers. Refer to Figure 9-75.

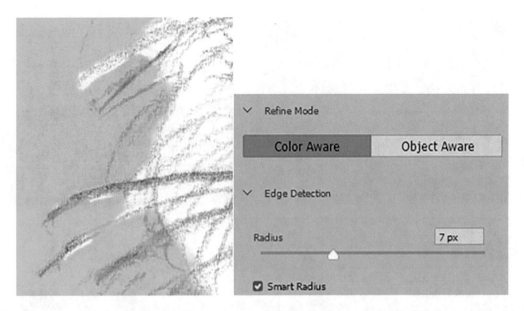

Figure 9-75. *Raising the radius to 7 px while in Refine mode, Color Aware, and Smart Radius are enabled*

Smart Radius automatically adapts the radius to the image's hard and soft edges and may not feather as close. Also, selection results may differ based on whether the Refine mode is Color Aware or Object Aware. Refer to Figure 9-75.

Adobe recommends using this setting when dealing with a transition from hair to shoulders in photos. But you can see this best at higher radius settings. Refer to Figure 9-76.

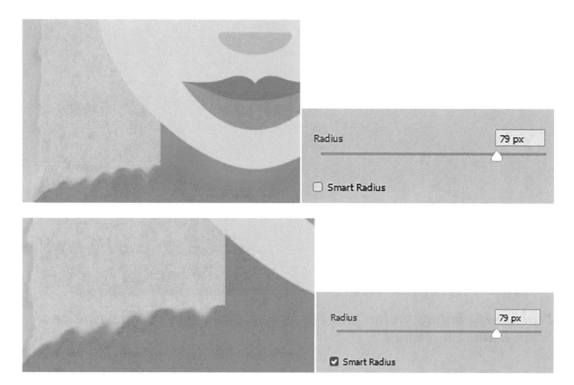

Figure 9-76. *Smart Radius may appear more apparent in color photos where the hair touches the solders and applies a higher radius*

Coming back to the picture of the cats, set the Radius back down to 0 and disable Smart Radius.

Global Refinements

The Global Refinements settings refine the entire selection. Refer to Figure 9-77.

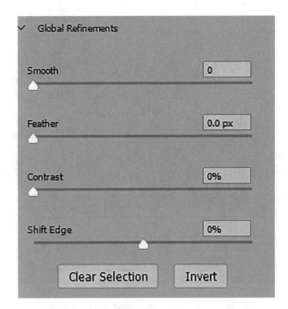

Figure 9-77. *Properties panel Global Refinements*

The **Smooth** slider smooths out jagged or abrupt edges in the selection. The range is 0–100. Refer to Figure 9-78.

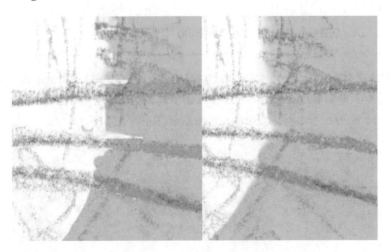

Figure 9-78. *When higher numbers of smoothing are applied, the area around the whiskers is blurred*

The **Feather** slider softens the selection edge similarly to edge detection. The range is 0.0 px – 1000 px. Refer to Figure 9-79.

Figure 9-79. *Global Refinements feather creates an overall more blurry selection*

Tip   If you plan to output to a mask rather than a selection, keep the Feather slider at 0 and later feather using the actual Layers Mask Properties panel. This is a less destructive option, which is discussed in Chapter 12.

The **Contrast** slider increases the contrast of the selection edge and makes it crisp. The range is 0%–100%. Be aware that using Radius, Smooth, and Feather in combination with this slider reverses the selection's sharpness. Refer to Figure 9-80.

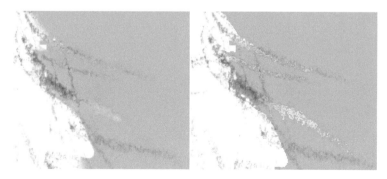

Figure 9-80. *Global Refinements contrast sharpens the selection slightly around the fur at higher settings*

The **Shift Edge** slider contracts the selection edge with negative a percent or expand it with a positive percent (–100%–0–100%). If set to 0%, then there is no edge shift. Contracting the selection can help remove unwanted background colors from the selection edge. Refer to Figure 9-81.

Figure 9-81. *Global Refinements Shift Edge can either contract or expand the selection*

Change the **Shift Edge** to 100% to expand your selection. This affects the other selections, but that is all right since the background is white and not complex. Refer to Figure 9-81.

Clear Selection removes the current selection, and you must create it again. Refer to Figure 9-82.

Figure 9-82. *Global Refinements Clear Selection and Invert buttons*

Invert inverts the selection as you do with Ctrl/Cmd+I or Select ➤ Inverse. Click Invert again to return to the current selection. Refer to Figure 9-82 and Figure 9-83.

Figure 9-83. *Invert the selection or Invert again to return to the original setting*

Continue to refine the selection around the cat's whiskers. Again, use the Refine Edge Brush tool (R) and Brush tool (B). Refer to Figure 9-84.

Figure 9-84. *Refine the selection around the fur with the various Select and Mask Brush tools*

Output Settings

This is the last section in the Properties panel.

The **Decontaminate Colors setting** removes color fringe from the image and uses colors within the selection. Refer to Figure 9-85.

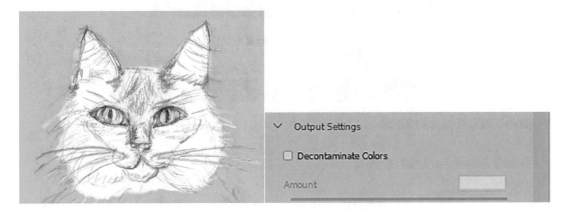

Figure 9-85. *Properties panel Output Settings Decontaminate Colors*

Note This setting is grayed out if you are working on a layer with no pixels.

The Amount slider removes the color fringed from the image. The range is 0%–100%. It is active when Decontaminate Colors is enabled. Refer to Figure 9-86.

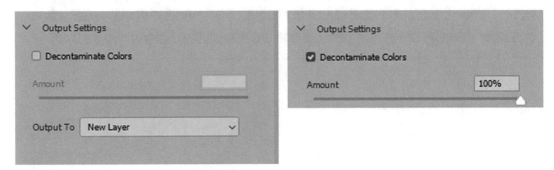

Figure 9-86. *The Amount slider is enabled when the Decontaminate Colors check box is enabled*

Leave Decontaminate Colors disabled. Refer to Figure 9-86.

Output To is explained in Chapter 7 and in this chapter, see Focus Area dialog box section. Refer to Figure 9-87.

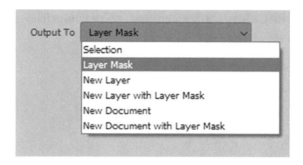

Figure 9-87. *Output To Selection menu*

The following are the options.

- Selection

- Layer Mask

- New Layer

- New Layer with Layer Mask

- New Document

- New Document with Layer Mask

Note   When Decontaminated Colors is enabled, you cannot output as a selection or a layer mask by itself; only new options are accessible. Refer to Figure 9-88.

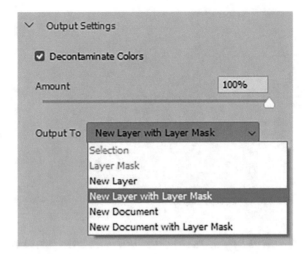

Figure 9-88. *Some options may not be available if you enable Decontaminate Colors*

On the lower right of the Properties panel, refer to Figure 9-89.

Figure 9-89. *Properties panel Reset icon, OK, and Cancel button*

- **Reset** resets the entire workspace.

- **OK** confirms the selection and type of output.

- **Cancel** exits the workspace without making any changes to the selection.

Choose **Selection** from the Output to List. Refer to Figure 9-90.

Figure 9-90. *Properties panel Choose Output To selection for this example*

Click OK. The new selections appear on the canvas. Refer to Figure 9-91.

Figure 9-91. *The selection appears around various cats and furniture in the sketch*

Once you leave the Select and Mask workspace, if you realize you need to add to the selection, choose any Selection tool from the Tools panel, and in the options panel, click the Select and Mask button to continue refining the selection. Refer to Figure 9-92.

Figure 9-92. *Choose a selection tool from the Tools panel, and then choose Select and Mask*

In the main Photoshop area, create a new layer from the Layers panel menu while the selection is active. Refer to Figure 9-93.

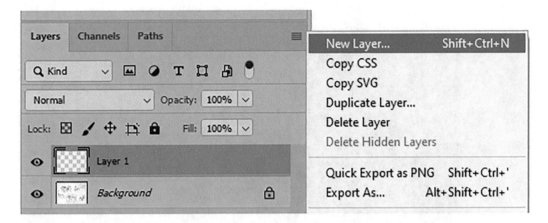

Figure 9-93. *In the Layers panel menu, create a new layer to paint on*

Paint inside the selection on the cat's face on the right. Use the Brush tool to paint a brown-gray color from the Foreground Color Picker in the Tools panel. I used the R:62, G:62, and B: 62 settings. Refer to Figure 9-94.

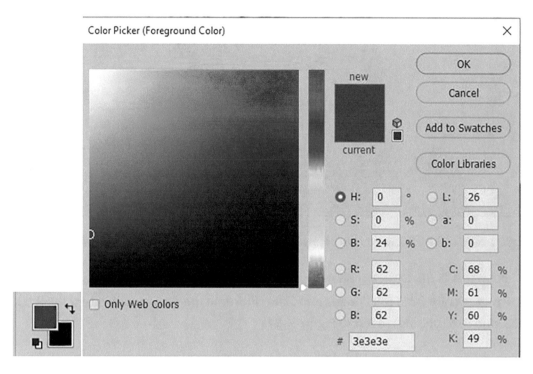

Figure 9-94. *Paint inside the selection of the cat's head on a new layer*

When you are done painting, change the Blending mode of layer 1 to **Overlay** to darken the line features of the cat's face. Refer to Figure 9-95

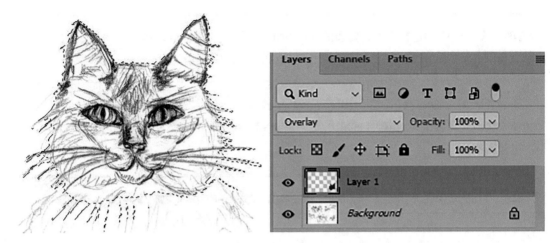

Figure 9-95. *The Blending mode is applied to the painted area on the cat's face on layer 1, and the lines are much darker*

Darkening the lines can either make the image stand out when printed or help a program like Adobe Illustrator detect lines more accurately if you plan to do an Image Trace.

Paint in the other selection areas with the same color on or around the cats. This affects those lines with the layer blending mode, but not the other cats in the upper area outside of the selection. Refer to Figure 9-96.

Figure 9-96. *Notice the lower cats in the sketch have darker lines applied but the upper lines are lighter and unaffected*

Note   You could use these selections for colorizing certain areas as well, but with different layer blending modes and opacities as in Chapter 8.

Select ➤ Deselect (Ctrl/Cmd+D). Save your document as a .psd. You can check out my final example in scan9_2_final.psd, where I saved the selection in the Channels panel.

Note   This is a complex selection. To learn how to save it for your own projects, read Chapters 10, 11, and 12.

Summary

This chapter explored two more selection tools that you can use to clean up your sketches. You discovered that Focus Area is a simplified form of the Select and Mask workspace. However, Select and Mask is better at finer selections of thin hair and fur lines. The previous chapters looked at the most frequently used selection tools for photos and scanned sketches. There are a few more in the next three chapters. You also learn ways to save your selection if you close your file and want to return to refining the selection another day.

CHAPTER 10

Shape Tools, Pen Tools, and Creating Paths

This chapter teaches you how to use the Shape tools or a Pen tool to create a path that can later be made into a selection for other projects.

Later, in following chapters, you'll look at a few additional ways to create and then save your selections in a document so that you can return to them another day.

This chapter discusses a few final tools that you can use to create a path and save that path in the Window ➤ Paths panel. In Chapter 11, you save that path as a selection in your Channels panel. Refer to Figure 10-1.

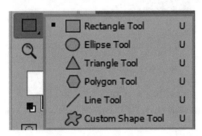

Figure 10-1. *Shape tools in the Tools panel*

The following are the Shape tools.

- Rectangle tool (U)

- Ellipse tool (U)

- Triangle tool (U)

- Polygon tool (U)

- Line tool (U)

- Custom Shape tool (U)

© Jennifer Harder 2022
J. Harder, *Accurate Layer Selections Using Photoshop's Selection Tools*,
https://doi.org/10.1007/978-1-4842-7493-4_10

To modify the path and its points, let's look at the Path Selection tool. Refer to Figure 10-2.

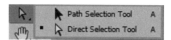

Figure 10-2. *Path Selection tools in the Tools panel*

- Path Selection tool (A)

- Direct Selection tool (A)

Finally, you look at the various Path Creation tools. Refer to Figure 10-3.

Figure 10-3. *Pen tools in the Tools panel*

- Pen tool (P)

- Freeform Pen tool (P)

- Content-Aware Tracing tool (P)

- Curvature Pen tool (P)

- Add Anchor Point tool

- Delete Anchor Point tool

- Convert Point tool

Note   This chapter does not cover the Frame tool (K) because it is for image linking or embedding within a .psd document. It is not a Shape tool for creating selections around a sketch. Refer to Figure 10-4.

Figure 10-4. *Frame tool in the Tools panel*

Note   If you want to know more about the Photoshop Frame tool, check out my Springer Nature video at `https://link.springer.com/video/10.1007/978-1-4842-6674-8`.

This chapter's projects are in the Chapter 10 folder.

Shape Tools

As you have seen, each selection you make may not have been one exact or perfect geometric shape. While working with the basic selection tools in Chapter 3, there may have been times when you wondered why there is no star-shaped marquee tool or a triangular marquee tool. At that point, you were only making very crude selections. Refer to Figure 10-5.

Figure 10-5. *Rectangular Marquee tool in the Tools panel*

In Chapter 5, you saw that you could make more angular selections with the Polygonal Lasso tool, but once you closed the selection, it did not leave a lot of time to edit that selection, and maybe you wanted it to be a precise geometric shape. Refer to Figure 10-6.

Figure 10-6. *Lasso tools in the Tools panel*

Likewise, in Chapter 6, you saw that you could make selections with Type with the Type Mask tools, but you could not create your own custom selections other than using the fonts to create a mask. Refer to Figure 10-7.

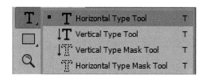

Figure 10-7. *Type tools in the Tools panel*

While they are useful for creating scalable vector shape layers, Shape tools also allow you to create paths that can be easily converted to selections. Let's talk about that procedure next as you look at each shape tool.

Rectangle Tool (U)

The first shape tool that is present in the Tools panel shapes list is the Rectangle tool. If you look at your options panel to the right of the Preset tools, the Pick Tool mode area should be currently set to Shape. Generally, when this Tool mode is set to Shape, the purpose is to create a Shape layer. Refer to Figure 10-8.

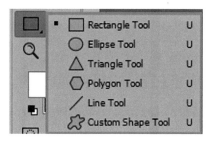

Figure 10-8. *Rectangle tool and its options in the options panel*

File ➤ Open scan10_1_rectangle.psd. It is a sketch of some rectangular-shaped brooches and a rectangular gemstone. Refer to Figure 10-9.

Figure 10-9. *Sketch of brooches and a gemstone*

Make an Image ➤ Duplicate of the file for practicing as you have in previous chapters. Click OK in the dialog box to confirm the copy.

Using the Rectangle tool, click at a point where you want to start your rectangle and hold down the mouse and drag out to the right and down around the rectangular-shaped brooch to create a Vector Rectangle layer. Refer to Figure 10-10.

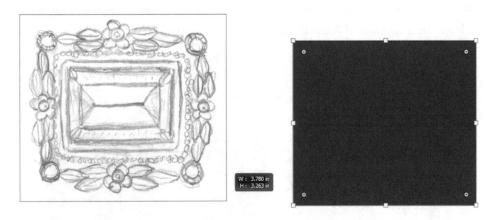

Figure 10-10. *The Shape layer covers the brooch*

In the Layers panel is the vector shape layer; in this case, Rectangle. Refer to Figure 10-11.

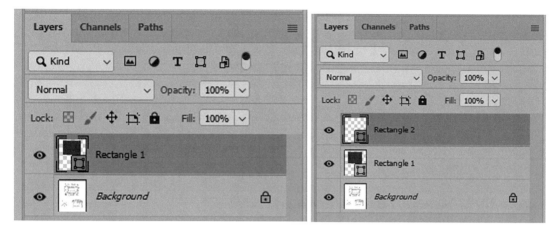

Figure 10-11. *Shape layers in the Layers panel*

You could continue to drag out multiple rectangles. Each would be on its own layer, but vector shape layers are not selections, and they are not very useful for cleaning up your sketches as they cover the sketch with a fill and/or a stroke.

However, you can Ctrl/Cmd-click the layer's thumbnail as you saw in Chapter 6, and you can load the selection of the rectangle. Refer to Figure 10-12.

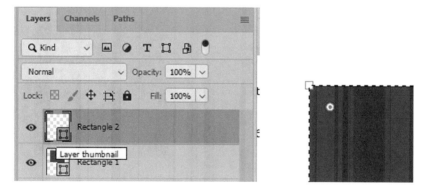

Figure 10-12. *Loading a Shape layer in the Layers panel*

Note   In this case, you cannot right-click to select the pixel because it is a vector shape layer. Technically, no pixels are present, only shape paths, and the entire layer with that option is selected rather than the rectangle. As you can see with the vector shape layer, the other problem is that it blocks the selection. So, you must turn off the layer's eye to hide it. In addition, you may not want to have this shape layer present in your document, so you must use the layer's trash can to delete it each, thus removing the "saved" path. Refer to Figure 10-13.

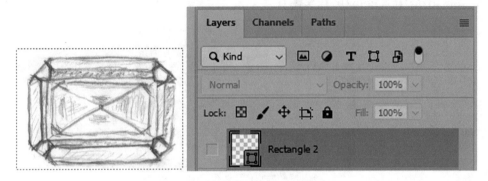

Figure 10-13. *The gem is revealed with the selection around it when the layer eye is turned off in the Layers panel*

Choose **Delete layer** in the Layers menu to delete the vector shape rectangle layers. Look at the background layer again. Refer to Figure 10-14.

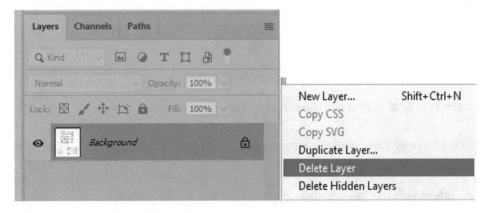

Figure 10-14. *Delete the Shape layers in the Layers panel*

How is this better than the Rectangular Marquee tool? I'll answer that question as you start examining the options panel.

Rectangle Tool Options

Look from left to right in the options panel shown in Figure 10-15.

***Figure 10-15.** Rectangle tool options in the options panel*

As with many of the tools you looked at in previous chapters, the Rectangle tool has an area where you can save and manage your **Presets**. Refer to Chapter 2 if you need to review how to do this. Refer to Figure 10-16.

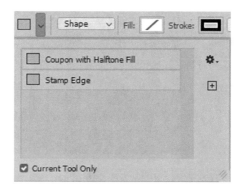

***Figure 10-16.** Rectangle tool presets in the options panel*

The next section in the options panel allows you to change **Tool mode**. Refer to Figure 10-17.

***Figure 10-17.** Tool mode options in the options panel*

Before you draw out a path or shape, pick one of the following options from the drop-down list.

- **Shape** allows the created shape to be a vector shape layer.

- Only the **path** of the shape appears in the Window ➤ Paths panel and does not create a layer.

- **Pixel** creates a rasterized shape on the currently selected layer with the current Tools panel foreground color. The shape is now in pixel form and is not as scalable as a vector shape. Always create a shape on a new blank layer, not on the background layer; otherwise, it covers the selected layer's pixels. Refer to Figure 10-18.

Figure 10-18. *The Shape in a normal layer in the Layers panel*

This book is not concerned with the shape or pixel modes because they do not assist you in creating selections, so set the Tool mode to **Path**, which sets any other shape tools. So, you do not have to switch each tool's modes when you get to that section in the chapter.

Looking at the options panel again, the options have now changed for paths. Refer to Figure 10-19.

Figure 10-19. *When Path is selected in the options panel, the options change*

Drag out another rectangle from left to right and down to go over the rectangular-shaped brooch. Refer to Figure 10-20.

Figure 10-20. *Drag a rectangle path around the brooch*

No vector shape layer appears in the Layers panel, yet the path is present and selected on the canvas. Refer to Figure 10-21.

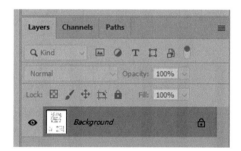

Figure 10-21. *No Shape layer appears in the Layers panel*

Where is the path stored? In the Window ➤ Paths panel as a work path. Click the Paths panel tab if you need to make the selection visible. Refer to Figure 10-22.

Figure 10-22. *A work path appears in the Paths panel*

Note When you create a vector shape layer, a path is stored in the Paths panel but hidden when creating another shape layer. Only when vector shape layers are selected in the Layers panel, do the paths appear again in the Paths panel. If you want to see both paths of multiple layers, Shift-click each of them in the Layers panel and look at the Paths panel at the same time. Refer to Figure 10-23.

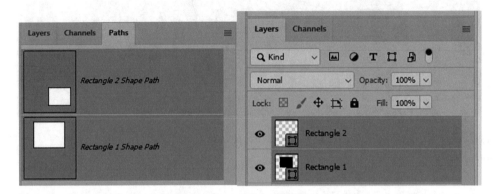

Figure 10-23. *Shape layers also have paths in the Paths panel*

While in the Tool mode and the work path is selected, you can continue to drag another rectangular path, which is added to the current work path. Refer to Figure 10-24.

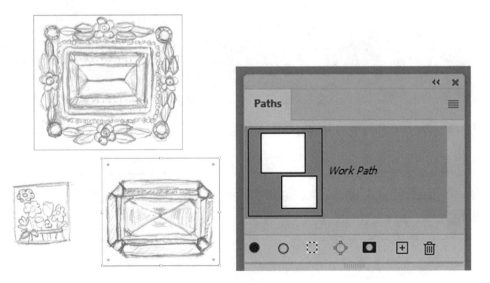

Figure 10-24. *Two paths around brooches and how they appear in the Paths panel*

Saving a Path

If you deselect the path, the paths could be lost by clicking the gray area below the path in the Paths panel and then drawing a new path. Refer to Figure 10-25.

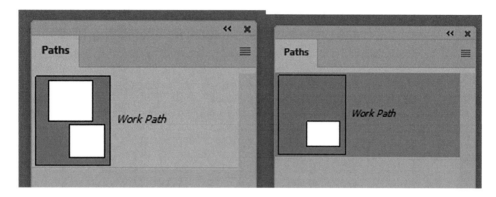

Figure 10-25. *If a work path is not saved, it is erased the next time you draw a path*

To ensure that the work path is saved, double-click the name **Work Path** and either accept the default name path 1 in the Save Path dialog box or type a new name and click OK to confirm. Refer to Figure 10-26.

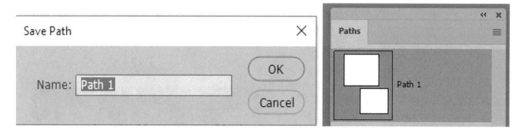

Figure 10-26. *Save a path using the Paths panel*

Note   To add a blank path area before drawing any paths, click the create path icon. Refer to Figure 10-27.

Figure 10-27. *Create a blank path before you start drawing paths in the Paths panel*

Note   To delete a path, click the delete path trash can on the lower right and click Yes to the warning message. Refer to Figure 10-28.

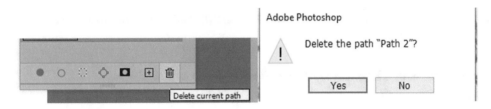

Figure 10-28. *Delete a path in the Paths panel*

You return to the Paths panel off and on throughout the chapter, but for now, keep path 1 selected.

Rectangle Tool Options Continued

With path 1 selected using the options panel, look at the Make section. You can easily change that shape into a selection. Refer to Figure 10-29.

Figure 10-29. *Selections can be made in the Make section of the options panel*

The Make section of the options panel is active when paths are present. Click the **Selection** button. The Make Selection dialog box appears and then choose the following options. Refer to Figure 10-30.

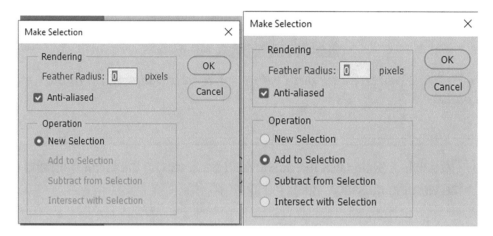

Figure 10-30. *Make Selections dialog box options are inactive or active depending on what is selected*

Rendering with a **Feather Radius** is from 0 pixels to 250 pixels.

Anti-alias smooths the selection.

Operation only allows New Selection when only path 1 is selected, even if more than one path is on the current path layer. However, if one selection is preset before the paths are created, you can draw another path and click the Selection again to add, subtract, or intersect with the selection. (You can review these operations further in by referring to the Rectangular Marquee tool in Chapter 3.) Refer to Figure 10-30 and Figure 10-31.

Figure 10-31. *A selection was already present when the path was turned into a selection, so it could add to the selection*

Click OK, and the path is now a selection. In the Paths panel, path 1 is deselected. You only see the selection on the canvas. Refer to Figure 10-32.

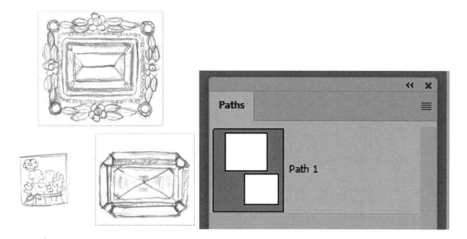

Figure 10-32. *Two selections made from the paths in the Paths panel*

Let's return to the options panel.

Mask creates a vector mask path. You look at it further in Chapter 12. Refer to Figure 10-33.

Figure 10-33. *Mask and Shape buttons. The Mask button creates a mask layer.*

Shape reverts to creating a vector shape layer. It is not covered moving forward. Refer to Figure 10-11 and Figure 10-33.

Remember to use the History panel to undo anything while creating a mask or shape layer. For now, create a single rectangle path on path 1. Refer to Figure 10-34.

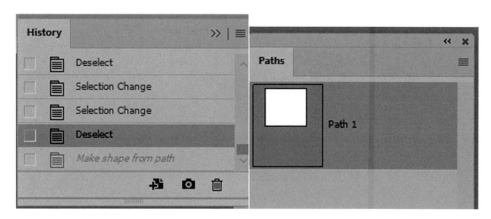

Figure 10-34. *Use your History panel to move back a few steps to reset the path*

The next set of options can assist in creating or combining selections.

I now demonstrate some possible paths you could create depending on the purpose of your path selection. However, you can follow along by creating a new path layer for practice. Refer to Figure 10-35.

Figure 10-35. *Path Operations, Path Alignment Path Arrangement, and Set Additional Path and Shape options drop-downs in the options panel*

Path Operations

From the **Path Operations** drop-down list, you can choose various operations to combine for paths. Refer to Figure 10-36.

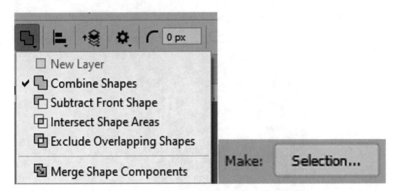

Figure 10-36. *Path Operations drop-down list in the options panel used with the Selection button to create selections*

New layer is grayed out because it is not an option for paths.

Let's discuss how to work with **Combine Shapes**. Drag out two paths that overlap on path 1 with this option selected. Click path 1 in the Paths panel to make sure both paths are selected, then click the Selection button. In the Make Selection dialog box, click OK, and the selection is combined. Refer to Figure 10-37.

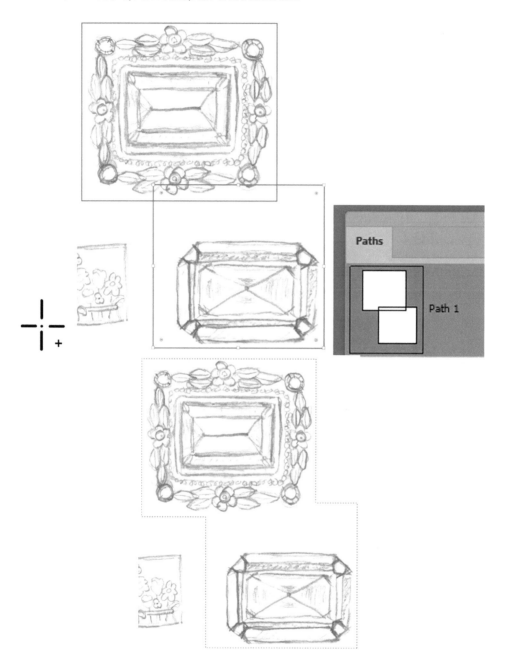

Figure 10-37. *The pointer changes to a plus symbol. When you drag out the paths, you can see them in the Paths panel and then how they appear with the selection around them, which is combined.*

Select ➤ Deselect Ctrl/Cmd+D to deselect the selection.

Next, let's discuss how to work with **Subtract Front Shape**. While path 1 is deselected, drag out two paths that overlap on a new work path with this option selected for this second path. Refer to Figure 10-38.

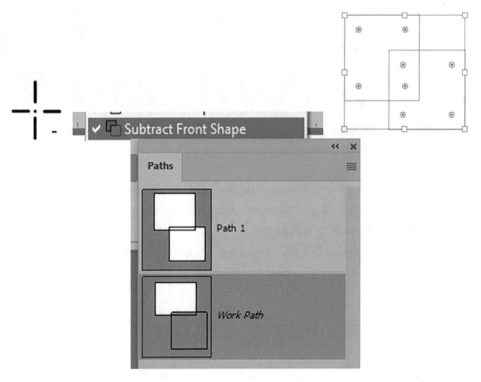

Figure 10-38. *The pointer changes to a minus symbol. When you drag out the paths, you can see them in the Paths panel.*

Click **Work Path** in the Paths panel to make sure both paths are selected, click the Selection button, click OK to confirm the message in the dialog box, and only the selection of the back part of the two paths appears.

You can see it more clearly in Quick Mask mode (Q). You can then save it as path 2 by double-clicking the work path. Refer to Figure 10-39.

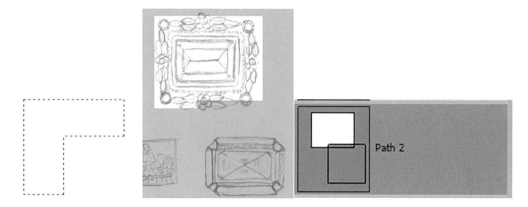

Figure 10-39. *The selection and how the subtracted selection appears in Quick Mask mode and the Paths panel*

However, if you have already created the path by clicking the **Create new path** icon first as in the "path 3" example and then repeating the same steps with the **Subtract Front Shape** option, of creating rectangles.

This time on path 3, you will create an inverse selection. Refer to Figure 10-40.

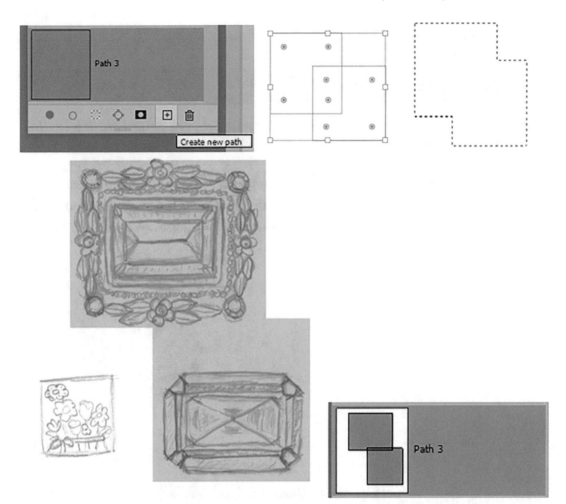

Figure 10-40. *A slightly different path happens with the Subtract Front Shape option when you save the path first. This time, it is an Inverse, and you can see how that looks in Quick Mask mode.*

So, the selection order for paths is very important when using this setting.

Select ➤ Deselect Ctrl/Cmd+D to deselect the selection.

Now let's discuss how to work with **Intersect Shape Areas**. Click **Create new path** to create path 4. Drag out two paths that overlap on a new path 4 with this option selected for both. Refer to Figure 10-41.

Figure 10-41. *Create a new path in the Paths panel and draw out paths with the Intersect Shape Areas option*

In the Paths panel, make sure both paths are selected, then click the Selection button. Click OK to confirm the message in the dialog box, and only the selection in the middle of the two paths appear. You can see this better in Quick Mask mode (Q). Refer to Figure 10-42.

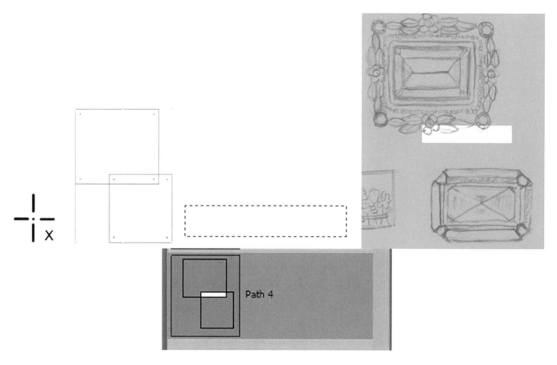

Figure 10-42. *The pointer changes to an X symbol. When you drag out the paths, you can see them in the Paths panel and how they appear as a selection and in Quick Mask mode.*

Select ➤ Deselect Ctrl/Cmd+D to deselect the selection.

Let's discuss how to work with Exclude Overlapping Shapes. Click **Create new path** to create path 5. Drag out two paths that overlap on a new path 5 with this option selected for both. Refer to Figure 10-43.

Figure 10-43. *Create a new path in the Paths panel and draw out paths with the Exclude Overlapping Shapes option*

In the paths panel, make sure both paths are selected, then click the Selection button. Click OK to confirm the message in the dialog box. Now the two paths appear, but the section in the center is excluded. You can see this better in Quick Mask mode (Q). Refer to Figure 10-44.

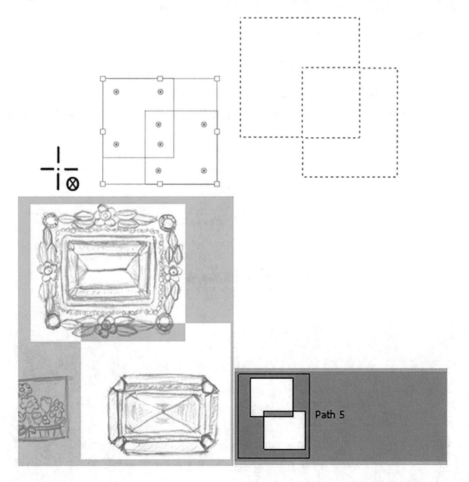

Figure 10-44. *The pointer changes to an X inside a circle symbol. When you drag out the paths, you can see them in the Paths panel and how they appear as a selection and in Quick Mask mode.*

Select ➤ Deselect Ctrl/Cmd+D to deselect the selection.

Merge Shape Components turns a live shape or path into a combined path. Click back to path 1. Refer to Figure 10-45.

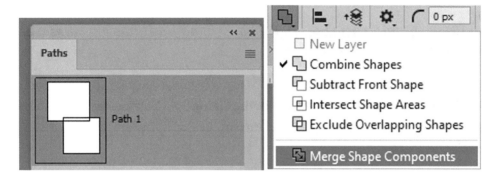

Figure 10-45. *Merge Shape Components is chosen while a path is selected*

Based on one of the earlier path operations for example use Path 1. When Combined Shapes is selected, click Yes in the message to make a single path rather than two. You could use this to simplify your paths before pressing the Selection button in the options panel. Refer to Figure 10-46.

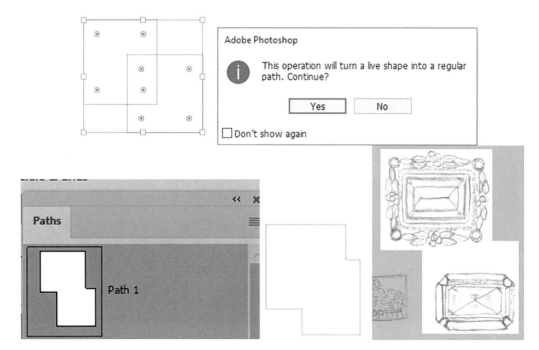

Figure 10-46. *The paths are merged, and you can see how that appears as a selection and in Quick Mask mode*

Now use the History panel and Reset Path operations back to combined shapes as they were before on path 1. Refer to Figure 10-47.

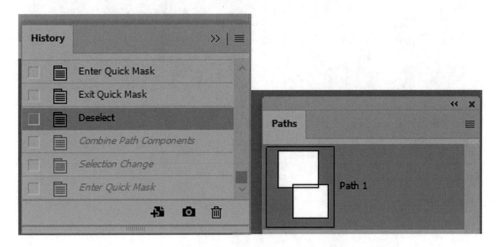

Figure 10-47. *Use your History panel if you need to undo a merged path right away*

Path Alignment

When two or more newly created paths are selected in the Paths panel, you can align them.

With no other path layers selected, draw out two rectangular paths that are not touching each other on a new work path layer. To ensure that both paths are selected, you can either click off your work path in the Paths panel gray area below the path and then on the path again in the panel. Or drag a marquee around the two paths with the Path Selection tool from the Tools panel to select both. Refer to Figure 10-48.

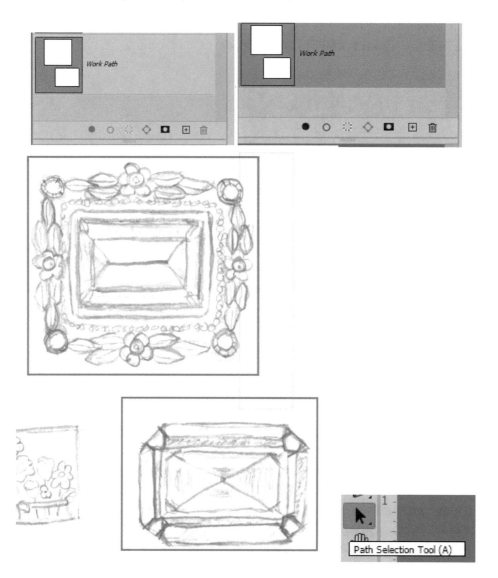

Figure 10-48. *When paths are selected, you can align them*

We'll talk more about that tool later.

Double-click the work path in the Paths panel to save it as path 6.

Now review the options in the Path Alignment drop-down list. Refer to Figure 10-49.

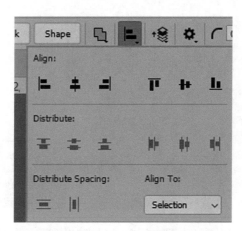

Figure 10-49. *Path Alignment options in the options panel*

Align includes Left Edges, Horizontal Centers, Right Edges, Top Edges, Vertical Centers, and Bottom Edges.

For path 6, while the two paths are selected, click Align Right Edges, and the selections are aligned to the right. Refer to Figure 10-50.

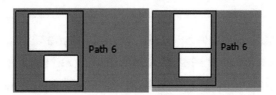

Figure 10-50. *When two paths are selected after the path is saved, they can be aligned*

With three or more paths created on a new work path and then saved (e.g., with a name like path 7), you can access the Distribute options. Refer to Figure 10-51.

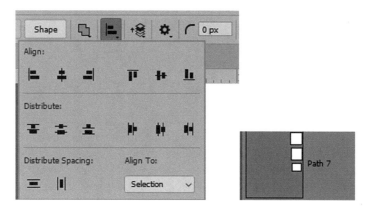

Figure 10-51. *When three or more paths are created right away after the path is saved, you have access to a few more options while the paths are selected*

Distribute includes Top Edges, Vertical Centers, Bottom Edges, Left Edges, Horizontal Centers, and Right Edges.

Distribute Spacing either vertically and horizontally.

Align to either the selection or the canvas.

Note   Distribute and Distribute Spacing may be grayed out with two paths, and only Align is available. Another reason it may be grayed out is if you did not create the paths one after the other on a new work path and saved the new path layer with a path name; for example, path 7. If you return later and add more paths that you want to align, the options are gray again. So, either create all the paths you need right away and align them or, as you did when using the Crop tool, View ➤ Rulers drag out guides and the Move tool to assist you in aligning paths. Then use the Path Selection tool (A) to move or scale the paths using the bounding box handles and snap to guides. Refer to Figure 10-52.

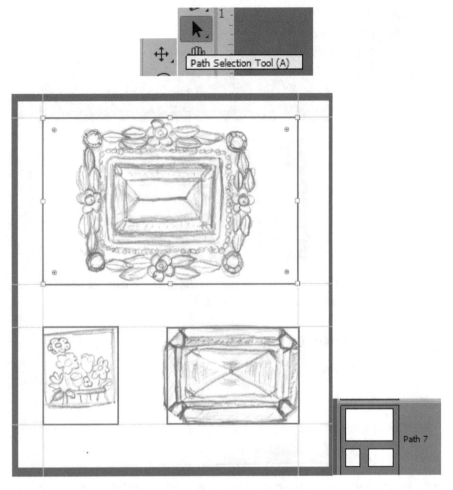

Figure 10-52. *Another way to align paths is to use Photoshop's Rulers and Guides to snap to while you use your Move tool to move the guides, then the Path Selection tool to scale the paths*

Path Arrangement

The next drop-down menu, Path Arrangement, is grayed out unless you select a path separately with the Direct Selection tool or one path with the Path Selection tool. Refer to Figure 10-53.

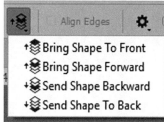

Figure 10-53. *Arrange single paths on the Paths layer if one needs to be in front or behind another for a certain type of selection*

When a single path is selected, you can use this to

- Bring Shape To Front

- Bring Shape Forward

- Send Shape Backward

- Send Shape To Back

While these are paths and not shape layers, you may need to adjust their order to make a better selection when working with or combining different shaped paths.

Set Additional Shape and Path Options

How you preview the path or drag it out can be set here. Some of these settings may be familiar to you from Chapter 3 with the Rectangular Marquee tool options. Refer to Figure 10-54.

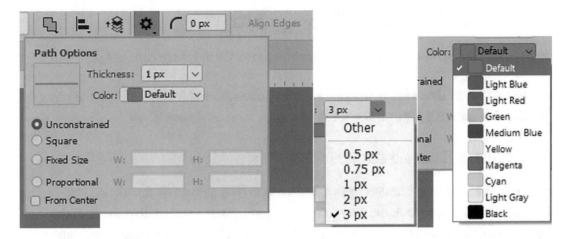

Figure 10-54. *Additional Path Options*

Let's go over some of the Path options.

Path Thickness previews how the path appears. In this case, you can see a 1 px line. You can increase the size to see it better, but it does not change the path and a physical stroke as it is only a preview.

Color sets the color of the path from the list. In this case, the default color is blue, but you may need to set it to another color on artwork where it is difficult to see the path.

Unconstrained makes a rectangle any size you want when you drag out a path.

Square drags square paths. Alternatively, you can hold down the Shift key as you drag. Refer to Figure 10-55.

Figure 10-55. *A square path*

Fixed Size constrains the width and/or height. Refer to Figure 10-56.

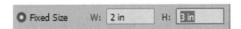

Figure 10-56. *Path options set a Fixed Size in width and height*

Proportional is like a fixed ratio where you can constrain the proportions; for example, 2:1 or 1:1. Refer to Figure 10-57.

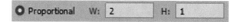

Figure 10-57. *Path options set a Proportional ratio in width and height*

From Center drags the path from a center point rather than the left. It is the same as holding down the Alt/Option key while you drag. Refer to Figure 10-54.

Set Radius of Rounded Corners

If you want to create a rounded rectangle selection, you cannot do it with the Rectangular Marquee tool. Before you create a path, enter a radius, like 60 px, in the Set Radius of Rounded Corners text box. Then drag out a rounded rectangular path. Then Press the Selection button. Click OK in the Make Selection dialog box. Refer to Figure 10-58.

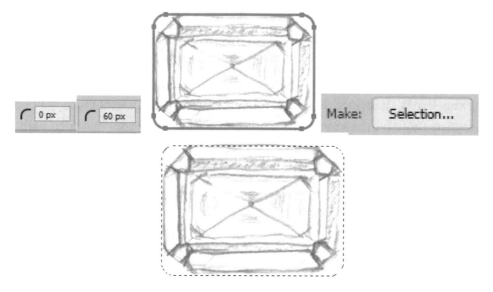

Figure 10-58. *Set a radius, and you can create a rounded rectangle selection*

Note   I always reset the round corner back to 0 px after I am finished using this tool to be ready for the next time I need to make a rectangle.

Another Way to round corners on a path afterward and refine it is to drag on the circle corner radius handles inward or outward to create a radius. A larger radius makes a tighter selection. Refer to Figure 10-59.

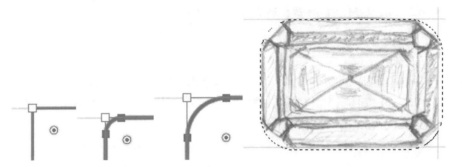

Figure 10-59. *Create a rounded rectangle and adjust the radius on the path before you make a selection*

Tip   If you need to affect only some sides of a rounded rectangle, you can do that. In this case, do not drag out the rectangle tool. Click the canvas to bring up the Create Rectangle dialog box. Unlink the Radii and set different pixel settings for Top Left, Top Right, Bottom Left, and Bottom Right. Click the link icon again to reset or click OK to confirm the setting. Refer to Figure 10-60.

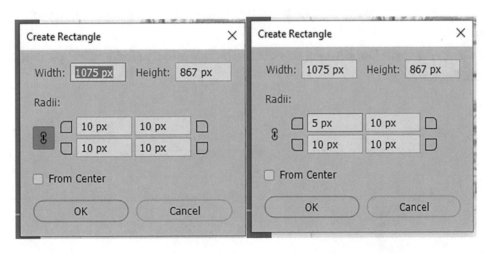

Figure 10-60. *Create a rectangle path in the Create Rectangle dialog box*

Align Edges is grayed out. Refer to Figure 10-61.

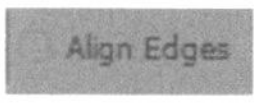

Figure 10-61. *Aligned Edges is inactive for paths*

Note   Align Edges is disabled because it aligns vector shape edges to the pixel grid, which is not part of the topic. I do not discuss it further because it is not relevant to this chapter.

At this point, you could use any of these paths you created to make selections and assist in cleaning up the sketch.

File ➤ Save (Ctrl/Cmd+S) your document. See my example scan10_1_rectangle_final.psd.

Let's take a brief look now at the other tools in this list. I am only pointing out the differences, so refer to this section of the Rectangle tool if you need to review the options.

Ellipse Tool (U)

Like the Ellipse Marquee tool (M) seen in Chapter 3, you can use the Ellipse tool to create circle and oval selections.

Open scan10_2_ellipse.psd, which is a gemstone and two brooches. Refer to Figure 10-62.

Make an Image ➤ Duplicate of this file to practice and try similar settings as you did with the Rectangle tool.

Figure 10-62. *A sketch of a Gemstone and two brooches*

Drag out a path or multiple paths with the ellipse as you did with the Rectangle tool, and they are added to the Paths panel as a work path. Refer to Figure 10-63.

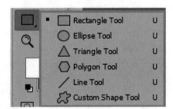

Figure 10-63. *The Ellipse tool in the Tools panel*

Use the path bounding box handles to scale the ellipse to get the paths closer to the brooch shapes. Refer to Figure 10-64.

Figure 10-64. *Shape tools in the Tools panel*

Double-click the path name in the Paths panel and click OK in the dialog box to save as path 1. Refer to Figure 10-65.

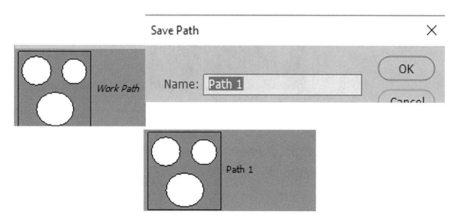

Figure 10-65. *Path created on a work path in the Paths panel*

Circle Tool Options

Many of the same tools you find with the Rectangular tool (U) in the options panel, so I point out the main differences. Look from left to right in Figure 10-66.

Figure 10-66. *Ellipse tool options in the options panel*

You can add or manage a **tool preset**. Refer to Figure 10-66.

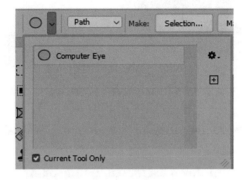

Figure 10-67. *Tool presets in the options panel*

Choose a **Tool mode**. Refer to Figure 10-68.

Figure 10-68. *Tool mode should be set to Path when working with paths and selections*

Note   If you already set the Tool mode to Path with the Rectangle tool, all the following tools are set to that mode.

Make

Click the **Selection** button while a path is selected and enter the Make Selection dialog box to confirm the selection. Click OK. Refer to Figure 10-69.

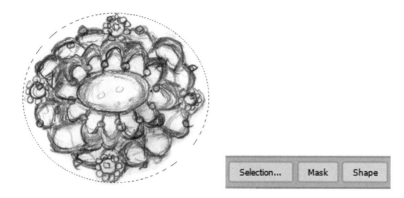

Figure 10-69. *Ellipse Selection is made when the Selection button is clicked*

Refer to the Rectangle tool for more information on the **Mask** and **Shape** buttons. Refer to Figure 10-69.

Path Operations is a drop-down list for combining paths and then selections. Refer to Figure 10-70.

Figure 10-70. *Path Operations, Path Alignment, and Path Arrangement option drop-down lists in the options panel*

Path Alignment is a drop-down list for aligning two or more paths.

If only one path in the Paths panel is selected with the Path Selection tool, you can use the **Path Arrangement** options to move the path over or under another intersecting path. Refer to Figure 10-70 and Figure 10-71.

Figure 10-71. *Path and Direct Selection tools in the Tools panel*

Refer to the Rectangle tool for more information on **Set Additional shape and path options.** However, note that if you want to set a circle path, you can select **Circle (draw diameter or radius)** or hold down the Shift key while dragging out the circle. Refer to Figure 10-72.

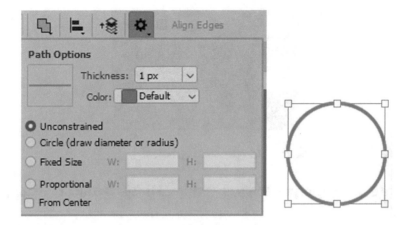

Figure 10-72. *Path options in the options panel*

Enable **From Center** if you want to drag out the path from the center rather than from the left edge or hold down the Alt/Option key. Refer to Figure 10-72.

Note   **Align Edges** is disabled; see the Rectangle tool note. Refer to Figure 10-72.

Tip   Click the canvas if you want to set a path to a set size without dragging out a circle, and then click OK to the width and height settings. Refer to Figure 10-73.

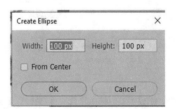

Figure 10-73. *Use the Create Ellipse dialog box to set some ellipse settings without dragging out a path*

After making various paths and creating selections, save the file and repeat similar steps of experimenting with the next set of tools. See the scan10_2_ellipse_final.psd file.

Triangle Tool (U)

The Triangle tool was recently added to the Tools group. Its main purpose is to create triangle shapes, but you can create a triangle selection. Refer to Figure 10-74.

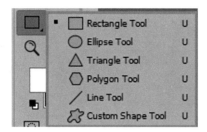

Figure 10-74. *The Triangle tool in the Tools panel*

Open scan10_3_triangle_polygon.psd. Create an Image ➤ Duplicate Copy. Refer to Figure 10-75.

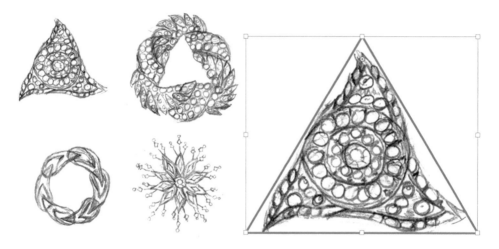

Figure 10-75. *Four Brooches are in this sketch. Drag a triangle path around the brooch in the upper left.*

Drag out a Triangle path around the brooch on the upper left. Refer to Figure 10-75. Use the path handles if you need to adjust the path. Refer to Figure 10-75.

Save the path in the Paths panel by double-clicking it and save as path 1. Refer to Figure 10-76.

Figure 10-76. *Save the work path as path 1*

Triangle Tool Options

Most of the options are the same in the options panel as the Rectangle tool, so I only discuss the key differences. Looking from left to right, refer to Figure 10-77.

Figure 10-77. *Triangle options in the options panel*

You can add or manage a **tool preset**. Refer to Figure 10-77.

You can also set the **Tool mode** to Path. Refer to Figure 10-78.

Figure 10-78. *Tool mode Path setting*

Make

Click the **Selection** button while a path is selected and enter the Make Selection dialog box to confirm the selection. Click OK. Refer to Figure 10-79.

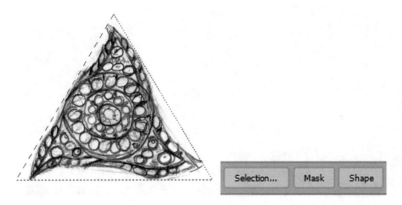

Figure 10-79. *A triangle selection is made with the Selection button*

Refer to the Rectangle tool for more information on **Mask** and **Shape** buttons. Refer to Figure 10-79.

Path Operations is a drop-down list for combining paths and then selections. Refer to Figure 10-80.

Figure 10-80. *Path Operations, Path Alignment, and Path Arrangement option drop-down lists in the options panel*

Path Alignment is a drop-down list for aligning two or more paths.

If only one path in the Paths panel is selected with the Path Selection tool, you can use the **Path Arrangement** options to move the path over or under another path. Refer to Figure 10-80 and Figure 10-81.

Figure 10-81. *Path and Direct Selection tools in the Tools panel*

Refer to the Rectangle tool for more information on **Set Additional shape and path options.** However, note that if you want to set an equal-sided path, you can select **Equilateral** or hold down the Shift key while dragging out the triangle. Refer to Figure 10-82.

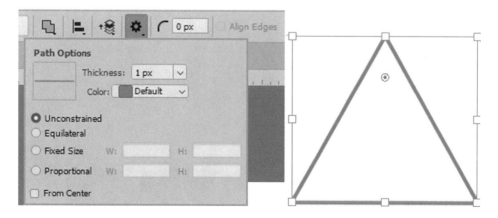

Figure 10-82. *Path options in the options panel and an equilateral triangle*

Enable **From Center** if you want to drag out the path from the center rather than from the left edge or hold down the Alt/Option key. Refer to Figure 10-82.

Set Radius of Rounded Corners

If you want to create a rounded triangle selection, enter a radius, such as 20 px, in the Set Radius of Rounded Corners text box. Then drag out a rounded triangle path. Press the selection button. Click OK in the Make Selection dialog box. Refer to Figure 10-83.

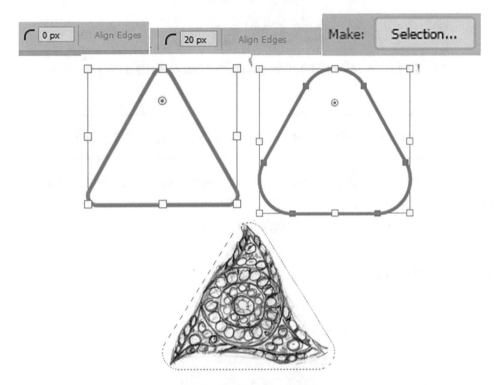

Figure 10-83. *Set the Radius and create a rounded triangle and make a Selection with the Selection button*

Or you can drag on the corner radius handle and alter the radii afterward for a more refined selection.

Note   I always reset the round corner back to 0 px after I am finished using it, so the tool is ready next time.

You can also create a triangle by clicking the canvas, entering your settings into the dialog box, and clicking OK. Refer to Figure 10-84.

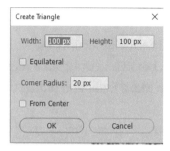

Figure 10-84. *Create a triangle before you drag out a path using the dialog box*

Note   Align Edges is disabled; see the Rectangle tool note. Refer to Figure 10-77.

As you see later in this chapter, you can combine different paths with different geometric shapes on the same path layer.

Keep the copy of the scan10_3_triangle_polygon.psd file open for now.

Polygon Tool (U)

The Polygon tool is great for creating shapes with many sides. Likewise, you can also make a path and then a selection with many sides as well. Refer to Figure 10-85.

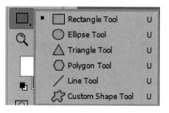

Figure 10-85. *Polygon tool in the Tools panel*

On path 1, while it is selected, drag out a polygon shape. Refer to Figure 10-86.

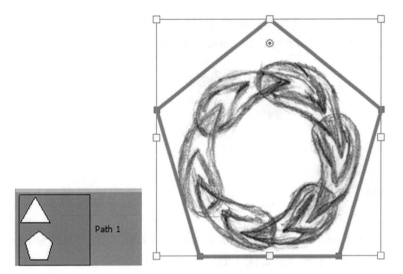

Figure 10-86. *Drag out a Polygon shape, and when path 1 is selected, it appears on the path*

Choose Edit ➤ Undo Ctrl/Cmd+Z right away, as you can see that this requires a six-sided polygon. Mine is five-sided. Let's find the right setting in a moment. Refer to Figure 10-87.

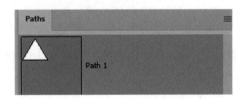

Figure 10-87. *The polygon did not have enough sides, so it was removed and is no longer in path 1*

Polygon Tool Options

Most of the options are the same in the options panel as the Rectangle tool. So, I only go describe the key differences.

Look at the options panel from left to right. Refer to Figure 10-88.

Figure 10-88. *Polygon tool options in the options panel*

You can add or manage a **tool preset**. Refer to Figure 10-88.

You can also set the **Tool mode** to Path. Refer to Figure 10-89.

Figure 10-89. *Tool mode Path setting*

Make

Click the Selection button while a path is selected and enter the Make Selection dialog box to confirm the selection. Click OK. Refer to Figure 10-90.

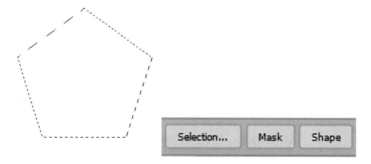

Figure 10-90. *A polygon selection is created from a path using the Selection button*

Refer to the Rectangle tool for more information on the **Mask** and **Shape** buttons. Refer to Figure 10-90.

Path Operations is a drop-down list for combining paths and then selections. Refer to Figure 10-91.

Figure 10-91. *Path Operations, Path Alignment, and Path Arrangement option drop-down lists in the options panel*

Path Alignment is a drop-down list for aligning two or more paths.

If only one path in the Paths panel is selected with the Path Selection tool, you can use the **Path Arrangement** options to move the path over or under another path. Refer to Figure 10-91 and Figure 10-92.

Figure 10-92. *Path and Direct Selection tools in the Tools panel*

Refer to the Rectangle tool for more information on **Set Additional shape and path options**. However, note that if you want to set an equal-sided path, you can select **Symmetric** or hold down the Shift key while dragging out the triangle. Refer to Figure 10-93.

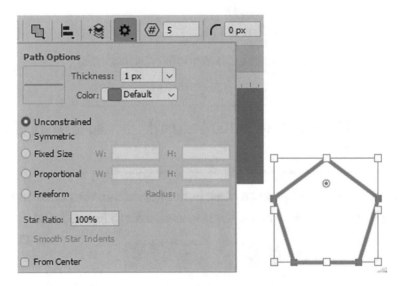

Figure 10-93. *Path options in the options panel and a symmetric polygon*

Freeform allows no constraints on the direction while dragging. Optionally, you can set a radius that creates a smaller shape. Refer to Figure 10-93.

Star Ratio is set to 100% for the Polygon shape, but if you want to create a star, choose a different percentage such as 50%. Refer to Figure 10-94 and Figure 10-95.

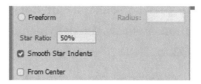

Figure 10-94. *options for Star Ratio*

If you enable **Smooth Star Indents**, the indents are round instead of sharp. Refer to Figure 10-95.

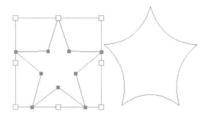

Figure 10-95. *A star without and with Smooth Star Indents*

Note   Reset the Star Ratio back to 100% again if you need to return to creating polygon selections.

Enable **From Center** if you want to drag out the path from the center rather than from the left edge or hold down the Alt/Option key. Refer to Figure 10-96.

Figure 10-96. *Set the number sides from 5 to 6*

Set the number of sides or points on a star. The default is 5, but you can set as low as 3 to create a triangle path (See Triangle tool) or up to 100 for a starburst. Refer to Figure 10-96.

Set the number of sides to 6 for the leaf broach and drag around the outside a polygon on path 1. Refer to Figure 10-97.

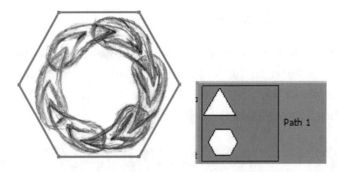

Figure 10-97. *This polygon has six sides, which conforms better to the sides of the brooch*

Now set the sides to 10 in the options panel. Refer to Figure 10-98.

Then set the star ratio in the paths option to 50%.

Drag around the outside of the star brooch. Use your handles to rotate when the pointer changes to a curve and scale. It will not be a perfect path, but you can use your Direct Selection tool later to move individual points as required.

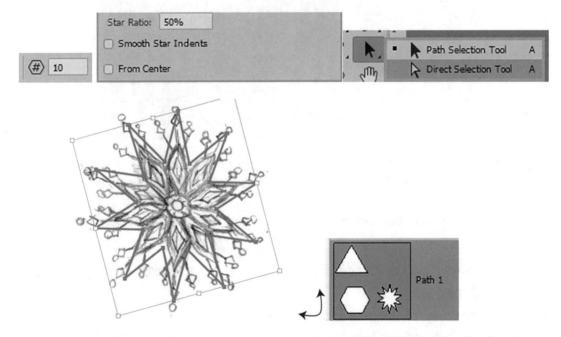

Figure 10-98. *Once you have a star path with ten sides in path 1, you can scale and rotate the path with your Path Selection tool to go around areas of the sketch*

Remember to reset your star ratio to 100% if you want to return to drawing other Polygons.

Set Radius of Rounded Corners

If you want to create a rounded star or rounded polygon points on your selection, first enter a radius, such as 20 px, in the Set Radius of Rounded Corners text box. Then drag out a rounded polygon or star path. Press the Selection button. Click OK in the Make Selection dialog box to confirm. Refer to Figure 10-99.

Figure 10-99. *Create a rounded path instead by setting the corner radius, and then create the selection. You can see how this appears in Quick Mask mode.*

You can see the selection better in Quick Mask mode (Q). Refer to Figure 10-99.

Note   I always reset the rounded corner to 0 px after I am finished using it, so the tool is ready next time.

Or you can click without dragging on the canvas and set similar settings in the Create Polygon dialog box and click OK to confirm. Refer to Figure 10-100.

Figure 10-100. *Use the Create Polygon dialog box to create a path instead of dragging*

Note   **Align Edges** is disabled; see the Rectangle tool note. Refer to Figure 10-88.

At this point, you could continue to practice adding more paths that you can turn into selections for refining your artwork or saving your document. See the scan10_3_triangle_polygon_final.psd file.

Line Tool (U)

By default, the line tool creates small hairline paths. You can drag out a line. However, it does not allow you to make a small selection from a single line when clicking the Selection button. Refer to Figure 10-101.

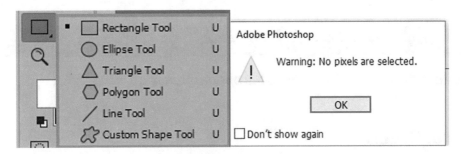

Figure 10-101. *Line tool in the Tools panel*

Open the scan10_4_line_custom.psd file.

Make an Image ➤ Duplicate of the file. It is an image of two brooches and a heart scent bottle necklace pendent. Refer to Figure 10-102.

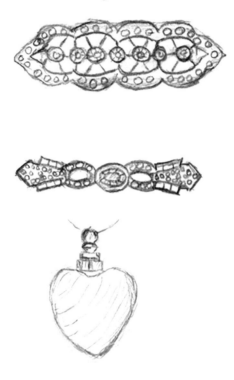

Figure 10-102. *A sketch of two brooches and a heart-shaped bottle*

If you add arrowheads and a line weight to make the line tool work correctly, you have something that Photoshop can turn into a selection. Most of the options are the same in the options panel as the Rectangle tool, so I only discuss the key differences. Refer to Figure 10-103.

Figure 10-103. *Line tool options in the options panel*

Line Tool Options

Look from left to right in the options panel shown in Figure 10-103.

Add or manage a **tool preset.**

Set the **Tool mode** to Path. Refer to Figure 10-104.

Figure 10-104. *Tool mode set to Path in the options panel*

Make

Click the **Selection** button and enter the Make Selection dialog box to confirm the selection. Click OK. Refer to Figure 10-103.

Refer to the Rectangle tool for more information on the **Mask** and **Shape** buttons. Refer to Figure 10-103.

Path Operations is a drop-down list for combining paths and then selections. Refer to Figure 10-105.

Figure 10-105. *Path Operations, Path Alignment, and Path Arrangement option drop-down lists in the options panel*

Path Alignment is a drop-down list for aligning two or more paths.

If only one path in the Paths panel is selected with the Path Selection tool, you can use the **Path Arrangement** options to move the path over or under another path. Refer to Figure 10-105 and Figure 10-106.

Figure 10-106. *Path and Direct Selection tools in the Tools panel*

Refer to the Rectangle tool for more information on **Set Additional shape and path options**. **Live Shapes Controls** must be enabled to show the hairline. However, note that if you want to use this tool to create a selection, you also need to enable the **arrowhead** check boxes separately or collectively of **Start** and **End**. Refer to Figure 10-107.

Figure 10-107. *Path options in the options panel*

Arrowhead settings also need the following.

- **Width:** arrowheads width

- **Length:** arrowheads length

- Concavity: (optional) (0%–100%) sets the curve as the base of the head where it meets the line (e.g., 20%)

Refer to Figure 10-107.

Figure 10-108. *An arrowhead with a concavity of 20%*

Weight sets the thickness of the line. Set it to 20 px and then drag out the line path and look at the results and as you did with the Rectangle tool, use the Selection button to turn it into a selection. Refer to Figure 10-109.

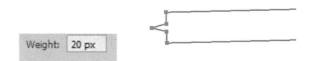

Figure 10-109. *Weight of 20 pixels for an arrowhead*

Now create a path selection for a brooch. Refer to Figure 10-110.

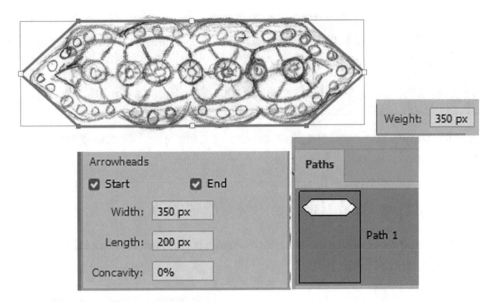

Figure 10-110. *Line tool with various path settings in the options panel. Once the shape is dragged out, you can see it in the saved path in the Paths panel.*

Drag around the upper brooch with a **weight** of 350 px.

In the **Path options,** I set the arrow heads to **Start** and **End** with a **Width:** 350 px, **Length:** 200 px, and **Concavity:** 0%.

Press the Selection button while a path is selected and click OK in the dialog box message to see the result. Save as path 1. Refer to Figure 10-103 and Figure 10-111.

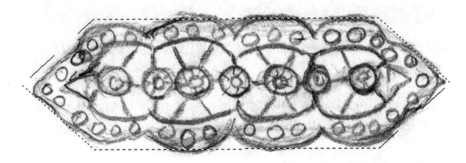

Figure 10-111. *The Line tool was able to create an angled selection*

Select ➤ Deselect (Ctrl/Cmd+D) to remove the selection.

> **Note**   Reset to 0px and turn off the arrowhead Start and End options if you need to set it back to a thin hairline.
>
> Align Edges is disabled; see the Rectangle tool note. Refer to Figure 10-103.

Keep this copy of the scan10_4_line_custom.psd file open because you add more paths next.

Custom Shape Tool (U)

The Custom Shape tool creates custom paths from shapes that reside in the Window ➤ Shapes panel. Refer to Figure 10-112.

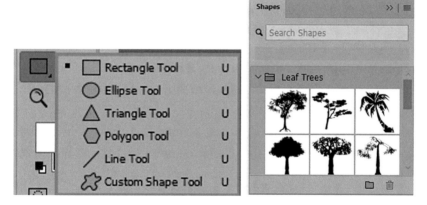

Figure 10-112. *Custom Shape tool in the Tools panel and the stored Shapes in the Shapes panel*

Let's access them from the options panel bar. Most options are the same in the options panel as the Rectangle tool, so I only discuss the key differences.

Custom Shape Tool Options

Look from left to right in the options panel shown in Figure 10-113.

Figure 10-113. *The Custom Shape tool options in the options panel*

Add or manage a **tool preset**. Refer to Figure 10-113.

Set the **Tool mode** to Path. Refer to Figure 10-114.

Figure 10-114. *Tool mode set to Path in the options panel*

Make

Press the **Selection** button while a path is selected and enter the Make Selection dialog box to confirm the selection. Click OK. Refer to Figure 10-111.

Refer to the Rectangle tool for more information on **Mask** and **Shape** buttons. Refer to Figure 10-113.

Path Operations is a drop-down list for combining paths and then selections. Refer to Figure 10-115.

Figure 10-115. *Path Operations, Path Alignment, and Path Arrangement option drop-down lists in the options panel*

Path Alignment is a drop-down list for aligning two or more paths.

If only one path in the Paths panel is selected with the Path Selection tool, you can use the **Path Arrangement** options to move the path over or under another path. Refer to Figure 10-115 and Figure 10-116.

Figure 10-116. *Path and Direct Selection tools in the Tools panel*

Refer to the Rectangle tool for more information on **Set Additional shape and path options**. However, note that if you want to set an equal-sided path, you can select **Defined Proportions** to match the defined shape or hold down the Shift key while dragging out the custom shape. **Defined Size** constrains the size of the shape or sets a **Fixed Size**. Refer to Figure 10-117.

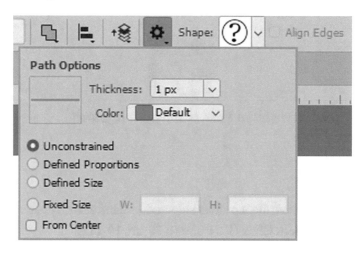

Figure 10-117. *Path options in the options panel*

Enable **From Center** if you want to drag out the path from the center rather than from the left edge or hold down the Alt/Option key. Refer to Figure 10-117.

Choose a **Shape** like the heart card from the drop-down list that you want to use a selection. Refer to Figure 10-118.

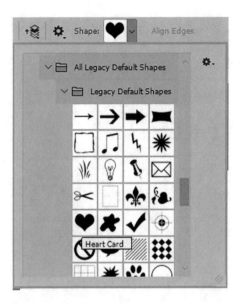

Figure 10-118. *Shape options in the options panel and the heart card selected*

Note   You may have to open a few folders in the hierarchy to find the type of shape for the path you want. In this case, if you have never used the Shapes panel, you may need to first go to the Shapes panel menu and click Legacy Shapes and More. Refer to Figure 10-119.

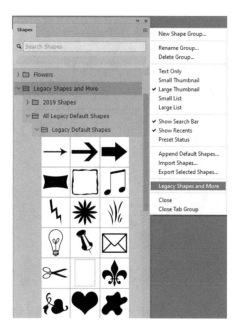

Figure 10-119. *Shape panel to load legacy shapes*

Return to the options panel, select All Legacy Default Shapes ➤ Legacy Default Shapes, and locate the heart card. Refer to Figure 10-120.

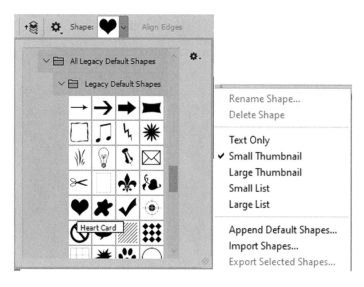

Figure 10-120. *Locate the heart card shape and use the menu options to see the shapes more clearly*

You can also click the gear menu to choose how you want to view the shapes. For example, **Large Thumbnail** makes the shapes larger for viewing. You can pull on the lower right edge of the menu to give you more viewing area. Refer to Figure 10-120.

Once you select the heart card shape, drag out the path around the sketch of the heart scent bottle. It's OK if it is not a perfect selection. Refer to Figure 10-121.

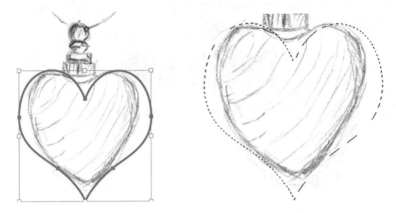

Figure 10-121. *Drag the heart path around the heart in the sketch*

Click the **Selection** button. Click OK in the Make Selection dialog box, and the custom selection is created.

Note   Align Edges is disabled; see the Rectangle tool note. Refer to Figure 10-113.

Select ➤ Deselect (Ctrl/Cmd+D) to remove the selection.
Save the path as path 2 in the Paths panel by double-clicking on the Paths name.
Save your document, but keep it open for now.

Create Custom Shapes

If you are interested in creating custom shapes to add to the Shapes panel and later use paths and selections, check out https://helpx.adobe.com/photoshop/using/drawing-shapes.html for more information.

Path Selection Tools

So far, you have looked at the Paths panel and how to save and add custom shapes to a current path layer and then save the path. However, after creating a path, you may want to modify it so that it more neatly fits around an area you are planning to turn into a selection. Two tools can help you modify your path: the Path Selection tool and the Direct Selection tool. Refer to Figure 10-122.

Figure 10-122. *Path Selection tool in the Tools panel*

Path Selection Tool (A)

When path 1 in the Paths panel is active, you can use the Path Selection tool to do the following.

- Select a single path for a selection.

- Drag a marquee around several paths or all paths that you want to include for your selection.

- Shift-click to select several paths.

- Use the bounding box handles to scale the section. Hover over a bounding corner until the pointer turns to diagonal arrows, then drag. Refer to Figure 10-123.

- Rotate the path using the bounding box handles when it changes to rounded arrows. Refer to Figure 10-123.

Figure 10-123. *Scale or rotate a path using the bounding box handles when the pointer changes to scale or rotate mode*

Round the corners of the current path, hover on the round corner dots, and drag them in to increase the radius or out to decrease it. Refer to Figure 10-124.

Figure 10-124. *Drag on the circle in or out to alter the radius*

To Duplicate a path while the path is selected, hold down the Alt/Option key and drag a copy of the path. Refer to Figure 10-125.

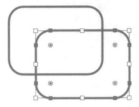

Figure 10-125. *Duplicate a path*

Press the Backspace/Delete key if you need to delete a single path. You may get an informational warning. Click Yes to the message, and the path is removed. Refer to Figure 10-126.

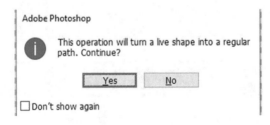

Figure 10-126. *An informational message appears when you delete a path. Click Yes to confirm.*

On path 2 of the open file, select the heart with the Path Selection tool and move the right and left handles in and the bottom bounding box handle to scale the heart path. Refer to Figure 10-127.

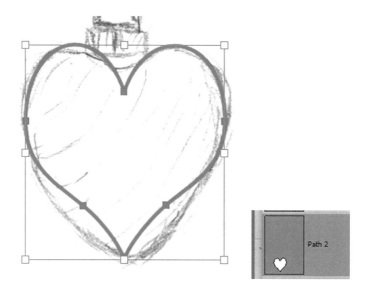

Figure 10-127. *Scaling the heart around the sketch with the bounding box handles*

Path Selection Tool Options

Look at the options panel from left to right. Refer to Figure 10-128.

Figure 10-128. *Path Selection tool options in the tool panel*

Because this chapter works with paths and not shape layers, some options in the options panel are inactive or do not apply to our current topic, so I focus on those that do.

You can create or manage a **tool preset**. Refer to Figure 10-128.

When you **Select** a path, you can choose from **Active Layers** or **All Layers** from the list. However, because these paths are not on any layer, this choice does not matter. Refer to Figure 10-129.

Figure 10-129. *Select has two options in the options panel*

Also, the following are grayed out and do not apply to paths: **Set Shape Fill Type, Set Shape Stroke Type Color, Set Shape Stroke Width. Set Shape Stroke Type, Set Shape Width, Set Shape Height.** Refer to Figure 10-128.

You can use the next options, however, which are the same as the Shape tools. Refer to the Rectangle tool if you need more information. Refer to Figure 10-130.

Figure 10-130. *Path Operations, Path Alignment and Path Arrangement Option dropdown lists in the options panel*

Path Operations is a drop-down list for combining paths and then selections.

Path Alignment is a drop-down list for aligning two or more paths.

If only one path in the Paths panel is selected with the Path Selection tool, you can use the **Path Arrangement** options to move the path over or under another path.

Note   Align Edges is disabled; see the Rectangle tool note. Refer to Figure 10-128.

Set Additional Path Alignment options lets you see the thickness and color of the path preview line. Refer to Figure 10-131.

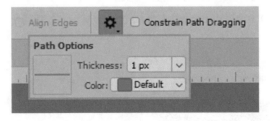

Figure 10-131. *Path options in the options panel*

Constrain Path Dragging lets you use legacy path segment dragging. This option is disabled by default. Refer to Figure 10-131.

Direct Selection Tool (A)

When you need to select a single point on the path to drag and move, use the Direct Selection tool. There is no real difference with the options in the options panel here. Refer to Figure 10-132.

Figure 10-132. *The options in the options panel for the Direct Selection tool are the same as the Path Selection tool*

Here are some tips for working with the tool.

- If you Shift-click, you can select multiple points on a path. Or Alt/Option-click to select the entire path.

- Press the Backspace/Delete key if you need to delete a single point. As with the Path Selection tool, you may receive an informational message. Click Yes, and the point is removed. Then press Backspace/Delete while the other points are selected, and they are removed as well.

While on path 2 on the heart, use the Direct Selection tool to move individual points so that the heart path conforms to the selection.

Click Yes to the informational message because you want this to be a regular path. Refer to Figure 10-133.

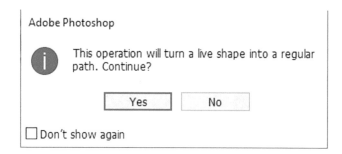

Figure 10-133. *An informational message appears if you alter the path*

Move the path segment handles if you need to adjust the closed path. Refer to Figure 10-134.

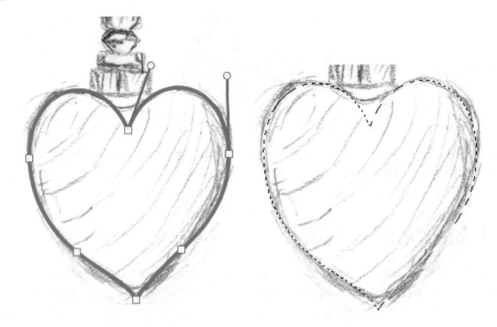

Figure 10-134. *Alter the path by moving points with the Direct Selection tool, then create a selection*

Return to the Custom Shape tool to access its options panel. Refer to Figure 10-135.

Figure 10-135. *Because the Path Selection tools do not have a selection button, switch to a shape tool to access the Selection button*

Click the Selection button in the options panel, and you should have a much tighter selection. Refer to Figure 10-135.

Save your document. You can see the scan10_4_line_custom_final.psd file.

Note   For extra practice, return to the star shape in the earlier file and use the path selection and direct selection to adjust the path around the star. Make a copy of the scan10_3_polygon_final.psd file if you don't have the path already created. Refer to Figure 10-136.

Figure 10-136. *The altered path on the star brooch is much more refined after I use the Direct Selection tool*

Path Creation Pen Tools

The last set of tools that you look at in this chapter are the Path Creation tools or Pen tools. You can use these tools to modify a currently selected path or create your own path. I first talk about the basic pen tools that are frequently used and then return to the newer, more specialized pen tools at the end. Refer to Figure 10-137.

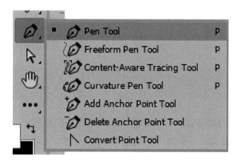

Figure 10-137. *Pen tools in the Tools panel*

Pen Tool (P)

Use the Pen tool to create custom paths.

Open scan10_5_pentool.psd. Refer to Figure 10-138.

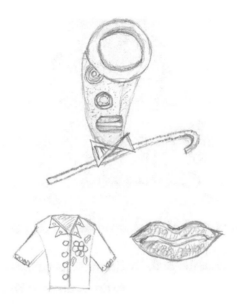

Figure 10-138. *A sketch of three brooches: clown, shirt, and lips*

Make an Image ➤ Duplicate of the file to practice on.

On the shirt brooch, you can make an angular selection around the edge of the shirt.

Like the Magnetic Lasso tool in Chapter 5, you can use the Pen tool to create points and path segments. Initially, your Pen tool pointer appears with an asterisk beside it. Refer to Figure 10-139.

Figure 10-139. *The Pen tools cursor's appearance before clicking the first point*

With the Pen tool, click a starting point and click at another location to add another point and path segment. If you need to make a straight line, hold down the Shift key while you click to constrain to 45° angles. Refer to Figure 10-140.

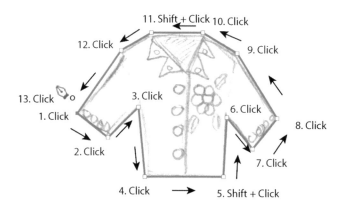

Figure 10-140. *With the Pen tool, click around the shirt to create a path*

When you reach the end of the path (in this case, point 13, which was point 1), you can close it when the path pointer changes to an O. Refer to Figure 10-140.

Save the work path as path 1 by double-clicking the work path's name and clicking OK to confirm. And deselect the path in the Paths panel so it is not active, and you can start a new work path. Refer to Figure 10-141.

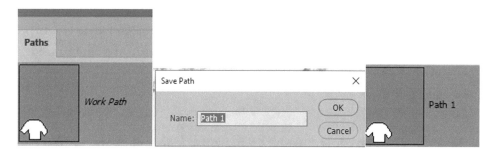

Figure 10-141. *Save your work path in the Paths panel*

Now try this on the upper area of the lips brooch.

For curved lines, first, click (point 1) on the left side of the lip.

Then click and drag downward at the next point (point 2) in the upper middle so that direction lines appear and the line curves upward; this is a smooth point. Refer to Figure 10-142.

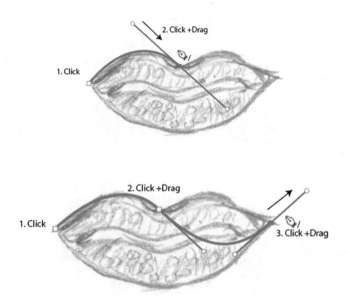

Figure 10-142. *Click and drag points around the lips to create a path*

Then click point 3 at the right side of the lip, dragging upward to create an S curve. Refer to Figure 10-142.

In this case, I want to go in the opposite direction. So, Edit ➤ Undo (Ctrl/Cmd+Z) that last step.

On the second point, hold down the Alt/Option key. This changes that point to a sharp angle or convert a corner, which would create a straight line on the next click. Refer to Figure 10-143.

Click and drag at point 3 downward to change direction, but make it still curved. Refer to Figure 10-143.

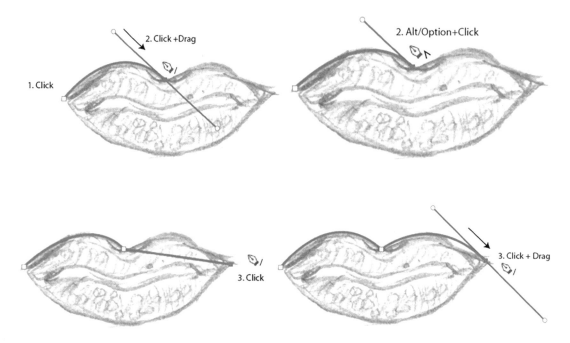

Figure 10-143. *The path needs to change direction to get over the next curve on the lip while still on the third point*

As you are creating points, if you need to stop and modify the placement of a point, hold down the Ctrl/Cmd key and the pointer change to the Direct Selection tool so you can move the point. Release the Ctrl/Cmd key to return to the Pen tool. Refer to Figure 10-144.

Figure 10-144. *Use your Direct Selection tool to move points*

Note   If you stop the working path and it is open, and need to rejoin. When you hover over a point, the pointer changes to the connecting merge icon. You can click that point, and then the point you want to join turns into an O. Click it to close the path. Refer to Figure 10-145.

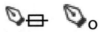

Figure 10-145. *Pointer changes when joining breaks in a path*

In your project, you may continue clicking around your path. However, on the lips for Alt/Option-click the third point to change direction. Refer to Figure 10-146.

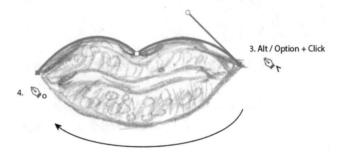

Figure 10-146. *Closing the path of the lips*

When you reach the end of the point back at point 1, the pointer changes to an O. You can close the path on the fourth click and drag upward to complete the curve. Refer to Figure 10-147.

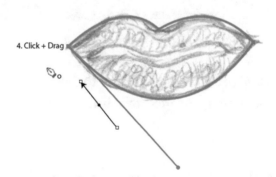

Figure 10-147. *As the path closes, I can adjust the curve of the lips*

Later, when the path is closed, you can use your Direct Selection tool to modify the points by dragging the points or modifying the direction lines by dragging on them. Refer to Figure 10-147.

Double-click your path in the Paths panel. Save your work path as path 2. Refer to Figure 10-148.

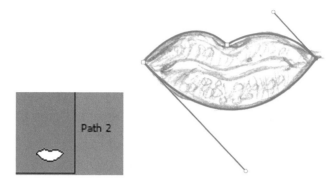

Figure 10-148. *The saved path and the path with its direction handles*

You can also use a few other point tools to modify the points, which you look at in a moment. As with the Rectangle tool (U) and path selection tools, many panel options are similar, so I point out a few differences.

Pen Tool Options

Look from left to right in the options panel shown in Figure 10-149.

Figure 10-149. *Pen tool options in the options panel*

Create or manage a **tool preset.** Refer to Figure 10-149.

Tool mode set it to path from the drop-down list. Refer to Figure 10-149.

Make

While a path is selected, click the **Selection** button, and enter the Make Selection dialog box to confirm the selection Click OK. Refer to Figure 10-149 and Figure 10-150.

Figure 10-150. *A selection created from the path with the Selection button*

Refer to the Rectangle tool for more information on the **Mask** and **Shape** buttons. Figure 10-149.

Path Operations is a drop-down list for combining paths and then selections. Set it to Combine Shapes, or you may get inverse paths. Refer to the Rectangle tool for more information. Refer to Figure 10-151.

Figure 10-151. *Set your path operations to Combine Shapes for this path when you create it*

Path Alignment is a drop-down list for aligning two or more paths. Refer to the Rectangle tool for more information. Refer to Figure 10-151.

If only one path in the Paths panel is selected with the Path Selection tool, you can use the **Path Arrangement** options to move the path over or under another path. Refer to Figure 10-151 and Figure 10-152.

Figure 10-152. *Path and Direct Selection tools in the Tools panel*

Set Additional pen and path options sets the path **thickness** and **color**. Refer to Figure 10-153.

Figure 10-153. *Path options in the options panel*

Rubber Band shows the path extension while drawing. It is disabled by default.

Auto Add/Delete automatically add or delete point when over a path. Adobe recommends disabling this setting when you are starting a new path over the existing one. Refer to Figure 10-153.

Align Edges is disabled (see the Rectangle tool note). Refer to Figure 10-153.

Your path is closed. Use the next three tools to modify the path further.

Add Anchor Point Tool

Use to add an anchor point to the path when you click somewhere on the path. Then you can use your Direct Selection tool to move the point if you need to adjust the path. Refer to Figure 10-154.

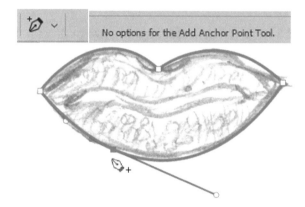

Figure 10-154. *Add a point with the Add Anchor Point tool*

This tool has no Presets or options in the options panel.

Note   With Auto Add/Delete enabled, after you have closed the path with the Pen tool, you can hover over a segment and then click to add a point.

Delete Anchor Point Tool

Use to delete an anchor point from a path when you click a point somewhere on the path. Refer to Figure 10-155.

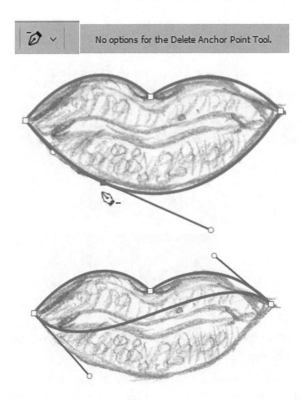

Figure 10-155. *Delete a point with the Delete Anchor Point tool*

This tool has no presets or options in the options panel.

Once a point is removed, you may need to use your Direct Selection tool to adjust the path. Refer to Figure 10-156.

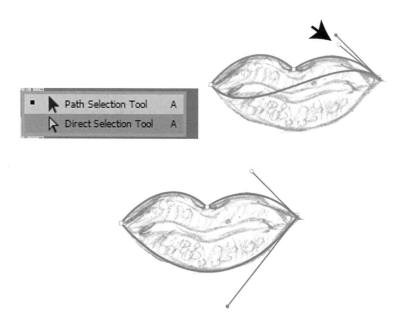

Figure 10-156. *To reset the path after a point is deleted, you may need to use your Direct Selection tool to read the direction handles*

In this case, I clicked on the point on the right of the lip and then dragged the lower direction line downward until it went around the lip. Refer to Figure 10-156.

Note   With Auto Add/Delete enabled, after you have closed the path with the Pen tool, you can hover over a segment and then click to delete a point.

Convert Point Tool

Changes the point from smooth segments to corner segments when you click it with the Convert Point tool. Refer to Figure 10-157.

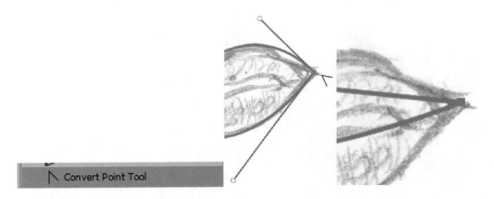

Figure 10-157. *The Convert Point tool can turn a curved point into a sharp corner point*

Or, if it is a corner point and segments, you can click and drag on the point to bring the direction lines back to make it smooth. Refer to Figure 10-158.

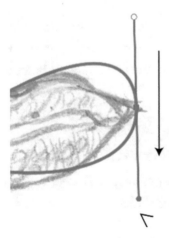

Figure 10-158. *The Convert Point tool can also change a sharp corner point back into a smooth curve*

If you only want one direction line adjusted independently to a corner, click one direction line, and drag with the Convert Point tool. Refer to Figure 10-159.

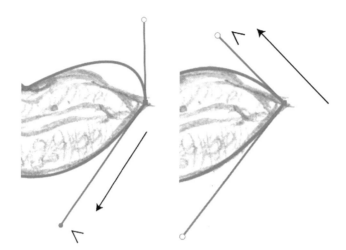

Figure 10-159. *Each direction line handle can be adjusted separately with the Convert Point tool*

Otherwise, on a smooth point, use the Direct Selection tool to keep the point smooth, but move one direction line to adjust the curve. Holding down the Shift key allows you to move the direction line at 45° angles. Refer to Figure 10-160.

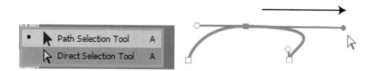

Figure 10-160. *Use the Direct Selection tool instead to keep a smooth curve but still adjust the direction line handles*

This tool has no Presets or options in the options panel. Refer to Figure 10-161.

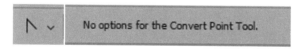

Figure 10-161. *No options of the Convert Point tool in the options panel*

Save your document to save the paths should you want to use the selections. See the scan10_5_pentool_final.psd file.

Three other Pen tools are also available. You look at these specialized tools next.

For the next three tools, File ➤ Open scan10_6_addtional_pen_tools.psd. It is a collection of three bottles.

Image ➤ Duplicate the file and click OK in the dialog box to confirm the copy. Refer to Figure 10-162.

Figure 10-162. *A sketch of various bottles*

Freeform Pen Tool (P)

Use this tool to create freehand shapes or paths. Refer to Figure 10-163.

Figure 10-163. *Freeform Pen tool*

As you would with a Lasso or Magnetic Lasso tool, you can drag around the sketch of the bottle on the left until you reach the starting point again, and the pointer adds an O to indicate the closing point. Refer to Figure 10-164.

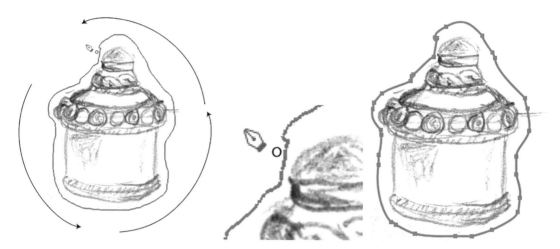

Figure 10-164. *Create a path around the bottle on the left with the Freeform Pen tool*

The path with points is created. You can then use the Pen tools to edit and modify the path. The options panel is the same as the Pen tool (P) and Rectangle tool (U), so I point out the differences.

Freeform Pen Tool Options

Look from left to right in the options panel shown in Figure 10-165.

Figure 10-165. *Freeform Pen tool options in the options panel*

Create or manage a **tool preset.** Refer to Figure 10-165.
Tool mode is set to **Path** in the drop-down list. Refer to Figure 10-165.

Make

While the path is selected, click the **Selection** button and enter the Make Selection dialog box to confirm the selection click OK. Refer to Figure 10-165 and Figure 10-166.

Figure 10-166. *The Selection button creates a loose selection around the bottle*

Refer to the Rectangle tool for more information on the **Mask** and **Shape** buttons. Refer to Figure 10-165.

Path Operations is a drop-down list for combining paths and then selections. Set it to Combine Shapes, or you may get inverse paths. Refer to the Rectangle tool for more information. Refer to Figure 10-166.

Figure 10-167. *Set your path operations to Combine Shapes for this path when you create it*

Path Alignment is a drop-down list for aligning two or more paths. Refer to the Rectangle tool for more information.

If only one path in the Paths panel is selected with the Path Selection tool, you can use the **Path Arrangement** options to move the path over or under another path. Refer to Figure 10-167 and Figure 10-168.

Figure 10-168. *Path and Direct Selection tools in the Tools panel*

Set Additional pen and path options sets the path thickness and color. Refer to Figure 10-169.

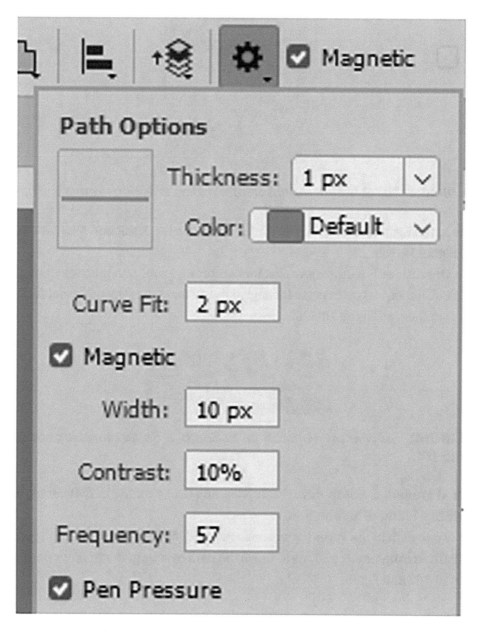

Figure 10-169. *Path options in the options panel*

Curve Fit sets the tolerance allowed when fitting Beziers along the path. The range is 0.5–10 px.

Magnetic changes from the lasso-like setting to the Magnetic Lasso settings, as seen in Chapter 5. You can set the **Width:** Set distance from edge to consider for path at 1–256. **Contrast:** set the contrast of edge to consider for path at 1%–100%. **Frequency:** at which points are added to the path at 0–100. **Pen pressure:** enable if you are using a tablet pressure to change the pen width.

Use the History panel to remove the path. Re-create it by enabling the magnetic options and slowly drag around the bottle letting the path snap to the line, and you see that it is a much closer path. Refer to Figure 10-170 and Figure 10-171.

Figure 10-170. *Go back a step in the History panel to enable the Magnetic setting*

Figure 10-171. *With the Magnetic pointer, drag around the path again to close the path until the pointer icon changes to an O symbol*

As you drag, you can release the mouse, and then you can use the Backspace/Delete if you need to move back a few points and start again.

Double-click to close the path or wait until you see the close path icon O on the pointer.

Tip   Remember to use your Zoom tool first to zoom in closer and the Hand tool (spacebar) while working with the Pen tool if you need to see a more accurate path while working. Refer to Figure 10-172.

Figure 10-172. *Zoom tool (Z) and Hand tool (H)*

Align Edges is disabled; see the Rectangle tool note. Refer to Figure 10-165.

Save your path (double-click the name in the Paths panel) as path 1, and then you'll use the next tool. Refer to Figure 10-173.

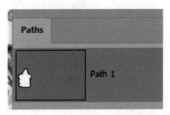

Figure 10-173. *Save your work path as path 1*

Curvature Pen Tool (P)

Use this tool if you need to draw paths with a lot of curves and straight segments quickly. As you click the Pen tool, it attempts to change to curved or straight surfaces. Refer to Figure 10-174.

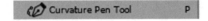

Figure 10-174. *Curvature Pen tool*

Try this on the middle bottle. Refer to Figure 10-175.

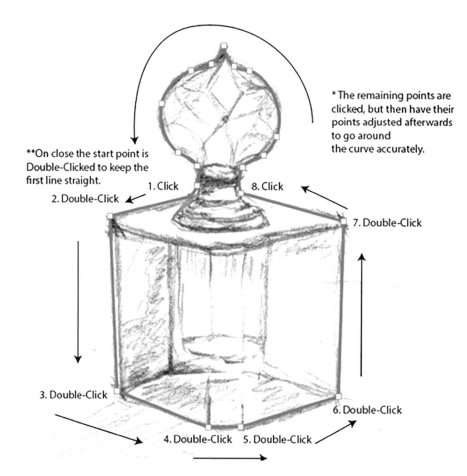

Figure 10-175. *Example of how to use the Curvature Pen tool*

Since every sketch is different, here are some tips for using this tool.

- Click the first point, then double-click the next point or any points when you want to transition from a smooth to a corner point.

- Press the Backspace/Delete key to go back to a point, click Yes to the warning message, and click the same point again to continue the path.

- Close the path or press the Esc key to keep the path open.

- Once the path is closed, drag on the handles to adjust the path further and move points.

- Double-click points once the path is closed to make them corner points.

- Click the line segments to add more points.

At first, you may find this tool a bit tricky to use but keep practicing. You can always drag the path to your trash can icon in the Paths panel and try again if you make a mistake. It makes a smoothed transition path with minimal points. Refer to Figure 10-176.

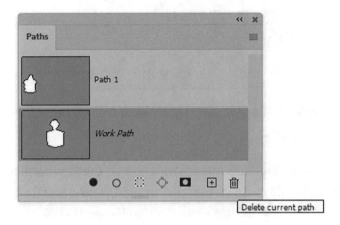

Figure 10-176. *If you make a mistake, you can always delete the current work path and try again*

Curvature Pen Tool Options

The options panel is the same as the Pen tool (P) and Rectangle tool (U). So, I point out the differences. Look from left to right in Figure 10-177.

Figure 10-177. *Curvature Pen tool options in the options panel*

Create or Manage a **Preset tool**. Refer to Figure 10-177.

Tool mode is set to Path in the drop-down list. Refer to Figure 10-177.

Make

When selecting a path, press the **Selection** button, enter the Make Selection dialog box to confirm the selection, and click OK. Refer to Figure 10-177 and Figure 10-178.

Figure 10-178. *A selection is created when the Selection button in the options panel is pressed*

Refer to the Rectangle tool for more information on the **Mask** and **Shape** buttons.

Path Operations is a drop-down list for combining paths and then selections. Refer to the Rectangle tool for more information. Refer to Figure 10-179.

Figure 10-179. *Set your path operations to Combine Shapes for this path when you create it*

Path Alignment is a drop-down list for aligning two or more paths.

If only one path in the Paths panel is selected with the Path Selection tool, you can use the **Path Arrangement** options to move the path over or under another path. Refer to Figure 10-179 and Figure 10-180.

Figure 10-180. *Path and Direct Selection tools in the Tools panel*

Set Additional pen and path options sets the path thickness and color. Refer to Figure 10-181.

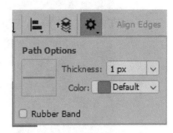

Figure 10-181. *Path options in the options panel*

Rubber Band shows the path extension by drawing; it is disabled by default.

Align Edges is disabled; see the Rectangle tool note. Refer to Figure 10-181.

Save your path (double-click the name in the Paths panel) as path 2, and then you'll use the last Pen tool. Refer to Figure 10-182.

Figure 10-182. *Save your path in the Paths panel as path 2*

Content-Aware Tracing Tool (P)

The Content-Awaare Tracing tool lets you create vector paths and selections by hovering over the edges of your image and clicking. It is a good option for grayscale sketches and color art.

If you don't see this tool in your Tools panel, you can enable the Content-Aware Tracing tool in Edit ➤ Preferences ➤ Technology Previews and then close and restart Photoshop. Refer to Figure 10-183.

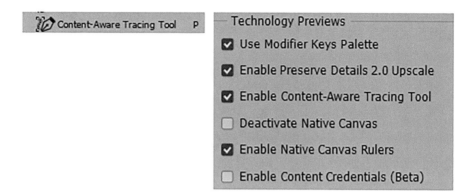

Figure 10-183. *Enable Content-Aware Tracing Tool in Preference Technology Preview*

The options panel is the same as the Pen tool and Rectangle tool. However, there are some key differences on the right-hand side of the bar, which I point out.

Content-Aware Tracing Tool Options

Look from left to right in the options panel shown in Figure 10-184.

Figure 10-184. *Content-Aware Tracing tool options in the options panel*

Create or manage a **tool preset**. Refer to Figure 10-184.

Tool mode is set to Path from the drop-down list. Refer to Figure 10-184.

Make

Press the **Selection** button, enter the Make Selection dialog box to confirm the selection, and click OK. Refer to Figure 10-184.

Refer to the Rectangle tool for more information on the **Mask** and **Shape** buttons. Refer to Figure 10-184.

Path Operations is a drop-down list for combining paths and then selections. Set it to Combine Shapes, or you may get inverse paths. Refer to the Rectangle tool if you need more information. Refer to Figure 10-185.

Figure 10-185. *Set your path operations to Combine Shapes for this path when you create it*

Path Alignment is a drop-down list for aligning two or more paths.

If only one path in the Paths panel is selected with the Path Selection tool, you can use the **Path Arrangement** options to move the path over or under another path. Refer to Figure 10-185 and Figure 10-186.

Figure 10-186. *Path and Direct Selection tools in the Tools panel*

Set Additional pen and path options sets the path thickness and color. Refer to Figure 10-187.

Figure 10-187. *Path options in the options panel*

This next section of options is different from the other Pen tools. Refer to Figure 10-188.

Figure 10-188. *Create, Extend and Trim paths as you connect the anchor points of the path*

The **Creates paths from currently detected edges** option creates your selection path. Hover over to see the selection and then click the highlighted selection to create a path. Refer to Figure 10-188.

The Extend currently selected paths with detected edges option is used as you hold down the Shift key and clicking to extend the path. Refer to Figure 10-188.

The Trim traced paths option deletes an area of the path. Click and drag in one direction to remove larger areas of the path. Refer to Figure 10-188.

The Tracing modes option detects whether the edges are detailed, normal, or simplified. Adjust these options depending on how detailed or textured the sketch is before processing the tracing. Refer to Figure 10-189.

Figure 10-189. Adjust your tracing modes, detail percent, or auto trim to refine your selection

Detail adjusts the number of detected edges 1%–100%. Photoshop displays a preview of the edges it sees. A higher percent increases the number of edges detected, while a lower percent decreases the amount of edge detection. Refer to Figure 10-189.

Auto Trim automatically trims the selected path and detected edge to minimize gap when extending traced paths. Refer to Figure 10-189.

Align Edges is disabled; see the Rectangle tool note. Refer to Figure 10-184. Depending on your sketch, this tool can be a bit tricky to use at first. You may find the Pen tool or Freeform tool with Magnetic enabled might be easier for you to use on your projects. However, I do recommend practicing with this tool.

Try this on the bottle on the right. First, let's discuss a few tips that work for me.

Hold down the Shift key while going around the bottle, clicking to keep adding to the path. Remember this is the same as the Extend Currently Selected Paths with detected edges icon in the options panel. Refer to Figure 10-190.

Figure 10-190. Hold down the Shift key so that you can keep on expanding your selection so that the points and lines do not break

Click slowly and do not rush. First, observe how the line preview shows how the next click is placed as a stripe. Move your pointer a bit, hover in a new location until you get the path you want, and then Shift-click. Refer to Figure 10-191.

Figure 10-191. *Use your preview to gauge where you click next*

Use Different Zoom Levels while using the Zoom tool may assist you in how this tool identifies the edge. Staying slightly distant at about 66.7% from the object before I started, I could get around my sketch.

Click when you reach the end of the path to close it.

You can see the final path here with notes on the various clicking points. It did create quite a few, but the selection was quite accurate.

You may want to use the Quick Mask mode (Q) in Chapter 6 to further clean up and refine the selection. Refer to Figure 10-192.

Figure 10-192. *The results of using the Content-Aware Tracing tool on the bottle on the right side. A selection was created with the Selection button and how it appears in Quick Mask mode and saved as path 3 in the Paths panel.*

I saved my work path as path 3. You can review these paths in the scan10_6_addtional_pen_tools_final.psd file. Refer to Figure 10-192.

Save your document.

Finally, let's return to the Paths panel and look at a few additional features.

Paths Panel: Saving Your Path and Other Options

When you create a work path using one of the tools, you can save it in the Paths panel by double-clicking it, naming it, and clicking OK in the dialog box. Refer to Figure 10-193.

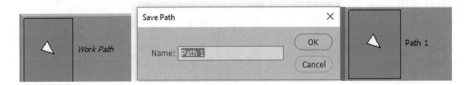

Figure 10-193. *Save your paths in the Paths panel so that you do not override them*

You can rename the path any time by double-clicking the path name. Enter a new name and then click away from the name to confirm. Refer to Figure 10-194.

Figure 10-194. *Rename your paths when you need to give them meaningful names*

Some additional things to note in the lower half of the Paths panel, look at the first icon on the right.

Fill path on a new layer with foreground color as you did with a selection

Stroke a path as you would with a brush on a new layer. Refer to Figure 10-195.

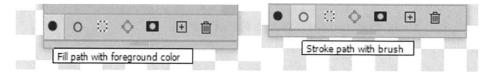

Figure 10-195. *When a path is selected, you can use the Fill and Stroke options from the Paths panel*

The following are other related selection and path settings.

Load Path as a selection is much faster than using the Selection button as you don't enter the dialog box. Click this when on a new layer, and the selection is instantly loaded. Refer to Figure 10-196.

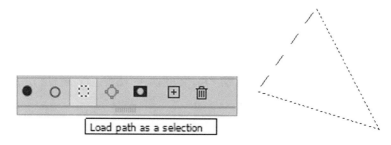

Figure 10-196. *Load a Selected path Quickly from the Paths panel in one click*

Make work path from selection means if you have a selection already active, refer to Figure 10-196, you can covert it to a path for saving in the Paths panel. Saving selections is discussed further in Chapter 11. Refer to Figure 10-197.

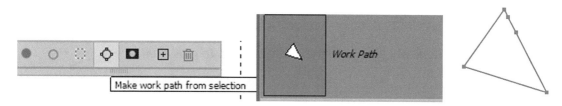

Figure 10-197. *Make a work path from a current selection*

In some situations, you may want to save an inverse selection as a path, as you saw when working with the Rectangle tool. If you have a selection active, choose Select ➤ Inverse (Shift+Ctrl/Cmd+I) and choose **Make work path from selection.** In this case, rather than the gray area surrounding the white selection, this path is the reverse, gray with white surrounding it. And you could then load the path as a selection later for a project if you need to continue to clean up a certain area surrounding your original selection. Refer to Figure 10-198.

Figure 10-198. *Inverse work path*

Add a Mask changes the current selection into a mask on a selected layer or the current path into a vector mask. You look at masks in Chapter 12. Refer to Figure 10-199.

Figure 10-199. *Add a layer or vector mask to a layer from the Paths panel*

Let's review the last two buttons.

Create new path creates additional paths to keep your selections separate. Use the Path Selection tool to select a path. Refer to Figure 10-200.

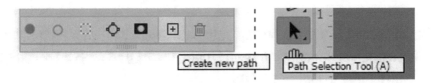

Figure 10-200. *Create a new path layer that you can copy paths onto to separate*

Then Edit ➤ Cut, followed by **Create new path**, and then Edit ➤ Paste to move the selection to a new work path. Refer to Figure 10-201.

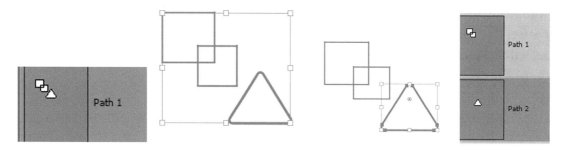

Figure 10-201. *Path Selection tool to select one path and cut to a new path layer to separate it*

Or make a copy of the path by dragging the path over the **Create new path** icon. Refer to Figure 10-202.

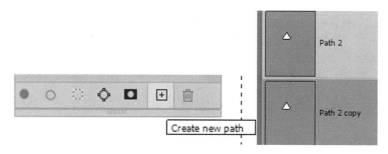

Figure 10-202. *Duplicate a path*

Tip   You can select two paths on separate path layers with your Path Selection tool by Shift-clicking both paths to reveal them. Click **Load path as a selection** to combine paths. Refer to Figure 10-203.

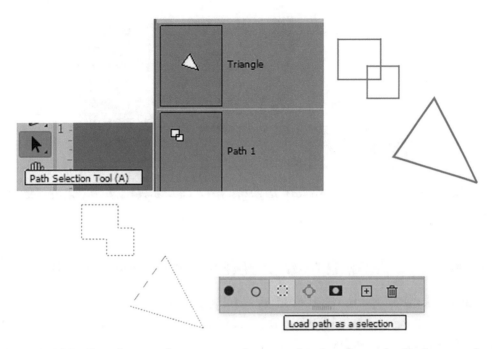

Figure 10-203. *Load more than one path as a selection from the Paths panel using the Path Selection tool*

Delete current path lets you either click the button or drag a path over the icon without seeing the warning message. Refer to Figure 10-204.

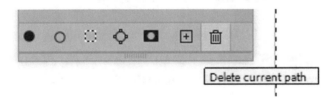

Figure 10-204. *Delete current path from the Paths panel*

Remember, now that you have saved paths in the various files in this chapter. Using the various method described in this chapter, you can then turn them into selections at any time. As a selection, you could paint with your Brush tool or use the Edit ➤ Fill dialog box to fill the selection with color, such as a white foreground from the Tools panel. Refer to Figure 10-205.

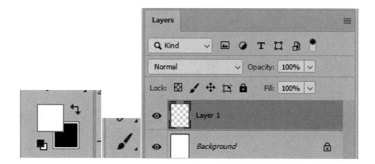

Figure 10-205. *Use your Brush tool to paint on a new layer when your selection is loaded*

Paint Bucket Pattern and Gradients for Filling in Selection

There are a few other options you could try to fill your selection. These are my suggestions; you may want to try on your own and experiment with and further colorize your art. Refer to Figure 10-206.

Figure 10-206. *Gradient tool and Paint Bucket tool*

Use the **Paint Bucket tool (G)**. On a new layer, click to fill the area with a foreground color from the Tools panel or switch to Pattern and choose a pattern from the list, which is also in the Window ➤ Patterns panel, as seen in Chapter 2. Refer to Figure 10-207.

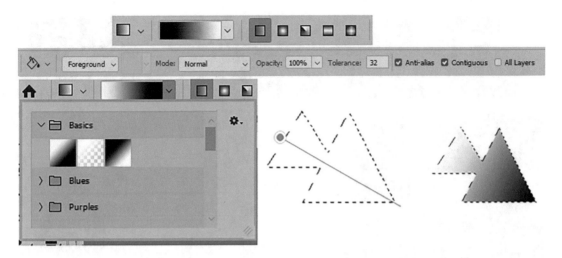

Figure 10-207. *Paint Bucket tool options in the options panel. Rather than fill a selection with the foreground color, try filling with a pattern instead.*

Click to fill the selection with a pattern.

For information on how to use the Paint Bucket tool, you can check out `https://helpx.adobe.com/photoshop/using/filling-stroking-selections-layers-paths.html`.

Use the Gradient tool (G) while the selection is active on a new layer, click and drag at an angle with your pointer across the selection. Use Gradients in the options panel, which are stored in the Gradients panel. Refer to Figure 10-208.

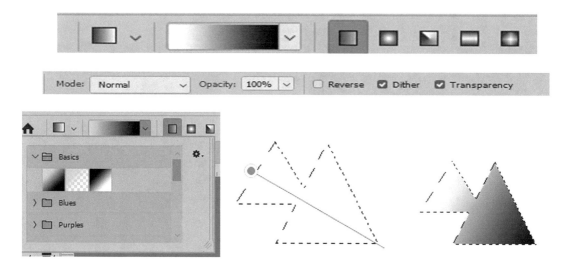

Figure 10-208. *Gradient tool options in the options panel fill your selection with a gradient*

For more information on working with the Gradient tool, check out `https://helpx.adobe.com/photoshop/using/gradients.html`.

Note   Patterns and gradients can also be used with masks and fill and adjustment layers. I talk about that briefly in Chapter 12.

Summary

This chapter covered a lot of tools for creating paths and then saving or storing the paths in the Paths panel. You then saw how you could turn any path quickly into a selection. You also discovered that you don't have to fill your selections with a solid color. Alternatively, you could use patterns and gradients. In the next chapter, you are saving your selections in the document's Channels panel and then loading them again should you accidentally deselect them while working on a complex selection.

CHAPTER 11

Channel Selections from Paths

This chapter shows you how to save a selection from the Paths panel in the Channels panel so that it can be reused and saved as a selection.

The last chapter looked at paths—how they can be saved in a document and how they can be made into selections. However, there may be other situations where you want to save a selection that you created, but it did not start off as a path. How that is done and where these selections are saved are explored next.

Open the scan11_1_selections.psd file.

Note   The projects for this chapter are in the Chapter 11 folder.

Go to Image ➤ Duplicate to make a copy to practice with. Click OK to the message dialog box to confirm the copy. Refer to Figure 11-1.

© Jennifer Harder 2022
J. Harder, *Accurate Layer Selections Using Photoshop's Selection Tools*,
https://doi.org/10.1007/978-1-4842-7493-4_11

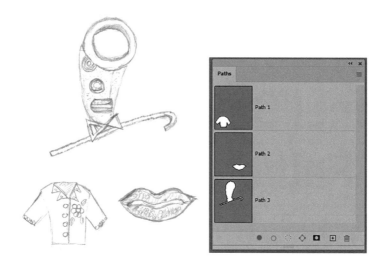

Figure 11-1. *Sketch of three brooches. A path is created and saved in the Paths panel*

Let's return to the brooches that we were working on in the last chapter. I created a path in the Paths panel for each of them to use in this example.

Paths Panel Review

In Chapter 10, toward the end of the chapter, you saw in the Paths panel that it had several button icons. Refer to Figure 11-2.

Figure 11-2. *Icons at the bottom of the Paths panel*

The third from the left is the **Load a path as a selection** button. This loads the currently selected path from the Paths panel without having to go through the Selection button or its dialog box with the Shape and Pen tools. Refer to Figure 11-3.

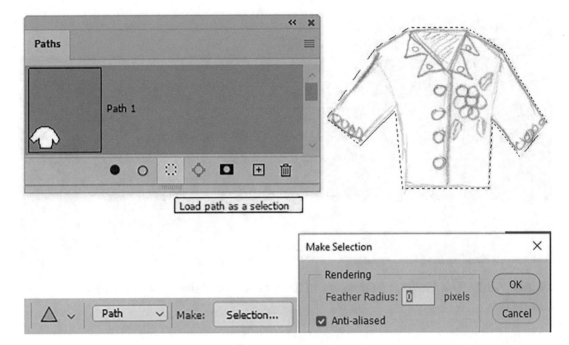

Figure 11-3. *Loading a Path from the Paths panel is faster than loading it using a Shape or Pen tool button*

You can also load a path as a selection with the **Make Selection** option in the Paths panel menu. This brings up the Selection button dialog box seen in Chapter 10. Refer to Figure 11-4.

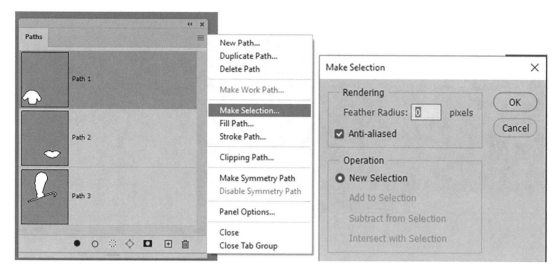

Figure 11-4. *The Paths panel menu also lets you enter the Make Selection dialog box*

Note   The Make Symmetry Path option in the menu is for Symmetry Painting when using the Brush tool and Eraser tool and is not a topic in this book, but you can learn more at `https://helpx.adobe.com/photoshop/using/paint-symmetry.html`.

---

1.   With path 3 selected, click the **Load path as a selection** button. Refer to Figure 11-5.

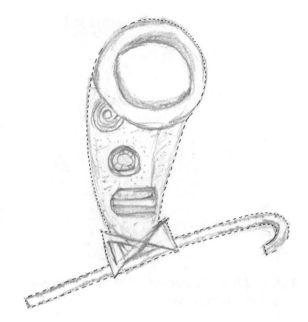

Figure 11-5. *Click the Load path as a selection icon in the Paths panel to load path 3 quickly*

Note   If you think that this resultant selection from the path is a bit too close to the shape as with any selection, you can modify the selection and choose Select ➤ Modify ➤ Expand or any of the Modify options, depending on your project. Remember that if you use Feather, you have a softer edge which you may not want when cleaning up stray marks around your selection. For this selection, I leave it as is. Refer to Figure 11-6.

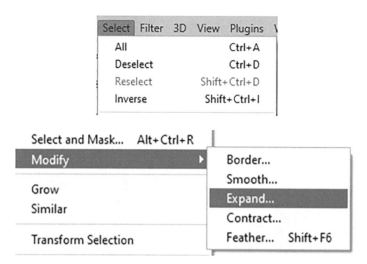

Figure 11-6. *Modify any loaded path with the Select menu, even if it was created with the Paths panel*

While the selection is active around the clown brooch, you can then save it using Select ➤ Save Selection. Refer to Figure 11-7.

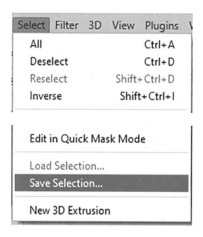

Figure 11-7. *Use the Select menu to save a selection*

The Save Selection dialog box opens. Refer to Figure 11-8.

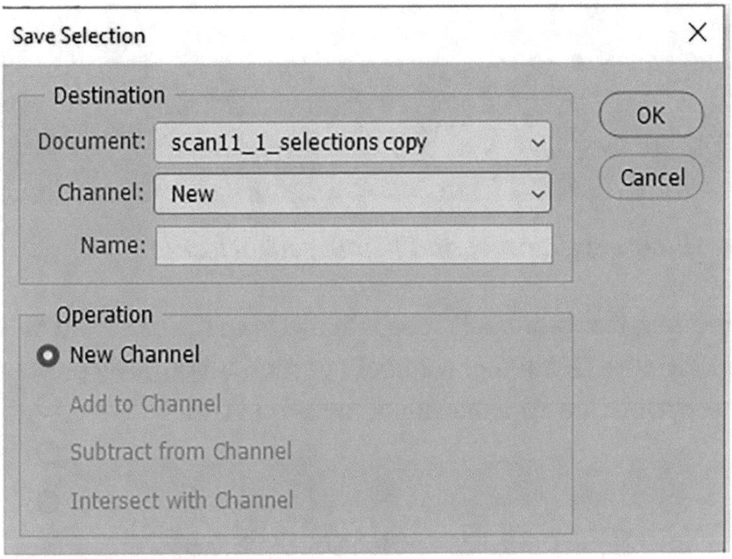

Figure 11-8. *Options in the Save Selection dialog box*

You have a few options that you must either select or enter in the dialog box.

In the Destination fields, consider which **Document** you plan to save the selection in.

You can select the current document, which is displayed by default, or a new document. In this case, I want to save it in the current document. Refer to Figure 11-9.

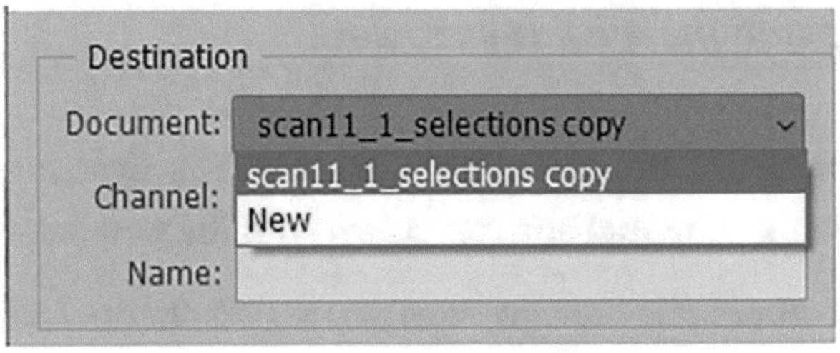

Figure 11-9. *Set a Destination for your selection*

The selection is saved in the Channels panel. By default, it is a new Channel/selection, but if another channel is already present, you could add it to that channel as well. Refer to Figure 11-10.

The **Name** of the selection appears in the Channels panel area. Refer to Figure 11-10.

Figure 11-10. *Choose a Channel and Name your selection*

Under **Operation**, if only one selection is active from the path, you must set it as a **New Channel**. However, if another channel selection was already present and you selected it, other options are available. Refer to Figure 11-11.

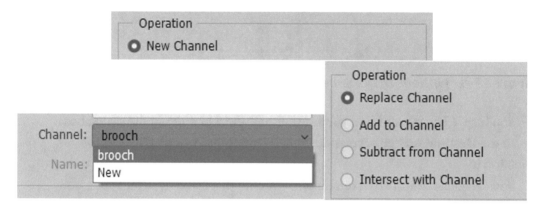

Figure 11-11. *Depending on whether you select a new channel or one already present, different operations will be available*

- **New Channel** switches to **Replace Channel**. This overrides the selection in that channel and replaces it with the new selection.

- **Add to Channel a**dds the new selection to that channel with an original selection.

- **Subtract From Channel** subtracts the new selection from the current selection in that channel.

- **Intersect with Channel** intersects the new selection with the current selection in that channel.

To learn more about these selection options, refer to Chapter 3, where you looked at similar selection options for the Rectangular Marquee tool. Refer to Figure 11-12.

Figure 11-12. *Most selection tools like the Rectangular Marquee have similar add, subtract, and intersect options*

Cancel exit without saving the channel. Refer to Figure 11-10.

After you have given your new selection a name, click **OK** to exit the dialog box. Refer to Figure 11-13.

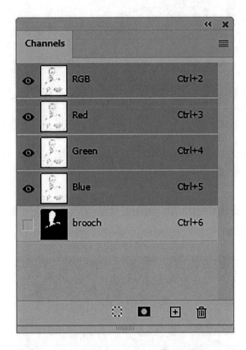

Figure 11-13. *A channel selection appears in the Channels panel*

In the Window ➤ Channels panel, you see a type of masked shape selection in black and white this is the saved selection. It appears below the RGB, Red, Green, and Blue channels but does not interact with them because the eye is turned off.

If you turn the eye on while the other channels are selected but it is unselected, you enter what is similar to Quick Mask mode (Q). Refer to Chapter 6 if you need to review this. Refer to Figure 11-14.

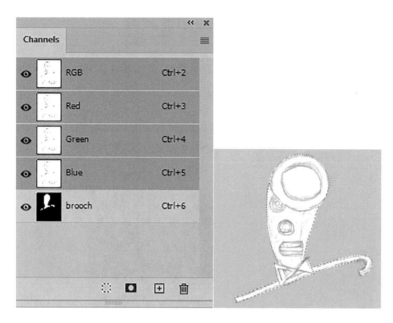

Figure 11-14. *When the eye of the channel is turned on, you can go into Mask mode only for that Channel*

However, if you look at the History panel, it shows you are not in Quick Mask mode. You are in the Mask mode for that channel, which you can edit. Refer to Figure 11-15.

Figure 11-15. *In the History panel, you can see you are not in Quick Mask mode (Q)*

Note   You can still enter Quick Mask mode (Q) at the same time, but this creates a temporary channel in the Channels panel, as it always does when you enter the Quick Mask mode. However, in this case, it's not the mask you want to edit. When you exit Quick Mask mode back to Standard mode, it disappears. In your project, if you were exiting Quick Mask mode after creating a selection, you can then choose Select ➤ Save Selection to Save it as a Selection in the Channels panel. Refer to Figure 11-16.

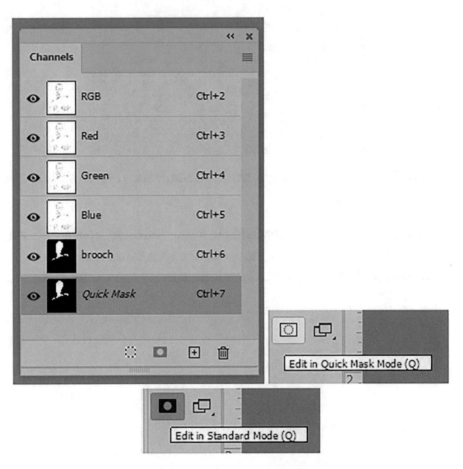

Figure 11-16. *Quick Mask mode creates a temporary channel in the Channels panel that you can enter an exit from the Tools panel or by pressing Q*

Altering the Channel/Selection

Returning the current saved selection. While in its Mask mode, choose Select ➤ Deselect (Ctrl/Cmd+D) to deselect the section. Refer to Figure 11-17.

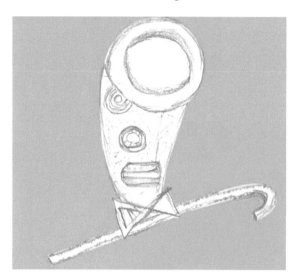

Figure 11-17. *Deselect your selection while on the brooch channel Mask mode in the Channels panel*

Now that it is saved, you can do that without losing your current selection. You want to be able to edit the mask, and keeping the selection on gets in the way.

Select the brooch channel but keep the RGB channel eyes on. Refer to Figure 11-18.

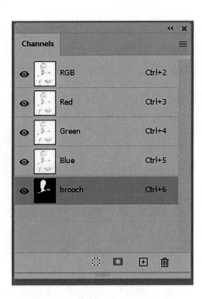

Figure 11-18. *Select the brooch channel, but make sure the RGB channels are still turned on*

Now use your Brush tool. In the Tools panel, switch the foreground and background color (X), set to default black and white (D), and paint within the mask on the channel to alter the selection. White adds to the selection, and black adds to the mask. Refer to Figure 11-19.

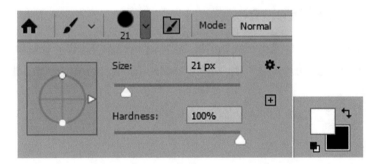

Figure 11-19. *Use your Brush tool as you do in Quick Mask mode to alter your brooch Channel while it is selected in the Channels panel*

I added to the selection any line that needed to be part of the selection and masked out some white areas that the path originally missed, like the inside of the clown's bowtie, which was hollow.

Remember to vary your brush size and keep your hardness at 100% unless you want to feather the selection. Use your Zoom tool and Hand tool (spacebar) along with the Brush tool if you need to get closer to make a more refined mask. Refer to Figure 11-20.

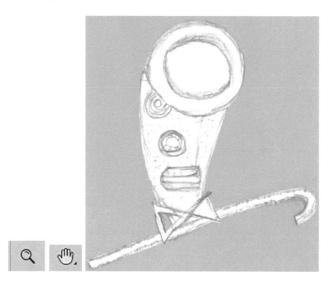

Figure 11-20.   *Using your Zoom tool and Hand tool may help you while you modify the selection with the Brush tool*

Invert a Channel/Selection

You can also inverse or invert the channel/selection in the Channel panel.

While it is selected, press Ctrl/Cmd+I. The selection appears around the shape. Refer to Figure 11-21.

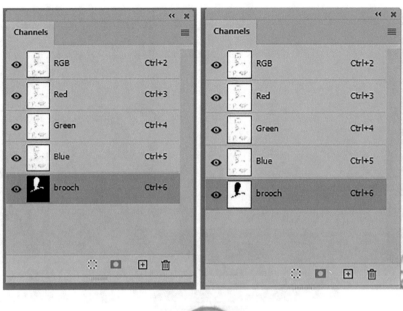

Figure 11-21. *Invert your selection using the Channels panel while the brooch channel is selected*

You can then drag the channel over the Create New Channel button, and a copy is created. Refer to Figure 11-22.

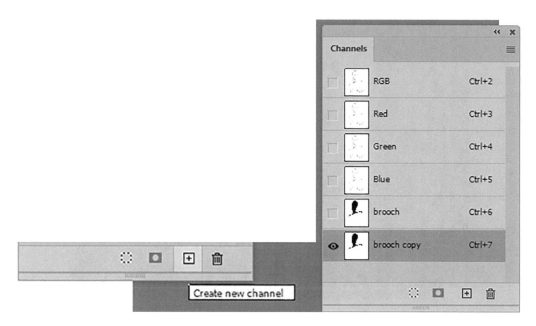

Figure 11-22. *Duplicate a channel by dragging it over the Create New Channel icon in the Channels panel*

While the copy is the only channel selected in the Channels panel, press Ctrl/Cmd+I again. You create an inverse that is like the original selection. Refer to Figure 11-23.

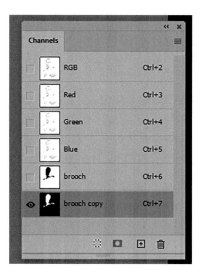

Figure 11-23. *Invert the brooch copy channel, so you have two selection options*

You can double-click both channel names one at a time to rename them to keep organized. Name the first brooch "brooch invert" and the next "brooch original". Refer to Figure 11-24.

Figure 11-24. *Rename the two channels in the Channels panel*

Having an inverse and the original selection available may be useful when sometimes you need to clean around the outside of the sketch on a new layer and then return to the inside of the sketch to use the stamp tool. Remember, however, that if you alter one of the Channels/Selections at this point, they will not be identical, and some parts of each selection will overlap, causing you to cover areas you don't want to, so you may have to create a new inverse or original to correct that.

Delete a Selection

If you don't require a selection, drag the Channel to the trash can icon to delete it. Refer to Figure 11-25.

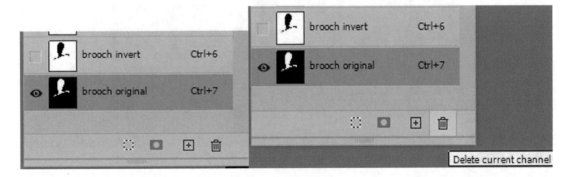

Figure 11-25. *Delete a Current Channel if it is not required or you made a mistake*

Edit ➤ Undo (Ctrl/Cmd+Z) the last step so that you do not delete the brooch original selection.

Channel Options

As you may have observed, only when the channel is selected and not RGB channels then the channel/selection appear as a mask in black and white. I prefer to have both selected with the red mask so I can see what I am erasing. So, make sure to select the RGB channel as well as the brooch original channel. Refer to Figure 11-26.

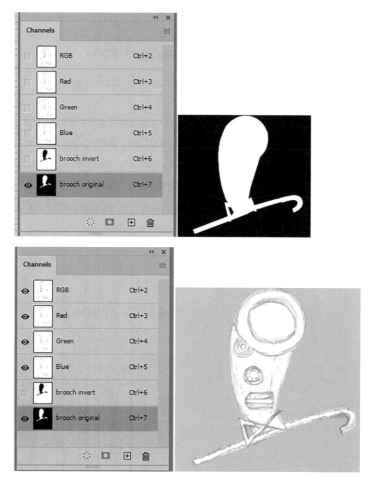

Figure 11-26. *Viewing the brooch original channel with the RGB channels turned off and then on. The brooch invert channel was left off*

If you need to change the red channel masking option, you can change it from the Channels panel menu. Select Channel Options to define what the color indicates.

- Masked Areas

- Selected Areas

- Spot Color (if you do a lot of print work with special colors)

Refer to Figure 11-27.

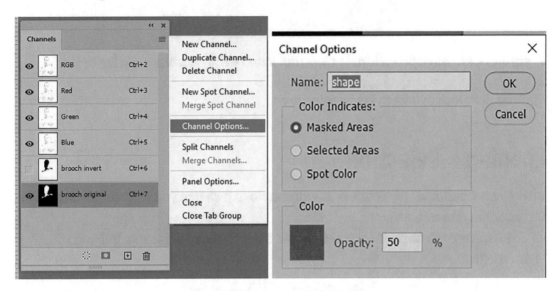

Figure 11-27. *Channel Options can be accessed in the Channel panel's menu and dialog box*

You can also change the color using the color picker and alter the opacity. I usually leave it at the default settings, but there may be a situation where red is not the ideal mask color for your artwork.

Note   Another way to save a copy of the current selection is to click **Save selection as channel**. By default, the name is Alpha 1, but this is only available if a selection is active and loaded. Refer to Figure 11-28.

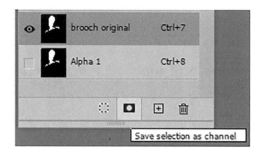

Figure 11-28. *Save Selection As Channel icon in the Channels dialog box*

Next, let's look at how to load a selection.

Loading a Selection

After you have altered a selection, you can then load it so that you can start cleaning up the selection on a new layer.

With the brooch original selected, choose Select ➤ Load Selection. Refer to Figure 11-29.

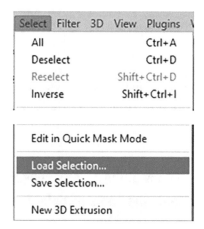

Figure 11-29. *Load Selection in the Select menu*

This opens the Load Selection dialog box. Refer to Figure 11-30.

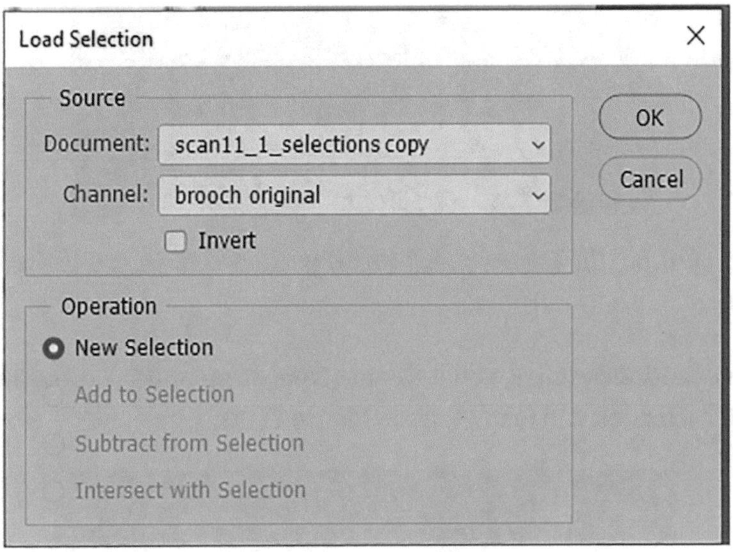

Figure 11-30. *The Select menu Load Selection dialog box*

The **Source** field area shows you what Document to Pick. You can select the current **Document,** or you can select from the drop-down list if another one that is currently open that you want to select a channel from. Refer to Figure 11-30.

Choose the currently selected **Channel**, or if there is more than one in your document, you can choose it from the list. Refer to Figure 11-31.

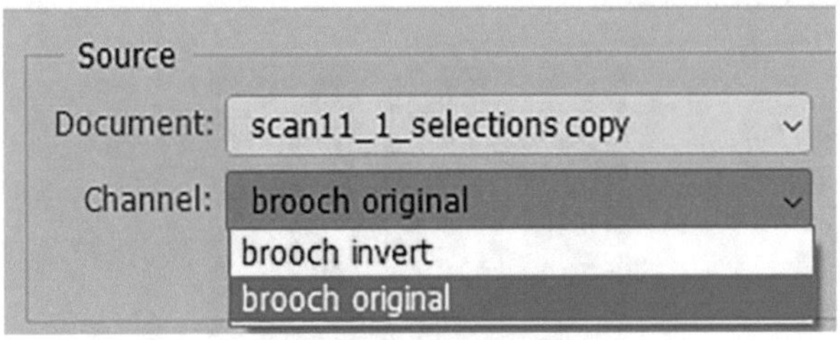

Figure 11-31. *Choose a Channel from the Load Selection dialog box*

You can also enable **Invert** to invert the selection rather than doing it later on; by default, it is deselected. Refer to Figure 11-32.

Figure 11-32. *Enable the Invert check box if you need to invert the selection when loading*

If no other selection is active, you have one **Operation** option—**New Selection,** and only the current selection will load. Refer to Figure 11-33.

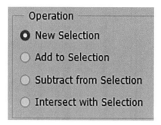

Figure 11-33. *Choose New Selection from the Load Selection dialog box*

However, if another selection is currently active before you load a selection, then you can also refer to Figure 11-34.

- Add to Selection

- Subtract from Selection

- Intersect with Selection

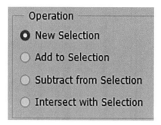

Figure 11-34. *Operation options of new, add, subtract, and intersect for loading selections*

Click OK to confirm. The selection is loaded. Refer to Figure 11-35.

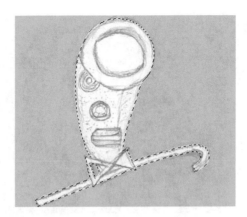

Figure 11-35. *The selection is loaded and in Mask mode*

Click the RGB channel and to get out of Mask mode.

Turn off the eye in the **brooch original** to see only the selection. Refer to Figure 11-36.

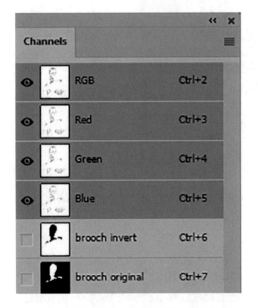
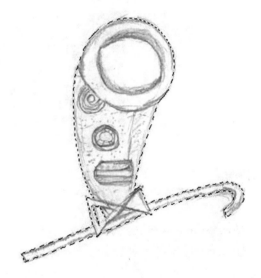

Figure 11-36. *Select only the RGB channels. Only the selection is now active on the background layer in your Layers panel*

If you want to load the selection quickly, click the **Load channel as selection** icon. Turn off the eye after loading and return to the RGB channel. Refer to Figure 11-37.

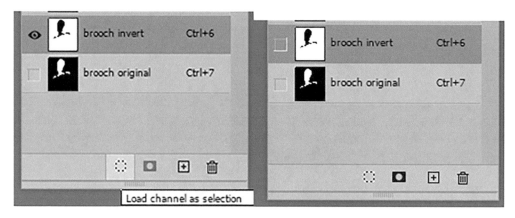

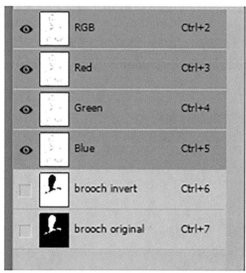

Figure 11-37. *Load different selections from the Channels panel depending on what area of the sketch you are cleaning up*

Now your selections are saved and loaded.

On a new layer, you can continue to paint, Clone Stamp, and erase in (load the **brooch original** channel) or around your selection (load the **brooch invert** channel). You can save your file (Ctrl/Cmd+S), close it, and load the selection again if you need to edit it later. Refer to Figure 11-38.

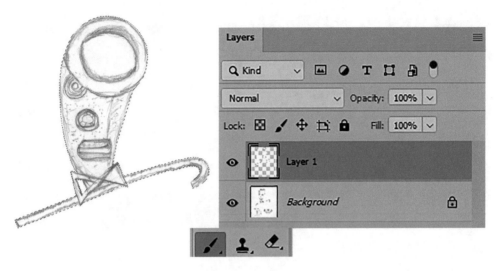

Figure 11-38. *While your selection is active, use your Brush tool, Clone Stamp tool, and Eraser tool to clean up on a New Layer (layer 1) in your Layers panel*

You can see how it looks in the scan11_1_selections_final.psd file.

Tip   Though not a topic for this book, you can use your saved channel/selections in other areas of Photoshop, for example, color blending. There are two areas that are not often explored by beginner users: Image ➤ Calculations and Image ➤ Apply Image. You can learn more about that topic at `https://helpx.adobe.com/photoshop/using/channel-calculations.html`.

Summary

This chapter showed how to save a selection, edit, duplicate, and create an inverse all in the Channels panel and then how to load them. The next chapter explores another way to store selections as masks on a layer.

CHAPTER 12

Save a Selection as a Layer Mask

This chapter shows you how to use the saved selections or paths and create a mask that can be altered or refined in a variety of ways.

In the last chapter, you looked at saving and loading your selections from the Channels panel. While it is convenient to save complex selections in this panel, you may want to have the selection as part of a specific layer. This is known as a *layer mask*. A mask blocks areas you do not want to see and reveals the areas you want to keep. If the mask is on its own layer, it is much easier to access and edit from the Layers panel than reload it each time from the Channels panel.

Note   This chapter's projects are in the Chapter 12 folder.

Chapter 9 looked at Select and Mask. Besides creating a selection, you saw that you could instantly create a layer mask from a selection from the output area. Refer to Figure 12-1.

© Jennifer Harder 2022
J. Harder, *Accurate Layer Selections Using Photoshop's Selection Tools*,
https://doi.org/10.1007/978-1-4842-7493-4_12

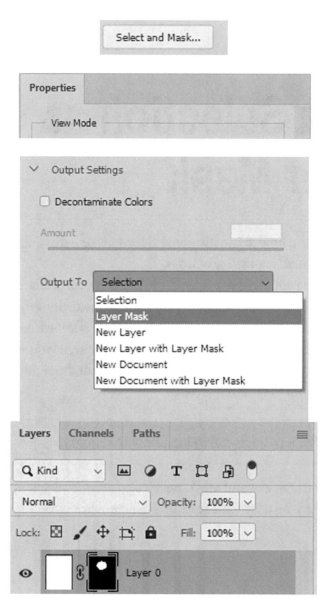

Figure 12-1. *The Select and Mask workspace allows you to output layer masks*

The mask could be on the current layer, a new layer, or a new document.

However, whether a selection is active or inactive, you do not need to enter the Select and Mask workspace to create a mask. You can save that selection as a mask by clicking the **Add a mask** icon at the bottom of the Layers panel. Refer to Figure 12-2.

Figure 12-2. *Add a mask from the bottom of the Layers panel*

Open the scan12_1.psd file. It is a colored pencil drawing of some apples. It contains a selection in the Channels panel. Go to Image ➤ Duplicate to make a copy to practice on. Refer to Figure 12-3.

Figure 12-3. *Colored sketch of apples in a bowl*

Go to the Channels panel, and with the **apples** channel selected with the eye off, choose the Load channel as a selection icon. Refer to Figure 12-4.

Figure 12-4. *Load the channel as a selection from the Channels panel while selected*

In the Layers panel with the background layer selected and in red mask mode, click the **Add a mask** icon. Refer to Figure 12-5.

Figure 12-5. *Add a layer mask to your background layer in the Layers panel and it becomes layer 0 and transparent around the masked area*

This adds a mask to a background layer as layer 0 and you exit mask mode. Refer to Figure 12-6.

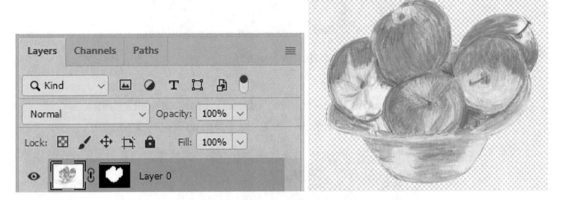

Figure 12-6. *Add a layer mask to your background layer in the Layers panel, and it becomes layer 0 and transparent around the masked area*

However, on a normal layer, the name of that layer remains, such as layer 1. Currently, the area surrounding the apples and the bowl is transparent.

Alternatively, you could add a layer mask while the selection is active, and from the main drop-down menu, choose Layers ➤ Layer Mask ➤ **Reveal Selection**. Refer to Figure 12-7.

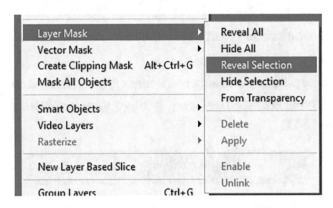

Figure 12-7. *The Layer menu has suboptions for the layer mask*

The following are the other choices.

- **Reveal All** creates a white layer mask and ignores the selection. The whole image is visible. Refer to Figure 12-8.

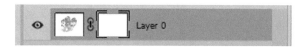

Figure 12-8. *Reveal All produces a blank mask*

- **Hide All** creates a layer mask that is a black layer mask and ignores the selection. None of the image is visible. Refer to Figure 12-9.

Figure 12-9. *Hide All adds a solid mask that blocks the whole image*

- **Hide Selection** creates an inverse using the selection. In this case, the apples and bowl are masked, but the background is visible. Refer to Figure 12-10.

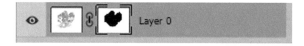

Figure 12-10. *Hide Selection reveals only the area around the selection*

- **From Transparency** creates a black mask from a transparent layer. In this case, there are no other layers, so this option is grayed out. Refer to Figure 12-11.

Figure 12-11. *From Transparency creates a mask on a transparent layer and fills the image area with the white foreground color*

There are three types of masks that Photoshop can create on various layers.

- Layer mask
- Vector mask
- Clipping mask

Let's look at the layer mask first.

Layer Masks

A layer mask can be applied to most layers in Photoshop, including the following.

- Normal and background layers

- Fill and adjustment layers

- Type layers

- Shape layers

- Smart Objects layers

- Group folders

Note   Frame Layers can also have layer masks; however, this is not a topic of this book. If you need more information on this topic, see my note on my Springer Nature video on Frames in Chapter 10.

As you saw, when a selection is active and the **Add a mask** icon in the Layers panel is clicked, the selection, as in the Channels panel, appears in white with a surrounding black which is the mask. Refer to Figure 12-12.

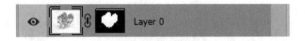

Figure 12-12. *The layer mask appears next to the thumbnail of the image*

Edit the Layer Mask

As you saw in the Channels panel in Chapter 11, you can edit the mask using the Brush tool (B) or Eraser tool (E).

In this case, after you select your Brush tool, remember to press D to reset the default colors to black and white in the Tools panel and use X to switch and toggle between hiding (black) and revealing (white). Refer to Figure 12-13.

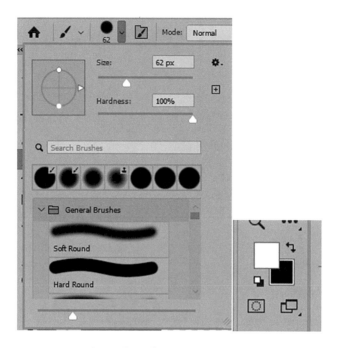

Figure 12-13. *Use your Brush tool with its various options to paint white or black on the mask area*

Make sure that when you select your layer, the mask is selected, and a border appears around the selected mask. If the layer thumbnail is selected by accident, with a border around it, and you start erasing or brushing with the Brush tool, you alter the image, which is not what you want to do. Refer to Figure 12-14.

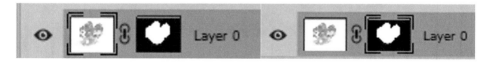

Figure 12-14. *In the Layers panel in the left screenshot, the border appears around the image thumbnail. In the right screenshot, the border appears around the layer mask*

If you think you may have done that, go back in the History panel as many steps as you need to or close the file without saving it and start again, this time with the layer's mask selected. That is another good reason to always make an Image ➤ Duplicate of your sketches when working on them.

When you open the file, make sure your mask is selected. Refer to Figure 12-15.

Figure 12-15. *Keep your mask selected as you edit the mask*

The mask is linked to the layer. If you move the layer with the Move tool, both move together. Refer to Figure 12-16.

Figure 12-16. *Linked masks and images can be moved around together on the canvas using the Move tool*

You can unlink the mask, and it can be moved independently from the layer. Refer to Figure 12-17.

Figure 12-17. *Depending on what is selected when the image and the layer masks are unlinked, they can move separately*

Generally, you want to keep them linked so that you can keep the mask selection in the same location as your sketch. Use your History panel to undo these move steps and keep the layer and layer mask linked. Refer to Figure 12-18.

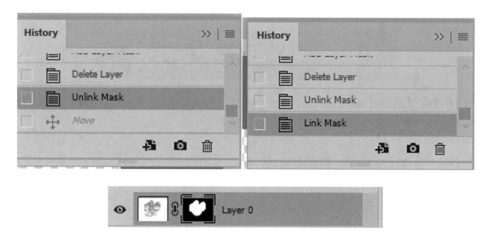

Figure 12-18. *Use your History panel to go back to before you moved the layer mask, and then in the Layers panel, link the Mask and Image together again*

Use your Brush tool to clean up areas on the layer mask. Remember to use your Zoom tool (Z) and Hand tool (H) (spacebar) if you need to move around the image.

I added a Solid Color fill layer, set the color to white in the color picker, and dragged it behind the sketch. Refer to Figure 12-19.

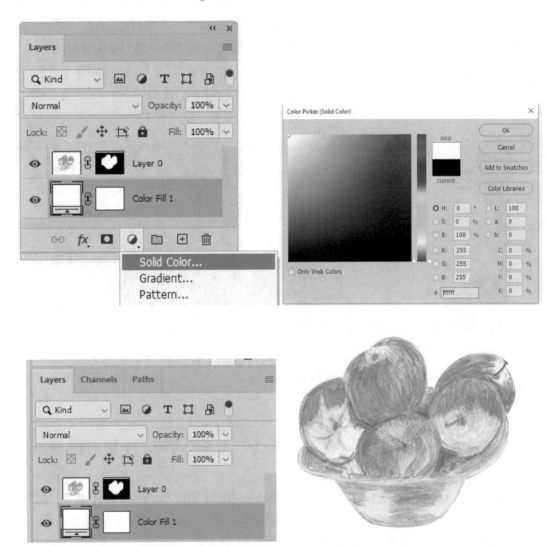

Figure 12-19. *A solid fill color adjustment layer can add a clean background behind a sketch*

This cleans up the sketch quite a bit from the original.

Now you could reselect the mask on layer 0 and continue to refine it as it might be easier to see any other areas you need to erase or show with a solid background. Refer to Figure 12-19.

Tip   If you need to see a mask. In the Layers panel on the selected layer, Alt/Option-click the layer mask to display the Layer Mask channel to check if all the areas are covered while painting. Then click back on the layer thumbnail in the Layers panel to return to the main image. Refer to Figure 12-20.

Figure 12-20. *View the layer mask on its own or in red mask mode when you need to clean up a selection further on a layer*

Note   Alt/Option+Shift-click the layer mask allows you to see the red mask mode for the layer. Refer to Figure 12-20.

Using these two modes is very helpful when you have little paper grains or imperfections that you may have missed adding to the mask when you created a selection with the Magic Wand tool. With your Brush tool, you can paint in black over those areas to conceal them.

Masks can be helpful for gutter shadow removal as well, as you see later in the chapter.

Save your document as a .psd. We will continue with this image later in the chapter.

Mask Layer Properties

The mask has properties that you can access in the Window ➤ Properties panel. Refer to Figure 12-21.

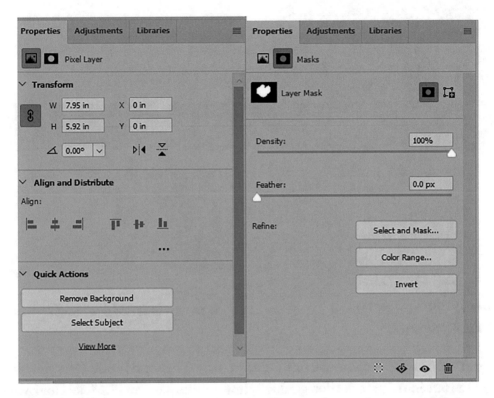

Figure 12-21. *The Properties panel has Pixel Layer (Image)options and the layer mask*

When you click the mask icon in the Properties panel in the upper left, a thumbnail of the current mask appears to the left, and to the right of it is an icon that indicates that the layer mask is selected.

The next button icon lets you **Add a vector mask**, which you look at later in the chapter. Refer to Figure 12-22.

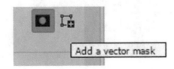

Figure 12-22. *Add a vector mask from the Properties panel*

The Density slider ranges from 0%–100%. It is like the Opacity slider but only affects the mask, not the whole layer. 100% makes the black area completely transparent. 0% hides the mask completely. Refer to Figure 12-23.

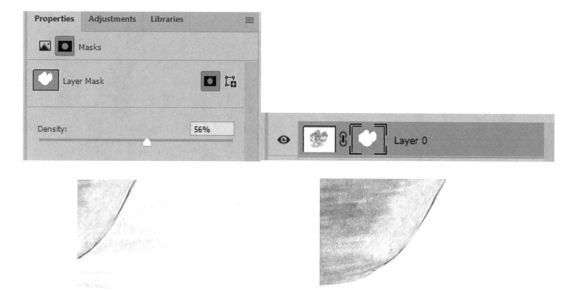

Figure 12-23. *Adjust the density of the mask to see what is hidden. Lower values turn the mask gray*

Feather has a slider range of 0 px to 1000 px. Like Select and Mask, it lets you feather or blur the outside of the selection gradually inward. However, unlike Select and Mask, it is non-destructive to the mask, and you can adjust the feather setting at any time. By default, it is set to 0 px. Refer to Figure 12-24.

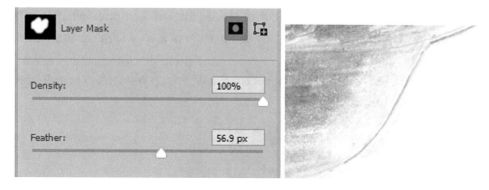

Figure 12-24. *Adjust Feather so that the mask becomes blurry and you can see a fuzzy edge*

Tip   Another way to add feathering to your mask is to use the Gradient tool to drag out a gradient, or you can also use the Filter ➤ Blur ➤ Gaussian Blur within the layer mask while it is selected. However, using the Feather option in the layer mask can create more refined Vignettes. Refer to Figure 12-25.

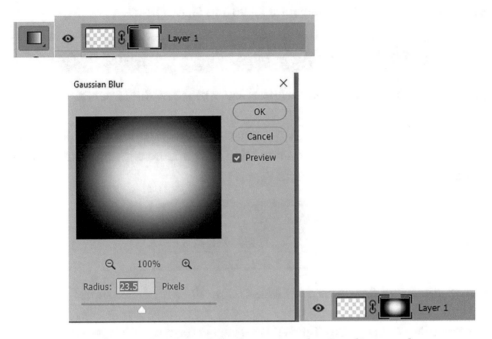

Figure 12-25. *Masks can be altered further using the Gradient tool or a Filter to blur*

The Properties panel for the mask also includes a **Refine** area. Refer to Figure 12-26.

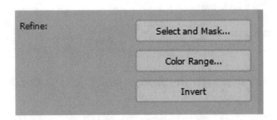

Figure 12-26. *The Properties panel layer mask Refine options*

Here you can enter the **Select and Mask** workspace to further refine your mask selection. Chapter 9 explains that it could be used for complex selections which involve

517

hair and fur. You can refer to that chapter if you need to review it. This time try applying a mask to a layer rather than a selection.

The Color Range button lets you enter its dialog box to create or alter a selection mask based on the selected colors. You can see more on that dialog box in Chapter 8.

Invert inverses the selection. Likewise, as you did in the Channels panel, you can Ctrl/Cmd+I on the mask, which creates the same effect. Click Invert again to change it back to the original state. Refer to Figure 12-26 and Figure 12-27.

Figure 12-27. *The inverted and original layer mask in the Layers panel*

At the bottom of the Properties panel, you can **Load Selection from Mask** while the mask is selected. You can do the same thing by Ctrl/Cmd clicking on the layer mask thumbnail in the Layers panel. Refer to Figure 12-28.

Figure 12-28. *Load Selection from Mask using the Properties panel*

Use Select ➤ Deselect (Ctrl/Cmd+D) to deselect the mask for now.

Apply Mask this applies the mask to the layer and merges it, thus removing anything surrounding the mask or the black area. Edit ➤ Undo (Ctrl/Cmd+Z) if you need to undo that step and keep the mask. Refer to Figure 12-29.

Figure 12-29. *Apply the Mask to the Image from the Properties panel*

Disable/Enable Mask This lets you turn the mask on and off so that you can see what it looks like before and after. Alternatively, you can access this option if you right-click the mask and choose from the pop-up menu. Refer to Figure 12-30

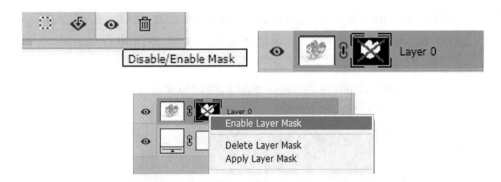

Figure 12-30. *Disable or enable the layer mask using the properties panel or right-click the layer mask*

Delete Mask this deletes the mask from the layer, but the layer remains. Edit ➤ Undo (Ctrl/Cmd+Z) if you need to undo that step and keep the mask. Refer to Figure 12-31.

Figure 12-31. *Delete the layer mask using the Properties panel*

The Properties panel menu also has a few additional mask and selection options. Refer to Figure 12-32.

Figure 12-32. *Options in the Properties panel menu*

- **Mask Options** lets you change the Layer Mask Display Options Color (via the Color Picker when clicking the color swatch) and Opacity. Refer to Figure 12-33.

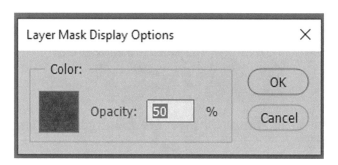

Figure 12-33. *Layer Mask Display Options dialog box*

If a selection is active while the mask layer is also active, you can use the following options.

- Add Mask to Selection

- Subtract Mask from Selection

- Intersect Mask with Selection

Note   These three options do not alter the mask. Only combine the mask and the new selection as a new selection. Refer to Figure 12-32.

Drag out an ellipse with the Elliptical Marquee tool. Make sure the layer mask is selected and choose **Add Mask to Selection**. Refer to Figure 12-34.

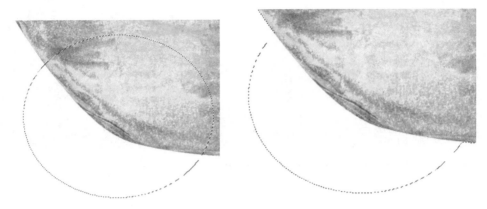

Figure 12-34. *Add Mask to Selection using the Properties panel*

While black is the foreground color in the Tools panel, press the Delete/Backspace key on your keyboard. This then adds to the current layer mask. Refer to Figure 12-35.

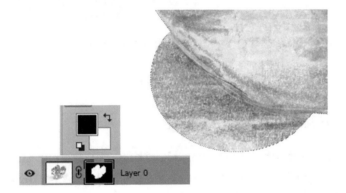

Figure 12-35. *The selection is added to the layer mask, and more of it is revealed, depending on the foreground color*

Edit ➤ Undo (Ctrl/Cmd+Z) if you need to undo that step and keep the original mask. Then Select ➤ Deselect (Ctrl/Cmd+D).

Moving and Copying Layer Masks

Masks can be dragged from one layer to another.

You can copy the mask to another layer if you hold down the Alt/Option key while dragging. You may want to do this with adjustment layers, for example, levels, where you want to affect the same region but alter the color.

Click Yes to replace the current mask in the adjustment layer. Refer to Figure 12-36.

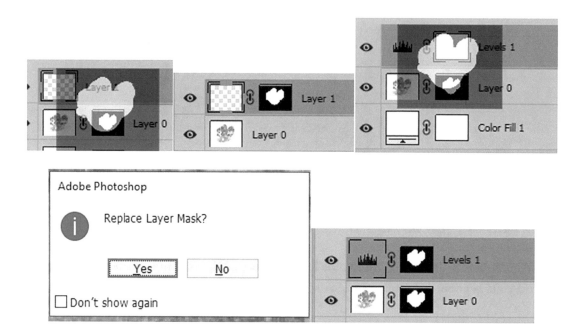

Figure 12-36. *Moving and copying layer masks from one layer to the next*

Save (Ctrl/Cmd+S) your document at this point.

Layer Mask on Adjustment Layers

Chapter 2 introduced adjustment layers and how they can clean up an entire sketch. However, until this point, you may not have been aware that you could alter the adjustment layer's layer mask as well.

Levels, Black & White, and Brightness/Contrast are useful for improving areas of your image in combination with blending modes. You can see how this knowledge could be very useful in the clean-up process in the transparent paper issue with the elephant from Chapter 2. Refer to Figure 12-37.

Open the elephant12_2.psd file and go to Image ➤ Duplicate to make a copy of it.

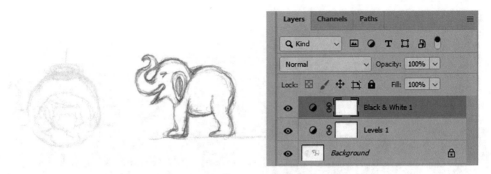

Figure 12-37. *The elephant sketch has some of the reverse image appearing on the left. I can only remove some of it using the adjustment layers*

In this case, I used adjustment layers to clean up the elephant as best as I could. Some of the the vase on the reverse side of the paper still showed through. I intended to keep the elephant's midtone grays, but I can only move the siders so far without affecting the vase's visibility. I could create a new blank layer, use the Brush tool, and cover it with white paint, or fill a selection with white using Edit ➤ Fill. However, let's try something else.

Use the elliptical marquee tool to drag an ellipse around the faded vase. Refer to Figure 12-38.

Figure 12-38. *An elliptical marquee around the reverse vase image*

Then from the Layers panel, choose a solid color fill layer. Refer to Figure 12-39.

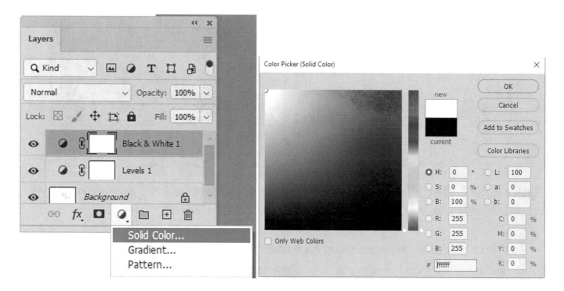

Figure 12-39. *Use the Layers panel to add a solid color fill adjustment layer*

Change the color in the color picker to white and click OK.

This covers the vase, and you can use the solid fill/color fill of white. Refer to Figure 12-40.

Figure 12-40. *Solid Color Fill 1 is added as a mask to the layer to hide the vase*

Paint with the Brush tool over any other stray lines you want to cover using the layer mask. Refer to Figure 12-41.

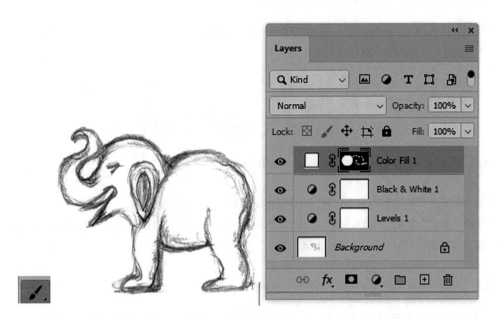

Figure 12-41. *Paint on your mask to reveal or show areas of the sketch*

You can then return to your levels 1 adjustment layer. In the Properties panel, darken the lines further if you need to by moving the shadow slider. Refer to Figure 12-42.

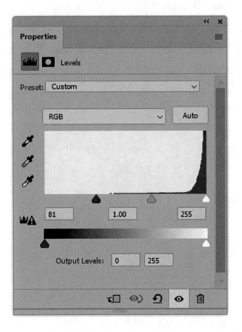

Figure 12-42. *Make adjustments to the levels in the Properties panel to darken the lines*

Use your Layers panel menu to flatten the image at this point if you need to or leave all the Layers intact. Refer to Figure 12-43.

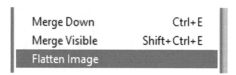

Figure 12-43. *Layers panel menu options*

You can see how this looks in my elephant12_2_final.psd file.

When you use a mask with brushes, you can clean one area. These changes apply to the adjustment layer.

Gutter Shadow and Adjustment Layers with Masks

With the ability to alter the mask, you can decide which areas need more color correction than others. A good example is with black-and-white drawings where you need to remove unneeded colors like yellows, or gutter shadows, that may be part of the Line drawing.

Look at my original scanned sketch from Chapter 6.

Open the scan12_3.psd file and look at the changes I made.

The original had a bad gutter shadow on the left that you can see with only the background layer turned on. Refer to Figure 12-44.

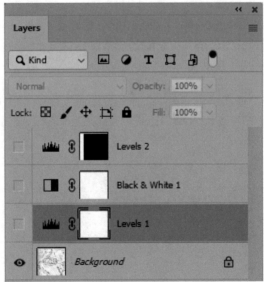

Figure 12-44. *This original image had some yellowing and gutter shadow issues*

However, as I added the Levels and Black & White adjustment layers, the image started to improve and was not as yellow, but there were still some remnants of the gutter shadow on the left. Refer to Figure 12-45.

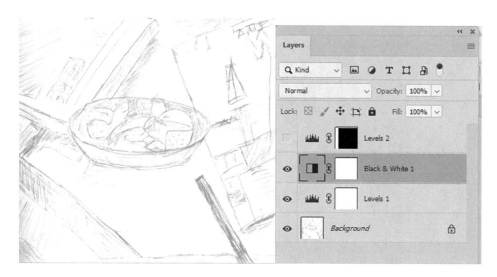

Figure 12-45. *Adjustment layers can help in correcting sketches, but sometimes one adjusment layer is not enough*

To correct this, I then dragged out a rectangle using the Rectangular Marquee tool on the left side of the sketch to where I felt the darkness began and ended. Refer to Figure 12-46.

Figure 12-46. *Use your Rectangular Marquee tool to create a selection for your adjustment layer*

From the Layers panel, I added another levels adjustment layer. It became levels 2, and this time moved the sliders for the RGB and output levels in the Properties panel until I felt that it blended in with the rest of the image and removed the gutter shadow. Refer to Figure 12-47.

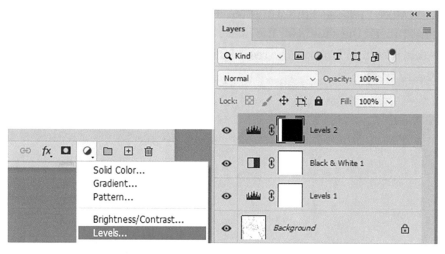

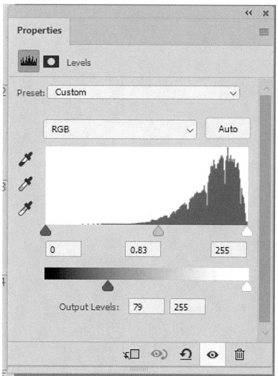

Figure 12-47. *Adding another adjustment layer or level creates an altered mask so that only the selected area can be altered using the Properties panel*

You can see how this blends in shadows better into lighter and darker areas. Remember, your sketches may differ from mine, so you may need to use other adjustment layers or different shaped selections to further clean up your gutter shadows, but the principles are still the same. Separate Selections on different adjustment layers assist in refining your artwork. You may need to change the blending modes or opacity of the adjustment layers to get the seamless results you want. Refer to Figure 12-48.

Figure 12-48. *The gutter shadow is barely noticeable and now blends in with the rest of my sketch*

Once I cleaned up the gutter, I added a solid color fill of white and then clicked the Invert button in the Properties panel to change the layer mask to black. Refer to Figure 12-49.

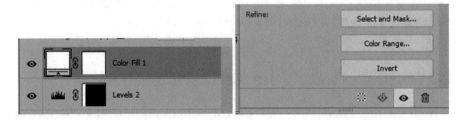

Figure 12-49. *Use the white color fill and click Invert to invert the mask*

Then I painted on the layer mask with the Brush tool to clean it up further. Refer to Figure 12-50.

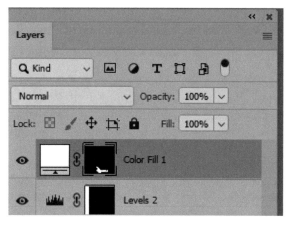

Figure 12-50. *Painting in white using the Color Fill adjustment layer covered up additional smudges on my image that I wanted to remove*

Removing Some Lines with Adjustment Layers and Masks

In the case of lines from lined paper with the cat, you may only want to remove the lines within the cat as you did in Chapter 2, but this time not the lines surrounding it.

Again, a layer mask on the Black & White layer could help you do that, as you can see in the cat12_4_final.psd file. Refer to Figure 12-51.

Figure 12-51. *Painting on the Black& White adjustment layer mask allowed me to keep the lines out of the cat and have them only appear around the cat*

Colorize with Masks and Adjustment Layers

In other situations, other adjustment layers such as Curves, Exposure, Hue/Saturation, Channel Mixer, or Selective Color may be equally as helpful.

For example, Hue/Saturation is very useful if you need to re-colorize an area of a picture as you did with the boat in Chapter 8.

Look at the scan12_4_final.psd file. I completed it, but you can follow these steps in another file.

Once you have a selection, use the Color Range dialog box instead of painting on a normal layer, choose the **Hue/Saturation** adjustment layer, and turn the selection into a mask. Refer to Figure 12-52.

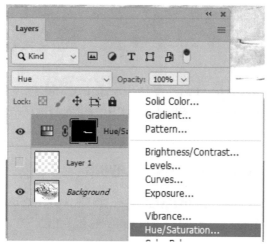

Figure 12-52. *Use the Hue/Saturation adjustment layer to colorize a selection and add the selection to the adjustment layer*

Enable the Colorize option in the Properties panel, moving the Hue, Saturation, and Lightness sliders until you get the color you want. Refer to Figure 12-53.

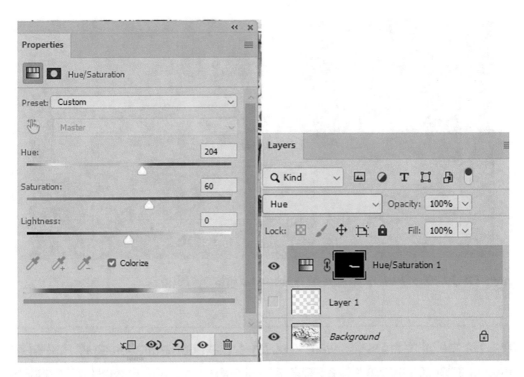

Figure 12-53. *Enable Colorize in the Properties panel Hue/Saturation to alter the color of only that area of the mask and change the blending mode*

Then set the adjustment layers Blending mode to Hue. Refer to Figure 12-53.

Later you can then alter the mask with your Brush tool or Eraser tool if you have any other areas you need to color with a similar hue. Refer to Figure 12-54.

Figure 12-54. *The hull of the boat is now a different blue*

Tip   For the other areas you want to colorize, use Hue/Saturation again, but with a different selection turned into a mask, and choose a different hue using the sliders in the Properties panel.

Besides Solid Color Fill, using **Gradient**, **Pattern**, and **Gradient Map**, let you access the Gradient and Patterns panels. Rather than using the Paint Bucket and the Gradient tool, I find that fill and adjustment layers in combination with masks are non-destructive and may be better when you need to quickly manipulate or change the pattern or gradient options. If you are creating comic book art and want to incorporate a pattern or a gradient into your design, I recommend alternative options. Refer to Figure 12-55.

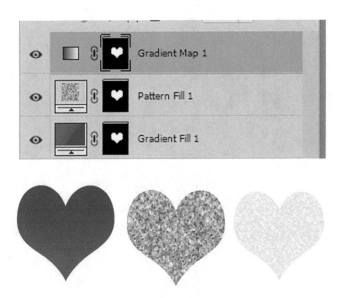

Figure 12-55. *You can alter your layer masks and selections with gradients and patterns using fill and adjustment layers*

Clipping Masks and Adjustment Layers

In some situations, cleaning up one area of a sketch may unintentionally affect the colors in another area of the sketch. In these situations, a *clipping mask* is applied to a separate area of the scan to better blend it might be required. However, you may or may not need to paint on the mask itself.

You can see an example of how that looks from an original file I used to create my collection of cat sketches in Chapter 9. Refer to Figure 12-56.

Open the scan12_5_final.psd file.

Figure 12-56. *Separate scans were made of each cat Image and then complied into one Photoshop (.psd) document*

Here you can see multiple clipping masks adjusted the levels for each cat layer separately. Then I applied an overall Black & White adjustment layer to adjust the overall coloring. Refer to Figure 12-57.

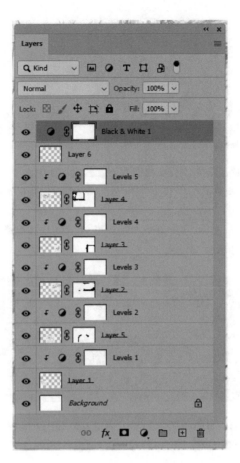

Figure 12-57. *The Layers panel contains many levels of adjustment layer clipping masks for each image*

Apply a clipping mask in your own projects when an adjustment layer with a layer mask is selected. Alt/Option-click between it and the lower layer. Alternatively, while the adjustment layer is selected from the main menu, choose Layer ➤ Create Clipping Mask (Alt/Option+Ctrl/Cmd+G). Refer to Figure 12-58.

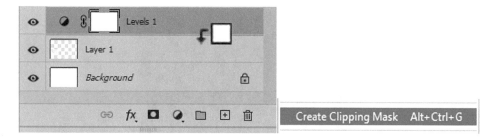

Figure 12-58. *Enable a clipping mask in the Layers panel and notice how the pointer changes between the layers when Alt/Option is pressed before clicking*

To release, Alt/Option-click between the two layers, or choose Layer ➤ Release Clipping Mask. Refer to Figure 12-59.

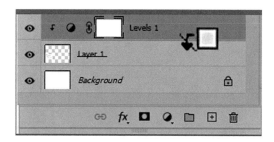

Figure 12-59. *Disable a clipping mask in the Layers panel notice how the pointer changes between the layers when Alt/Option is pressed before clicking*

A clipping mask applies only that adjustment to that area of the layer and not over other sketches on other layers. Refer to Figure 12-60.

Later a Black & White adjustment layer was applied overall to remove any yellowing. Refer to Figure 12-56 and Figure 12-57.

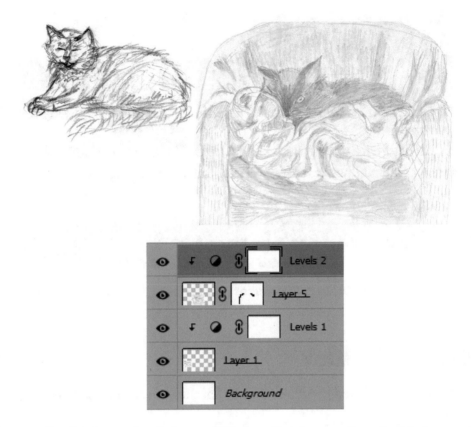

Figure 12-60. *Each cat sketch has a different clipping mask so that it does not alter the levels of the other layer and darken or lighten another image too much*

Note   In the Properties panel, there are no additional settings for a clipping mask.

Vector Mask

A *vector mask* can also be added to the same layer. They can be linked or unlinked. Refer to Figure 12-61.

Figure 12-61. *Add a vector mask to the layer in the layer in the Layers panel*

If you Ctrl/Cmd-click the mask icon in the Layers panel, you can add a blank to the vector mask without adding the layer mask first. Refer to Figure 12-62.

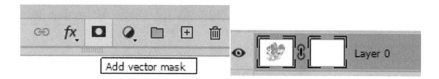

Figure 12-62. *If you want to add a vector mask, Ctrl/Cmd on the mask icon*

Adding A Vector Mask

Open the scan12_1_finished.psd file and make another copy (Image ➤ Duplicate) to work on again.

This time in the Paths panel, select the apples path. Now click the **Add a vector mask** icon in the Layers panel. Refer to Figure 12-63.

Figure 12-63. *Use the Paths panel with a selected path and then the Layers panel to add the vector mask*

Or you can create the vector mask from a selected path in the Paths panel. From the menu, choose Layer ➤ Vector Mask ➤ Current Path. Refer to Figure 12-64.

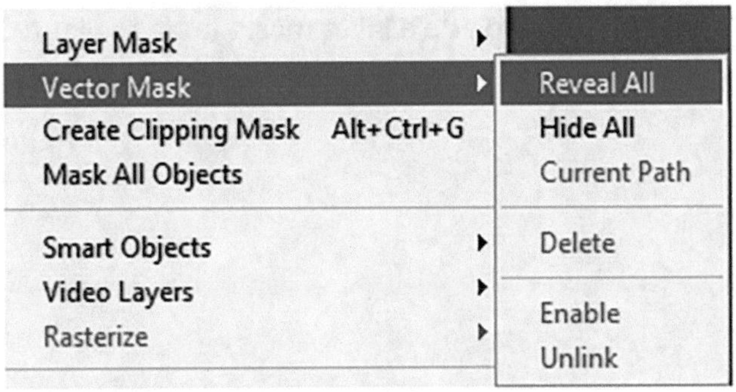

Figure 12-64. *Use the Layer menu to add a vector path*

Note   Reveal All create a blank vector mask and Hide All a blank inverse vector mask, both not based on any selected path. Refer to Figures 12-64 and 12-65.

Figure 12-65. *Reveal All or Hide All options for a vector mask*

To see how the vector mask properties work, I right-click and disable the layer mask. Refer to Figure 12-66.

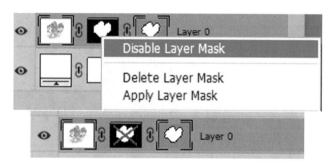

Figure 12-66. *Disable the layer mask on layer 0 by right-clicking on it and choosing the option from the pop-up menu*

Vector Mask Properties

The Properties panel contains the settings for the vector mask. If only the vector mask is present, then you have the option to add a layer mask. Refer to Figure 12-67.

Figure 12-67. *Vector Mask options and menu*

Vector masks are path-based and produce cleaner selections. However, you can still adjust their density and feathering, but you do not have access to the Refine section.

The Density slider affects the area surrounding the path. It has the same range as a layer mask. Refer to Figure 12-68.

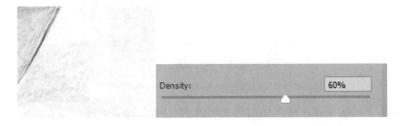

Figure 12-68. *Adjust the density of a vector mask in the Properties panel*

The Feathering slider affects the inside of the selection. It does not go far beyond the border of the path. By default, it is set to 0 pixels and has the same range as a layer mask. Refer to Figure 12-69.

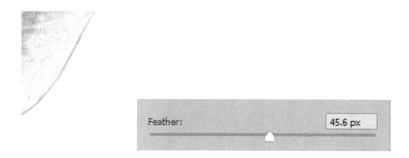

Figure 12-69. *Adjust the Feather of a vector mask in the Properties panel*

You can also **load**, **apply**, **enable/disable**, and **delete** a vector mask as you did a layer mask using the options and the bottom of the Properties panel. Refer to Figure 12-67.

Edit a Vector Mask

Like a layer mask, a vector mask can also be **added**, **subtracted**, and **intersected** with a current active selection using the Properties panel menu. Make sure Vector Mask is selected before you choose this option.

Drag a rectangular marquee over the base of the bowl with the vector path selected. Refer to Figure 12-67 and Figure 12-70.

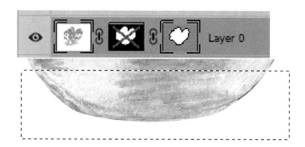

Figure 12-70. *Drag out a rectangular marquee while the vector mask is selected*

From the Properties panel menu, choose Add Vector Mask to Selection. Refer to Figure 12-71.

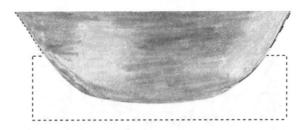

Figure 12-71. *Add vector mask to selection*

To add this selection to create a new path, in the Paths panel, click **Make work path from selection**. Refer to Figure 12-72.

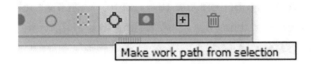

Figure 12-72. *In the Paths panel, while the selection is active, click Make work path from selection*

Drag the current vector mask on layer 0 to the **Delete vector mask** icon (trash can) in the Layers panel. Click OK to confirm the warning message. Refer to Figure 12-73.

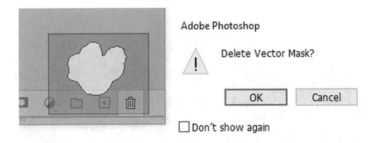

Figure 12-73. *Delete the current Vector Path from layer 0 in the Layers panel and click OK to the warning*

Select the newly drawn work path in the Paths panel. Refer to Figure 12-74.

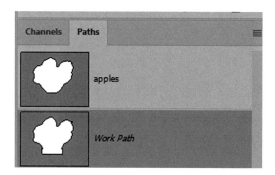

Figure 12-74. *Select the work path in the Paths panel*

Select any Shape or Pen tool from the Tools panel. With the tool mode of the path selected in the options panel, click the Mask button to add the new vector mask to the layer (layer 0). Refer to Figure 12-75.

Figure 12-75. *Use a Shape tool to add a new Vector Mask to layer 0*

Inverse a Vector Mask

Can a vector mask be inversed? Notice that the Refine: Invert button is not available when a vector path is selected in the Properties panel. Refer to Figure 12-76.

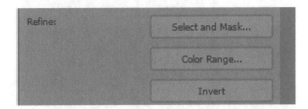

Figure 12-76. *In the Refine area in the Properties panel, the Invert button is disabled for the vector mask*

To invert, you must first inverse the path before you apply it as a vector mask.

While the current vector mask is selected and present in the Paths panel, click the Load path as a selection icon in the Paths panel. Refer to Figure 12-77.

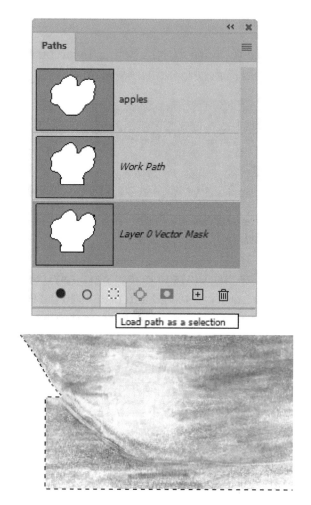

Figure 12-77. *Load the vector mask path as a selection from the Paths panel*

To inverse the selection choose Select ➤ Inverse (Shift+Ctrl/Cmd+I).

Then in the Paths panel, click the **Make work path from selection** icon. Refer to Figure 12-78.

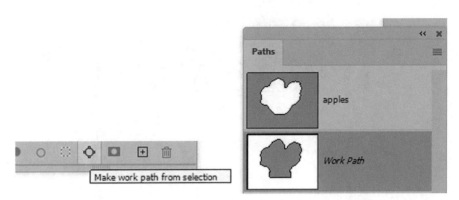

Figure 12-78. *From the Paths panel, choose to make work path from selection to create the inverse path*

In the Layers panel, drag the current layers vector mask to the **Delete vector mask** icon. Click OK for any message. Refer to Figure 12-79.

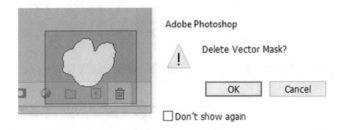

Figure 12-79. *Delete the current vector path on layer 0 and click OK to the warning*

Click a Shape or Pen tool in the Tools panel. With the tool mode of the path selected, click the Mask button. Refer to Figure 12-80.

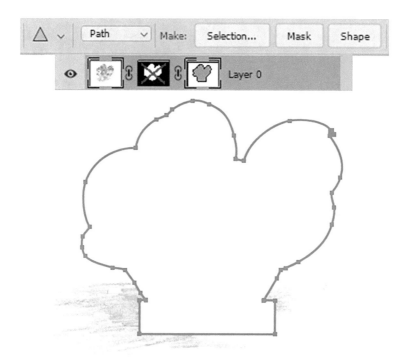

Figure 12-80. *Use a Shape tool to turn the inverse path into a vector mask*

You now have an inverse vector mask, and only the surrounding is visible.

To return to your original vector mask at the beginning of the section.

Delete the inverse vector mask you created on layer 0 and add the selected apples path as a vector mask. Refer to Figure 12-81.

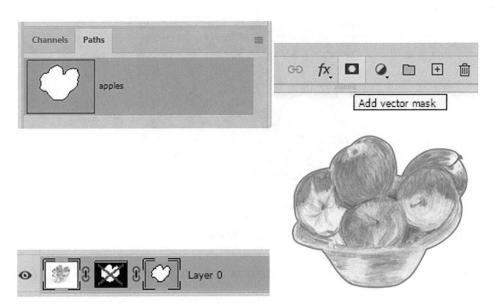

Figure 12-81. *Add the original apples path back to layer 0 as a vector mask using the Paths and Layers panels*

As with other paths, you can use your Path Selection tool and Direct Selection tools to alter the vector mask while the mask's path is selected. Refer to Chapter 10 on how to use these tools. Refer to Figure 12-82.

Figure 12-82. *Path Selection and Direct Selection tools can alter a vector mask path*

A vector mask can also be a clipping mask and be applied to adjustment layers. Refer to Figure 12-83.

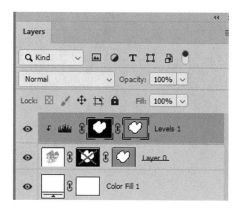

Figure 12-83. *Adjustment layers can use vector paths as well*

Save the document. You can see my final example in scan12_1_finished2.psd.

Vector Masks and Fill Adjustment Layers

If you apply a vector mask for solid color, gradient, or pattern fills, the layer becomes a shape layer, but keeps the adjustment layer name and layer mask. Refer to Figure 12-84.

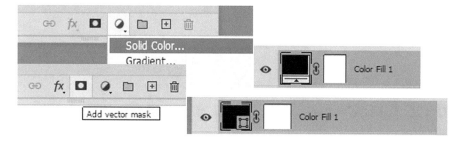

Figure 12-84. *Adding a vector mask to a solid color fill turns it into a shape layer with a layer mask*

Shape Layers

As with fill adjustment layers, for shape layers, only the thumbnail image, which is vector shape, and the layer mask are available. Refer to Figure 12-84.

554

Applying Masks to Group, Folders, Type Layers, and Smart Object Layers

While not relevant to the topic, group folders, type layers, and Smart Object layers can also have vector and layer masks applied for non-destructive editing. A group folder allows you to keep several layers together and apply one layer mask and/or a vector mask to them collectively. The layers within the group folder can have separate masks as well. A new feature for version 2022 allows you create a group folder from a selection when you choose from the Layers Panel or Layer ➤ Mask All Objects. It will generate masks for all the objects detected within your layer with just a single click. You can then add your layers to the folder. Refer to Figure 12-85.

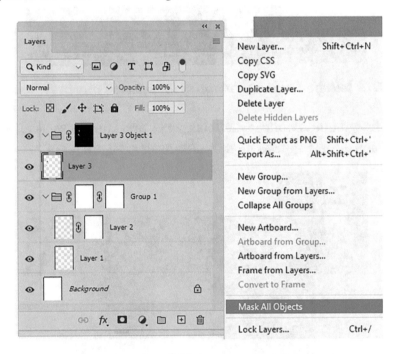

Figure 12-85. *Group Folder with Layer and Vector Masks in the Layers Panel*

From Chapter 6, remember that you can use your Horizontal and Vertical Type tools to create a Type selection. Refer to Figure 12-86.

Click and type on a selected layer mask.

Figure 12-86. *Use a Type Mask tool to add text to a mask*

Then confirm the selection by clicking the Commit button in the options panel. Refer to Figure 12-87.

Figure 12-87. *A selection appears on top of the selected mask*

While the foreground is white in the Tools panel, press the Backspace/Delete key on the keyboard, and the text appears on the mask. Refer to Figure 12-88.

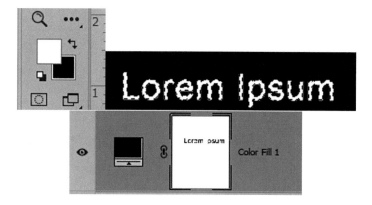

Figure 12-88. *This makes the text become a mask, and you can see the background layer of white through the letters*

If you want to learn more about **Smart Object layers** and **Smart Filters** and how they can assist you with non-destructive scaling and masks, check out https://helpx.adobe.com/photoshop/using/create-smart-objects.html.

With the altered copy of the images you have created so far, from the Layers panel, choose Flatten Image and then make sure that the sketches are saved either in a .psd or .tiff file format. This reduces their file size. Then you can continue to work with sketches in Illustrator starting in Chapter 13. Refer to Figure 12-89.

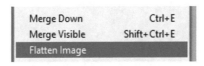

Figure 12-89. *Flatten Images to save file space that you plan to trace over in Illustrator*

Summary

This chapter looked at how selections can be turned into layer masks, vector masks, and clipping masks. Using normal layers and adjustment layers, you modified those masks using your Brush tool or Eraser tool. Now that you know more about creating selections and refining your artwork, it's time to move on to Adobe Illustrator and turn your sketches into vector artwork.

CHAPTER 13

Placing Your Artwork into Illustrator

Once you clean up a Photoshop file, you are ready to place it into Illustrator. In this chapter, I demonstrate how to do that.

The previous chapters focused on cleaning up artwork in Photoshop. You have worked with my files or your own to remove unwanted areas of your drawing, whether through cropping or using a selection and related tools to control where your brush, eraser, or clone stamps appear on various layers.

In some situations, you may want to print your artwork from Photoshop. However, there may be other situations where you want to trace your artwork to vectorize it and scale it to another size. This and the following chapters show you how that is done in Adobe Illustrator. Refer to Figure 13-1.

Figure 13-1. *Adobe Illustrator app in the Creative Cloud Desktop console*

If you have a Creative Cloud subscription, then along with Photoshop, you should have access to this app. If using the Creative Cloud Desktop console, make sure that you have installed the most recent version of the program. Currently, I am using Adobe Illustrator CC 2022 or (Version 26). Refer to Figure 13-2.

© Jennifer Harder 2022
J. Harder, *Accurate Layer Selections Using Photoshop's Selection Tools*,
https://doi.org/10.1007/978-1-4842-7493-4_13

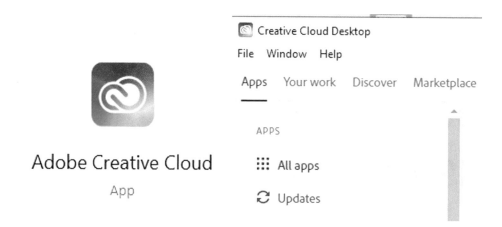

Figure 13-2. *Locate your Adobe Illustrator application in the Creative Cloud Desktop console*

Also, if you are not sure whether you can or cannot run Illustrator on your computer, then make sure to check out the system requirements at `https://helpx.adobe.com/illustrator/system-requirements.html`.

Once Adobe Illustrator is installed from your Creative Cloud console, click the Open button to run the application. Refer to Figure 13-1.

This book focuses on specific tools and panels in Adobe Illustrator as they relate to modifying sketches. Refer to my other books and related videos if you need additional information on working in Illustrator for general purposes or on websites.

- ***Graphics and Multimedia for the Web with Adobe Creative Cloud*** (Apress, 2018)
  `https://link.springer.com/book/10.1007/978-1-4842-3823-3`

- **Illustrator Path Finder Effects** (2020)
  `https://link.springer.com/video/10.1007/978-1-4842-6581-9`

- **Introduction to 3D Design with Adobe Photoshop and Illustrator** (2019)
  `https://link.springer.com/video/10.1007/978-1-4842-5396-0`

- **Introduction to Color Theory with Photoshop and Illustrator** (2019)
  `https://link.springer.com/video/10.1007/978-1-4842-4974-1`

Note   A few settings have changed since the video was created for some panels, but it does give a basic overview of working in Illustrator with color.

- **Introduction to Adobe's CC Libraries in Illustrator and InDesign** (2020)
  https://link.springer.com/video/10.1007/978-1-4842-6092-0

Note   This video is part 2 of the one mentioned in Chapter 2. There have been a few changes since the libraries were introduced, but the provides information on how to work with graphic assets in Illustrator.

Creating a Document

Once Illustrator opens, you are presented with your recent and past projects. However, if you have never created a project in Illustrator before, click the **New file** button or File ➤ New (Ctrl/Cmd+N) from the main menu. Refer to Figure 13-3.

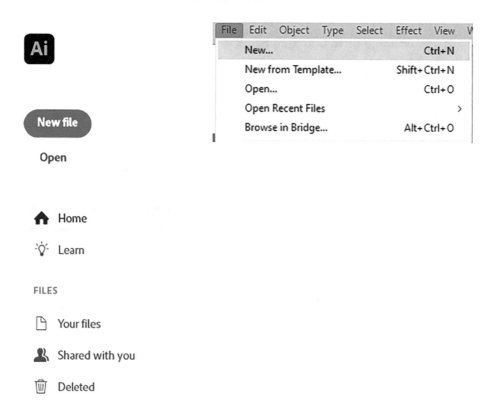

Figure 13-3. *Create a new document when you open Adobe Illustrator*

The New Document dialog box opens. Refer to Figure 13-4.

Figure 13-4. *New Document dialog box in Adobe Illustrator*

Across the top are various preset option tabs: Recent, Saved, Mobile, Web, Print, Film and Video, Art, and Illustrator.

For my portfolio, I generally choose the **Print** Setting and then choose the blank document Preset of **Letter** 612×792 pt. Refer to Figure 13-5.

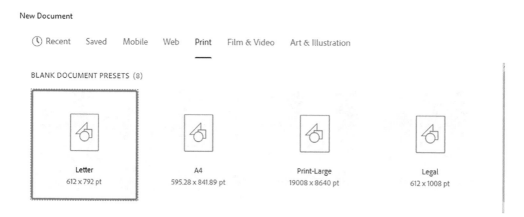

Figure 13-5. *The New Document Letter preset*

This places the preset details on the right-hand side for an Untitled document.

I keep the default settings. However, for your project, you can always make the artboard larger by adjusting the width and height to whatever paper size your printer is using, or choose a different blank document preset on the left.

Note   If you see the units of measurement are in points, you can change them to Inches in the drop-down next to the width field. As well, there are other units of measurement options such as centimeters and pixels. Refer to Figure 13-6.

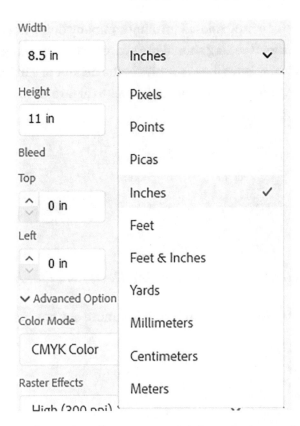

Figure 13-6. *Change the units of measurement from points to inches*

You can also choose whether you want the artboard's orientation to be **Portrait** or **Landscape** and the number of **artboards**, which I leave at 1 for this file. Refer to Figure 13-7.

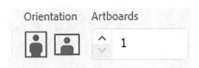

Figure 13-7. *Set the document orientation and the number of artboards*

Note   While you can have multiple artboards for various projects in one file during drawing or tracing, this can sometimes, for a beginner, be confusing to know which artboard you stored a graphic on. I usually start with one artboard, and if I need another, I can always add it later after the document is created.

If you are working for a professional printing company doing document layout work, you may need to set a **Bleed** setting should the artwork go off the edge of the page.

However, for this work, leave these settings at the default of 0 in for the top, bottom, left, and right, and keep the link icon enabled. Refer to Figure 13-8.

Figure 13-8. *Bleed settings at default in New Document dialog box*

In the **Advanced Options** area, you have a few more options. Refer to Figure 13-9.

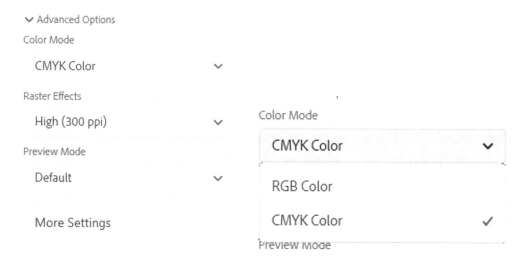

Figure 13-9. *Advanced Options in the New Document dialog box for Color mode*

- **Color Mode**: The print default is CMYK Color. You can change this to RGB Color if your focus is not print.

- **Raster Effects**: You want to make sure that the quality of the artwork is at least 300 ppi (pixels per inch) for print and tracing, so keep the setting at High (300 ppi) should there be any rasterized graphics on your artboard. However, for your work, you may want a lower setting of Medium (150 ppi), Screen (72 ppi), or 36 ppi. Refer to Figure 13-10.

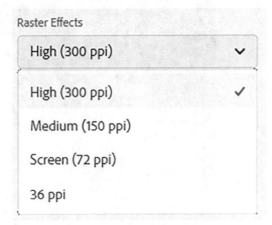

Figure 13-10. *Raster Effects*

- **Preview Mode**: Keep it at the default for creating vector artwork. Other options include Pixel and Overprint. Refer to Figure 13-11.

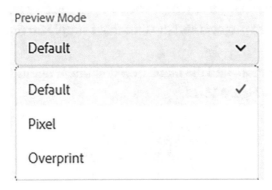

Figure 13-11. *Preview Mode*

- **More Settings**: The same settings as the New Document dialog box. It also allows you to organize multiple artboards. You can ignore that button and just click **Cancel** if you open the dialog box. Refer to Figure 13-12.

More Settings

Name: Untitled-2

Profile: [Custom]

Number of Artboards: 1

Spacing: 0.2778 in   Columns: 1

Size: Letter

Width: 8.5 in   Units: Inches

Height: 11 in   Orientation:

	Top	Bottom	Left	Right
Bleed:	0 in	0 in	0 in	0 in

▼ Advanced

Color Mode: CMYK

Raster Effects: High (300 ppi)

Preview Mode: Default

Templates...   Create Document   Cancel

Figure 13-12. *More Settings*

While Illustrator has many free templates, and you can buy from Adobe Stock, this book focuses on our own projects and the files that I supply for the chapters. Refer to Figure 13-4.

Click the **Create** button, and the blank new document opens with the assigned preset settings. Refer to Figure 13-13.

Figure 13-13. *Click the Create button to create your new document with prests*

Setting up the Workspace

As in Photoshop, it's good to set up a workspace here to have all the tools and panels you need while you work. I generally use the **Essentials Classic** workspace in the menu bar or Window ➤ Workspace ➤ Essentials Classic. Refer to Figure 13-14.

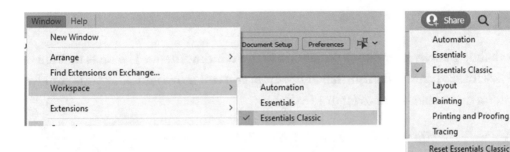

Figure 13-14. *Choose your workspace so that you have all the panels and tools you require*

Note If you have used Essentials Classic, you may have altered it. So, from the Workspace menu choose, **Reset Essentials Classic** so that it looks Figure 13-15.

Figure 13-15. *The layout of the Essentials Classic workspace in Illustrator*

You are modifying the workspace to add some additional panels, so you can always create a **New Workspace** based on these changes afterward. Refer to Figure 13-14.

Panels

Like Photoshop panels, Illustrator's panels are in the Window menu. The ones that are currently visible are checked. Also, like Photoshop, you can move and dock your panels to keep them organized. Refer to Figure 13-16.

Figure 13-16. *Access all the panels from the Window menu, and you can dock them on the right*

Next, let's go over the main panels.

Control

The Control panel bar is very similar to the options panel bar across the top in Photoshop. However, it only changes or alters its control options when a new selected shape, path, or object is present. Most tool options in Illustrator are in the Properties panel. Refer to Figure 13-17.

Figure 13-17. *The Control panel changes as different objects are selected*

Toolbars

The Toolbars panel features the Essentials Classic workspace, which gives you access to all the tools. This is what I prefer. Many of the tools are hidden in other workspaces, but they can be accessed from the dotted ellipse **Edit Toolbar** button at the bottom of the Toolbars panel. Refer to Figure 13-18.

***Figure 13-18.** Many tools are available in the Toolbars panel*

I click the top of the panel's right-pointing double arrows to see the options as two columns rather than a single column. Refer to Figure 13-19.

Figure 13-19. *Make the Toolbars panel two-column by clicking the upper arrows*

In the Window menu, I set this panel to **Advanced** to ensure that all the tools are present. Refer to Figure 13-20.

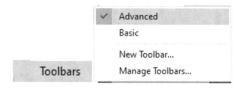

Figure 13-20. *Toolbars settings in the Window menu*

Let's look at some essential tools for tracing later in the chapter and others in the following chapters. There are other Essentials Classic workspace panels that you may use, depending on what you are trying to accomplish.

For the initial placement of your sketches, you could use layers.

Layers

The Layers panel is for placing through linking or embedding your .tiff or .psd file on the artboard and keeping your paths and sketches organized.

The panel allows you to place your sketches and objects on a layer or sublayer. Layers can be locked to prevent movement while working on other layers. Likewise, you can move your objects from one layer to the next, create additional layers, name your layers, and delete layers. On a layer, you can select single, multiple, or grouped objects. You look at many of these panel options in more detail as you work on various projects in this chapter and later chapters. Refer to Figure 13-21.

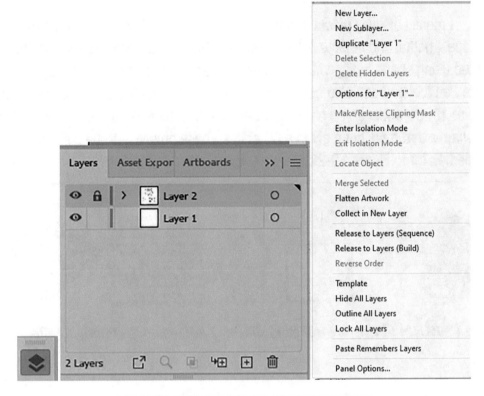

Figure 13-21. *Layers panel collapsed and open, Layers panel menu, and Layer Options dialog box*

Note   I mostly discuss placed Photoshop **sketches** in this chapter. Later you look at shapes, paths, and objects. When I refer to **shapes**, I am talking about paths created using shape tools, which you see in Chapter 15. **Paths** are also created by the Pen tool and can also be irregular shapes with anchor points, also noted in Chapter 15. **Objects** can be paths, but they can also be in references to text boxes and shapes that have been given a 3D effect. These objects can be collectively grouped. Refer to Figure 13-22.

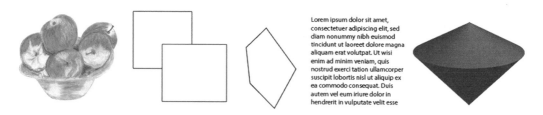

Figure 13-22. In Illustrator, a sketch, shapes, path, text object with 3D effect

Links

Choose Window ➤ Links if you do not see this panel in your workspace. The Links panel allows you to choose whether you are working with linked or embedded images that you plan to Image Trace or trace over with your Pen tools, as you see in Chapters 14 and 15. Refer to Figure 13-23.

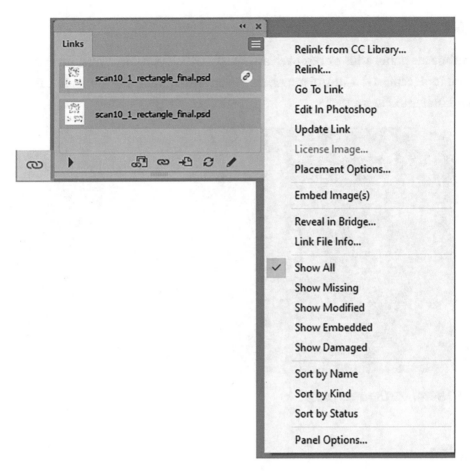

Figure 13-23. *Links panel menu and embedded file*

Note   Linking Photoshop files to an Illustrator file keeps the Illustrator file small. However, if you move the Photoshop file, it can become unlinked upon opening. Embedding the Photoshop files within the Illustrator file can help you avoid broken links, but it does increase the Illustrator's file size, and it makes it more awkward to update the sketch if you go back and make a change.

Artboards

The Artboards panel adds or removes artboards, which you can adjust further using the Artboard tool (Shift+O), Control panel, and Properties panel. Currently, this file has one artboard. Refer to Figure 13-24.

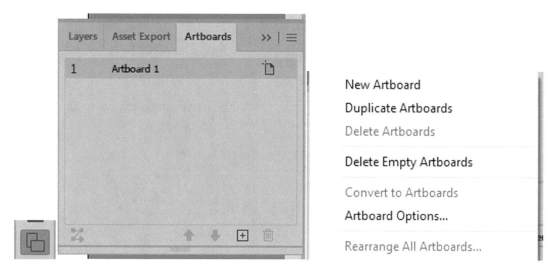

Figure 13-24. *Artboards panel*

Libraries

As with Photoshop, you can use the Libraries panel to import or export sketches and graphic assets that you may have stored in Creative Cloud Library files and move them from one app to the other. If you need to learn more on that topic, you can check out the video that I mentioned earlier. Refer to Figure 13-25.

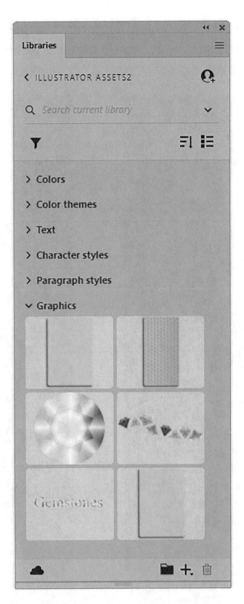

Figure 13-25. *The Libraries panel contains many assets, and some may come from Photoshop*

Properties

The Properties panel often combines other Window panels while working on a selected image sketch, path, or object. In some situations, it functions like the Properties panel in Photoshop. However, when certain tools are selected, it acts more like Photoshop's options panel. In addition, at the bottom of the panel, it supplies various **Quick Actions** buttons so that you do not have to hunt through the main menu to do a basic task quickly. Refer to Figure 13-26.

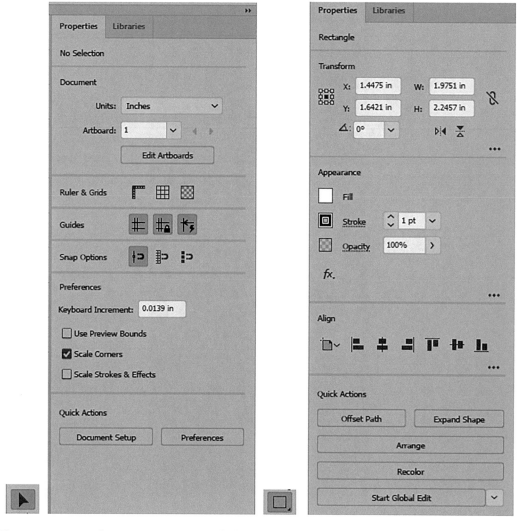

Figure 13-26. *The Properties panel changes as you select or draw with various tools*

Once you have created paths and shape objects beside the Control and Properties panel, you can use the following other panels to assist you with your vector artwork. Remember that the Properties panel often combines these following panels when a shape or path is selected.

Color

The Color panel allows you to color objects that are selected. You select a color using an eyedropper tool or slider if Show Options from the menu is activated. Refer to Figure 13-27.

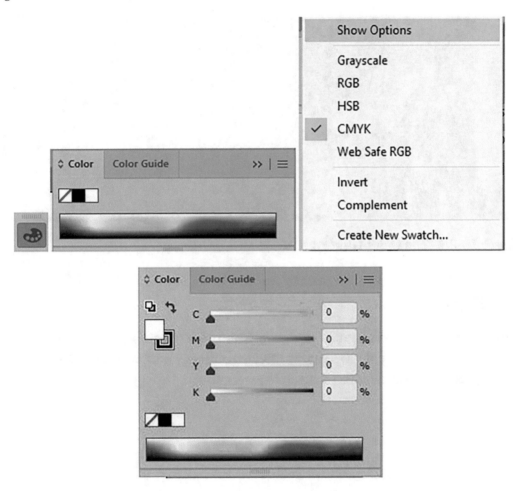

Figure 13-27. *The Color panel with menu and options*

From this panel, you can also choose other color spaces and make minor color adjustments and create swatches for the Swatches panel.

Color Guide

The Color Guide panel allows you to modify your color or colors using various harmonies or color themes that it creates. I investigate this tool in more depth in my Introduction to Color Theory video and in Chapter 17. Refer to Figure 13-28.

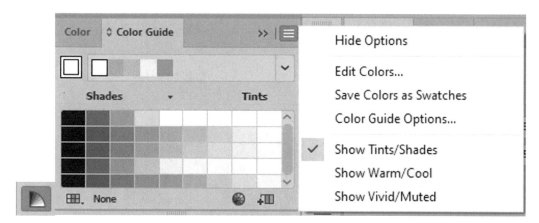

Figure 13-28. *The Color Guide panel*

Swatches

The Swatches panel stores swatches, gradients, and patterns that you can use to modify your artwork. You can apply swatches to selected objects. Additional Swatches are stored in the Window ➤ Swatch Libraries. Refer to Figure 13-29

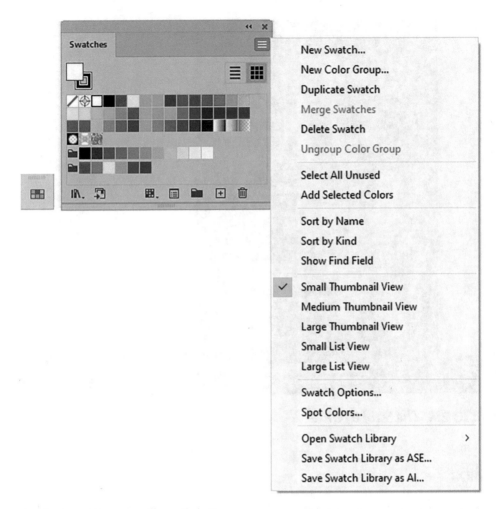

Figure 13-29. *The Swatches panel*

Strokes

While you can stroke your selected paths with a color, gradient, or pattern, the Strokes panel allows you to adjust the weight of the stroke, cap, corner, limit, and alignment on the path. The stroke can be dashed or have arrowheads added to the start and endpoints, which can be scaled and aligned. You can also alter the profile of the line in this panel or the Control panel. If you want to see more or fewer options, you can change this setting in the Stroke panel's menu by selecting Show/Hide options. Refer to Figure 13-30 and Chapter 16 for more details on strokes.

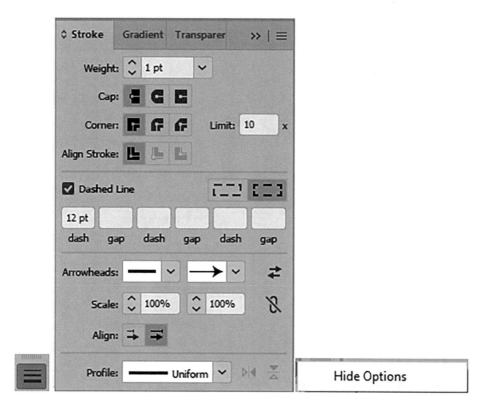

Figure 13-30. *The Stroke panel*

Brushes

Stroked paths can be further altered by selecting a different brush from the Brushes panel. Lines can be more exact or like Photoshop brush strokes. These brushes fall into different categories: Calligraphic, Scatter, Art, Bristle, and Pattern. Extra brushes are stored in the Window ➤ Brush Libraries. Refer to Figure 13-31 and Chapter 16 for more details on brushes.

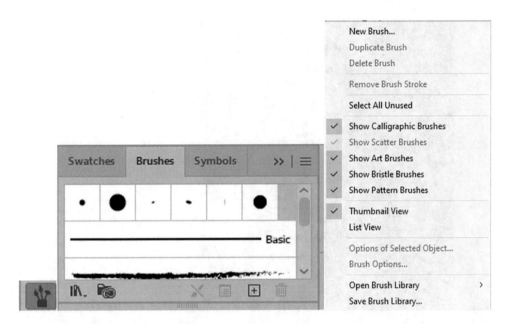

Figure 13-31. *The Brushes panel*

Gradient

The Gradient panel adds various gradients— linear, radial, and free-form—to the object and paths that are altered with the Gradient tool (G). You can access your saved gradients from the Swatches panel, and additional gradients are in Window ➤ Swatch Libraries. Refer to Figure 13-32.

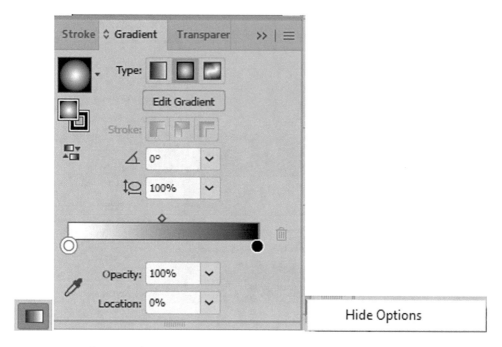

Figure 13-32. *The Gradient panel*

Transparency

The Layers panel in Illustrator does not have Opacity options. You must use the Transparency panel to apply **blending modes**, **opacity**, and **opacity masks** to your selected objects separately or as grouped objects. Refer to Figure 13-33.

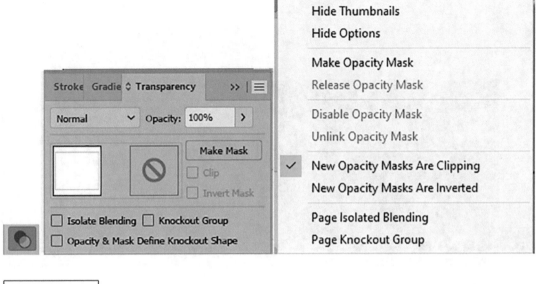

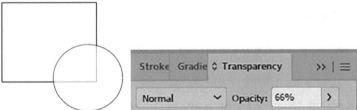

Figure 13-33. *The Transparency panel*

Appearance

The Appearance panel allows you to create overlapping combinations of strokes, fills, opacities, and some effects, which are like Photoshop filters and effects (*fx*). Once created and selected, these Appearance collections can be stored in the Graphic Styles panel. Refer to Figure 13-34.

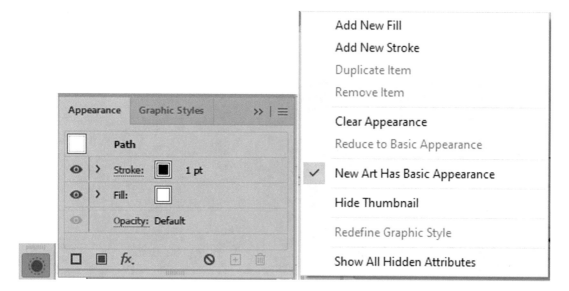

Figure 13-34. *The Appearance panel*

Graphic Styles

The Graphic Styles panel stores all the Graphic (Appearance) Styles you created or accessed from the Illustrator Window ➤ Graphic Style Libraries. You can then apply these styles to a selected path or object. Refer to Figure 13-35.

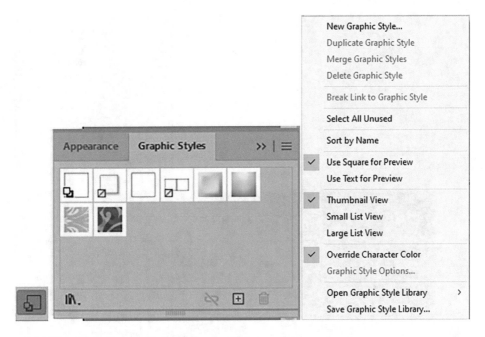

Figure 13-35. *The Graphic Styles panel*

Note   Photoshop contains its own Layer Styles panel as well. However, Photoshop can only access those for their own layers and cannot be applied directly to Illustrator objects. You can learn more on that topic from my videos on Creative Cloud Libraries.

Symbols

Once graphic styles are applied to a path or objects, they can be made into symbols that are stored in the Symbols panel. Symbols are like templates as they can be used repeatedly in a document and save space as they are referenced rather than a duplicate copy. Additional symbols are in Window ➤ Symbol Libraries. Refer to Figure 13-36.

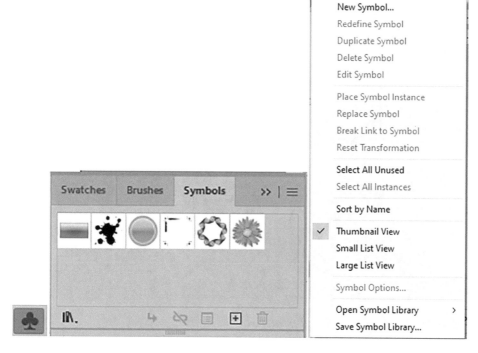

Figure 13-36. *The Symbols panel*

Symbols can also be useful in other Adobe programs, like Adobe Animate for character animations, or Photoshop as Smart Object layers. These graphics can be imported using Edit ➤ Copy in Illustrator. Then, go to the other app and choose Edit ➤ Paste onto a new layer. Alternatively, through the CC Libraries panels, you can import into those apps symbols as Graphics assets.

Asset Export

Although not relevant to this book, if you plan to export your graphics for the web, the Asset Export panel can help you do that quickly. By dragging artwork into the panel and adjusting the settings, you can export your graphics as PNG, JPG, SVG, and.PDF. I discuss this panel in *Graphics and Multimedia for the Web with Adobe Creative Cloud*. Refer to Figure 13-37.

Figure 13-37. *The Asset Exports panel*

Some of the other panels you want to add to your Essentials Classic workspace are in the Window menu.

Transform

The Transform panel can assist you in scaling your selected sketch, paths, or objects on the artboard and has many similar settings as Photoshop's Edit ➤ Transform for scaling and rotation, skewing. Depending on the type of path, additional properties may be available that also affect strokes, patterns, and other effects applied to the objects. Refer to Figure 13-38.

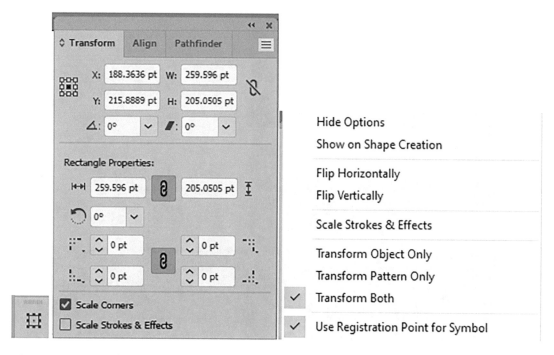

Figure 13-38. *The Transform panel*

Align

Like Photoshop's options panel for layers, the Align panel offers options for the alignment of placed sketches or objects. Refer to Figure 13-39.

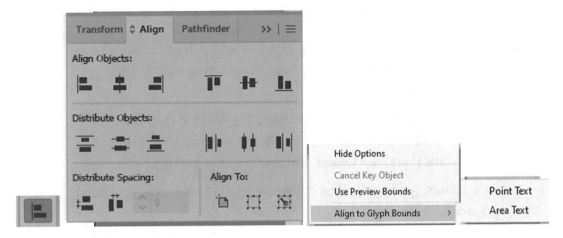

Figure 13-39. *The Align panel*

To keep organized, you can use this panel to align more than one sketch or path on the artboard when they are selected and distribute when three or more are selected. Refer to Figure 13-40.

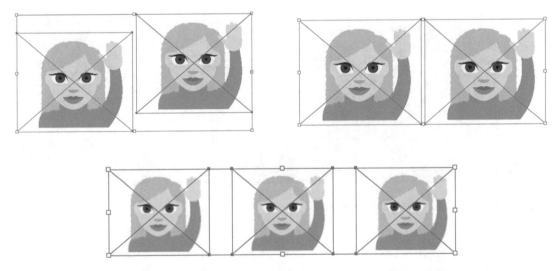

Figure 13-40. *Sketches unaligned, using the Align panel, two selected sketches Vertical Align Bottom setting, and three selected sketches with Horizontal Distribute Center setting*

The following are some of the options.

- **Align Objects**: Horizontal Align Left, Horizontal Align Center, Horizontal Align Right, Vertical Align Top, Vertical Align Center, Vertical Align Bottom

- **Distribute Objects**: Vertical Distribute Top, Vertical Distribute Center, Vertical Distribute Bottom, Horizontal Distribute Left, Horizontal Distribute Center, Horizontal Distribute Right

- **Distribute Spacing**: Vertical Distribute Space, Horizontal Distribute Space, and Spacing Value

- **Align To**: Artboard, Selection, or Key Object

Pathfinder

Like in Photoshop, the Pathfinder panel offers several pathfinder options for combining shapes and paths. Refer to Figure 13-41.

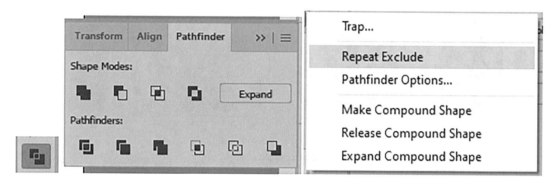

Figure 13-41. *The Pathfinder panel*

- **Shape Modes**: Unite, Minus Front, Intersect, Exclude and Expand button for working with created Compound Shapes

- **Pathfinders**: Divide, Trim, Merge, Crop, Outline, and Minus Back

You'll look at how this panel can be used with objects in Chapter 16.

Note   Optionally, the Transform and Align panels can be accessed from the Properties panel via the ellipse icons for more options when a sketch, path, or object is selected. Refer to Figure 13-42.

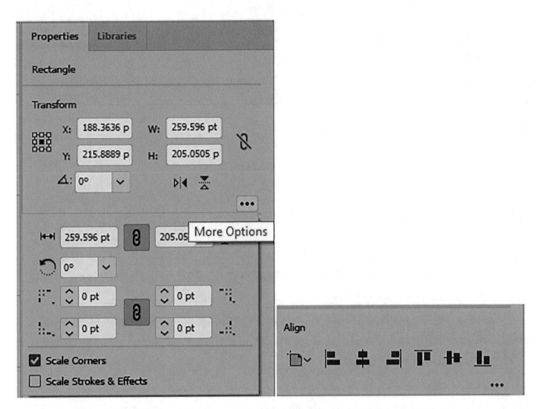

Figure 13-42. *In the Properties panel, additional panels and options are found by clicking the ellipse button*

Magic Wand Panel

This panel features options for the Magic Wand tool for selecting objects based on fill, stroke color, stroke weight, opacity, and blending mode. You'll look at the tool later in this chapter. Refer to Figure 13-43.

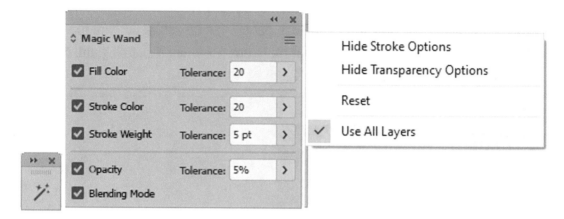

Figure 13-43. *The Magic Wand panel*

Other panels are explored over the next few chapters.

Essential Tools

As you can see, the Toolbars panel contains many tools. This book does not discuss all the tools, but I find some more relevant to drawing and sketching than others. I present them in this and the following chapters.

When you start a project in Illustrator, you want to select your placed sketch or sketches and be able to move them around on the artboard or scale them. Here are a few tools you should know about first.

Note   The Properties panel options change depending on what tools you use to select sketches on the artboard.

Selection Tool (V)

Since there is no Move tool (V), as in Photoshop, use this tool to move and drag your embedded or linked sketches or paths around on the artboard. You can Shift-click or Drag around your selected images to marquee them and select more than one. Refer to Figure 13-44 and Figure 13-45.

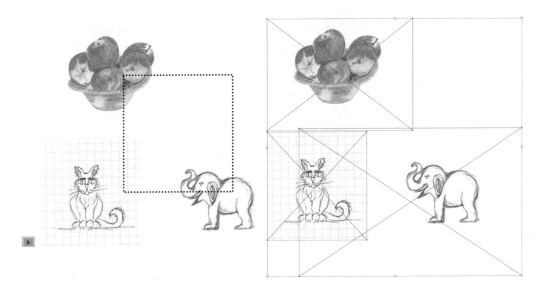

Figure 13-44. *A marquee selection is made with the Selection tool, and the three sketches are selected*

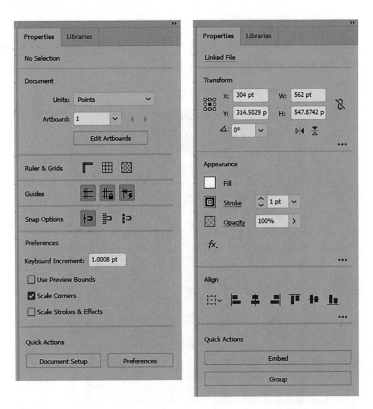

Figure 13-45. *The Properties panel changes when nothing is selected with the Selection tool to when an object is selected*

595

This tool is also like the Path Selection tool (A) in Photoshop, and you can press Alt/Option and drag to duplicate a shape. Refer to Figure 13-46.

Figure 13-46. *Duplicate a sketch or object*

Tip   With an object or sketch selected, you can press the Backspace/Delete key to remove it.

Double-click this tool in the Toolbars panel to access the Object ➤ Transform ➤ Move (Shift+Ctrl/Cmd+M). Refer to Figure 13-47.

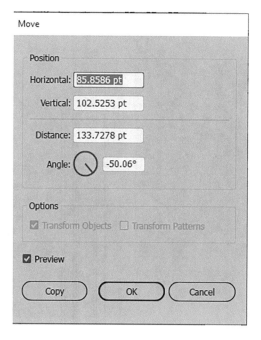

Figure 13-47. *The Move dialog box*

In this dialog box, you can adjust the object's horizontal and vertical position and the distance and angle or create a copy of that object in the new position. Some options affect not only the transformation of the object but also the pattern if the object contains a pattern.

Direct Selection Tool (A)

The Direct Selection tool selects individual points on a path, not a placed sketch, and is like the Photoshop tool for selecting points on a path. Double-click this tool to access the Move dialog box (Figure 13-47) and choose options to move a single anchor point. Likewise, you can use the Properties panel to modify the points, as you see later when you work with the Pen tool in Chapter 15. Refer to Figure 13-48.

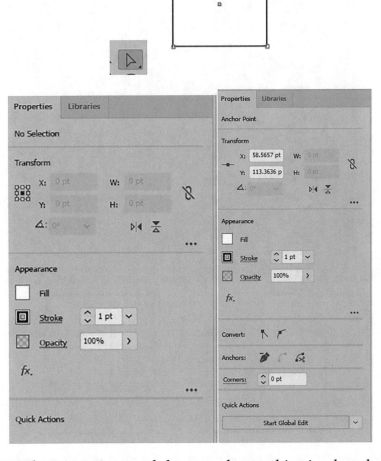

Figure 13-48. *The Properties panel changes when nothing is selected with the Direct Selection tool to when an anchor point is selected*

597

Group Selection Tool

The Group Selection tool selects points in a grouped object or shape with multiple clicks. Double-click on this tool to get access to the Move dialog box. Refer to Figure 13-49.

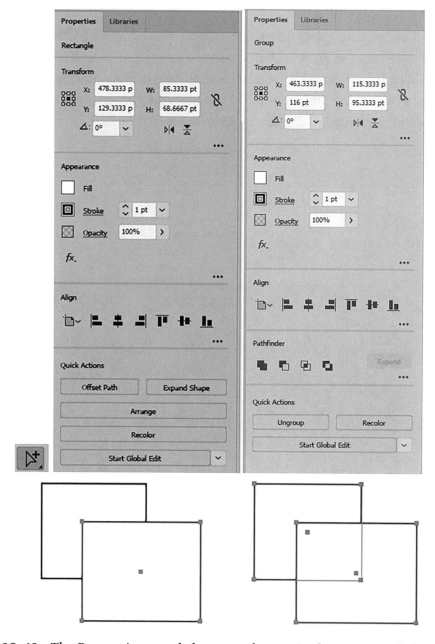

Figure 13-49. *The Properties panel changes when a single or grouped shapes are selected with the Group Selection tool*

Note   A Grouped Object is created when two or more objects are selected, and you choose Object ➤ Group (Ctrl/Cmd+G). To ungroup while selected choose Object ➤ Ungroup (Shift+Ctrl/Cmd+G).

Magic Wand Tool (Y)

The Magic Wand tool lets you select objects of the same color, stroke weight, stroke color, opacity, or blending mode by clicking the object. Refer to Figure 13-50.

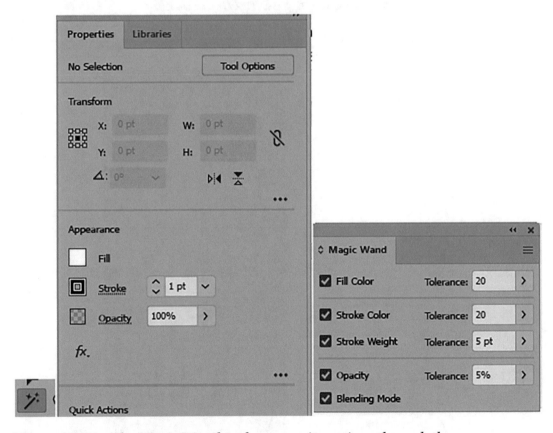

Figure 13-50. *The Magic Wand tool accesses its options through the Properties panel*

Note   These options can be adjusted using the Window ➤ Magic Wand panel or the Properties panel by clicking the Tool Options button. Refer to Figure 13-51.

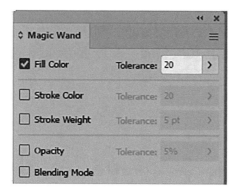

Figure 13-51. *Magic Wand tool settings altered in the panel*

When paths are selected, the Properties panel changes. Refer to Figure 13-52.

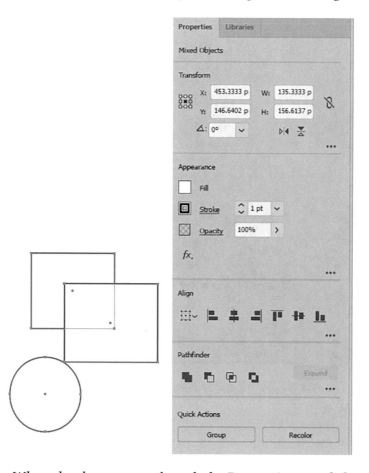

Figure 13-52. *When the shapes are selected, the Properties panel changes to Mixed Objects*

Tip   Shift-click if you want to select two or more placed sketches.

Lasso Tool (Q)

The Lasso tool lets you select objects, anchor points, or path segments by dragging around all or part of the object. This is a good tool for selecting sketches or objects that are not aligned or selecting multiple points that you cannot as quickly with the Direct Selection tool (A). Refer to Figure 13-53.

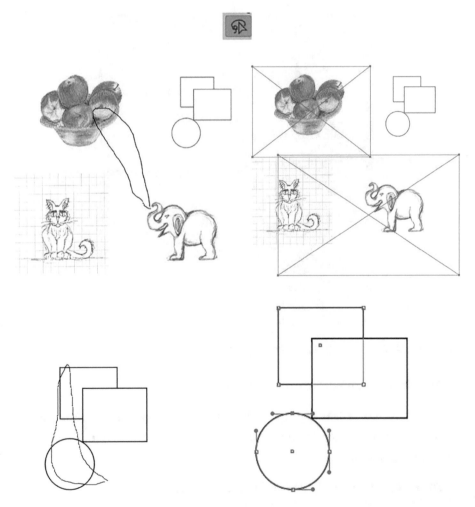

Figure 13-53. *Use your Lasso tool to make more complicated selections of sketches or path anchor points*

Note   This tool contains no additional features.

To Deselect objects or sketches when using any of these selection tools, click a blank area of the artboard with that tool.

The Select Menu

Besides these selection tools, there are a few additional ways you can select multiple items on the artboard using the Select menu. Refer to Figure 13-54.

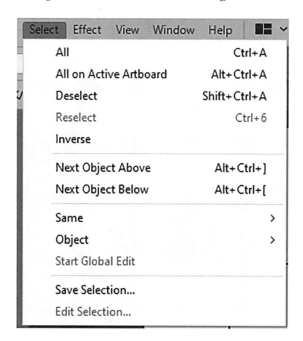

Figure 13-54. *Illustrator select menu options*

- **All** selects all objects on the artboard or artboards.

- **All on Active Artboard** selects all objects on the active artboard and not on inactive ones. In this case, there is only one artboard, so it is active by default.

- **Deselect** deselects all selected objects on the artboard.

- **Reselect** reselects deselected objects.

- **Next Object Above** selects the object above the selected object.

- **Next Object Below** selects the object below the selected object.

- **Same** allows you to select items with similar attributes such as
  Appearance, Appearance Attribute, Blending Mode, Fill & Stroke,
  Fill Color, Opacity, Stroke Color, Stroke Weight, Graphic Style, Shape,
  Symbol Instance, and Link Block Series (threaded text boxes). In
  version 2022 you now can also select similar text attributes as well.
  Refer to Figure 13-55.

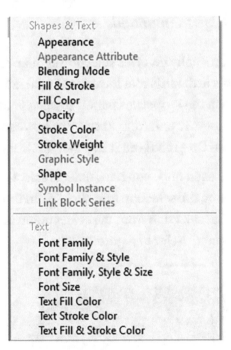

Figure 13-55. *Select ➤ Same Commands*

- **Object** allows you to select objects All on Same Layer, Direction
  Handles, Bristle Brush Strokes, Brush Strokes, Clipping Masks, Stray
  Points, All Text Objects, Point Type Objects, and Area Type Objects.
  Depending on the selection, the Properties panel options change.
  Refer to Figure 13-56.

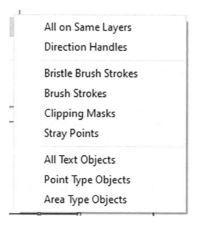

All on Same Layers
Direction Handles

Bristle Brush Strokes
Brush Strokes
Clipping Masks
Stray Points

All Text Objects
Point Type Objects
Area Type Objects

Figure 13-56. *Select ➤ Object Commands*

Start Global Edit usually involves selecting similar objects or assets on multiple artboards that have the Global Edit (Adobe Sensei) applied via the Properties panel. You can learn more about this in Chapter 17 and from `https//helpx.adobe.com/illustrator/how-to/global-editing-sensei.html`.

- **Save Selection** is used once you have objects selected and you are ready to save. Name the selection and click **OK** in the dialog box, and you can access that selection from the select menu after the objects have been deselected. Refer to Figure 13-57.

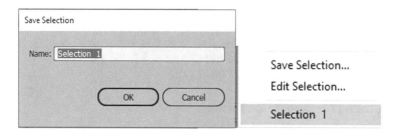

Figure 13-57. *Save Selection dialog box and selection appears in the Select menu*

- **Edit Selection** lets you modify the name of the selection or delete the selection setting from the list. Click OK after deleting a selection. Refer to Figure 13-58.

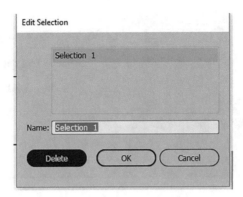

Figure 13-58. *Edit Selection dialog box lets you edit and remove selections*

Arrange and Align

Once you have objects selected, you can use your Align panel to align them, or one of the options from **Object ➤ Arrange**. If you need to move a sketch over or under another, you can Bring to Front, Bring Forward, Send Backward, or Send to Back. Refer to Figure 13-59.

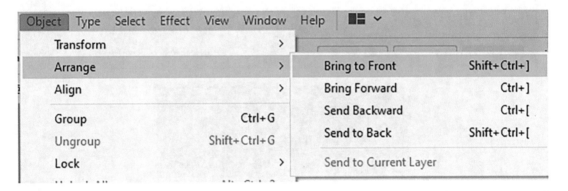

Figure 13-59. *Object ➤ Arrange commands*

Note   These are in the Properties panel Quick Actions area. Click the Arrange button to access them. Refer to Figure 13-60.

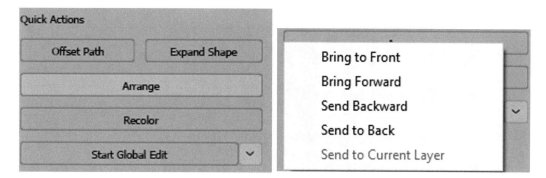

Figure 13-60. *Properties panel Quick Actions allows you to access menu commands*

Object ➤ Align your sketches and objects using similar options as the Align panel. Refer to Figure 13-61.

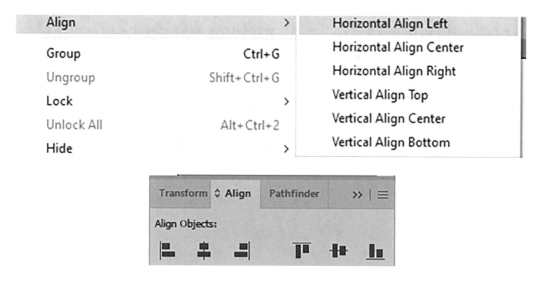

Figure 13-61. *The Align panel has the same commands as Object ➤ Align*

Transform Your Sketch with Tools

Once you have a sketch selected, you may need to scale it to fit on the artboard.

Using your Selection tool (V), you can scale a selected sketch easily using the bounding box handles or Move dialog box. And on corner points, you can rotate as well. Refer to Figure 13-62.

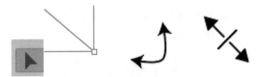

Figure 13-62. *Use the Selection tool to rotate or scale a sketch*

However, besides scaling either your sketch or an object, you can also use any of the following tools from the Toolbars panel for further transformation.

Free Transform (E)

The Free Transform tool contains various suboptions: **Constrain Proportions**, **Free Transform**, **Perspective Distort**, and **Free Distort**. In most situations, for your sketches, you likely just use the Free transform option for scaling. As the pointer changes when you hover or the bounding box, different options or rotate, skew and scale are possible. Refer to Figure 13-63.

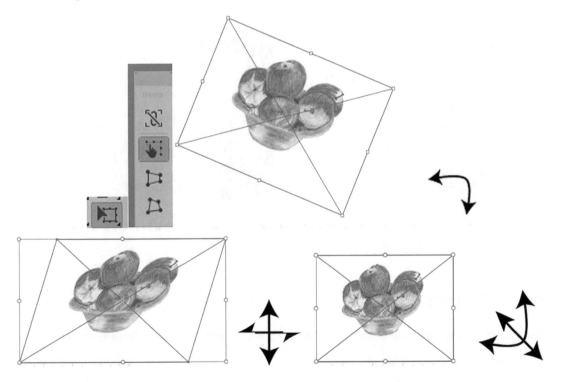

Figure 13-63. *The Free Transform tool and its suboptions can assist you in rotation, shearing, and scaling*

Hold down the Shift key while dragging to constrain proportions or click the **constrain** option. Refer to Figure 13-64.

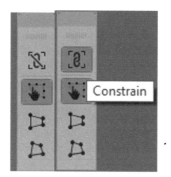

Figure 13-64. *Set the Constrain settings to keep the proportion ratio the same when you scale*

More options like **Perspective Distort** and **Free Distort** are available for paths rather than placed sketches. Refer to Figure 13-65.

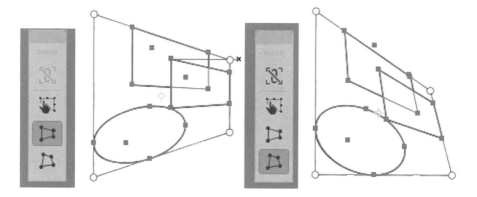

Figure 13-65. *Distorted shapes in the Perspective Distort and Free Distort setting in the Free Transform tool*

Rotate Tool (R)

The Rotate tool allows you to rotate a sketch or object around a set center point as you drag.

Here are some additional tips.

- To move the center point, hold down the Alt/Option key as you click in a new location, and you enter the Rotate dialog box to alter the rotation in a set manner, which rotates the objects and transforms patterns if they are present. Refer to Figure 13-66.

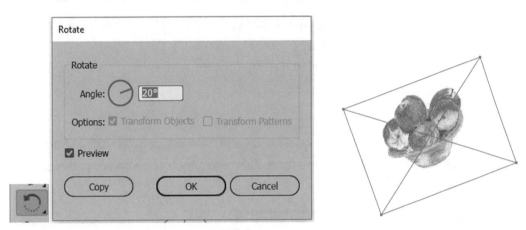

Figure 13-66. *The Rotate tool, the Rotate dialog box, and a rotated sketch*

- If you Alt/Option-drag on the object itself, you create a rotated copy, or you can use the **Copy** button in the dialog box. Refer to Figure 13-67.

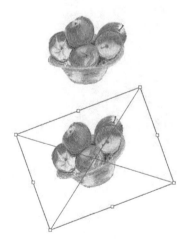

Figure 13-67. *A copy was rotated rather than the originally placed sketch*

- Alternatively, you can double-click the tool in the Toolbars panel to enter the Rotate dialog box, which is the same as Object ➤ Transform ➤ Rotate. The Transform panel allows you to rotate as well.

- Hold down the Shift key while dragging to rotate at 45° angles.

Note   For this and the following dialog boxes, make sure the Preview checkbox is enabled to see the transformation.

Reflect Tool (O)

The Reflect tool allows you to reflect on a horizontal, vertical, or angle axis a sketch or object around a set center point as you drag. This also affects the object's patterns if they are present. Refer to Figure 13-68.

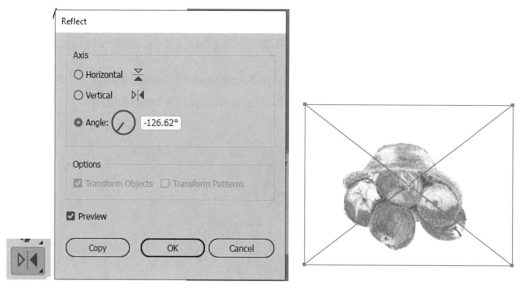

Figure 13-68. *The Reflect tool, the Reflect dialog box, and a reflected sketch*

Here are some additional tips.

- To move the center point and enter the Reflect dialog box, hold down the Alt/Option key and click in a new location.

- Alt/Option-drag on the object to create a reflected copy, or you can use the **Copy** button in the dialog box. Refer to Figure 13-69.

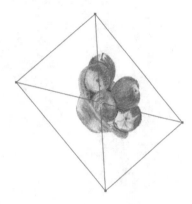

Figure 13-69. *A copy was reflected rather than the originally placed sketch*

- Alternatively, double-click the tool in the Toolbars panel to enter the Reflect dialog box. This is the same as Object ➤ Transform ➤ Reflect.

- Hold down the Shift key while dragging to reflect at 45° angles.

Scale Tool (S)

The Scale tool allows you to scale a sketch or object around a set center point that is either Uniform or Non-Uniform with different horizontal and vertical percentages (1%–100%) as you drag. If present, this scaling can also affect corner scaling radii, strokes, effects, and patterns. Refer to Figure 13-70.

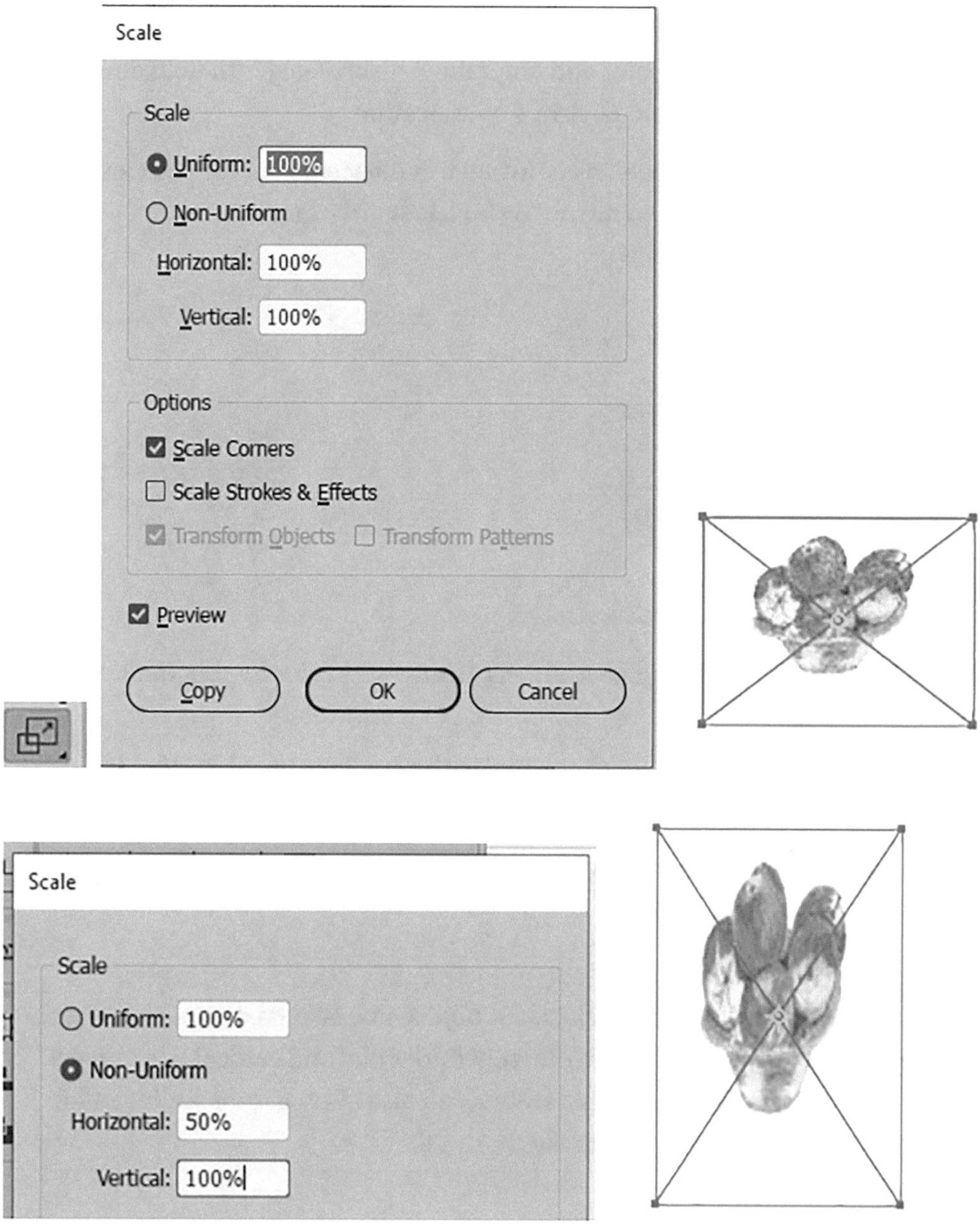

Figure 13-70. *The Scale tool, the Scale dialog box, and a non-uniform scaled sketch*

Here are some additional tips.

- Hold down the Alt/Option key and click in a new location to move the center point. You then enter the Scale dialog box, which allows you to alter the scale settings.

- Alt/Option-drag on the object to create a scaled copy, or use the **Copy** button in the dialog box. Refer to Figure 13-71.

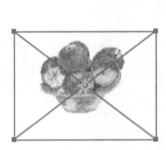

Figure 13-71. *A copy was scaled rather than the originally placed sketch*

- Alternatively, double-click the tool in the Toolbars panel to enter the Scale dialog box, and this is the same as Object ➤ Transform ➤ Scale.

- Hold down the Shift key while dragging to scale proportionately.

Shear Tool

The Shear tool allows you to shear a sketch or object around a set center point as you drag. Refer to Figure 13-72.

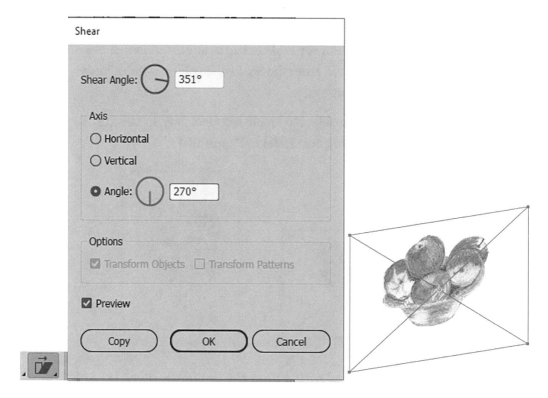

Figure 13-72. The Shear tool, the Shear dialog box, and a sheared sketch

Here are a few additional tips.

- To move the center point, hold down the Alt/Option key as you click in a new location, and you enter the Shear dialog box, which allows you to alter the setting for the Shear angle and the horizontal, vertical, and angle axis. This can affect the object's patterns if present.

- Alt/Option-drag on the object to create a shear copy, or use the **Copy** button in the dialog box.

- Double-click the tool in the Toolbars panel to enter the Shear dialog box. This is the same as Object ➤ Transform ➤ Shear. Note that the Transform panel also allows you to shear.

- Hold down the Shift key to shear either on the horizontal or vertical axis.

Additional Transformations

In the Object ➤ Transform menu, there are a few additional transform options. Refer to Figure 13-73.

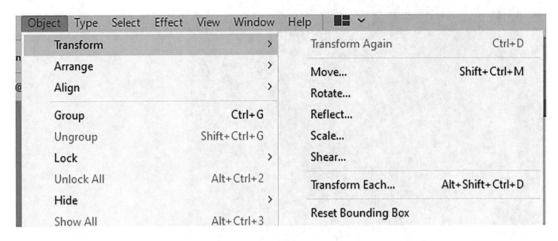

Figure 13-73. *Object ➤ Transform Commands*

The **Transform Again** (Ctrl/Cmd+D) command is used to transform a shape or copy of the shape and repeat that same transformation.

The **Transform Each (Alt/Option+Shift+Ctrl**/Cmd+D) dialog box lets you scale, move, rotate, and set various options of transformation and reflection all in one dialog box from a set reference point. Depending on the options that are enabled, the transformation may affect the object's patterns and strokes, effects, and corners. The **Random** option creates a more random rotation. You can either transform the current item or a copy using the **Copy** button. Refer to Figure 13-74.

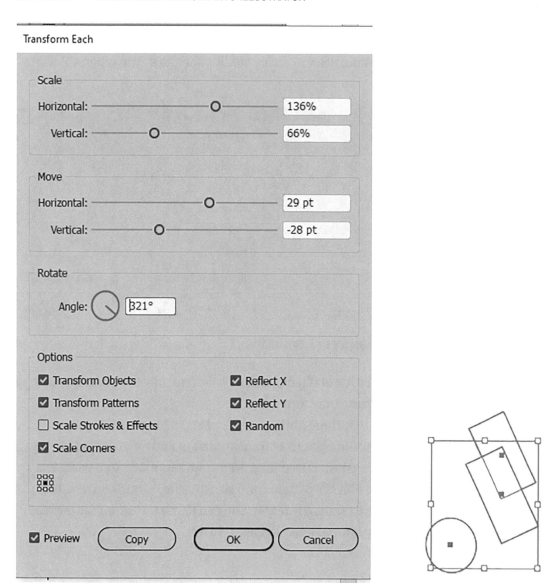

Figure 13-74. *The Transform Each dialog box and some shapes affected by the transformation settings*

The **Reset Bounding Box** resets the bounding box. It is used with more complex paths after they have been rotated. Refer to Figure 13-75.

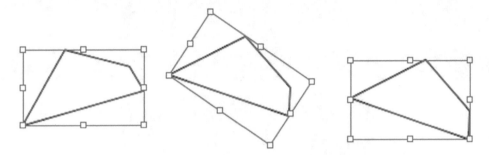

Figure 13-75. *Reset the bounding box on complex paths*

The next few chapters look at a few more options that apply to creating artwork and the paths in the Object menu.

Essential Tools Continued

Let's discuss other tools you should be aware of in the Toolbars panel.

Artboard Tool (Shift+O)

The Artboard tool works with the Artboard panel. It lets you alter the size of the current artboard should you need to make it larger or smaller in either the Control or Properties panel. It also sets additional artboard options, such as renaming or reordering if there is more than one. To exit artboard mode, click another tool in the Toolbars panel or click Exit in the Properties panel. Refer to Figure 13-76.

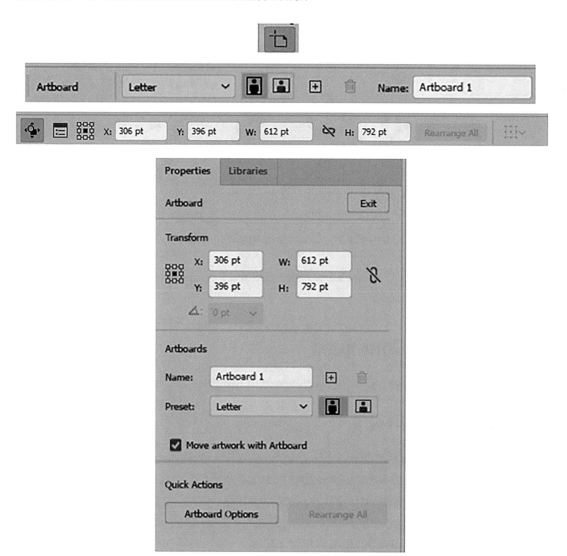

Figure 13-76. *The Artboard tool and its options in the Control and Properties panels*

Zoom Tool (Z)

The Zoom tool is the same as in Photoshop. Use it to zoom in and out of areas. Hold down the Alt/Option key to change to a minus symbol to zoom out. Ctrl/Cmd++ (plus), Ctrl/Cmd+- (hyphen) and Ctrl/Cmd+0 key commands work as well. Refer to Figure 13-77.

Figure 13-77. *The Zoom tool in the Tools panel*

Hand Tool (H)

The Hand tool is the same as in Photoshop. Use the Hand tool when you need to move around your artwork without moving it. You can hold down the spacebar on your keyboard to change any current tool into the Hand tool and drag it around the artboard. Refer to Figure 13-78.

Figure 13-78. *The Hand tool in the Tools panel*

Fill and Stroke

If you need to switch colors, use the Fill and Stroke tool. Press D for the default and X if you want to toggle or switch between altering the fill or the stroke. Shift+X allows you to swap the colors. Refer to Figure 13-79.

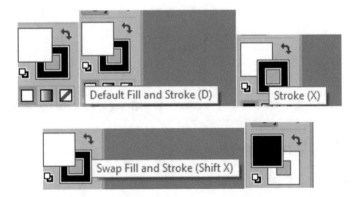

Figure 13-79. *Fill and Stroke Settings can be altered when the border is around the fill or stroke*

Note   As in Photoshop, you can double-click Fill or Stroke to enter Color Picker. Refer to Figure 13-80.

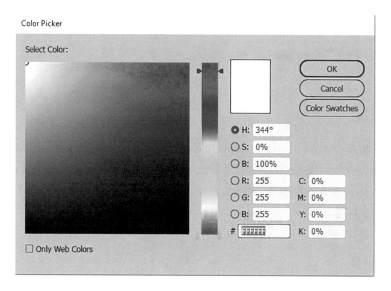

Figure 13-80. *Enter the Color Picker to change the color of the selected fill or stroke*

Set Color, Gradient, or None

In the Toolbars panel below Fill and Stroke, you can set whatever is currently selected.
Refer to Figure 13-81.

Figure 13-81. *Adobe Illustrator set a color, gradient, or none for the fill and stroke*

- **Color** for the selected fill or stroke (<)

- **Gradient** for the selected fill or stroke (>)

- **None** or no color for the selected fill or stroke (/)

Tip   If you cannot see certain tools in the Toolbars panel. It might be because you are using a different workspace than mine, or you may need to click the **Edit Toolbar** options button to see if any of the hidden tools are present in the list and drag and add them to the Toolbars panel. Refer to Figure 13-82.

Figure 13-82.   *Edit Toolbar adds tools to the Toolbars panel*

Currently, all tools should be in the Toolbars panel and grayed out in this area.

Upcoming chapters explore the Pen and Shape tools and other tools to create more accurate paths.

Note   The next exercise's project files are in the Chapter 13 folder.

PLACE A FILE

Open the Untitled Document that you created earlier in the chapter.

1.   Go to File ➤ Place (Shift+Ctrl/Cmd+P).

2.   Locate the file you want to place. This exercise uses the apple13_1.psd image, which is the cleaned-up version from Chapter 12. Click the Place button to confirm. Refer to Figure 13-83.

File name: apple13_1.psd ∨   All Formats (*.AI;*.AIT;*.PDF;*.D ∨

Place   Cancel

Figure 13-83. *Place an image into Illustrator from the Place dialog box*

3. The pointer icon will temporarily change to a small thumbnail preview of the file before you click on the artboard to place it, this is known as the place gun which can hold one or more selected files. While the place gun is loaded, click the artboard. Note: If you discover you selected the wrong image, click another tool in the Toolbars panel to cancel the place, or while selected on the artboard, click the Backspace/Delete key on your keyboard to remove it.

4. Once placed on the artboard, you can check the Window ➤ Links panel to see that it is linked if you open the lower details area under the triangle. Refer to Figure 13-84.

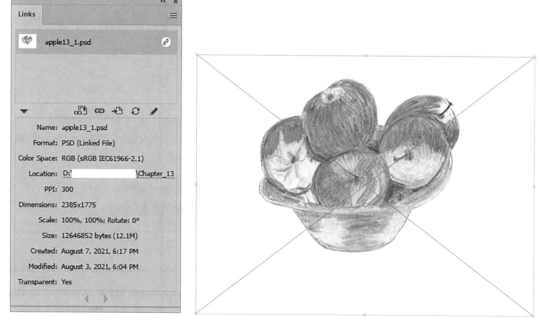

Figure 13-84. *Look at the lower details in the Links panel to see if the file is linked or embedded*

5. Your placed file should appear on layer 1. You can tell it is selected because of the bounding box around the sketch and the blue square on the right of layer 1 in Layers. You can lock this layer next to the eye so that the image is not editable. Refer to Figure 13-85.

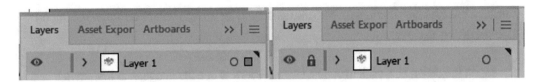

Figure 13-85. *Use the Layers panel to lock your layer so that the placed file cannot move*

6.   Click the lock to unlock the layer, and select the image again with the Selection tool (V). Refer to Figure 13-86.

Figure 13-86. *The placed file is selected in layer 1 and on the artboard*

Embed this graphic so that if you accidentally move the file to another folder, it cannot become unlinked. This increases the file size a bit.

7.   From the Links panel, choose Embed Image(s). Refer to Figure 13-87.

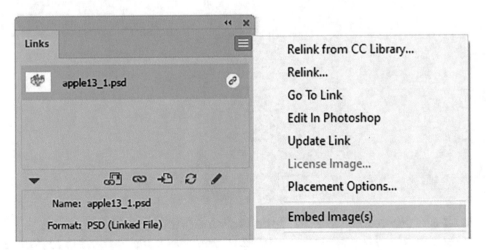

Figure 13-87. *The Links panel menu creates an embedded image*

Because this was not a flattened (.psd) file containing layers, you enter the Photoshop Import Options dialog box first.

8. In the dialog box, click to enable show preview to see the image, and then from the options, choose **Flatten Layers to a Single Image** as you do not want to convert the layer to objects.

9. Click OK to confirm. Refer to Figure 13-88.

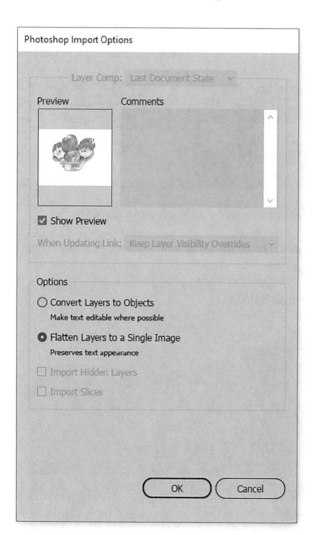

Figure 13-88. *Photoshop Import Options dialog box opened because the document contained unflattened layers, and now you have the option to flatten them before you embed them*

The image is now embedded. There is an icon beside it, and it is confirmed in the details below the panel under the triangle.

10.   Create another layer using the **Create New Layer** button at the bottom of the Layers panel (layer 2 and lock layer 1). You can use this layer 2 later for tracing with the Pen tool in Chapter 15. Refer to Figure 13-89.

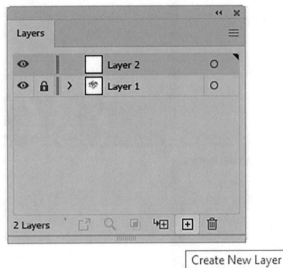

Figure 13-89. *Create a new blank layer in the Layers panel*

Notice that the page looks better in landscape rather than portrait. You can change that now.

11.   Using your Artboard tool, change the orientation to **Landscape** in the Control panel area. Then **exit** Artboard mode from the Properties panel. Refer to Figure 13-90.

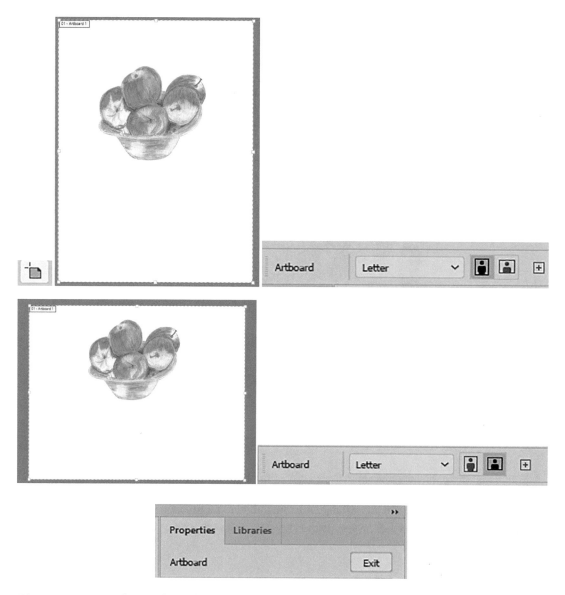

Figure 13-90. *The Artboard tool settings in the Control panel and the Properties panel exits the Artboard mode*

As with Photoshop, I like to see rulers so that if I need to drag out guides for alignment, you can do that too.

12.   From the View menu choose View ➤ Rulers ➤ Show Rulers (Ctrl/Cmd+R). This turns the rulers on. Refer to Figure 13-91.

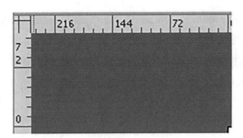

Figure 13-91. *Point unit rulers are added around the artboard*

13. To ensure that they are set to Inches, go to Edit ➤ Preferences ➤ Units and set the general setting from Points to **Inches**. Click **OK** to confirm, and the rulers should now be set to inches. Refer to Figure 13-92.

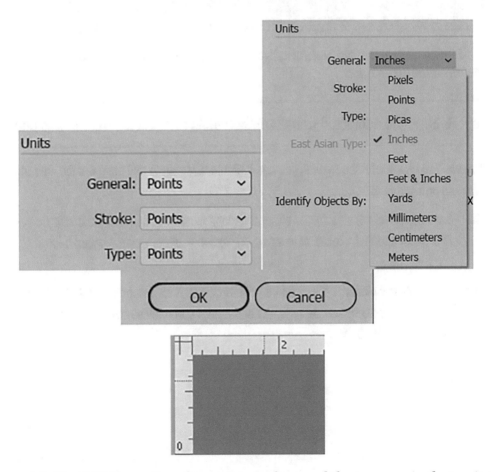

Figure 13-92. *Edit the unit preferences to inches, and they appear in that unit of measurement around the artboard*

14. Unlock layer 1 if you need to scale and move your artwork with the Selection tool to fit on the page using the bounding box handles. It's OK if some of the white area extends outside of the artboard. Hold down the Shift+Alt/Option keys as you drag outwards to scale from the center. Refer to Figure 13-93.

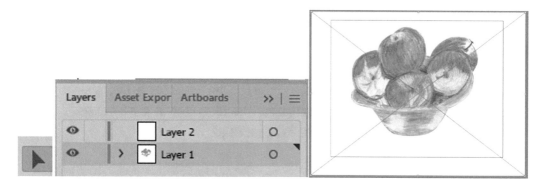

Figure 13-93. *Scale the embedded sketch to fit on the artboard, with some of the white area extending over*

Note   Refer to the additional transformation tools discussed earlier in this chapter.

When you are happy with the results, you can lock the layer again and save the file, and the artwork is now ready to trace.

15. Save (Ctrl/Cmd+S) your file as either an Adobe Illustrator AI (.ai) or Illustrator EPS (.eps) and find a location to save your file on your computer. I called mine 13_trace.ai.

When I first create my sketch, I prefer an (.ai) file format as it allows me to retain the most up-to-date Illustrator effects and settings, but some print companies may request an (.eps) instead. Refer to Figure 13-94.

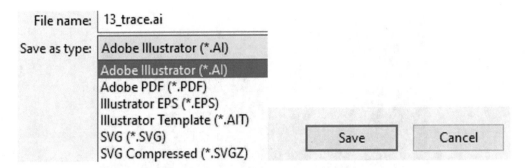

Figure 13-94. *Save your file for tracing*

16. Click the Save button in the Save dialog box and click OK in Illustrator Options
as shown in Figure 13-95.

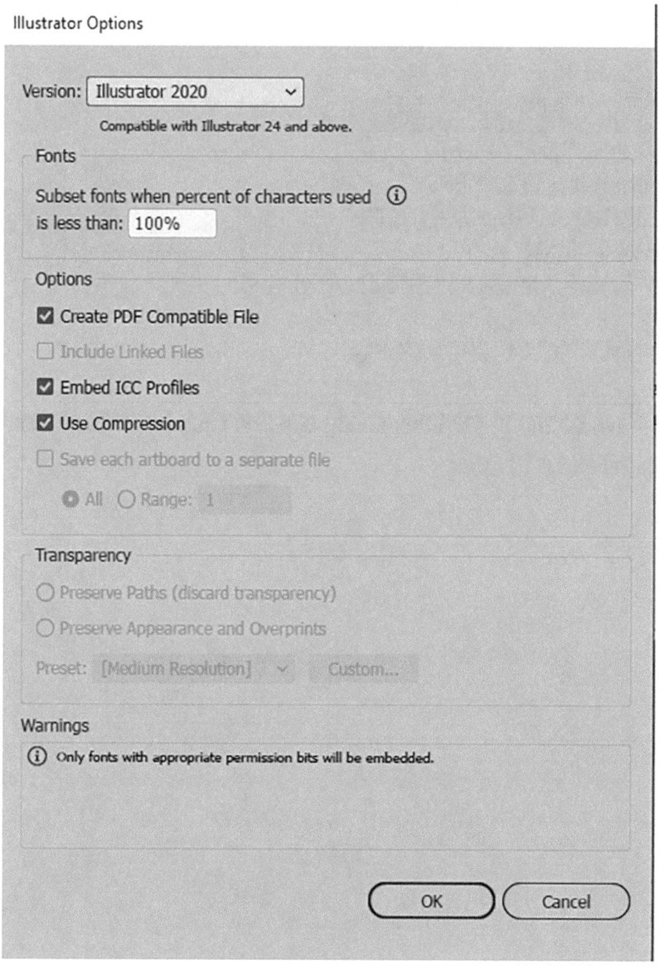

Figure 13-95. *Illustrator Options dialog box for altering the file settings*

17. After you save your file, go to File ➤ Close (Ctrl/Cmd+W) to exit the document, or you can keep it open for the next chapter.

Summary

This chapter covers some basic panels and tools that are part of the Essentials Classic workspace and how they prepare your sketches for tracing. The next chapter uses the Image Trace panel and Control bar panel settings to trace over various sketches.

CHAPTER 14

Image Trace

In this chapter, you learn how to use the Image Trace panel to clean up your artwork and look at options for tracing with the Control bar and Image Trace panel.

In the last chapter, you looked at setting up a document for image tracing or tracing with the Pen tool, as you see in Chapter 15. In this chapter, you continue with the apples sketch and look at other sketches while learning how to adjust and apply settings for your image. Then you see which presets and settings from the Image Trace panel work best for your projects.

To begin working with image trace, I recommend using either a color photograph or a colored sketch for the widest range of options, which gives photographic realism in creating tiny little paths. While black-and-white sketches can be used for some presets, there are limitations due to the lack of color.

Note Projects for this chapter are in the Chapter 14 folder.

Open the 14_trace.ai file. File ➤ Save As (Shift+Ctrl/Cmd+S) to practice with or in case you need to return at some point and try other Image Trace settings on another copy. I called mine 14_trace2.ai. Refer to Figure 14-1.

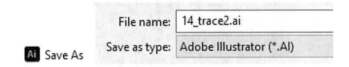

Figure 14-1. *Save As dialog box settings*

© Jennifer Harder 2022
J. Harder, *Accurate Layer Selections Using Photoshop's Selection Tools*,
https://doi.org/10.1007/978-1-4842-7493-4_14

Click Save in the dialog box. Refer to Figure 14-2.

Figure 14-2. *In the Save As dialog box, click the Save button to save a copy of the file*

Click OK to the various Illustrator options, as you saw in Chapter 13. This keeps 14_trace2.ai open. Close the original.

In this case, the .psd file was embedded and is on layer 1. However, whether the .psd file is embedded or linked, you have various options in the Control panel when the sketch is selected with the Path Selection tool. Refer to Figure 14-3.

Figure 14-3. *The apple sketch as it appears on the current layer in the Layers panel*

Note   Because there is no History panel in Illustrator, make sure to use
Edit ➤ Undo (Ctrl/Cmd+Z) as many times as required when you need to go back
a step, or **Edit ➤ Redo** (Ctrl/Cmd+Shift +Z) when you need to go forward a step
again. Window ➤ Version History has to do with Version History of the Creative
Cloud documents but cannot assist you in going back a step in your current
document.

Control Panel Options

While the embedded apple sketch is selected, let's look from left to right at the area in the
Control panel that applies to the image trace. Refer to Figure 14-4.

Figure 14-4. *Control panel options*

The name of the embedded file appears where the original link was when I hover
over the link. Refer to Figure 14-5.

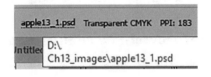

Figure 14-5. *The original link to the embedded file*

It was converted during the embedding to a transparent CMYK. Originally it was
RGB mode, but because the Adobe Illustrator document was CMYK mode, it changed.
If it had any transparent areas, they would have been retained. Notice that the PPI is **183**
and not 300ppi. That is because I scaled up the image up in Chapter 13. Remember, the
sketch is in a raster pixel state, so the pixels do not remain at 300 if scaled upward, so
keep this in mind if you are scanning a document that you are planning to enlarge to a
very large size. Scan it at 600 ppi or higher. In this case, let's leave it as-is since this is not
a photograph that I am expecting precise realism, but a colored sketch.

Next, the **Unembed button** allows you to relink the linked file by locating it through the Unembed dialog box. If you choose to do that, locate the file in the Chapter 13 folder or wherever you have stored it, select it, and click **Save** in the dialog box. The file would be linked again. However, in this case, you want the sketch to be embedded for image trace, so you can ignore that button for this chapter. Refer to Figure 14-6.

Figure 14-6. *Unembed button in the Control panel*

In other situations, if the file is linked, then the **Edit in Photoshop** button would not be grayed out. This allows you to enter Photoshop and edit the currently linked placed graphic. Refer to Figure 14-7.

Figure 14-7. *Edit in Photoshop button in the Control panel lets you go to Photoshop for further editing*

This is helpful if you discover that when you placed the document in Illustrator, you missed a few stray lines or a dark shadow around the edge of the image that needed to be removed.

The **Image Trace** button and **preset** drop-down list automatically trace the image and convert it into a Tracing object with whatever default settings are present in the Image Trace panel. Refer to Figure 14-8.

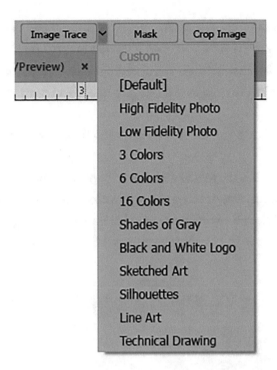

Figure 14-8. *Image Trace button and drop-down list in the Control panel*

When you click Image Trace, you are presented with a warning. Illustrator recommends that you Object ➤ Rasterize the image first to lower the resolution and make the tracing faster. Refer to Figure 14-9.

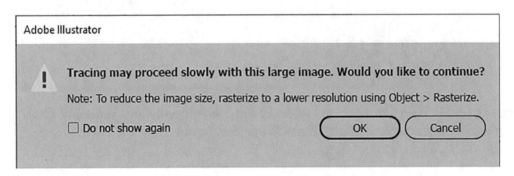

Figure 14-9. *Alert Message when the Image Trace button is clicked*

Clicking **OK** starts the tracing anyway, but at a slower speed depending on the Image and may not get the results you want if the file is very large. Clicking **Cancel** and then choosing Object ➤ Rasterize speeds up the process, but you should only do that after scaling the embedded image to the size you need. You look at that and each of the presets later.

The **Mask** button allows you to create a Clipping Mask path. You can ignore this button for now.

You may notice that the current sketch has a lot of white space around it. Rather than going back to Photoshop, the **Crop Image** button removes some of the white areas around an embedded sketch. When you click this button, it changes the Control panel and the Properties panel to the Cropping setting. Refer to Figure 14-10.

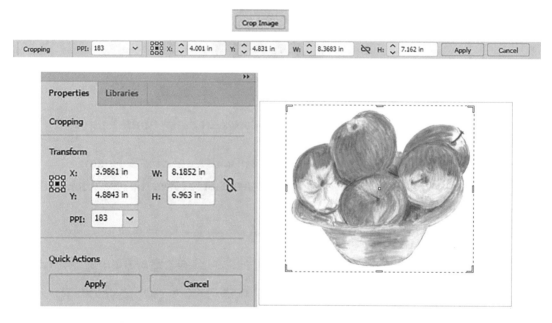

Figure 14-10. *The Crop Image button in the Control panel lets you enter Crop mode, showing similar options in the Properties panel*

Cropping the Sketch

Let's crop the sketch now.

Click the **Crop** button to enter Crop mode. Drag the bounding box handles around the area you want to crop. Your area does not have to be the same as mine.

Note   You can also lower the resolution, but by default, it is whatever the current resolution is, so leave that area at the current setting of 183 ppi. Refer to Figure 14-11.

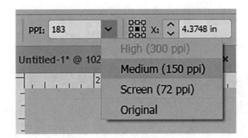

Figure 14-11. *You can alter the resolution from the Control panel*

Click the **Apply** button to confirm or Cancel to exit without saving changes. Refer to Figure 14-12.

Figure 14-12. *Click the Apply button in the Control panel to apply the crop*

Note   Upon doing this crop you will lose the name link to the file, and it be removed as well in the Control Panel depending on what version of Illustrator you are using. Refer to Figure 14-13.

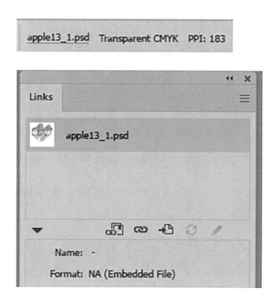

Figure 14-13. *Links Panel, the link name has been removed from the embedded file*

Before you image trace an item, you can lower the opacity 0% to 100% using the **Opacity** slider. However, by doing so, you capture less detail when you image trace your graphic. By default, I recommend leaving it at 100%, but if you are trying to create a certain faded effect, you may want to experiment with lower percentage settings. Refer to Figure 14-14.

Figure 14-14. *Set Opacity in the Control panel*

Rasterize the Sketch

Choose Object ➤ Rasterize so that you can speed up the tracing for later or increase the resolution. In your case, if the file is small, you can skip this step. You enter the Rasterize dialog box. Refer to Figure 14-15.

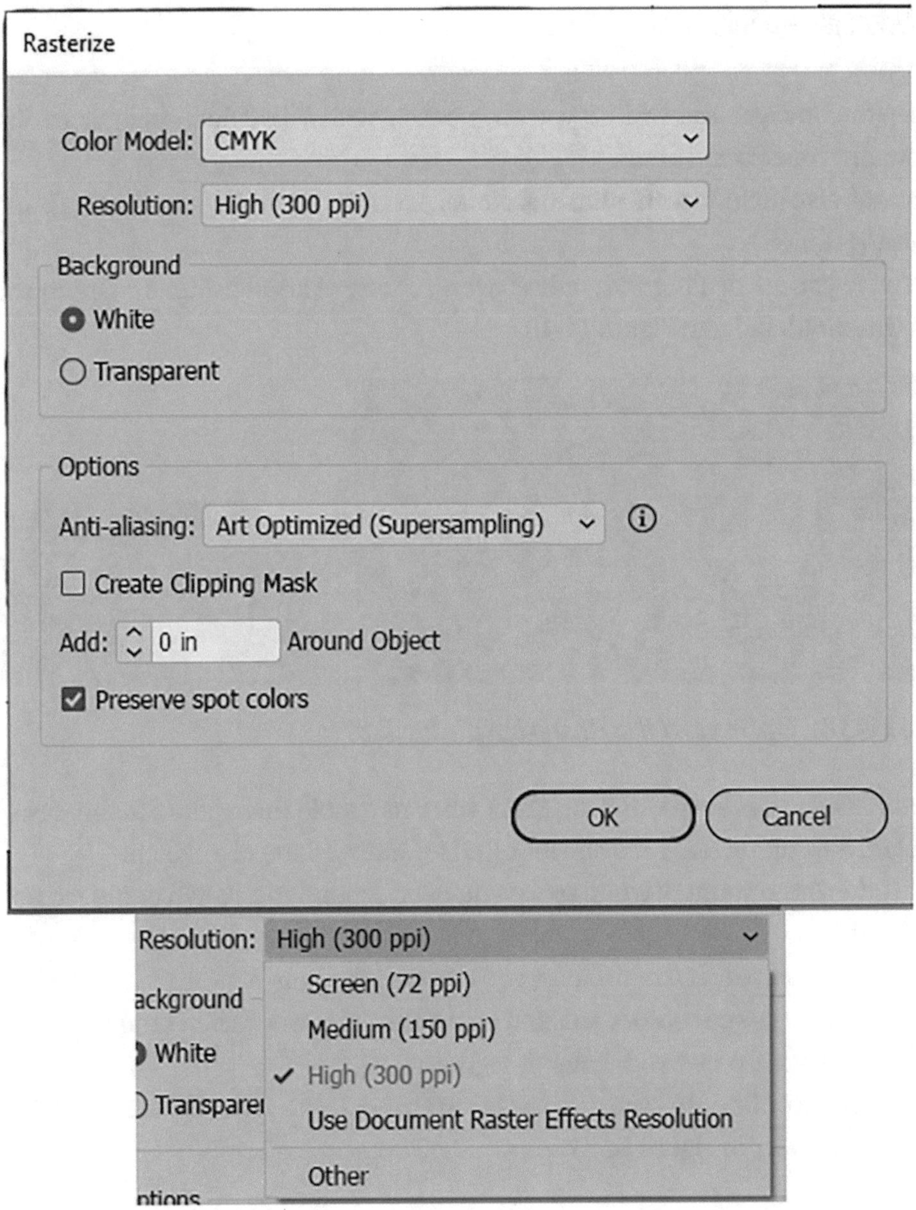

Figure 14-15. *Rasterize dialog box*

In the dialog box, keep the **Color Model** at CMYK, even though there are other options for grayscale and bitmap. You can choose several resolution options, but Keep the **Resolution** at High (300 ppi) to upscale and return to the original resolution.

Note   Use Document Raster Effects Resolution and whatever the Illustrator file resolution is—in this case, 300 ppi.

Keep the **Background** white if you are working with a .psd document or an object that contains transparent areas.

Options also include **Anti-aliasing**: None, Art Optimized (Supersampling), and Text Optimized (Hinted).

Because you are dealing with only artwork, choose Anti-aliasing: Art Optimized (Supersampling). Refer to Figure 14-16.

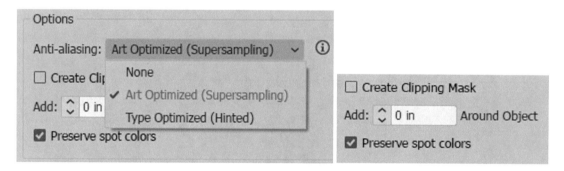

Figure 14-16. *Options in the Rasterize dialog box*

If you need to **Create a Clipping Mask** you can enable this option; in this case, keep it disabled. A Clipping Mask may be required for hiding parts of a sketch.

Add adds the amount of white space you need around the sketch or object. Refer to Figure 14-16.

In this case, leave it at 0 in because you cropped the image.

I leave **Preserve spot colors** enabled by default. This way, when unique spot colors are present, they are preserved. Refer to Figure 14-16.

Click **OK** to confirm that the artwork is rasterized. It has returned to 300 ppi in the Control panel. Refer to Figure 14-17.

Figure 14-17. *Click OK to exit the Rasterize dialog box and the resolution of the embedded image is increased*

After the divider on the Control panel, the additional options do not specifically relate to this topic. I point them out briefly next. You saw some of them in Chapter 13. Refer to Figure 14-18.

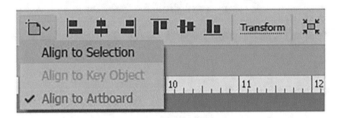

Figure 14-18. *Additional Settings in the Control panel*

- **Align to Artboard:** Use this if you need to align more than one object to a selection or the artboard itself.

- **Align panel options:** Horizontal Align Left, Horizontal Align Center, Horizontal Align Right, Vertical Align Top, Vertical Align Middle, Vertical Align Bottom. These are all in the Align panel and the Properties panel when more than one object is selected.

- **Transform panel:** access to the panel and all its settings.

- **Isolate Selected Object:** Assists you in selecting only that sketch, path, or object. Go into Isolation mode as seen in the Layers panel and on the graphic itself. To exit this mode, click the upper-left arrow below the horizontal ruler until all the arrows disappear and deselect the object, returning to the main layers. Refer to Figure 14-19.

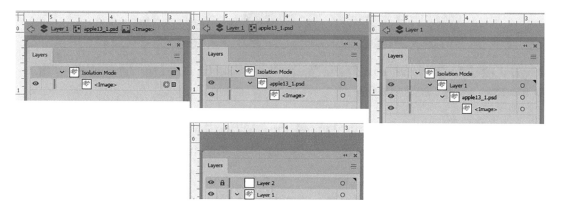

Figure 14-19. *Use the Control and Layers panel to isolate the object and leave Isolation mode*

The area on the far right has a few icons.

- **Align selected art to** the **pixel grid**.

- **Align art to Pixel Grid on Creation and Transformation**.

- **Advanced Options for snap to Pixel** (currently grayed out).

- **Snap to Pixel** panel menu settings for various tools in the Control panel. By default, all the checks in the menu (other than **Dock to Bottom**) are highlighted. Refer to Figure 14-20.

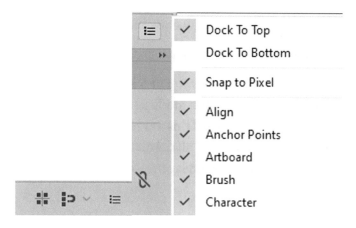

Figure 14-20. *Additional Control panel settings*

Make sure the embedded image is again selected with the Selection tool.

Image Trace

In Illustrator, there are several ways to access the Image Trace options.

- The Control panel (refer to Figure 14-23)

- The Properties panel using the **Quick Actions** ➤ Image Trace (refer to Figure 14-21)

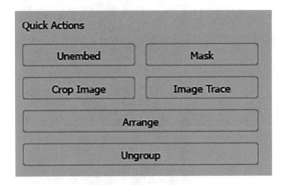

Figure 14-21. *Quick Actions in the Properties panel*

- Object ➤ Image Trace using the current default settings when clicking Make or Make and Expand (refer to Figure 14-22)

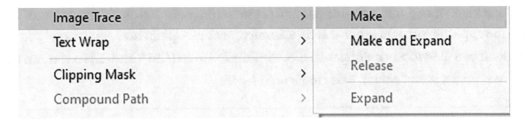

Figure 14-22. *Image Trace commands*

- Window ➤ Image Trace panel (refer to Figure 14-24)

I find that having the Image Trace panel open while I work in the Control panel is the best option to control the exact tracing.

Image Trace from the Control panel has 11 created presets. You look at them via the Image Trace panel. Refer to Figure 14-23.

Figure 14-23. *Image Trace presets in the Control panel*

Image Trace Panel Options

In the Image Trace panel, some additional preset settings are across the top as icons. I use the apple picture and other sketches as references to explain how each preset setting works. If you plan to work along with me, use Edit ➤ Undo (Ctrl/Cmd+Z) so you can try the next preset one at a time. Refer to Figure 14-24.

Note   If you get the warning message regarding Object ➤ Rasterize as you click Setting, click OK in the message.

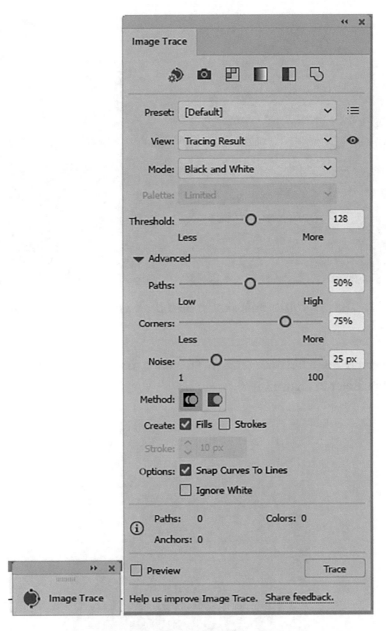

Figure 14-24. Image Trace panel collapsed and open

I zoomed in with my Zoom tool (Z) to see the detail of each Image Trace preset.

Auto-Color automatically creates a posterized color trace of about 25 colors; however, it may be more or less depending on your sketch and the colors it contains. Fewer colors simplify the paths and designs. Refer to Figure 14-25.

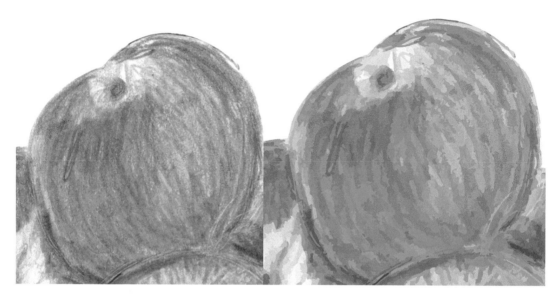

Figure 14-25. *The original apple sketch and then applied with the Auto-Color preset*

High Color creates a full tone range of 85 colors; there is more detail, like a photo or original sketch. Refer to Figure 14-26.

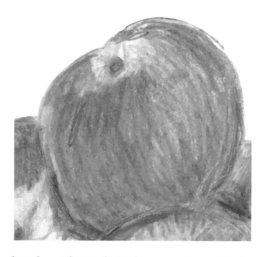

Figure 14-26. *Apple sketch with High Color preset applied*

Low Color creates a very low color range, the pallet is limited to 2 to 30 colors, and details are more sketchy and semi-photorealistic. Refer to Figure 14-27.

Figure 14-27. *Apple sketch with Low Color preset applied*

Grayscale creates a sketch with tones of gray and 0 to 100 gray shades. You could use a color or grayscale pencil sketch with this option. One of the drawings from Chapter 3 is seen in the 14_trace_3.ai file, which I did not expand so that you can look at the custom settings after I applied the grayscale preset. Refer to Figure 14-28.

Figure 14-28. *Apple sketch and abstract sketch with grayscale preset applied*

Black and White is the preset is for black and white only and can be altered by the threshold of 0-255; the default is the midtone of 128. This preset is best for one color artwork drawn with a black felt tip pen, and there is a little transition between the black and any additional gray tones or colors. It could be the start of a pattern or logo. See the 14_trace_4.ai file to see the Image Trace Settings for the square pattern. Refer to Figure 14-29.

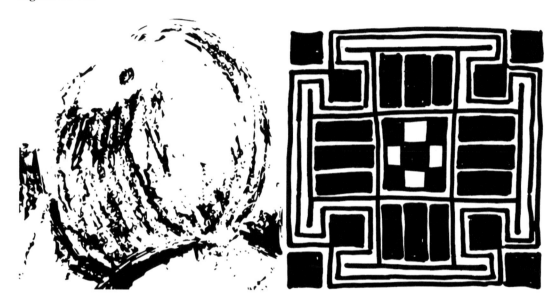

Figure 14-29. *Apple sketch and pattern sketch with black-and-white preset applied*

Outline creates little black-and-white stroke outlines of the pattern and almost a stippling effect with long lines. However, with line drawings made with a dark pen with no other grayscale contrast, you can see that by adjusting the preset's threshold, you can retain many of the details. See the 14_trace_5.ai file for the building sketch. Refer to Figure 14-30.

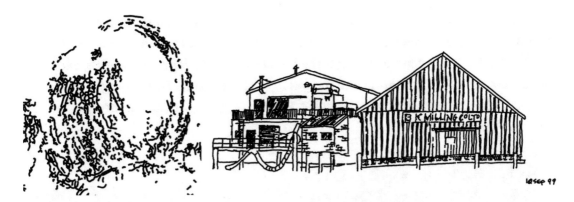

Figure 14-30. *Apple sketch and building pen sketch with Outline preset applied*

In the **Presets** drop-down menu, you find the same presets as in the Control panel. **[Default]** is the preset is the same as Black and White for sketches of one solid color. Refer to Figure 14-29.

The **High Fidelity Photo** preset is the same as high color and is good for color photos and colored sketches. Refer to Figure 14-26.

The **Low Fidelity Photo** preset has a lower color range than High Fidelity Photo with a full tone but has more color range than low color. It is good for color photos and colored sketches. Refer to Figure 14-31.

Figure 14-31. *Apple sketch with Low Fidelity Photo preset applied*

3 Colors has a limited pallet of three colors. The path is very simplified, and Illustrator draws out what it thinks are the three prominent colors within the image. They may not be the colors you want, but you can alter that by adjusting the type of pallet and the colors slider. This preset and the next two are very good for drawing with a felt tip pen, and you have a limited color pallet. See the 14_trace_7.ai file for the eye sketch. Refer to Figure 14-32.

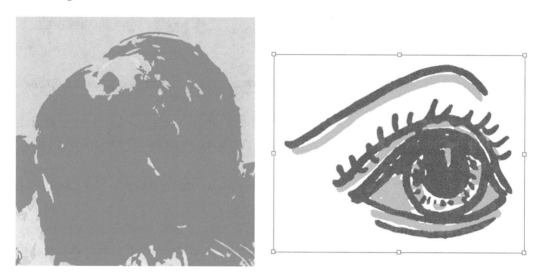

Figure 14-32. *Apple sketch and eye sketch with 3 color preset applied*

6 Colors has a limited pallet of six colors. The path is very simplified, and Illustrator draws out what it thinks are the six prominent colors within the image. They may not be the colors you want, but you can alter them by adjusting the pallet type and the number of colors using the slider. See the 14_trace_7.ai file for the circle pattern sketch. Refer to Figure 14-33.

Figure 14-33. *Apple sketch and circle pattern sketch with 6 Color preset applied*

16 Colors has a limited pallet of sixteen colors. The path is very simplified, and Illustrator draws out what it thinks are the 16 prominent colors within the image. They may not be the colors you want, but you can alter them by adjusting the pallet type and the number of colors using the slider. See the 14_trace_7.ai file for the heptagon sketch. Refer to Figure 14-34.

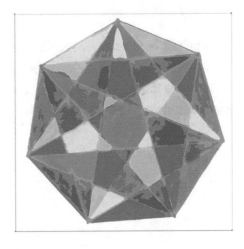

Figure 14-34. *Apple sketch and heptagon sketch with 16 Color preset applied*

The **Shades of Gray** preset is the same as Grayscale and is good for color or black-and-white sketches. Refer to Figure 14-28.

The **Black and White Logo** preset is the same as Black and White and is good for artwork that is one color and has no additional grayscale or color tones. Refer to Figure 14-29.

The **Sketched Art** preset is very similar to Black and White. However, it contains a slightly different setting than in the options that ignore white areas when tracing. While this setting is not always the best solution for grayscale and color drawings, it can be useful to trace solid color sketches with a pen and do not want the white paper areas to appear as part of the trace and sets the fill to none. I find that in this sketch, it is a better option than the Outline preset as the lines are finer. See the 14_trace_6.ai file for building sketch. Refer to Figure 14-35.

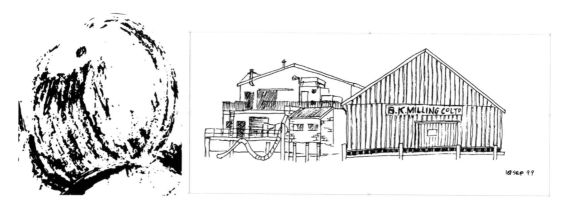

Figure 14-35. *Apple sketch and building pen sketch with Sketched Art preset applied*

The **Silhouettes** preset is similar to Black and White; however, its settings allow you to fill all or most of the entire drawing with a black. This is good for solid color drawings with a crisp line and a dark fill area, such as a single-color logo or areas drawn with a black marker. Refer to Figure 14-36.

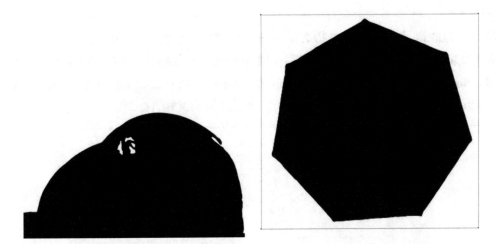

Figure 14-36. *Apple sketch and heptagon sketch with Silhouettes preset applied*

The **Line Art** preset is the same as Outline and creates little black-and-white strokes. Refer to Figure 14-30.

The **Technical Drawing** preset is like Outline and creates little black-and-white strokes, but they are finer and similar to stippling. Refer to Figure 14-37.

Figure 14-37. *Apple sketch with Technical Drawing preset applied*

Note   Each time you switch to a different preset, the options and sliders adjust in
the Image Trace panel. If you alter any of the sliders outside of the normal presets,
you create a Custom preset, which you can save, and manage (delete or rename)
from the Manage Presets pop-out menu. Refer to Figure 14-38.

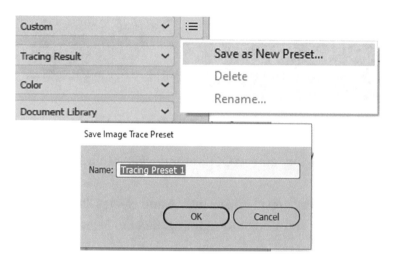

Figure 14-38. *Create and save your own custom presets*

The **View** viewing options let you preview the **Tracing Result**, the **Tracing Result
with Outlines**, **Outlines**, **Outlines with Source Image**, **Source Image**. The **eye** on
the upper right allows you to press and hold to view source image and is like a show
and hide feature. I generally keep my setting on the default Tracing Result. Refer to
Figure 14-39.

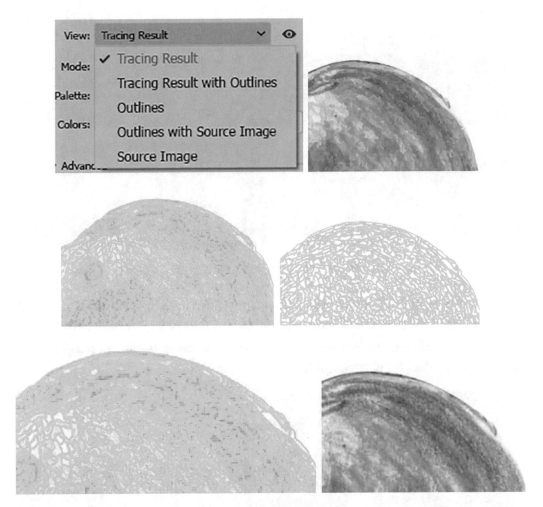

Figure 14-39. *View options from the Image Trace panel and how they preview as you select them one at a time*

Mode features color modes for tracing. From the list, you can choose **Black and White**, **Grayscale**, and **Color**. They change to different slider settings, other than the threshold for Black and White. They are for Grayscale (Grays) and Color (Colors). Refer to Figure 14-40.

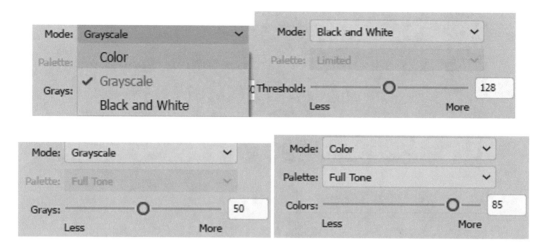

Figure 14-40. *Color mode settings in the Image Trace dialog box*

The **Palette** drop-down list assists with tracing. Only when Color mode is activated is this drop-down list available. **Automatic** allows 0 to 100 colors. **Limited** allows 2 to 30 colors. **Full Tone** allows 0 to 85 colors, although you can move the slider up to 100 for a higher range of colors for photographic work. Refer to Figure 14-41.

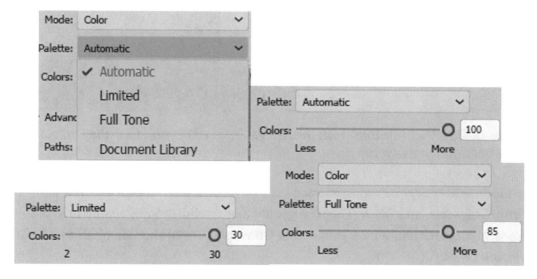

Figure 14-41. *Palette and colors options for the Image Trace panel*

So, to create a Custom preset when the Colors slider appears, you can choose a color accuracy in a percentage of a range from 0 to 100. Less means the color options are simplified and less like the true sketch or photo, compared to a Pallet with a Full Tone of 5 to 85. Refer to Figure 14-42.

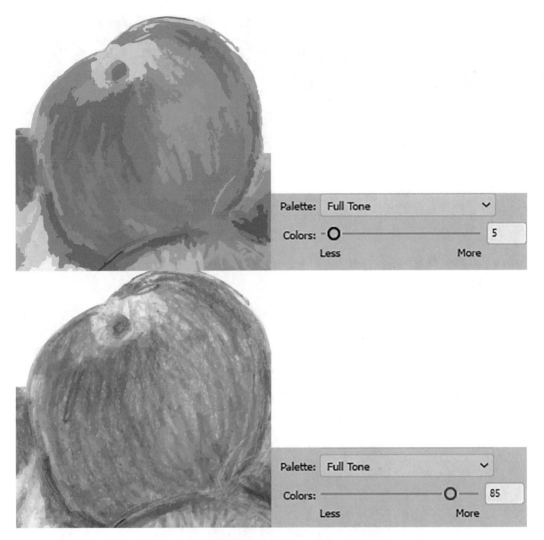

Figure 14-42. *Moving the colors slider creates less or more detail on the apple*

Another Palette is **Document Library**. This sets the colors to **All,** or those collections or Color Groups are in the Swatches panel that you may have by default or a group that you created with the Color Guide panel, which you see in Chapter 17. The color group could even be a former color theme created with Adobe Color that you created via that panel link using the Creative Cloud Desktop App and then imported from your Libraries panel into the Swatches panel. Refer to Figure 14-43.

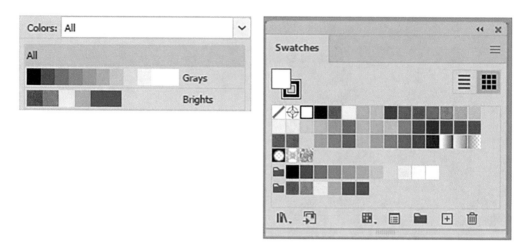

Figure 14-43. *The Palette for the Document Library comes from the Swatches panel*

Note   Chapter 17 shows how to colorize your traced and expanded artwork using the Window ➤ Color Guide panel to edit colors and give you better control of the order of select colors. Refer to Figure 14-44.

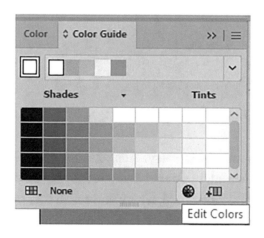

Figure 14-44. *You can achieve more selective colors with the Color Guide panel*

The **Threshold** slider controls the Black and White mode, the level of darkness or lightness that Illustrator Traces. Less More 0-255. Pixels darker than the threshold are converted to black and lighter pixers are converted to white. Refer to Figure 14-45.

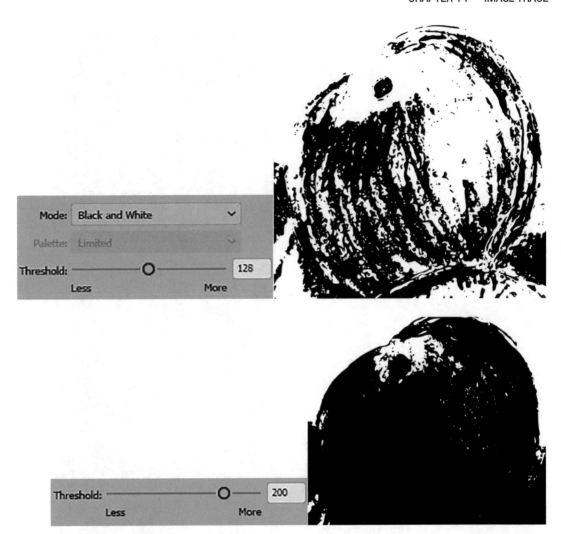

Figure 14-45. *Adjusting the Black and White threshold in the Image Trace panel*

Based on Color mode and Palette change, this option changes to **Grays** (Less More 0%-100%) and **Colors** (Less More 0%-100%) or (2-30). Refer to Figure 14-46.

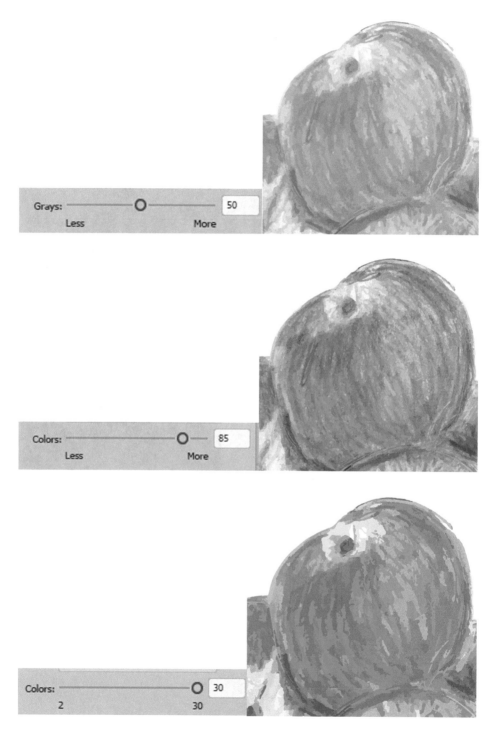

Figure 14-46. *Grays and Color Setting sliders in the Image Trace panel*

Advanced reveals a few more advanced sliders and settings you can alter separately or collectively. Refer to Figure 14-47.

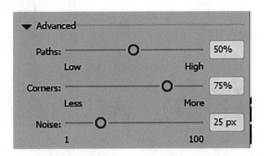

Figure 14-47. *Advanced Options of Paths, Corners, and Noises in the Image Trace panel*

Paths (Low to High, 1%–100%) focus on path fitting. A higher value means a tighter fit. Figure 14-48 is a close-up example of a low-fidelity photo with tracing result outlines.

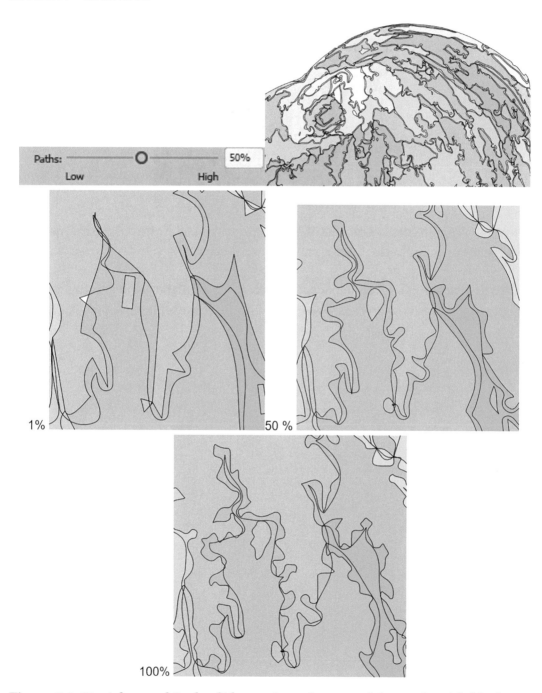

Figure 14-48. *Advanced Paths slider settings close-up of the apple with black outlines*

Corners (Less/More 0%–100%) focuses on corner emphasis. a higher value means more corners for a sharp bend. Refer to Figure 14-49.

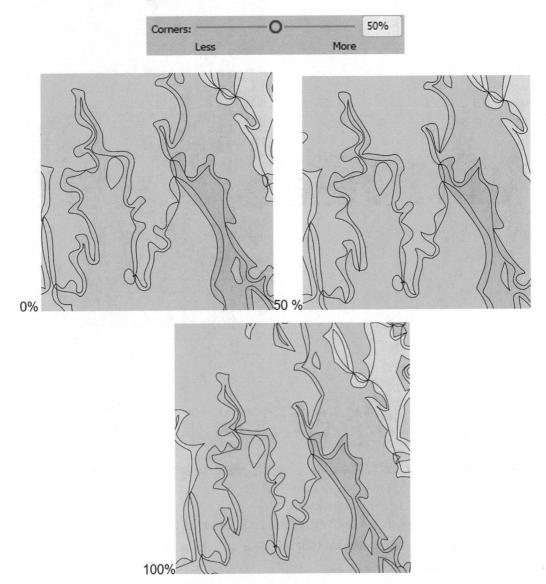

Figure 14-49. *Advanced Corner slider settings close-up of the apple with black outlines*

Noise (1 px to 100 px) reduces noise by ignoring areas of specified pixel size. A higher value means less noise and some details may be removed. Adobe recommends that you set a higher value for high-resolution images and a lower value for low-resolution graphics. Refer to Figure 14-50.

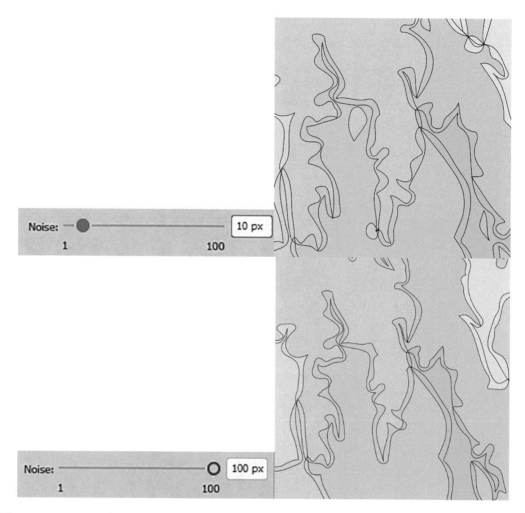

Figure 14-50. *Advanced Noise slider settings close-up of the apple with black outlines*

Method has two options. **Abutting** (creates cutout paths that are edge to edge). **Overlapping** (creates stack paths that slightly overlap). Some presets set one or the other automatically. Refer to Figure 14-51.

Figure 14-51. *Method Settings in the Image Trace panel*

Create enables the creation of **Fills** or Filled regions depending on the preset. However, you can enable **Strokes** or stroked paths. Strokes lets you set the **Maximum width** in pixels that are recognized and converted to stroked paths. If larger, they become outlined areas during the trace. Refer to Figure 14-52.

Figure 14-52. *Setting an area with fills and then strokes using the Image Trace panel increases the path thickness*

These settings are available for Black and White mode. In Grayscale or Color presets, this area is grayed out. Refer to Figure 14-53.

Figure 14-53. *Not all modes can access these options*

Options: Snap Curves To Lines replaces slightly curved lines with straight lines within the range of 0° to 90°. **Ignore White** sets white fills to none when enabled. This option is grayed out if Method is set to Overlapping. Refer to Figure 14-54.

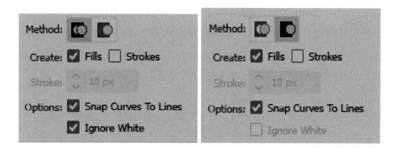

Figure 14-54. *Options setting in the Image Trace dialog box*

Information on **Paths, Anchors,** and **Colors** changes as the tracing results are altered when you set different presets and create custom presents. Refer to Figure 14-55.

Figure 14-55. *Information on the Paths, Anchors, and Colors in the Image Trace dialog box*

Preview shows the results of current settings. Clicking the **Trace** button confirms the trace settings. Refer to Figure 14-56.

Figure 14-56. *View a preview of the image trace or click Trace to confirm settings*

Note   Adobe is always making changes and alterations to its panels, and with products like Adobe Sensei, it's always trying to find ways to improve its products, including Image Trace. You can share feedback with them if you have a suggestion. Refer to Figure 14-56.

Trace, Change, and Expand a Drawing

Once the **Trace button** has been enabled in the Image Trace panel, you can continue reviewing and improving your image trace. At this point, you probably have played with quite a few settings and want to reset Image Trace so that you can continue with the next steps. Refer to Figure 14-56.

Use Ctrl/Cmd+0 to zoom out if you need to see the full image again.

If you need to get out of Image Trace, choose Object ➤ Image Trace ➤ Release. Refer to Figure 14-57.

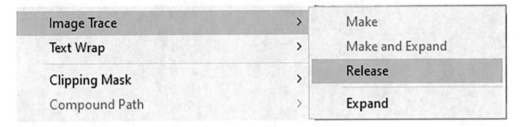

***Figure 14-57.** Release your sketch from Image Trace*

In the Image Trace panel, use the High Fidelity Photo preset. Refer to Figure 14-58.

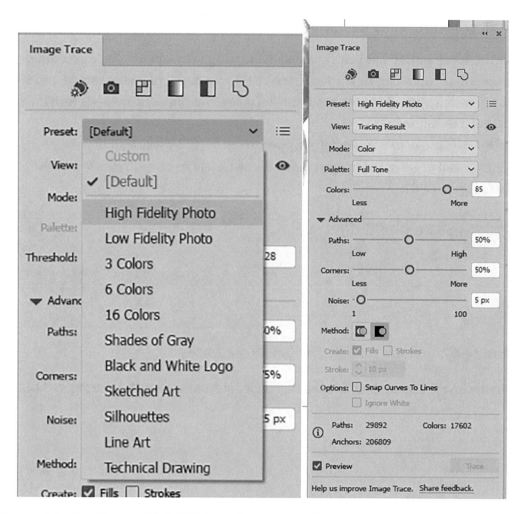

Figure 14-58. *Choose High Fidelity Photo preset from the Image Trace panel*

Click OK to any warning message and wait until the tracing is complete. In my case, I wanted the sketch to be as realistic as possible and as close to the original artwork.

When you are happy with the result, click the **Expand** button in the Control panel, and the tracing is confirmed, and the original sketch is removed from the Links panel. This is the same as Object ➤Image Trace ➤ Expand. Refer to Figure 14-57 and Figure 14-59.

Figure 14-59. *Click the Expand button in the Control panel to confirm the image trace*

Note   Choose Edit ➤ Undo right away if you realized you made a mistake after clicking Expand.

After Expansion, the Image Trace panel is disabled. Refer to Figure 14-60.

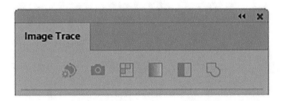

Figure 14-60. *The Image Trace dialog box is disabled when there is nothing to trace*

The resultant paths are grouped, as you can see when you click them with the Selection tool (V) and look at the message to the left of the Control panel; it says Group. Refer to Figure 14-61.

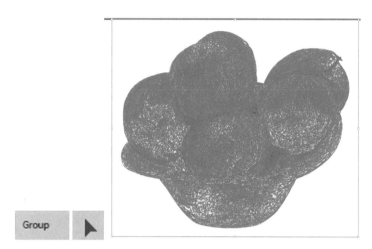

Figure 14-61. *All the group paths are selected with the Selection tool*

I generally keep the paths grouped so I can move them together because they are so complex. But if for some reason you need to ungroup the paths, choose Object ➤ Ungroup; this allows the paths to move separately. Leave the paths in this chapter as a group.

In this case, you want to remove the white background surrounding the apples and bowl, so click the white background with your white Direct Selection tool (A). Refer to Figure 14-62.

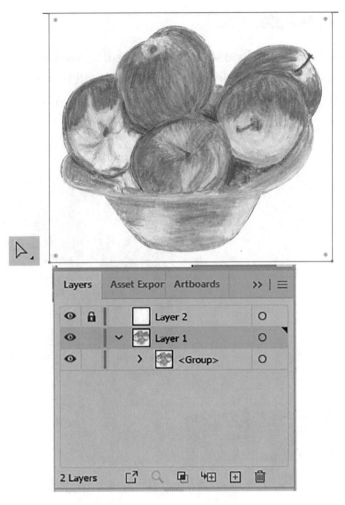

Figure 14-62. *Use your Direct Selection tool to remove the white background and then look at the result in the Layers panel*

Now click the Backspace/Delete key to remove the white background. Only the colored bowl and apples remain.

Save your document at this point. The Layers panel shows that it is on layer 1 and is a group with many sublayers.

Now that this image is a vector file, you can scale it up or down using the bounding box handles while holding down the Shift key to scale proportionately, or use one of the tools in Chapter 13 without worry that it loses quality or resolution.

Simplify a Vector Path

Let's discuss what you need to do to simplify the paths due to a large file size.

Once a copy of the file is expanded and vectorized, it can be simplified using Object ➤ Path ➤ Simplify. Click the ellipse dots to see more options in the dialog box. Refer to Figure 14-63.

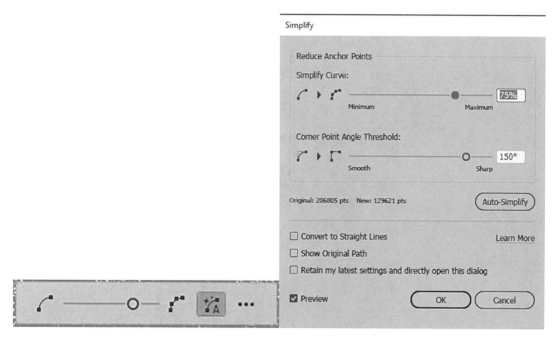

Figure 14-63. *Basic and Advanced settings in the Simplify dialog box*

Moving the sliders to reduce the anchor points to **Simplify the Curve (minimum)** or to increase **(maximum)** or **Corner Point Angle Threshold (smooth)** or to increase **(sharp)** while the **Preview** Check is enabled, reduce, or add points in some paths and make the file smaller or larger. However, in some situations, the paths may become too simplified, causing small gaps and breaks. Refer to Figure 14-63 and Figure 14-64.

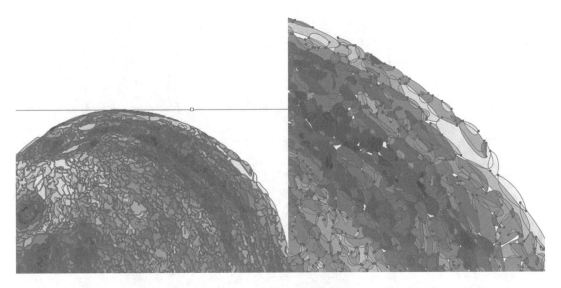

Figure 14-64. *When paths become too simplified on a complex drawing, unwanted white gaps can appear*

For this project, I clicked **Cancel** and exited the dialog box. I did not alter the graphic. However, for your own projects, after adjusting the settings, click OK to confirm. Refer to Figure 14-63.

Adding Effects to Your Sketch Before You Image Trace

Are there any other ways you could affect my image before you use Image Trace in Illustrator? Yes, here is an idea you might want to explore.

Remember how Photoshop has filters? You saw a few of them in Chapter 2. In Illustrator, the Filter Gallery is in the Effect menu (Effect ➤ Photoshop Effects Effect Gallery). Some of these filters are stored in the Effects Gallery or when you select one of the Photoshop Effects submenus other than Blur, Pixelate, or Video. After you apply a filter effect from the Gallery as you would in Photoshop and click OK. Refer to Figure 14-65.

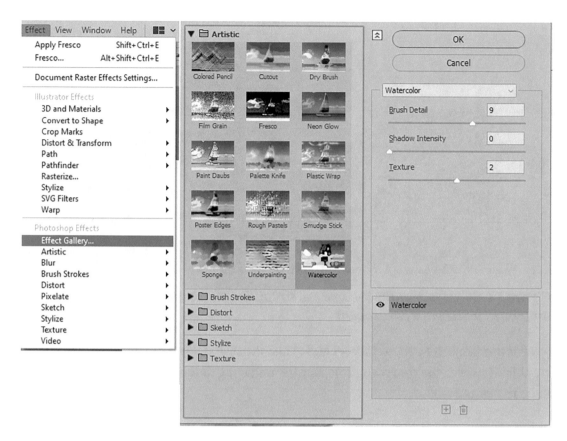

Figure 14-65. *Illustrator's Photoshop Effects Effect Gallery can enhance your sketch before an image trace*

Note   Effects for Blur and Pixelate are not in the Effect Gallery as they may produce undesirable results, so you may want to experiment with those effects on your own.

The effects are stored in the Appearance area of the Properties panel. Refer to Figure 14-66.

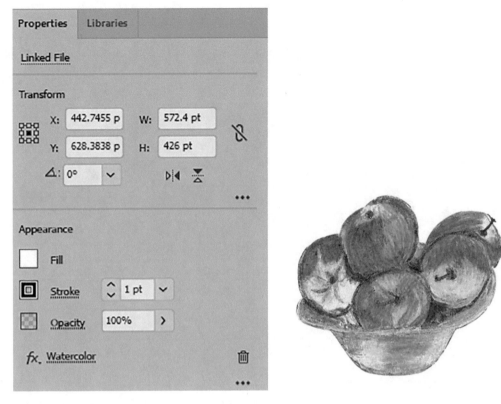

Figure 14-66. *Effect stored in the Appearance area and the apples with the Watercolor effect added*

You could then choose to image trace your embedded sketch, which applies that effect to your image trace after clicking the Expand button.

Summary

This chapter used the Image Trace panel to transform a sketch into vector artwork that you can scale without losing the resolution. You discovered that you could modify not only your paths but the sketches as well, using various presets and effects. The next chapter explains how to create your own paths over artwork should you want to manually redraw portions of a sketch or the entire sketch.

CHAPTER 15

Working with the Pen Tools

In this chapter, you learn how to work with the Shape and Pen tools in areas in which Image Trace did not do such a good job.

As you saw in the previous chapter, Image Trace works very well for photo-realistic images when you want to capture details of a sketch or photo or transform it into grayscale or color vector artwork. It also works very well when you have a pen or felt tip pen drawings with solid boundaries and little variation in color, such as one or three-color projects. However, sometimes what you draw in a sketch is not exactly your final goal. Image Trace tries to re-create exactly what it sees. Although it has artificial intelligence, it cannot read minds or see your exact vision. Sometimes a drawing is a starting point that you want to simplify down to become a well-designed logo. Other times it is a rough sketch that simply is a basic concept or a rough draft that needs adjustments and colorization. Only once you are in the Illustrator app can you control the way the lines move or alter them, so they are exactly what you envision.

This chapter is about creating path lines and curves manually based on a rough sketch. Many of the topics about creating paths should be familiar to you from Chapter 10, where you created various paths with Shape and Pen tools while using various selection tools. However, rather than using these paths to create selections or masks for clean-up, this time, you are using them to create objects and shapes that are part of the final vector Illustration.

Note This chapter contains projects that are in the Chapter 15 folder.

© Jennifer Harder 2022
J. Harder, *Accurate Layer Selections Using Photoshop's Selection Tools*,
https://doi.org/10.1007/978-1-4842-7493-4_15

Selection Tool Review

First, let's review Chapters 13 and 14. Use your Selection tool (V) to select, rotate, or scale an entire path, object, or shape. With ungrouped objects, you can Shift-click to select or drag a marquee around the objects you want to select with the Selection tool to move them as a group. You can then group them using Object ➤ Group (Ctrl/Cmd+G). Refer to Figure 15-1.

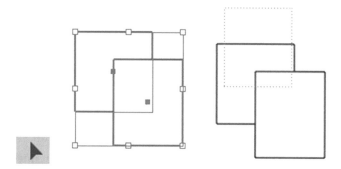

Figure 15-1. *Select more than one shape with the Selection tool either using the Shift key or marquee around a shape*

You can also Alt/Option-drag a selected shape to create copies of shapes.

Direct Selection Tool Review

The Direct Selection tool (A) selects or manipulates individual anchor points on a path. Also, you can Shift-click points or drag a marquee to select multiple paths or points, and they can be moved by either dragging that point. Or you can also nudge them using the arrow keys on your keyboard. Refer to Figure 15-2.

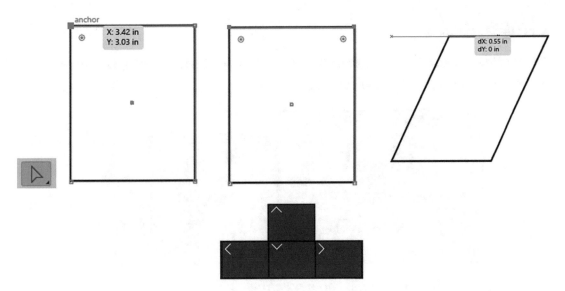

Figure 15-2. *Use the Direct Selection tool to move selected points or use your arrow keys to nudge the points*

Group Selection Tool Review

You can select more than one path within a group using the Group Selection tool when you click multiple times on a grouped object with the tool. Or Shift-click that path again to deselect it. Refer to Figure 15-3.

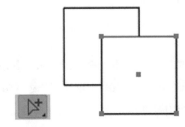

Figure 15-3. *The Group Selection tool lets you select one shape within a group*

To delete points or paths, you can select a point or path and press the Backspace/Delete key on your keyboard.

Take time to review Chapter 13 for any additional information on those tools.

Shape Tools

This section looks at Shape tools and how they affect the Control panel, Transform panel, and Properties panel. Refer to Figure 15-4.

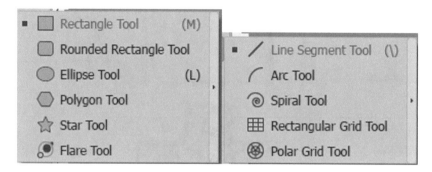

Figure 15-4. *Shape tools in the Toolbars panel*

The following are the main Shape tools in the Toolbars panel.

- Rectangle tool (M)
- Rounded Rectangle tool
- Ellipse tool (L)
- Polygon tool
- Star tool
- Line Segment tool (\)
- Arc tool

Later, I briefly discuss the following Shape tools, which are less frequently used. Although they do not help with manual drawing directly, you could use them afterward to create some graphic enhancements.

- Flare tool
- Spiral tool
- Rectangular Grid tool
- Polar Grid tool

Working with Shape Tools

Create a new blank document as you did in Chapter 13: File ➤ New (Ctrl/Cmd+N).

In the New Document dialog box, use the Print and Letter presets (612×792 pt or 8.5×11 inches), Color Mode: CMYK, and Resolution: 300 ppi. Click the Create button.

If you don't see your rulers, then go to View ➤ Rulers ➤ Show Rulers.

Right-click the upper ruler and set the units of measurement to inches, or from Edit ➤ Preferences ➤ Units General, as you saw in Chapter 13. Refer to Figure 15-5.

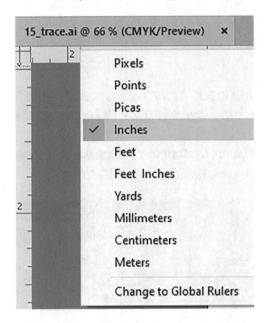

Figure 15-5. *Set the ruler's units of measurement to inches*

When learning to use shapes, I find that practicing dragging them out on layer 1 of the Layers panel of a blank document helps me feel more comfortable with how shape tools and shapes operate.

If you run out of room in the Layers panel, lock layer 1, click the eye to hide the content and create a new layer (layer 2) and continue to draw some more basic shapes. Refer to Figure 15-6.

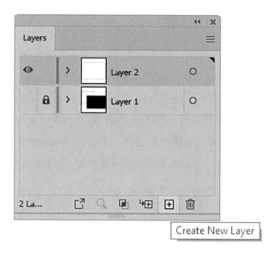

Figure 15-6. *Create more layers in the Layers panel when you need practice with your shape tools and lock the layers you are finished working on*

You can rename your layers by double-clicking the name and entering a new name to organize your practice layers. Refer to Figure 15-7.

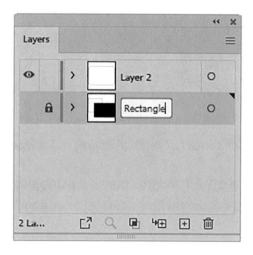

Figure 15-7. *Rename the layers to keep organized*

Note   When a shape is selected, the Properties panel already contains an area with the Transform panel included, but sometimes additional options are not visible. You can see these extra options either by clicking the ellipsis **More Options**

button or displaying the Window ➤ Transform panel so that you can see how the panel changes based on the type of shape after it is selected. Refer to Figure 15-8.

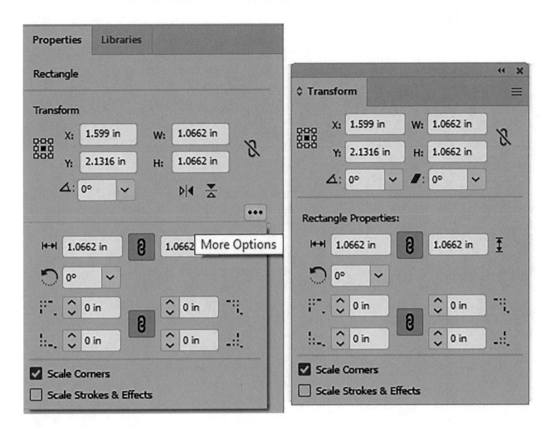

Figure 15-8. *More Options for a shape in the Properties panel or the Transform panel*

Like Photoshop, Illustrator has Shape tools too. However, unlike Photoshop, where the shape is drawn and appears as a Vector Shape layer, in Illustrator, vector shapes are not layer-dependent. They can be moved from layer to layer at any time using your Layers panel.

Move Shapes

You can move shapes by doing one of the following.

- Go to Edit ➤ Copy (Ctrl/Cmd+C) and select a new layer and then choose Edit ➤ Paste (Ctrl/Cmd+V) on another layer.

- Drag the selected shape to another layer via the Layers panel. A
  highlighted square on the right-hand side **indicates selected art**.
  Drag that square, which represents the shape, to the next layer. Refer
  to Figure 15-9.

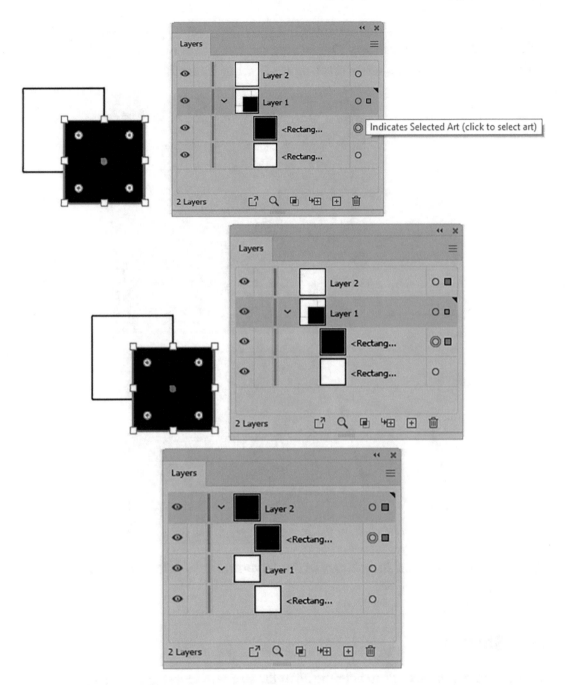

Figure 15-9. *Move selected shape up in the Layers panel from layer 1 to layer 2*

For your workflow, this helps create order when drawing since you may want some paths to be above or below others. Or you may want to lock or hide some paths while working with others, as you see in this chapter. Refer to Figure 15-10.

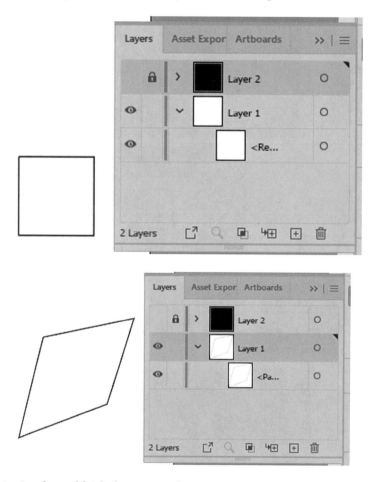

Figure 15-10. *Lock and hide layers in the Layers panel while you modify other shapes*

Color Shapes

While creating shapes, you can alter the fill or the stroke of that shape using your selected fill and stroke in the Toolbars panel. Review the key commands from Chapter 10 on that topic. Refer to Figure 15-11.

- Press X to see fill or stroke.

- Hold Shift+X to switch the color between fill or stroke.

- Press D to set the default fill and stroke. Refer to Figure 15-11.

- Use the Swatches panel to set new colors besides black and white or double-click the fill or stroke to enter the Color Picker. Click **OK** to exit and confirm the new color. Refer to Figure 15-11.

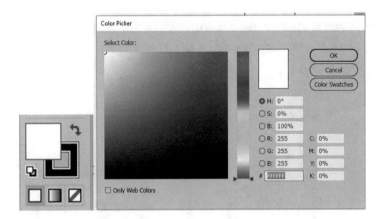

Figure 15-11. *Set the default color for Fill and Stroke or set new colors using Color Picker*

For now, set the fill and stroke to default (D), and use your new blank document to practice drawing each shape along with me. Refer to Figure 15-11.

Create a new layer in the Layers panel for each shape as you practice. Then lock the last one before you move on to the next shape tool. Refer to Figure 15-7.

Rectangle Tool (M)

The Rectangle tool lets you do the following.

- Drag out a rectangular or square shape while you hold down the Shift key.

- Hold Shift+Alt/Option and drag the square shape from center point. Refer to Figure 15-12.

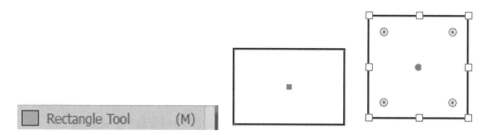

Figure 15-12. *The Rectangle tool lets you create rectangles and squares*

You can then scale and rotate the rectangle using the bounding box handles or use the round corner handles by dragging them in or outwards to create a different rounded radius. Refer to Figure 15-13.

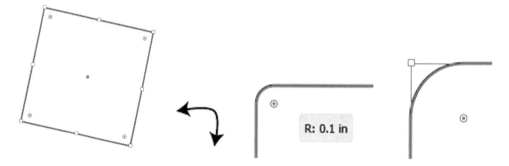

Figure 15-13. *Rectangles rotated with the bounding box or use round corner handles to change the corner radius*

While the tool is selected, you can click the artboard first to enter the Rectangle dialog box to set the width and height, which can be proportionate and constrained or unconstrained by checking the link icon. Then click OK to confirm the preset size. It appears on the artboard. Refer to Figure 15-14.

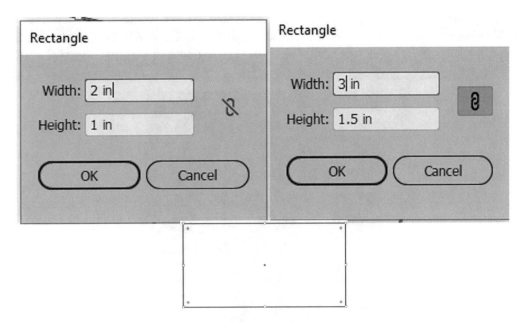

Figure 15-14. *The Rectangle dialog box presents a few options to change width and height and constrain proportions before adding the rectangle to the artboard*

When you are tracing over a sketch, you are scaling manually and relying on the Control panel and Properties panel. They display all the options you want to adjust, and you can manually type them into the text boxes. Both panels are used in tandem, and much of it references the other shape tools as well. Refer to Figure 15-15.

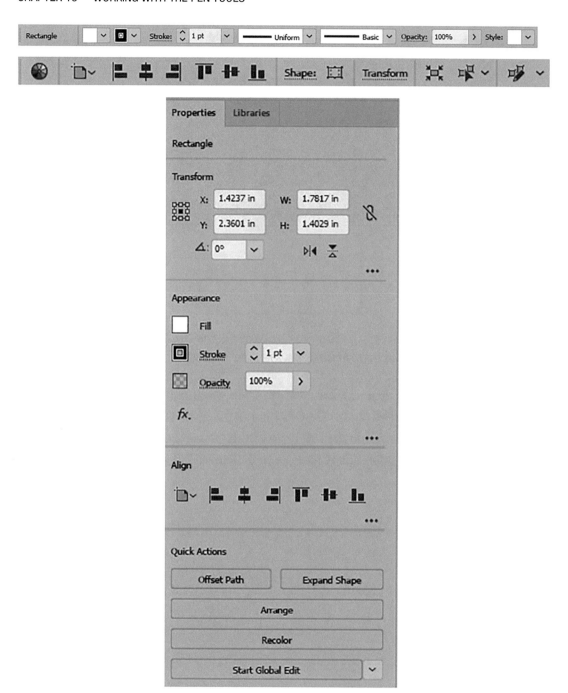

Figure 15-15. *Once a shape is created, the Control and Properties panel present many options for modifying that shape*

Rectangle Shape Options

Once a rectangle is created, you can alter the following options in the Control panel.

Fill Color with swatches in the Swatches panel that can be accessed from the drop-down list. Alternatively, if you hold down the Shift key while clicking the drop-down menu, you bring up the slider options to select a color. These same options can be accessed from the Appearance areas of the Properties panel. Use the toggle buttons to access swatch and slider options. Refer to Figure 15-16.

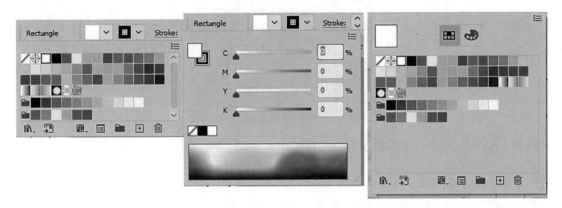

Figure 15-16. *In the Control panel for the Fill or Stroke panel, you have access to the Swatches or Color panel. The same options are in the Properties panel*

Stroke Color with swatches in the Swatches panel that can be accessed from the drop-down list. Alternatively, if you hold down the Shift key while clicking the drop-down menu, you bring up the slider options to select a color for the stroke. The same options can be accessed from the Appearance areas of the Properties panel. Use the toggle buttons to access swatch and slider options. Refer to Figure 15-16.

Stroke opens the Stroke panel and various options. Alternatively, these can be accessed from the Appearance areas of the Properties panel. Refer to Figure 15-17.

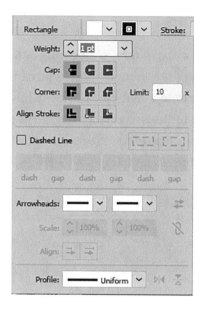

Figure 15-17. *Stroke settings accessed from the Control panel*

This panel is discussed in more depth in Chapter 16. Stroke properties can include **weight**, line end **cap** options, **corner** options, miter **limit**, stroke **alignment**, **dashed line** options, **arrowheads** that can be **scaled** and **aligned**, and **variable-width profile** and **orientation**.

Stroke Weight sets the weight of the stroke in point sizes, either in the Stroke panel or using the drop-down menu or entering your own number in the text box. The arrows on the left of the menu let you scale the point size up or down. Alternatively, these can be accessed from the Appearance areas of the Properties panel. Refer to Figure 15-18.

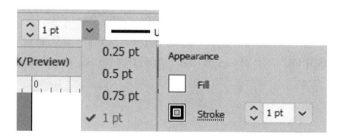

Figure 15-18. *Stroke weight settings in the Control and Properties panel*

The **variable-width profile** adjusts how the stroke path around the shape appears. By default, it is set to Uniform. You can access them from the Strokes panel as well. Refer to Figure 15-19.

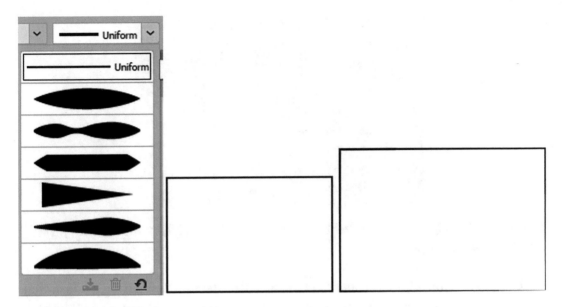

Figure 15-19. *Select a variable-width profile from the Control panel to alter the path*

The **brush definition** option may alter when you set the variable-width profile. You can use different brush styling in the Window ➤ Brushes panel. By default, it is set to Basic. This area is explored more in Chapter 16. Refer to Figure 15-20.

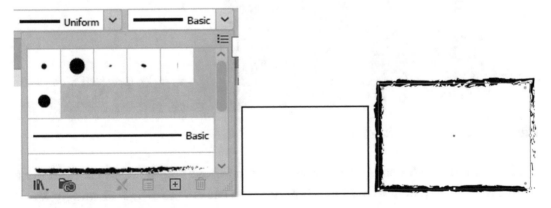

Figure 15-20. *Select a brush definition from the Control panel or Brushes panel to alter the path*

Opacity opens the Transparency panel and provides various options for the selected shape, including Blending mode. Alternatively, these options can be accessed from the Appearance areas of the Properties panel. Refer to Figure 15-21.

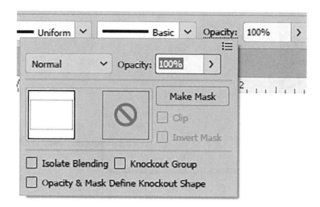

Figure 15-21. *Opacity and other options can be accessed from the Control panel and Transparency panel*

Opacity lets you adjust the opacity of a shape (0%–100%). Alternatively, these options can be accessed from the Appearance areas of the Properties panel and set additional effects *(fx)* and Appearance options. For now, leave the opacity of your shapes at 100%. Refer to Figure 15-22.

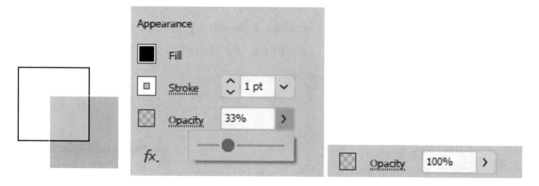

Figure 15-22. *Adjust the opacity*

The **Graphic Styles panel** lets you choose from various graphic styles accessed from the Graphic Styles panel. To reset the Graphic Styles back to the default fill and stroke, click the Default Graphic Style while the object is selected. Refer to Figure 15-23.

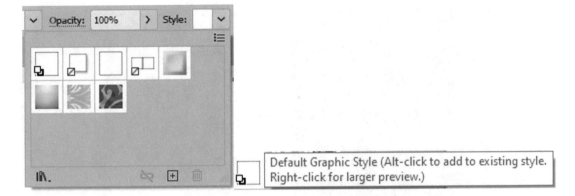

Figure 15-23. *Access Graphic Styles from the Control panel*

Recolor Artwork opens a portion of the options of the Color Guide panel. You look at this in more detail in Chapter 17, but when grouped objects and shapes are selected, this can be a very useful area to assist in recoloring artwork. Alternatively, you can access these options in the Properties panel under Quick Actions: Recolor. Refer to Figure 15-24.

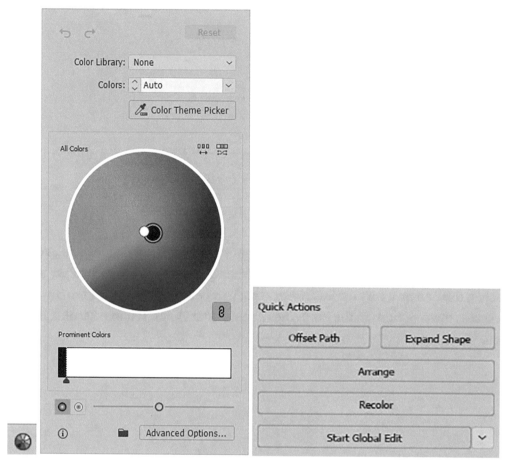

Figure 15-24. *Recolor artwork using the Control panel or Properties panel*

See Chapter 14 for more information on **Align to Artboard**. This option aligns the shape to either the selection or the artboard. Refer to Figure 15-25.

Figure 15-25. *Align artwork to a selection or artboard by altering the settings in the Control panel*

Align Options aligns one or more shapes' horizontal align (left, center, right) and vertical align (top, center, bottom). Alternatively, you can access these options in the

Properties panel under the Align area, and access additional align options under the ellipse button **More Options**. See Chapter 10 for more details. Refer to Figure 15-26.

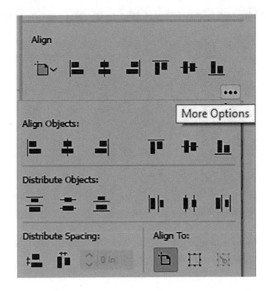

Figure 15-26. *More Align options are under the More Options button in the Properties panel*

Shape Properties opens additional properties in the Window ➤ Transform panel for Rectangles. It provides options for scaling width and height, rotation, and the radii of rounded corners, which you can adjust collectively or separately when unlinked. You can also adjust the corner type separately. Refer to Figure 15-27.

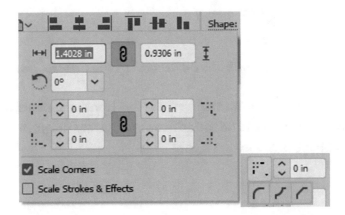

Figure 15-27. *Each shape has slightly different properties that can be accessed from the Control panel*

Scale Corners is enabled by default, and you also have the option **to Scale Strokes & Effects** if present. Alternatively, you can access these options from the Properties panel when clicking the More Options button in the Transform area. Refer to Figure 15-28.

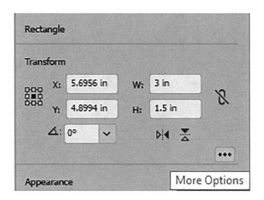

Figure 15-28. *You can access the Shapes properties in the Transform area of the Properties panel under the More Options button*

Note   When drawing a new shape, you may, before you draw the shape in this area of the Control panel, see an additional icon for hiding or showing the **Shape widget**. Refer to Figure 15-29.

Figure 15-29. *Shape Widget options on and off in the Control panel*

The **Transform panel** opens the main area of the Transform panel where you can scale position x and y coordinates on the artboard, width and height, angle, or skew. You can review this in Chapter 13. Refer to Figure 15-30.

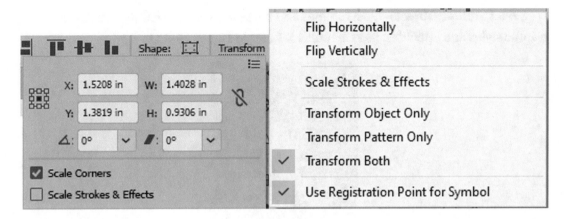

Figure 15-30. *From the Control panel, you can access the Transform panel and its menu options*

Scale Corners and **Scale Strokes & Effects** are also available in the Transform menu. Alternatively, you can access these options from the Properties panel in the Transform area, which lets you flip the shape vertically and horizontally without having to access the menu on the upper right of the panel. Refer to Figure 15-31.

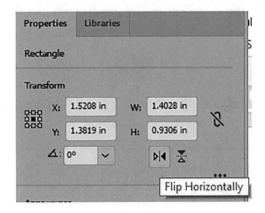

Figure 15-31. *The Properties panel has options to flip horizontally or vertically a selected shape*

Isolate selected objects isolates an object or shape on the sublayer to make edits. See Chapter 14 for more information. Refer to Figure 15-32.

Figure 15-32. *The Isolate selected objects Icon in the Control panel*

Select Similar Objects selects shapes and paths with similar colors and strokes or graphic styles and opacities. See Chapter 13. Refer to Figure 15-33.

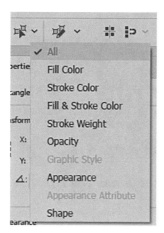

Figure 15-33. *Select Similar Objects Options from the drop-down menu in the Control panel*

You can edit various shapes together. This feature is in the Properties panel under Quick Actions ➤ Start Global Edit. You look at this in more detail in Chapter 17. Refer to Figure 15-34.

Figure 15-34. *Globally edit on all artboards from the Control panel*

Note   The other for alignment and menu icons in the Control panel are referenced in Chapter 14. Refer to Figure 15-35.

Figure 15-35. *Alignment and Control options in the Control panel*

Shape Expansion and Conversion

When manipulated with the Direct Selection tool, shapes become general paths. Often a message appears after the manipulation that says the shape was expanded. Refer to Figure 15-36.

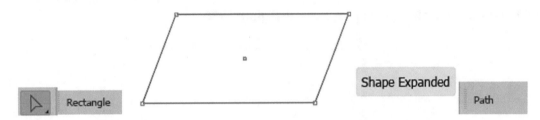

Figure 15-36. A shape is expanded and altered to become a path using the Direct Selection tool and is no longer considered a rectangle by Illustrator

It is no longer a rectangle shape but a closed path.

In the Properties panel, additional Quick Actions allow you to **Offset the path**, which creates an additional larger path or **Expand Shape**. If you click Expand Shape, the rectangle becomes a path and no longer has some of the rectangle shape properties in the Transform panel. Refer to Figure 15-37.

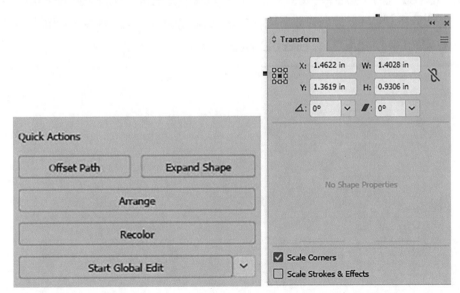

Figure 15-37. Quick Actions to expand a shape, no shape properties are in the Transform panel

Use ➤ Edit Undo (Ctrl/Cmd+Z) if you need to undo that step to return to a shape path.

Basic paths can also be converted to shapes if you need to give them some shape properties using **Object ➤ Convert to Shape**. However, if the shape has been manipulated, so it no longer resembles a rectangle, it may be regarded as a polygon, which you see later in this chapter. Refer to Figure 15-38.

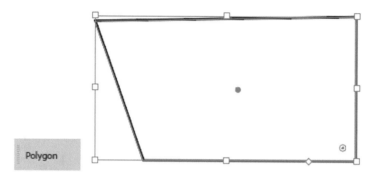

Figure 15-38. *The path was converted to a polygon shape*

Note   You can also arrange the order of the shapes when selected to higher or lower on the sublayers or use the Object ➤ Arrange commands from the Properties panel as seen in Chapter 13. Refer to Figure 15-39.

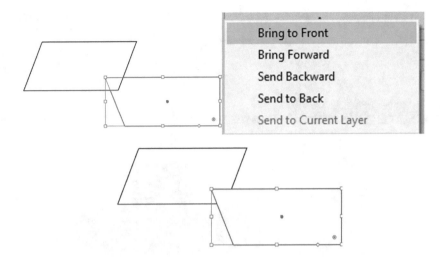

Figure 15-39. *Move a path over or under another using one of the Object ➤ Arrange commands*

Rounded Rectangle Tool

This tool creates a rounded rectangle. The Rounded Rectangle tool lets you do the following.

- Hold down the Shift key while dragging out a rounded square.

- Hold Shift+Alt/Option while you drag from the center of the shape.

- Press the up and down arrow keys while dragging to change the corner radius gradually. The left and right arrow keys let you square or round corners quickly. Refer to Figure 15-40.

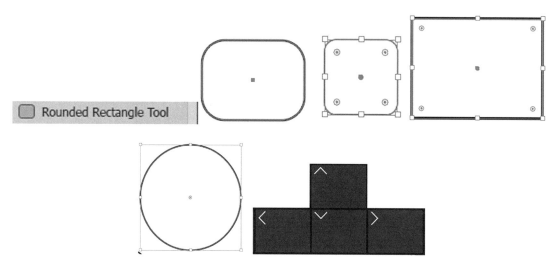

Figure 15-40. *The rounded rectangle can also be a rounded square. You can alter the radius using the arrow keys on your keyboard*

Rounded Rectangle Options

The Rounded Rectangle tool's options are in the Control and Properties panels. Most are the same as the Rectangle tool's options, so refer to that section in this chapter for more information. However, I'll point out a few key differences.

Before dragging out a rounded rectangle, enter it in the Rounded Rectangle dialog box by clicking on the artboard. You can automatically set the corner radius. Refer to Figure 15-41.

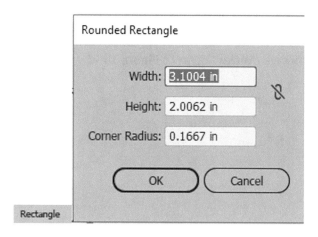

Figure 15-41. *The Rounded Rectangle dialog box lets you set a Corner Radius for all four sides*

The corner options and properties can also be automatically set. Refer to Figure 15-42.

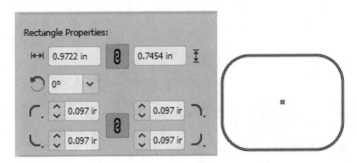

Figure 15-42. *Adjust Rectangle Properties in the Transform panel*

You can then change the corner types in one or all corners. Refer to Figure 15-43.

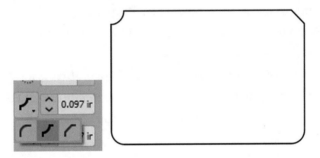

Figure 15-43. *Set a new corner type or radius for each corner*

Ellipse Tool (L)

The Ellipse tool lets you do the following.

- Create an oval or circle when you hold down the Shift key while dragging.

- Use Shift+Alt/Option to drag from the center. Refer to Figure 15-44.

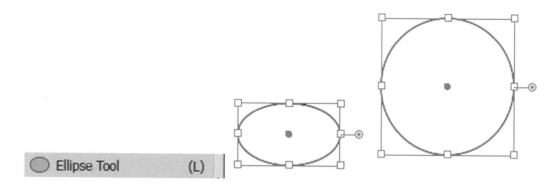

Figure 15-44. *The ellipse can be an oval or a circle*

Ellipse Options

The Ellipse tool's options are in the Control and Properties panels. Most are the same as the Rectangle tool's options, so refer to that section in this chapter for more information. However, I'll point out a few key differences.

Click the artboard. Instead of dragging out an ellipse, choose a setting in the Ellipse dialog box. Like the Rectangle tool, you can set the width and height and constrain or not constrain the proportions using the link icon. Refer to Figure 15-45.

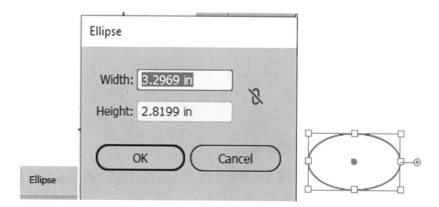

Figure 15-45. *The Ellipse tool dialog box and a created ellipse*

You can set a pie start and end angle, and then invert the pie shape. Refer to Figure 15-46.

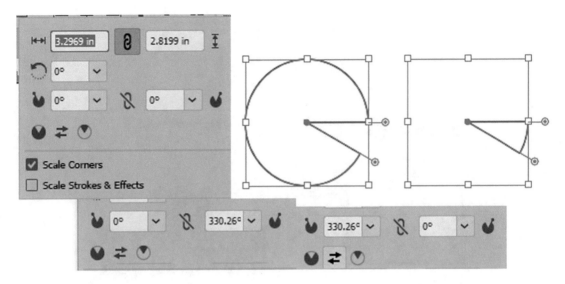

Figure 15-46. *Ellipse properties in the Transform panel and create a pie shape, and invert it*

This same step can also be done by dragging on the right handles connected to the ellipse. Refer to Figure 15-46.

Polygon Tool

The Polygon tool allows you to do the following.

- Create polygons with multiple sides from 3 up to 1000.

- Drag to create a polygon while rotating or hold the Shift key and drag to prevent rotation.

- Shift+Alt/Option to drag from the center. Refer to Figure 15-47.

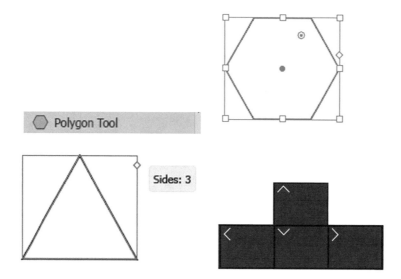

Figure 15-47. *Create a polygon with multiple sides using the bounding box slider or your arrow keys as you drag*

The diamond icon on the right side of the bounding box lets you drag to move it up or down to decrease or increase the number of sides on the polygon. Refer to Figure 15-47.

When you are dragging out a polygon if you press the up and down arrow keys on your keyboard, you can add or remove sides on your polygon while dragging it out. Refer to Figure 15-47.

Polygon Options

The Polygon tool's options are in the Control and Properties panels. Most are the same as the Rectangle tool's options, so refer to that section in this chapter for more information. However, I'll point out a few key differences.

To set the sides before dragging out, click the artboard with the tool to enter the Polygon dialog box, change the radius, and enter the number of sides. Refer to Figure 15-48.

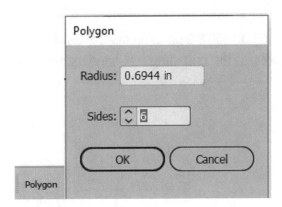

Figure 15-48. *The Polygon dialog box lets you set a radius and sides before you create the polygon*

In the Transform panel via Shape in the Control panel or through the Properties panel, you can set the number of sides after selection. Set an angle, a collective **Corner Type**, **Corner Radius**, **Polygon Radius**, and **Polygon Side Length**. Refer to Figure 15-49.

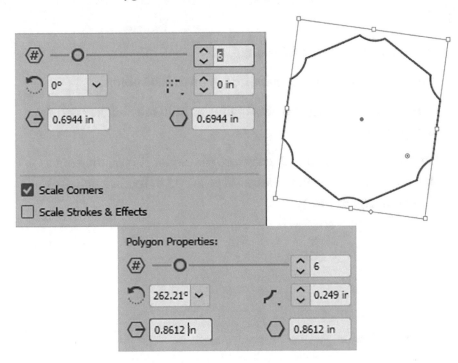

Figure 15-49. *Polygon Properties in the Transform panel let you alter the sides*

Note   If you want the polygon's side to be disproportionate, after creating, scale with the Selection tool and the bounding box handles. Refer to Figure 15-50.

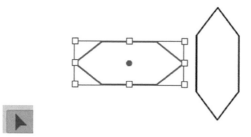

Figure 15-50. Use the Selection tool to scale the Polygon vertically or horizontally with your bounding box handles

Star Tool

The Star tool allows you to do the following.

- Create stars with multiple sides from 3 up to 1000 points.

- Drag to create a polygon while rotating or hold the Shift key and drag to prevent rotation.

- Hold Shift+Alt/Option and drag from the center. As you drag out a star, press the up and down arrow keys to add or remove points from it. Refer to Figure 15-51.

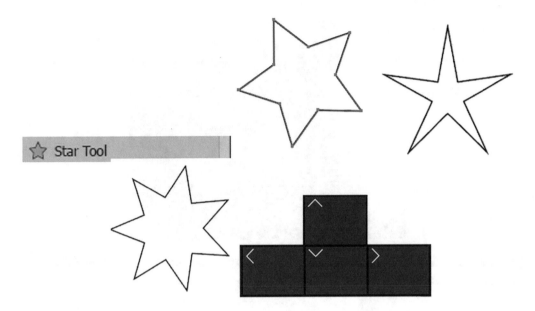

Figure 15-51. *Use the Star tool and your arrow keys to create a star with multiple sides*

Star Options

The Star tool's options are in the Control and Properties panels. Most are the same as the Rectangle tool's options, so refer to that section in this chapter for more information. However, I'll point out a few key differences.

To set the points before dragging out a star, click the artboard with the tool to enter the Star dialog box. There change the Radius 1 and Radius 2 and then enter the number of points. Refer to Figure 15-52.

711

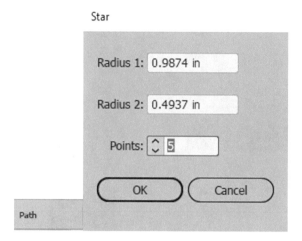

Figure 15-52. *The Star Radius dialog box lets you set the two radii and the number of points for the star*

You see that there is no shape link or properties in the Transform panel for the star. Refer to Figure 15-53.

Figure 15-53. *The Star has no shape properties in the Transform panel and is a path as seen in the Control panel*

Let's go over rounding the star's or polygon's corners as you did in Chapter 10.

After selecting it with the Selection tool, select the Direct Selection tool but do not select any specific point on the star. You then see the rounding corner handles. Refer to Figure 15-54.

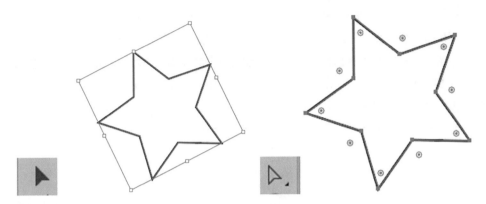

Figure 15-54. *Alter the stars' points with the Selection and Direct Selection tools*

This brings up new options in the Control panel, called **Corners and Corner Radius**. You can enter a new radius number in the corner or drag on the corner handles to set your radius manually. Refer to Figure 15-55.

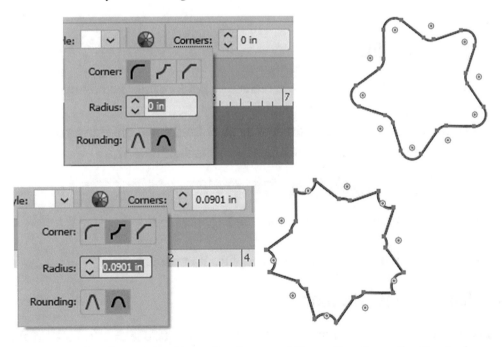

Figure 15-55. *Set the corner Type, Radius, and Rounding from the Control panel*

In the corner pop-out menu, there are a few alternate corner stylings and rounding as well. Refer to Figure 15-55.

Note   When you select a single point with the Direct Selection tool (A), individual anchor point corners can be adjusted with corners if a radius is present, in this case, for the star. You see point adjustment in more detail when you explore the Pen tool(P). Refer to Figure 15-56.

Figure 15-56. *Set different corners for points on a star when you select each point separately with the Direct Selection tool*

Line Segment Tool (\)

The Line Segment tool is very useful when creating random lines that mimic brush strokes for hair or pencil lines from sketches.

Drag out a line to whatever length, then let go or hold down the Shift key while dragging, and constrain the line to 45° angles. Refer to Figure 15-57.

Figure 15-57. *Drag out a line with the Line Segment tool*

A single line with no connective points or paths is created.

Line Segment Tool Options

The Line Segment Tool options are in the Control and Properties panels. Most are the same as the Rectangle tool's options, so refer to that section in this chapter for more information. However, I'll point out a few key differences.

When you click the artboard with this tool in the Line Segment Tools Options dialog box, you can set the Length, Angle, and if the line has a fill should you want to connect it later. By default, this option is disabled. Refer to Figure 15-58.

714

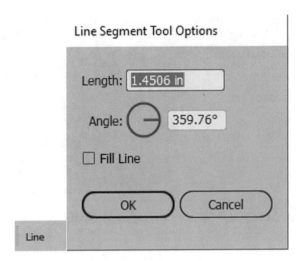

Figure 15-58. *Line Segment Tool Options dialog box*

In the Transform panel, or via Shape in the Control panel or through the Properties panel, you can adjust the length and rotation of the selected line. Refer to Figure 15-59.

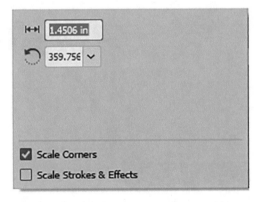

Figure 15-59. *Line Segment properties in the Transform panel*

Note   If you discover you added a fill by accident to the line, you can always set Fill to none in the Control panel and leave Stroke at black. Refer to Figure 15-60.

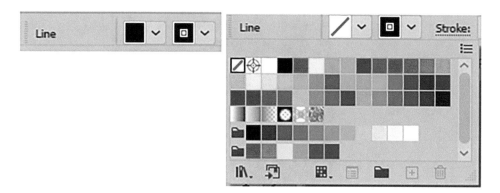

Figure 15-60. *In the Control panel, set line fill to None*

Arc Tool

The Arc tool is very similar to the Line Segment tool; however, it allows you to create an arched line when you drag or scale it proportionately when you hold down the Shift key. Refer to Figure 15-61.

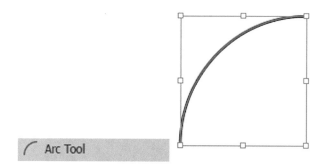

Figure 15-61. *Use the Arc tool to drag out an arc*

It is useful for creating various brush strokes or curves for hair or fur.

Arc Segment Tool Options

The Arc Segment Tool Options are in the Control and Properties panels. Most are the same as the Rectangle tool's options, so refer to that section in this chapter for more information. However, this tool has no additional shape options or properties, so use your dialog box to adjust for each arc.

To adjust the arc manually before you drag, click the artboard to enter the Arc Segment Tool Options dialog box. Refer to Figure 15-62.

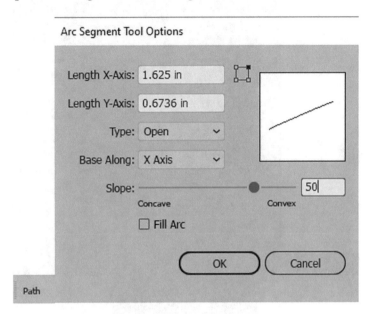

Figure 15-62. *Arc Segment Tool Options dialog box*

Here you can set **Length X-Axis**, **Length Y-Axis**, **anchor reference point** or **start position**, **Type:** open or closed, **Base Along:** X axis or Y axis, and **Slope:** Concave or Convex, which is adjusted using the slider (–100 to 100). You can choose to **fill the arc**, but by default, this option is disabled.

Lesser-used Shape Tools

There are a few additional shape tools that are used less frequently for re-creating sketches or drawings. I consider them more as decorative accents that could be later added to a drawing or logo. I talk about them here briefly. Each can be dragged (Shift and drag) to create a shape. Like the Rectangle tool, it can be accessed when you click the artboard.

Flare Tool

As you see in some photographs, the Flare tool is a specialized tool that creates a lens flare. You can add this afterward to an Illustration, but otherwise, it has no other practical use in this book. Refer to Figure 15-63.

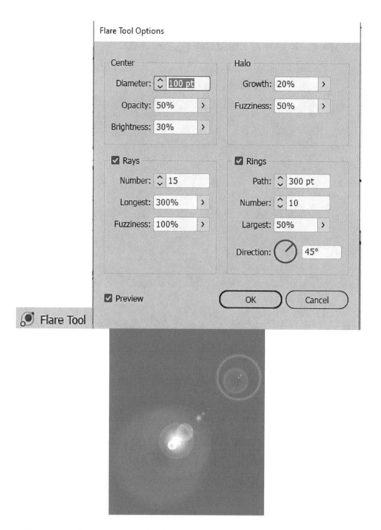

Figure 15-63. *Flare Tool Options dialog box with the preview on a blue background*

Note   You can alter the overall opacity and gradient using either the Control or Properties panel after the flare is created. Refer to Figure 15-64.

Figure 15-64. *Flare has opacity, colors, Gradient Type, and Edit the Gradient options*

Spiral Tool

This tool is similar to the Arc tool. It creates unique spirals or snail shells that either move clockwise or counterclockwise style. You can set the radius, decay (loose with a lower percent or tight with a higher percent, 80% is the default), and the number of segments. While dragging, use the up and down arrow keys on your keyboard to add or subtract segments. Refer to Figure 15-65.

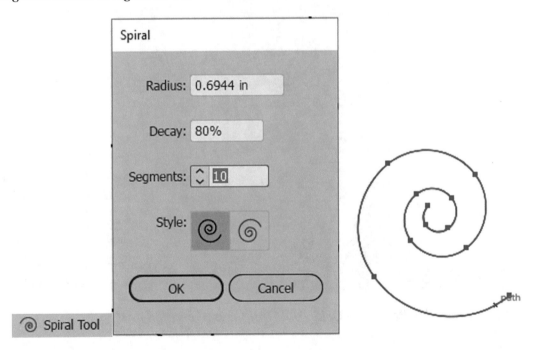

Figure 15-65. *The Spiral tool dialog box and a created spiral*

The Spiral, like the arc, is regarded as a path and has no additional properties in the Transform panel. Refer to the Rectangle tool if you need to review options in the Control or Properties panel.

Rectangular Grid Tool

The Rectangular Grid tool creates a grouped number of lines that appear as a grid. This grid simulates graph paper or bars but does not assist in redrawing most illustrations. However, it can create colored squares with the Live Paint Bucket and Live Paint Selection tool, which are covered in Chapter 16. However, you can enable the Fill Grid check box if a current fill exists in the Toolbars panel. Refer to Figure 15-66.

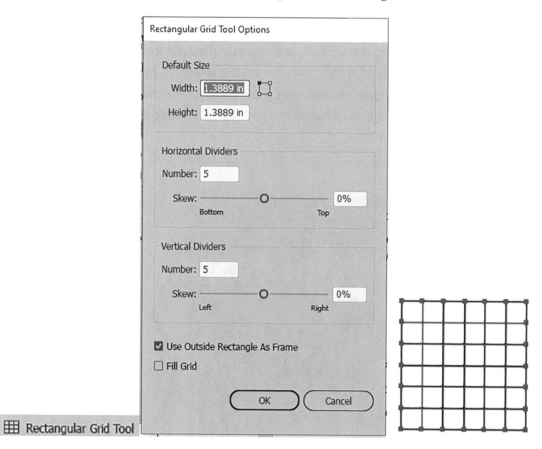

Figure 15-66. *The Rectangle Grid Tool Options and created grid*

Like the Arc, it's regarded as a path, or in this case, a grouped path, and has no additional properties in the Transform panel. Refer to the Rectangle tool if you need to review options in the Control or Properties panel.

Polar Grid Tool

The Polar Grid tool creates a grouped number of lines that appear as a circular grid. This grid could simulate a target or a spider's web, but it does not assist in redrawing most illustrations. However, it can create colored areas with the Live Paint Bucket and Live Paint Selection tools, which are discussed in Chapter 16. Refer to Figure 15-67.

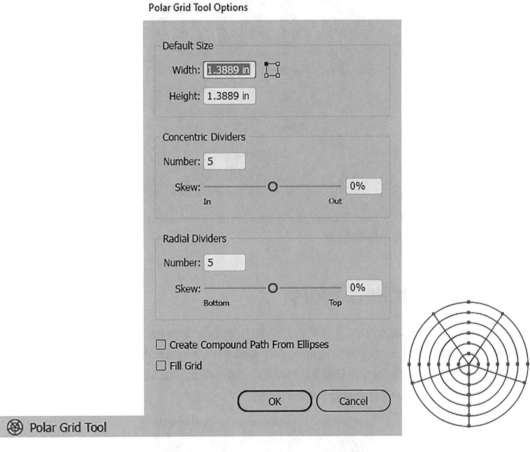

Figure 15-67. *The Polar Grid Tool Options and a created circular grid*

Like the Rectangular Grid, it's regarded as a grouped path and has no additional properties in the Transform panel. Refer to the Rectangle tool if you need to review options in the Control or Properties panel.

Once you have completed drawing the practice shapes, File ➤ Save (Ctrl/Cmd+S) your document as an (.ai) file.

Look at the 15_shape_examples.ai file if you need to see some examples to compare your work with my layer order. Refer to Figure 15-68.

Figure 15-68. *In the Layers panel, I organize all my shape examples on various layers to reference them anytime*

Working with Pen Tools

In Chapter 10, you created paths in Photoshop using the Pen tool for selection and masks. Now you can create paths that you fill and stroke with color.

Most of the settings for the Pen tool are the same as in Photoshop. Let's review some of the differences as well. Refer to Figure 15-69.

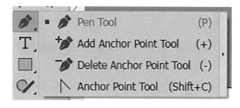

Figure 15-69. *The Pen tools in the Toolbars panel*

1. Create a File ➤ New Document for practice. You can practice on one or more layers, and as you fill one layer, you can always lock that layer and practice on a new one. You can refer to the following Figures for guidance or create your own paths.

Pen Tool (P)

The Pen tool draws straight or curved arc paths. Let's go over some tips and review the Pen tool.

Click and then click another place on the artboard to create a straight path with corners.

Shift-click when you want to create a straight line or one at 45 ° increments. Refer to Figure 15-70.

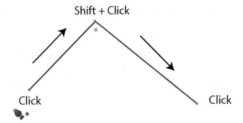

Figure 15-70. *With the Pen tool, create a path of straight lines and corner points*

Click and drag to create a curve. Then click and drag to create another curve. Refer to Figure 15-71.

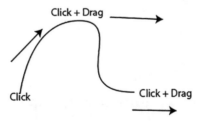

Figure 15-71. *Create a smooth anchor point and paths*

Shift-click and drag create a curve at angles of 45° increments.

Alt/Option-click a point after dragging again to make a corner point or wait for the Icon to change to the Anchor Point icon and click that point to create a corner point. Refer to Figure 15-72.

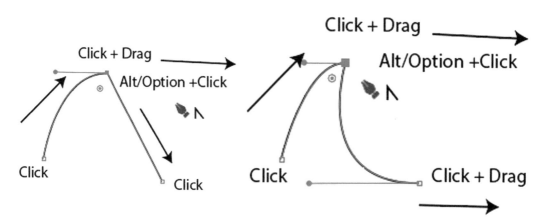

Figure 15-72. *Make a corner point and change direction on a path*

Note   The Anchor Point tool lets you further adjust the direction handles after closing the path.

When you reach the end of the path, the cursor changes to an O. You can click or click and drag to close the path. Refer to Figure 15-73.

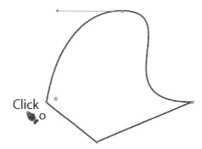

Figure 15-73. *Close an open path with the Pen tool*

If a path is broken, you can join two paths by clicking one point and then the other. Refer to Figure 15-74.

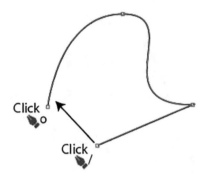

Figure 15-74. *Reconnect a broken path*

You can temporarily change to the Direct Selection tool (A) while creating a path by holding down the Ctrl/Cmd key. Click in the artboard to deselect the path without closing it. Refer to Figure 15-75.

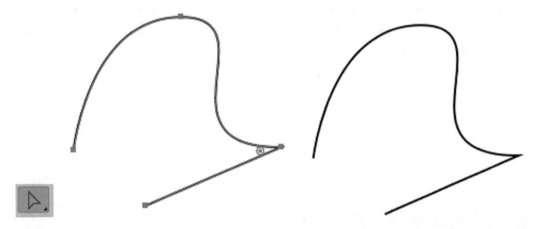

Figure 15-75. *Keep a path open with the Direct Selection tool and deselect the path*

Add Anchor Point Tool (+)

With a closed path, you can use **Add Anchor Point Tool (+)** to click in an area of a path to add a point and then hold down the Ctrl/Cmd key to select that point then drag it to the new location. Refer to Figure 15-76.

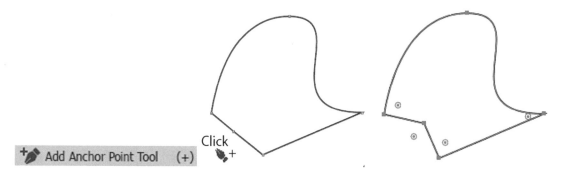

Figure 15-76. *Add Anchor Point tool adds a point to the path*

Delete Anchor Point Tool (-)

Use the **Delete Anchor Point Tool** (-) to click a point on a path to remove it. Doing so may distort the path, and you may need to use either your Direct Selection tool or your Anchor Point tool to adjust. Refer to Figure 15-77.

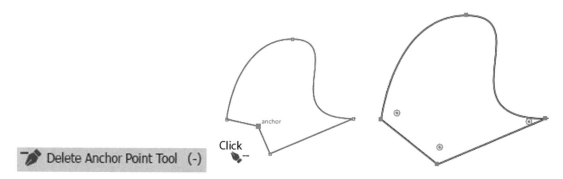

Figure 15-77. *Delete Anchor Point tool deletes a point but keeps the path closed*

Anchor Point Tool (Shift+C)

To convert a curved smooth point to a straight point, click a point with the **Anchor Point tool** (Shift+C) and click and drag on the same point to make the straight point curved and then click on the handles and drag to straighten it. Refer to Figure 15-78.

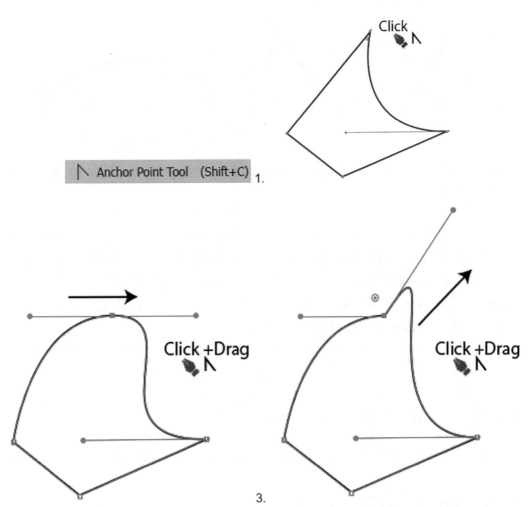

Figure 15-78. *Alter the path using the Anchor Point tool to make smooth and corner points*

This tool can also help you adjust any points that appear to be twisted while creating a path by clicking the twisted anchor point.

You can also drag on the line segment itself to make a curve. Refer to Figure 15-79.

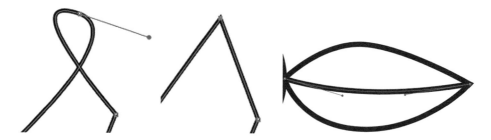

Figure 15-79. *Use the Anchor Point tool to correct twists or pull on a segment to make it curved*

Remember, you can use the Spacebar to change to the Hand tool (H) if you need to move around while making anchor points without moving them on the artboard by mistake. Use your Zoom tool (Z) if you need to get closer to your path so you can easily select points. Refer to Figure 15-80.

Figure 15-80. *The Hand tool and Zoom tool*

File ➤ Save the document as an (.ai) file of the practice paths you have created so far.

Curvature Tool (Shift+~)

This tool is in many ways like Photoshop's Curvature Pen tool in operation that you saw in Chapter 10. You can use it to create smooth and rounded curves quickly by clicking and dragging, and then close the path. Refer to Figure 15-81.

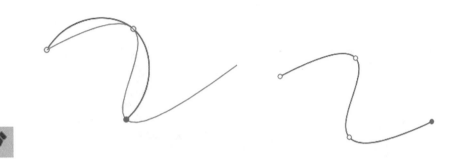

Figure 15-81. *Drawing paths with the Curvature tool*

With this tool, you can hover over a sketch and then click out the path while adding smooth corner points, drag out the curve to see the rubber band preview. Refer to Figure 15-82.

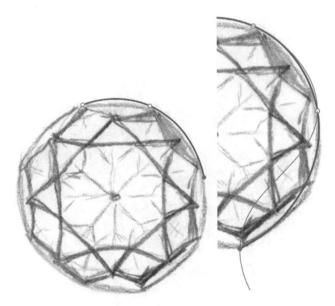

Figure 15-82. *Clicking out the path points with a rubber band preview*

To create a corner point, double-click or press the Alt/Option key while clicking a point.

Any path can use the Curvature Pen tool, even if it was not created with the tool.

While this tool is active, you can double-click a point to make them straight or curved. Refer to Figure 15-83.

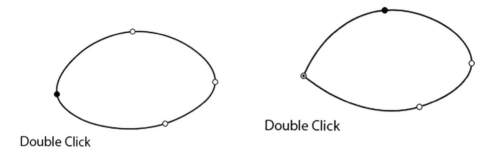

Figure 15-83. *Double-click a point to make it smooth or curved*

Click a point to move it or click a point and press the Backspace/ Delete key to remove it and then click the Point again to continue the path.

To close a path, when you reach the original start point, the pointer icon changes to an O, and then click. You can also drag an endpoint over a start point on an open path to close it. Refer to Figure 15-84.

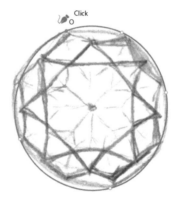

Figure 15-84. *Closing a path with the Curvature tool*

Press the Esc key to stop creating the path if you do not want to close it.

Note   While working, if you cannot see the rubber band preview, then go to Edit ➤ Preferences ➤ Selection & Anchor Display ➤ Enable Rubber Band. Make sure it is checked for Pen and Curvature tool and click OK to exit the dialog box. Refer to Figure 15-85.

Enable Rubber Band for: ☑ Pen Tool ☑ Curvature Tool

Figure 15-85. *Preference setting for the Rubber Band Preview for Pen and Curvature tool*

PRACTICE WITH THE CURVATURE TOOL

You may need to practice with the Curvature tool a few times until you feel comfortable with the tool.

Open the 15_trace_curvature.ai file to practice on layer 3 to create a curved path around the gemstone sketch.

In this example, I drew the path on layer 2 and locked it so you can compare. I used a pink Stroke and a Fill of None to see the path and compare. Refer to Figure 15-86.

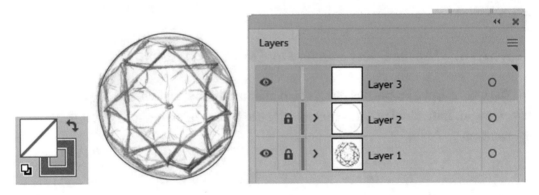

Figure 15-86. *Practice on your own layer with the Curvature tool. My layer 2 is hidden in the Layers panel*

Later in this chapter, I show you some ways to work efficiently while tracing your own paths.

Direct Selection Tool for Individual Points

When an individual point on a path is selected, you can move the point, but on curved smooth points, you can also drag or hold the Shift key and drag one of the handles to adjust one side of the curve. Refer to Figure 15-87.

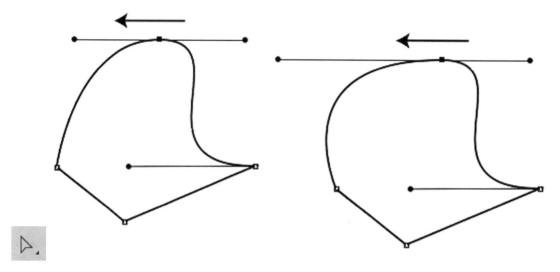

Figure 15-87. *Use the Direct Selection tool to alter a curve on a path*

The Control and Properties panels also offer additional ways to modify the path when an individual point is clicked with the Direct Selection tool (A). Refer to Figure 15-88.

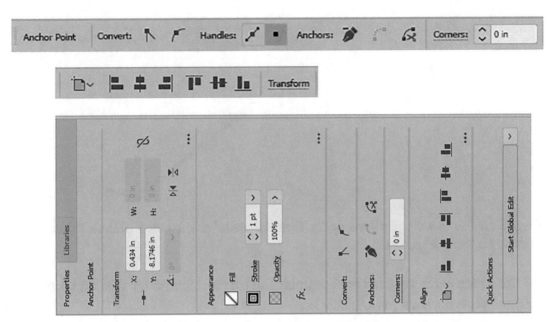

Figure 15-88. *The Control panel and Properties panel have options for Anchor points*

Let's focus on the Control panel looking from left to right.

Convert converts selected anchor points from a smooth curve to a corner point or back to smooth. Refer to Figure 15-89.

Figure 15-89. *Convert a single anchor point to corner or smoothed in the Control panel*

Handles lets you show or hide multiple direction handles for selected anchor points. Refer to Figure 15-90.

Figure 15-90. *Hide or show handle options in the Control panel*

Anchors allows you to **remove selected anchor points**. If two open points or endpoints are selected, you can **join** them. Refer to Figure 15-91.

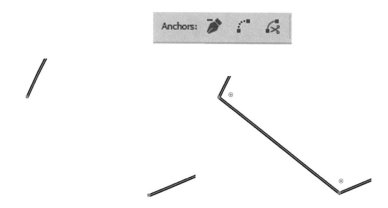

Figure 15-91. *Anchor options in the Control panel allow you to delete, join or cut anchor points and paths*

Cut a path at the selected anchor points, select the line with the Direct Selection tool, and press the Backspace/Delete key.

Corners alters the individual corner radii and points. Refer to Figure 15-92.

Figure 15-92. *Set Corners and Radius in the Control panel*

You can also **align** selected points and use the **Transform panel** to move the point on the x and y axes in set increments. Refer to Figure 15-93.

Figure 15-93. *Align and move points in set increments using the Control and Transform panels*

Path Commands

Object ➤ Path also has a few extra commands that can help you work with your paths; you looked at **Object ➤ Path ➤ Simplify** in Chapter 14 to reduce the number of anchor points on a path. However, there are a few more that may be helpful for your projects. Refer to Figure 15-94.

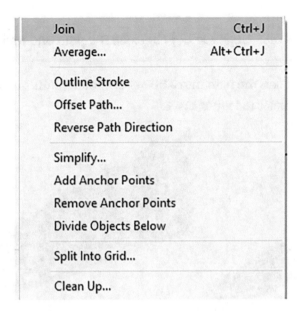

Figure 15-94. *Object ➤ Path Commands in the main menu*

Use **Join** to connect two selected paths.

Average brings two paths together at the horizontal or vertical axis or both. Use the Average dialog box to set the axis and click OK to confirm. Refer to Figure 15-95.

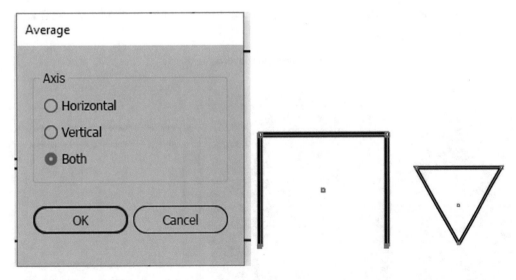

Figure 15-95. *Use the Average dialog box to move two selected points together*

Tip   You could then use Object ➤ Join to close the path and make it one point.

Outline Stroke makes the path into a fill or compound path. You could then apply a stroke to the new fill. Refer to Figure 15-96.

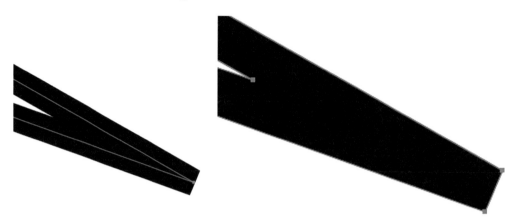

Figure 15-96.   *Outline a stroke to make it a path*

Offset Path creates another path **Offset** from the original. In the dialog box, you can also alter the type of **Joins** (miter, round, beveled) or **Miter limit** for a point on sharp lines so that it does not appear to be cut off. Select the Preview check box to see the result. Refer to Figure 15-97.

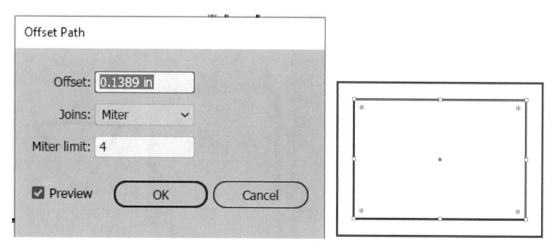

Figure 15-97.   *Offset Path dialog box and the new path is previewed*

Tip   Use a negative number in the offset to inset a path (e.g., –0.5 in).

Reverse Path Direction is more apparent when you want the strokes to move in one direction, such as simulated brush strokes. Refer to Figure 15-98.

Figure 15-98.   *Reverse the directions on the path to make it appear the brush stroke is going in the other direction*

Add Anchor Points adds additional anchor points between the originally selected anchor points. Refer to Figure 15-99.

Figure 15-99.   *Add anchor points to a path*

Remove Anchor Points removes selected anchor points but does not delete the path segment.

Divide Objects Below divides the upper selected path or shape with the unselected object below. What is not within the lower path is deleted. Refer to Figure 15-100.

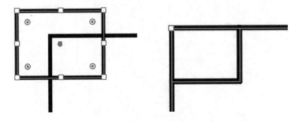

Figure 15-100.   *Divide Objects Below remove a part of the upper shape or object*

Like the Rectangular Grid tool, **Split Into Grid** transforms a rectangle into a grid using the dialog box and enabled preview. Refer to Figure 15-101.

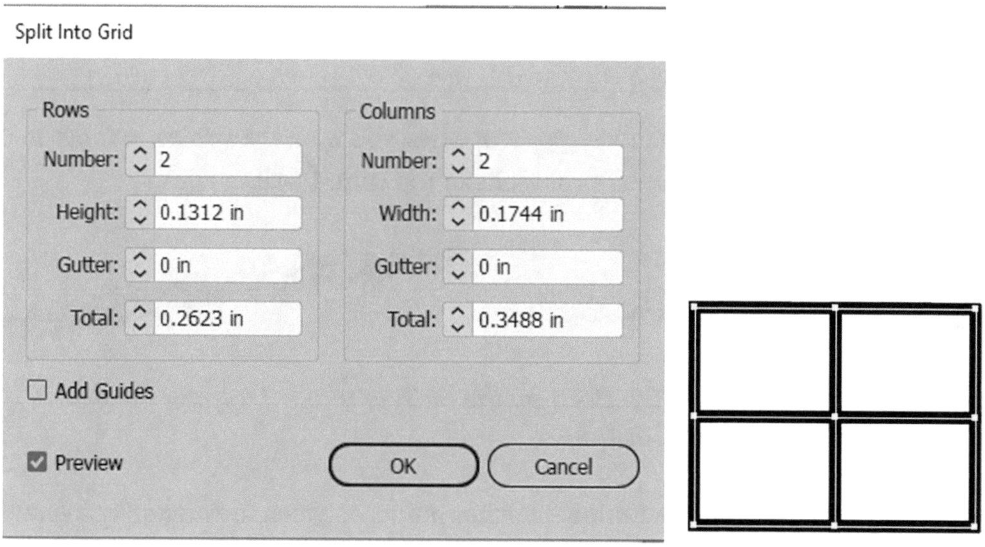

Figure 15-101. *Split Into Grid dialog box and the preview of the created grid*

The **Clean Up** dialog box assists in cleaning up accidental stray points on the unlocked layers. Disable any options that you do not want to delete. Refer to Figure 15-102.

Figure 15-102. *Clean Up dialog box to Delete Stray Points, Unpainted Objects, and Empty Text Paths*

Chapter 16 looks at a few additional tools that help you clean up your paths and adjust further.

SHAPE AND PEN TOOLS PROJECT

You have seen what the Shape and Pen tools have to offer during practice.

1. File ➤ Open 15_trace.ai.

2. File ➤ Save As (Shift+Ctrl/Cmd+S) to make a copy of the file to practice on to review what you have learned so far about Shape and Pen tools. I saved mine as 15_trace_final.ai, should you need to review it and compare later.

3. In the Layers panel, I placed my sketches on layer 1, grouped them, and locked the layer. These are sketches of brooches from Chapter 10. I placed (Shift+Ctrl/Cmd+P) them on the artboard and then embedded and cropped the sketches one at a time. You can review how to do this in Chapter 13 when I placed an apple image.

4. I created a new blank layer 2, which is the layer that you can create shape paths and pen paths on. Refer to Figure 15-103.

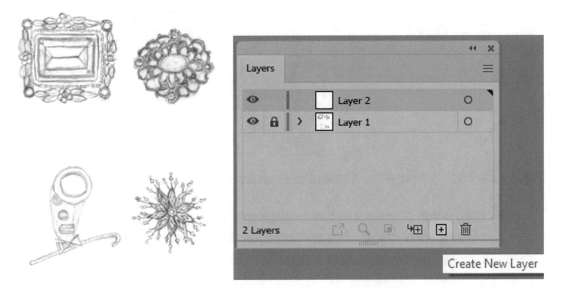

Figure 15-103. *Four Grouped brooch sketches are on layer 1 and locked in the Layers panel with a tracing layer 2*

5.   Use the Zoom tool to zoom in on the upper left rectangular brooch.

6.   Make sure your stroke and fill are set to default (D). Select the Rectangle tool and drag a rectangle over the gem area. Refer to Figure 15-104.

Figure 15-104. *Draw a rectangle with the Rectangle tool over the sketch with the default colors in the Toolbars panel*

As you create a path or shape on layer 2, notice that if you use a fill, it covers the shape and some areas that you want to see.

7.   In this example, set the Fill in the Toolbars panel to None. Refer to Figure 15-105.

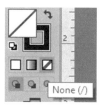

Figure 15-105. *Set the fill to None while you trace out your new paths and shapes*

8.   Use a very thin line when making the initial path. In the Control panel, set the weight to 1pt or less. Keep the line variable-width profile at Uniform and the brush definition at Basic. Refer to Figure 15-106.

Figure 15-106. *Use these settings for tracing*

Chapter 16 looks at those areas as ways to accent your artwork, but for now, you want to keep the lines simple while tracing.

Layer Options for Paths

Make sure the layer color for your path selection guides does not clash with the art because it may be difficult to see while tracing.

1. Double-click layer 2 to enter the Layer Adjustment panel if you need to change the color. Light Blue or Red show up clearly in sketches, but Black or Yellow are difficult to see in some lines or against some backgrounds. Click OK in the dialog box to confirm and exit. Refer to Figure 15-107.

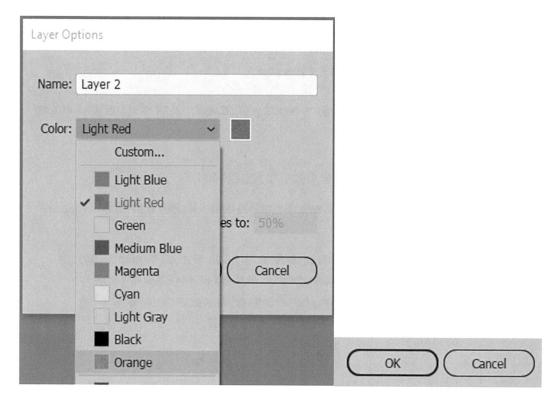

Figure 15-107. *Path colors are important when you need to see a path, so set it in the Layer Options dialog box for the layer*

At this point, you could continue to either use other shapes or use the Pen tool. However, here is one of the best ways to trace over some shapes.

2. Drag the Sketch layer (layer 1) over the Tracing layer (layer 2). Refer to Figure 15-108.

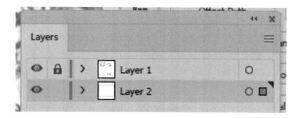

Figure 15-108. *Drag your layer 1 over the top of layer 2 in the Layers panel*

3. Use the Zoom tool while holding down the Alt/Option key or Ctrl/Cmd+0 to zoom out.

4. Temporarily unlock layer 1, and then select the grouped sketches with the Selection tool. Refer to Figure 15-109.

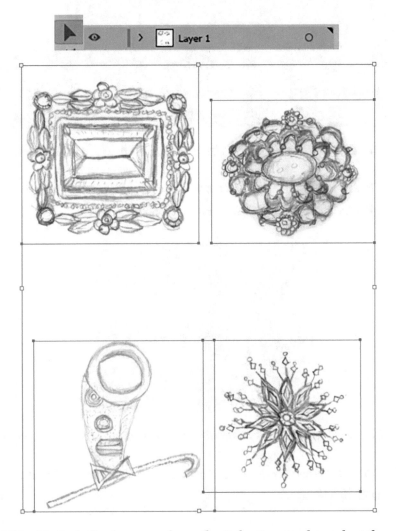

Figure 15-109. *Unlock the layer and use the Selection tool to select the grouped sketches*

5. With the Transparency panel and the sketches selected, choose a different Blending mode so that you can see the tracing lines showing through. I used **Darken** mode. Refer to Figure 15-110.

743

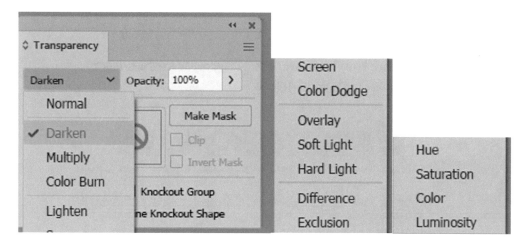

Figure 15-110. *Transparency panel drop-down menu to set the mode to Darken*

6. Lock layer 1 so the sketch cannot move. Continue to trace out the shapes on layer 2, which is below layer 1 now. Refer to Figure 15-111.

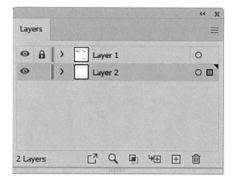

Figure 15-111. *Lock layer 1 in the Layers panel and continue to trace on layer 2*

Now you can still see the rectangular path, and it is not covered while you draw. Refer to Figure 15-112.

Figure 15-112. *The rectangle shape can be seen on the sketch*

Blend Modes Applied Sketches or Objects

So why did you do these last steps with blending modes? While it may not seem important right now, as you add more lines and layer fills, there will be points during creation at which you want to compare your current strokes and fills with your original path. Rather than turning on and off your sketch on layer 1 in the Layers panel this saves you time as you can see the sketch lines as you fill the paths with color as the sketch and lines blend because of the blending mode.

As you saw in Photoshop, working with layers in different blending modes can affect the underlying layer. In Illustrator, they affect the underlying object when applied to the selected object above it. Objects are not layer-dependent. Other blending modes, like Multiply or Overlay, may work as well, depending on how your sketch's colors interact with the strokes and fills you are using for the path. Refer to Figure 15-113.

Figure 15-113. *When a sketch has a blending mode applied, you can still see the shape's fill below while you continue to trace*

It does not matter what the colors of the stroke or fill are if you can trace around the areas of the shape that you need for your sketch.

1.   Leave the shape's fill at none and a black stroke and use various shape tools to create rectangles and ellipses. Refer to Figure 15-105.

2.   Scale and rotate the shapes using the bounding box handles.

If you need to create a duplicate of a shape, select it and Alt/Option-drag.

Next, let's look at some tips to help you complete the paths for the brooch.

When you select more than one shape, use the Align panel to center shapes or distribute them. Refer to Figure 15-114.

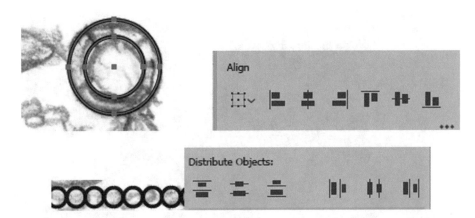

Figure 15-114. *Use your Align Options in either your Properties or Align panel to center objects as well you can space selected objects out using the Distribute Objects options*

By using the Line Segment tool, you can create thin facet lines for the gemstone. Refer to Figure 15-115.

Figure 15-115. *Use the Align tool to create facets for the gemstone and group them*

Use Object ➤ Arrange commands as you work to bring some shapes over others. When you add a color fill later, the order is very important.

If you have several paths that you want to keep together, first choose Object ➤ Group so that you can move the entire selection using the Selection tool (V) when you click and drag. Refer to Figure 15-115.

You can then Alt/Option-drag out similar grouped shapes, which saves you time replicating areas of the drawing.

With Grouped objects, you can use your Group Selection tool to select and then Backspace/Delete unwanted shapes. Refer to Figure 15-116.

Figure 15-116. *The Group Selection tool can help you select a single shape within a group and delete it*

Select a group with the Selection tool (V) and use your keyboard arrow keys to nudge it into place. Refer to Figure 15-117.

Figure 15-117. *Use your Selection tool and keyboard arrow keys to nudge your groups into place*

Use your Star tool, Ellipse tool, and Line tool to create a rounded star for the flower petals. Refer to Figure 15-118.

Object ➤ Group these flower paths and Alt/Option-drag to make copies. Note that you may need to rotate the lower flower using your bounding box handles one so that the petals align better. Refer to Figure 15-118.

Figure 15-118. *Create a flower with the star and line tools and then group it, make copies, and rotate the lower center flowers*

Use the Pen tools and the Direct Selection tool to create and modify a path and anchor points for leaves and gemstone prong. You can select each piece with the Selection tool, Alt/Option-drag to replicate, then Object ➤ Group the leaves as well. Refer to Figure 15-119.

Figure 15-119. *After drawing the prong and leaves, you can replicate and group them into sets*

Note   As you draw paths with the Pen tool, avoid connecting to line segments in other groups. I often use more than one layer for tracing and then locking layers to avoid creating unwanted paths with more complex drawings. Refer to Figure 15-120.

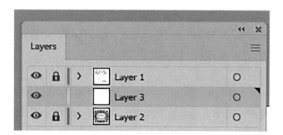

Figure 15-120. *Use multiple layers to trace when you are worried about paths joining while using the Pen tool*

Choose Object ➤ Transform ➤ Reflect to make a copy. This helps you create the vertical reflection of the leaf pattern. Refer to Figures 15-119 and 15-121.

Figure 15-121. *The Reflect dialog box can help you create horizontal and vertical reflections of paths*

You do not have to trace exactly over the sketch. The sketch is there to give you a rough idea as to where paths should be placed. The interpretation of that is up to you.

You can use Illustrator to get the paths and shapes exact either by selecting paths and using the Align panel on objects, grouped objects, or scaling the bounding boxes.

Some shapes may need to be rounded further by changing the radii, such as rectangles around the gemstone and flower border, to create a rounded border effect like the original brooch. Refer to Figure 15-122.

Figure 15-122. *Paths with layer 1 turned on and paths with layer 1 turned off*

You can see how these paths on Layer 2 now look with the sketch on layer 1 hidden.

Later, as you build more paths and fill with color in Illustrator, many lines are hidden, making the sketch more realistic and refined.

Remember to use Object ➤ Arrange if certain shapes need to be sent behind or in front of others.

Alhough using the Shapes and Pen tools is more work than the Image Trace panel, you can see how this could be the start of a minimalistic line drawing or a logo for a jewelry company.

File ➤ Save (Ctrl/Cmd+S) your document.

As additional practice, you can try tracing over the other three pieces of jewelry as well, also on layer 2. You can see how this looks in the 15_trace_final.ai file. Refer to Figure 15-123.

Figure 15-123. *Practice using your Shape and Pen tools to trace the other three brooches*

Summary

This chapter discussed using Shape tools and Pen tools to create artwork. It also offered additional ways to select and adjust a path using Object ➤ Path Commands. You looked at the importance of layer order and how sketches with applied blending modes can assist in drawing paths. In the next chapter, you continue to work with your paths and modify them with a few additional tools in the Toolbars panel that Illustrator offers.

CHAPTER 16

Illustrator Tools

This chapter shows how to use a few additional Illustrator tools that can help you re-create your artwork further.

The previous chapter looked at the basic functions of Shape and Pen tools and how they are used for tracing over your artwork.

While working on your paths, at some point, you want to refine some paths that contain color or remove parts of paths. Although the Pen, Selection, Direction Selection, and Group Selection tools do a good job modifying paths, Illustrator has some unique tools that you can use for more accurate tracing, line segment joining, removal of segments, and painting fills. Refer to Figure 16-1.

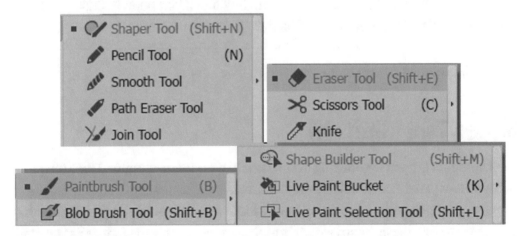

Figure 16-1. *You can select several tools to edit your artwork from the Toolbars panel*

The following tools are in the Toolbars panel.

- Shaper tool (Shift+N)

- Pencil tool (N)

© Jennifer Harder 2022
J. Harder, *Accurate Layer Selections Using Photoshop's Selection Tools*,
https://doi.org/10.1007/978-1-4842-7493-4_16

- Smooth tool

- Path Eraser tool

- Join tool

- Eraser tool (Shift+E)

- Scissors tool (C)

- Knife

- Paintbrush tool (B)

- Blob Brush tool (Shift+B)

- Shape Builder tool (Shift+M)

- Live Paint Bucket (K)

- Live Paint Selection tool (Shift+L)

Note   Use Edit ➤ Undo (Ctrl/Cmd+Z) with any tool if you need to undo a step. Projects for this chapter are in the Chapter 16 folder.

Let's look at the first tool in the list.

Shaper Tool (Shift+N)

The Shaper tool is great for drawing over a sketch. It creates a simplified path shape quickly so that you do not need to worry about creating basic shapes like the ellipse, rectangles, and polygons. It is a three-in-one tool, so you do not need to switch tools. When you draw on the artboard with this tool and then release the mouse as you close the path, the shapes are transformed from a crude line to a shape with a black stroke and a light gray fill. Refer to Figure 16-2.

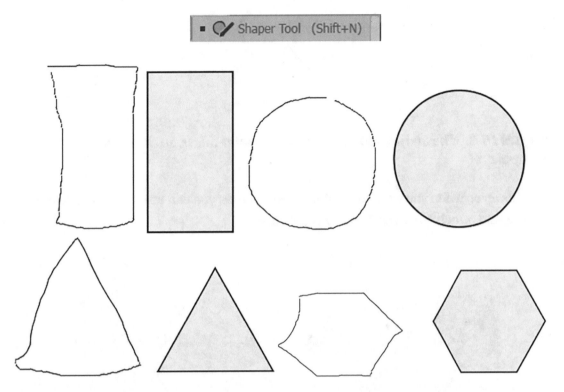

Figure 16-2. *Crude drawings of shapes can be recognized by the Shaper tool as basic shapes*

In a File ➤ New Document, try drawing some of these shapes using the Shaper tool to practice with.

Note   Although this tool is useful for basic shapes, it does not do well with more complex paths like stars or random paths. These disappear when you close the path. In this case, use your Pencil tool (N) instead, which you look at later in the chapter. Refer to Figure 16-3.

Figure 16-3. *The Shaper tool does not know what this is, so the drawing disappears*

However, when you want to combine basic shapes, you can use this tool to delete, merge, and punch out areas. Refer to Figure 16-4.

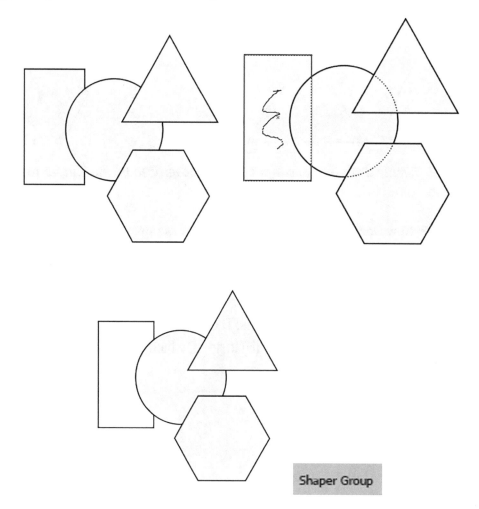

Figure 16-4. *Overlapped shapes when you scribble with the Shaper tool turn them into a Shaper Group*

Once you have drawn the shapes and moved them into place with your Selection tool, use Object ➤ Arrange commands to adjust the order.

You can then return to the Shaper tool to scribble over overlapping areas.

If the scribble is within one shape and only on the fill, the area is punched out or removed, creating a Shaper Group. You can confirm this when you select the shapes with the Selection tool and look in the Control panel for the description on the left.

Note   Do not draw a straight line when trying to punch out or combine shapes. Always draw a scribble, or the tool thinks you are drawing a line segment. Also, all the shapes do not need to be selected; you only need to overlap to become part of the Shaper Group.

If the scribble is across intersecting areas of two or more shapes, the intersecting areas are punched out or merged, and a Shaper Group is created. Refer to Figure 16-5.

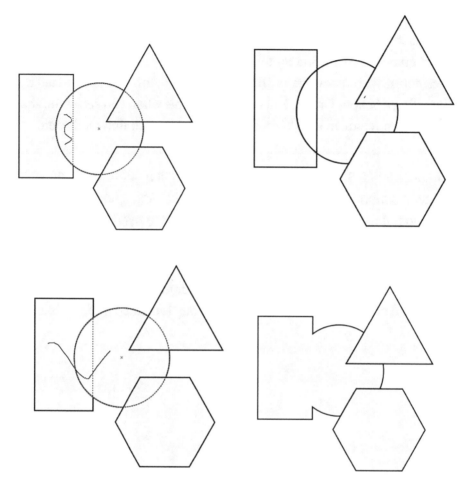

Figure 16-5. *If you scribble inside two intersecting areas, you punch out a hole, but over two shapes, then you merge them*

Shaper Tool and Colored Shapes

If a shape is colored, it can affect how the selection is altered.

For example, if a scribble originates from the shape in the front, from a non-overlapping area to an overlapping area, the shape in the front is punched out, but the stroke remains. Refer to Figure 16-6.

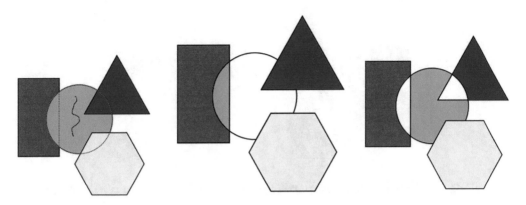

Figure 16-6. *With colored shapes depending on what area you scribble in, different areas are punched out*

The shapes are merged from an overlapping area to a non-overlapping area, with the color of the merged area being that of the scribble origin point. It is like using the Pathfinders panel to merge shapes, which you see later in the chapter. Refer to Figure 16-7.

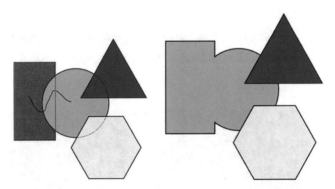

Figure 16-7. *Scribbling over an overlapping area can result in a merge of color; in this case, the overlapping color merged as I scribbled toward the left*

The shapes are merged if the scribble originates from the shape in the back, from a non-overlapping area to an overlapping area. The color of the merged area is the scribble origin point. Refer to Figure 16-8.

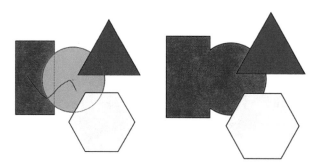

Figure 16-8. *Scribbling over the overlapping area can result in a merge of color; in this case, the underlying color merged as I scribbled toward the right*

Shaper groups can be expanded into a Grouped path by clicking the Expand button in the Control panel or Properties panel in the Quick Actions. Refer to Figure 16-9.

Figure 16-9. *Expand a Shaper Group*

If there more than one Shaper Group is present, it can be merged with the other. Click Continue if you see a warning message. Refer to Figure 16-10.

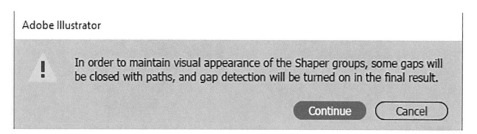

Figure 16-10. *When you try to merge two Shaper Groups, you may get a warning*

You can also use gap detection if small gaps are detected for painting, but look at that further when looking at the Shape Builder tool, Live Paint Bucket, and Live Paint Selection tools. Gaps in this case preview in a Light Red when hovered over when using these tools. Refer to Figure 16-11.

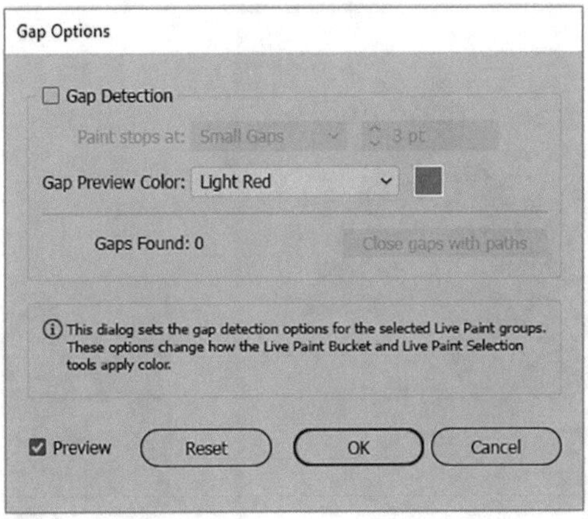

Figure 16-11. *Gap Options dialog box*

To edit shapes in the Shaper Group, select the group with the Selection tool, then the Shaper tool, which is currently in Face Selection mode, and click the Down arrow on the bounding box. It changes to an Up arrow, and you are in Construction mode. Refer to Figure 16-12.

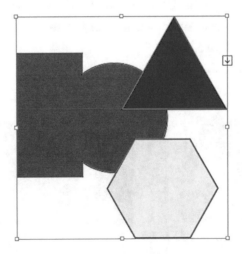

Figure 16-12. *Shaper Group in Face Selection mode*

You can then continue to scribble on areas of the shape to merge or punch out. Refer to Figure 16-13.

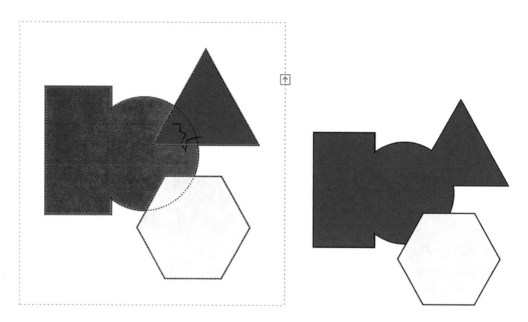

Figure 16-13. *Shaper Group in Construction mode*

Double-clicking a shape in this Construction mode allows you to drag and move it within the bounding box area. You can also alter the shapes and scale them with the bounding boxes. Refer to Figure 16-14.

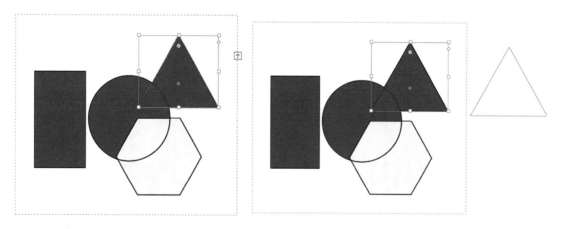

Figure 16-14. *Moving a shape in Construction mode and then outside of the Shaper Group*

To remove a shape from the shaper group, drag it outside of the bounding box area. Refer to Figure 16-14.

You can compare your drawing results with my 16_shaper_tool.ai file.

Later, you can use this tool with the **Shape Builder tool** for more editing and creating complex paths and Live Paint tools, which you see later in the chapter.

Pencil Tool (N)

The Pencil tool lets you draw more complex paths. You can use it as you would a brush to draw a path and then the path has a stroke of black and a fill of none. Refer to Figure 16-15.

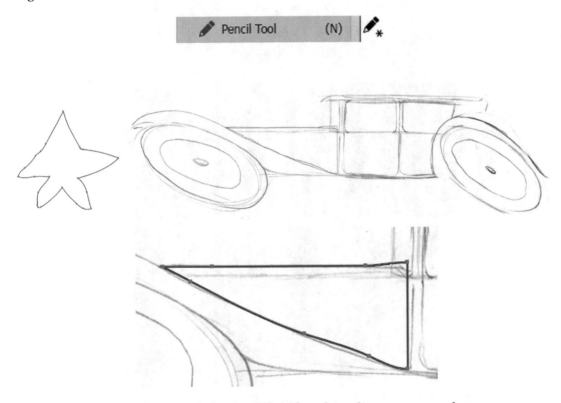

Figure 16-15. *Working with the Pencil tool to draw lines on a new layer over a sketch*

File ➤ Open 16_pencil_tool.ai if you need a file to practice with or use your own drawing to practice with the next few tools.

You can adjust the Pencil tool options in the Toolbars panel.

Pencil Tool Options

The **Fidelity** slider can be set to a high Accurate setting to a loose Smooth setting and controls how far you must move your mouse before Illustrator adds new anchor points to the path and has a range of 0.5 to 20 pixels. By default, the slider is in the center. Refer to Figure 16-16.

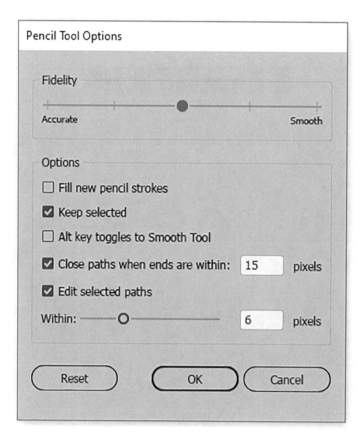

Figure 16-16. *Pencil Tools Options dialog box*

The following describes the other options.

- **Fill new pencil strokes:** If you want to fill in the path as you draw, enable this setting; by default, it is unselected. If enabled, you must have a fill selected in the Toolbars panel for this setting to work.

- **Keep selected:** After the line is drawn, it remains selected. Keep this option enabled so that you can use other tools to quickly modify the path.

- **Alt/Option key toggles to Smooth tool:** If this option is enabled, you can hold down your Alt/Option key afterward to smooth the path.

- **Close paths when the ends are within a set number of pixels:** This can be set up or down depending on how high or low a tolerance you need before the paths join to close the path with the endpoints. By default, it is set to 15 pixels.

- **Edit selected paths within a set number of pixels:** Determines how close your pointer must be to an existing path to edit the path with the Pencil tool.

If you make changes, click **OK** or press the **Reset** button before leaving to reset the alterations. Click **Cancel** without making changes.

When you draw with the Pencil tool, you can hold down the Shift key to create a straight line constrained to 45° angles rather than a free-form line. Refer to Figure 16-17.

Figure 16-17. *Draw a straight line with the Pencil tool, release the Shift key to return to free-form drawing*

Hold down the Alt/Option key. You still create a straight line, but you have 360° to move in while drawing this time. Release the Alt/Option or Shift key to return to regular freeform pencil as you draw.

The Ctrl/Cmd key allows you to temporarily switch to the Selection tool so you can move parts of the lines on the artboard. Refer to Figure 16-18.

Figure 16-18. *Hold down the Ctrl/Cmd key when moving a path while using the pencil tool*

If you have an open selected path, you can continue to connect to the line if the (/) appears beside the tool's pointer until you close the path when O appears by the pointer as with the Pen tools. Paths not selected do not join with the new path drawn. It is its separate path. Refer to Figure 16-19.

Figure 16-19. *As you join paths, the pointer changes near the start point to close it*

The Pencil tool can also edit paths. While a path is selected, you can draw between two points to alter the path. You can hold down the Alt/Option key as you drag to create a new straight area for the path. Refer to Figure 16-20.

Figure 16-20. *Edit a selected path with the pencil tool, and the path is selected. Hold down the Alt/Option key for a straighter path*

Smooth Tool

The Smooth tool acts in some ways like the Object ➤ Path ➤ Simplify command you looked at in Chapter 14. However, you are controlling the exact area that you want to reduce and simplify the number of points this time. Refer to Figure 16-21.

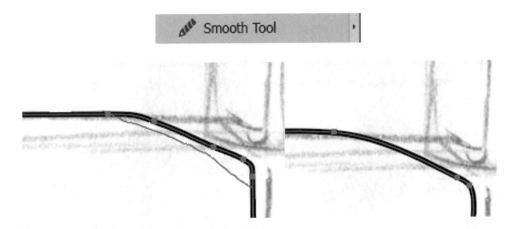

Figure 16-21. *Smooth tool to reduce points along a path*

By dragging over various areas of the path, you can reduce the number of points and smooth the curve. This, however, may alter the path slightly.

Smooth Tool Options

Double-clicking the Smooth tool in the Toolbars panel reveals the Smooth Tool Options dialog box, which lets you adjust **Fidelity** from Accurate to Smooth. Refer to Figure 16-22.

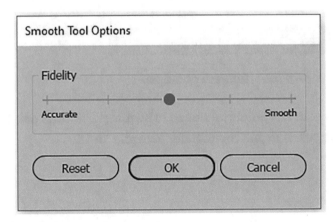

Figure 16-22. *Smooth Tool Options dialog box*

You can also reset it to the default center of the slider with the **Reset** button.

Path Eraser Tool

The Path Eraser tool selects and erases areas of a selected path, creating an open path as you drag along that area of the path between points. Refer to Figure 16-23.

Figure 16-23. *Path Eraser tool removes part of a path and makes it an open path*

There are no other options for this tool. Later in the chapter, you look at a few other options for path removal and division.

Join Tool

The Join tool is like command Object ➤ Path ➤ Join or a similar option in the Control panel. When points are selected with the Direct Selection tool, you can choose **Connect selected endpoints**. Refer to Figure 16-24.

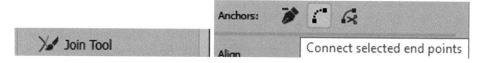

Figure 16-24. *The Join tool joins an open path*

When an open path has points that need to be joined, you can paint with this tool's brush between the points to join them. Refer to Figure 16-25.

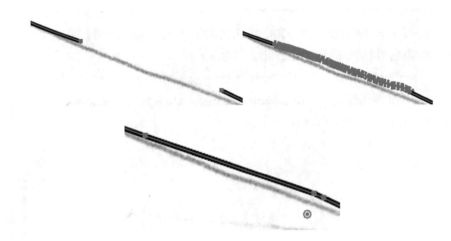

Figure 16-25. *The line is joined using the Join tool*

There are no other options for this tool.

Eraser Tool (Shift+E)

While the Path Eraser tool is good for erasing paths, the Eraser tool is used for dividing and erasing part of an object whether selected or not. Refer to Figure 16-26.

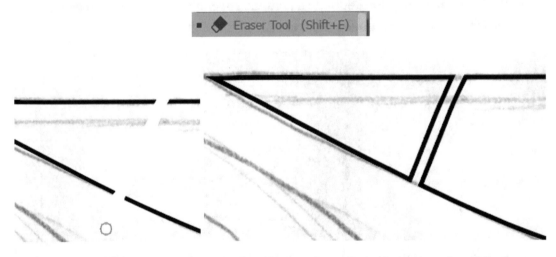

Figure 16-26. *The Eraser tool can break a path or shape into two closed paths*

Note   To prevent non-selected objects from erasing, select the object that you want to erase and then start using the Eraser tool.

Hold down the Shift key while dragging to make straight, horizontal, vertical, and diagonal erase lines. Refer to Figure 16-27.

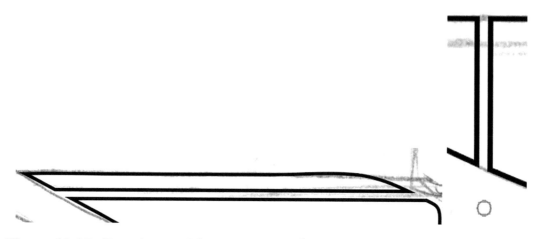

Figure 16-27. *Drawing straight erases using the Eraser tool*

Hold down the Alt/Option key to do a marquee, to erase a rectangular area or Shift+Alt/Option to do a marquee square erase. Refer to Figure 16-28.

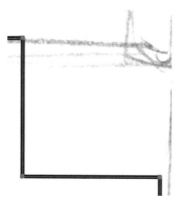

Figure 16-28. *A square marquee erase with the Eraser tool*

To decrease or increase the eraser size, you can use your keyboard's left and right brackets. Refer to Figure 16-29.

Figure 16-29. *Change the Brush size of the Eraser tool using your keyboard brackets*

Eraser Tool Options

To alter the settings, double-click the tool in the Toolbars panel to enter the Eraser Tool Options dialog box. Refer to Figure 16-30.

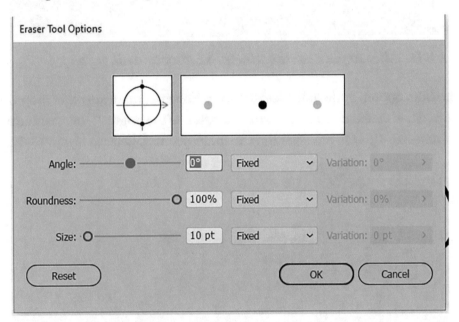

Figure 16-30. *Eraser Tool Options dialog box*

Like the Eraser tool brush options in Photoshop, you can set the **angle** (–180-0-180) of the eraser, the **roundness** (0%–100%), and the **size** of the Eraser head (1pt-1296pt). It is previewed in the **preview windows**. The preview on the left lets you alter the brush angle (dragging the arrowhead) and roundness (dragging the black dots in or out from the center) rather than using the sliders. Refer to Figure 16-31.

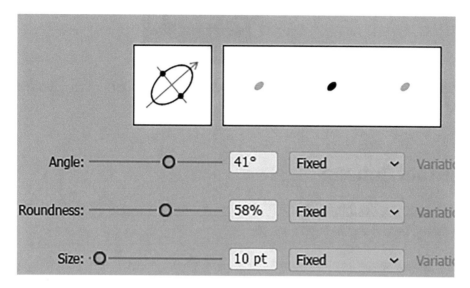

Figure 16-31. *Alter Angle and Roundness in Eraser tool dialog box*

Each slider option, by default, is set to **Fixed**. However, there are other drop-down list options when enabled which allow for **Variation** of the **angle** 0°–180°, **roundness** 0%–16%, and **size** 0 pt–155 pt, depending on initial settings. Refer to Figure 16-32.

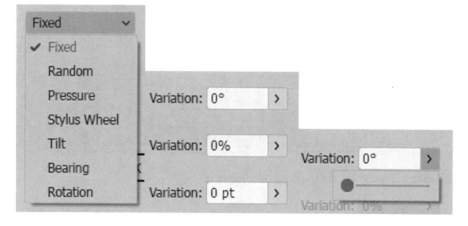

Figure 16-32. *Set the type of brush variation for angle, roundness, and size*

This **Random** option creates random variation; for example, if the size is 15 pt and the variation is 5 pt, the size could vary between 10 pt and 20 pt. Based on the settings, they preview in the dialog box. Refer to Figure 16-33.

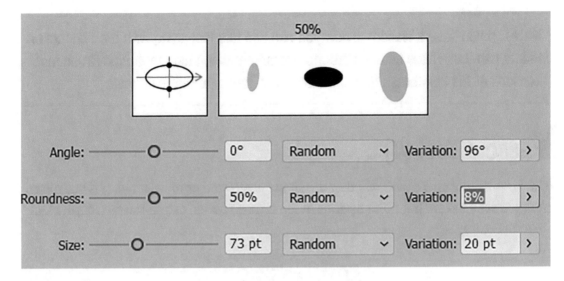

Figure 16-33. *Variation is set to Random in the dialog box*

The **Pressure** option can be used with a graphics tablet and a drawing stylus. Best used with the Size options. For example, enter a value in the Variation text box for roundness to specify how much more or less the original value the brush characteristic varies. If the Roundness value is 75% and the Variation is 25%, the lightest stroke is 50%, and the heaviest stroke is 100%. A lighter pressure makes the brush stroke more angular.

If you have a **Stylus Wheel**, the size varies based on the options you set.

The **Tilt** option affects angle, roundness, and size based on the drawing stylus's tilt. Best used for roundness options. It is available only if you have a graphics tablet that can detect the direction in which the pen is tilted.

The **Bearing** option affects angle, roundness, and size based on the drawing stylus's pressure. It is most useful when used to control the angle of calligraphic brushes, especially when you're using the brush like a paintbrush. It is available only if you have a graphics tablet that can detect how close to vertical the pen is.

The **Rotation** option affects angle, roundness, and size is based on how the drawing stylus pen tip is rotated. This option is most useful when used to control the angle of calligraphic brushes, especially when you're using the brush like a flat pen. It is available only if you have a graphics tablet that can detect this type of rotation.

Click **Reset** if you need to Reset the dialog box back to the default settings. Click **OK** to confirm settings, or click **Cancel** and exit without saving your settings. Refer to Figure 16-30.

Note   If you have a Wacom stylus, you can use this tool along with the Pen tool or Paintbrush tool. These settings are more apparent when using the Blob Brush tool. You look at the Paintbrush tool and Blob Brush tool later in the chapter.

Scissors Tool (C)

The Scissors tool cuts a path whether the shape is selected or unselected. It is like the cut points at selected anchor point options in the Control panel, as you saw in Chapter 15. Refer to Figure 16-34.

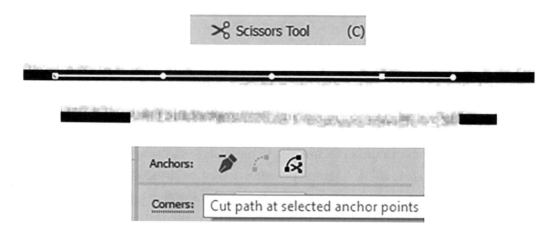

Figure 16-34. *Using the Scissors tool to cut out part of a closed path to make it open*

1. Select a path with the Selection tool (V).

2. Click the path, two points, so that you can delete part of a segment from the path.

3. Press the Backspace/Delete key twice on your keyboard to remove that area of the path and points.

Note   If you get a warning message when you click the first point, click OK in the message. Click the next anchor point or part of the segment you want to cut. Refer to Figure 16-35.

Adobe Illustrator

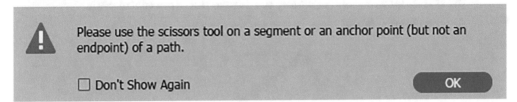

Please use the scissors tool on a segment or an anchor point (but not an endpoint) of a path.

☐ Don't Show Again   OK

Figure 16-35. *Warning you may see while creating a path with the Scissor tool*

Knife Tool

The Knife tool cuts or divides an area of a selected or unselected path or object out on a curve but keep a closed path. Refer to Figure 16-36.

✏ Knife

Figure 16-36. *The Knife tool*

1. Select a path or shape with the Selection tool (V).

2. Then drag the knife around the area beyond the path you want to remove, make sure that you go beyond the path a bit on both sides. Refer to Figure 16-37.

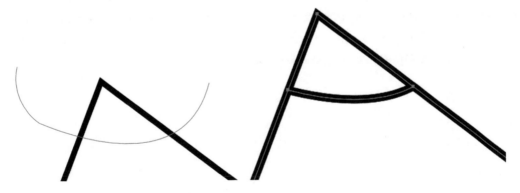

Figure 16-37. *Drag around a part of the path with the knife tool to carve it out*

3. When you release the mouse, this creates an area that is separated from the original shape.

4. With the Selection tool, you can drag that path away and then press the Backspace/Delete key to remove that area of the path. Refer to Figure 16-38.

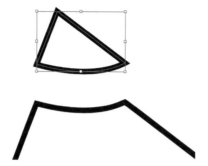

Figure 16-38. *The path carved with the Knife tool is separate*

Tip   Hold down the Alt/Option key if you need to cut a straight path with the Knife tool.

There are other options in the Pathfinders panel that can perform divisions.

Pathfinders Panel

Photoshop selections and paths can be united and divided. When working with shapes in Illustrator, the Pathfinders panel can merge or divide paths. In Illustrator, the **Shape modes** (Unite, Minus Front, Intersect, Exclude) can create compound shapes when you hold down the Alt/Option key on your keyboard. Refer to Figure 16-39.

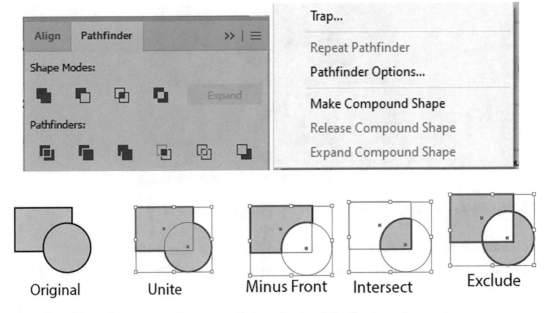

Figure 16-39. *Using the Shape modes in the Pathfinder panel to create compound shapes*

To expand the selected Compound Shape, press the **Expand** button. This splits or merges the path destructively. Refer to Figure 16-40.

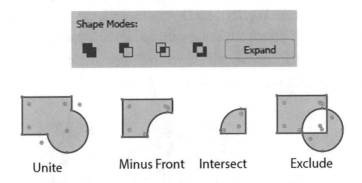

Figure 16-40. *Compound shapes expanded*

The other **Pathfinders** (Divide, Trim, Merge, Crop, Outline, and Minus Back) cannot create compound shapes. They alter the two paths automatically and are destructive. Refer to Figure 16-39 and Figure 16-41.

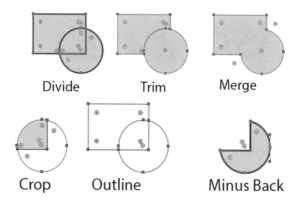

Figure 16-41. *Pathfinders options in the Pathfinder panel*

However, there is a way to get around that destructive issue with Illustrator Pathfinder Effects. I explain that in more detail in my video, *Illustrator Pathfinder Effects* (`https://link.springer.com/video/10.1007/978-1-4842-6581-9`).

It should be noted that while working with paths, you may encounter two other kinds of paths.

Object ➤ Compound Path

A Compound path is created after using one of the Pathfinders like minus front without holding down the Alt/Option key. It creates a hole through the path that you can see the artboard through. You can create this same path without the pathfinder by selecting a shape that overlaps another. Select both shapes and choose Object ➤ Compound Path ➤ Make. Refer to Figure 16-42.

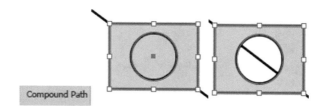

Figure 16-42. *An example of a created compound path that you can see through*

Or choose Object ➤ Compound Path ➤ Release to release the paths.

Object ➤ Clipping Mask

A clipping mask hides the surrounding areas of a shape. When selected with the lower shape, the upper shape can be turned into a clipping mask by choosing Object ➤ Clipping Mask ➤ Make. Object ➤ Clipping Mask ➤ Release releases the paths. Refer to Figure 16-43.

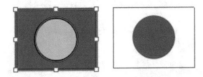

Figure 16-43. *An example of a created clipping mask that hides the rectangle shape behind*

As you saw in Chapter 12, Photoshop has layer clipping masks that perform a similar function. However, in Chapter 18, you briefly look at Photoshop's **clipping path** and why it is needed in programs like Adobe InDesign to hide backgrounds around a sketch.

Paintbrush Tool (B)

The Paintbrush tool is in many ways like the Pencil tool (N) for path creation. However, its main purpose is not to create closed paths but new open paths created each time the mouse button is released. The paths can be altered later while selected when you choose options from the Control panel and the Stroke panel and Brushes panel. Refer to Figure 16-44.

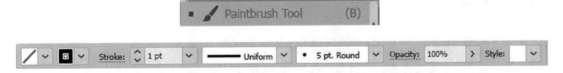

Figure 16-44. *The Paintbrush tool and some options in the Control panel you can set before you start to paint*

Paintbrush Tool Options

When you double-click the tool in the Toolbars panel, you can enter the Paintbrush Tool Options dialog box. Notice that the brush definition by default is set to 5pt. Round and not Uniform.

The **Fidelity** slider can be set to a highly Accurate setting to a loose Smooth setting. By default, the slider is in the center. Refer to Figure 16-45.

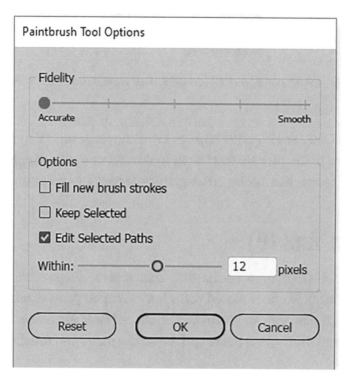

Figure 16-45. *Paintbrush Tool Options dialog box*

The following describes the other options.

- **Fill new brush strokes**: If you want to fill in the path as you draw, enable this setting; by default, it is disabled. If enabled, you must have a fill selected in the Toolbars panel for this setting to work.

- **Keep selected**: By default, after the line is drawn and the mouse is released, it becomes deselected as you start a new path. Keep this option enabled if you need to keep the path selected while drawing.

- **Edit selected paths within a set number of pixels**: Determines how close your pointer must be to an existing path to edit the path with the Paintbrush tool.

If you make changes, click **OK** or click the **Reset** button before leaving to reset the alterations. Click **Cancel** without making changes. Refer to Figure 16-46.

To decrease or increase the Paintbrush tool size, you can use your keyboard's left and right brackets. After a path has been painted, while selected, you can still use the brackets to increase or decrease the stroke width. Refer to Figure 16-46.

Figure 16-46. *Alter the Paintbrush size*

Hold down the Alt/Option key as you drag to create a closed path rather than an open path, and a small O appears next to the pointer. Refer to Figure 16-47.

Figure 16-47. *Close the path with the Paintbrush tool*

The Ctrl/Cmd key allows you to temporarily switch to the Selection tool (V) so you can move your path. Ctrl/Cmd+Alt/Option lets you duplicate the complete path when you drag. Refer to Figure 16-48.

Figure 16-48. *Change the pointer to the Selection tool when you hold down the Ctrl/Cmd key*

If you have two paths or path ends selected, you can continue connecting the two lines by dragging between them, and then they become one path. Refer to Figure 16-49.

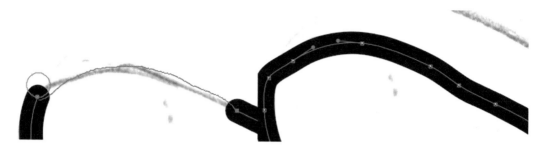

Figure 16-49. *Join two paths with the Paintbrush tool*

When you draw with the Paintbrush tool, you can hold down the Shift key to create a straight line constrained to horizontal or vertical rather than a free form line. Refer to Figure 16-50.

Figure 16-50. *Draw a straight path with the Paintbrush tool*

The Paintbrush tool can also edit paths. While a path is selected, first with the Direct Selection tool and then the Brush tool, you can draw between two points to alter the path. As before, you can hold down the Alt/Option key as you drag to create a new straight area for the path. Refer to Figure 16-51.

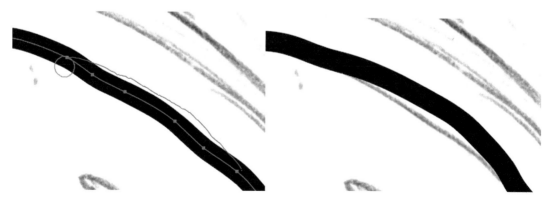

Figure 16-51. *Edit the selected path with the Paintbrush tool*

Blob Brush Tool (Shift+B)

The Blob Brush tool has similar features to the Eraser tool and the Paintbrush tool. Refer to Figure 16-52.

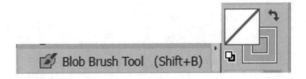

Figure 16-52. *Blob Brush tool paints fill even though color set in the stroke*

However, rather than paint a stroke like the Paintbrush tool, it is meant to paint a colored fill that, has no stroke. You see this when you select it with the Direct Selection tool. It merges fills of the same color and creates separate fills when they are different colors. Gaps that are not filled in are part of a compound path. Refer to Figure 16-53.

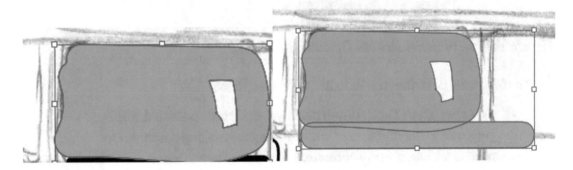

Figure 16-53. *The Blob Brush tool after painting if there is a gap is a Compound Path*

Hold down the Shift key while dragging to make straight horizontal or vertical Blob Brush fills.

To decrease or increase the brush size, you can use your keyboard's left and right brackets.

Blob Brush Tool Options

The Blob Brush Tool Options dialog box is accessed from the Toolbars panel. Refer to Figure 16-54.

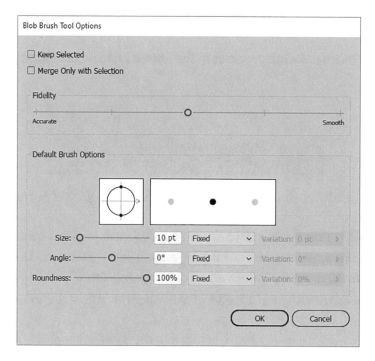

Figure 16-54. *Blob Brush Tool Options dialog box*

The following describes the Blob Brush tool's options.

- **Keep Selected:** This is deselected by default but if selected, allow you to keep the fill selected while adding to it during painting. On mouse release, if I stop painting, a new fill is created when the fill is a different color than the first; otherwise, it merges with the same last fill. This option is useful for viewing all paths that are included in the merged path while painting.

- **Merge Only with the Selection:** Merge only with the selected object. It is disabled by default, so even unselected paths can merge during painting.

- **Fidelity:** See the Pencil tool in this chapter for more information.

- **Default Brush Options:** For more information on size, angle, and roundness with different variations, see the Eraser tool discussion.

Click **OK** to confirm your settings, or click **Cancel** to exit without making changes.

To prevent non-selected objects from being painted, select the object that you want to paint and then start using the Blob Brush tool. The topmost fill merges with the lower and all intersecting fills. If they are the same colors and do not overlap a different color while painting with your brush, the compound path is filled in; otherwise, a new path is created during overlap. Also, the created fills should have a stroke of none, or they cannot merge. Refer to Figure 16-55.

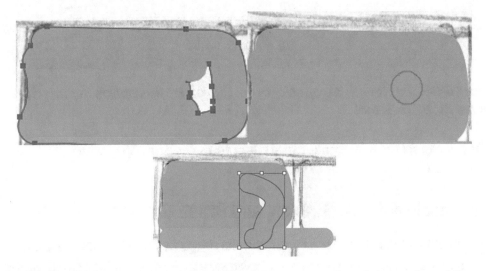

Figure 16-55. *Do not overlap other colors if you want the Blob Brush to fill in an area with a similar color*

Attributes can be adjusted, such as **Opacity**, to a fill to make it more transparent. These settings can be applied while painting if already set, in the Appearance panel, Properties panel, or Control panel. Refer to Figure 16-56.

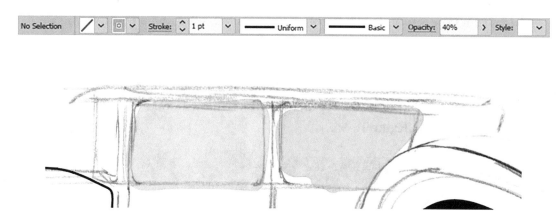

Figure 16-56. *Paint with an opacity of 40% if you set this option before painting with the Blob Brush tool*

Or you can set the opacity afterward when you select the object with the Selection tool.

Swatches, Gradients, Strokes, and Brush Options

While adjusting paths, there are a few additional things that you can alter to improve your paths, besides just choosing a color in the Swatches panel. Colors, Gradient, and Patterns are stored in the Swatches panel. When a shape is selected, depending on whether the stroke or fill is active in the Toolbars panel, you can click a swatch or use the Control or Properties panel to apply the swatch directly to the Stroke or Fill. Refer to Figure 16-57.

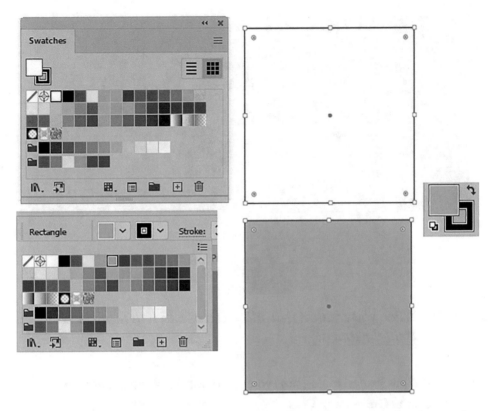

Figure 16-57. *Use the Swatch panel or Control panel to set a color for a selected fill or stroke*

Creating a New Swatch

If you create a new swatch color using the **Color panel**, you can add it to the panel by doing the following.

1. Click the New Swatch button icon while active in the Toolbars panel to add it to the list. Refer to Figure 16-58.

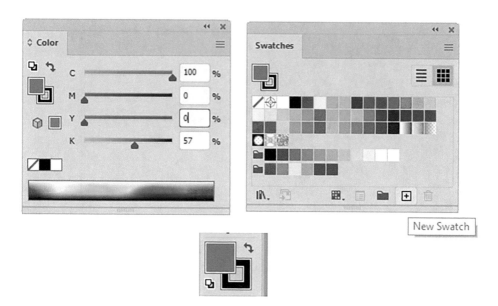

Figure 16-58. *When you create a new fill, you can add it to the Swatches panel to store in your current document*

2. In the New Swatch dialog box, you can name the swatch, deselect the **Global Option** and Click **OK** to the dialog box settings, and it is added to the Swatches panel. Refer to Figure 16-59.

3. To delete a swatch, select the swatch and click the trash can icon in the Swatches panel. Refer to Figure 16-59.

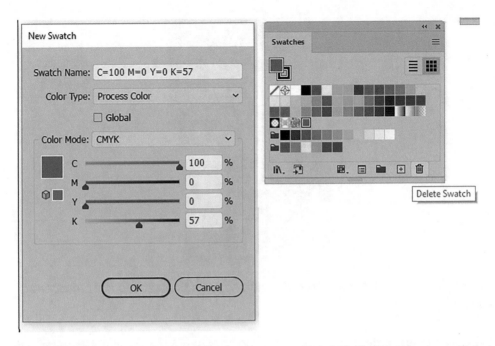

Figure 16-59. *After you create a Swatch, name it, and click OK. The swatch is in the Swatches panel, but you can delete it using the Trash Can Icon*

Creating a New Gradient

You can use the Gradient panel to create gradients that you can then add to your Swatches panel.

Double-click a gradient slider to change the color of the current gradient. You can then set it Linear or Radial. Refer to Figure 16-60.

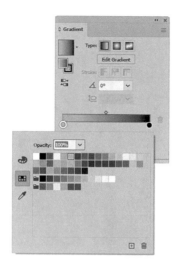

Figure 16-60. *In the Gradient panel, each slider has access to the Swatches panel colors*

When the new gradient appears in the Toolbars panel in the Swatches panel, click New Swatch, name it, and click **OK** for it to appear in the Swatches panel. Refer to Figure 16-61.

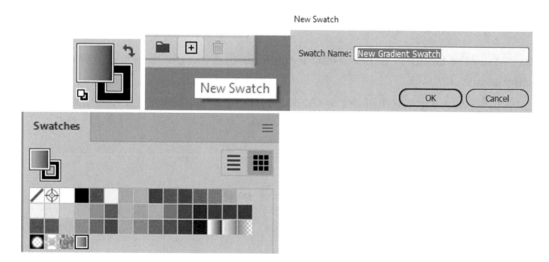

Figure 16-61. *Adding a Gradient to the Swatches panel*

Stroke Panel Options

Access to the Stroke panel is through the Control or Properties panels and can be changed on selected Shapes and Objects. Refer to Figure 16-62.

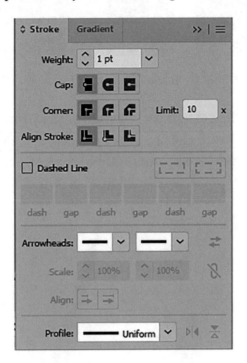

Figure 16-62.   *The Stroke panel*

The stroke **Weight** is set in points. Higher numbers make the stroke thicker and lower numbers thinner. The lowest weight number you want to set for printing purposes is 0.25pt; otherwise, the line may be difficult to see. Choose a weight size from the drop-down list or type in your own number.

Cap is how an open path's anchor point is rounded off. The options are Butt, Round, and Projecting Cap. Refer to Figure 16-63.

Figure 16-63.   *Stroke Cap Options of Butt, Round, and Projecting*

Corners is how the corner edges of a shape are rounded off. The options are Miter, Round, and Bevel Join. Refer to Figure 16-64.

Figure 16-64. *Stroke Corner Options of Miter, Round, and Bevel Join*

The miter **Limit** (1–500) creates a flat (beveled) or sharp (mitered) point corner based on weight, number input, and line angle. The default is 10. If the angle is very sharp, the point of the corner is sometimes lost and flattened; increasing the meter limit to 20 adds the sharp point back to the corner. Refer to Figure 16-65.

Figure 16-65. *Adjusting the Miter Limit from 10 to 20 to maintain a sharp stroke*

Align Strokes is based on where the Stroke sits on the path. The options are Center, Inside, or Outside. By default, and for printing purposes, I usually leave it at Center. Refer to Figure 16-66.

Figure 16-66. *Align strokes on path: Center, Inside, and Outside*

Dashed Line enables this setting to create a path with dashed and gap segments. You can set three dash options and three gap options that repeat along the path. The icons on the right of the check box lets you **preserve the exact dash and gap lengths** or **align the dashes to the corners and path ends, adjusting lengths to fit** if the shape is scaled. Refer to Figure 16-67.

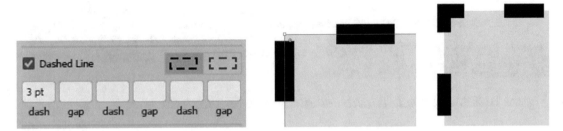

Figure 16-67. *Dashed strokes on a path*

Tip   Change the cap in the Stroke panel to alter the type of dash ends.

The **Arrowheads** option adds arrowheads to the start, end, or both sides of the line. There are 39 arrowhead options you can choose from the drop-down list. The arrowhead start and end can be swapped if they are different to change the line direction. Start and end can be scaled separately or together when the link is enabled. The arrowheads can be aligned beyond the end of the path or at the end of the path. Refer to Figure 16-68.

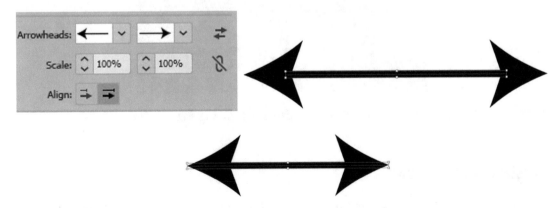

Figure 16-68. *Choose various options for arrowheads, including alignment in the Stroke panel*

The **Profiles** option lets you adjust how the stroke path around the shape appears for the variable-width profile. By default, it is set to Uniform, and you can access them from the Strokes panel. They can be flipped horizontal (along) or vertical (across). Some profiles allow you to access none, one, or both options. This is like Object ➤ Path ➤ Reverse Path Direction. Uniform is the default. Refer to Figure 16-69.

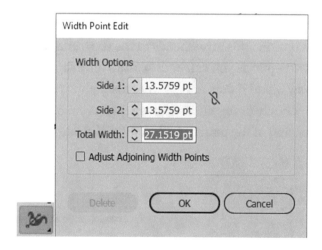

Figure 16-69. *Set a new variable-width profile for the stroke*

If you want more information on adjusting a stroke's variable-width profile using the Width tool (Shift+W) and its dialog box and adding a profile to your collection, check out https://helpx.adobe.com/illustrator/using/stroke-object.html. Refer to Figure 16-70.

Figure 16-70. *Width tool and Width Point Edit dialog box*

Brushes Panel Options

Brushes in the Control panel can be applied to the strokes around a path. They fall into five main categories. Refer to Figure 16-71.

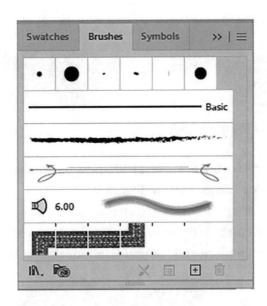

Figure 16-71. *Brush tool panel*

Calligraphic brushes create strokes that resemble those drawn with the angled point of a calligraphic pen and are drawn along the center of the path. When you use the Blob Brush tool, you can paint with only the calligraphic brush and automatically expand the brush stroke into a fill shape that merges with other filled objects of the same color that intersect or are adjacent in stacking order. Refer to Figure 16-72.

Figure 16-72. *Calligraphic and Scatter Brushes*

Scatter brushes disperse copies of an object (such as an arrow or shapes) along the path. Refer to Figure 16-72.

Art brushes stretch a brush shape (such as Rough Charcoal) or object shape evenly along the length of the path, which is useful for paint-like effects. Refer to Figure 16-73.

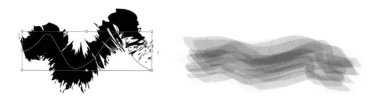

Figure 16-73. *Art and Bristle brushes*

The **Bristle brush** creates brush strokes with the appearance of a natural brush with bristles such as watercolor effects. Refer to Figure 16-73.

Pattern brushes paint a pattern—made of individual tiles—that repeats along the path. Pattern brushes can include up to five tiles for the sides, inner corner, outer corner, beginning, and end of the pattern and are useful for borders. Refer to Figure 16-74.

Figure 16-74. *Pattern brush*

You can apply brush strokes when the path is selected from the Brushes panel or access them from the Control panel. Additional brushes can be accessed from the Window ➤ Brush Libraries, located on the lower left of the Brushes panel. Refer to Figure 16-75.

Figure 16-75. *More brushes in the Brushes Library*

Note   You may get an alert if you delete a brush stroke from the Brushes panel. In this case, click **Remove Strokes**, and the path is set back to the default stroke settings. Refer to Figure 16-76.

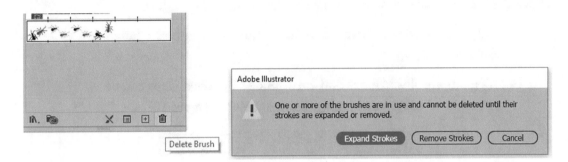

Figure 16-76. *If you delete a brush from the Brushes panel and that brush has been applied somewhere in your document, you may receive a warning to either expand or remove the strokes*

If you want to further explore how to create and modify brushes, check out `https://helpx.adobe.com/illustrator/using/brushes.html`.

Live Shape Tools

Along with the Shaper tool (Shift+N), these next three tools work together to create live shapes and paths that you can edit. Select with the Selection tool first the multiple shapes you want to work with before you select the Shape Builder tool. Refer to Figure 16-77.

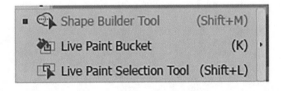

Figure 16-77. *Create Live Shapes with the Shape Builder and Live Paint tools in the Toolbars panel*

Shape Builder Tool (Shift+M)

The Shape Builder tool is used for creating complex shapes by merging and erasing simple and compound paths. You can then click between gaps to highlight regions that you want to fill with the Live Paint Bucket. The tool highlights edges and regions of the selected art so that you can merge and combine to form new shapes.

- Edges are sections of paths that do not intersect any other path of a selected object.

- Regions are closed areas that are bounded by edges. Gaps can be considered a region when highlighted. Refer to Figure 16-78.

Figure 16-78. *The Shape Builder tool*

1. In the next example, use the 16_live_paint.ai file to practice.

Open the 16_live_paint.ai file. Using the Ellipse, Rectangular, and Line Segment tools, I traced some sketches with a 1 pt uniform basic stroke and a fill of None. Refer to Figure 16-79.

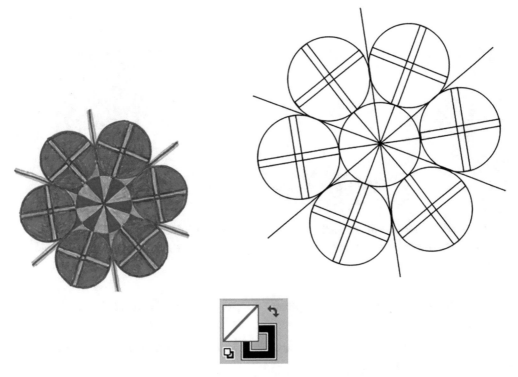

Figure 16-79. *This sketch was traced and made into paths with various shape tools with a fill of none and a stroke of black*

I then marquee selected the entire path and Object ➤ Grouped. While it was selected, I clicked a region with the Shape Builder tool.

File ➤ Save As (Shift+Ctrl/Cmd+S) to make a copy of the file if you want to follow along.

On layer 2, choose Select ➤ All (Ctrl/Cmd+A).

With the Shape Builder tool, click in a region that you want to color. The area is highlighted in gray. Refer to Figure 16-80.

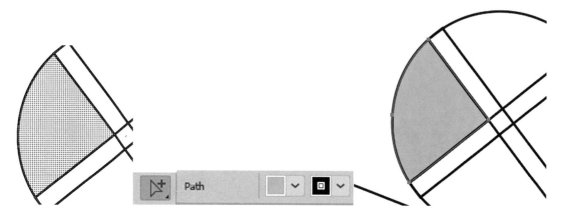

Figure 16-80. *Use the Shape Builder to select an area to fill, select with the Group Selection tool and choose a new swatch fill from the Control panel to fill the wedge with*

This made this area an entirely separate shape. You can fill this region with a new color.

To do that, select this region with the Group Selection tool and choose a new fill from the Control panel. Refer to Figure 16-80.

You could then continue and select other regions, areas, or gaps with the Shape Builder tool and continue to fill these regions. Refer to Figure 16-81.

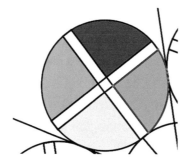

Figure 16-81. *Continue to add fills to the new shapes created with the Shape Builder*

Shape Builder Tool Options

When you double-click the tool in the Toolbars panel, you can enter the Shape Builder Tool Options dialog box. Refer to Figure 16-82.

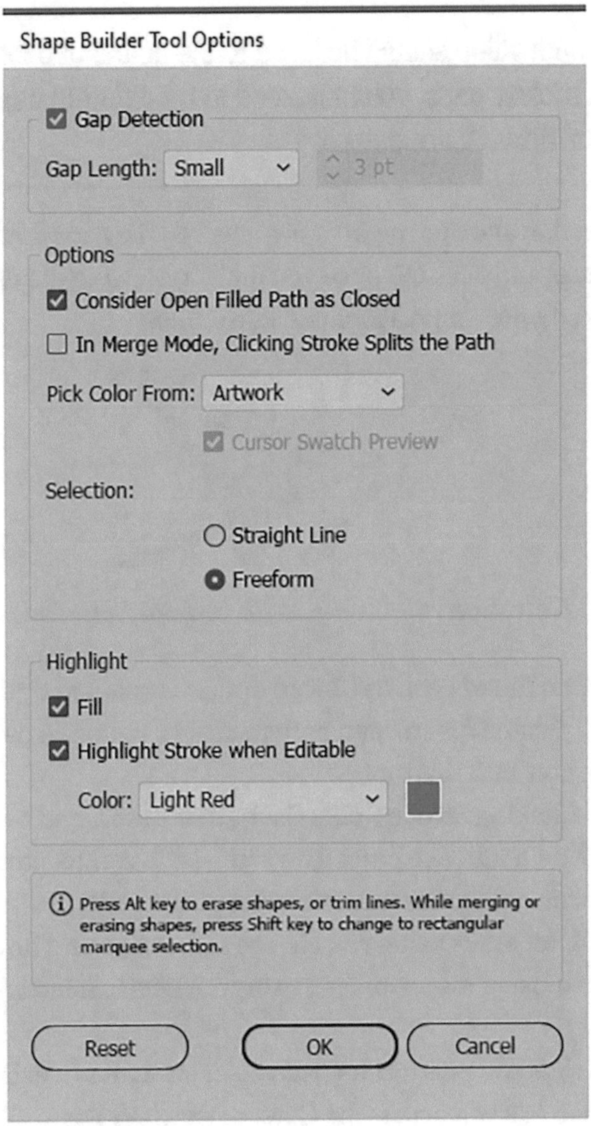

Shape Builder Tool Options

Gap Detection

Gap Length: Small ⌄   ⌃ 3 pt

Options
☑ Consider Open Filled Path as Closed
☐ In Merge Mode, Clicking Stroke Splits the Path

Pick Color From: Artwork ⌄
                ☑ Cursor Swatch Preview

Selection:
              ○ Straight Line
              ● Freeform

Highlight
☑ Fill
☑ Highlight Stroke when Editable
Color: Light Red ⌄ ▪

ⓘ Press Alt key to erase shapes, or trim lines. While merging or
   erasing shapes, press Shift key to change to rectangular
   marquee selection.

Reset   OK   Cancel

Figure 16-82. *Shape Builder Tool Options*

Let's go over the Shape Builder Tool options.

Gap Detection, when enabled, sets the gap length using the drop-down menu of Small (3 pt), Medium (6 pt), Large (12 pt), or Custom (0.01 pt–72 pt) for an exact gap length.

Note   The gap length value should be close to the actual gap length in the artwork. To detect trickier gaps, you may need to try different gap length values until the gaps in the artwork are detected.

A small gap detection allowed me to easily select all the gaps that I planned to color. So, select these settings and click OK once you finish reviewing the options in the dialog box and continue to edit the shape. Refer to Figure 16-83.

Figure 16-83.   *Gap Detection allows me to fill in gaps between shapes with a fill*

The **Consider Open Filled Path as Closed** option is enabled by default, and an invisible edge is then created for an open path to make a region. A path is created by clicking inside the region with this tool.

In Merge Mode, Clicking Stroke Splits the Path is deselected by default. This setting splits a parent path into two parts. The first path is created from the edge on which you click. The second path is the remaining portion of the parent path, excluding the first path. The pointer alters when you choose this option and hover over a highlighted line. When the paths are moved using the Direct Selection tool, you can see an open path.

Pick Color From lets you pick a color from color swatches or existing artwork. The **Color Swatches** option lets you access the Cursor Swatch Preview. When enabled, it allows you to preview and select colors. Refer to Figure 16-84.

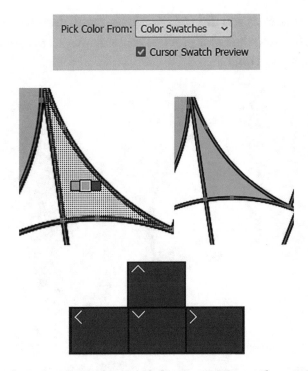

Figure 16-84. *With Color Swatches and the Cursor Swatch preview, I can then choose colors from the swatches panel using my arrow keys to fill my regions*

To change colors in the preview, use the right and left arrow keys on your keyboard to access colors from the Swatches panel. This option lets you change the color of a fill. Refer to Figure 16-84. You can also change the color of a stroke by first selecting the **In Merge Mode, Clicking Stroke Splits the Path** option.

With the **Artwork** option, you do not have access to the Swatches panel for selection and rely on the current artwork's colors during the merge. Refer to Figure 16-85.

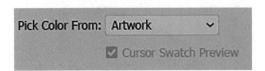

Figure 16-85. *Artwork color setting relies on the current colors in the artwork to pick colors*

The **Selection** between regions can be made by dragging out a **Straight Line** or a **Freeform** (squiggle) to create the merge. Freeform is the default so that you can still draw straight lines while you edit your artwork. Refer to Figure 16-82.

To merge some shapes as you did with the Shaper tool, draw a squiggle across more than one region. Notice that the color preview is not displayed to clearly see the merge of the shapes. Refer to Figure 16-86.

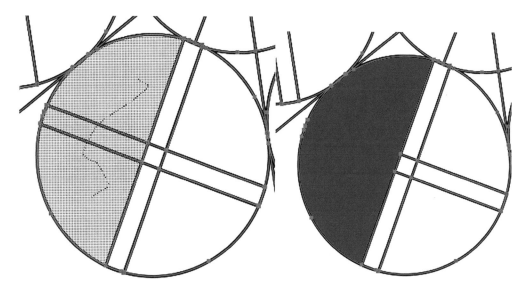

Figure 16-86. *Scribble over two or more paths to merge them*

Use Edit ➤ Undo (Ctrl/Cmd+Z) to undo this last step if this was not your intent. Next, let's go over the Highlight options.

Fill is selected by default. The path or region can merge and is highlighted in a gray preview when you hover over the region. When not hovering, the color appears normal. Refer to Figure 16-82.

Highlight Stroke When Editable is selected by default so the stroke can be edited. Refer to Figure 16-85 and Figure 16-87.

Figure 16-87. *The stroke is highlighted if this option is selected*

The **Info** dialog box reminds you that, while working with the tool, when you hold down the Alt/Option instead of combining paths and regions, you can now erase shapes or trim lines as you scribble over them. If you hold down the Shift key, you can change from selecting with the pointer to using the rectangular marquee selection as you drag over shapes to merge or erase. Refer to Figure 16-88.

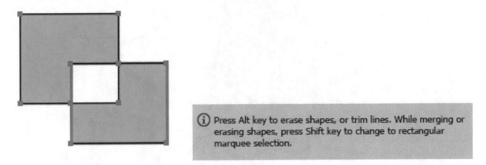

Figure 16-88. *Use the Shape Builder tool to erase part of a path when the Alt/ Option key is held down when you scribble*

The **Reset** button lets you reset your settings back to the Adobe default if you alter them.

Click **OK** to confirm settings, or click **Cancel** without changing settings. Refer to Figure 16-82.

You can continue using the Shape Builder tool, your Group Selection tool, and your Control panel to fill in the colors or continue with the next tool, Live Paint Bucket.

Live Paint Bucket (K)

Once you have used the Shape Builder tool to create your shape regions, you can continue to use the Live Paint Bucket for Painting Live Shapes or gaps where there is no fill. Refer to Figure 16-89.

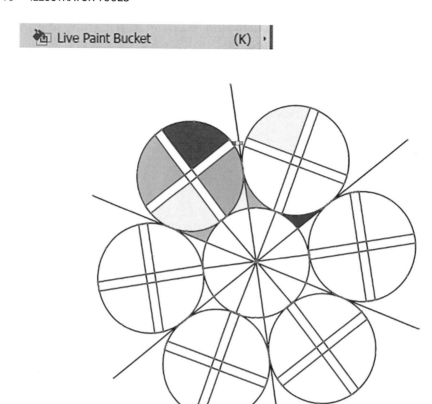

Figure 16-89. *Use the Live Paint Bucket tool to continue to colorize the regions*

Live Paint Bucket Options

Double-clicking the Live Paint Bucket tool in the Toolbars panel opens its Options dialog box. Refer to Figure 16-90.

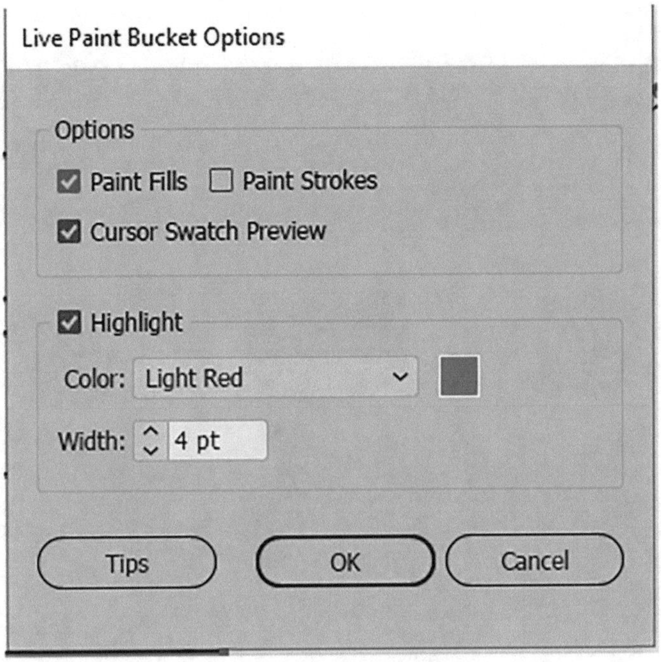

Live Paint Bucket Options

Options
☑ Paint Fills   ☐ Paint Strokes
☑ Cursor Swatch Preview

☑ Highlight
Color: Light Red   ⌄
Width: ↕ 4 pt

Tips   OK   Cancel

Figure 16-90. *Live Paint Bucket Tool Options dialog box*

Let's go over the options.

Paint fills lets you fill in regions with fill colors.

Paint strokes lets you add color to strokes.

With the **Cursor Swatch Preview** enabled, as with the Shape Builder tool, you have the option to preview and select colors. Use the right and left arrow keys on your keyboard to access colors from the Swatches panel and click to add a color. Refer to Figure 16-91.

Figure 16-91. *Choose what color to paint a region with the Cursor Swatch Preview and the arrow keys on your keyboard, and then click in the regions to add the color*

Highlight shows the preview highlight color as a stroke in a **Color** you set in the dialog box and a set **Width** of 4 pt, which can be increased or decreased.

The **Tips** button guides you on how to use the Live Paint Bucket more efficiently. Click **Next** to see Tip #2 or **Previous** to go back to Tip #1. Click **OK** to exit when you have reviewed the two tips. Refer to Figure 16-92.

Figure 16-92. *Basic Tips provided with the Live Paint Bucket Options dialog box*

Try some of these steps and tips with your own image or my image. Or Try the Live Paint Bucket with the Rectangular Grid tool or Polar Grid tool and fill in the selected grid squares and regions with colors. Refer to Figure 16-93.

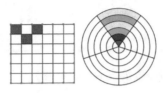

Figure 16-93. *Adding Live Paint to various grids*

1. Click regions with the Live Paint Bucket tool to color and then switch colors using your arrow keys.

2. Hold down the Shift key if you want to color the Strokes or edges.

3. You can see with my example how I continued to color it in the 16_live_paint_final.ai file on **Layer 2 final** in the Layers panel. Refer to Figure 16-94.

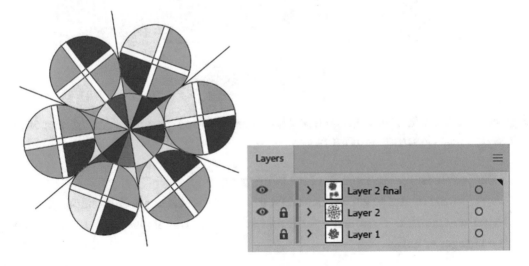

Figure 16-94. *Live Paint was added to select regions and gaps to create a colorful design*

Object ➤ Live Paint Commands

Object ➤ Live Paint has a few commands you can use: Refer to Figure 16-95.

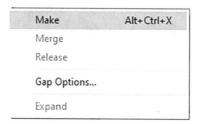

Figure 16-95. *Additional commands available for Live Paint*

Make (Alt/Option+Ctrl/Cmd+X) makes a Live Paint group.

Merge merges select live paint paths as you add them to the current paths. This same option appears in the Control panel and Properties panel. Click Continue if you see a warning message. Refer to Figure 16-96.

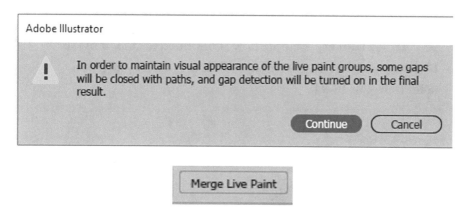

Figure 16-96. *When you merge two Live Paint Groups, you may get this warning message, click Continue to confirm*

Release releases paths from the Live Paint group.

Gap Options relates to gap detection (see Shaper tool earlier in this chapter).

Expand expands and confirms paths and takes them out of Live Paint mode, making them no longer editable.

Live Paint Bucket Selection Tool (Shift+L)

The Live Paint Bucket Selection tool selects Live Shapes areas and regions before adding a color. Refer to Figure 16-97.

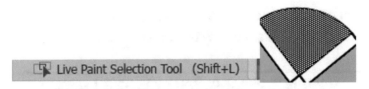

Figure 16-97. *Live Paint Selection tool and a selected region*

Live Paint Selection Options

You can double-click this tool in the Toolbars panel to enter the Live Paint Selections Options dialog box. The options include Select Fills, Select Strokes, and set the Preview Highlight Color and Width as you did with the Live Paint Bucket tool. Refer to Figure 16-98.

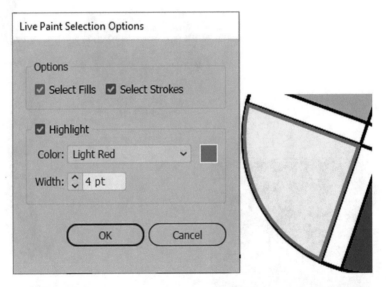

Figure 16-98. *Live Paint Selection Options dialog box and a highlighted area*

When a Live Paint Object is selected with the Selection tool (V), you can expand the Grouped Live Paint from the Control panel. Then it is no longer in Live Paint mode. Refer to Figure 16-99.

Figure 16-99. *Selected Live Paint groups can be expanded using the button in the Control panel*

For additional ways, you can use the Live Paint group, check out https://helpx.
adobe.com/illustrator/using/live-paint-groups.html.

PUT INTO PRACTICE WHAT YOU HAVE LEARNED

Take some time to practice. This example uses one of the brooches sketched in the previous
lesson. It is now colorized. The example also uses a stylized car and a little gnome character.
Both could be used to start a still frame in character animation.

Open 16_practice_tool.ai, and File ➤ Save As a Copy if you want to edit it. Refer to
Figure 16-100.

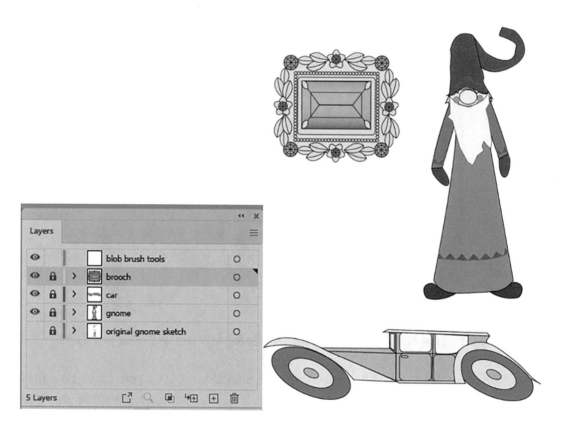

Figure 16-100. *Various sketches and paths are organized on different layers with
one blank layer for practice not locked*

I added a fill to select areas of the brooch using colors from my Swatches panel to colorize
parts with a new fill. You can select solid colors or create gradients from the Swatches panel.

I went to the Swatches Library, added a Color Group of Gold 2 from the Metal Library, and selected those colors for my brooch design. I also acquired other Color Groups from the **Neutral** and **Gradient ➤ Stone and Brick**. I prefer to create my own gradients, but you can use one from the Gradients library.

Click one color group in a library to add it to the Swatches panel. Refer to Figure 16-101.

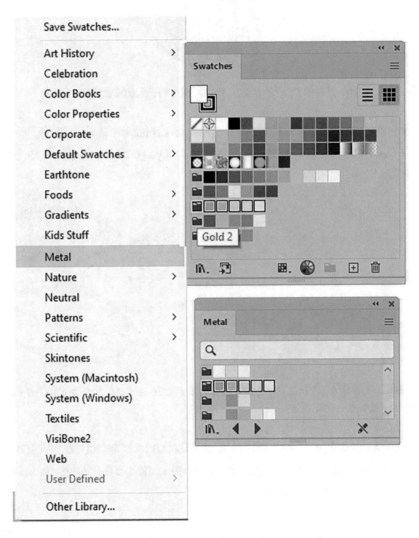

Figure 16-101. *Add new swatches to your Swatches panel*

<u>Outline Mode</u>

During construction and colorization of the brooch, I realized that some paths were in front and others were hidden behind it. Refer to Figure 16-102.

Figure 16-102. *One of the paths on the leaf was hidden behind it*

A good command to use when working with paths you cannot see is View ➤ Outline or (Ctrl/Cmd+Y). It sets you into Outline View mode so that you only see the paths. Refer to Figure 16-103.

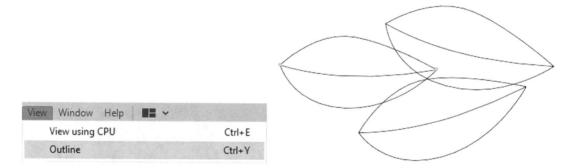

Figure 16-103. *Outline Viewing mode helps me to see all the paths so I can select the underlying ones*

Then you can use one of your Selection or Group Selection tools, select the path and choose from the Object ➤ Arrange option (e.g., Bring to Front) to move a path Infront or in other situations Back. Refer to Figure 16-104.

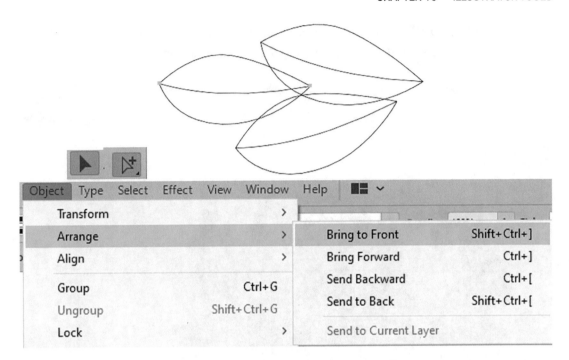

Figure 16-104. *Use Object ➤ Arrange when you need to move a path forward or back a step or two*

To exit this mode and see the result, choose View ➤ Preview. In this example, the line is in front. Refer to Figure 16-105.

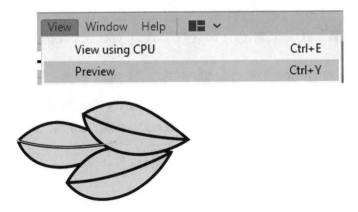

Figure 16-105. *Return to Preview mode to see your artwork in color. The line moved to the front of that group*

I used my Group Selection tool to select multiple grouped shapes (click twice to select more shapes in the group) to color them quickly using the Control panel. Refer to Figure 16-106.

Figure 16-106. *When objects are part of a group, you can color them quickly*

After Choosing colors and gradients, you can enhance it in other ways.

For example, on a new layer called **blob brush tools**. Use the Blob Brush tool and subtly paint over areas with varying sizes of brushes and changes in opacity to make the brooch appear shinier and more realistic. Refer to Figure 16-107.

Figure 16-107. *Paint with swatches on the blank layer using your Blob Brush tool*

Use your Eraser tool to remove selected areas of the fill you do not want.

I prefer to paint on a new layer and lock my lower layers while painting. That way, I do not destroy my lower layers if I need to alter. Or Backspace/Delete selected paths that the Blob Brush tool created.

You can refer to my 16_practice_tool_final.ai file if you want to compare my brush techniques to your own.

Note   An alternative is to use Live Paint Bucket to fill regions of your paths with color and then use the Blob Brush on a separate layer to paint.

Now with the Blob Brush and Eraser tools paint over areas of the car. And then gnome. Refer to Figure 16-108.

Figure 16-108. *Finished example of the brooch, gnome, and car*

In the 16_practice_tool_final.ai file, I incorporated a different **brush definition** on the **blob brush tools** layer to give the beard fuzziness. Refer to Figure 16-109.

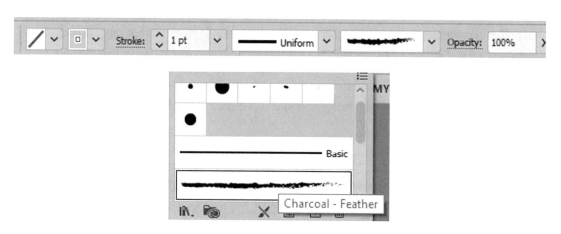

Figure 16-109. *Use your Paintbrush tool and select a different brush stroke brush definition*

Use your **Paintbrush tool (B)** to paint the beard with the Charcoal- Feather brush and add a bit of hair under his hat. You can see what that looks like in my file. Refer to Figure 16-110.

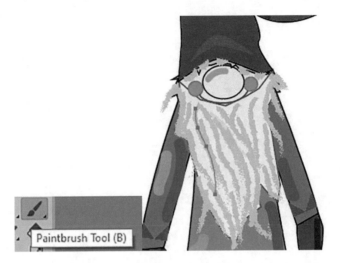

Figure 16-110. *Use your Paintbrush tool to add different brush stroke paths for hair on the gnome's beard*

After you have completed your embellishments, save (Ctrl/Cmd+S) your document.

Summary

This chapter looked at a few additional tools that you can use to improve your artwork. You learned how to apply color and brush effects to your artwork using tools such as the Blob Brush tool and Live Paint Bucket tool. The next chapter looks at adjusting the colors using the Color Guide panel, Global Colors, and Global Edits.

Adjusting Colors and Saving Artwork

This chapter demonstrates how to adjust your colors quickly and discusses file formats for saving your artwork for your portfolio.

In the previous chapter, you saw how to color artwork using the Swatches panel and the Blob Brush tool and the Live Paint Bucket tool. This chapter looks at editing colors on strokes and fills after they have been applied and how this could be applied globally to artwork.

Note To learn more about color and how it works, check out my *Introduction to Color Theory with Photoshop and Illustrator* video so that you can see some of these color harmonies and themes in action.

Projects for this chapter are in the Chapter 17 folder.

First, let's look at a few basic ways this can be done.

Eyedropper Tool (I)

A simple way to alter color, from one shape to another, is to use the Eyedropper tool. Refer to Figure 17-1.

Figure 17-1. *The Eyedropper tool in the Toolbars panel*

© Jennifer Harder 2022
J. Harder, *Accurate Layer Selections Using Photoshop's Selection Tools*,
https://doi.org/10.1007/978-1-4842-7493-4_17

When you select a shape with the Selection tool (V) and then click another unselected shape with the Eyedropper tool, those appearance attributes are applied to the selected shape. Refer to Figure 17-2.

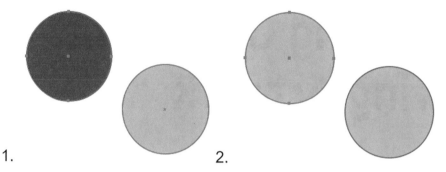

Figure 17-2. *The Eyedropper tool allows you to select attributes from an unselected object*

Eyedropper Options

You can check which attributes can be applied to another shape or object when you double-click the tool in the Toolbars panel to enter the Eyedropper Options dialog box. As in Photoshop, with its Eyedropper tool, you can set the **Raster Sample Size** to Point Sample, 3×3 Average, and 5×5 Average. You can select what the Eyedropper picks up and then what the Eyedropper applies. Refer to Figure 17-3.

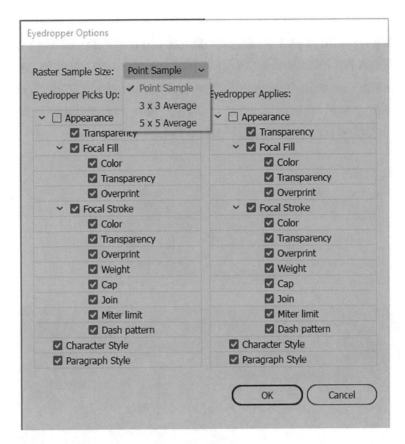

Figure 17-3. *Eyedropper Options dialog box*

The following are the options that can be transferred.

- **Transparency**: Applied to the object overall, which is opacity, and could include blending modes

- **Focal Fill**: Color (Solid, Gradient, or Pattern), Transparency, and Color Overprint

- **Focal Stroke**: Color (Solid, Gradient, or Pattern), Transparency, Overprint, Weight, Cap, Join, Miter Limit, and Dash Pattern

- **Character Style** and **Paragraph Style**: For text-related objects and fonts

Tip   You may have an object or shape that has (*fx*) applied because the
Eyedropper does not include this option to pick up and then apply to another
object. A workaround is to save your Appearance as a New Graphic Style in the
Graphic Styles panel for your open document. Then click and apply that graphic
style to the selected object. Refer to Figure 17-4.

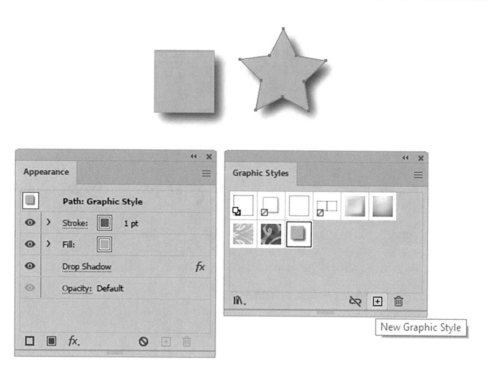

Figure 17-4.   *When you want to apply a Graphic Style to another object, store it in*
the Graphics Styles panel after building it using the Appearance panel

Edit Colors

Another way to edit colors on shapes is to use the options under Edit ➤ Edit Colors.
Some of these options allow for direct conversion without additional settings in
dialog boxes, while others alter specific areas of color in a customizable way. Refer to
Figure 17-5.

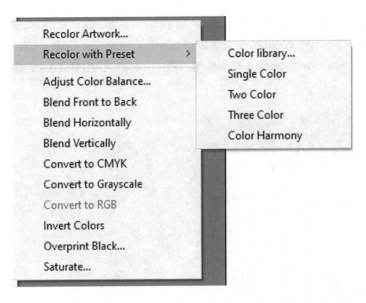

Figure 17-5. *Edit Colors options*

If you want to follow along with me, you can create your own shapes and paths or use the paths in the 17_pratice.ai file and File ➤ Save As a copy.

Recolor Artwork...

This brings up a basic version of the Recolor Artwork dialog box. Later you look at the advanced version of the panel. You can find a link to this dialog box in the Properties panel when you click the Quick Actions **Recolor** button or through the Control panel icon. Refer to Figure 17-6.

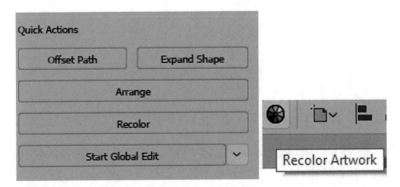

Figure 17-6. *The Properties panel Quick Actions and Control panel have the Recolor Artwork option*

When a shape or path is selected, there are some options you can choose. In this example, the star has two colors: yellow and black. Currently, **Color Library** is set to None. However, you can choose a different color library from the drop-down list. Refer to Figure 17-7.

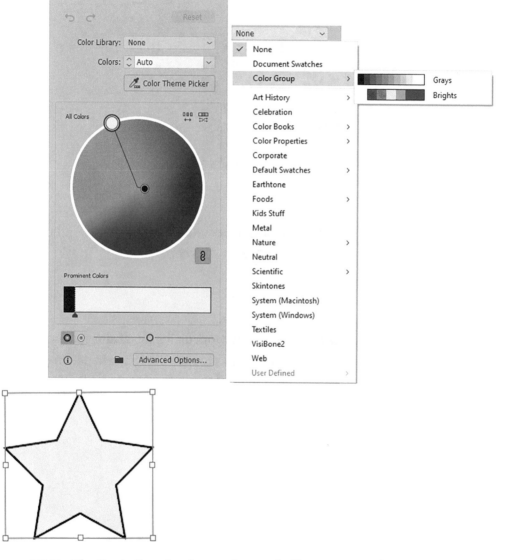

Figure 17-7.   *The Basic Recolor Artwork panel allows you to choose the color library option to reassign new swatches to your artwork*

Color Group ➤ Brights, for example, makes a color more prominent (in this case, red) and limits the number of colors in your selection. Refer to Figure 17-8.

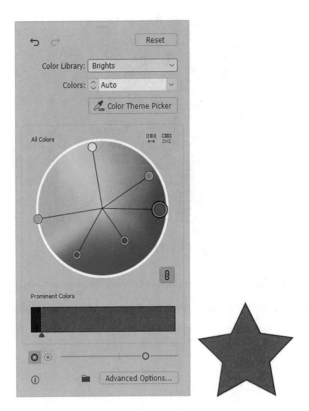

Figure 17-8. *The Brights library changed the color of the currently selected object path*

Because the star is only two colors, this is not really a concern, but in more colorful designs, major color shifts may occur when you set a limit with other libraries. At this point, if you want to revert, you can click the **Reset** button in the upper right or use the **undo** and **redo changes** icons in the upper left. Refer to Figure 17-8.

From the next drop-down list, **Colors,** you can further limit your color choices for a shape from one to five colors or keep all colors. By default, it is set to Auto. Refer to Figure 17-9.

Figure 17-9. *Limit the number of colors during recolor*

The **Color Theme Picker** option lets you click or drag over multiple objects to extract and apply color themes from the reference images or artworks. Refer to Figure 17-10.

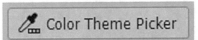

Color Theme Picker: click or drag (over multiple) to extract and apply color themes from reference images or artworks

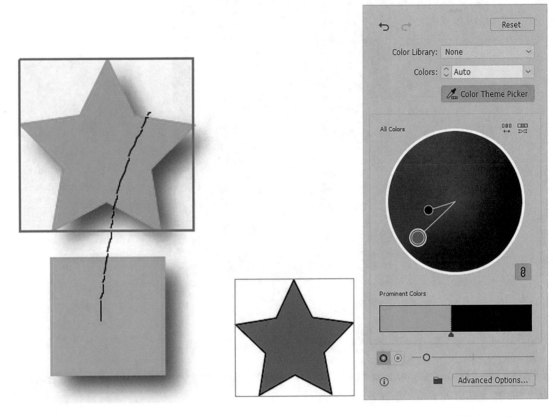

Figure 17-10. *Enable the Color Theme Picker button to access colors from other Objects for your currently selected object and change its color*

When you do this, the areas in **All Colors** and the **Prominent Colors** change. In this example, there are two new colors: cyan and dark blue. Click the **undo changes** icon in the upper left to go back a step to return to the Brights library. Refer to Figure 17-11.

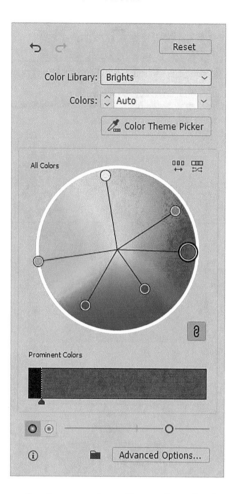

Figure 17-11. *Undo, or redo changes in color using the icons in the upper areas of the Basic Recolor dialog box*

All Colors has a few other options that then let you **Change Color Order Randomly** and **Change Saturation and Brightness randomly**. Refer to Figure 17-12.

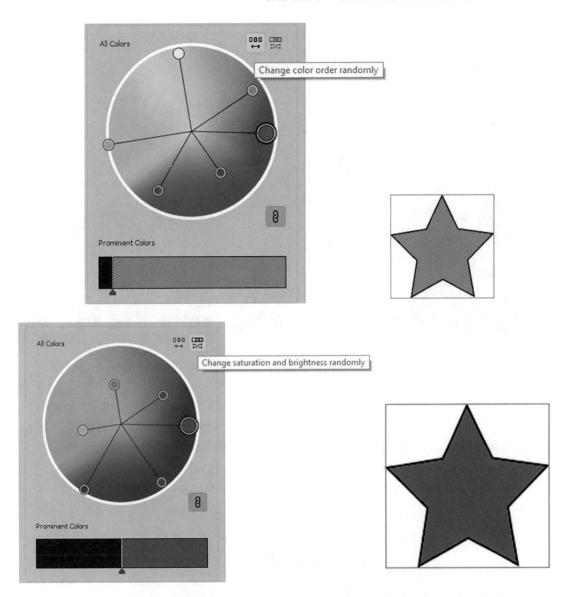

Figure 17-12. *Change the color order or Saturation/Brightness randomly for your objects*

You can then move the color points by dragging them, set a new prominent color, or select another point and right-click to choose **Set as Base Color** to alter the color wheel further. Refer to Figure 17-13.

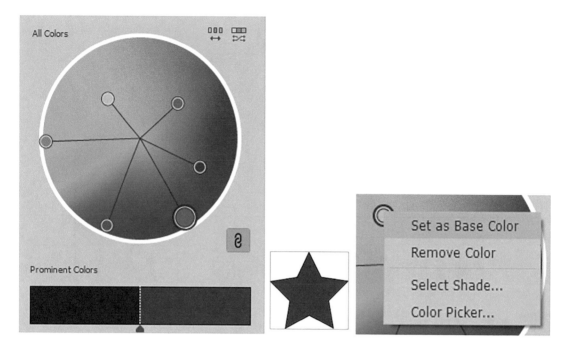

Figure 17-13. *Reset the base color in the All Colors area*

Other options from this menu include **removing a color point** or selecting a new color point, and altering the color with **Select Shade** or **Color Picker**. If you double-click a color point, you can enter Color Picker this way as well. Refer to Figure 17-14.

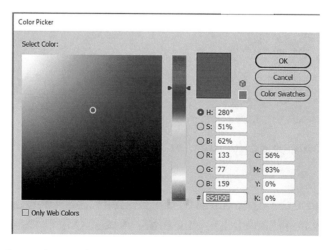

Figure 17-14. *The Color Picker dialog box lets you set a new color point*

Next to the color wheel, you can **link or unlink Harmony Colors** individually so that you can move them separately around and then relink them together again to move as one group. Refer to Figure 17-15.

Figure 17-15. *Link or unlink color points so you can move them freely of the other points*

Moving the **Prominent Colors** slide edges next to a color patch left or right also causes a color shift in your artwork and increases or decreases the color's weight in your artwork. Refer to Figure 17-16.

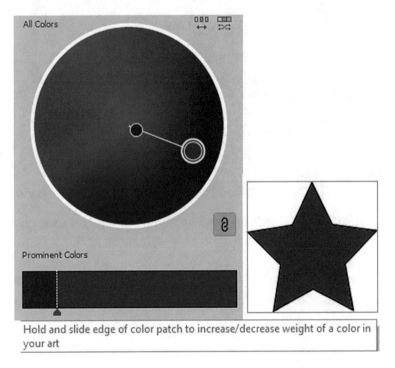

Figure 17-16. *Adjust your prominent colors using the slider*

Lower on the dialog box, there are two icons: one allows you to **show saturation and hue on the color wheel** (default) and **show brightness and hue on the color wheel**. Changing this does not shift the current color of your artwork.

However, moving the slider allows you to adjust the brightness or saturation of your colors in your artwork, depending on which color wheel setting you choose. Refer to Figure 17-17.

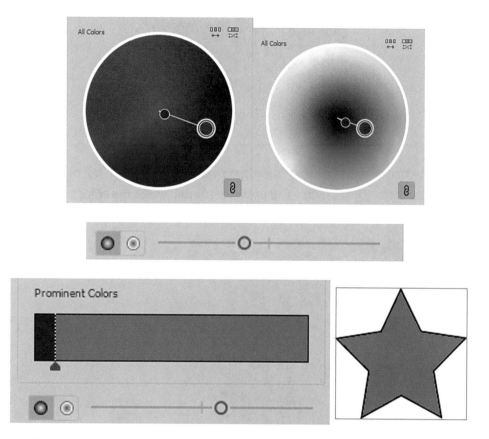

Figure 17-17. *Alter hue, saturation, and brightness based on icon choice and slider*

Save All Colors (from the color wheel) or **Save Prominent Colors** (from the slider bar) directly to the Swatches panel. In this case, it is a color group of two. Refer to Figure 17-18.

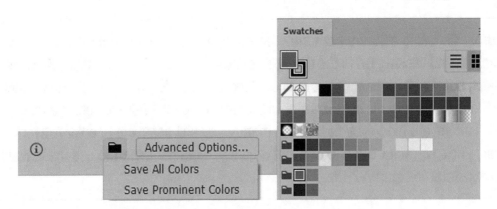

Figure 17-18. *Save your colors created in the basic Recolor dialog box in the Swatches panel*

You look at the **Advanced Recolor Options** later in the chapter. You can click away from the dialog box to exit it.

See the Adobe help section at `https://helpx.adobe.com/illustrator/using/recolor-artwork.html` for more information.

Recolor with Preset ➤

This submenu has several options that allow you to color a selected shape or path quickly without entering the Recolor Artwork dialog box. Refer to Figure 17-19.

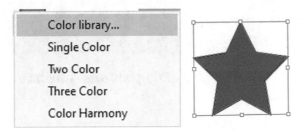

Figure 17-19. *Recolor your artwork with several preset options*

Color library... allows you to recolor using a limited color group that is in the Swatches library. This does not include Gradients or patterns, only solid color swatches.

Note   Choosing a library from the drop-down menus, for example, Art History ➤ Ancient, and clicking OK in the dialog box cause you to enter the Recolor Artwork dialog box. Click OK to confirm, or click Cancel to exit. However, by clicking Cancel in the Color Library dialog box (refer to the left of Figure 17-20, where the dialog box buttons are hidden by the Library menu), you still enter the Recolor Artwork dialog box, so click Cancel to exit that area if you did not intend to use these dialog boxes. Refer to Figure 17-20.

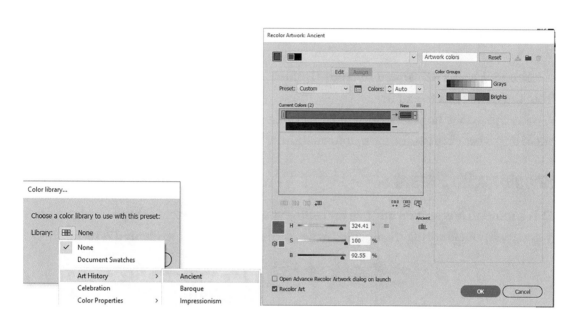

Figure 17-20. *Use the Color Library dialog box and Advanced Recolor options to change your artwork's color*

Single Color, Two Color and Three Color presents a similar dialog box allowing you to select one, two, or three colors from select swatches libraries to colorize the artwork. This may be useful when you are dealing with a very strict color palette. Whether you click OK or Cancel, you enter the Recolor Artwork dialog box, which you look at later in the chapter. Refer to Figure 17-21.

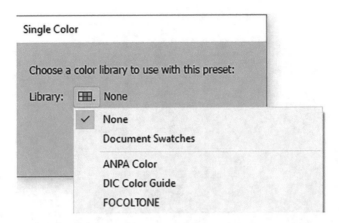

Figure 17-21. *Choose a swatch from a select library when creating artwork with one to three colors*

Color Harmony directly enters the Recolor Artwork dialog box. Refer to Figure 17-20.

Adjust Color Balance

Adjust Color Balance adjusts color on a layer, like Image ➤ Adjustments in Photoshop. In this case, you are adjusting the object. You can adjust the **Color mode** of the selected object to Grayscale, RGB, CMYK, or Global (affects swatches that have been set to global). The RGB adjustment only works if you are in a document set to RGB color mode. If you are in a document with CMYK mode, that option is unavailable. Select **Convert** if you need to ensure the path is in that color mode. Move the sliders to make the adjustments to the CMYK values. The **Adjust Options** can be set to change the **Fill, Stroke,** or both. Select the **Preview** to see the changes to the selected shape. Click **OK** to confirm the color change. Refer to Figure 17-22.

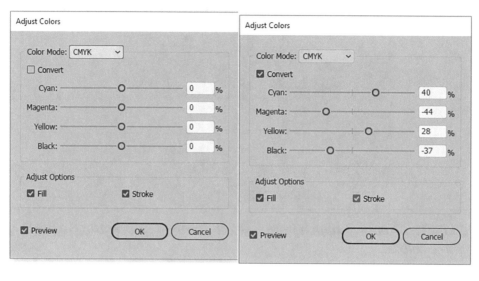

Figure 17-22. *Adjust Colors dialog box and the changes made to the objects when the sliders are moved*

Blend Front to Back

For this option to work, you must have at least three shapes selected that are overlapping. This fills the intermediate objects with graduated blends between the frontmost and backmost filled objects. Any less, and you receive a warning message. Click OK and make sure you have at least three shapes or objects selected. Refer to Figure 17-23.

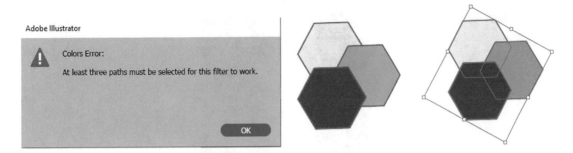

Figure 17-23. *Blend front to Back needs at least three shapes or objects to work correctly*

The start and end colors are then blended into the middle color.

Blend Horizontally

When three or more shapes with fills and strokes are lined up horizontally, you can blend using the leftmost and rightmost colored objects to blend the intermediate color. Refer to Figure 17-24.

Figure 17-24. *Blend three or more shapes in a horizontal direction*

Blend Vertically

When three or more shapes with fills and strokes are lined up vertically, you can blend using the topmost and bottommost colored objects to blend the intermediate color. Refer to Figure 17-25.

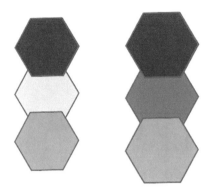

Figure 17-25. *Blend three or more shapes in a vertical direction*

Convert to CMYK

This converts the current colors of the shapes or objects to CMYK mode. This is useful when you may have copied the shapes from a document in RGB mode to a CMYK mode document. Though the conversion may be automatic during the transfer, it is usually a good idea to apply this setting anyway, in case you should run into color-related errors later if you plan to print the artwork. Additionally, before I print, I always double-check that my document is in CMYK mode through File ➤ Document Color Mode ➤ CMYK Color. Refer to Figure 17-26.

Figure 17-26. *Check the current Document Color mode for your file*

Convert to Grayscale

This converts the current colors of the shapes or objects to grayscale or shades of gray. Your document may be in RGB or CMYK mode, but for artistic reasons, you want to see how your artwork appears in a monochrome of grays. If you plan to show a color copy and a grayscale copy of the artwork, always keep a backup copy of the color version either on a separate layer or artboard before you convert a copy to grayscale. Seeing your artwork in grayscale is also good should you plan to print out your artwork to your laser printer, and you want to preview the most accurate transitions. Refer to Figure 17-27.

Figure 17-27. *Convert your shapes or objects to grayscale*

Convert to RGB

This converts the current colors of the shapes or objects to RGB mode. This is useful when you may have copied the shapes from a document in CMYK mode to an RGB mode document. Though the conversion may be automatic during the transfer, it is usually a good idea to apply this setting anyway, in case you should run into visual color errors later if you plan to use your artwork in animation or as a graphic on your website. I always double-check that my document is in RGB mode through File ➤ Document Color Mode ➤ RGB Color. Refer to Figure 17-26.

Invert Colors

When a shape or grouped shapes with fills and strokes are selected, this allows you to automatically convert the colors to the opposite complementary color as they are on the color wheel, red to cyan, orange to blue, yellow to dark blue, green to magenta and so on. Refer to Figure 17-28.

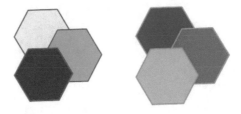

Figure 17-28. *Colors of shapes and objects can be inverted*

Note   From your Color panel, you can select a single shape and use the Invert or Complement menu option to perform a similar basic color change on the stroke or fill. Refer to Figure 17-29.

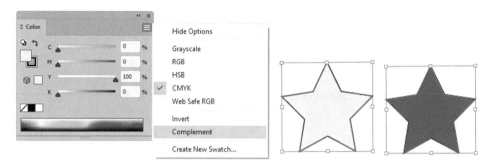

Figure 17-29. *Invert or Complement a single shape's stroke of fill from the Colors panel*

Overprint Black (Advanced Users)

In some CMYK printing situations, you need to ensure that the black of a stroke contains CMY colors along with black so that if there is a shift of colors on the offset press, this does not cause tiny white gaps in the artwork. Usually, this is not required for laser or Inkjet printing at home, but maybe a setting requested by a professional offset prepress person. They may need you to add or remove black from your selected artwork if they notice there could be a printing issue. For example, sections within a logo area that may be next to or overlapping additional spot colors. When applied by clicking OK in the Overprint Black dialog box, the Overprint appears in the Appearance panel and can be reset via the Window ➤ Attributes panel. Refer to Figure 17-30.

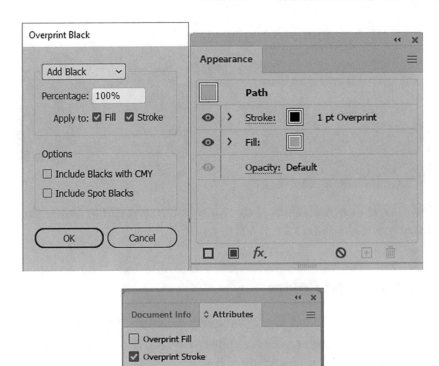

Figure 17-30. *Overprint Black dialog box settings and how they appear in the Appearances panel and Attributes panel if required as an advanced setting for print work*

In most situations, a print company uses professional software to correct overprints or traps. Nevertheless, you should discuss with them and research if you are planning on using spot colors to ensure your artwork looks consistently at its best if printing a large amount. Go to `https://helpx.adobe.com/illustrator/using/overprinting.html` to learn more.

Saturate

The Saturate dialog box lets you desaturate or saturate your selected shapes and objects by moving the slider left or right. Select Preview to see the color change. Click OK to confirm. Refer to Figure 17-31.

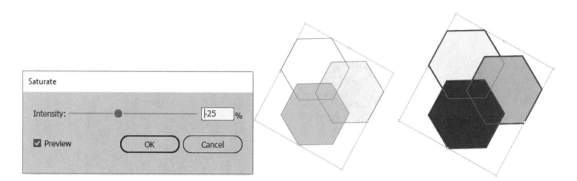

Figure 17-31.   *The Saturate dialog box changes the amount of saturation for the objects as you move the sliders from left to right*

Other Ways to Blend Colors

Additional blends can be created when shapes are selected. One is Window ➤ **Transparency Blending Modes**, which applies to the fill, stroke, or both using the Appearances panel. Refer to Figure 17-32.

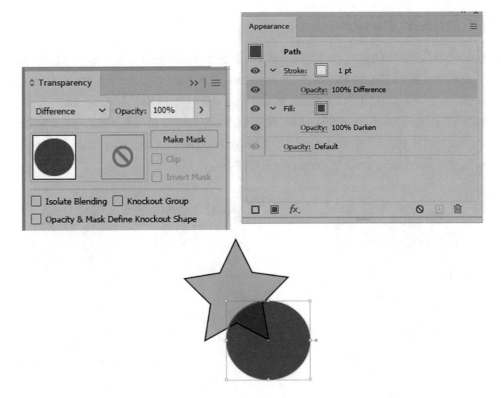

Figure 17-32. *Use the Transparency panel to create a blend of colors*

In my *Illustrator Pathfinder Effects* video, I look at different blends using the Pathfinder effects *(fx)* (https://link.springer.com/video/10.1007/978-1-4842-6581-9).

Note   If you want to explore more complex blending that involves shapes, objects, symbols as well as colors, refer to https://helpx.adobe.com/illustrator/using/blending-objects.html. Refer to Figure 17-33.

Figure 17-33. *Use the Blend tool when you want to blend both color and objects at the same time*

Color Guide Panel

One of the best ways to affect multiple colors on grouped objects or symbols is to use the Window ➤ **Color Guide Panel**. I demonstrate this panel in my *Introduction to Color Theory* video, and I go into more detail about this panel later in this chapter.

Open 17_practice2.ai, and Save As a copy to work on. This file contains the geometric drawing from Live Paint Expanded and the brooch on the artboard and stored as a symbol in the Symbols panel. Refer to Figure 17-34.

Figure 17-34. *You can use these kinds of vector files and easily recolor them with the Color Guide panel*

Tip   If you plan to alter multiple copies of your artwork, always make sure to save a backup copy of the original file. Likewise, for smaller pieces, you can save copies as symbols in the Window ➤ Symbols panel. Using the Color Guide panel, you can test different color group options until you find the exact color arrangement you are looking for. Refer to Figure 17-35.

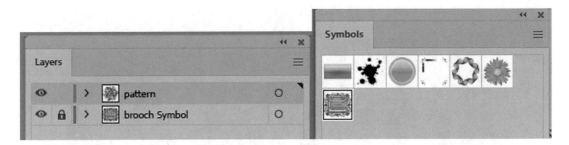

Figure 17-35. *Once you create an object, you can store it in the Symbols panel for safekeeping*

Let's look at it first without any of the objects or symbols selected and keep the **brooch symbol** layer in the Layers panel locked for now. Refer to Figure 17-35

Make sure that the Toolbars panel is set to white fill and a black stroke. Refer to Figure 17-36.

In the Swatches panel, click the Brights folder color group so that you can see a full range of six colors. And then look at the Color Guide panel. Refer to Figure 17-36.

Figure 17-36. *The Swatch panel contains a color group, while the Color Guide is set with a base fill of white from the Toolbars panel*

This panel has two parts to it.

- The panel that shows the shades and tints

- An icon to enter the **Edit Colors** dialog box

To recolor artwork, the object or grouped object needs to be selected to be altered. However, you can still use the Color Guide panel to create your color groups when the artwork is not selected.

The square swatch in the first row next to the drop-down list allows you to set your **base color**, which is white in this example. Refer to Figure 17-37.

Figure 17-37. *Reset the base color in the Color Guide panel from Harmony Rules*

However, it could be the selected color of either the Stroke or Fill in the Toolbars panel.

Or you can click a color in the Harmony Rules drop-down list to choose a new base color.

Click the red swatch. Refer to Figure 17-37.

Then click the drop-down itself. Choose from the drop-down list various Harmony Rules options of up to six colors. These are all possible colors that you can use as color groups in all your artwork. Refer to Figure 17-38.

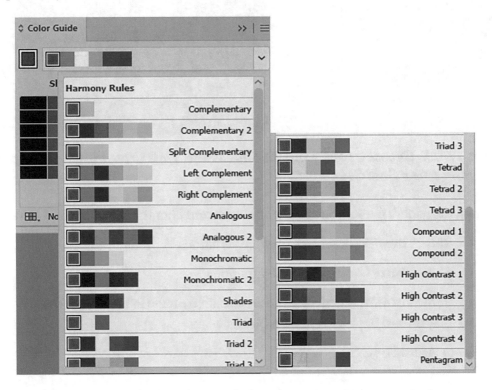

Figure 17-38. *In the Color Guide panel, there are many Harmony Rules to choose from*

> **Note**   Harmony rules are a big part of learning about color theory, and knowing which colors work well together is a science in itself. If you are not sure whether your taste in color is good or bad, don't worry. As a beginner, you can rely on Illustrator's harmonies and learn as you practice and observe color combinations.

Or you can set the base color again by selecting a shade or a tint and then click the **Set Base Color** as the current color button to alter the Harmony Rules again to a new collection. Refer to Figure 17-39.

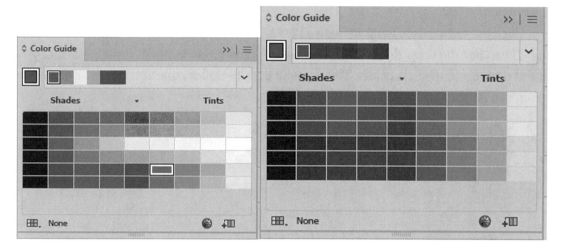

Figure 17-39.   *Choose a color from the Shades and Tints to create new Harmony Rules from a new Base Color*

From the panel's menu, you can choose to see and filter the colors by the following.

- **Show Tints/Shades**: black to white variations

- **Show Warm/Cool**: red to blue variations

- **Show Vivid/Muted**: decrease the saturation on the left to reduce the gray toward brighter colors on the right

Refer to Figure 17-40.

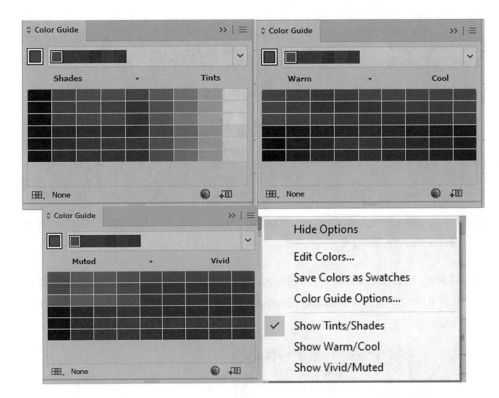

Figure 17-40. *Organize colors by Shades/Tints, Warm/Cool, or Muted/Vivid in the Color Guide panel*

I usually keep it set to Show Tints/Shades.

Color Guide Options

If you want to adjust this range further from the menu, you can choose Color Guide Options. This allows you to increase or decrease the number of steps between colors 3 and 20 and the variation of color using the slider (0%–100%), less to more between those steps. As you make changes here, the options change in the Color Guide panel. The default is four steps, and the variation is set to 100%.

Click OK to confirm your changes, or click Cancel to exit without changing the options. Refer to Figure 17-41.

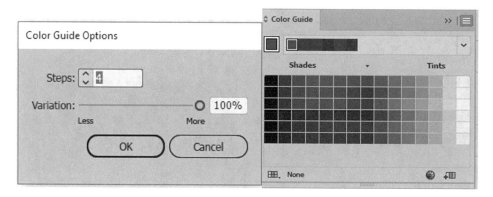

Figure 17-41. Color Guide Options dialog box and how the Color Guide appears if set to 7 steps rather than 4

On the lower half of the Color Guide dialog box, you have an option that limits the color groups to colors in a **swatch library**. By default, it is set to None. Refer to Figure 17-42.

Figure 17-42. Choose from a library to limit the number of colors in the Color Guide

For now, keep the library at the None setting.

If no shapes or objects are selected, you can click the **Edit Colors** icon. Refer to Figure 17-43.

Figure 17-43. *The Edit Colors icon at the bottom of the Color Guide*

The **Save Color group to Swatches panel** icon on the lower right. When clicked, it saves the color group you created, and it appears in the Swatch panel. Refer to Figure 17-44.

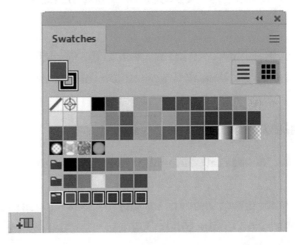

Figure 17-44. *Add the colors you create in the Color Guide to the Swatches panel*

Another way to create a color group is to Ctrl/Cmd-click or Shift-click, select colors out of harmony, and click the **Save color group to Swatch panel** button. Refer to Figure 17-45.

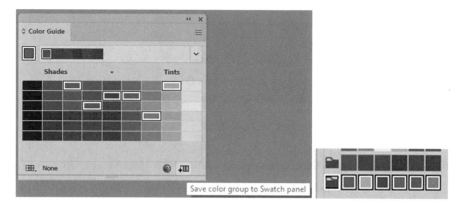

Figure 17-45. *Save a random group of colors from the Color Guide to the Swatches panel*

You can delete any swatches you do not need in the Swatches panel or continue to add more. However, I keep the default Grays and Brights groups that Illustrator created.

Edit Colors Dialog Box

This part of the chapter focuses on editing the color groups, not assigning a color to an illustration.

Again, select the color group folder of Brights in the Swatches panel

Click the Edit Colors icon on the Color Guide to enter the dialog box. Refer to Figure 17-46 and Figure 17-47.

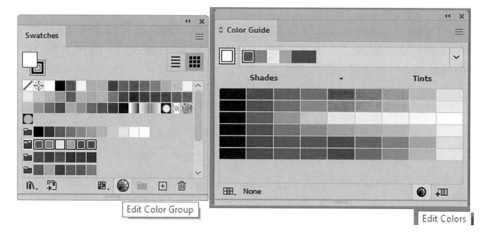

Figure 17-46. *Edit Colors dialog box through the Swatches panel or Color Guide dialog box*

Note   If you want to edit the color group click the Edit Color Group icon in the Swatches panel to edit that color group directly. Refer to Figure 17-46.

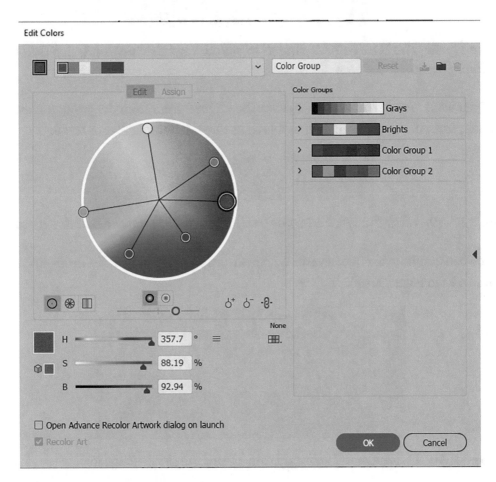

Figure 17-47. *Edit Colors dialog box*

You can then see that the highlighted color in the drop-down is considered the base color.

When you click a color in the list and then the Active Colors box on the left, you can set a new base color and scheme. Refer to Figure 17-48.

Figure 17-48. *The Base color is altered to yellow, and the current Active Colors in the Color Group*

If you want to revert, make sure to click the original color from the group folder originally from the Swatches panel; in this case, the red. Refer to Figure 17-49.

Figure 17-49. *Click the original color (red) if you want to make it active again*

You can continue to choose various colors from the Harmony Rules drop-down menu. Refer to Figure 17-50.

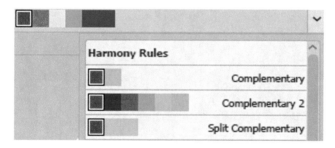

Figure 17-50. *Choose new Harmony Rules from the drop-down list*

There are often two or more Harmony Rules options available. This new group (Triad 2) can be added to the Color Groups on the right by naming the group and clicking the **New Color Group** icon. This is done to prevent this new collection from being overwritten should you want to edit a collection again. Refer to Figure 17-51.

Figure 17-51. *Create a New Color Group from the currently active colors*

Note   If you are editing a selected color group, you know this is happening because the selected name on the right becomes italic. Refer to Figure 17-52.

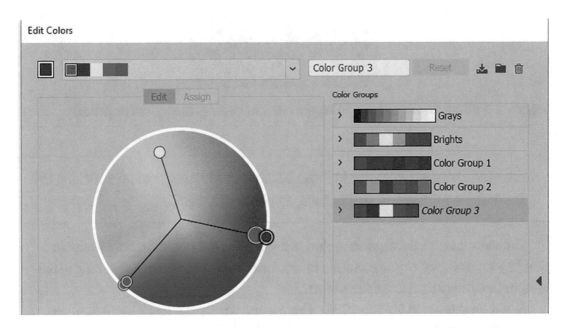

Figure 17-52. *If you edit a color group while selected, its name becomes italic*

Afterward, you can click Save Changes to Color Group or Delete Color Group to remove it. Click the icon to save changes. Refer to Figure 17-53.

Figure 17-53. *Save your changes to the Color Group after you make changes*

You can later rename the color group by double-clicking the name to prevent it from being overwritten. I called the group Color Group Triad. Refer to Figure 17-54.

Figure 17-54. *Rename your color group so you can identify it*

Always click the New Color Group icon to create a new color group as you find one that you like to add to your collection. You may want to see the full list of colors on some groups when you click the triangle and right-click the swatch to **remove color**. Refer to Figure 17-55.

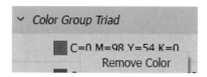

Figure 17-55. *Remove a color from the current color group if not required*

Note   The changes you make to these color groups are not final until clicking OK in the dialog box. However, in this case, do not close it yet.

You see a more visual representation of these color harmonies in action later in the chapter. However, as you continue to tour this dialog box, you can see some of the options have more than five color points.

Select Brights Again from the Color Groups and Save as a New Color Group icon. Refer to Figure 17-56.

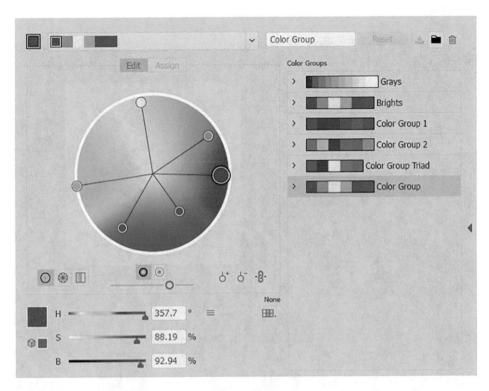

Figure 17-56. *Create a copy based on the Bright Color Group*

With a copy of the color group, you can continue to edit in several ways.

These color points in the **Edit** tab can be moved and dragged and spun to new locations, creating different hues or moving them in and out to adjust saturation. Refer to Figure 17-57.

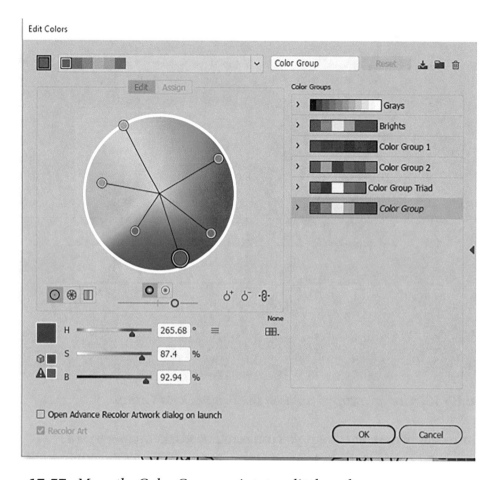

Figure 17-57. *Move the Color Group points to edit the color group*

Notice that now when no object is selected, the Assign tab and the recolor artwork check box are grayed out. You look at that area later in the chapter.

As you work with the colors in this area of the wheel, you can choose how you want to view the color as you edit them.

Display Smooth Color Wheel displays the color of hue saturation and brightness in a smooth continuous circle. You can see a gradation of continuous color, and it is hard to see specific colors. Refer to Figure 17-58.

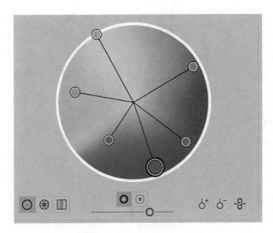

Figure 17-58. *Display Smooth Color Wheel setting*

Display Segmented Color Wheel displays colors in segmented patches, you can see individual colors more clearly, but it does not give the same color range as the smooth color wheel. Refer to Figure 17-59.

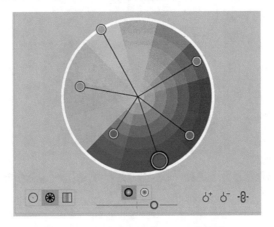

Figure 17-59. *Display Segmented Color Wheel setting*

Display Color Bars are useful when you have a lot of points on the wheel. Color bars have a different option than the wheel for allowing you to **randomly change color order**, **randomly change saturation brightness,** and **unlink harmony colors** so that you can drag and rearrange them. Then you can **relink**. Refer to Figure 17-60.

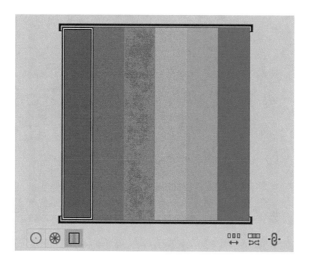

Figure 17-60. *Display Color Bars setting that are currently linked*

Clicking a color bar in the lower corner lets you see the color picker and allows you to edit the color and its linked colors. Unlink if you only want to edit a select bar. Refer to Figure 17-60 and Figure 17-61.

Figure 17-61. *Edit each bar when you open the color picker in the lower corner and select a new color*

Let's return to Display Smooth Color Wheel.

Show Saturation and Hue on Wheel works with a smooth or segmented color wheel, which I prefer to work with. Refer to Figure 17-62.

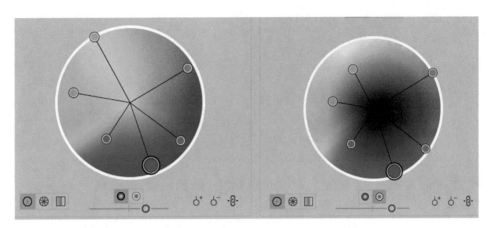

Figure 17-62. *Show colors by saturation or by brightness and hue on the color wheel*

Show Brightness and Hue on Wheel works with a smooth or segmented color wheel. Refer to Figure 17-62.

Slider adjusts brightness or saturation depending on what show option was selected prior. Refer to Figure 17-62.

Add a Color tool points allows you to click and add more colors to your artwork to recolor it. Refer to Figure 17-63.

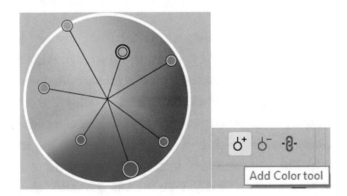

Figure 17-63. *Add color tool lets you add another color point*

Remove Color tool points allows you to click and remove a selected color point from your artwork. Refer to Figure 17-64.

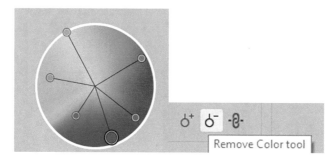

Figure 17-64. *Remove a selected color point from the wheel with the Remove Color tool*

Unlink Harmony Colors links or unlinks to move colors separately on the wheel. When done moving, make sure to link again, so the position is locked again. Refer to Figure 17-65.

Figure 17-65. *Link or unlink the harmony colors to move them independently*

Specify the mode of the color adjustment slider. The color area below indicates the currently selected swatch color or base color, and you can use the drop-down menu to change the mode. The **cube** under the swatch means that a color is "out of web color range," while the **warning alert triangle** means the color is "out of gamut" or cannot be reproduced within the current color space. You can click either one to ensure that your color is both web-safe and in gamut. Currently, the mode is **HSB** (Hue Saturation Brightness). But, you can alter it by clicking the menu icon and choosing another color mode, such as **RGB**, **CMYK**, **Web RGB** for limited RGB colors (for web design in Hexadecimal), **Tint** (only available for global swatches), **Lab**, or **Global Adjust** (Saturation, Brightness, Temperature, Luminosity). Refer to Figure 17-66.

For now, I leave it at HSB.

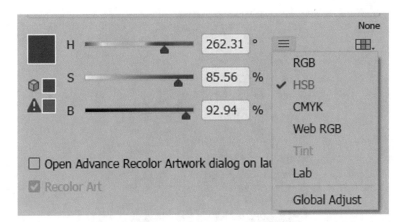

Figure 17-66. *Set your color adjustment slider to different modes*

Limit the color group to colors in the Swatch library. You can work with different swatch libraries to limit color. However, I leave it at None.

Open Advanced Recolor artwork dialog box on launch is left deselected by default.

After renaming and saving your group, click **OK** to exit the dialog box. Click Yes to any alert that may occur. Refer to Figure 17-67.

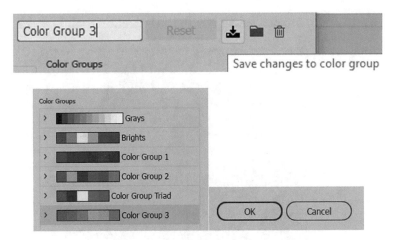

Figure 17-67. *Save the new Color Group you create after it has been altered and click OK in the Edit Colors dialog box*

Color Groups with five or more colors are added to the Swatches panel. Refer to Figure 17-68.

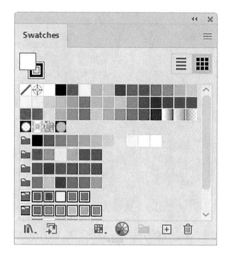

Figure 17-68. *The new color groups are saved in the Swatches panel*

Save (Ctrl/Cmd+S) your work in the document.

Recolor Artwork Dialog Box

When you have artwork to recolor, select it with the Selection tool. Refer to Figure 17-69.

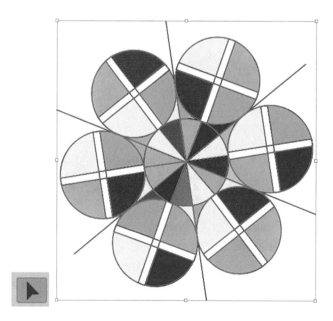

Figure 17-69. *Use the Selection tool to select the Grouped Object*

Click the Edit or Apply icon in the Color Guide panel to enter the Recolor Artwork dialog box. Refer to Figure 17-70.

Figure 17-70. *The Color Guide icon changes to Edit or Apply Colors*

You then have access to the **Assign tab** first, and the Recolor Artwork Preview check is available. Refer to Figure 17-71.

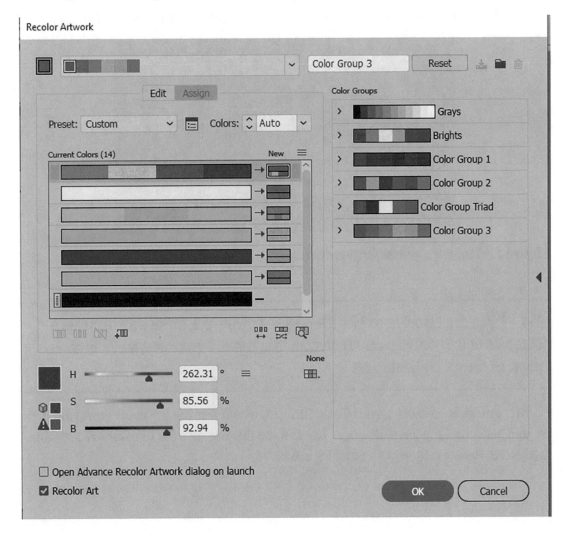

Figure 17-71. *Recolor Artwork dialog box with Assign tab active*

You saw this same dialog box when you selected the artwork and Choose Edit ➤ Edit Colors ➤ Recolor Artwork and then click the Advanced Options button in the dialog box and when editing with Recolor with Preset. Refer to Figure 17-72.

Figure 17-72. *Advanced Options button in the Basic Recolor Artwork dialog box*

If you preset to limit your artwork to a library with one, two, or three colors or color harmony, via that path, you still have the option to reset this when you choose the Recolor Artwork option through in the Color Guide panel. Refer to Figure 17-73.

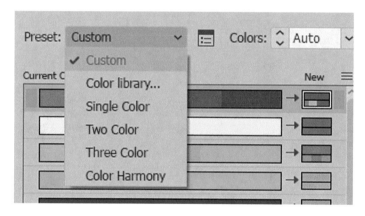

Figure 17-73. *Set a preset for your artwork*

Tip   If you don't want to recolor the original artwork yet, make sure to create a duplicate or uncheck Recolor Art. If more than one of the same symbols is on a page, all recolor the same way.

My artwork is recoloring with Color Group 3, which was the last color group that I created before exiting the dialog box. You can see this because the Recolor Art checkbox is selected. Refer to Figure 17-71 and Figure 17-74.

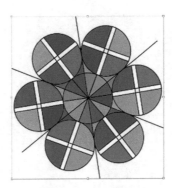

Figure 17-74. *The object has now been recolored because Color Group 3 was currently selected*

In the Recolor Artwork dialog box, you can still access all the same settings as in the Edit Color dialog box, including the **Edit tab** if you need to continue creating or saving color groups and adjusting harmonies while working on your selected artwork.

Assign Tab

In the Assign tab, I leave my preset at Custom. For your project, you may pick another preset. You can choose from the same presets in the Edit menu, such as Color Library, Single Color, Two Color, Three Color, and Color Harmony. Refer to Figure 17-73 and Figure 17-75.

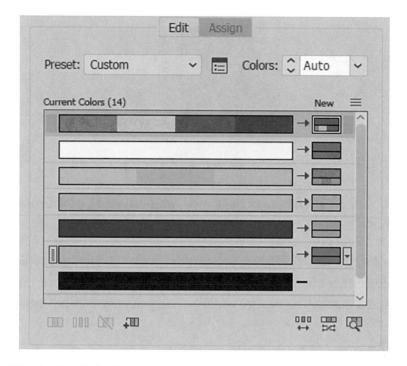

Figure 17-75. *Assign Tab Options*

Color Reduction Options

 The next button beside the Preset drop-down lets you refine your color reductions options further. Refer to Figure 17-76.

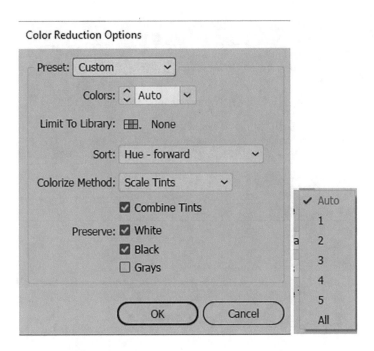

Figure 17-76. *Color Reduction Options dialog box*

The same **Preset** setting as in the Assign tab.

Colors are also in the Assign tab, where you can set a range of colors for Auto, 1 through 5, or all present colors.

Limit to Library allows you to limit your color choices to a specific swatch library.

Sort determines how the original colors are sorted in the current color columns. Refer to Figure 17-77. You have the following options.

- None

- Hue- forward (default)

- Hue – backward

- Lightness – dark to light

- Lightness -light to dark

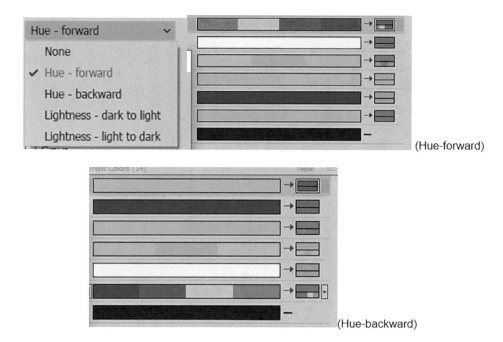

Figure 17-77. *Change the order of the colors*

Colorize Method sets the types of variations allowed for the new colors. Refer to Figure 17-78.

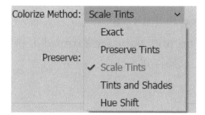

Figure 17-78. *The Colorize Method has several options in the drop-down list*

Exact replaces each current color with the specified new color.

Preserve Tints is for non-global colors. For spot or global colors, it applies the current color's tint to the new color. Use this setting when all the current colors in the row if are tints of the same or similar global color. For best results, when using Preserve Tints, also select the **Combine Tints** checkbox.

The default **Scale Tints** setting replaces the darkest current color in the row with the newly specified color. Other current colors in the same row are replaced with a lighter tint.

Tints and Shades replace the current color with the average lightness and darkness with the newly specified color. If the current colors are lighter than the average, they are replaced with a lighter tint of the new color. Likewise, if current colors are darker than the average, they are replaced by adding black shades to the new color.

Hue Shift sets the most typical color in the Current Colors row as a key color and replaces the key color with the new color. The other current colors are replaced by colors that differ from the new color in brightness, saturation, and hue by the same amounts that the current color differs from the key or main color.

Combine Tints sorts all tints of the same global color into the same Current Colors row, even if colors are not limited. Use this option only when the selected art contains global or spot colors applied at tints less than 100%. Adobe recommends for best results, use in combination with the Preserve Tints colorization method. When unselected, color reduction combines tints of the same global color before it combines different non-global colors. Refer to Figure 17-79.

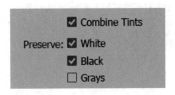

Figure 17-79. *In the Color Reduction dialog box, Combine Tints is selected with some of the Preserve options*

Preserve preserves **whites**, **blacks**, and **grays** of the original artwork. White and black are selected by default, but for other art, you may need to preserve the shades of gray. If a color is preserved, it appears in the Current Colors column as an excluded row. Refer to Figure 17-79 and Figure 17-80.

Figure 17-80. *Black is preserved as a color and cannot be altered if the preserve setting is enabled*

For now, click Cancel to exit as you do not want to reduce colors yet. Refer to Figure 17-81.

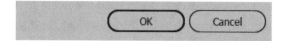

Figure 17-81. *Click Cancel if you do not want to save changes in the Color Reduction Options dialog box*

Leave the Color setting in the Assign tab at Auto. Refer to Figure 17-82.

Figure 17-82. *Leave the color setting at Auto if you do not want to reduce the colors in the Color Group*

Currently, you are looking at the current colors (14). The new settings to the right are assigned based on the earlier Color Group choices. Refer to Figure 17-83.

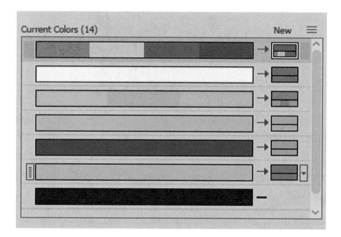

Figure 17-83. *Current colors and new colors that replace, some are displayed*

Above the rows and columns is the same **Sort** menu you saw on the Color Reduction Options dialog box.

I keep it at **Custom**. But you can try other Sort settings if you wish to see if your artwork changes. Refer to Figure 17-84.

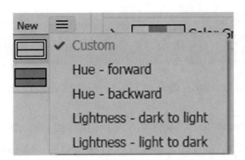

Figure 17-84. *Sort your colors using the menu or leave them in the Custom setting*

If you want to revert to follow along, click the **Reset** button to reset your artwork and then on Color Group 3. You can find this library in the 17_paractice _2.ai file if yours is different from mine. Refer to Figure 17-85.

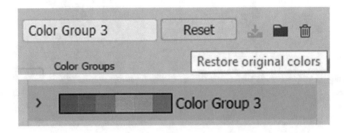

Figure 17-85. *Reset your color group if you do not like the edits you made*

The handle on the left of each color row allows you to drag and move all colors to another row. Refer to Figure 17-86.

Figure 17-86. *Drag a color to another row*

Some rows have more than one color. Dragging them to another row adds that color or colors to that row.

You can't Edit ➤ Undo this move other than resetting everything.

Rather, it is better if you find that you made a mistake selecting that color in the row, drag it back to the blank white area right away. Refer to Figure 17-87.

Figure 17-87. *Drag that color back to its row right away to undo this color step*

If you don't want some of the colors in your illustration to be recolored, click the arrow to make it a line. This way, those areas of color stay as they are. Click the line again to change it back to an arrow so that it can be recolored. Refer to Figure 17-88.

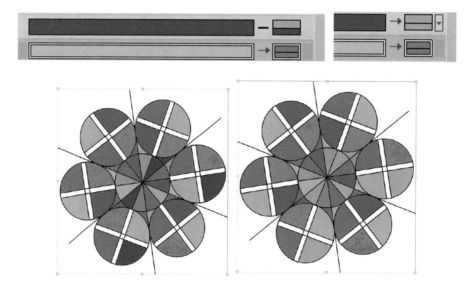

Figure 17-88. *Color you do not want to change can be unlinked when you click the arrow*

Next, you can double-click a new color on the right (in this case, the khaki yellow, which I do not like) to edit it with the color picker. Refer to Figure 17-89.

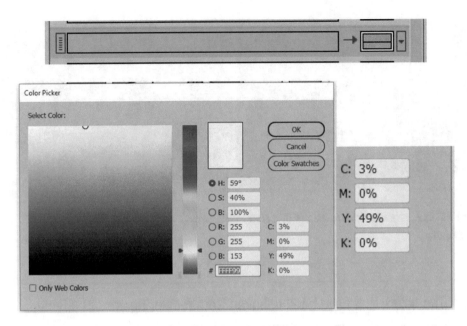

Figure 17-89. *Find a better color using Color Picker to alter colors you do not like in your artwork*

Click OK to confirm the new lighter color and exit the dialog box. Refer to Figure 17-90.

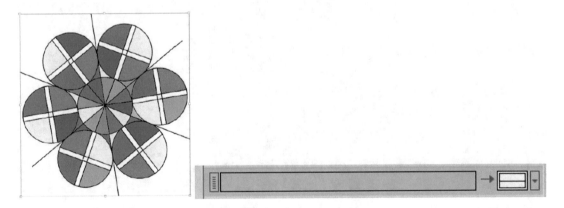

Figure 17-90. *The replacement color is much brighter*

Then Drag to swap new colors on the right for another and shift the order. Refer to Figure 17-91.

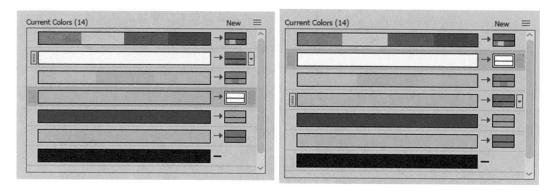

Figure 17-91. *Swap the new colors that you want to replace and assign to other colors*

Note   The colors that have been unlinked from recoloring are not affected.

The drop-down arrow beside each new color is the same Colorize Method as the Color Reduction Options dialog box, which lets you adjust the colors further. Refer to Figure 17-92.

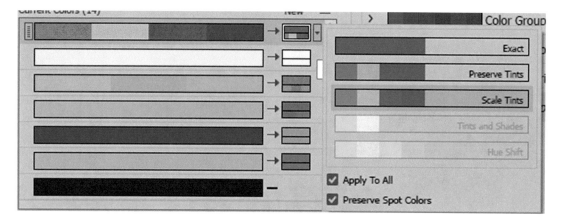

Figure 17-92. *Choose a new Colorize Method for all or some of the colors*

The default in my case was **Scale Tints**; however, in some situations, during experimentation on other projects, depending on the artwork, I find that **Preserve Tints** gives a softer effect. The **Exact** setting in other situations was posterized.

When **Apply to All is** checked, that means all colors are affected by the change. If unchecked, then separately.

If you want to **Preserve Spot Colors**, then make sure that is checked as well. If unchecked, any spot colors are converted to process, but you can access **Tints and Shades** and **Hue Shift** options. Refer to Figure 17-93.

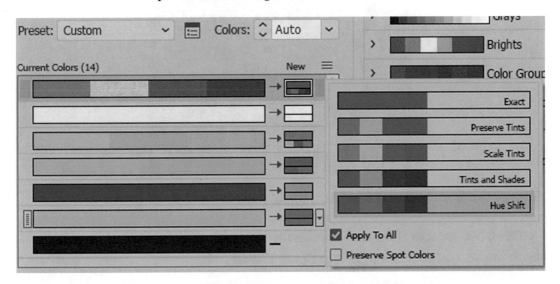

Figure 17-93. *By unchecking Preserve Spot Colors, you can access the disabled Colorize Methods of Tints and Shades and Hue Shift*

Once you have chosen an option from the list, then click the new color to confirm it. Refer to Figure 17-94.

Figure 17-94. *Click the New Color to Confirm the Colorize Method*

For your project, these options may recolor in a way that you find more or less pleasing; it depends on what colors you use.

For now, I check **Preserve Spot Colors** and the setting on **Preserve Tints** and click the new color to confirm. Refer to Figure 17-95.

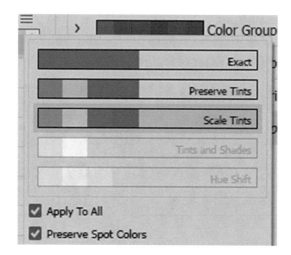

Figure 17-95. *Reset your Colorize Method back to the default*

When two or more of the current colors are selected on different rows, you can access the next set of buttons. Refer to Figure 17-96.

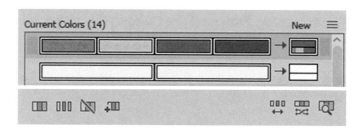

Figure 17-96. *Select more than one of the current colors to access various color options in the Assign tab of the Recolor Artwork dialog box*

Note   You can also drag your new selected color up or down in the list to reassign it to a different row of current colors then swap it with the new color you hover over.

You cannot undo **Merge colors into a row** directly unless you reset. So, the most direct way to correct it is to drag the color back to the original row. Refer to Figure 17-97.

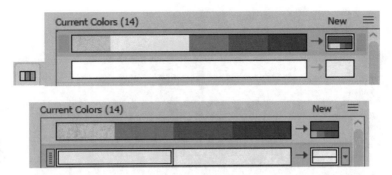

Figure 17-97. *Merge the selected color into a row. Drag it out to put it back in the original row*

Separate colors into different rows is used when you have two colors that you want to separate into two rows. A new row is created using one of the currently unused colors due to the earlier restriction. Refer to Figure 17-98.

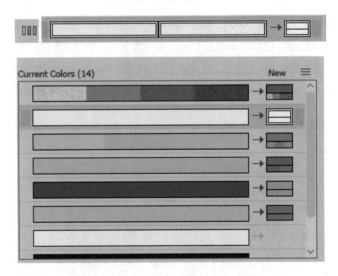

Figure 17-98. *Separate colors into different rows*

To reset this, drag the color back to the original row and then right-click the blank new color to remove it if present. This removes any unused or unlinked colors. Refer to Figure 17-99.

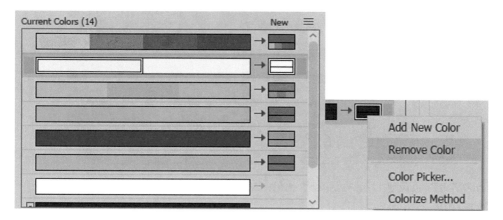

Figure 17-99. *Some Additional new colors not required can be removed by right-clicking them*

Note   If you find that the white is not removed and locked, you may have to go into your color reduction option and uncheck Preserve White, if this color is not present in your artwork. Click OK, and then the white is removed. You can always go back into this area if you need to reset the Preserve White. Refer to Figure 17-100.

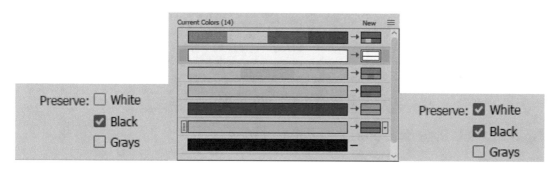

Figure 17-100. *If you can't remove the white from the current colors, uncheck it in the Preserve section of the Color Reduction Options*

Exclude selected colors so they will not be recolored. Select the color and choose this option if you want to exclude a certain color in a row. Refer to Figure 17-101.

Figure 17-101. *Exclude a selected color so it cannot be recolored*

This moves it onto its own row with the new color removed from recoloring or unlinked. Refer to Figure 17-102.

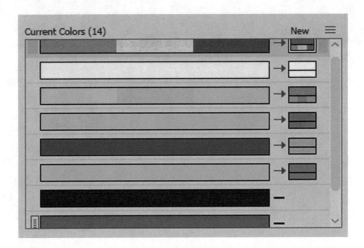

Figure 17-102. *The magenta is now excluded from being recolored*

If you want it to be part of the original group, you need to drag it back. Refer to Figure 17-103.

Figure 17-103. *Color added back to the original row*

Then remove the extra white layer again.

New row adds a new row.

Or you can right-click any blank new area or row to add a new color row. Drag a color onto that row You can then change it to unlink if you want to exclude that color from change. Refer to Figure 17-104.

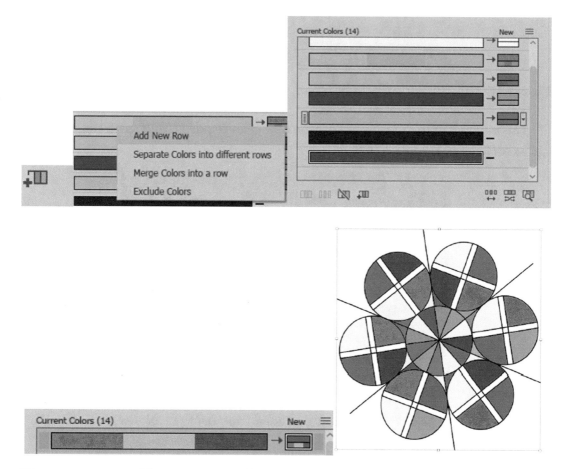

Figure 17-104. *Add a new row and drag a current color onto that row like the red to exclude it from being changed*

If you like your color group, make sure to save it as a new color group. Refer to Figure 17-105.

Figure 17-105. *Save your new Color Group*

Click OK to exit the dialog box for a moment and confirm your artwork and your artwork is colorized.

Random Color Change

In the 17_practice_2_final.ai file, I copied my pattern layer by dragging it over my new layer icon in the Layers panel and then locked and hid that layer. I then selected the group selection on the pattern copy layer with my Selection tool to continue my tour of the recolor artwork dialog box. Refer to Figure 17-106.

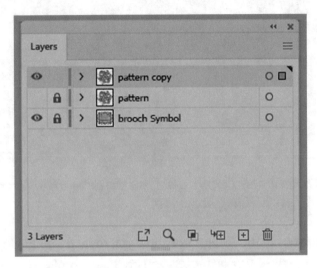

Figure 17-106. *Use your Layers panel to create a backup of your object when creating a new recolor, so you do not override the original*

From the Color Guide panel, re-enter the recolor artwork dialog box. As you see, sometimes, when you want to continue coloring, when you enter the box again, your artwork may be colored again in a way you do not expect, even in the same color group. That is why I always recommend keeping a backup copy when working with this panel, as it can be difficult to control color order afterward and may be difficult to reset. Refer to Figure 17-107.

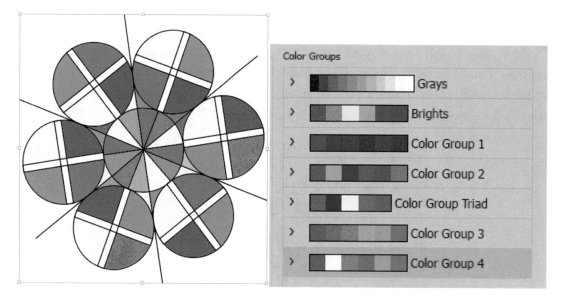

Figure 17-107. *The new color group colorizes the artwork differently when you enter the Recolor Artwork dialog box again*

The next two buttons in the **Assign tab** allow you to do the following.

Randomly change the color order lets you create new color combinations. Refer to Figure 17-108.

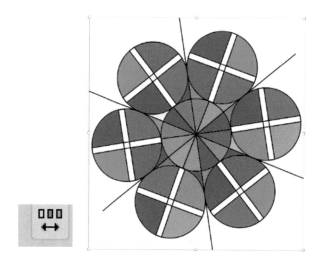

Figure 17-108. *Click this icon to randomly change the color order of your selected group*

Randomly change the saturation and brightness makes colors darker or lighter. Refer to Figure 17-109.

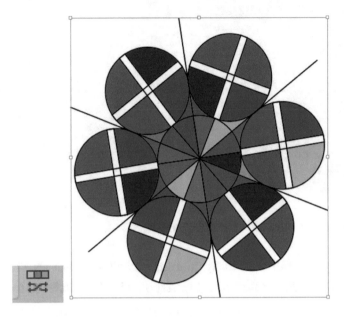

Figure 17-109. *Randomly change the saturation and brightness of your selected group*

Click on colors to find them in the artwork. If you have a lot of colors in your artwork, this is very useful for finding where the exact locations are that may need to be altered differently from the rest of the artwork. The cursor pointer changes so you can select different colors in your rows. When you are done, click this icon again to see the artwork as it currently is. Refer to Figure 17-110.

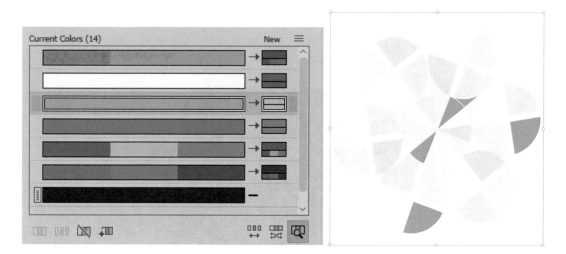

Figure 17-110. *Find selected colors in your artwork*

If you are happy with the recolor results and checked recolor art, click OK to finish the re-colorization. However, for now, stay in the dialog box. Refer to Figure 17-111.

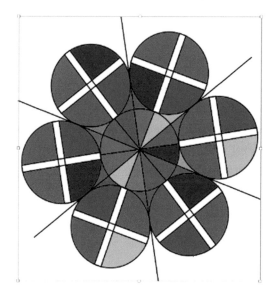

Figure 17-111. *View recolorized artwork*

Again, the lower color area can alter your colors. Correct any "out of gamut" colors by clicking the warning triangle in the lower swatch color area. Refer to Figure 17-112.

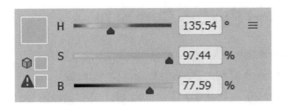

Figure 17-112. *Correct colors that are out of gamut if they affect your design*

In the end, your colors and arrangement for this second pattern may look different than mine.

When done, you can save your current color group. Click OK to exit the recolorize area or recolor artwork. Refer to Figure 17-113.

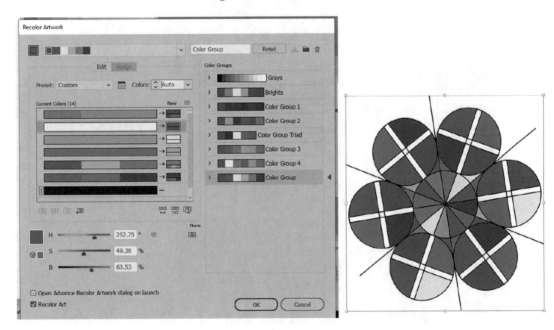

Figure 17-113. *Altered color groups change the results in the Recolor Artwork dialog box*

Your artwork should now be recolored. Save your file.

You can compare your colors to mine in the 17_practice_2_final.ai file. If you want, you could then turn your graphic into a symbol.

First, let's look at how colors are globally updated in all instances on the artboard.

Global Colors and Saving Symbols

Let's update the colors in the color group globally.

Open the 17_practice_3.ai file. Do not select anything.

In your Swatches panel, select the first swatch color group 5 and double-click it to enter the Swatch Options. Refer to Figure 17-114.

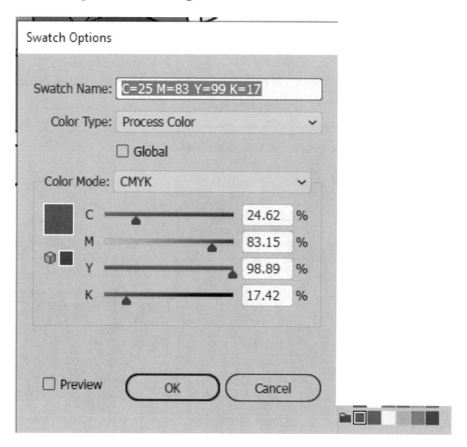

Figure 17-114. *Swatch Options dialog box for selected swatch*

Check the global checkbox in the Swatch Options dialog box and click OK. Refer to Figure 17-115.

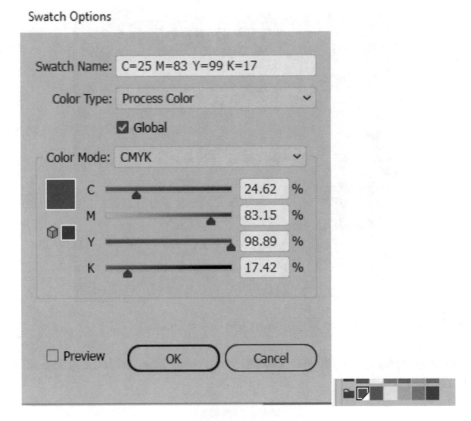

Figure 17-115. *Select Global in Swatch Options*

The swatch is now shown with the global symbol in the Color Guide. Refer to Figure 17-116.

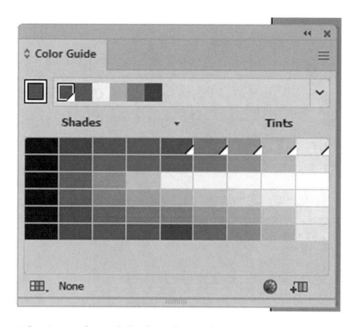

Figure 17-116. *The Swatch is global in the Color Guide*

Repeat these steps to set all your colors in that color group with the global settings. Refer to Figure 17-117.

Figure 17-117. *Set your swatches in your Color Group to Global*

Now reselect your artwork. From the Color Guide, enter the Recolor Artwork dialog box again. Your colors on your original artwork may shift when you enter the Recolor Artwork dialog box. Select the Color Group 5 and click OK to exit. Refer to Figure 17-118.

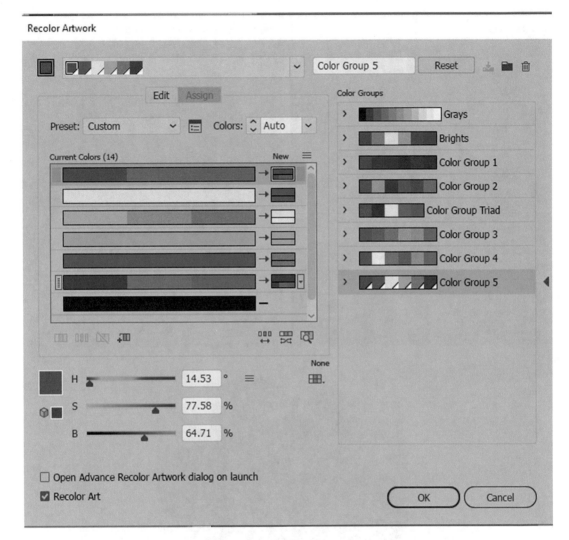

Figure 17-118. *Global swatches are visible in the Recolor Artwork dialog box*

Now, if you double-click a global swatch in the Swatches panel and alter the color in the dialog box using the sliders, it updates on the selected shape. Refer to Figure 17-119.

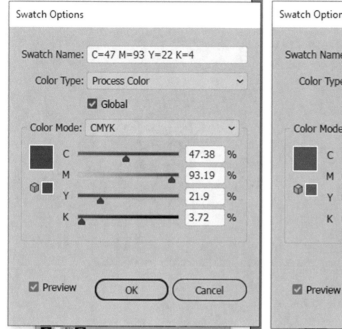

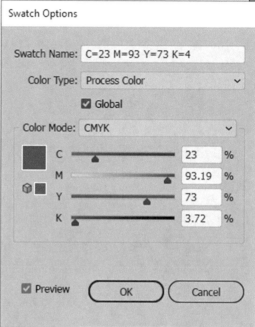

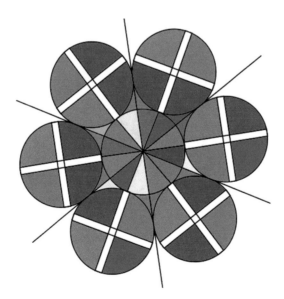

Figure 17-119. *Once a Global Swatch is assigned, you can then move the slider in the dialog box to alter that color*

Click OK to confirm, or click Cancel to not save the color changes.

Note   Any shape that uses global swatch updates throughout the document if its color is altered. You can see how that looks in the 17_practice_3_final.ai file.

While recoloring artwork can be challenging, once mastered, it can add variety to your illustrations.

Note   The color groups are stored in the Swatches panel. They can be saved in your Libraries panel as color themes if they have between one and five colors. With more than five, they need to be saved as separate colors or themes. If you want to continue to explore Adobe color themes with my video and the color wheel, make sure to check out `https://color.adobe.com/create/color-wheel`. In this version of Creative Cloud, Adobe is adjusting its panel layout. You can access this link through the Creative Cloud Desktop ➤ Web ➤ Adobe Color and Click the Launch Button to Launch in your Browser.

Saving Symbols of Your Artwork for Later Use

If you want to save your graphic as a symbol, let's try that now.

Select your grouped path with your Selection tool (V) and click the new symbol icon in your Symbols panel. Refer to Figure 17-120.

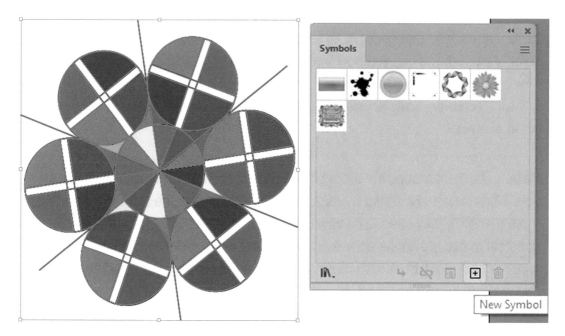

Figure 17-120. *Save your artwork as a symbol*

Symbol Options

Open the Symbol Options dialog box, and name the symbol. Refer to Figure 17-121.

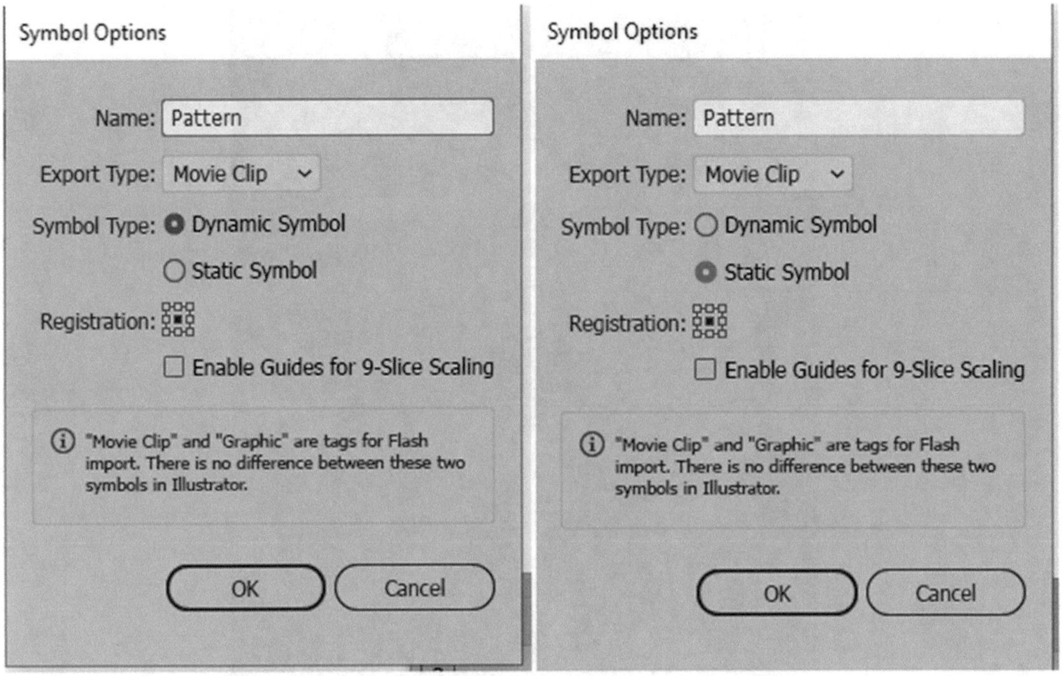

Figure 17-121. *Symbol Options dialog box*

To use a symbol between a program like Adobe Animate (formerly Flash) and Illustrator, you can set an Export Type. Since you are only working in Illustrator, it does not really matter whether you set it to **Movie Clip** or **Graphic**. But you never know where your artwork may be used, so I generally keep it at Movie Clip because it might be part of moving animation.

In Illustrator, I keep **Symbol Type** as a **Static Symbol**, but **Dynamic Symbols** can have alternations.

Leave registration at the center and keep disabled the **Enabled Guides for 9-slice Scaling** unless you plan to use the Symbol in Animate.

Click OK. The symbol is added to the Symbol panel. You can edit it further using the Control panel. Refer to Figure 17-122.

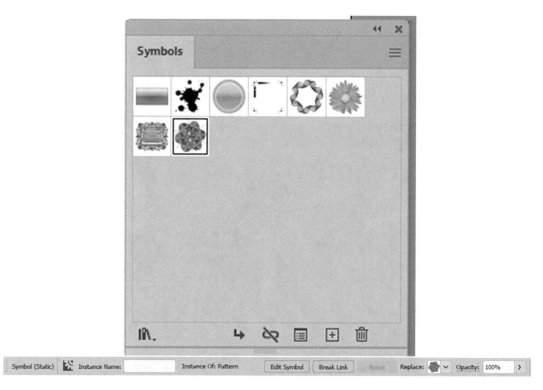

Figure 17-122. *A symbol is now on the artboard and saved in the Symbols panel. You can edit that Symbol using the Control panel*

A detailed overview of Symbols is at https://helpx.adobe.com/illustrator/ using/symbols.html.

Using Static Symbol, when you drag another copy of the symbol onto the artboard and choose recolor artwork from Color Guide, both symbol instances update identically. The original master symbol colors update in the Symbols panel.

Note   If you do not want the Symbol to update in the Symbols panel, you must choose the Break Link button from the Control panel before entering the Recolor Artwork dialog box and save it as a new symbol after recoloring.

Save your document. You can see how it looks in the 17_practice_3_final.ai file.

For additional practice, try using the Recolor Artwork dialog box on the brooch symbol to unlock the layer in the Layers panel and see how that affects the colors and gradients using different color groups. Refer to Figure 17-123.

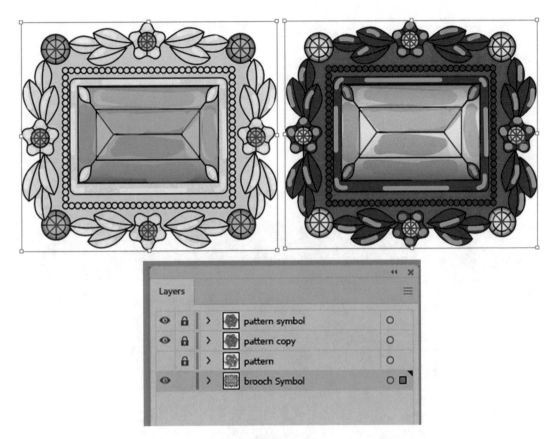

Figure 17-123. *Try to recolor the brooch Symbol when you unlock that layer in the Layers panel*

Or try some color alterations on the gnome and car from Chapter 16. Using the 17_practice_tools_final.ai file, I grouped the blob brushes with each character and put them on their own layers so that you could recolor the entire object at the same time. Refer to Figure 17-124.

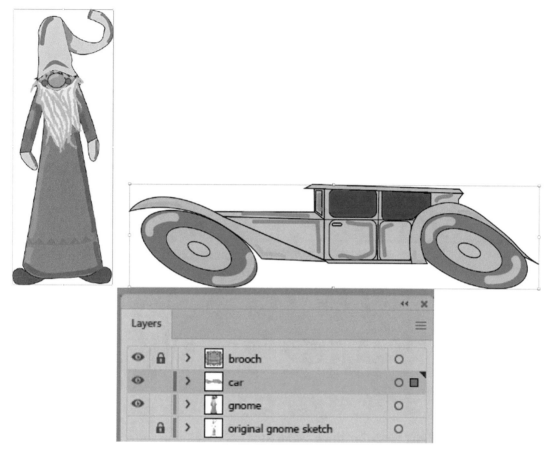

Figure 17-124. *You can create a different gnome or car coloration with the Recolor Artwork dialog box*

Edit Colors and Recolor Artwork After Image Trace

Colors can be altered on simple or complex artwork or created using the Image Trace panel after expansion, as you see with the apple from Chapter 14 (17_practice_apples.ai.)

When selected, you can alter or limit the colors with Recolor Artwork. However, the larger number of colors and more detail, the more time it takes to alter the colors. In this case, sort all 17,735 colors down to six new colors. Refer to Figure 17-125.

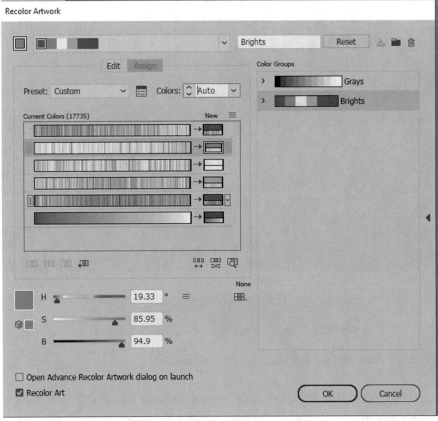

Figure 17-125. *Recolor your Image Trace with fewer colors in the Recolor Artwork dialog box*

As with the other drawings, you can choose to limit your colors using the Swatches libraries.

Global Edit

As you saw, colors, when applied to more than one artwork, can then be set to global colors. However, artwork can also be globally edited via the Control panel options or Properties panel options, which is helpful when you have similar pieces on more than one artboard and need to adjust them quickly. You can match such things as items with a similar appearance and size. **On Artboards** lets you select All, Portrait, Landscape, or Square. You can also set the **Range** of the artboard you want to edit. **Include Objects On Canvas** is enabled by default. Refer to Figure 17-126.

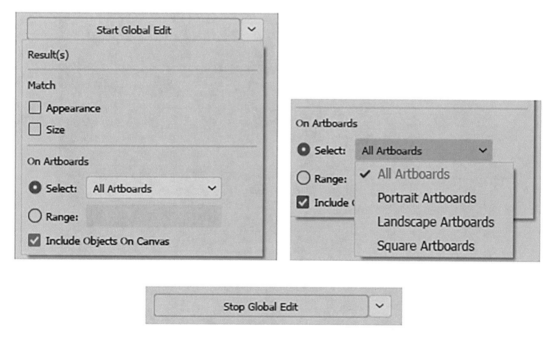

Figure 17-126. *Start a Global Edit in your artwork*

Click Start to locate similar items, and then as you move one object or scale it with your Selection tool, the other object moves as well. Click Stop Global Edit when you want to edit the objects separately. Refer to Figure 17-127.

Figure 17-127. *Global-scale both objects on different artboards*

Save Artwork in Other formats

You should make sure that your artwork is saved in either an .ai or .eps format for print and archiving. In other situations, like for an online portfolio or to send your artwork to a client, using File ➤ Save As a PDF is a good choice because people can view your files online. And you can set basic security to prevent others from printing your artwork if you only want it to be viewed. Refer to Figure 17-128.

File name:	Untitled-3.ai
Save as type:	Adobe Illustrator (*.AI)
	Adobe Illustrator (*.AI)
	Adobe PDF (*.PDF)

Figure 17-128. *Save your file as a PDF for print or your online portfolio*

You can use the Window ➤ Asset Export panel to save small graphics for the web when you need to create PNG, JPG, SVG, or PDF files. Refer to Figure 17-129.

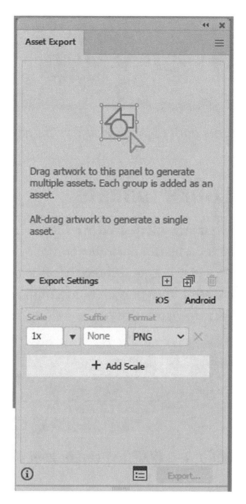

Figure 17-129.   *Use the Asset Export panel to save some of your objects for a website*

If you want to know more about saving your artwork for the web, make sure to check out my other book, *Graphics and Multimedia for the Web with Adobe Creative Cloud* (Apress, 2018).

Summary

This chapter covered ways to edit your artwork to achieve many different color variations on the same design as you edit colors and recolor artwork. The last chapter explores possible directions to take your artwork, next using other Adobe applications for page layout, animation, and video.

Conclusion

Once your artwork is saved in Illustrator, where can you use it in other projects or Adobe programs? Let's explore some possibilities in this chapter.

Now that you have saved your artwork in Photoshop and Illustrator formats, consider where you could take your artwork next in the digital Adobe Creative Cloud. This chapter talks about the possibilities of using other Adobe applications and the next direction for your artwork. Possible directions may include print, 3D designs, video production, or web design for your online portfolio. Refer to Figure 18-1.

Note   This chapter contains projects that are in the Chapter 18 folder.

© Jennifer Harder 2022
J. Harder, *Accurate Layer Selections Using Photoshop's Selection Tools*,
https://doi.org/10.1007/978-1-4842-7493-4_18

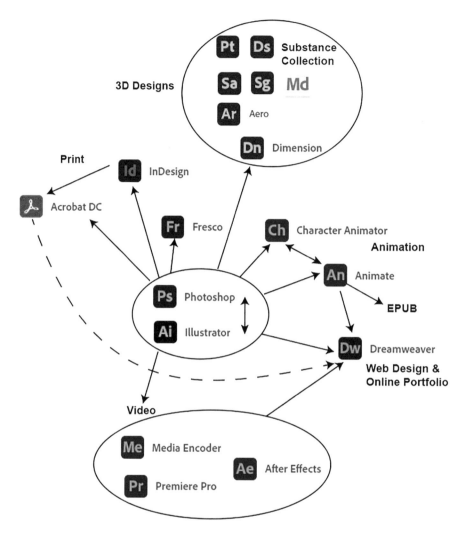

Figure 18-1. *After completing your refining and redrawing of your sketches in Photoshop and Illustrator, you may want to use them in other Adobe software apps*

Adobe Photoshop

Continuing with print, such as for a comic book in an Illustrator project, you could return to Photoshop to copy and paste your vector drawing back as a Smart Object layer. Refer to Figure 18-2.

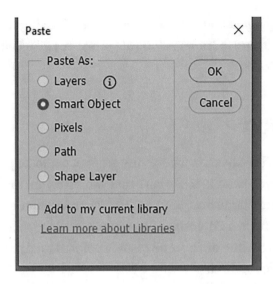

Figure 18-2. *Pasting an Illustrator graphic as a Smart Object layer into Photoshop*

You could then add layer style effects (*fx*), add masks, and Smart Filters to further adjust the drawing. Refer to Figure 18-3.

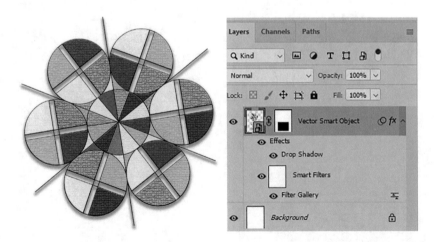

Figure 18-3. *Smart Objects can have layer styles, masks, and Smart Filters applied*

Other enhancements could be made in Adobe Fresco. You could create your own video or a GIF animation of your sketches in Photoshop. I present these options in my book *Graphics and Multimedia for the Web with Adobe Creative Cloud* (Apress, 2018).

Another possibility is you could even rasterize your drawings in Photoshop and later make it into a skin or texture for other Adobe 3D programs, like Dimension, Aero, or the newer Substance collection.

Adobe InDesign

If the artwork is part of the layout in a book, the graphic could be placed into an InDesign file. (.indd). Note that you want to make sure that you save your .psd; or if a .tiff file, add a clipping path for some Photoshop graphics. Unlike an Illustrator .ai file with clean, transparent areas around it, a Photoshop file, especially those that have been flattened (.psd, .tiff, or .eps), has a white or, in some cases, a colored background surrounding the main image. Refer to Figure 18-4.

Figure 18-4. *A page layout with illustrations in InDesign on a light-blue background—on the left, no clipping path, on the right, a clipping path*

This presents a problem when you want to remove most of that background or have text flow around the image. Though this book does not cover InDesign in detail, if you are a person who frequently uses that program, I give some steps here to follow along. Also, InDesign now has an option that helps you detect a path and its edges which you will see as well.

Create a Clipping Path in Photoshop and Import It into InDesign

Let's look at the apple from Chapter 12 and return to Photoshop.

1. File ➤ Open 18_apples_no_ClippingPath.psd and make an Image ➤ Image Duplicate.

    In this case, the file has been flattened to the background layer, but I kept the path I drew earlier called **apples**. In your project, you must create your own path.

2. Once the path is created and selected from the Paths panel menu, choose Clipping Path. Refer to Figure 18-5.

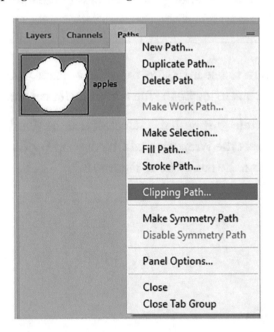

Figure 18-5. *Creating a clipping path in Photoshop using the Paths panel menu*

3. The Clipping Path dialog box opens. Refer to Figure 18-6.

Figure 18-6. *Clipping Path dialog box*

4. The current path appears, and then set Flatness to 1 for device pixels because you want a close edge. Then click OK to confirm. Refer to Figure 18-6.

5. Save (Ctrl/Cmd+S) your file. I saved my file as 18_apples_ ClippingPath.psd.

Note You can use this same setting for a .tiff or a Photoshop .eps file and then save your document.

6. If you know how to use InDesign, then File ➤ Place your .psd file. Use the dialog box to locate the file and place it over some text.

7. In InDesign, while the graphic is selected, use the Window ➤ Text Wrap panel to set the Wrap Around Object Shape option Third button icon from the left. Refer to Figure 18-7.

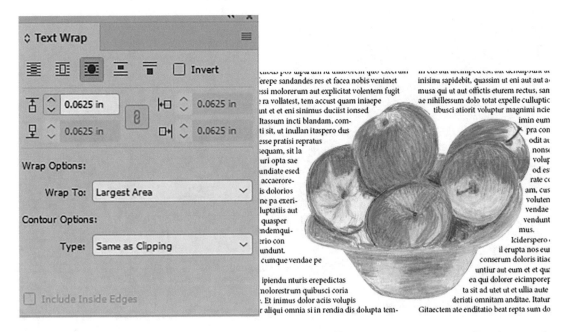

Figure 18-7. *The Text Wrap panel in InDesign allows you to set your clipping path for the selected image you can see the result on the right*

8. Add some offset area to the top, left, bottom and right. Set as Wrap To: **Largest Area** and Contour Options Type: **Same as Clipping**. This contours the shape of the text around the image and removes any excess white areas around the apples.

    Likewise, for an Illustrator (.ai) file, since there are no Clipping Path pre-settings, once placed, you could use the Contour Options Type: Detect Edges setting, which allows the text to go around a complex illustration like Image Trace in Chapter 14. Refer to Figure 18-8.

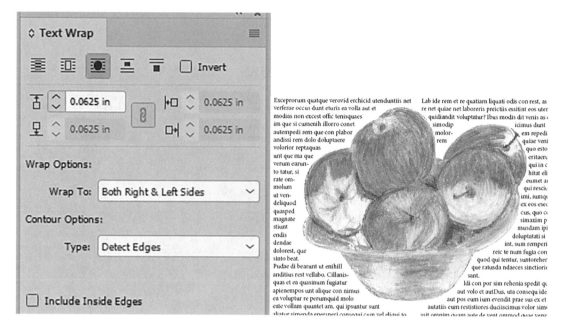

Figure 18-8. *An Illustrator file can also use the Text Wrap panel within InDesign*

9.   You can look at these examples in my file 18_clipping_path.indd file.

Later, in InDesign, a completed book could be exported as a multipage PDF file, which could be printed or placed on a website. Another suggestion is to use your artwork as part of a group of data merge files for conferences and mailings. I talk about this in my book *Data Merge and Styles in Adobe InDesign CC 2018* (Apress, 2017) and my video, *Beginning Data Merge with Adobe InDesign CC* (`https://link.springer.com/ video/10.1007/978-1-4842-4538-5`), which demonstrates how to set up data merges.

Adobe Animate and Character Animator

If you plan to create an animation for stills of characters for the web, a program like Adobe Animate or Character Animator might be the next step in the animation process. For Animate, you can directly Import to Stage graphics layers from Photoshop or Illustrator or add them into separate frames. I explore these animation options in *Graphics and Multimedia for the Web with Adobe Creative Cloud*. Illustrator also lets you copy a shape or symbol and paste it into Animate either as a bitmap or from an .ai file using the importer preferences. Refer to Figure 18-9.

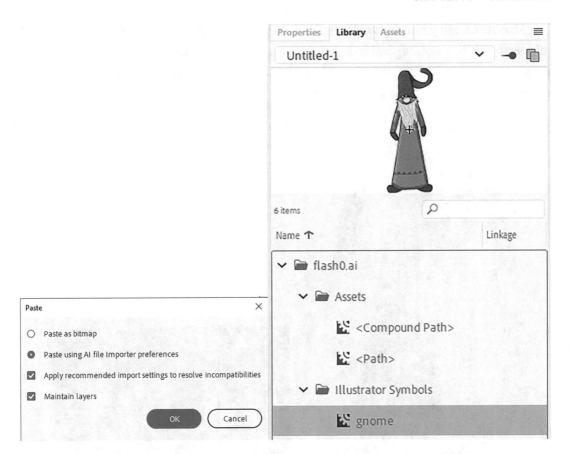

Figure 18-9. *Paste a symbol into Animate, and it is stored in the Libraries panel*

With dynamic symbols, you have the same options. It is pasted on the stage, and a copy is stored in its Library panel for reuse, as you would with symbols in Illustrator. However, regardless of whether you copy shapes or symbols, if effects were applied to them in Illustrator, but these effects are not available in Animate, you may lose some detail and Animate may generate a warning message. Refer to Figure 18-10. In some situations, it may be better to paste as a bitmap instead to rasterize the shape.

```
Warnings generated while copying/importing in Untitled-1:
* Blend Modes(Layer) is not supported in HTML5 Canvas document, and has been converted to Normal in an instance of Movieclip <Compound Path>.
* Blend Modes(Layer) is not supported in HTML5 Canvas document, and has been converted to Normal in an instance of Movieclip <Path>.
```

Figure 18-10. *Animate generates an output warning if it can't handle certain blending modes or filters and then alters them to compensate*

Also, if you are planning to create characters that are moving using the Bone tool and armature layers, it is good to save your vector artwork arms, legs, feet, body, and head as separate symbols so that you can connect the parts later in Animate to give your character movement. Refer to Figure 18-11.

Figure 18-11. *Using Illustrator, save parts of your illustration as separate dynamic symbols if you create an animation in Animate*

In Animate, the animation stills or armature layers could be incorporated into a GIF animation, a video clip H.264 (.mp4) video, a JavaScript (HTML 5 canvas), a SVG that could be used on a website, or an OAM file that could be used in InDesign for an EPUB document.

From Adobe Animate, you can export SVG files for Character Animator. There is more information on this at `https://helpx.adobe.com/adobe-character-animator/using/projects.html`.

In Character Animator you can import .psd and .ai files as well as, jpg, .png, .eps and .svg which you can later use to create H.264 (.mp4) videos.

Adobe Dreamweaver and Your Website

For your website, you may want to incorporate and link your images into a .gif animation or a gallery that you create using Bootstrap and Adobe Dreamweaver or another web page creation program. I talk about Dreamweaver in more detail in *Graphics and Multimedia for the Web with Adobe Creative Cloud*. Use Photoshop's Export options such as Save for Web (Legacy) to save your files in web-safe file formats like .gif (stills and animation), .jpg, and .png that you can link to your web page.

In Illustrator, you can use File ➤ Export as well to save in similar raster formats, as mentioned in Chapter 17, using the Asset Export panel. In my other book, I discuss export formats such as an SVG for animations that change on hover or other JavaScript settings.

Adobe Media Encoder, Premiere Pro, and After Effects

You can import your .jpg and gif animations into Media Encoder to make them into H.264 (.mp4) video clips. I talk about this in more detail in my other book.

However, in a more professional video, you may want to add tracks to your images in Premiere Pro and incorporate other effects with the After Effects program. For more information on that topic, go to `https://helpx.adobe.com/premiere-pro/using/importing-still-images.html`.

Summary

This final chapter briefly looked at what could be the next step in your Illustrator sketches project. Once you digitize your sketches, there is a whole range of possibilities you can explore. You can continue to edit and refine your sketches in Photoshop and Illustrator.

The process starts with an idea, a willingness to pursue your dreams, however difficult it seems at first, learn how to draw and use Adobe software, then the guidance, and support from those around you, whether they be instructors, your family, or friends. With that motivation, you can achieve what you didn't think possible and make it a reality.

Index

A, B

Adobe Animate/Character
    Animator, 914–916
Adobe Photoshop
    layer styles/masks/smart filters, 909
    smart object layer, 909
    websites, 917
Adobe Scan app, 23–25
Artwork, illustrator, *see* Illustrator app

C

Channels panel, 477
    alter selection
        brooch channel, 489
        brush tool, 489
        deselection, 488
        zoom tool/hand tool, 490
    delete selection, 493
    inverse/invert selection
        brooch channel, 490, 491
        copy channel, 492
        duplication, 492
        rename option, 493
    load selection
        brooch selection, 496
        brush/clone stamp/eraser tool, 501
        dialog box, 497
        focus area dialog box, 497
        icon selection, 499, 500
        invert check box, 498
        operation option, 498

RGB channels, 499
    select menu, 496
    options panel, 494–496
    save selection, 496
Clone stamp tool (S)
    adjusting settings, 82
    aligned check box, 81
    angle/overlay mode, 79
    brush settings, 76, 77
    eraser tool, 83
    flatten image, 84
    healing tools, 84
    layers panel menu, 83
    mode/opacity/pressure flow rate/
        airbrush/angle, 80, 82
    options menu, 78
    options/preset picker, 76
    sample/pressure size settings, 83
    show overlay, 80
    sketches, 75
    stamp tool and pressure, 81
    working process, 81
Color adjustment/artwork, 823
    adjust balance, 839, 840
    artwork format, 905, 906
    asset export panel, 906, 907
    blend front/back, 840
    CMYK mode document, 842
    edit options, 826, 827
    eyedropper tool (I), 823–826
    grayscale, 842
    guide panel (*see* Guide (Color) panel)

© Jennifer Harder 2022
J. Harder, *Accurate Layer Selections Using Photoshop's Selection Tools*,
https://doi.org/10.1007/978-1-4842-7493-4

M, N

Printed in the United States
by Baker & Taylor Publisher Services